D1441998

Handbook of Occupational Health Psychology

Handbook of
Occupational
Health Psychology

Edited by
James Campbell Quick
and Lois E. Tetrick

American Psychological Association
Washington, DC

Published by
American Psychological Association
750 First Street, NE
Washington, DC 20002
www.apa.org

To order
APA Order Department
P.O. Box 92984
Washington, DC 20090-2984
Tel: (800) 374-2721; Direct: (202) 336-5510
Fax: (202) 336-5502; TDD/TTY: (202) 336-6123
Online: www.apa.org/books/
Email: order@apa.org

In the U.K., Europe, Africa, and the Middle East, copies may be ordered from
American Psychological Association
3 Henrietta Street
Covent Garden, London
WC2E 8LU England

Typeset in New Century Schoolbook by World Composition Services, Inc., Sterling, VA

Printer: United Book Press, Baltimore, MD
Cover Designer: Naylor Design, Washington, DC
Project Manager: Debbie Hardin, Carlsbad, CA

The opinions and statements published are the responsibility of the authors, and such opinions and statements do not necessarily represent the policies of the American Psychological Association.

Library of Congress Cataloging-in-Publication Data
Handbook of occupational health psychology / edited by James Campbell Quick and Lois E. Tetrick.
   p. cm.
  Includes bibliographical references and index.
  ISBN 1-55798-927-3
    1. Industrial psychiatry—Handbooks, manuals, etc.   2. Clinical health psychology—Handbooks, manuals, etc.   3. Psychology, Industrial—Handbooks, manuals, etc.   I. Quick, James C.   II. Tetrick, Lois E.

RC967.5 .H358 2002
616.89—dc21

2002022843

British Library Cataloguing-in-Publication Data
A CIP record is available from the British Library.

Printed in the United States of America
First Edition

Contents

Contributors

Joyce A. Adkins, U.S. Department of Defense, Washington, DC
Dean Baker, University of California–Irvine
Julian Barling, Queen's University, Kingston, Ontario, Canada
Karen L. Belkić, University of Southern California School of Medicine, Alhambra
Joel B. Bennett, Organizational Wellness and Living Systems, Fort Worth, TX
Pascale Carayon, University of Wisconsin–Madison
Frank T. Conway, State of Wisconsin, Worker's Compensation Division, Madison
Royer F. Cook, The ISA Group, Alexandria, VA
Cary L. Cooper, University of Manchester, Manchester, England
Michael D. Coovert, University of South Florida, Tampa
Kelly DeRango, W. E. Upjohn Institute for Employment Research, Kalamazoo, MI
Philip Dewe, Birkbeck College, University of London
Simon Folkard, University of Wales–Swansea
Luisa Franzini, University of Texas, Houston
Michael R. Frone, State University of New York at Buffalo
Julie A. Fuller, Bowling Green State University, Bowling Green, OH
Amanda Griffiths, University of Nottingham
Catherine A. Heaney, Ohio State University, Columbus
Beth A. Jones, Yale University School of Medicine, New Haven, CT
Ben-Tzion Karsh, University of Wisconsin–Madison
Stanislav V. Kasl, Yale University School of Medicine, New Haven, CT
Paul A. Landsbergis, Mount Sinai School of Medicine, New York
Lennart Levi, Karolinska Institute, Sollentuna, Sweden
Debra L. Nelson, Oklahoma State University, Stillwater
Michael O'Driscoll, University of Waikato, Hamilton, New Zealand
Kenneth R. Pelletier, University of Maryland School of Medicine, Baltimore
Thomas G. Pickering, Mount Sinai School of Medicine, New York
James Campbell Quick, University of Texas at Arlington
Ruth E. Quillian-Wolever, Duke University Medical Center, Durham, NC
Peter L. Schnall, University of California–Irvine
Joseph E. Schwartz, State University of New York–Stony Brook
Norbert K. Semmer, University of Berne, Switzerland
Arie Shirom, Tel Aviv University
Bret L. Simmons, University of Alaska–Fairbanks
Carlla S. Smith, Bowling Green State University, Bowling Green, OH
Michael J. Smith, University of Wisconsin–Madison
Charles D. Spielberger, University of South Florida, Tampa
Lois E. Tetrick, University of Houston, TX

Töres Theorell, National Institute for Psychosocial Factors and Health, Stockholm, Sweden

Lori Foster Thompson, East Carolina University, Greenville, NC

Peter R. Vagg, University of South Florida, Tampa

Carol F. Wasala, University of South Florida, Tampa

Howard M. Weiss, Purdue University, West Lafayette, IN

Mark E. Wolever, Chapel Hill, NC

Dov Zohar, Technion–Israel Institute of Technology, Haifa

Foreword

It is widely accepted that a broad range of physical, biological, and chemical exposures can damage health and well-being—for example, bacteria, viruses, ionizing radiation, short asbestos fibers, lead, mercury, and organic solvents. It is harder to demonstrate, and to find acceptance for, the notion that psychosocial influences brought about by social and economic conditions and conveyed by processes within the central nervous system or human behavior can have corresponding effects (Karasek & Theorell, 1990; Kompier & Levi, 1994; Levi, 1971, 1972, 1979, 1981, 2000a, 2000b; Levi & Andersson, 1974; Shimomitsu, 2000).

Nearly two and a half millennia ago, Socrates came back from army service to report to his Greek countrymen that in one respect the Thracians were ahead of Greek civilization: They knew that the body could not be cured without the mind. "This," he continued, "is the reason why the cure of many diseases is unknown to the physicians of Hellas, because they are ignorant of the whole" (quoted by Dunbar, 1954, p. 3). About two millennia later Paracelsus emphasized that "true medicine only arises from the creative knowledge of the last and deepest powers of the whole universe" (p. 3). Perhaps these assertions represent an early, intuitive understanding of what we today refer to as ecological, cybernetic, and systems approaches.

During the past century and the present one, we have relinquished as an ideal the mastery of the whole realm of human knowledge by one person, and our training as specialists has made it difficult for us to accept the ideal of intelligent cooperation (Dunbar, 1954). This training has tended to keep each of us so closely limited by our own field that we have remained ignorant even of the fundamental principles in the fields outside our own.

This superspecialization and fragmentation are becoming increasingly problematic against the background of ongoing rapid changes in public health conditions in the Western world. Most of the major killers are now chronic, degenerative diseases. They are highly complex in their etiology, pathogenesis, manifestations, and effects. They are not easily accessible to purely medical interventions.

At the same time, it seems likely that much of the morbidity and premature mortality is preventable. This, however, requires action beyond the health and health care sector and may involve the empowerment of the grassroots sectors. Sectors outside the traditional health and health care field, but still of major importance for our health and well-being, include education, employment, work environment, economic resources, housing, transportation and communication, leisure and recreation, social relations, political resources, safety and security, and equality.

Taking occupational factors as an example, we find that work-related stress, its causes and consequences, are all very common in the 15 European Union (EU) member states. More than half of the 160 million workers report working at a very high speed (56%) and under tight deadlines (60%). More than one third have no influence on task order, and 40% report having monotonous tasks. Such work-related "stressors" are likely to have contributed to the present spectrum of ill health: 15% of the workforce complain of headaches, 23% of neck and shoulder pains, 23% of fatigue, 28% of "stress," and 33% of backache, and many complain of other diseases, even to life-threatening ones (European Foundation, 2001).

Such a "causality" may imply a range of relationships. It can mean that a certain exposure is necessary—enough for a certain disease to develop (such as the exposure to lead causing lead poisoning). An exposure may also be sufficient—no additional influences or vulnerabilities are necessary. Or exposure may be contributory and neither necessary nor sufficient. The question also remains about whether an exposure really causes a specific disease or if it "just" aggravates it, accelerates its course, or triggers its symptoms. If we keep all these options in mind, it becomes clear that work-related exposures may, but need not, be a prerequisite for the development of specific occupational diseases, a *sine qua non*. On the other hand, it becomes equally clear that they may contribute to a wide variety of morbidity and mortality, a much wider spectrum than is usually realized.

How, then, can disease be prevented and health and well-being promoted at work and elsewhere? In theory, this can be achieved in accordance with principles spelled out in the EU Framework Directive (89/391/EEC), according to which employers have a

> duty to ensure the safety and health of workers in every aspect related to the work, on the basis of the following general principles of prevention:
> - avoiding risks;
> - evaluating the risks which cannot be avoided;
> - combating the risks at source;
> - adapting the work to the individual, especially as regards the design of workplaces, the choices of work equipment and the choice of working and production methods, with a view, in particular to alleviating monotonous work and work at predetermined work rate and to reducing their effects on health;
> - *developing a coherent overall prevention policy* [italics mine] which covers technology, organisation of work, working conditions, social relationships and the influence of factors related to the working environment. (89/391/EEC)

To implement this, strategies need to address the root causes (primary prevention), to reduce their effects on health (secondary prevention), and also to treat the resulting ill health (tertiary prevention; e.g., Quick, Quick, Nelson, & Hurrell, 1997).

Article 152 of the European Treaty of Amsterdam states that "a high level of human health protection shall be ensured in the definition and implementation of *all* Community policies and activities" [italics added].

As pointed out in the European Commission's Guidance (Levi, 2000a), work-related disease prevention programs can aim at a variety of targets and be based on various philosophies. If the condition at work—the "shoe"—does not "fit" the worker—the foot—one political approach is to urge the "shoe factories" to manufacture a wide variety of shoes in different sizes and configurations to fit every, or almost every, conceivable foot. Whenever possible, the instructions to the shoe factories should be *evidence-based*—in other words, based on measurements of a representative, random sample of all feet, all shoes, and of the existing fit. This is a first—diagnostic—step in a primary prevention approach on a *population* level.

Another approach, again based on primary prevention, aims at finding the right shoe for each individual foot—promoting "the right person in the right place."

A third, complementary approach is that the owner of each foot should have access to and be encouraged to use a "lasting device" to adjust available shoes to fit his or her feet. The emphasis is on *empowerment*, on active, responsible workers, able, willing, and encouraged to make adjustments of their working conditions, to improve the work–worker fit.

All three approaches can aim at an improved fit in general terms or can address the *inequity* of various feet in various shoes.

So far, in the EU and elsewhere, most work-stress prevention approaches are oriented toward secondary or tertiary prevention only (Malzon & Lindsay, 1992). Most of these approaches involve, for example, the provision of on-site fitness facilities, smoking cessation programs, dietary control, relaxation and exercise classes, health screening, psychological counseling, or sometimes some combination of these packaged as a multimodular program available to employees (Cartwright, Cooper, & Murphy, 1995; Kompier & Cooper, 1999). This "band-aid" approach would correspond to offering "corn plaster" only to the owners of sore feet—or pain killers, tranquilizers, or psychotherapy to deal with the outcomes of the lack of fit between the worker and his or her conditions of work.

This in no way implies a criticism against secondary and tertiary prevention approaches, particularly not as long as the latter constitute a part of a larger *package* that includes primary prevention also.

An obvious difficulty with primary prevention lies in the fact that "one size does not fit all." It follows that we need a multifaceted approach to stressor prevention and to promotion of healthy workers in healthy companies. An attempt to design such an approach has been made by the U.S. National Institute for Occupational Safety and Health in its National Strategy for the Prevention of Work-Related Psychological Disorders (Sauter, Murphy, & Hurrell, 1990). It addresses

- *Workload and work pace:* Avoiding both under- and overload, allowing recovery from demanding tasks and increasing control by workers over various work characteristics;
- *Work schedule:* Designing schedules to be compatible with demands and responsibilities outside the job and addressing flex time, job sharing, and rotating shifts;
- *Job future:* Avoiding ambiguity in opportunities for promotion and career or skill development and in matters pertaining to job security;
- *Social environment:* Providing opportunities for employee interaction and support; and

- *Job content:* Designing job tasks to have meaning, to provide stimulation, and to provide an opportunity to use existing skills and develop new ones.

A key question, of course, concerns what is, indeed, preventable in terms of exposures and inequities in exposures to occupational stressors. Many tasks are intrinsically stressful but still need to be performed for the public good—for example, night work in an emergency ward. It can be debated how much of the reactions to these stressors depend on excessive occupational demands and how much on individual vulnerabilities of the worker. In practice, however, there is an abundance of occupational exposures that the great majority of the labor force would experience as noxious and pathogenic. It is in the interest of all parties on the labor market to prevent, as far as possible, workers from being exposed to them. If, for one reason or another, this turns out to be unfeasible, a complementary approach is to try to reduce exposure time or to buffer or otherwise decrease the noxious effects.

Secondary or tertiary prevention can also involve improving the workers coping repertoire. If "deep and troubled waters" cannot be eliminated, the attempt is to teach people to "swim"—to cope. Coping is a cognitive and behavioral process of mastering, tolerating, or reducing internal and external demands (Lazarus & Folkman, 1984). It can be *problem*-focused (trying to change the actual exposures), emotion-focused (trying to modify the resulting emotions), or both.

All this is presented and discussed in considerable depth by the eminent scientists in the chapters of this important volume. This handbook is an essential resource for scholars, researchers, and practitioners in occupational health psychology who aim to make workplaces healthier for all concerned. It is also an essential resource for those in public health and medicine who are concerned with health issues in working environments.

LENNART LEVI

References

Cartwright, S., Cooper, C. L., & Murphy, L. R. (1995). Diagnosing a healthy organization: A proactive approach to stress in the workplace. In L. R. Murphy, J. J. Hurrell, Jr., S. L. Sauter, & G. P. Keita (Eds.), *Job stress interventions* (pp. 217–233). Washington, DC: American Psychological Association.

Dunbar, F. (1954). *Emotions and bodily changes.* New York: Columbia University Press.

European Foundation. (2001). *Third European survey on working conditions.* Dublin: European Foundation for the Improvement of Living and Working Conditions.

Karasek, R., & Theorell, T. (1990). *Healthy work. Stress, productivity, and the reconstruction of working life.* New York: Basic Books.

Kompier, M., & Cooper, C. (1999). *Preventing stress, improving productivity—European case studies in the workplace.* London: Routledge.

Kompier, M., & Levi, L. (1994). *Stress at work: Causes, effects, and prevention. A guide for small and medium sized enterprises.* Dublin: European Foundation.

Lazarus, R. S., & Folkman, S. (1984). *Stress, appraisal, and coping.* New York: Springer.

Levi, L. (1971). *Society, stress and disease—The psychosocial environment and psychosomatic diseases, Vol. I.* London: Oxford University Press.

Levi, L. (1972). Stress and distress in response to psychosocial stimuli. Laboratory and real-life studies on sympathoadrenomedullary and related reactions. *Acta Medica Scandinavica, 191,* 528.

Levi, L. (1979). Psychosocial factors in preventive medicine. In D. A. Hamburg, E. O. Nightingale, & V. Kalmar (Eds.), *Healthy people. The Surgeon General's report on health promotion and disease prevention. Background papers* (pp. 207–252). Washington DC: U.S. Government Printing Office.

Levi, L. (1981). *Society, stress and disease—Working life, Vol. IV.* Oxford,UK: Oxford University Press.

Levi, L. (2000a). *Guidance on work-related stress. Spice of life or kiss of death?* Luxembourg: European Commission.

Levi, L. (2000b). Stress in the global environment. In J. Dunham (Ed.), *Stress in the workplace, Past, present and future* (pp. 1–18). London: Whurr.

Levi, L., & Andersson, L. (1974). *Population, environment and quality of life. A contribution to the United Nation's World Population Conference.* Stockholm: Royal Ministry of Foreign Affairs.

Malzon, R., & Lindsay, G. (1992). *Health promotion at the worksite. A brief survey of large organizations in Europe* (European Occupational Health Series No. 4). Copenhagen: WHO Regional Office for Europe.

Quick, J. C., Quick, J. D., Nelson, D.L., & Hurrell, J. J., Jr. (1997). *Preventive stress management in organizations.* Washington, DC: American Psychological Association.

Sauter, S. L., Murphy, L. R., & Hurrell, J. J., Jr. (1990). Prevention of work-related psychological distress: A national strategy proposed by the National Institute of Occupational Safety and Health. *American Psychologist, 45,* 1146–1158.

Shimomitsu, T. (2000). Work-related stress and health in three post-industrial settings— EU, Japan, and USA. *Journal of Tokyo Medical University, 58,* 327–469.

Preface

The American Psychological Association (APA) has a long history of concern for safe and healthy work, beginning with APA President Hugo Münsterberg's interest in industrial accidents during the early years of the 20th century. Each of the editors of this volume have had long-standing professional and personal concerns for safe and healthy work. We are delighted that the APA has chosen to publish the *Handbook of Occupational Health Psychology* to explore the unique concerns and issues in this emerging specialty in the science and practice of psychology. We see the volume as a good fit with the *ILO Encyclopaedia of Occupational Health and Safety* and *Maxey-Rossneau-Last's Public Health and Preventive Medicine*, each of which addresses much broader concerns with industrial work environments and with human health.

We are also delighted to have been involved with the collaboration between the APA and the National Institute of Occupational Safety and Health (NIOSH) since the late 1980s. NIOSH identified job-related psychological disorders as among the top 10 occupational health concerns in the early 1980s. However, the concern was preceded by Lennart Levi's chapter on work stress and psychologically healthy work in *Healthy People: The Surgeon General's Report on Health Promotion and Disease Prevention* (1979). We are delighted that Dr. Levi has written the foreword for this international handbook.

References

Healthy people: The surgeon general's report on health promotion and disease prevention. (1979). Washington, DC: U.S. Government Printing Office.

Stellman, J. M. (Ed.). (1997). *ILO encyclopaedia of occupational health and safety.* Geneva, Switzerland: International Labour Office and Rand McNally.

Wallace, R. B., Doebbeling, B. N., & Last, J. M. (Eds.). (1998). *Maxcy-Rosenau-Last public health and preventive medicine.* (14th ed.) Stamford, CT: Appleton & Lange.

Acknowledgments

We would like to thank our international advisory board, the members of which helped us in a variety of ways as we framed, then developed, the handbook. We thank Donna Ross for her invaluable administrative support throughout the entire project, beginning with her role as editorial office manager during the founding years of the *Journal of Occupational Health Psychology*. She has been a wonderful support. We would like to thank Gary VandenBos, Julia Frank-McNeil, Judy Nemes, Vanessa Downing, and other APA staff members who so ably encouraged, nurtured, and supported our editorial efforts.

Jim thanks President Robert Witt, Executive Vice President and Provost George C. Wright, Dean of Business Daniel D. Himarios, and many colleagues at the University of Texas at Arlington (UTA) for their active support and commitment to his work over the years in occupational health psychology. He is especially appreciative to UTA for the 2000–2001 Faculty Development Leave, which supported this work and his complimentary new research on executive health, and to Michael Moore for his guidance and support to make that happen.

Lois thanks the Department of Psychology at the University of Houston for their support of this project and of the occupational health psychology minor. In addition, she thanks Jim and all of the authors of the handbook for their valuable contributions, support, and responsiveness throughout the publication process.

THE HANDBOOK OF OCCUPATIONAL HEALTH PSYCHOLOGY ADVISORY BOARD

Cary L. Cooper, PhD, CBE, University of Manchester, Manchester, England
Lennart Levi, MD, PhD, Karolinska Institute, Sollentuna, Sweden
Teruichi Shimomitusu, MD, PhD, Tokyo Medical University
Arie Shirom, PhD, Tel Aviv University
Carlla S. Smith, PhD, Bowling Green State University, Bowling Green, OH
Charles D. Spielberger, PhD, University of South Florida, Tampa
Craig Stenberg, PhD, Duke University, Durham, NC

The Past, Present, and Future of Occupational Health Psychology

Occupational health psychology is a relatively young specialty within the science and practice of psychology. This handbook is designed to consolidate and organize the emerging knowledge in the field from the interdisciplinary perspectives of an international group of scholars and researchers. Part I includes five chapters designed to provide historical, contemporary, and future-oriented perspectives on this emerging specialty after first discussing prevention and public health in occupational settings. These five chapters reflect the interdisciplinary nature of occupational health psychology, with a strong blend of psychology and public health. In addition to considering health and safety risks and organizational wellness, this part concludes with an emphasis from positive psychology.

Chapter 1 by Tetrick and Quick offers a public health and prevention framework for occupational health psychology. The authors suggest that occupational health psychology should develop, maintain, and promote employees' health and the health of their families. The prevention model presented and elaborated throughout the structure of the handbook classifies preventive interventions as primary, secondary, or tertiary. Primary interventions focus on people who are not yet at risk. Secondary interventions focus on people who are suspected to be at risk for illness or injury, such as smokers. Tertiary interventions focus on those with health problems and are largely therapeutic or curative in nature. Several subsequent chapters in the handbook elaborate and include variations on this prevention framework.

Chapter 2 by Barling and Griffiths reflects the European and North American heritage in occupational health psychology, dating back to the work of Friedrich Engels at the dawn of the Industrial Revolution in Manchester, England. The authors focus on the origins of the field from the perspectives of people, ideas, events, and institutions, showing how far occupational health psychology has come in a comparatively short period of time. Barling and Griffiths give separate treatment to the early developments in the United States and early influences from Europe, with an emphasis on working populations. The chapter also includes a section that addresses unemployment and nonwork.

Chapter 3 by Smith, Karsh, Carayon, and Conway presents the traditional perspective of occupational safety and health. The authors begin with a summary of relevant safety and health agencies, laws, and regulations. Then they present a model of occupational safety and health performance. The major components of the model include person factors, task activities, the physical work environment, technology/tools/machinery, organizational structure, and supervision. The model reflects the interdisciplinary nature of occupational safety and health and the potential factors that can contribute to employees' health. In addition to the model, this chapter provides descriptions of known workplace hazards and references to various resources for obtaining information on such hazards, developing hazard inspection programs, and ways of controlling workplace hazards once they are identified.

Chapter 4 by Bennett, Cook, and Pelletier presents an integrated framework for comprehensive organizational wellness. In reviewing the literature on health promotion programs in organizations, the authors review eight core themes in conceptualizations of organizational health. They conclude that much of the literature suggests a "cross-level mimicry"—that is, the process of health promotion at the individual level and at the organizational level are parallel. The second part of this chapter describes four practitioner models of health promotion. Finally, the literature on effectiveness of health promotion and disease management programs is summarized.

The final chapter in this first part, chapter 5, by Nelson and Simmons presents an overview of definitions of health expanding the construct to be more than just the absence of illness as is typical of medical models of health. Rather, a more holistic model of health is presented. Incorporating both a positive as well as a negative perspective of health, Nelson and Simmons then review four of the major theories of work stress, proposing that the concept of eustress and distress are necessary to understand employees' health. They conclude the chapter with a thrust from positive psychology, offering suggestions for the prevention of distress and the generation of eustress.

1

Prevention at Work: Public Health in Occupational Settings

Lois E. Tetrick and James Campbell Quick

People spend a significant proportion of their lives at work, and often their jobs bring meaning and structure to their lives (Jahoda, 1982). In fact, work may dominate the lives of many individuals (Cox, 1997). Because work is a central aspect of many peoples lives, it generally is recognized that individuals should have a safe and healthy work environment. Employees should not have to worry about injury or illness, and legislation has been introduced in many industrialized countries including the United States, the Netherlands, Sweden, and European Union to help ensure this (Kompier, 1996). The focus of much of the early work on occupational safety and health was on workers' exposures to physical hazards in the work environment. Increasingly, however, the workplace is viewed as the logical, appropriate context for health promotion not just the prevention of injuries and illness (Cooper & Cartwright, 1994; Cox, 1997). This broader perspective is concerned with healthy people and healthy organizations, especially considering the recent changes in the organization of work as well as changes in the people in the workforce (Levi, Sauter, & Shimomitsu, 1999). The purpose of this chapter is to examine the context of this broader perspective in which occupational health psychology is emerging and integrate occupational health psychology with the public health model. We conclude with future directions for occupational health psychology.

Healthy Organizations

In considering healthy organizations, one must consider the question of healthy for whom? Many definitions of organizational health have focused on the organization itself. For example, Miles (1965) defined a healthy organization as one that survives but also continues to cope adequately over the long haul, continuously developing and expanding its coping abilities. Cooper and Cartwright (1994) extended this by including the health of employees when they described a healthy organization as one that is financially successful and has a healthy workforce. A healthy organization is able to maintain a healthy and satisfying work environment over time even

3

in times of market turbulence and change. Similarly, Quick (1999) indicated that high productivity, high employee satisfaction, good safety records, few disability claims and union grievances, low absenteeism, low turnover, and the absence of violence characterized a healthy work environment. One could further extend the consideration of organizational health to the community in which the organization is located. Such an extension makes clear the public health perspective of occupational health psychology and its focus on prevention. Prevention programs aimed at improving the health of organizations benefit both the organization and the people in them because they reflect a value placed on people, human activities, and human relationships (Rosen, 1986; Schein, 1990).

Healthy People

In 1946 the World Health Organization defined health as not just the absence of disease but as a state of complete physical, mental, and social well-being. The Ottawa Charter of the World Health Organization in 1986 defined health as a resource for everyday life, not the object of living. Health is a positive concept including social and personal resources as well as physical capabilities (Nutbeam, 1990). It also has been conceptualized as the ability to have and to reach goals, meet personal needs, and cope with everyday life (Raphael et al., 1999). The United States is among the countries that set national health objectives for its people, both with regard to health-related behavior, disease prevention, and health and safety in the workplace (U.S. DHHS, 1990).

Occupational Health Psychology

The purpose of occupational health psychology is to develop, maintain, and promote the health of employees directly and the health of their families. The primary focus of occupational health psychology is the prevention of illness or injury by creating safe and healthy working environments (Quick et al., 1997; Sauter, Hurrell, Fox, Tetrick, & Barling, 1999). Key areas of concern are work organization factors that place individuals at risk of injury, disease, and distress. This requires an interdisciplinary, if not transdisciplinary, approach (Maclean, Plotnikoff, & Moyer, 2000) across multiple disciplines within and beyond psychology. For example, such psychology specialties as human factors, industrial and organizational psychology, social psychology, health psychology, and clinical psychology affect occupational health psychology, as do other disciplines such as public health, preventive medicine, and industrial engineering (Schneider, Camara, Tetrick, & Stenberg, 1999). Integration of these disciplines with a primary focus on prevention is the goal of occupational health psychology. Therefore, the focus is on organizational interventions rather than individual interventions, such as counseling (Quick, 1999).

The challenge to occupational health psychology in promoting healthy organizations and healthy people can be more fully appreciated by examining changes that are occurring in workplaces and in the workforce. These changes shape the nature of occupational risks to which people are exposed and the context within which they work. Key changes that relate to occupational health psychology are described in the following sections.

The Changing Nature of Work

One of the more notable and sweeping changes in the nature of work concerns the process of globalization, which has increased the international competition to which organizations are subject, increased the stress for companies and individuals alike, and decreased people's job security. Globalization has been accompanied by greater global interdependency. For example, advances in the high technology sectors helped fuel job creation in Europe during the late 1990s. However, when the restructuring and downturn came in 2000, the interdependencies across economies put many people out of work. Although the U.S. economy accounted for about 35% of world economic activity after World War II, its global role moved back toward its historical place of about 16% as the European and Japanese economies were rebuilt. However, by 2000, U.S. gross domestic product (GDP) accounted for almost 30% of world output, up from 26% in 1992. Further, U.S. companies make almost 50% of all world corporate profits, which is a 33% increase in a decade. During the Thatcher and post-Thatcher eras in the United Kingdom, there has been an Americanization of that economy.

Within the U.S. economy, there has been a substantial shift in the number of jobs in various sectors, with fewer jobs in manufacturing and more jobs in service industries. The Bureau of Labor statistics reflect that for the period 1988 to 1998, the occupational groups with the slowest growth and thus the sharpest decline in percentage of overall employment were agriculture, forestry, and fishing occupations and the precision production, craft, and repair occupational groups. Operators, fabricators, and laborers as well as clerical workers experienced slower than average growth while very rapid growth was seen among the professional specialty occupations and the executive, administrative, and managerial occupational groups. An important result of this shift is that employees are potentially exposed to different occupational hazards, including psychosocial stressors in the work environment that have been linked to ill-health.

This shift to a service economy also has increased the number of self-employed people (Aronsson, 1999) and the number of other forms of flexible employment such as home-based work, temporary work, and contract work (Benach, Fernando, Platt, Diez-Roux, & Muntaner, 2000). Benach et al. (2000) reported that the International Labour Organization estimates that 25% to 30% of workers globally are underemployed in that they are working substantially less than full-time and want to work longer or they are earning less than a living wage. It is not clear what effects these alternative employment relations may have on individuals' health. It is well-established that unemployment is related to ill-health and it has been suggested that because these new forms of flexible employment are likely to share some of the same unfavorable characteristics of unemployment, there is potential for health-damaging effects (Benach et al., 2000). In addition, data suggest that people have a number of different jobs in their life times. The percentage of people who hold multiple jobs at the same time has increased somewhat, gradually declining for men and rapidly raising for women (*Safe Work in the 21st Century*, 2000). This pattern of employment relations suggests that people's exposure to work environments may be very dynamic, making it difficult from an epidemiological perspective to identify the sources of ill-health (Berkman & Kawachi, 2000; see also chapter 18, this volume).

In addition to these structural changes in work, the organization of work has undergone significant changes. *Organization of work* refers to the management systems, supervisory practices, production processes, and their influence on the way work is performed (Sauter et al., 1999). Among these changes are globalization, increased competition and economic pressures, technological innovations, and increased complexity of organizational structures and task interdependence. Globalization has been suggested to create several issues relative to the health and well-being of individuals (Frumkin, 1998). Globalization may result in relocation or displacement of employees. This resulting unemployment, fear of unemployment, and migration can result in stress and negative effects on the health of workers as well as their families. In addition, countries differ in their occupational health and safety standards and the extent to which these standards are enforced; this creates potentially healthy and unhealthy work environments, depending on the context. The increased diversity resulting from globalization also may be stressful, perhaps as a result of difficulty in communication or conflict among cultural values or norms, thus negatively affecting employees' health.

The need to maintain a competitive edge has resulted in several organizations of work practices, such as lean production, total quality management, and advanced manufacturing techniques and increased use of technology. These practices were developed to provide organizations with a means of responding more quickly and efficiently to production demands with better quality. Typically these systems increase the cognitive demands on employees, their responsibilities, and the interdependence among employees. Wall and Jackson (1995) indicated that these demands can result in stress that can lead to negative health effects.

The changes in the organization of work and global competition have resulted in increased downsizing and restructuring of organizations (Burke & Nelson, 1998; Tetrick, 2000). The health and safety effects of downsizing and restructuring have been found to be negative for the victims, the survivors, and the managers who implemented the downsizing efforts. The most common effect was depression (de Vries & Balasz, 1997; Tetrick, 2000). These findings were consistent with a 1996 American Management Association Survey that found job elimination was related to increased disability claims, with the largest increase in claims being stress-related (e.g., mental or psychiatric problems, substance abuse, hypertension, and cardiovascular disease).

The Changing Workforce

The workforce is becoming more diverse with respect to the age of workers, the continued entry of women into the workforce, the composition of the workforce by race and ethnicity, and the increased participation of individuals with disabilities in the workforce. Each of these factors are discussed next.

Age

The Institute of Medicine's Committee to Assess Training Needs for Occupational Safety and Health Personnel in the United States (*Safe Work in the 21ˢᵗ Century,* 2000) reported an absolute decline in the number of workers under age 25 and a growth of workers 25 to 54 during the 1990s, using Bureau of Labor statistics. This shift at least partially reflected the baby boom generation and the shift to an older population characteristic of Western industrialized society (Roberts & Tracy, 1998). Roberts and Tracy's (1998) review pointed out that there have been relatively few studies of age, work productivity, and health. One study by Ilmarinen (cited in Roberts & Tracy, 1998) found three domains of risk factors that either singly or in combination increased the likelihood of a decline in work capacity. The first domain was work content; the common element among these risk factors was physical demands. The second domain was the nature of the work environment, which included accident hazards, extreme temperatures or changes in temperature, and general physical working conditions. The third domain was psychosocial factors, including role conflict, poor supervision, fear of failure, time pressure, lack of control, lack of development, and lack of recognition. There was an additive effect of multiple risk factors, but it appeared that changes to working conditions could be adjusted to maintain work capacity. However, as the Institute of Medicine's Committee to Assess Training Needs for Occupational Safety and Health Personnel in the United States pointed out, workers over 55 are one third less likely to be injured on the job. If they are injured, though, they take on average two weeks longer to recover than younger workers.

Gender

Women have been in the workforce for decades, with the most recent decade experiencing a slowing in the growth rate. However, by 1998 women accounted for 46% of the labor force. Although there may be some unique work environment factors that put women at increased risk for ill-health such as exposure to radiation, a major focus of research has been on work–family issues. This may reflect the fact that, as of 1998, 72.2% of women participating in the labor force had children with 62.2% of women participating in the labor force having children under 3 years of age (*Bureau of Labor Statistics Current Population Survey,* 1998). Flexible working arrangements (e.g., flexiplace, flexitime) have been implemented to reduce the work–family conflict; however, these may have generated other stressful working conditions such as disappearing boundaries between work and family (Lewis & Cooper, 1999) or less safe work environments (Fairweather, 1999). These work–family issues have been demonstrated to create stress and thus result in decreased health.

Race and Ethnicity

Paralleling globalization, the U.S. labor force has experienced a change in the racial and ethnic composition of the workforce mirroring changes in the population. Based on the 2000 census, the United States is more diverse both racially and ethnically than ever (Schmitt, 2001) and in some areas white non-Hispanic individuals have become the minority (Purdum, 2001). Therefore, it would be expected that the proportion of white non-Hispanics in the workforce will continue to decline as it has for the past decade (*Bureau of Labor Statistics,* 1998). This increased diversity in the workforce is being reflected within the workplace, with implications for health and human resources. There is a body of research that indicates differential disease rates for different racial and ethnic groups, and although this difference can be explained to a large degree by social economic status some differences remain (Williams, 1999). As an organization's workforce becomes more racially and ethnically diverse there is an increased need for considering alternatives for maintaining health care costs for organizations and potential accommodations for employees with disabilities.

Disabilities

During the past decade since the implementation of the Americans With Disabilities Act (1990), there has been a significant increase in the number of individuals with disabilities in the workplace. It is estimated that between 3% and 20% of the U.S. population is disabled (Andresen et al., 1999), and based on Behavioral Risk Factor Surveillance System data from 1993 to 1997, severe work disability may be on the increase. Andresen et al. (1999), however, noted that people who reported fair to poor health appeared to be decreasing (Andresen et al., 1999). Further analyses of the reasons for limited ability to work were common chronic conditions such as arthritis, back or neck problems, heart problems, and fractures or joint injuries. It is not clear whether any of these conditions were the result of work environment factors, although there is evidence for a link between work stress and musculoskeletal problems including back and neck problems (Griffiths, 1998; Warren, Dillon, Morse, Hall, & Warren, 2000) and heart problems (Bosma, Peter, Siegrist, & Marmot, 1998).

Disability also is related to depressive disorders, resulting in diminished quality of life, economic losses, and increased use of health services (Kouzis & Eaton, 1997). It also has been demonstrated that work impairment from psychiatric disorders indicated by lost workdays is similar across occupations, although effects on reductions in workdays or work cutback days are greater among professional workers (Kessler & Frank, 1997). Kessler and Frank's study (1997), based on the U.S. National Comorbidity Survey, found pure affective disorders, which included depression, were associated with the largest average number of lost work days and work cutback days. They projected this loss of work to be 4 million lost workdays in the United States per year and 20 million work cutback days. Because there is an established link between workplace stressors and depression, it is reasonable to assume that at least some of the lost workdays were a result of the work environment. A study of work-related illness conducted in Great Britain in 1995 estimated 19.5 million lost work days (Griffiths, 1998). Griffiths (1998) also reported 14% of the people in the United Kingdom who retired early did so because of ill-health and part of these ill-health conditions were believed to be the result of working conditions or at least made worse by working conditions. In fact, she reported that an estimated two million people in Great Britain were suffering from a work-related illness in 1990. With continued medical advances, it can be expected that individuals with work disability, whether work-related or not, may be more likely to return to work especially with reasonable accommodations being made by employers (Krause, Dasinger, & Neuhauser, 1998).

Prevention and the Public Health Model

The previous discussion serves to demonstrate the importance of safety and health in the workplace as a public health concern. There are two major schools of thought on prevention: population-based interventions and interventions for individuals at high-risk (Weich, 1997). These two schools set up what has been called the prevention paradox (Rose, 1992). Some people view population-based interventions as wasteful of scarce resources. However, high-risk interventions require knowledge of the causes or etiology of particular illnesses and may be too focused to address the problem. Maclean et al. (2000) indicated that more illness may be prevented by making minor changes for many people than by making major changes for those few who are at high risk. Weich suggested "a high risk approach to prevention on its own is incapable of reducing the prevalence of the common mental disorders to any significant extent" (p. 760). However, there is some support that individual-level intervention (counseling) had clear benefits on employees' well-being, and an organizational-level intervention (increased participation and control) did not (Reynolds, 1997). The public health model actually incorporates both the population-based and at-risk individual-based models of interventions.

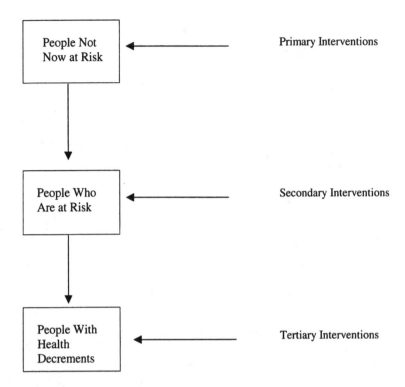

Figure 1.1. A prevention and public health model.

The public health model classifies interventions into three categories: primary interventions, secondary interventions, and tertiary interventions (Schmidt, 1994). Figure 1.1 presents a prevention and public health model showing health risk factors, asymptomatic disorders and diseases, and symptomatic disorders and diseases with the accompanying points of intervention (Wallace & Doebbeling, 1998). Primary interventions focus on prevention among people who are not at risk. This is essentially the population-based model where the intervention is applied to entire populations or groups, although Schmidt (1994) argued that all interventions must have an individual component and therefore needs to incorporate psychological theoretical approaches. Primary interventions are frequently used in health promotion and health education campaigns where the message is sent out to everyone whether they are at-risk or not, such as infomercials broadcast on television and radio about the negative health effects of smoking.

Secondary interventions focus on people who are suspected to be at risk for illness or injury. Such interventions may be administered to groups or individuals. Staying with the health promotion and health education campaigns example, a secondary intervention would be to target the message to a particular group of people who are at-risk, such as smokers. This would be akin to warning messages on packs of cigarettes.

Tertiary interventions focus on those who have experienced a loss in their health and attempt to restore them to health. Tertiary interventions are largely therapeutic and curative in nature. These interventions typically are individual-based, although they can be group-based such as the difference between individual therapy and group therapy. A natural progression from our previous example would be the provision of smoking cessation programs to smokers who had experienced loss of lung capacity.

As stated earlier, occupational health psychology focuses on primary interventions and from a public health and preventive medicine perspective primary prevention is always the preferred point of intervention (Wallace & Doebbeling, 1998). A prevention model is highly appropriate in occupational health psychology because it is systemic in nature and recognizes the life history and multifaceted complexity of many health problems (Ilgen, 1990; Quick, Quick, Nelson, & Hurrell, 1997). These sorts of health problems stand in contrast to the infectious and contagious illnesses for which the traditional public health model was developed, originally to prevent disease epidemics.

Therefore, occupational health psychology interventions address changes to organizations or systems, groups, and individuals. For example, changing the organizational culture to value learning would reduce stress from fear of making mistakes. Because the organizational culture affects everyone in the population, or organization in this case, it would change groups and individuals. The resultant decrease in stress at the individual level would improve the health of employees. Also, encouraging learning and development, which would be consistent with an organizational value for learning, would directly improve health (Mikkelsen, Saksvik, & Ursin, 1998). Learning organizations appear to place a premium on human resources and human development, rather than treating people as simple labor costs (Forward, Beach, Gray, & Quick, 1991; Leonard-Barton, 1992), and it is proposed that this creates healthy people and healthy organizations. Cooper and Cartwright (1994) concluded that healthy organizations will not need secondary and tertiary interventions. However, as Quick (1999) pointed out, there may be times when secondary or tertiary interventions may be needed because primary prevention was not feasible or individual factors create health concerns for only some people.

Several of the chapters in this handbook, especially in Parts I and II, take a primary prevention focus (see the introductory comments for each section for brief descriptions of each of the chapters). These chapters discuss the identification and development of healthy work environments and potential risk factors from which primary prevention strategies can be fashioned.

Occupational health psychology also involves secondary interventions. These interventions would typically focus on groups or individuals that are at risk for injury or illness. An example of an occupational health psychology secondary intervention at the group level might be the redesign of the work environment for a particular unit or department. It might be that the physical layout of a specific hospital unit does not allow the nurses to be within sight of the nursing station from all of the patient rooms. This creates an unsafe working condition because the nurse may not be able to call for help in an emergency without leaving the patient. Remodeling the unit could reduce this physical hazard, improving the health and safety of the nurses by removing the risk factor.

In occupational health psychology it is often difficult to distinguish between primary prevention and secondary interventions as interventions affect many, if not all, individuals in an organization. Therefore, some of the individuals that are affected may be at risk while others are not. However, in both primary and secondary interventions the focus is prevention of ill-health. Several of the chapters in both Parts I and II of this handbook address secondary interventions as well as primary prevention. In fact, some of the chapters in Part III inform secondary interventions.

Occupational health psychology recognizes the needs for tertiary interventions in cases in which individuals are injured, damaged, or are suffering on the job. Tertiary intervention in psychology is primarily the concern of clinical, counseling, and rehabilitation psychology. Occupational health psychology may be able to contribute to the multidisciplinary team in restoring the individual's health especially by modifying organization of work factors that have created the health problem for the individual where possible. Therefore, if an individual is injured or ill, the intervention would be at the individual level and the goal would be to restore the individual's health.

Chapters in Part III discuss some of the illnesses associated with the work environment and present reviews of interventions to restore the health of individuals. Because some of these interventions could target individuals who are not at risk or have not yet exhibited any symptoms of distress, technically they might fall under primary prevention or secondary interventions.

Future Directions

As a new specialty within the science and profession of psychology, occupational health psychology is still emerging. Concurrently many business scholars are recognizing the importance of healthy organizations and healthy people (Frost & Robinson, 1999). Frost and Robinson (1999) argued that emotional suffering, conflict, and pain are often endemic to organizational life for a variety of reasons. They suggest that some individuals serve the role of organizational heroes who metabolize the emotional toxins that may build up within the system often at a price to their own health. Schein (as interviewed by Quick & Gavin, 2000) conceptualized these processes within organizations as potentially homeopathic ones in which disorder and dysfunction are metabolized before they create disability on the part of the individual, the work group, or the organization. Occupational health psychology can help organizations develop immune systems to metabolize the psychosocial and emotional toxins that may build up in work environments. Crafting organizational roles or functions for psychologists and their allies to function as immune system agents at work can contribute to the overall health and vitality of the organization and the people within it. Although there are many ways this might be achieved, two seem especially important. These growth areas concern work and organizational design and organizational health centers.

Luczak (1992) made the case for "good work" design from an industrial engineering perspective. From an occupational health psychology perspective, the implications of his argument are that health and safety issues must be considered on the front end of work, job, and organizational design efforts. Luczak (1992) suggested that the traditional approach to the design of work, jobs, and organizations is technocentric in nature. That is, it places technology at the center of the design process with careful deliberation over economic considerations. The implication of this approach is that people are expected to accommodate and adjust themselves to the characteristics of the work environment. In contrast, Luczak's "good work" design approach is anthropocentric in nature, placing the individual at the center of the design process. This alternative view of work, job, and organizational design is highly consistent with the emphasis we have placed on primary prevention interventions. Thus, the design of work, jobs, and organizations should be healthy and adaptive for the people who enliven them with their work efforts. This direction for occupational health psychology requires collaboration with engineers and managers for it to be effective.

A second direction for occupational health psychology is through the pioneering concept of an organizational health center. This concept places a psychologist on the staff of a senior organizational leader to oversee the mental health and behavioral well-being of people throughout the organization. This elevates health and safety to the top levels in the organization. Adkins (1999) conceptualized the organizational health center as a mechanism for promoting organizational health, with its positive consequences for individual health and well-being. She pioneered the concept at the Sacramento Air Logistics Center, McClellan Air Force Base, California, during the 1990s, with the functions being prevention and intervention, training and development, and research, surveillance, and evaluation. The concept was adapted for the San Antonio Air Logistics Center, Kelly Air Force Base, Texas, to help with the largest federal industrial closure effort in U.S. national history. Preliminary indications have shown benefits in lives saved (i.e., only 1 suicide in a transferred workforce of 12,000 compared to 20 suicides in a comparable transferred industrial workforce of 8000; a .08/1000 rate compared to a 2.5/1000 rate), workplace violence prevented (i.e., no incidents), and costs avoided (i.e., more than $30 million in cost avoidance; Quick & Klunder, 2000). The cost-avoidance estimate is based on a total cost of $80,000 for each employee complaint processed by the U.S. Air Force. Using this case estimator and the number of cases expected during this closure period, civilian personnel found the number of actual cases to be 25% below what they estimated. The concept has resulted in the vice-commander of the Air Force Materiel Command placing a senior, active duty psychologist on his staff to oversee organizational health center activities.

Both the "good work" design efforts of Luczak (1992) and the organizational health center are potential mechanisms to metabolize the psychosocial and emotional toxins that may build up in work environments. In addition, both of these approaches can go beyond the prevention of illness and injury to the promotion of health within the organization. Also, these approaches clarify the importance of occupational health psychology's multidisciplinary approach to developing and maintaining healthy people and healthy organizations. It may be that these two directions are not mutually exclusive and the practice of occupational health psychology will evolve to incorporate both approaches.

Although there is a considerable empirical base for crafting interventions that enhance organizational and employee health, more research and better methodologies are needed. Several of the teams formed around the priority areas of the U.S. National Occupational Research Agenda (NIOSH, 2001) focus on the need for improved measurement and intervention methodologies as well as the need for surveillance and monitoring systems to identify potential risk factors associated with the organization of work. The chapters in Part IV address some of these issues, as do some of the other chapters (such as chapters 3, 4, 6, 9, 12, 14, and 16) in the handbook.

Conclusion

Theory and research have not fully integrated job and work design with employee health nor have studies directly addressed the linkages between employee health and organizational health. The practice of occupational health psychology requires a sound scientific basis for developing healthy organizations and healthy people. To this end, more theoretical development and supporting research is needed to define health not just as the absence of illness but as something more. Perhaps the efforts of positive psychology to understand optimum human functioning and happiness (Seligman & Csikszentmihalyi, 2000) has implications for occupational safety and health and the design of primary interventions to promote health in the workplace. Seligman (1998) chided psychology for focusing on disease to the exclusion of working toward building strength and resilience in people. It appears that occupational health psychology has heard this call and, as indicated in several of the chapters in this handbook, there is growing recognition that occupational health psychology is concerned with creating healthy people and healthy organizations, not just the prevention of injury and illness.

References

Adkins, J. A. (1999). Promoting organizational health: The evolving practice of occupational health psychology. *Professional Psychology: Research and Practice, 30*(2), 129–137.

Americans With Disabilities Act of 1990. (1990). Pub. L. No. 101-336.

Andresen, E. M., Prince-Caldwell, A., Akinci, F., Brownson, C. A., Hagglund, K., Jackson-Thompson, J., & Crocker, R. (1999). The Missouri disability epidemiology and health project. *American Journal of Preventive Medicine, 16,* 63–71.

Aronsson, G. (1999). Influence of worklife on public health. *Scandinavian Journal of Work Environment Health, 25*(6), 597–604.

Benach, J., Fernando, G. B., Platt, S., Diez-Roux, A., & Muntaner, C. (2000). The health-damaging potential of new types of flexible employment: A challenge for public health researchers. *American Journal of Public Health, 90*(8), 1316–1317.

Berkman, L. F., & Kawachi, I. (Eds.). (2000). *Social epidemiology.* New York: Oxford University Press.

Bosma, H., Peter, R., Siegrist, J., & Marmot, M. (1998). Two alternative job stress models and the risk of coronary heart disease. *American Journal of Public Health, 88*(1), 68–74.

Bureau of Labor Statistics Current Population Survey, March Supplements. (1998). Washington, DC: U.S. Department of Labor.

Burke, R. J., & Nelson, D. (1998). Mergers and acquisitions, downsizing, and privatization: A North American perspective. In M. K. Gowing & J. D. Kraft & J. C. Quick (Eds.), *The new organizational reality: Downsizing, restructuring, and revitalization* (pp. 21–54). Washington, DC: American Psychological Association.

Cooper, C. L., & Cartwright, S. (1994). Healthy mind; Healthy organization—A proactive approach to occupational stress. *Human Relations, 47*(4), 455.

Cox, T. (1997). Workplace health promotion. *Work & Stress, 11*(1), 1–5.

de Vries, M. F. R. K., & Balasz, K. (1997). The downside of downsizing. *Human Relations, 50,* 11–50.

Fairweather, N. B. (1999). Surveillance in employment: The case of teleworking. *Journal of Business Ethics, 22*(39–49).

Forward, G. E., Beach, D. E., Gray, D. A., & Quick, J. C. (1991). Mentofacturing: A vision for American industrial excellence. *Academy of Management Executive, 5,* 32–44.

Frost, P., & Robinson, S. (1999). The toxic handler. *Harvard Business Review, 77,* 97–106.

Frumkin, H. (1998). Free-trade agreements. In J. M. Stellman (Ed.), *Encyclopaedia of occupational health and safety* (Vol. I, pp. 20.13–20.17). Geneva: International Labour Office.

Griffiths, A. (1998). Work-related illness in Great Britain. *Work & Stress, 12*(1), 1–5.

Ilgen, D. R. (1990). Health issues at work: Opportunities for industrial/organizational psychology. *American Psychologist, 45,* 273–283.

Jahoda, M. (1982). *Employment and unemployment: A social psychological analysis.* Cambridge: Cambridge University Press.

Kessler, R. C., & Frank, R. G. (1997). The impact of psychiatric disorders on work loss days. *Psychological Medicine, 27,* 861–873.

Kompier, M. A. J. (1996). Job design and well-being. In M. J. Schabracq, J. A. M. Winnubst, & C. L. Cooper (Eds.), *Handbook of work and health psychology* (pp. 349–368). New York: John Wiley & Sons.

Kouzis, A. C., & Eaton, W. W. (1997). Psychopathology and the development of disability. *Social Psychiatry Psychiatric Epidemiology, 32,* 379–386.

Krause, N., Dasinger, L. K., & Neuhauser, F. (1998). Modified work and return to work: A review of the literature. *Journal of Occupational Rehabilitation, 8*(2), 113–139.

Leonard-Barton, D. (1992). The factory as a learning laboratory. *Sloan Management Review, 34,* 23–39.

Levi, L., Sauter, S. L., & Shimomitsu, T. (1999). Work-related stress—It's time to act. *Journal of Occupational Health Psychology, 4*(4), 394–396.

Lewis, S., & Cooper, C. L. (1999). The work–family research agenda in changing contexts. *Journal of Occupational Health Psychology, 4*(4), 382–393.

Luczak, H. (1992). "Good work" design: An ergonomic, industrial engineering perspective. In J. C. Quick, L. R. Murphy, & J. J. Hurrell, Jr. (Eds.), *Stress & well-being at work: Assessments and interventions for occupational mental health* (pp. 96–112). Washington, DC: American Psychological Association.

Maclean, L. M., Plotnikoff, R. C., & Moyer, A. (2000). Transdisciplinary work with psychology from a population health perspective: An illustration. *Journal of Health Psychology, 5*(2), 173–181.

Mikkelsen, A., Saksvik, P. O., & Ursin, H. (1998). Job stress and organizational learning climate. *International Journal of Stress Management, 5*(4), 197–209.

Miles, M. B. (1965). Planned change and organizational health: Figure and ground. In F. D. Carver & T. J. Sergiovanni (Eds.), *Organizations and human behavior: Focus on schools* (pp. 375–391). New York: McGraw-Hill.

National Institute for Occupational Safety and Health (NIOSH). (2001). *National occupational research agenda: Update 2001* (DHHS Publication No. 2001-147). Washington, DC: U.S. Government Printing Office.

Nutbeam, D. (1990). Health promotion glossary. *Health Promotion International, 13*(4), 349–364.

Purdum, T. S. (2001, March 3). Non-Hispanic Whites a minority, California census figures show. *New York Times,* pp. A1, A16.

Quick, J. C. (1999). Occupational health psychology: The convergence of health and clinical psychology with public health and preventive medicine in an organizational context. *Professional Psychology: Research and Practice, 30*(2), 123–128.

Quick, J. C., Camara, W. J., Hurrell, J. J., Johnson, J., V., Piotrkowski, C. S., Sauter, S. L., & Spielberger, C. D. (1997). Introduction and historical overview. *Journal of Occupational Health Psychology, 2*(1), 3–6.

Quick, J. C., & Gavin, J. H. (2000). The new frontier: Edgar Schein on organizational therapy. *Academy of Management Executive, 14,* 31–44.

Quick, J. C., & Klunder, C. (2000). Preventive stress management at work: The case of San Antonio Air Logistics Center (AFMC). *Proceedings of the Eleventh International Congress on Stress.* Yonkers, NY: American Institute of Stress.

Quick, J. C., Quick, J. D., Nelson, D. L., & Hurrell, J. J., Jr. (1997). *Preventive stress management in organizations.* Washington, DC: American Psychological Association.

Raphael, D., Steinmetz, B., Renwick, R., Rootman, I., Brown, I., Sehdev, H., Phillips, S., & Smith, T. (1999). The community quality of life project: A health promotion approach to understanding communities. *Health Promotion International, 14*(3), 197–209.

Reynolds, S. (1997). Psychological well-being at work: Is prevention better than cure? *Journal of Psychosomatic Research, 43*(1), 93–102.

Roberts, A., & Tracy, C. S. (1998). Health and productivity of older workers. *Scandinavian Journal of Work Environment Health, 24*(2), 85–97.

Rose, G. (1992). *The strategy of preventive medicine.* Oxford: Oxford University Press.

Rosen, R. H. (1986). *Healthy companies.* New York: American Management Association.

Safe Work in the 21st Century: Education and Training Needs for the Next Decade's Occupational Safety and Health Personnel. (2000). Washington, DC: Institute of Medicine, National Academy Press.

Sauter, S. L., Hurrell, J. J., Fox, H. R., Tetrick, L. E., & Barling, J. (1999). Occupational health psychology: An emerging discipline. *Industrial Health, 37,* 199–211.

Schein, E. H. (1990). Organizational culture. *American Psychologist, 45*(2), 109–111.

Schmidt, L. R. (1994). A psychological look at public health: Contents and methodology. *International Review of Health Psychology, 3,* 3–36.

Schmitt, E. (2001, April 1). U.S. now more diverse, ethnically and racially. *New York Times,* p. A20.

Schneider, D. L., Camara, W. J., Tetrick, L. E., & Stenberg, C. R. (1999). Training in occupational health psychology: Initial efforts and alternative models. *Professional Psychology: Research and Practice, 30*(2), 138–142.

Seligman, M. E. P. (1998, Jan.). Building human strength: Psychology's forgotten mission. *APA Monitor, President's Column.* Retrieved January 18, 2002, from www.apa.org/monitor/jan98/pres.html.

Seligman, M. E. P., & Csikszentmihalyi, M. (2000). Positive psychology: An introduction. *American Psychologist, 55,* 5–14.

Tetrick, L. E. (2000). Linkages between organizational restructuring and employees' well-being. *Journal of Tokyo Medical University, 58,* 357–363.

U.S. DHHS-PHS. (1990). *Healthy People 2000: National health promotion and disease prevention objectives.* Washington, DC: National Academy of Sciences.

Wall, T. D., & Jackson, P. R. (1995). New manufacturing initiatives and shopfloor job design. In A. Howard (Ed.), *The changing nature of work* (pp. 139–174). San Francisco: Jossey-Bass.

Wallace, R. B., & Doebbeling, B. N. (1998). *Maxcy-Rosenau-Last public health & preventive medicine* (14th ed.). Stamford, CT: Appleton & Lange.

Warren, N., Dillon, C., Morse, T., Hall, C., & Warren, A. (2000). Biomechanical, psychosocial, and organizational risk factors for WRMSD population-based estimates from the Connecticut upper-extremity surveillance project (CUSP). *Journal of Occupational Health Psychology, 5*(1), 164–181.

Weich, S. (1997). Prevention of the common mental disorders: A public health perspective. *Psychological Medicine, 27,* 757–764.

Williams, D. R. (1999). Race, socioeconomic status, and health: The added effects of racism and discrimination. In N. E. Adler, M. Marmot, B. S. McEwen, & J. Stewart (Eds.), *Socioeconomic status and health in industrial nations: Social, psychological, and biological pathways. Annals of the New York Academy of Sciences* (Vol. 896, pp. 173–188). New York: New York Academy of Science.

2

A History of Occupational Health Psychology

Julian Barling and Amanda Griffiths

Interest in questions about occupational health psychology is by no means a recent phenomenon. The question of how workplace practices and policies, supervision, and leadership affect employees' physical and psychological well-being has attracted a considerable amount of interest for much of the twentieth century. Recognition of the importance of the more intangible aspects of work and their effects on individual health, both psychological and physical, began to emerge in the nineteenth century, particularly after the Industrial Revolution. At that time, psychology was only a fledgling discipline; it was largely confined to purely experimental matters, making little contribution to applied issues. However, individuals from disciplines with a more substantial history—such as philosophy, politics, sociology, art, and literature—had begun to air concerns about the impact of the changing world of work on employees' physical and psychological health. The strange and dehumanizing world of factories and offices began to appear not only in the sociological and political commentaries of that time, but also in novels throughout much of Europe in the late nineteenth and early twentieth centuries, for example, in the writings of authors such as Kafka.

In this chapter, we trace the development of occupational health psychology in the twentieth century. In doing so, we take the position that the interactions between people, ideas, events, and institutions are critical. We will trace various events throughout the twentieth century and note how they influenced what today we refer to as occupational health psychology. We will also examine some of the institutions that have had a critical impact on the development of occupational health psychology. Throughout, we will introduce some of the people whose research, ideas, and personal efforts helped to create occupational health psychology as a recognizable

Financial support from the Social Sciences and Humanities Research Council of Canada to the first author is gratefully acknowledged. The second author acknowledges helpful correspondence from many colleagues in Europe, particularly from members of the European Academy of Occupational Health Psychology.

discipline and who may have begun to make a difference to the lives of working people.

One of the first to voice concern, in the mid-nineteenth century, was Friedrich Engels in *The Condition of the Working Class in England* (1845/1987), first published in German. He described in detail the physical and psychological health problems suffered by workers from many different trades. He believed the origins of these problems to be in the organization of work and its associated social and physical environments. Karl Marx subsequently wrote about the horrific ways in which industrial capitalism exploited employees in *Das Kapital* (1867/1999), the first volume of which he published himself. He famously described the "alienation" of workers when treated as commodities within a capitalist economic system where workplaces were increasingly characterized by specialization and division of labor. Many in Europe who subsequently became interested with the health effects of work organization have acknowledged an intellectual debt to both Marx and Engels: Both of the works referred to previously are still in print and widely read today.

However, despite these concerns, a considerable period of time elapsed before the effects of the organization of work (as opposed to the physical working environment) on health were subject to serious scientific attention. A more substantial investigation of the nature of the relationship between health and work from a psychological perspective began to emerge in publications from Northern Europe and the United States in the mid-twentieth century. This occurred partly as a result of the cross-fertilization of ideas between the disciplines of medicine, psychology, sociology, and management. It could be argued that it was from these developments that the discipline of occupational health psychology, as we now know it, emerged.

Writing a history of any newly emerging field presents particular challenges, notably in attempting to document the contribution of specific individuals or events. With the benefit of more hindsight—perhaps a century or two rather than a few decades—one might make a more informed judgment. But even 200 years may not be enough. Chou En-Lai, the former Chinese leader, when asked in the late 1970s for his opinion on the impact of the French Revolution (1789), is reputed to have responded, "I don't know. It's too soon to tell." It is clear that tracing influential early developments in an area as new as occupational health psychology presents an intriguing challenge, but one with which we nonetheless readily engage.

There are two further notes of caution. First, a significant proportion of the subject matter included in this analysis is largely restricted to that published in, or translated into, English. Second, perceptions of important conceptual frameworks in the discipline vary between North America and Europe and between the various countries of Europe. This chapter may be ambitious in trying to reconcile many different viewpoints and distill them in so few pages. In many ways, therefore, what is offered is *a* history rather than *the* history of occupational health psychology.

Early Developments in the United States

Although many developments relating to occupational health psychology throughout the twentieth century were positive from the perspective of employees, one of the earliest events in the United States was certainly not. We refer to the seminal work of Frederick Taylor whose work, *The Principles of Scientific Management* (1911), was to attract considerable attention for the remainder of the century. Taylor, initially a machine-shop foreman, proposed that low productivity was partly the result of management's ignorance of working processes. This ignorance allowed workers to deceive managers, to control those processes, and thus to determine the speed of work. He advocated, in the interests of financial economy, that tasks should be carefully analyzed, simplified, compartmentalized, and standardized and that worker influence should be removed. In effect this reduced the amount of skill required to complete tasks and removed all worker control and discretion. These principles appeared to make economic sense to many managers at the time and had a significant impact on management practice both inside and outside the United States. "Scientific management" was a critical development in the emergence of occupational health psychology because of its two inherent assumptions. First, as a forerunner of the industrial engineering approach, it separated "thinking" about work from "doing" work. Specifically, one class of employees, industrial engineers, would have the specialized skills (and as it later transpired, the organizational power) that would allow them to design the work of other people, whose only role was to perform whatever tasks were assigned to them. In this sense, scientific management may represent the first concerted effort to de-skill work. Second, scientific management demanded that consideration of employee emotions at work be eliminated, on the assumption that they interfered with productive work. As we shall see, at the end of the twentieth century, occupational health psychology would be embracing the very opposite of these two concepts.

Additional research in the United States that had a widespread influence in many countries included the experiments carried out in the 1920s at the Western Electric Company at Hawthorne (Mayo, 1933; Roethlisberger & Dickson, 1939). Using a Tayloristic framework, these studies explored the relationships between various working conditions (e.g., lighting, wages, or rest breaks) and productivity. But whatever changes were made, productivity usually rose. It was eventually concluded that receiving special attention, being aware that they were the focus of research, and guessing what the researchers were investigating affected the way workers behaved. It became apparent that workers' perceptions of, and feelings about, what was happening to them were important (the antithesis of the Tayloristic emphasis on removing emotions from the workplace). This effect was henceforth named the "Hawthorne effect." The significance of this development lay in the recognition of the importance of "human relations"— the social, psychological, and cultural aspects of work. It gradually became apparent that although Taylor's principles may have appeared to managers to make economic sense, "scientific management" was not necessarily followed by increases in productivity and was in fact often associated with negative attitudes and poor health outcomes. Two subsequent investigations into the physical and mental health problems experienced by automobile workers in the United States substantiated this view (Chinoy, 1955; Kornhauser, 1965). Such findings were also being documented in Europe. Before noting these, however, it is worth mentioning two other significant theoretical developments for occupational health psychology that arose from quite different streams of research in the United States. First, from a perspective of personality and clinical psychology, Abraham Maslow published his theory of self-actualization (1943), and some 20 years later applied it specifically to work organizations (1965). Although it has been generally underappreciated from the perspective of occupational health psychology, Maslow stated explicitly that only individuals who are psychologically healthy could be motivated to work, arguing that repressive environments, including work environments, would inhibit individuals from reaching their fullest potential.

Perhaps one of the other most salient developments in the twentieth century was the advent of job design theories. Credit for much of the initial thinking about those working conditions that influence job performance and mental health can be given to Frederick Herzberg (1966). He suggested that motivation and job satisfaction could be improved by improving people's work—for example, by enriching their jobs through increased skill use, challenge, or recognition. Although some of his research has been subsequently criticized, these basic suggestions about job enrichment remain useful, and his ideas stimulated a considerable amount of research on this topic. Some years later, Hackman and Oldham (1976, 1980) provided a more specific "job characteristics" model, rejuvenating research and thinking on the topic of job design.

Many other important theoretical contributions in the early development of occupational health psychology and social psychology are acknowledged to have originated at the University of Michigan. In 1948, Rensis Likert had established the Institute for Social Research (ISR) at the University of Michigan, and the institute's influence was to be felt for the rest of the century. It is the oldest institute for interdisciplinary research in the social sciences in the United States, currently employing about 350 individuals. Some of its earlier substantive contributions included Quinn and Staines's (1977) "quality of employment survey," and House's (1981) research on work stress and social support. The early theoretical contributions (e.g., person–environment fit) of what was known as the "Michigan School" (e.g., Caplan, Cobb, French, van Harrison, & Pinneau, 1975; Kahn, Wolfe, Quinn, Snoek, & Rosenthal, 1964; Katz & Kahn, 1966) was widely acknowledged in Europe. More recently, the influence of the ISR is maintained through, for example, its research program on the effects of unemployment, as well as on the factors that influence reemployment (e.g., Caplan, Vinoker, Price, & van Ryn, 1989; Kessler, Turner, & House, 1987; Vinokur, Schul, Vuori, & Price, 2000).

Early Influences From Europe

Research in Europe was demonstrating the dangers of scientific management. In Britain, for example, the negative effects of the disregard for workers' psychological well-being in job design in coal mines was explored in some detail by researchers from the Tavistock Institute of Human Relations in London (Trist & Bamforth, 1951). Trist (a psychiatrist) and Bamforth (a former miner with 18 years experience at the coal-face) described in considerable detail the psychological and social consequences of a particular change in coal-mining methods. They explored the relationship between the health and productivity of miners as a function of the social structure of the work system. Miners' work had changed from a "whole" task, skilled, autonomous system, to a mechanized, fractured system with isolated but heavily interdependent groups of workers. In this new system, miners were observed to experience high levels of anxiety, anger, and depression—problems that had previously been largely absent. Major disruptions in social support also were observed. Trist and Bamforth concluded (1951, p. 41) that it was "difficult to see how these problems can be solved effectively without restoring responsible autonomy to primary groups within the system and ensuring that each of these groups has a satisfying sub-whole as its work task, and some scope for flexibility in workplace." They concluded that the nature of demand and employee participation in decision-making were important for employee health.

At this time, although it is hard to trace, there was much cross-fertilization of ideas about work organization in the Nordic countries (e.g., Scandinavia and Finland). Many Nordic academics read fluently in several languages, including English. Trist and his colleagues from London, notably Fred Emery, collaborated closely with a Norwegian, Einar Thorsrud, who is often regarded as the founding figure of what would now be recognized as "occupational health psychology" in Norway. Thorsrud and Emery's empirical research on the empowering of work groups (essentially, an anti-Tayloristic approach) and their theory of psychological job demands were widely read and inspired many researchers in Denmark and Sweden (Thorsrud & Emery, 1970). Similarly, the sociologist Sverre Lysgård's writings on workers' collectives (1961) was influential. Also in Norway, a separate research group led by Holger Ursin began publishing work on stress-related psych-physiological mechanisms (Ursin, Baade, & Levine, 1978; Ursin, 1980). In Finland there had been a long-term interest in the mental health outcomes of work design. The Finnish Institute of Occupational Health, for example, acknowledged major influences from the United States, Germany, and the United Kingdom, with some of their psychologists visiting Trist and colleagues in London in the 1950s. In 1974, Finland employed its first practicing occupational health psychologist in the UPM Kymmene paper mill. In Denmark, an interest was also flourishing in the importance of working conditions and related interventions: Indeed, the translation of "occupational health psychology" in Danish is "work environment psychology." Much of the Danish interest was inspired by work in Sweden, where major direct challenges to Taylor's ideas are widely acknowledged to have emerged in the 1970s and 1980s, much of it published in English. We return to this work in more detail below.

Moving ahead for a moment, the publications that have probably had the most impact in occupational health psychology, and that demonstrated to a wide audience the inadvisability of adopting a Tayloristic approach to job design, were Robert Karasek's (1979) paper on job demands, job decision latitude, and mental health, and his subsequent paper on the importance of such factors for cardiovascular health in a prospective study of Swedish men (Karasek, Baker, Marxer, Ahlbom, & Theorell, 1981). A third publication, the influential book that Karasek coauthored with Töres Theorell titled *Healthy Work* (1990) brought the subject matter to an even wider audience. The historical importance of the job demands–job control theory lies not so much in the subsequent attempts at its validation by other workers but in the enormous amount of research that later focused on those psychosocial aspects of work that might be critical for psychological and physical health. Within a decade of the appearance of *Healthy Work,* research findings were suggesting that the factors responsible for psychological and physical health were the same as those associated with higher levels of job performance (e.g., Parker & Wall, 1998; Wall, Corbett, Martin, Clegg, & Jackson, 1990).

The work of Karasek and Theorell did not emerge in a vacuum. It followed directly from the strong tradition of research on, and thought about, work design and health in the Nordic countries. In those countries, activities typical of traditional industrial/organizational psychology, such as personnel selection and performance assessment, had been criticized (largely by the labor movement) and had not prospered, but research and practice concerned with work reform and worker well-being flourished.

It is widely acknowledged in Europe that many of the major intellectual developments that heralded interest in the relationship between work and health from a psychological and psychophysiological perspective, and that provided an empirical base for such concerns, emerged in Sweden and in Norway. Karasek and Theorell had worked, separately, in two key institutions in Sweden that had a major impact on the early development of occupational health psychology and under the guidance of two influential figures: Bertil Gardell (a psychologist) at the University of Stockholm, and Lennart Levi (a physician) at the Karolinska Institute in Stockholm.

Gardell is widely recognized in Europe as one of the founding figures of work and organizational psychology. He worked at the University of Stockholm from the 1960s, becoming professor of psychology, studying work reform. He described in detail how work (e.g., as advocated by Taylor) could lead to "alienation" and withdrawal, and published widely on the relationship between technology, autonomy, participation, and mental health (e.g., Gardell, 1971, 1977) and on the relationship between work reform research and social change (Gardell & Gustavsen, 1980). In a series of empirical studies, he and others in Sweden (e.g., Gunnar Aronsson and Gunn Johansson) established credibly throughout the 1970s and 1980s that, among other matters, machine-paced work, lack of control at work, monotonous work, and fragmented and isolated work all had adverse effects (e.g., Johansson, Aronsson, & Lindström, 1978). The importance of worker participation and control were particularly central to many of these investigations: Aronsson (1987) later published a book on the concept of control in work psychology.

Many of Gardell's ideas, before and after his unfortunate early death, were developed further by his colleagues and researchers in Sweden. Marianne Frankenhaeuser was one such collaborator, among the first to explore the psychophysiological mechanisms involved in the relationship between working conditions and ill-health as a means of broadening the "scientific" case for job redesign. She and her colleagues investigated the neuroendocrinological changes associated with various environmental conditions such as understimulation, low control, monotonous activity, or fast-paced work (Frankenhaeuser & Gardell, 1976; Frankenhaeuser, Lundberg, & Forsman, 1980; Frankenhaeuser & Johansson, 1986).

Also in Stockholm in the 1950s, Lennart Levi, a physician, had created his "stress" laboratory as part of the Karolinska Institute. He had previously spent some time working with Hans Selye in Montreal and his initial focus, largely experimental, was on the physiological aspects of stress. However, he gradually adopted a multidisciplinary focus, and began working with psychologists and sociologists in the 1960s on large-scale studies, some with Aubrey Kagan, of working conditions and their associations with various health indicators. Levi also explored the psychophysiological mechanisms associated with "stressful" conditions. He was influential in international circles, advancing the importance of the psychosocial work environment and systems-level thinking for worker health at a time when such notions, and social medicine in general, were not widely accepted by the medical establishment (Levi, 1971). Researchers at the Karolinska Institute conduct many studies on work stress as well as on stress in general. Levi later founded the Institute for Psychosocial Factors and Health, an independent government institute associated with the Karolinska Institute, in 1981, and became its first director.

Töres Theorell, one of Levi's younger colleagues, was a specialist in clinical cardiology with an initial interest in the role of life events. He went on to make a significant impact on the field, both with Karasek and with colleagues at the Karolinska Institute. On Levi's retirement in 1996, Theorell took over as director of the institute. The results of his work partly inspired The Whitehall Study, a longitudinal study on the relationship between working conditions and cardiovascular disease, carried out by Michael Marmot and colleagues in the United Kingdom. Marmot and Theorell pioneered the notion that differences in the psychosocial work environment may be partly responsible for the association between social class and the incidence of coronary heart disease (Marmot & Theorell, 1988).

Unemployment and Nonwork

So far, we have examined the issue of the organization of work and its effects on mental or physical health. A comprehensive study of the field of occupational health psychology today, however, would include not just a focus on psychosocial factors at work but also an understanding of the effects of nonwork and unemployment. Although research on the interdependence of work and nonwork has been conducted since the early 1980s, there is substantially more research on this topic than on unemployment. The primary focus of this research endeavor has been on the mutual effects of work on family, and family on work (Barling, 1990). In contrast, the effects of unemployment have been the focus of research for at least seven decades, with interest peaking after bouts of high unemployment.

The contribution of Marie Jahoda was substantial throughout most of this period. Jahoda's earliest research focused on the effects of unemployment on a particular group in Europe, the Marienthal community, which had previously experienced sustained industrial development (Jahoda, Lazarsfeld, & Zeisel, 1933). Much later, she provided a theory of the psychological meaning both of employment and unemployment, reasoning that neither of them exerts uniform effects; instead it is the quality of the employment and unemployment experience that is critical (Jahoda, 1982). Remarkably, her contribution did not end there, as was evident from her review of the effects of economic recession on psychological well-being in 1988, some 55 years after her initial research findings were first published. Indeed, on her death on April 28, 2001, at the age of 94, the byline of one obituary noted, "Psychologist who examined the corrosive effects of unemployment" (*Professor Marie Jahoda*, 2001).

Separately, research was being conducted within Australia and the United States. Although no individual researcher matched the length of Jahoda's career, the findings of Stan Kasl and Sidney Cobb (Kasl & Cobb, 1970; Kasl, Gore, & Cobb, 1975) helped to legitimize the study of unemployment in the United States, as did those of Peter Warr in the United Kingdom (1987). Similarly, like Jahoda's (1982) theory, the archival analyses of the Great Depression by Glen Elder (1974) helped to dispel the notion that unemployment exerted uniform negative effects. Research by Boris Kabanoff, Norman Feather, and Gordon O'Brien (e.g., Feather, 1990; O'Brien & Feather, 1990) advanced the breadth of occupational health psychology by providing a comprehensive understanding of the nature and effects of both employment and unemployment.

Other Significant Institutions

The U.S. National Institute for Occupational Safety and Health (NIOSH) is widely acknowledged as having played an important role in furthering the cause of occupational health psychology since the early 1990s. NIOSH is mandated by federal law in the United States to conduct research on working conditions that could be hazardous to employee mental or physical well-being. An additional mandate is to make recommendations and disseminate knowledge that could be used to prevent workplace injuries. NIOSH has made three substantial contributions to the field. First, Sauter, Murphy, and Hurrell (1990) published a seminal paper, based on extensive consultations with researchers, practitioners, and policy makers, that presented a comprehensive national strategy both to promote and to protect the psychological well-being of workers. Second, NIOSH entered into a cooperative agreement with the American Psychological Association (APA) to fund the initial development of graduate training in occupational health psychology in the United States. Several universities in the United States (e.g., Bowling Green State University, Clemson University, Kansas State University, Tulane University, and the Universities of Houston and Minnesota) received funding toward the design and delivery of modules on this subject. Third, NIOSH and the APA joined forces in the 1990s to host four major international conferences on the broad topic of work and well-being. These took place in 1990, 1992, 1995, and 1999. The number of attendees increased approximately ten-fold within the decade, as did the number of countries represented; at the 1999 conference, representatives from 25 countries participated. These conferences instituted something of a tradition: At the time this chapter goes to press, the next such conference is scheduled to be held in Toronto in March 2003.

In many countries, distinct institutions can be identified that have been influential in the development of occupational health psychology. We have already mentioned some from the United States and Sweden. But there are others. In the United Kingdom, for example, at least three separate research groups made an important contribution in early developments.

The Institute of Work, Health & Organisations, I-WHO, (formerly the Stress Research Group, and then the Centre for Organisational Health & Development) at the University of Nottingham has had a commitment to occupational health psychology as a distinct discipline since its beginnings in the early 1970s. Under the direction of Tom Cox, it made a notable contribution to the development of research, particularly in the fields of work stress (e.g., Cox, 1978) and workplace violence (e.g., Cox & Leather, 1994). Cox's approach was driven by transactional theories such as that of Richard Lazarus (e.g., Lazarus, 1966; Lazarus & Folkman, 1984) that highlighted the importance of cognitive and perceptual processes in people's reactions to their environments. However, the focus of his early work was more on the psychophysiological processes that might mediate between various aspects of the environment and health. Cox and his colleagues moved on to apply theory in the workplace via interventions using a risk-management paradigm (Cox, Griffiths, & Rial-Gonzalez, 2000). They acknowledged the significant influence of the Nordic emphasis on design, prevention, and systems-level—rather than individual-level—analysis. I-WHO has also been a leader in the field of postgraduate education in occupational health psychology since 1996 when it established the first (year-long) master's-level degree in the world devoted entirely to occupational health psychology.

The Institute for Work Psychology at Sheffield (formerly the Social and Applied Psychology Unit) has been one of the longest standing and most highly respected research institutions in the United Kingdom for research and education in work and organizational psychology. It has also made major contributions that are relevant to occupational health psychology, notably in terms of the relationship between work, well-being, and effectiveness (Warr, 1999). Peter Warr's "Vitamin Model" and his work on the relationship between work, well-being, and unemployment (Warr, 1987) were notable early examples, as was Toby Wall's research on the nature and consequences of job redesign (Wall, 1982).

At the University of Manchester Institute for Science and Technology (UMIST), Cary Cooper has promoted the general field of occupational health psychology through the development of a number of broadly based journals, including the *Journal of Organizational Behavior,* by bringing together numerous collections of the works of authors in various areas of occupational psychology as informative and influential edited collections, and by being a prolific and effective publicist for the subject.

There was clearly much activity in various institutions elsewhere in Europe in the 1970s and 1980s that was relevant to occupational health psychology's concerns, but much of what happened then is not as widely known as is deserved, simply because the significant authors operated and published in their native languages. But there is no doubt that some of these individuals have been influential. Winfried Hacker and his colleagues from Dresden (in the former East Germany), for example, undertook much-admired early research on working conditions and the psychophysiology of stress (Hacker, 1978; Hacker & Richter, 1980). There are other relevant contributors (e.g., Johannes Siegrist, also from Germany; Siegrist, 1996); but space precludes further discussion of their contribution. For these omissions, we apologize.

Professional Organizations and Their Activities

Several other recent developments warrant attention, because they point to the emergence of occupational health psychology as an institutionalized, mature discipline. One of these is the publication of two journals that are devoted specifically to occupational health psychology. *Work and Stress* has been edited by Cox at the University of Nottingham since its inception in 1987, and is currently in its 16th year. The *Journal of Occupational Health Psychology* has been published by the APA since 1996, first edited by James Campbell Quick, and from 2000 by Julian Barling. Like other journals, *Work and Stress* and the *Journal of Occupational Health Psychology* provide a forum for researchers and practitioners and for the dissemination of knowledge. The presence of two such international quarterlies lends further support to the notion that occupational health psychology has emerged as a distinct discipline.

The emergence of organizations for scientists and practitioners could be taken as further evidence of maturity of a field. The European Academy of Occupational Health Psychology was established in 1997 by Cox and coworkers in the United Kingdom (Amanda Griffiths), together with colleagues from Sweden (Sten-Olof Brenner, Curt Johansson, and Clemens Weikert) and Denmark (Einar Baldrussen). Its purpose is to promote research, practice, and education in the discipline, and has a separate forum devoted to each of those three endeavors. It hosted its first conference in Sweden in 1999, its second in the United Kingdom in 2000, and its third in Spain in 2001. As with the NIOSH/APA conferences, this tradition is expected to continue: At the time this chapter went to press, a fourth conference is planned in Austria for 2002.

The International Commission on Occupational Health ratified a new Scientific Committee in 1999 on Work Organization and Psychosocial Factors (ICOH-WOPS), with Raija Kalimo from the Finnish Institute of Occupational Health as its first chair and Michiel Kompier from the University of Nijmegen in the Netherlands as its second. Its remit is largely to promote occupational health psychology.

In 2000, an informal International Coordinating Group for Occupational Health Psychology (ICGOHP) was formed, its purpose being to promote and facilitate the development of research, professional practice, and education in occupational health psychology within an international framework. One particular task is the coordination of the scheduling of conferences serving the discipline. Informal meetings take place at major conferences where its role and membership are reviewed. The initial members of the ICGOHP, together with the bodies they represent are, Barling (*Journal of Occupational Health Psychology*), Mike Colligan (NIOSH), Cox (*Work and Stress*), Heather Fox (APA), Griffiths (European Academy of Occupational Health Psychology), Joe Hurrell (NIOSH), Gwendolyn Keita (APA), and Steve Sauter (NIOSH).

The very existence of regular international conferences bringing together researchers in occupational health psychology is another mark of a maturing discipline. In addition to the conference series sponsored by NIOSH and the APA as well as the series sponsored by the European Academy for Occupational Health Psychology, the International Commission on Occupational Health (ICOH) hosted its first special conference on Psychosocial Factors at Work in Copenhagen in 1998, and is planning a second in Japan in 2005. These conferences will be coordinated in the future whenever possible.

Recent Developments

One of the ultimate criteria for the contribution and maturity of occupational health psychology is that some of its central tenets (e.g., the importance of employee control and participation) have become enshrined in government legislation and advice for employers in many countries. The following examples demonstrate the developing situation.

One of the first countries to establish such legislation was Sweden. The Swedish Work Environment Act (1978) specified, among other things, that working methods, equipment, and materials should be adapted to fit people—both from a physiological and a psychological point of view. Sweden's Act of Co-determination (1977) had already given workers influence over job design, production methods, and the work environment, as well as the right to influence major decisions and planning processes via representation at board level (Gardell & Johansson, 1981). Somewhat later, in 1989, the European Commission published their framework directive titled, "Council Framework Directive on the Introduction of Measures to Encourage Improvements in the Safety and Health of Workers at Work" (European Commission, 1989). Every member state of the European Union (EU) was required to translate the requirements of this directive into their own national legislative frameworks by 1992. Major requirements were that employers should assess all major risks to employee health and that employees or their representatives should be consulted on all matters that might affect their health and safety. In the United Kingdom, some of these requirements were already in place, but those that were not were incorporated into the Management of Health & Safety at Work Regulations (1992, 1999). In the Approved Code of Practice for these Regulations (1999), it states, for example, that "employers should increase the control individuals have over the work they are responsible for" and that they should "adapt work to the requirements of the individual (consulting those who will be affected when designing workplaces" (paragraph 30d). In the United States, as mentioned previously, NIOSH advised employers that workers should be given the opportunity to participate in decisions that affect their jobs and task performance (Sauter et al., 1990).

Three workers in the field have received significant recognition in the United Kingdom, in the form of national honors, for their respective services to occupational health. Marmot and Cox received their honors in person from Queen Elizabeth II in 2000. In 2001, Cooper was similarly honored. Awards such as these are exceptional, and provide external confirmation of their recipients' significant contributions.

Given that occupational health psychology is still a newly emerging field, we hope that this brief introduction to its origins—people, ideas, events, and institutions—has demonstrated how far it has come in a short time. Whereas at the beginning of the twentieth century work was designed largely with managers' best interests at heart, increasingly we are witnessing a desire to promote and protect the psychological and physical health of workers themselves, through prevention and job design. If this level of progress continues throughout the twenty-first century, we can be cautiously optimistic that occupational health psychology will make a worthwhile and lasting contribution.

References

Aronsson, G. (1987). *Arbetspsykologi: Stress och kvalifikationsperspektiv* [The concept of control in work psychology]. Lund, Sweden: Studentlitteratur.

Barling, J. U. (1990). *Employment, stress and family functioning.* New York: Wiley.

Caplan, R., Cobb, S., French, J., van Harrison, R., & Pinneau, S. (1975). *Job demands and worker health.* Washington, DC: National Institute for Occupational Safety and Health.

Caplan, R. D., Vinokur, A. D., Price, R. H., & van Ryn, M. (1989). Job seeking, reemployment and mental health: A randomized field experiment in coping with job loss. *Journal of Applied Psychology, 74,* 759–769.

Chinoy, E. (1955). *Automobile workers and the American dream.* Garden City, NJ: Doubleday.

Cox, T. (1978). *Stress.* London: Macmillan.

Cox, T., Griffiths, A., & Rial-Gonzalez, E. (2000). *Research on work-related stress.* Luxembourg: Office for Official Publications of the European Communities, European Agency for Safety & Health at Work.

Cox, T., & Leather, P. (1994). The prevention of violence at work: Application of a cognitive behavioural theory. In C. L. Cooper & I. T. Robertson (Eds.), *International Review of Industrial & Organizational Psychology, 9,* 213–245. Chichester, UK: Wiley & Sons.

Elder, G. H. (1974). *Children of the Great Depression.* Chicago: University of Chicago Press.

Engels, F. (1987). *The condition of the working class in England.* London: Penguin Books. (Original work published 1845)

European Commission. (1989) Council framework directive on the introduction of measures to encourage improvements in the safety and health of workers at work. 89/391/EEC. *Official Journal of the European Communities, 32,* No L183, 1–8.

Feather, N. T. (1990). *The psychological impact of unemployment.* New York: Springer.

Frankenhaeuser, M., & Gardell, B. (1976). Underload and overload in working life: Outline of a multidisciplinary approach. *Journal of Human Stress, 2,* 35–46.

Frankenhaeuser, M., & Johansson, G. (1986). Stress at work: Psychobiological and psychosocial aspects. *International Review of Applied Psychology, 35,* 287–299.

Frankenhaeuser, M., Lundberg, U., & Forsman, L. (1980). Dissociation between sympathetic-adrenal and pituitary-adrenal responses to an achievement situation characterized by high controllability: Comparison between type A and type B males and females. *Biological Psychology, 10,* 79–91.

Gardell, B. (1971). Alienation and mental health in the modern industrial environment. In L. Levi (Ed.), *Society, stress and disease* (Vol. 1, pp. 148–180). Oxford: Oxford University Press.

Gardell, B. (1977). Autonomy and participation at work. *Human Relations, 30,* 515–533.

Gardell, B., & Gustavsen, B. (1980). Work environment research and social change: Current developments in Scandinavia. *Journal of Occupational Behaviour, 1,* 3–17.

Gardell, B., & Johansson, G. (1981). *Working life: A social science contribution to work reform.* Chichester, UK: Wiley & Sons.

Hacker, W. (1978). *Allgemeine arbeits—und ingenieurpsychologie* [General work and engineering psychology]. Bern, Switzerland: Huber.

Hacker, W., & Richter, P. (1980). *Psychische fehlbeanspruchung, psychische ermüdung, monotonie, sättigung und streß* [Psychological mis-strain, psychological fatigue, monotony, satiation, and stress]. Berlin: Deutscher Verlag der Wissenschaften.

Hackman, J. R., & Oldham, G. R. (1976). Motivation through the design of work: Test of a theory. *Organizational Behavior and Human Performance, 16,* 250–279.

Hackman, J. R., & Oldham, G. R. (1980). *Work redesign.* Reading, MA: Addison-Wesley.

Herzberg, F. (1966). *Work and the nature of man.* Cleveland, OH: World.

Jahoda, M. (1982). *Employment and unemployment: A social psychological analysis.* Cambridge: Cambridge University Press.

Jahoda, M. (1988). Economic recession and mental health: Some conceptual issues. *Journal of Social Issues, 44,* 13–24.

Jahoda, M., Lazarsfeld, P. F., & Zeisel, H. (1933). *Marienthal: The sociography of an unemployed community.* London: Tavistock.

Johansson, G., Aronsson, G., & Lindström. B.O. (1978). Social psychological and neuroendocrine stress reactions in highly mechanized work. *Ergonomics, 21(8),* 583–599.

Kahn, R., Wolfe, D. M., Quinn, K. P., Snoek, J. D., & Rosenthal, R. A. (1964). *Organizational stress: Studies in role conflict and ambiguity.* New York: John Wiley & Sons.

Karasek, R. A. (1979). Job demands, job decision latitude, and mental strain: Implications for job redesign. *Administrative Science Quarterly, 24,* 285–307.

Karasek, R. A., Baker, D., Marxer, F., Ahlbom, A., & Theorell, T. (1981). Job decision latitude, job demands, and cardiovascular disease: A prospective study of Swedish men. *American Journal of Public Health, 71,* 694–705.

Karasek, R., & Theorell, T. (1990). *Healthy work: Stress, productivity and the reconstruction of work life.* New York: Basic Books.

Kasl, S. V., & Cobb, S. (1970). Blood pressure changes in men undergoing job loss: A preliminary report. *Psychosomatic Medicine, 32,* 19–38.

Kasl, S. V., Gore, S., & Cobb, S. (1975). The experience of losing a job: Reported changes in health, symptoms and illness behavior. *Psychosomatic Medicine, 37,* 106–122.

Katz, D., & Kahn, R. (1966). *Social psychology of organizations.* New York: Wiley & Sons.

Kessler, R. C., Turner, J. B., & House, J. S. (1987). Intervening processes in the relationship between unemployment and health. *Psychological Medicine, 17,* 949–961.

Kornhauser, A. (1965). *Mental health and the industrial worker.* New York: Wiley & Sons.

Lazarus, R. S. (1966). *Psychological stress and the coping process.* New York: McGraw-Hill.

Lazarus, R. S., & Folkman, S. (1984). *Stress, appraisal and coping.* New York: Springer.

Levi, L. (1971). *Society, stress and disease.* (4 Vols.). Oxford: Oxford University Press.

Lysgård, S. (1961). *Arbeiderkollektivet: En studie i de underordnedes sosiologi* [Workers' collective: A study of the sociology of the subordinated]. Oslo, Bergen: Universitetsforlaget.

Marmot, M. G., & Theorell, T. (1988). Social class and cardiovascular disease: The contribution of work. *International Journal of Health Services, 18,* 659–674.

Marx, K. (1999). *Das Kapital.* Oxford: Oxford University Press. (Originally published in 1867).

Maslow, A. H. (1943). A theory of human motivation. *Psychological Review, 50,* 370–396.

Maslow, A. H. (1965). *Eupsychian management: A journal.* Homewood, IL: Irwin-Dorsey.

Mayo, E. (1933). *The human problems of an industrial civilization.* New York: MacMillan.

O'Brien, G. E., & Feather, N. T. (1990). The relative effects of unemployment and quality of employment on the affect, work values and personal control of adolescents. *Journal of Occupational Psychology, 63,* 151–165.

Parker, S. K., & Wall, T. (1998). *Job and work design.* Thousand Oaks, CA: Sage.

Professor Marie Jahoda. (2001, May 17). www.thetimes.co.uk/article/0,60-203019,00.html.

Quinn, R. P., & Staines, G. L. (1977). *The 1977 quality of employment survey.* Ann Arbor: University of Michigan, Institute for Social Research.

Roethlisberger, F., & Dickson, W. J. (1939). *Management and the worker.* Cambridge, MA: Harvard University Press.

Sauter, S. L., Murphy, L. R., & Hurrell, J. J. (1990). Prevention of work-related psychological disorders: A national strategy proposed by the National Institute for Occupational Safety and Health (NIOSH). *American Psychologist, 45,* 1146–1158.

Siegrist, J. (1996). Adverse health effects of high-effort/low-reward conditions. *Journal of Occupational Health Psychology, 1,* 27–41.

Taylor, F. W. (1911). *The principles of scientific management.* New York: Harper & Brothers.

Thorsrud, E., & Emery, F. E. (1970). *Mot en ny bedriftsorganisasjon* [Toward a new organization of enterprises]. Oslo: Tanum.

Trist, E. L., & Bamforth, K. W. (1951). Some social and psychological consequences of the longwall method of coal-getting. *Human Relations, 14,* 3–38.

Ursin, H. (1980). Personality, activation and somatic health. A new psychosomatic theory. In S. Levine & H. Ursin, (Eds.), *Coping and Health* (pp. 259–279). New York: Plenum Press.

Ursin, H., Baade, E., & Levine, S. (1978). *Psychobiology of stress: A study of coping men.* New York: Academic Press.

Vinokur, A. D., Schul, Y., Vuori, J., & Price, R. H. (2000). Two years after a job loss: Long-term impact of the JOBS program on re-employment and mental health. *Journal of Occupational Health Psychology, 5,* 32–47.

Wall, T. D. (1982). Perspectives on job redesign. In J. E. Kelly & C. W. Clegg (Eds.), *Autonomy and control in the workplace* (pp. 1–20). London: Croom Helm.

Wall, T. D., Corbett, M. J., Martin, R., Clegg, C. W., & Jackson, P. R. (1990). Advanced manufacturing technology, work design and performance: A change study. *Journal of Applied Psychology, 75,* 691–697.

Warr, P. B. (1987). *Work, unemployment, and mental health.* Oxford: Oxford University Press.

Warr, P. B. (1999). *Work, well-being and effectiveness: A history of the MRC/ESRC Social and Applied Psychology Unit.* Sheffield, UK: Sheffield Academic Press.

3

Controlling Occupational Safety and Health Hazards

Michael J. Smith, Ben-Tzion Karsh,
Pascale Carayon, and Frank T. Conway

According to the International Labour Organization (ILO, 1998), about 250 million workers worldwide are injured annually on the job, 160 million suffer from occupational diseases, and approximately 335,000 workers die each year from occupational injuries. In the United States alone, it was estimated that in 1992 the direct costs of occupational injuries and illnesses (e.g., medical, property damage) totaled $65 billion and the indirect costs (e.g., lost earnings, workplace training and restaffing, time delays) totaled $106 billion (Leigh, Markowitz, Fahs, Shin, & Landrigan, 1997). Although agriculture, commercial fishing, construction, and mining surpass manufacturing in the number of fatalities and serious injuries, manufacturing has a higher than average injury rate in developed countries.

This chapter will examine the causes of occupational injuries and illnesses and ways to reduce worker risk. It will provide direction for establishing effective detection and control methods. Additional resources are provided throughout the chapter for more detailed information about the subjects covered.

The Interdisciplinary Nature of Occupational Safety and Health

Occupational health and safety has its roots in several disciplines, including such diverse fields as engineering, toxicology, epidemiology, medicine, sociology, psychology, and economics. Occupational safety and health is a multidisciplinary endeavor requiring knowledge from diverse sources to deal with the interacting factors of people, technology, the work environment, and the organization of work activities. Any successful approach for the prevention of injuries and health disorders must recognize the need to deal with these diverse factors using the best available tools from various disciplines and to organize a systematic and balanced effort. Large companies have many resources that can be called on, but small companies do not have such resources and may need to contact local, state, and federal agencies for information, advice, and consultation.

Safety and Health Agencies, Laws, and Regulations

Factory safety laws were enacted in Europe in past centuries to protect workers, particularly women and children, in factories and mines. The basic European concepts were adopted in the United States by several states and took the form of factory laws and regulations, both for worker safety and the protection of women and children from unreasonable work. In addition many states developed laws for worker's compensation in case of injury. In 1969 and 1970 the U.S. Congress created two federal laws regulating safety and health, the Mine Safety and Health Act (1969, which is now the Federal Mine Safety and Health Act of 1977) and the Occupational Safety and Health Act of 1970 (OSH Act). These, as they have been amended, remain the primary federal legislation for ensuring workplace safety and health. The OSH Act requires that employers provide a place of employment free from "recognized" hazards to employee safety or health. The critical word is "recognized," because today's workplaces have many new materials and processes for which an understanding of the hazards is absent or unclear. This places a large responsibility on the employer to keep abreast of new knowledge and information about workplace hazards for their operations. Every developed country has an established law and accompanying regulations to ensure the safety and health of the workforce. These laws are enforced in various ways, but the heart of each law is a set of regulations or rules that specify unsafe working conditions that need to be resolved by the employer. Employers must take measures to ensure that the workplace complies with safe levels of exposures. There are several organizations at the international and national levels that address occupational safety and health.

International Labour Organization (ILO)

The ILO was created in 1919 and is a United Nations (UN) specialized agency that seeks the promotion of social justice and internationally recognized human and labor rights (http://www.ilo.org). The ILO formulates minimum standards of basic labor rights such as freedom of association, the right to organize, and collective bargaining. It also provides technical assistance in areas such as vocational training and vocational rehabilitation; employment policy; working conditions; and occupational safety and health. There is a branch concerned with occupational safety and health (http://www.ilo.org/public/english/protection/safework/intro.htm) that focuses on reducing the number and seriousness of occupational injuries and diseases; adapting the working environment, equipment, and work processes to the physical and mental capacity of the worker; enhancing the physical, mental, and social well-being of workers in all occupations;

encouraging national policies and programs of member states; and providing appropriate assistance to members. To achieve those aims, the ILO works with government and nongovernment agencies to design and implement policies and programs to improve working conditions. The ILO is currently working on a global program for occupational safety and health.

World Health Organization (WHO)

The constitution of the WHO was approved in 1946 (http://www.who.org). Its goal is good health for all people. To this end, the WHO directs international health activity, promotes technical cooperation, helps governments to strengthen their own health services, provides technical assistance, conducts research, and establishes international standards for biological and pharmaceutical products, among other things. It also provides information on global occupational safety and health issues (http://www.who.org/peh/Occupational—health/occindex.html), such as biological agents, noise, radiation, chemicals, occupational carcinogens, and allergenic agents. The WHO established the international statistical classification of diseases and related health problems in occupational health. The organization has a global strategy on occupational safety and health that includes 10 priority areas: (a) strengthening international and national policies for health at work and developing necessary policy tools; (b) developing healthy work environments; (c) developing healthy work practices and promoting health at work; (d) strengthening occupational health services; (e) establishing support services for occupational health; (f) developing occupational health standards; (g) developing human resources for occupational health; (h) establishing registration and data systems, developing information services, and raising public awareness; (i) strengthening research; and (j) developing collaboration in occupational health with other services.

European Agency for Safety and Health at Work

The European Agency for Safety and Health at Work (http://europe.osha.eu.int/) began in 1996 and is based in Bilbao, Spain. The agency has put forth numerous directives for employers in EU member states to follow. These include general safety requirement directives; directives regarding temporary workers, pregnant workers, and young people; and directives on manual handling, work equipment, and safety signs. The agency also conducts information campaigns, such as a recently launched campaign aimed at reducing the number of work-related back injuries and other musculoskeletal disorders. Other information about occupational health and safety in the EU can be found using HASTE (http://www.occuphealth.fi/e/eu/haste/), the EU health and safety database that lists databases from member states.

U.S. Occupational Safety and Health Administration
(OSHA)

OSHA (http://www.osha.gov) is part of the U.S. Department of Labor. OSHA has the responsibility for establishing federal workplace safety and health standards and enforcing them. Over the past three decades OSHA has developed hundreds of standards that have been published in the code of federal regulations (C.F.R.) C.F.R. Section 29, subsections 1900–1928, which cover general industry (1910), longshoring (1918), construction (1926), and agriculture (1928). The Website location http://www.osha-slc.gov/OshStd—toc/OSHA—Std—toc.html is a direct path to OSHA standards. The federal code of standards is revised periodically and new standards are added continually. Examples of current and proposed rules and standards include Process Safety Management of Highly Hazardous Chemicals (§ 1910.119), Personal Protective Equipment (§§ 1910.132–1910.139), and the proposed Safety and Health Program Rule. Recently, a new standard, the Ergonomic Program Standard was promulgated but rescinded by the U.S. Congress. It is important for employers to keep up with these new and revised standards. One way is to keep in frequent contact with the area office of OSHA and request that this office send updates of the standards. Another way is to subscribe to one or more of the many newsletters for occupational safety and health that provide current information and updates. Yet another is to access the OSHA Website (http://www.osha.gov), which provides information about current activities, regulations, and updates. There are occupational safety and health standards that cover the wide range of hazardous conditions and exposures. OSHA often relies on voluntary organizations to produce national standards for workplace health and safety. One such organization is the American National Standards Institute (ANSI). ANSI and OSHA have a working arrangement for developing standards in which ANSI provides technical support through its committees, and OSHA representatives provide health and safety information and research to the standard development and modification process. OSHA also can rely on the National Institute for Occupational Safety and Health (NIOSH) for criteria documents for standards as established by the OSH Act. NIOSH is an agency of the Department of Health and Human Services that conducts research on various safety and health problems, provides technical assistance to OSHA, and recommends standards for OSHA's adoption.

A Balance Model of Occupational Safety and
Health Performance

An important consideration in conceptualizing an approach to occupational health and safety is an understanding of the many various personal and workplace factors that interact to cause exposures and accidents. Any strategy to control these exposures and accidents should consider a range of factors and their influences on each other. A model of human workplace interaction was proposed by Smith and Sainfort (1989). This model has

---

Useful WEB Information Sources

American Association of Occupational Health Nurses.
  http//:www.aaohn.org
American Board of Industrial Hygiene. http//:www.abih.org
American College of Occupational and Environmental Medicine.
  http//:www.acoem.org
American Council of Government Industrial Hygienists.
  http//:www.acgih.org
American Industrial Hygiene Association. http//:www.aiha.org
American Psychological Association. http//:www.apa.org
Bureau of Labor Statistics. http//:www.bls.gov
Centers for Disease Control and Prevention. http//:www.cdc.gov
Department of Justice. http//:www.usdoj.gov
Department of Labor. http//:www.dol.gov
National Institute for Environmental Health Sciences.
  http//:www.niehs.gov
National Institute for Occupational Safety and Health.
  http//:www.niosh.gov
National Safety Council. http//:www.nsc.org
Occupational Safety and Health Administration.
  http//:www.osha.gov.

---

five components including the person, task activities, the environment, technology/tools/machinery, and the work organization and supervision. For each element of this model there can be hazardous exposures, for instance a machine with an unguarded drive shaft or a person using unsafe work methods. The elements of the model can also interact together to produce hazardous exposures, for example a high workload task that is performed in an environment with chemical exposures by an untrained worker is a combination of hazards. Or when the person uses machinery and tools that have hazardous characteristics and there is high work pressure to complete a task quickly. The model can serve as a template for analyzing tasks and hazards. Each one of the elements of the model has specific characteristics that can influence (create, enhance, modify) exposures to hazards and accident potential or disease risk. At the same time each element interacts with the others to increase risks or mitigate exposures.

The Person

There are a wide range of individual attributes that can affect exposure and accident potential. These include intellectual capabilities and aptitudes, perceptual–motor abilities, physical capabilities such as strength and endurance, current health status, susceptibilities to disease, and personality. Intelligence affects the ability for hazard recognition, and aptitude for training in hazard recognition and elimination. An important aspect of injury prevention is to have knowledgeable employees who can determine the potential danger of an exposure and respond appropriately. This requires some previous experience with a hazard or training about the nature of the hazard, its injury potential, and ways to control it. Employees must have the intelligence to learn and retain the information that they are given in training classes. There is a fundamental need for employees to have an adequate background and education to be able to apply their intelligence and acquire new knowledge through training. Of specific importance are observational, reading, listening, and language skills so employees can be trained and instructed properly. Physiological considerations such as strength, endurance, and susceptibilities to fatigue, stress, or disease are also important aspects of injury potential. Some jobs demand high energy expenditure and strength requirements. For these, employees must have adequate physical resources to do the work safely. Another attribute related to physical capacity is perceptual–motor skills and abilities such as eye–hand coordination. These skills come into play in the moment-by-moment conduct of work tasks and interactions with hazards. Although strength may influence the ability to do a specific component of a task, perceptual–motor skills are involved in all aspects of manual tasks. Thus, perceptual–motor skills affect the quality with which a task is carried out as well as the probability of a mistake that could cause an exposure or accident.

It is critical that a proper "fit" is achieved between employees and other elements of the model. This can occur with proper hazard orientation, training, skill enhancement, ergonomic improvements, and proper engineering of the tasks, technology, and environment.

Machinery, Technology, and Materials

There are characteristics of the machinery, tools, technology, and materials used by the worker that can influence the potential for an exposure or accident. One consideration is the extent to which machinery and tools influence the worker's use of the most appropriate and effective perceptual–motor skills and energy resources. The relationship between the controls of a machine and the action of that machine dictates the level of perceptual–motor skill necessary to perform a task. The action of the controls and the subsequent reaction of the machinery must be compliant and compatible with basic human perceptual–motor patterns. If not, significant interference with performance can occur, which may lead to improper responses that can cause accidents. In addition, the adequacy of feedback about the action of the machine affects the performance efficiency that can be achieved and the potential for an operational error. An excellent resource for determining if a machine is compliant with human factors is the *Handbook of Human Factors and Ergonomics,* edited by Gavriel Salvendy (1997).

The inherent characteristics of materials such as the flammability or toxicity will affect exposures and risk. More hazardous materials clearly have a greater probability of adverse safety or health outcomes if there is an exposure. Sometimes employees will be more careful when using materials that they know have a high hazard potential. But this can only be possible when they have adequate knowledge of the material's hazard level. When a material is very hazardous, often there are other, less hazardous materials available that can be substituted that will then reduce the extent of risk. The same is true for hazardous work processes. Proper substitution of better methods, materials, or machinery can decrease the risk of injury or illness. However, care must be taken to ensure that the material or process being substituted is really safer and that it "mixes" well with the entire product formulation or production–assembly process. This calls for an analysis of the "systemic" influences of changes.

Task Factors

The demands of a work activity and the way in which it is conducted can influence the probability of an exposure or accident. In addition, the influence of the work activity on employee attention, satisfaction, and motivation can affect behavior patterns that increase exposure and accident risk. Work-task considerations can be broken into the physical requirements, the mental requirements, and psychological considerations. The physical requirements influence the amount of energy expenditure necessary to carry out a task. Excessive physical requirements can lead to fatigue, both physiological and mental, which can reduce worker capabilities to recognize and respond to workplace hazards. Typically, relatively high workloads can be tolerated for only short periods of time. Longer exposure to heavy workloads or multiple exposures to shorter duration heavy workloads leads to diminished employee capacity to respond normally.

Other task considerations related to the physical work requirements include the pace or rate of work, the amount of repetition in task activities, and work pressure as a result of production demands. Task activities that are highly repetitive and paced by machinery, rather than employee-paced, tend to be stressful. Such conditions diminish an employee's attention to hazards and the capability to respond to a hazard because of boredom. These conditions may produce cumulative trauma disorders to the musculoskeletal system when the task activity cycle time is short and constant. Tasks with relatively low workload and energy expenditure can also produce problems as a result of the high frequency of muscle and joint motions, and boredom that leads to employee inattention to hazards.

Psychological task content considerations, such as satisfaction with job tasks, the amount of control over the work process, participation in decision making, the ability to use knowledge and skills, the amount of esteem associated with the job, and the ability to identify with the end products of the task activity can influence employee attention and motivation. They also can cause job stress. Job stress can affect employee ability to attend to, recognize, and respond to hazards, as well as the motivation needed to be concerned with personal health and safety considerations.

Job stress can bring about emotional disturbances that limit the employee's capabilities to respond, as well as general motivation. Task considerations are a central aspect in reducing worker fatigue and stress and in enhancing worker motivation for positive safety behavior. Tasks must be designed to fit the workforce capabilities and needs and to be compatible with the other elements of the balance model.

The Work Environment

The work environment exposes employees to materials, chemicals, and physical agents that can cause harm or injury if the exposure exceeds safe limits. Such exposures vary widely from industry to industry, from job to job, and from task to task. Exposures from the work environment influence the probability for an injury or illness, and the extent of exposure often determines the seriousness of the injury. The extent of environmental exposures is an important basis for determining the rates companies pay for worker's compensation insurance. The central concept is one of relative risk. The greater the number of hazards, and the more serious their potential to inflict injury or illness, then the greater the probability of an accident. The greater the probability of a serious accident, then the higher the insurance premium. The hazard potential of different environmental factors can be evaluated using various federal, state, and local codes and standards for worker protection and limits that have been established by scientific groups.

Environmental conditions can also hamper the ability of employees to use their senses (poor lighting, excessive noise) and thus reduce employees' abilities to respond or react to hazardous situations. The environment should be compatible with worker perceptual–motor, energy expenditure, and motivational needs to encourage hazard recognition, precautions, and the desire to do tasks in the proper way.

Organizational Structure

Several aspects of organizational design and management can have an influence on accident risk. These include management policies and procedures, the way in which work tasks are organized into plantwide activities, the style of employee supervision, the motivational climate in the plant, the amount of socialization and interaction between employees, the amount of social support employees receive, and management attitude toward safety. Research has shown that all of these can influence a company's health and safety performance (Cohen, 1977; Smith, Cohen, Cohen, & Cleveland, 1978). Management attitude has often been cited as the most critical element in a successful safety program (Cohen, 1977; Smith et al., 1978). If the individuals that manage an organization have a disregard for safety considerations, then employees tend not be very motivated to work safely. Conversely, if the management attitude is one in which safety considerations are paramount—even more important than production goals—

then managers, supervisors, and employees will put a great effort into health and safety considerations.

There are other organizational considerations that are important in safety performance that are related to management atmosphere and attitudes. For instance, a management structure that provides for frequent employee interaction with other employees, the style of the supervisor, and providing frequent social support all lead to an organizational climate that is conducive to cooperative efforts in hazard recognition and control. Such a structure also allows for the motivational climate necessary to encourage appropriate safety behavior.

A consistent factor in accident causation is work pressure for greater production, or faster output, or to quickly correct problems to continue production, or to reduce customer waiting time. Such work pressure issues were defined in a series of catastrophic accident disasters in the HBO documentary movie *Death on the Job* (1991). These case studies demonstrated how poor management decisions about production issues led to fatal employee, supervisor, or contract worker mistakes leading to disastrous results. As shown in this movie work pressure can be exacerbated by technology malfunctions, insufficient staffing, and improper work standards. Management emphasis on reducing costs, enhancing profits, and increasing stock price often stretch the limits of the capabilities of the workforce and technology. When breakdowns occur or operations are not running normally, employees tend to take risks to keep production online or to get it back online quickly. It is during these nonnormal operations that many accidents occur. Management must provide adequate resources to meet production goals and to accommodate nonnormal operations. Management must also establish policies to ensure that employees and supervisors do not take unnecessary risks to ensure production.

Defining Occupational Injuries and Diseases

Early in the 1980s, NIOSH defined the 10 most serious occupational disease and injury areas (CDC, 1983). These were occupational lung diseases, musculoskeletal injuries, occupational cancers, acute trauma, cardiovascular diseases, disorders of reproduction, neurotoxic disorders, noise-induced hearing loss, dermatologic conditions, and psychological disorders. In April of 1996, NIOSH developed the National Occupational Research Agenda (NORA; NIOSH, 1996a), which identified 21 priority research areas to target and coordinate occupational safety and health research. Eight of the 21 target areas focus on occupational diseases and injuries. This was an update of the "top 10 list" from the early 1980s. The new list identifies allergic and irritant dermatitis, asthma and chronic obstructive pulmonary disease, fertility and pregnancy abnormalities, hearing loss, infectious disease, low back disorders, musculoskeletal disorders of the upper extremities, and traumatic injuries (NIOSH, 1996b) as serious problems. More detail of each disease or condition is provided in Table 3.1 using excerpts from NIOSH (NIOSH, 1996b). Table 3.2 provides brief descriptions of vari-

Table 3.1. Descriptions of NIOSH's Top Eight Occupational Disease and Injury Categories

Disease or injury	Description
Allergic and irritant dermatitis	Allergic and irritant dermatitis (contact dermatitis) is overwhelmingly the most important cause of occupational skin diseases, which account for 15% to 20% of all reported occupational diseases. There is virtually no occupation or industry without potential exposure to the many diverse agents that cause allergic and irritant dermatitis.
Asthma and chronic obstructive pulmonary disease	Occupationally related airway diseases, including asthma and chronic obstructive pulmonary disease (COPD), have emerged as having substantial public health importance. Nearly 30% of COPD and adult asthma may be attributable to occupational exposure. Occupational asthma is now the most frequent occupational respiratory disease diagnosis. More than 20 million U.S. workers are exposed to substances that can cause airway diseases.
Fertility and pregnancy abnormalities	Although more than 1000 workplace chemicals have shown reproductive effects in animals, most have not been studied in humans. In addition, most of the four million other chemical mixtures in commercial use remain untested. Physical and biological agents in the workplace that may affect fertility and pregnancy outcomes are practically unstudied.
Hearing loss	Occupational hearing loss may result from an acute traumatic injury, but it is far more likely to develop gradually as a result of chronic exposure to ototraumatic (damaging to the ear or hearing process) agents. Noise is the most important occupational cause of hearing loss, but solvents, metals, asphyxiants, and heat may also play a role. Exposure to noise combined with other agents can result in hearing losses greater than those resulting from exposure to noise or other agents alone.
Infectious disease	Health care workers are at risk of tuberculosis (TB), hepatitis B and C viruses, and the human immunodeficiency virus (HIV). Social service workers, corrections personnel, and other occupational groups who work regularly with populations having increased rates of TB may also face increased risk. Laboratory workers are at risk of exposure to infectious diseases when working with infective material.

Low back disorders

Back pain is one of the most common and significant musculoskeletal problems in the world. In 1993, back disorders accounted for 27% of all nonfatal occupational injuries and illnesses involving days away from work in the United States. The economic costs of low back disorders are staggering. According to NIOSH (1996b), a recent study showed the average cost of a workers' compensation claim for a low back disorder was $8300, which was more than twice the average cost of $4075 for all compensable claims combined. Estimates of the total cost of low back pain to society in 1990 were between $50 billion and $100 billion per year, with a significant share (about $11 billion) borne by the workers' compensation system. Moreover, as many as 30% of American workers are employed in jobs that routinely require them to perform activities that may increase risk of developing low back disorders.

Musculoskeletal disorders of the upper extremities

Musculoskeletal disorders of the upper extremities (such as carpal tunnel syndrome and rotator cuff tendinitis) due to work factors are common and occur in nearly all sectors of our economy. More than two billion dollars in workers' compensation costs are spent annually on these work-related problems. Musculoskeletal disorders of the neck and upper extremities due to work factors affect employees in every type of workplace and include such diverse workers as food processors, automobile and electronics assemblers, carpenters, office data entry workers, grocery store cashiers, and garment workers. The highest rates of these disorders occur in the industries with a substantial amount of repetitive, forceful work. Musculoskeletal disorders affect the soft tissues of the neck, shoulder, elbow, hand, wrist, and fingers.

Traumatic injuries

During the period 1980 through 1992, more than 77,000 workers died as a result of work-related injuries. This means that an average of 16 workers die every day from injuries suffered at work. The leading causes of occupational injury fatalities over this 13-year period were motor vehicles, machines, homicides, falls, electrocutions, and falling objects. There were four industries—mining, construction, transportation, and agriculture—with occupational injury fatality rates that were notably and consistently higher than all other industries. In 1994, 6.3 million workers suffered job-related injuries that resulted in lost work time, medical treatment other than first aid, loss of consciousness, restriction of work or motion, or transfer to another job. The leading causes of nonfatal occupational injuries involving time away from work in 1993 were overexertion, contact with objects or equipment, and falls to the same level.

Source: NIOSH, 1996.

Table 3.2. Descriptions of Various Occupational Disorders and Diseases Not Included in Table 3.1

Disease or injury	Description
Occupational lung disease	The latent period for many lung diseases can be several years. For instance, for silicosis it may be as long as 15 years and for asbestos related diseases as long as 30 years. The lung is a primary target for disease related to toxic exposures because it is often the first point of exposure through breathing. Many chemicals and dusts are ingested through breathing. The six most severe occupational lung disorders include asbestosis, byssinosis, silicosis, coal workers pneumoconiosis, lung cancer and occupational asthma.
Asbestosis	This disease produces scarring of the lung tissue which causes progressive shortness of breath. The disease continues to progress even after exposures end and there is no specific treatment. The latent period is 10 to 20 years. The agent of exposure is asbestos, and insulation and shipyard workers are those most affected.
Byssinosis	This disease produces chest tightness, cough and airway obstruction. Symptoms can be acute (reversible) or chronic. The agents of exposure are dusts of cotton, flax and hemp, and textile workers are those most affected.
Silicosis	This is a progressive disease that produces nodular fibrosis that inhibits breathing. The agent of exposure is free crystalline silica, and miners, foundry workers, abrasive blasting workers and workers in stone, clay, and glass manufacture are most affected.
Coal miners' pneumoconiosis	This disease produces fibrosis and emphysema. The agent of exposure is coal dust. The prevalence of this disorder among currently employed coal miners has been estimated at almost 5%.
Lung cancer	This disease has many symptoms and multiple pathology. There are several agents of exposure including chromates, arsenic, asbestos, chloroethers, ionizing radiation, nickel and polynuclear aromatic hydrocarbon compounds.
Occupational cancers	There is some debate on the significance of occupational exposures in the overall rate of cancer ranging from 4 to 20% due to occupation, yet there is good agreement that such occupational exposures can produce cancer. There are many types of cancer that are related to workplace exposures and some of these include hemangiosarcoma of the liver; mesothelioma; malignant neoplasm of the nasal cavities, bone, larynx, scrotum, bladder, kidney and other urinary organs; lymphoid leukemia and erythroleukemia.

Traumatic injuries

Amputations

The vast majority of amputations occur to the fingers. The agents of exposure include powered hand tools and powered machines. Many industries have this type of injury as do many occupations. Machine operators are the single most injured occupation for amputations.

Fractures

Falls and blows from objects are the primary agents that cause fractures. The major sources of these injuries include floors, the ground and metal items. This suggests falling down or being struck by an object as the primary reasons for fractures. Truck drivers, general laborers and construction laborers were the occupations having the most fractures.

Eye loss

It was estimated that in 1982 there were over 900,000 occupational eye injuries. Most were due to particles in the eye such as pieces of metal, wood or glass, but a smaller number were caused by chemicals in the eye. A number of occupations are affected including those in woodworking, metalwork, construction and agriculture.

Lacerations

Over 2,000,000 lacerations occur each year with the majority to the fingers, followed by the arms, legs and head/neck. Lacerations occur primarily from being struck or stuck by an object or from striking against an object. The major agents of exposure include knives, sharp metal objects, saws, glass items, nails and machines.

Cardiovascular disease

These disorders include hypertensive disease, ischemic heart disease, other forms of heart disease and cerebrovascular disease. As with cancer, the specific contribution of occupational factors to the causation of CVD has been debated, but there is agreement that some workplace factors contribute to or cause CVD (See Smith and Sainfort, 1990 for a detailed discussion of psychosocial factors and their contribution). Four main occupational sources of CVD causation are agents that affect cardiopulmonary capacity, chemicals, noise and psychosocial stress.

Cardiopulmonary capacity reducers

Agents such as dusts, mists, heavy metals, silica and other trace elements make the lungs work much harder than normal and can induce congestive heart failure. Metal such as beryllium, antimony, lead and cobalt as well as silica and asbestos can produce heart disorders.

continued

Table 3.2. *(Continued)*

Disease or injury	Description
Cardiovascular disease Chemicals	Some chemicals act to sensitize the heart muscle and the smooth muscle of the blood vessels while others reduce the oxygen carrying capacity of the blood. These include nitroglycerin, carbon monoxide, carbon disulfide and halogenated hydrocarbons.
Noise	Studies have shown that noise can produce transient increases in blood pressure which may lead to CVD. This may be due to psychological factors related to stress reactions.
Psychosocial stress	Research from longitudinal studies of cardiovascular fitness have demonstrated a relationship between perceived job satisfaction and stress and cardiovascular illness. Epidemiological studies have shown that particular jobs with specific characteristics, such as high demands and low control, have a higher incidence of coronary heart disease. Organizational demands and relations, job task demands, social relationships at work, work schedule, work content features, discretionary control and participation and physical working conditions have all been shown to influence the level of job stress (Smith, Kalimo 1986; Lindstrom & Smith 1997).
Neurotoxic disorders	Neurotoxic disorders are produced by damage to the central nervous system, damage to the peripheral nervous system and intoxication. These cause deficits in attention, reasoning, thinking, remembering and making judgments. They may also cause peripheral neuropathy, neuroses and psychoses, personality changes, aberrant behavior, or reduced reaction time and motor skill. One of the first workplace related neurological disorders identified was lead poisoning which produced palsy in workers exposed to lead dust. NIOSH publishes a list of the materials known to have neurotoxic effects.
Psychological disorders	Psychological disorders related to working conditions include sleep disturbances, mood disturbances, reduced motivation to work or recreate, somatic and psychosomatic complaints, neuroses, psychoses and dysfunctional coping behavior. The effects of stress on an individual are influenced by the nature of the exposures and the individual's physical and psychological characteristics and coping behaviors which may accentuate or mitigate the exposure.

ous types of occupational diseases and injuries not included in Table 3.1 that were highlighted previously by the Centers for Disease Control and Prevention (CDC) and NIOSH.

As mentioned in the previous section, NORA is composed of 21 priority areas, among which 8 relate specifically to occupational illnesses or injuries. A common theme among the priority areas is the primary role played by psychological factors (in the form of psychosocial stressors, work organization interventions, job stress, etc.). Table 3.3 lists those priority areas that either directly or indirectly related to psychological factors.

Workplace Hazards

To list of all of the currently recognized and potential workplace hazards would take a document larger than this handbook—for example, the OSHA standards are multiple volumes of telephone-book size. The best sources to start accumulating hazard information pertinent to one's operations are the OSHA standards, NIOSH criteria documents, and government reports and publications. These are available on the Websites listed in this chapter and from the U.S. Superintendent of Documents in Washington, DC. The Websites have a great deal of useful information. There are also other excellent sources of information, such as the National Safety Council (NSC) *Safety Manual* (Volumes I, II, 2000), NIOSH's resource book, *The Industrial Environment: Its Evaluation and Control* (1973), which has been updated by the American Industrial Hygiene Association (Dinardi, 1997), and *Best's Loss Control Engineering Manual* (2002), to name a few. There are also other federal, state, and local agencies that can provide information on some aspects of occupational health and safety hazard information. At the federal level these include the Environmental Protection Agency (EPA), the National Institute for Environmental Health Sciences (NIEHS), and the CDC. All have Websites (www.cdc.gov, www.niehs.gov, www.epa.gov).

It is important to comprehend the breadth and nature of occupational hazard exposures. To do this workplace hazard sources are classified into broad categories that help explain their nature and potential controls. These are (a) physical agents such as noise and heat; (b) powered mechanical agents such as machinery and tools; (c) nonpowered mechanical agents such as hammers, axes, and knives; (d) liquid chemical agents such as benzene and toluene; (e) powdered materials such as pesticides, asbestos, sand, and coal dust; (f) gaseous or vaporous chemical agents such as nitrous oxide, carbon monoxide, and anhydrous ammonia; (g) heavy metals such as lead and mercury; (h) biological agents such as bacteria and viruses; (i) genetically engineered agents; and (j) other hazards such as wet working surfaces, unguarded floor openings, job stress, and the unsafe behavior of others.

These hazards enter the body through various routes, including inhalation into the lungs and nose, absorption through the skin and other membranes, ingestion into the throat and stomach, traumatic contact with various body surfaces and organs, and in the case of job stress through the cognitive mental processes. Descriptions of many of these hazards and

Table 3.3. NORA Priority Areas Involving Psychology

Priority area	Examples of the role of psychology
Emerging technologies	Provides the example that the new industry of recycling small household batteries is exposing workers to hazardous levels of mercury, which is a neurological poison.
Fertility and pregnancy abnormalities	Stresses that developmental disabilities such as mental retardation may, in some cases, be the result of, occupational exposures to chemicals.
Health services research	States that there are research opportunities to study the social consequences of injuries and illnesses and what psychological interventions are most effective in preventing posttraumatic stress syndromes for victims and witnesses of severe or fatal traumatic work injuries or violence at the worksite.
Indoor environments	Discusses social/psychological stressors that may be contributing to sick building syndrome.
Intervention effectiveness	Lists work organization changes and worker/management participatory safety and health programs as types of workplace safety interventions in need of more research. Other psychology-related issues focused on by the priority area include studying the barriers to the acceptance of new control technologies and the factors that motivate the voluntary adoption of protective work practices.
Organization of work	This priority area is concerned with, among other issues, job stress.
Social and economic consequences of workplace illness and injury	This priority area is concerned with studying social and psychological consequences of illness and injury.
Special populations at risk	Notes that psychosocial factors may place young workers at increased risk of injury in the workplace and that research is needed on the interaction between psychosocial stressors and other work factors such as musculoskeletal stressors or safety practices.
Surveillance research methods	States that one of the ways hazard surveillance systems could help improve worker safety and health is by identifying and quantifying exposure to occupational safety and health hazards associated with psychosocial factors.

Traumatic injuries	States that multiple factors and risks contribute to traumatic injuries, including the characteristics of workers, workplace/process design, work organization, economics and other social factors.
Low back disorders	Psychosocial stressors may be associated with the development of low back disorders, and thus psychosocial interventions may also help reduce the incidence of low back disorders.
Musculoskeletal disorders of the upper extremity	Psychosocial stressors may be associated with the development of upper extremity musculoskeletal disorders (UEMSDs), and thus psychosocial interventions may also help reduce the incidence of UEMSDs.

definitions of adverse exposure levels are contained in the NIOSH book, *Occupational Diseases: A Guide to Their Recognition and Control* (1977).

Traditional hazards such as unexpected energy release and chemicals are still major concerns in the workplace. The use of lasers, robots, microwaves, x-rays, and imaging devices have become more common. Their use makes many of the traditional problems of controlling energy release and limiting worker access to hazardous machine components even more challenging. These technologies will become even more problematic because of the complex nature of the mechanisms of energy release and because of the increased power of the forces involved. For instance, using x-rays for lithographic etching of computer chips could produce exposures that are substantially higher than conventional diagnostic x-rays. The safety precautions for this type of instrument have to be much better than current standards for diagnostic equipment. In addition, emerging hazards are appearing. Some will be the exotic products of genetic engineering and biotechnology, and others will be the products of scientists' ability to harness the laws of physics and chemistry with advanced engineering designs. These will become everyday tools used by thousands of workers, many whom will not be well-educated or knowledgeable of the tremendous power of the technology with which they will be working.

Although these physical and biological hazards will become more prevalent and dangerous than they are today, there will also be more physical and psychological work demands that can lead to psychological stress problems. Currently, the two fastest rising worker's compensation claims areas in the United States are cumulative musculoskeletal trauma and psychological distress (see CDC/NIOSH Website for more information). The rise in these problems can generally be related to two factors. First, there is greater media, worker, and employer awareness and knowledge about how the workplace can contribute to such problems. Second, there are huge increases in workplace automation that create conditions that produce these disorders. It is possible that dealing with these stress-induced problems may be even more difficult than dealing with the biological, chemical, and physical hazards.

Measuring Hazard Potential and Safety Performance

To successfully control occupational hazards and related illness and injuries, it is necessary to define their nature and predict when and where they will occur. This requires that some system of hazard detection be developed that can define the frequency of the hazard, its seriousness, and its amenability to control. Traditionally, two parallel systems of information have been used to attain this purpose. One system is hazard identification, such as plant inspections, fault-free analysis, and employee hazard reporting programs that have been used to define the nature and frequency of company hazards. In this case action is taken before an injury or illness occurs. The second system is after the fact in that it uses employee injury and company loss control information to define problem spots based on the extent of injuries and costs to the organization. When pre- and postinjury systems have been integrated, an organization has been successful in predicting high-risk plant areas or working conditions where remedial programs can be established for hazard control.

Hazard Inspection Programs

Hazard identification before the occurrence of an occupational injury is a major goal of a hazard inspection program. In the United States such programs have been formalized in terms of federal and state regulations that require employers to monitor and abate recognized occupational health and safety hazards. These recognized hazards are defined in the federal and state regulations that provide explicit standards of unsafe exposures. The standards can be the basis for establishing an in-plant inspection program, as they specify the explicit subject matter to be investigated and corrected.

Research has shown that inspections are most effective in identifying permanent fixed physical and environmental hazards that do not vary over time. Inspections are not very effective in identifying transient physical and environmental hazards or improper workplace behaviors, as these hazards may not be present when the inspection is taking place (Smith et al., 1971). A major benefit from inspections, beyond hazard recognition, is the positive motivational influence on employees. Inspections demonstrate management interest in the health and safety of employees and a commitment to a safe working environment. To capitalize on this positive motivational influence, an inspection should not be a punitive process of placing blame, confrontation, or punishment. Indicating the good aspects of a work area and not just the hazards is important in this respect. It is also important to have employees participate in hazard inspections as this increases hazard recognition skills and increases motivation for safe behavior. The first step in an inspection program is to develop a checklist that identifies all potential hazards. A good starting point is the state and federal standards. Many insurance companies have developed general checklists of OSHA standards that can be tailored to a particular plant. These are a good source when drawing up the checklist. A systematic inspection procedure is preferred. This requires that the inspector knows what to look for, where to look for it, and has the proper tools to conduct an effective assessment. It is important that the checklist be tailored to each work area after an analysis of that work area's needs has been undertaken. This analysis should determine the factors to be inspected, including (a) the technology, machinery, tools, and materials; (b) chemicals, gases, vapors, and biological agents; and (c) environmental conditions. The analysis will also determine (a) the frequency of inspection necessary to detect and control hazards; (b) the individuals who should conduct or participate in the inspection; and (c) the instrumentation needed to make measurements of the hazards. The hazards that require inspection can be determined by (a) the potential to cause an injury or illness; (b) the seriousness of the injury or illness; (c) the number of injuries and illnesses a specific workplace factor has been identified with; and (d) conditions defined by federal, state, and local regulations.

The frequency of inspections should be based on the nature of the hazards being evaluated. For instance, once a serious fixed physical hazard has been identified and controlled, it is no longer a hazard. It will only have to be reinspected periodically to be sure the fixed hazard is still being controlled. Random spotchecking is another method that can indicate whether the hazard control remains effective. Other types of hazards that are intermittent will require more frequent inspection to ensure proper hazard abatement. In many cases, monthly inspections are warranted, and in some cases daily inspections are reasonable. Inspections should take place when and where the highest probability of a hazard exists, and reinspection can occur on an incidental basis to ensure that hazard control is effectively maintained. The timing of inspections should be when work processes are operating and should be conducted on a recurring basis at regular intervals. According to the National Safety Council (1974), a general inspection of the entire premises should take place at least once a year, except for those work areas scheduled for more frequent inspection because of their high hazard level. Because housekeeping is an important aspect of hazard control, inspection of all work areas should occur at least monthly for cleanliness, clutter, and traffic flow.

A checklist can be used to identify each hazard, its nature, exact location, potential to cause serious damage, and possible control measures. During the walk through, employee input should be solicited. Photographs and videotapes of hazards are effective in documenting the nature and potential seriousness of hazards. Once the inspection is completed, a report is prepared that specifies pertinent information about the nature of the hazards, illness, and injury potential and abatement recommendations. This report needs to be detailed and provide step-by-step instructions for instituting hazard control procedures in a timely manner. It is not sufficient to simply write up the results; they should be shared with all concerned parties in a face-to-face meeting. This meeting will give the results greater significance and serve as the basis for further interaction and possible modification of recommendations. Such meetings will enhance employee understanding and allow for in-depth discussion of the findings and recommendations. This makes the entire inspection process more relevant to supervision and employees, and facilitates the favorable acceptance of the results and any subsequent recommendations.

Illness and Injury Statistics

There are four main uses of injury statistics: (a) to identify high risk jobs or work areas, (b) to evaluate company health and safety performance, (c) to evaluate the effectiveness of hazard abatement approaches, and (d) to identify factors related to illness and injury causation. An illness and injury reporting and analysis system requires that detailed information must be collected about the characteristics of illness and injuries and their frequency and severity. The OSH Act established illness and injury reporting and recording requirements that are mandatory for all employers, with certain exclusions such as small establishments and government agencies. Regulations have been developed to define how employers are to adhere to these requirements (www.osha.gov). The OSH Act requirements specify that any illness or injury to an employee that causes time lost from the job, treatment beyond first-aid, transfer to another job, loss of consciousness, or any occupational illness must be recorded on a daily log of injuries (OSHA 300 form). This log identifies the injured person, the date and time of the injury, the department or plant location where the injury occurred, and a brief description about the occurrence of the injury, highlighting salient facts such as the chemical, physical agent or machinery involved and the nature of the injury. An injury should be recorded on the day that it occurs, but this is not always possible with musculoskeletal disorders and other cumulative trauma injuries. The number of days that the person is absent from the job is also recorded on the employee's return to work. In addition to the daily log, a more detailed form is filled out for each injury that occurs (OSHA 301 form). This form provides a description of the nature of the injury, the extent of damage to the employee, the factors that could be related to the cause of the injury—such as the source or agent that produced the injury—and events surrounding the injury occurrence. A worker's compensation form can be substituted for the OSHA 301 form, because equivalent information is gathered on these forms.

The OSH Act injury and illness system specifies reporting a procedure for calculating the frequency of occurrence of occupational injuries and illnesses and an index of their severity. These can be used by companies to monitor their health and safety performance. National data by major industrial categories is compiled by the U.S. Bureau of Labor Statistics annually and can serve as a basis of comparison of individual company performance within an industry in the United States. Thus a company can determine whether its injury rate is better or worse than other companies in its industry. This industry-wide injury information is available on the OSHA Website (www.osha.gov).

The OSHA system uses the following formula in determining company annual injury and illness incidence. The total number of recordable injuries are multiplied by 200,000 and then divided by the number of hours worked by the company employees. This gives an injury frequency per 100 person-hours of work (injury incidence). These measures can be compared to an industry average.

$$\text{Incidence} = \frac{\text{Number of recordable injuries and illnesses} \times 200,000}{\text{Number of hours worked by company employees}}$$

where:

1. The number of recordable injuries and illnesses is taken from the OSHA 300 daily log of injuries.

2. The number of hours worked by employees is taken from payroll records and reports prepared for the Department of Labor or the Social Security Administration.

It is also possible to determine the severity of company injuries. Two methods are typically used. In the first, the total number of days lost because of injuries are compiled from the OSHA 300 daily log and are divided by the total number of injuries recorded on the OSHA 300 daily log. This gives an average number of days lost per injury. In the second, the total number of days lost are multiplied by 200,000 and then divided by the number of hours worked by the company employees. This gives a severity index per 100 person-hours of work. These measures can also be compared to an industry average.

Injury incidence and severity information can be used by a company to monitor its injury and illness performance over the years to examine improvement and the effectiveness of health and safety interventions. Such information provides the basis for making corrections in the company's approach to health and safety, and can serve as the basis of rewarding managers and workers for good performance. However, it must be understood that injury statistics give only a crude indicator of safety company performance and an even cruder indicator of individual manager or worker performance. Because injuries are rare events, they do not always reflect the sum total of daily performance of company employees and managers. Thus, although they are an accurate measure of overall company safety performance, they are an insensitive measure at the individual and departmental levels. Some experts feel that more basic information has to be collected to provide the basis for directing health and safety efforts. One proposed measure is to use first-aid reports from industrial clinics. These provide information on more frequent events than the injuries required to be reported by the OSH Act. It is thought that these occurrences can provide insights into patterns of hazards and behaviors that may lead to the more serious injuries, and that their greater number provides a larger statistical base for determining accident potential.

Controlling Workplace Hazards

Having identified and defined the workplace hazards, the next logical step is to eliminate or control them. There are three classes of interventions for achieving this, and these are not always mutually exclusive:

1. Elimination of the hazard,
2. Blocking employee access to the hazard, and
3. Warning the employee of the hazard and training the employee how to avoid it.

Engineering Controls (Eliminating and Blocking)

The simplest way to deal with a hazard is to get rid of it. This can be accomplished by redesigning a product, tool, machine, process, or environment, or through substitution of a nonhazardous or less hazardous material. For example, the loading of a mechanical punch press can be accomplished by placing a part directly onto the die with the employee's hand, which puts the hand directly into the point of operation. If the press should inadvertently cycle, the employee could injure his or her hand. To eliminate this hazard, a fixture can be designed that the employee can place the part onto and then slide the fixture with the part into the point of operation without putting his or her hand into the point of operation. This redesign removes the hand from the hazardous area of the machine. Another example is substituting a less hazardous chemical for a more hazardous chemical and thereby reducing the extent of risk or the level of exposure—for instance using toluene rather than benzene as a solvent.

The second class of engineering controls is blocking employee access to the hazard. This can be achieved by putting up a barrier that keeps the employee from entering a hazardous area. The best example of this is fencing off an area such as high voltage transformers. With this type of intervention, the hazard remains but is controlled. However, it is often the case that the hazardous area must be accessed for maintenance or other reasons. In this case, there are often secondary hazard controls to protect those who cross the barrier. For example, robots usually have a barrier around them to keep employees outside of their arc of swing so that they do not inadvertently come into contact with the robot's arm. But when the robot has to be programmed or maintained, then an employee has to go across the barrier to access the robot. A secondary control is to have the robot automatically shut down when the barrier is breached. This is a form of "interlock" that keeps the hazard inactive while employees are present in the danger zone. In the case of many hazards, such as the high voltage transformer, it may not be possible to have a secondary hazard control. Then an organization must rely on the knowledge, skills, and good sense of the employee or the person breaching the barrier.

Containment is a form of a barrier guard that is used primarily with very dangerous chemical and physical hazards. An example is the ionizing radiation from a nuclear reactor. This radiation at the core of the reactor is restrained from leaving the reactor by lead-lined walls, but if leakage should occur through the walls, then a back-up barrier contains the leakage. In the case of a "closed" system, the employee never comes in contact with the source (such as the reactor core) of the hazard. The system is designed through automation to protect the employee from the hazard source. Many chemical plants use the concept of a closed system of containment. The only time an employee would contact these specific deadly hazards would be in the case of a disaster in which the containment devices failed.

Another form of barrier control that looks something like a secondary hazard control is a guard. A guard is used when there is only a hazard during certain aspects of an operation. For example, when a power press is inactive, there is no hazard at the point of operation. But when it is activated, the punch bit is set in motion, and this becomes a hazard. Then guards are engaged that prohibit employee contact with the bit when this hazard is present. When using guards, there is a barrier to keep the employee from the area of the hazard only when the hazard is present. The guard allows access to the area of the hazard so that loading, unloading, and other job operations can be carried out near the energy source before and after activation. But when the energy is activated to transform the employee and machine actions into a product, then the guard is put in place to block the employee from access to the site of the action. This site alone is the source of the energy that could cause an injury or illness. In the case of the robot, the hazard area was quite large and a barrier had to be used; but in the case of a mechanical punch press the hazard area was limited to the point of operation that is quite small and feasible to use a guard. In the mechanical punch press case, constructing a constant barrier would make the work process impossible because the point of operation has to be accessed. Thus, a moveable guard is used.

Yet another engineering control that is important in dealing with workplace hazards is the active removal of the hazard before it contacts the employee during the work process. An example of this would be a local scavenger ventilation system that would suck the fumes produced by an operation such as welding or laser surgery away from the employees. This would exhaust the fumes into the air outside of the plant (surgery room) away from the employees. The ventilation systems must comply with federal, state, and local regulations in design and in the level of emissions into the environment. Thus, the fumes may need to be "scrubbed" clean by a filter before being released into the open environment. A related ventilation approach is to dilute the extent of employee exposure to airborne contaminants by bringing in more fresh air from outside the plant on a regular basis. The fresh air dilutes the concentration of the contaminant to which the employee is exposed to a level that is below the threshold of dangerous exposure. The effectiveness of this approach is verified by measuring the ambient air level of contamination and employee exposure levels on a regular basis. When new materials or chemicals are introduced into the work process, or when other new airborne exposures are introduced into the plant, the adequacy of the ventilation dilution approach to provide safe levels of exposure(s) must be reverified.

When engineering controls cannot provide adequate employee protection, then personal protective equipment must be worn by the employees. This is not a preferred method of control because the employee may still come in contact with the hazard because the hazard is not removed. It is a cardinal rule of safety and health engineering that the primary method of controlling hazards is through engineering controls. Human factors controls are to be used primarily when engineering controls are not practical, feasible, solely effective in hazard control, or cost-effective. It is recognized that human factor controls are often necessary as adjuncts (supplements) to engineering controls, and in some instances are the only feasible and effective controls.

Warnings and Instructions

Informing employees about workplace hazards has three aspects: (a) the right to know, (b) warnings, and (c) instructions. Federal safety and health regulations and many state and local regulations specify that an employer has the obligation to inform employees of hazardous workplace exposures to chemicals, materials, or physical agents that are known to cause harm. The requirements of reporting vary from locale to locale, and employers must be aware of the reporting requirements in their area. In general, an employer must provide information on the name of the hazard, its potential health effects, exposure levels that produce adverse health effects, and the typical kinds of exposures encountered in the plant. For each chemical or material or physical agent classified as toxic by OSHA, employers are required to maintain a standard data sheet that provides detailed information on its toxicity, control measures, and standard operating procedures for using the product. A list of hazardous chemicals, materials, and physical agents can be obtained from your local OSHA office or the OHSA Website at *www.osha.gov*. These standard data sheets (some are referred to as material safety data sheets) must be supplied by the manufacturer. These data sheets must be shared with employees who are exposed to specific hazardous products and must be available at the plant (location) as an information resource in case of an exposure or emergency. The motivation behind the right to know concept is that employees have a basic right to knowledge about their workplace exposures and that informed employees will make better choices and use better judgment when working with hazardous materials.

Warnings are used to convey the message of extreme danger. They are designed to catch the attention of the employee, to inform the employee of a hazard, and to instruct him or her in how to avoid the hazard. The American National Standards Institute (ANSI) has developed standards for the design of visual warnings that provide reasonable guidelines (Z535.1-535.4, 1991). Warnings are primarily visual, but can also be auditory, as in the case of a fire alarm. Warnings use sensory techniques that capture the attention of the employee, for instance the use of the color red has a cultural identification with danger or the use of loud, discontinuous noise that is culturally associated with emergency situations. After catching attention, the warning must provide information about the nature of the hazard. This provides the employee with an opportunity to assess the risk of ignoring the warning. Finally, the warning should provide some information about specific actions to take to avoid the hazard such as "stay clear of the boom," or "stand back 50 feet from the crane," or "stay away from this area."

Developing good warnings requires following the ANSI standards, using the results of current scientific studies, and good judgment. Considerations such as the educational level of employee and word comprehension, the placement of the warning, environmental distortions, wording of instructions, and employee sensory overload, just to name a few, must be taken into account. Even when good warnings are designed, their ability to influence employee behavior varies greatly. Even so, they do provide the employee with an opportunity to make a choice regarding exposure. Warnings should never be used in place of engineering controls and should always serve as an adjunct to other means of hazard control.

Instructions provide direction to employees that will help them to avoid or to more effectively deal with hazards. They are the behavioral model that can be followed to ensure safety. The basis of good instructions is the job analysis that provides detailed information on the job tasks, the environment, the tools, and materials used. The job analysis will identify high-risk situations. Based on verification of the information in the job analysis, a set of instructions on how to avoid hazardous situations can be developed. The implementation of such instructions as employee behavior will be covered in the next section under training and safe behavior improvement.

Promoting Safe Employee Behavior Through Training

Training workers to improve their skills and to recognize hazardous conditions is a primary means for reducing exposures and accidents. Cohen and Colligan (1998) found that safety and health training was effective in reducing employee risk. Training can be defined as a systematic acquisition of knowledge, concepts, or skills that can lead to improved performance or behavior. Eckstrand (1964) has defined seven basic steps in training: (a) defining the training objectives; (b) developing criterion measures for evaluating the training process and outcomes; (c) developing or deriving the content and materials to be learned; (d) designing the techniques to be used to teach the content; (e) integrating the learners and the training program to achieve learning; (f) evaluating the extent of learning; and (g) modifying the training process to improve learner comprehension and retention of the content. These steps provide the foundation for the application of basic guidelines that can be used for designing the training content and integrating the content and the learner.

In defining training objectives two levels can be established: global and specific. The global objectives are the end goals that are to be met by the training program. For instance, a global objective might be the reduction of eye injuries by 50%. The specific objectives are those that are particular to each segment of the training program, including the achievements to be reached by the completion of each segment. A specific objective might be the ability to recognize eye injury hazards by all employees by the end of the hazard education segment. A basis for defining training objectives is the assessment of company safety problem areas. This can be done using hazard identification methods such as injury statistics, inspections, and hazard surveys. Problems should be identified, ranked in importance, and then used to define objectives.

To determine the success of the training process, criteria for evaluation need to be established. Hazard identification measures can be used to determine overall effectiveness. Thus, global objectives can be verified by determining a reduction in injury incidence (such as eye injuries) or the elimination of a substantial number of eye hazards. However, it is necessary to have more sensitive measures of evaluation that can be used during the course of training to assess the effectiveness of specific aspects of the training program. This helps to determine the need to redirect specific training segments if they prove to be ineffective. Specific objectives can be examined through the use of evaluation tools. For instance, to evaluate the ability of workers to recognize eye hazards, a written or oral examination can be used. Hazards that are not recognized can be emphasized in subsequent training and retraining.

The content of the training program should be developed based on the learners' knowledge level, current skills, and aptitudes. The training content should be flexible enough to allow for individual differences in aptitudes, skills, and knowledge, as well as for individualized rates of learning. The training content should allow all learners to achieve a minimally acceptable level of health and safety knowledge and competence by the end of training. The specifics of the content deal with the skills to be learned and the hazards to be recognized and controlled.

There are various techniques that can be used to train workers. Traditionally on-the-job training (OJT) has been emphasized to teach workers job skills and health and safety considerations. The effectiveness of such training will be influenced by the skill of the supervisor or lead worker in imparting knowledge and technique, as well as their motivation to successfully train the worker. First-line supervisors and lead workers are not educated to be trainers and may lack the skills and motivation to do the best job. Therefore, OJT has not always been successful as the sole safety training method. Because the purpose of a safety training program is to impart knowledge and to teach skills, it is important to provide both classroom experiences to gain knowledge, as well as OJT to attain skills.

Classroom training is used to teach concepts and improve knowledge, and should be carried out in small groups (not to exceed 15 employees). A small group allows for the type of instructor–student interaction needed to monitor class progress, provide proper motivation, and determine each learner's comprehension level. Classroom training should be given in an area free of distractions to allow learners to concentrate on the subject matter. Training sessions should not exceed 30 minutes, after which workers can return to their regular duties. There should be liberal use of visual aids to increase comprehension and make the training more concrete and identifiable to the learners. In addition, written materials should be provided that can be taken from the training session for study or reference away from the classroom. For OJT the major emphasis should be on enhancing skills through observation and practice. Key workers with exceptional skills can be used as role models and mentors. Learners can observe these key workers and pick up tips from them. They then can practice what they have learned under the direction of the key workers to increase their skill, obtain feedback on their technique, and be motivated to improve. Once the learner and the training program have been integrated, it will be necessary to evaluate the extent of learning. This can be done by testing learner knowledge and skills. Such testing should be done frequently throughout the training process to provide the learners with performance feedback and to allow for program redirection as needed. Knowledge is best tested by written examinations that measure acquisition of facts and concepts. Pictorial examinations (using pictures or slides of working conditions) can be used to determine hazard recognition ability. Oral questioning on a frequent basis can provide the instructor with feedback on the class comprehension of materials being presented but should not be used for individual learner evaluation because many learners are not highly verbal and could be demotivated by being asked to recite. Skills testing should take place in the work area under conditions that control hazard exposures. Skills can be observed during practice sessions to determine progress under low-stress conditions.

The final stage in a training program, having determined the success of the program, is to make modifications to improve the learning process. Such modifications should be done on a continuous basis as feedback on learner performance is acquired. In addition, at the end of the program it is necessary to determine if the company objectives have been met. If so, should the objectives be modified? The answers to these questions can lead to modifications in the training program.

Hazard Reduction Through Improved Work Practices

A large number of the hazards in the workplace are produced by the interaction between employees and their tools and environment. These hazards cannot be completely controlled through hazard inspection and machine guarding. They can be controlled by increasing employee recognition of the hazards and by proper worker behavior. Such behavior may be an evasive action when a hazard occurs or it may be the use of safe work procedures to ensure that hazards will not occur. There are very few hazard control efforts that are not in some way dependent on employee behavior. Making employees aware of hazards is meaningless if they do not choose to do something about them. For example, when controlling chemical exposures personal protective equipment is useless if it is not worn. Likewise an inspection system is useless if hazards are not reported or not corrected when reported. Thus, taking positive action (behavior) is central to hazard control. It is often true that there are no ideal engineering control methods to deal with a certain hazard. In such a case, it is usually necessary to use proper work practices to avoid hazardous exposure when engineering controls are not feasible. Likewise, even when engineering control will work successfully it is necessary to have employees use good work practices to get the engineering controls to work properly.

Conard (1983) has defined work practices as employee behaviors that can be simple or complex, which are related to reducing a hazardous situation in occupational activities. There are a series of setups that can be used in developing and implementing work practices for eliminating occupational hazards: (a) the definition of hazardous work practices; (b) the definition of new work practices to reduce the hazards; (c) training employees in the desired work practices; (d) testing the new work practices in the job setting; (e) installing the new work practices using motivators; (f) monitoring the effectiveness of the new work practices; (g) redefining the new work practices; and (h) maintaining proper employee habits regarding work practices. In defining hazardous work practices there are a number of sources of information that should be examined. Injury and accident reports such as the OSHA 301 Form provide information about the circumstances surrounding an injury. Often employee or management behaviors that contributed to the injury can be identified. Employees are a good source of information about workplace hazards. They can be asked to identify critical behaviors that may be important as hazard sources or as hazard controls. First-line supervisors are also a good source of information because they are constantly observing employee behavior. All of these sources should be examined; however the most important source of information is in directly observing employees at work.

There are a number of considerations when observing employee work behaviors. First, observation must be an organized proposition. Before undertaking observations, it is useful to interview employees and first-line supervisors and examine injury records to develop a checklist of significant behaviors to be observed. This should include hazardous behaviors as well as those that are used to enhance engineering control or to directly control hazards. The checklist should identify the job task being observed, the types of behaviors being examined, their frequency of occurrence, and a time frame of their occurrence. The observations should be made at random times so that employees do not change their natural modes of behavior when observed. The time of observation should be long enough for a complete cycle of behaviors associated with a work task of interest to be examined. Two or three repetitions of this cycle should be examined to determine consistency in behavior with an employee and among employees. Random times of recording behavior is most effective in obtaining accurate indications of typical behavior. The recorded behaviors can be analyzed by the frequency and pattern of their occurrence as well as their significance for hazard control. Hot spots can be identified. All behaviors need to be grouped into categories in regard to hazard control efforts and then prioritized.

The next step is to define the proper work practices that need to be instilled to control the hazardous procedures observed. Sometimes the observations provide the basis for desired good procedures. Often, however, new procedures need to be developed. There are four classes of work practices that should be considered: (a) hazard recognition and reporting; (b) housekeeping—which concerns the cleanliness of the work areas; (c) doing work tasks safely; and (d) emergency procedures. The recognition of workplace hazards requires that the employee be cognizant of hazardous conditions through training and education and that the employee actively watches for these conditions. Knowledge is useless unless it is applied. These work practices ensure the application of knowledge and the reporting of observed hazards to fellow workers and supervisors. Housekeeping is a significant consideration for two reasons. A clean working environment makes it easier to observe hazards. It is also a more motivating situation that enhances the use of other work practices.

The most critical set of work practices deals with carrying out work tasks safely through correct skill use and hazard avoidance behaviors. This is where the action is between the employee and the environment and must receive emphasis on instilling proper work practices. There are situations that occur that are extremely hazardous and require the employee to get out of the work area or to stay clear of the work area. These work practices are often life-saving procedures that need special consideration because they are used only under highly stressful conditions, such as emergencies.

Each of these areas needs to have work practices spelled out. These should be statements of the desired behaviors specified in concise, easily understandable language. Statements should typically be one sentence long and should never exceed three sentences. Details should be excluded unless they are critical to the proper application of the work practice. Having specified the desired work practices employees should be given classroom and on-the-job training to teach them the work practices. Training approaches discussed earlier should be applied. This includes classroom training as well as an opportunity for employees to test the work practices in the work setting. To ensure the sustained use of the learned work practices it is important to motivate workers through the use of incentives. There are many types of incentives, including (a) money, (b) tokens, (c) privileges, (d) social rewards, (e) recognition, (f) feedback, (g) participation, and (h) any other factors that motivate employees such as enriched job tasks. Positive incentives should be used to develop consistent work practice patterns. Research has demonstrated that the use of financial rewards in the form of increased hourly wage can have a beneficial effect on employee safety behaviors and reduced hazard exposure (Hopkins, Conard, & Smith; 1986; Smith, Anger, Hopkins, & Conrad, 1983).

Safety Programs

The preceding materials provide the basis for developing an effective company hazard control program. However, there are a number of other elements to consider in developing a safety program or upgrading your current program. These include organizational policies, managing various elements of the program, motivational practices, hazard control procedures, dealing with employees, accident investigations, and injury recording. Aspects of each of these have already been discussed and in this section they are integrated into an effective safety program. There has been considerable research into the necessary elements for a successful safety program (see Cohen, 1977) and how these elements should be applied. One primary factor emerges from every study on this subject. A safety program will not be successful unless there is a commitment to the program by top management. This dictates that there be a written organizational policy statement on the importance of safety and the general procedures the corporation intends to use to meet this policy. Having such a policy is just the first step toward effective management commitment.

Smith et al. (1978) has shown that it takes more than a written policy to ensure successful safety performance. It takes involvement on the part of all levels of management in the safety program. From the top managers it means that they must get out onto the shop floor often and talk to employees about plant conditions and safety problems. This can be on a scheduled basis, but seems to be more effective on an informal basis. For middle managers there is a need to participate in safety program activities such as monthly hazard awareness meetings or weekly toolbox meetings.[1] This does not necessitate active presentations by these managers, but it does mean active participation in group discussions and in answering worker questions. These activities bring the upper and middle managers in touch with potential hazard sources and educates them to shop floor problems. It also demonstrates to employees that management cares about their safety and health.

Another aspect of management commitment is the level of resources that are made available for safety programming. Cohen (1977) in reviewing successful programs found that organizational investment in full-time safety staff was a key feature to good plant safety performance. The effectiveness of safety and health staff was greater the higher they were in the management structure. The National Safety Council (1974) has suggested that plants with less than 500 employees and a low to moderate hazard level can have an effective program with a part-time safety professional. Larger plants or those with more hazards need more safety staff.

Along with funds for staffing, successful programs also make funds available for hazard abatement in a timely fashion. Thus, segregated funds are budgeted to be drawn on when needed. This gives the safety program flexibility in meeting emergencies when funds may be hard to get quickly from operating departments. An interesting fact about companies with successful safety programs is that they are typically efficient in their resource utilization, planning, budgeting, quality control, and other aspects of general operations, and that they include safety programming and budgeting as just another component of their overall management program. They do not single safety out or make it special; instead they integrate it into their operations to make it a natural part of daily work activities.

Organizational motivational practices will influence employee safety behavior. Research has demonstrated that organizations that exercise humanistic management approaches have better safety performance (Cohen, 1977; Smith et al., 1978). These approaches are sensitive to employee needs and thus encourage employee involvement. Such involvement leads to greater awareness and higher motivation levels conducive to proper em-

---

[1]A toolbox meeting is a "formal," structured meeting either before the work starts or after work in which the supervisor presents an issue regarding safety and discusses this with the employees on the crew. Topics for discussion and materials are most often organized by the safety department. Some organizations such as the National Safety Council have packages of materials and discussion points that can be purchased and used by smaller corporations that do not have safety departments. There are typically handouts for employees that provide the highlights of the presentation and pertinent details.

ployee behavior. Organizations that use punitive motivational techniques for influencing safety behavior have poorer safety records than those using positive approaches. An important motivational factor is encouraging communication between various levels of the organization (employees, supervisors, managers). Such communication increases participation in safety and builds employee and management commitment to safety goals and objectives. Often informal communication is a more potent motivator and provides more meaningful information for hazard control.

An interesting research finding is that general promotional programs aimed at enhancing employee awareness and motivation, such as annual safety awards dinners and annual safety contests are not very effective in influencing worker behavior or company safety performance (Smith et al., 1978). The major reason is that their relationship in time and subject matter to actual plant hazards and safety considerations is so abstract that workers cannot translate the rewards to specific actions that need to be taken. It is hard to explain why these programs are so popular in industry because they are so ineffective. Their major selling points are that they are easy to implement and highly visible, whereas more meaningful approaches take more effort.

Another important consideration in employee motivation and improved safety behavior is training. There are two general types of safety training that are of central importance: (a) skills training and (b) training in hazard awareness. Training is a key component to any safety program because it is important to employee knowledge of workplace hazards and proper work practices, and it provides the skills necessary to use the knowledge and the work practices. Both formal and informal training seem to be effective in enhancing employee safety performance. Formal training programs provide the knowledge and skills for safe work practices, and informal training by first-line supervisors and fellow employees maintain and sharpen learned skills.

All safety programs should have a formalized approach to hazard control. This often includes an inspection system to define workplace hazards, accident investigations, record keeping, a preventive maintenance program, a machine guarding program, review of new purchases to ensure compliance with safety guidelines, and housekeeping requirements. All contribute to a "safety climate" that demonstrates to workers that safety is important. However, the effectiveness of specific aspects of such a formalized hazard control approach have been questioned (Cohen, 1977; Smith et al., 1978). For instance, formalized inspection programs have been shown to only deal with a small percentage of workplace hazards (Smith et al., 1971). In fact, Cohen (1977) indicated that more frequent informal inspections may be more effective than more formalized approaches. However, the significance of formalized hazard control programs is that they establish the groundwork for other programs such as work practice improvement and training. In essence, they are the foundation for other safety approaches. They are also a source of positive motivation by demonstrating management interest in employees by providing a clean workplace free of physical hazards. Smith et al. (1978) has demonstrated that sound environmental conditions are a significant contribution to company safety performance and to employee motivation.

Conclusion

Reducing occupational injuries and illnesses requires a multifaceted approach that can define hazards, evaluate risks, establish means to control risks, and incorporate management, supervision, and employees actively in the process. This chapter has defined various workplace hazards to provide a starting point for determining risks. In addition, it has described programs and methods to involve employees and managers in defining and controlling the identified risks. These specific methods for defining hazards, assessing the level of risk, engaging employees in hazard recognition and control, and organizational structures for safety programs are the major elements of an occupational hazard control program that can lead to improved organizational safety.

References

Best's Loss Control Engineering Manual. (2002). Oldwick, NJ: A. M. Best.

Centers for Disease Control (CDC). (1983). Leading work-related diseases and injuries— United States; Musculoskeletal injuries. *Morbidity and Mortality Weekly Report, 32,* 189–191.

Cohen, A. (1977). Factors in successful occupational safety programs. *Journal of Safety Research, 9,* 168–178.

Cohen, A., & Colligan, M. J. (1998). *Assessing occupational safety and health training: A literature review.* Cincinnati, OH: National Institute for Occupational Safety and Health.

Conard, R. (1983). *Employee work practices.* Cincinnati, OH: U.S. Department of Health and Human Services, National Institute for Occupational Safety and Health.

Death on the Job. (1991). Burbank, CA: Half Court Productions.

DiNardi, S. R. (1997). *The occupational environment: Its evaluation and control.* Fairfax, VA: American Industrial Hygiene Association Press.

Eckstrand, G. (1964). *Current status of the technology of training* (AMRL Doc. Tech. Rpt. 64-86). Washington, DC: U.S. Department of Defense.

Federal Mine Safety & Health Act of 1977. (1977). Pub. L. No. 91-173, as amended by Pub. L. No. 95-164.

Hopkins, B. L., Conard, R. J., & Smith, M. J. (1986). Effective and reliable behavioral control technology. *American Industrial Hygiene Association Journal, 47*(12), 785–791.

International Labour Organization (ILO). (1998). Occupational safety and health. Retrieved 1998, from http://www.ilo.org/public/english/90travai/sechyg/intro.htm.

Kalimo, R., Lindstrom, K., & Smith, M. J. (1997). Psychosocial approach in occupational health. In G. Salvendy (Ed.), *Handbook of human factors and ergonomics* (pp. 1059–1084). New York: John Wiley & Sons.

Leigh, J. P., Markowitz, S. B., Fahs, M., Shin, C., & Landrigan, P. J. (1997). Occupational injuries and illness in the United States. *Archives of Internal Medicine, 157,* 1557–1568.

National Safety Council. (1974). *Accident prevention manual for industrial operations* (7th ed.). Chicago: Author.

NIOSH. (1973). *The industrial environment: Its evaluation and control* (NIOSH Publication No. 74-117). Washington, DC: U.S. Government Printing Office.

NIOSH. (1977). *Occupational diseases: A guide to their recognition.* Washington, DC: U.S. Government Printing Office.

NIOSH. (1996a). National occupational research agenda. Available at http://www.cdc.gov/niosh/norhmpg.html.

NIOSH. (1996b). *National occupational research agenda—Disease and injury priority areas.* Retrieved March 29, 2002, from http://www.cdc.gov/niosh/diseas.html

Occupational Safety and Health Act of 1970. (1970). Pub. L. No. 91-596, S. 2193 (Dec. 29).

Salvendy, G. (1997). *Handbook of human factors and ergonomics.* New York: John Wiley and Sons.

Smith, M. J. (1986). Occupational stress. In G. Salvendy (Ed.), *Handbook of human factors* (pp. 844–860). New York: John Wiley & Sons.

Smith, M. J., Bauman, R. D., Kaplan, R. P., Cleveland, R., Derks, S. Sydow, M., & Coleman, P. J. (1971). *Inspection effectiveness.* Washington, DC: Occupational Safety and Health Administration.

Smith, M., Anger, W. K., Hopkins, B., & Conrad, R. (1983). Behavioral–psychological approaches for controlling employee chemical exposures. In *Proceedings of the Tenth World Congress on the Prevention of Occupational Accidents and Diseases.* Geneva: International Social Security Association.

Smith, M. J., Cohen, H. H., Cohen, A., & Cleveland, R. (1978). Characteristics of successful safety programs. *Journal of Safety Research, 10,* 5–15.

Smith, M. J., & Sainfort, P. C. (1989). A balance theory of job design and for stress reduction. *International Journal of Industrial Ergonomics, 4,* 67–79.

4

Toward an Integrated Framework for Comprehensive Organizational Wellness: Concepts, Practices, and Research in Workplace Health Promotion

Joel B. Bennett, Royer F. Cook, and Kenneth R. Pelletier

Two recent trends affect how organizations design and manage work. First, organizations are adapting more complex, nonbureaucratic models, pursuing multiple and disparate goals, and restructuring through upsizing, downsizing, and outsourcing (Gowing, Kraft, & Quick, 1998). These changes create pressures that have a negative impact on employee health. As a result, new models of organizational well-being that balance health and productivity are needed (Cooper, 1999; Karasek, 2001). Second, the changing nature of work occurs in tandem with the development of management models, which treat organizations as complex systems that undergo rapid cycles of change (e.g., "emergent" organizations; Hock, 1999; Stacey, Griffin, & Shaw, 2001; Syvantek & Brown, 2000).

This chapter seeks to help occupational health psychologists respond to these trends. First, it reviews the literature within three areas of comprehensive organizational health, distinguishing key postulates and insights. Second, it encourages occupational health psychologists to create a more interdisciplinary and dynamic approach to wellness. We borrow from academic, popular, and business literatures to speak to the cross-disciplinary role of occupational health psychologists and the importance of spanning fields that border occupational health psychology (e.g., health management, occupational medicine, managerial studies, training, and development). The final section of the chapter discusses ideas for future exploration of an integrated model of organizational wellness.

Three Streams of Organizational Health: Concept, Practice, and Health Promotion

The following review targets three perspectives or streams of research and practice. The first focuses on the concept of the "healthy workplace" and the idea that some workplaces are generally healthier than others (e.g., Jaffe, 1995). This stream aspires to a holistic view of organizations that learn about, maintain, and enhance health across multiple dimensions. The second stream involves practice-oriented and consultative models that promote organizational health. The third stream focuses on comprehensive or multifactor health promotion and disease management programs. Although the different streams speak to a comprehensive view of organizational wellness, they tend to emphasize different levels of health (individual, job, or organizational); this chapter discusses concepts and practices across these levels and suggests that occupational health psychologists must play a more proactive role in assessing relationships and integrating strategies among these levels.

The failure to work from an integrative model often limits the contributions of one of the streams. For example, organizational-level change strategies can have unintended and negative effects on health and stress (Hochschild, 1997; Landsbergis, Cahill, & Schnall, 1999). Conversely, employee-level participation in health promotion is limited and positive outcomes short-lived when either upper management or the workplace social environment is not supportive (Israel, Parker, Godenhar, & Heany, 1996).

Occupational health psychologists can also play a role in integrating wellness initiatives with financial management of health care. Significant advances in such integration have recently occurred in the field of health and productivity management (Goetzel & Ozminkowski, 2000), to be reviewed later. There is also growing recognition that financial health correlates with investments in employee well-being (Goetzel, Guindon, Turshen, & Ozminskowski, 2001). Lau and May (1998) assessed the financial health of companies identified as "the best companies to work for" according to several quality-of-work life criteria (opportunity for career growth, a culture of support and openness; Levering & Moskowitz, 1994). Compared to other well-established, financially stable companies, the "best companies" had higher levels of sales and asset growth and return on assets.

The reviews of the three streams presented in the following sections are not exhaustive but instead are intended to provide a broad set of references as a basis for synthesis and integration.

The Healthy Company: Conceptual Approaches

> There must be criteria for a healthy organization. I don't know what they are or if anybody has listed them, but it is imperative to do this.
> —Abraham Maslow (1965/1998, p. 25)

> If we view organizations as adaptive, problem-solving, organic structures, then inferences about effectiveness have to be made on the basis of the processes through which the organization approaches problems. . . . In other words, no single time-slice of organizational performance can provide valid indicators of organizational health.
> —Warren Bennis (1962/1993, p. 49)

There are two types of definitions of organizational health: criteria and process. Maslow emphasized organizational criteria (cf., Beckhard, 1997; Powell, 1999). Bennis focused on processes or adaptations (cf., Beer, 1980; Morgan, 1998). Since Maslow and Bennis, many definitions of a "healthy company" have been developed. Such definitions include lists of qualities (e.g., adaptability, high performance, and flexibility; Quick & Quick, 1984), theoretical models that situate corporate health as an outcome of psychological processes (Guthrie & Olian, 1990), or box-and-arrow causal models with many factors (e.g., management systems: Danna & Griffin, 1999; health care utilization: Peterson & Wilson, 1998). Other models describe the related concepts of flexibility (Mayrhofer, 1997), individual-organizational fit (James, 1999), or fitness (Anderson, 1999).

Although there is wide variation in how conceptual models define health, authors from disparate areas have used common themes to synthesize concepts. Figure 4.1 provides a schematic overview of these overlapping themes. They are (a) *multidimensional assessments* in core areas of health; (b) *multilevel descriptions* of health that include the individual, group, and organization; (c) *self-assessment* whereby organizations continuously monitor health levels, use feedback, make changes, and reassess; (d) *effort in health promotion* through singular or multipronged programs that are accessible to employees; (e) awareness of and responsiveness to the *degree of fit or congruence* across levels, as well as between the organization and its surrounding environment; (f) awareness of and responsiveness to *core tensions* that require balancing and moderation; and (g) awareness of and response to stages or phases of general *development and regression*.

Eight Core Themes in Conceptions of Organizational Health

Each theme is briefly reviewed, with references to empirical studies or measures that illustrate the theme. The reader will note a tendency, across themes, to move from an individual emphasis that highlights criteria definitions (themes 1 and 2) to an organizational emphasis that highlights more dynamic and complex definitions (themes 6 and 7). There is overlap in themes, which speaks to the need for an integral model. For example, self-assessment (theme 3) plays an important role in health promotion and other themes. Analysis of each theme also yields basic postulates of organizational health (Table 4.1). These postulates may provide a foundation for future studies as well as for training occupational health psychologists in integrative organizational wellness.

Theme 1: Multidimensional View of Organizational Health

Many researchers assume that there are several dimensions of health. Fleisher, Brown, and Fleisher (1996) proposed six dimensions and described "comprehensive organizational wellness" at individual and group levels.

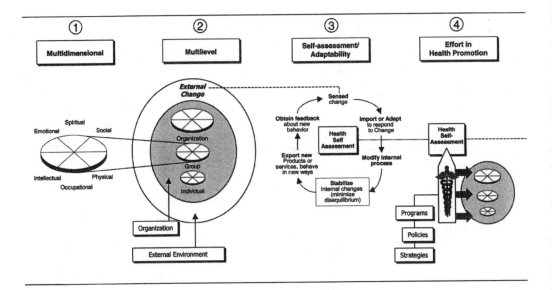

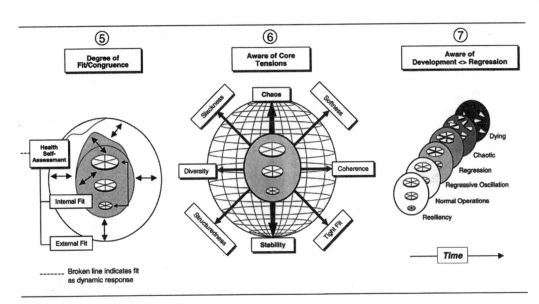

Figure 4.1.   Seven core themes in conceptions of organizational health.

Researchers have also developed multidimensional assessments for individual health (wellness and lifestyle questionnaires), although there has been little research that assesses their discriminant validity or explores these dimensions at group- or organizational-levels. Psychometric studies have demonstrated reliability of the Perceived Wellness Survey, which assesses intellectual, social, physical, emotional, spiritual, and psychological wellness (e.g., Adams, Bezner, Drabbs, Zambarano, & Steinhardt, 2000).

Table 4.1.   Postulates and Key References of Organizational Health
(From the Conceptual Literature)

Theme	Postulate of organizational health (key reference)
1 Multidimensional	A healthy organization considers multiple dimensions of employee well-being (e.g., social, emotional, physical, spiritual). See Fleisher et. al. (1996), Adams et al. (2000).
2 Multilevel	A healthy organization considers multiple levels of health (across individual, groups, departments, as well as the entire organization) and is aware of cross-level relationships across these areas. See Kidwell, Mossholder, & Bennett, 1997; Soderfeldt et al., (1997).
3 Self-assessment/ adaptability	Using information from the two previous factors, a healthy organization is committed to continually monitoring its state of health and to adjust and adapt to maintain optimal levels of well-being across levels and dimensions of health. See Bennis (1962/1993); Schein (1965).
4 Effort in health promotion	A healthy organization makes an ongoing effort to provide programs and policies that increase the well-being of employees. See O'Donnell (2001) and any issue of the *American Journal of Health Promotion.*
5 Fitness/congruence	A healthy organization maintains levels of relative fitness or congruence at two levels: (a) between the organization and the external environment (market, economy, and social community), and (b) between components within the organization (i.e., communication between individuals, groups, and executive levels). See Brown & Eisenhardt (1998); Kelly & Allison (1999); Kozlowski & Salas (1997).
6 Core tensions	A healthy organization is aware of and addresses the various tensions involved in maintaining levels of optimal health (e.g., serving internal and external customers). See Mayrhofer (1997).
7 Regression/ development	A healthy organization maintains an awareness of cycles of growth, regression, and deterioration in overall organizational vitality. This awareness is used to make adjustments in health efforts (5) and respond to different levels of incongruence (6) and tension (7). See Kilburg, Stokes, & Kuruvilla (1998).

A number of health risk appraisals assess multiple dimensions of health, such as TestWell (National Wellness Institute, 2001), the Health Promoting Life Style Profile (Megel et al., 1994; Walker, Sechrist, & Pender 1987), and the Computerized Lifestyle Assessment (Stein & Skinner, 1998). These measures include subscales on nutrition, emotional health, drug use, sleep, exercise, health responsibility, interpersonal support, stress management, and spirituality. Future research should assess the divergent–convergent validity of such measures and how they may be applied at the level of group or team health.

Theme 2: Multilevel Descriptions of Organizational Health

The separate dimensions of health described previously have received attention at individual, group, and organizational levels, but often under different labels. Social health has been explored at the individual level as social support (e.g., Loscocco & Spitze, 1990) and at the group level as cohesiveness (Kidwell, Mossholder, & Bennett, 1997; Wech, Mossholder, Steel, & Bennett, 1998). Social health is also defined at organizational levels, where it may be reflected in policies concerning social responsibility to workers (*social capital*; Cohen & Prusak, 2001), surrounding communities (Schwartz & Gibb, 1999), and the natural environment (*sustainability*; *Reflections,* 2000). Intellectual or cognitive health has been assessed as beliefs and information processing surrounding health care (e.g., Christensen, Moran, & Wiebe, 1999). The concept of cognitive health should become increasingly important as businesses place more emphasis on intellectual capital (knowledge management; Agor, 1997; Bassi, 1997) and view such capital as a sign of organization health (Mayo, 2000). Recent studies suggest a relationship between spirituality or religious involvement and health, and that work climates that honor or respect employee spirituality may also be more productive (Mitroff & Denton, 1999; Seybold & Hill, 2001). Additional research should explore how indexes of spiritual health may be extended to organizational levels (see Macdonald, Friedman, & Kuentzel, 1999). Multilevel statistical models have also recently been applied in the study of how organizational-level factors affect individual health (Bennett & Lehman, 1999; Kidwell, Mossholder, & Bennett, 1997; Soderfeldt et al., 1997; Van-Yperen & Snijders, 2000).

Theme 3: Self-Assessment of Health and Adaptability

An organization's capacity to self-monitor internal health as well as changes in the environment is key to sustained wellness. Bennis (1962/1993, pp. 60–63) specified three criteria for organizational health that have self-assessment at their core: (a) *adaptability,* (b) a *clear sense of identity,* and (c) a *capacity to test reality.* Based on Bennis's work, Schein (1965) proposed the "adaptive-coping" cycle. When an effective company (a) senses a change in the environment, it (b) imports relevant information and (c) changes processes to accommodate the change, while (d) maintaining relative stability. Those processes (e) lead to new services or products and to (f) obtaining feedback on the success of the change (Schein, 1965, p. 99).

Others have stressed the importance of self-assessment and adaptability in the organizational stress literature (Beer, 1980; Quick & Quick, 1984), in organizational development, and, most recently, in the field of organizational complexity (Pascale, Milleman, & Gioja, 2000). For example, a healthy or "adaptive" employee who senses increased strain would take preventive action and seek out social support to replenish the store of adaptive energy.

Occupational health psychologists can also play an important role in assessment by using and refining extant measures of healthy work climate or culture. The 69-item Worksite Health Climate Scale assesses whether workers feel their organization values health, has supportive supervisors and coworkers, and has clear organizational norms for practicing healthy behaviors (Ribisl & Reischl, 1993). The shorter 10-item Organizational Wellness Scale asks employee's perceptions about healthy work climate, coworker respect and openness, and organizational supports for wellness (Bennett & Lehman, 1997). Other self-assessment measures include the Organizational Health Scale (Miles, 1969) and the Organizational Health Inventory (Hoy & Woolfolk, 1993). Future research should assess the validity and reliability of these measures and explore whether they moderate the negative effects of organizational stress and the positive effects of health promotion.

Theme 4: Effort in Health Promotion

The literature on health promotion (O'Donnell, 2001) suggests three main strategies through which an organization makes efforts at health promotion: specific programs, human resource policies, and managerial–environmental strategies. Effort may be defined as the frequency, intensity, or availability of each of these strategies or the degree to which all strategies are used. First, organizations may provide specific health promotion programs (e.g., health-risk appraisals, smoking-cessation classes, etc.) or combine these into multicomponent programs. Second, human resource policies and training programs may be seen as investments in "human capital" (Barrier, 1997; Guthrie & Olian, 1990)—for example, employee assistance programs, diversity training, and so forth. Third, management practices can emphasize supportive climates and otherwise reduce strain through job and environmental designs (Stokols, 1992; Warr, 1999).

Theme 5: Degree of Fit or Congruence

The concept of fit has been discussed at the individual level as well as an intraorganizational and extraorganizational dynamic. At the individual level, person–environment fit (P–E fit) models describe how individual values, needs, and abilities fit or are congruent with the organization's values (culture), demands, and resources (Caplan, 1987; Peterson & Wilson, 1998). Empirical studies have supported models of P–E fit. Lack of fit between cognitive ability and job complexity was associated with increased substance abuse (Oldham & Gordon, 1999), and fit between environmental demands for creativity and creative abilities was associated with less job strain (Livingstone, Nelson, & Barr, 1997).

Intraorganizationally, congruence across individual, group, and organizational levels enhances learning and adaptability (Kozlowski & Salas, 1997). An organization is more likely to promote learning when its structure is congruent—that is, it keeps employees informed, allows employees to learn quickly, and enables them to transfer knowledge across organizational levels. The concept of the people-centered organization applies organizational design strategies, policies, and workflows to maximize congruence across levels (Overholt, Connally, Harrington, & Lopez, 2000). Overholt developed the Organizational Flexibility Profile to assess how well organizational components fit together (Overholt et al., 2000).

Extraorganizational fit or congruence refers to an organization's competitive success in the economic environment, profit revenue, or economic health. These economic perspectives have been recently grafted from biological models. For example, Anderson's "fitness landscape" model depicts fitness as the organizations ability to survive: "The more offspring an organism contributes to the next generation, the fitter it is" (Anderson, 1999, p. 224). To be economically healthy and maintain competitiveness, organizations continually work out tradeoffs between internal goals and processes and external demands and constraints. Rand (1999) argued that economic health requires that managers have a clear view of organization structure, as well as alignment of organizational elements. "The relational organizational structure will provide managers at all levels with the visibility required to see the condition of their revenue-producing processes . . . and insure its economic health" (Rand, 1999, p. 113). These ideas about fitness have been extended into actual practices in business strategy (Brown & Eisenhardt, 1998; Kelly & Allison, 1999).

Theme 6: Awareness and Responsiveness to Core Tensions

Organizations are rarely in a state of perfect congruence, and tensions naturally arise in the course of adaptation to the environment. Healthy organizations manage "adaptive tensions" as part of their self-assessment of health (Theme 3) and maintenance of fitness (Theme 5). A core idea in complexity theory is that healthy organizations are rarely in a state of equilibrium but live more "on the edge of chaos." The current theme reviews some of the core tensions (disequilibria) as outlined by Mayrhofer (1997). The cardinal tension that informs organizational health is Stability ↔ Chaos, also referred to as relative predictability–unpredictability, certainty–uncertainty, or security–insecurity. In the current model, this cardinal tension informs the other three described later. Chaos occurs with too much diversity, softness, and slack; excessive stability arises with too much coherence, structure, and tight fit.

Diversity ↔ Coherence refers to the need to maintain some uniformity or coherence through rules and norms, while accommodating different people and divergent environmental demands. G. Powell (1998) addressed diversity ↔ coherence in terms of employee selection processes. If organizations only select employees who fit with the culture, cohesiveness is preserved but at the cost of deemphasizing multicultural values and diverse knowledge, skills, and abilities. Softness ↔ Structuredness refers to the idea that a healthy organization is neither too structured, bureaucratic, nor hierarchical, nor overly flexible and innovative. Quinn (2000) explained that organizational form is not an end in itself but should come in the service of creating a productive community "which is both structured and spontaneous" (p. 51).

Organizational Slack ↔ Tight Fit shows that organizational resources (time, hardware, and human resources) are either (a) available only in specified amounts and on an as-needed basis in an attempt to remain lean and cut costs (tight fit), or (b) available in more abundant supply and in different configurations to improve quality, avoid stressors in specific areas, and promote innovation (organizational slack). Cheng and Kesner (1997) found that as a firm allocates resources to internal operational efficiency, increases in slack decrease management ability to respond to environment changes. They conclude that managers might have to be selective in their attempts to store up slack resources for use in turbulent times.

Different types of stress occur when management places a tight rein on resources. Stress rises in highly demanding work environments over which employees have little control (Karasek et al., 1998) or where work pressures exist in the absence of supportive elements (Vagg & Spielberger, 1998). A growing concern for many companies is tight fit for time (Lawson, 2001). Time pressures, workaholic norms, or "Type A" organizations (Cunningham, 1997) can have negative effects on employee well-being (Bonebright, Clay, & Ankenmann, 2000).

Theme 7: Awareness and Responsiveness to Organizational Development and Regression

This last theme concerns the general organizational lifecycle and borrows the metaphors of growth, aging, regression, and dying (e.g., Cameron, Sutton, & Whetton, 1988). Specifically, we refer to a model developed by Kilburg and colleagues and depicted at far right in Figure 4.1 (Ginsberg, Kilburg, & Gomes, 1999; Kilburg, Stokes, & Kuruvilla, 1998). Following from earlier themes of adaptation and tension the model suggests that "organizations must manage both internal and external regressive forces by creating or using internal balancing forces in order to prevent dysfunctional regression that can dramatically and adversely influence performance" (Ginsberg et al., 1999, p. 443).It is important to note that organizational regression has potential consequences for the individual (stress, behavioral health problems), work group (conflict), organization (downsizing), and community (increased poverty).

Summary and Application of Seven Core Themes:
Cross-Level Mimicry

The seven themes were derived from a broad reading of the literature on organizational health. They may be best considered as rubrics for research and practice rather than a set of health criteria. Our goal is to build an integral model, to increase occupational health psychologists' awareness of bordering fields (management, training, medicine), and to provide terms and references to increase occupational health psychologists' roles in these fields. A key insight from this synthesis is that processes at one level are either mimicked or are replicated at another level. For example, individual ability to cope with stress is mirrored in the organization's capacity to adapt to changes in the economy and broader environment (fitness). Similarly, individual ability to monitor health levels is mirrored by the organization's ability to do the same. In short, there is an ongoing relationship between individual, group, and organizational processes of health. This insight is at the core of the approaches described next.

The Healthy Company:
Practice Models–Practitioner Approaches

> Health promotion proponents can state with greater conviction that how people behave, whether in preventing a problem before it begins or better managing disease when it occurs, has enormous cost saving impli-cations. . . . The good news is that we know better than we did 10 or 20 years ago how to modify risk. Likewise more research continues to surface showing how these interventions positively impact costs.
>
> —Thomas Golaszweski (2000, p. 53)

Most companies will not use and commit to healthy organizational practices unless those practices help cut costs and improve productivity. Practitioners can establish a strategic alignment between healthy practices, cost containment, and productivity goals through health-promotion ap-proaches (Heany & Goetzel, 1997), cultural interventions (Rosen, 1996). Before reviewing these approaches, it helps to understand the relationship between behavioral risks and health care costs.

Introduction to Modifiable Health Risks and
Cost Expenditures

Recently, research studies have shown that workers who live less than healthy lifestyles represent significant cost risks to their employers. The Health Enhancement Research Organization (HERO) has conducted the largest of these studies (www.the-hero.org). The HERO sample consisted of 46,026 employees of six large employers: Chevron; Health Trust, Inc.; Hoffman-La Roche, Inc.; Marriott Corporation; the state of Tennessee, and the state of Michigan. Each of these employers was a client of the StayWell Company of St. Paul, Minnesota, and the MEDSTAT Group, Inc., of Ann Arbor, Michigan. All employees completed a health-risk appraisal (HRA), which was linked with files for health claims. Results that show relationships between HRA and health claims are reported in two studies (Anderson et al., 2000; Goetzel et al., 1998).

Results from this study show that employees at high risk for 7 of 10 risk categories had significantly higher expenditures when compared with those at lower risk. The difference between those with and without a risk was highest for those reporting depression (70.2% higher) and stress (46.3% higher). Moreover, employees at high risk for stress accounted for the largest incremental expenditures of any high-risk category ($6.2 million, or 7.9% of total health care expenditures). This was a result of the relatively high prevalence of stress (18.5% of the sample) combined with its high impact. These findings should be very useful to occupational health psychologists in that—from a cost perspective—they suggest mental health risks may be even more important than other types of health risks (e.g., cardiovascular-related). Moreover, because workplace programs may be cost-effective for improving stress (Murphy, 1996), depression (Simone et al., 2001), and alcohol abuse (Sturm, Zhang, & Schoenbaum, 1999), they have relevance for managed care (e.g., Terry, 1998).

Although high alcohol use was actually associated with lower health costs, Anderson et al. (2000) suggested that this may be a function of heavy drinkers avoiding the health care system over the short term. In an attempt to address this problem, several researchers have been developing workplace prevention programs to encourage responsible drinking and early self-referral for counseling (Bennett & Lehman, 2001; Cook, Back, & Trudeau, 1996; Heirich & Sieck, 2000; Snow & Kline, 1995). Anderson et al. (2000) also pointed out the large discrepancy between rates of depression in the HERO sample (2%) and in the general population (11%; Kessler & Underwood, 1993). They suggested that underreporting of depression was a result of employee denial or stigma. Here, too, occupational health psychologists may find ways to reduce stigma associated with mental illness (Corrigan & Penn, 1999; Sayce, 2000).

The four practitioner models described next each emphasize highly interrelated elements that are common to the others. These common elements (and emphases) are linking health with productivity (health and productivity management or HPM), managing risk (behavioral risk management), building healthy cultures (R. Allen & Allen, 1987), and leadership development (Rosen, 1996). We also describe recent efforts in industry to recognize and reward companies for attempting to build healthy companies. Such efforts have the potential of shaping the design and delivery of practice models.

Health and Productivity Management

Broadly defined, HPM has three goals: (a) integration and coordination of different types of services that employees can access to promote health or when they are sick, injured, or balancing work–life issues, (b) increase of productivity (on-the-job, morale, turnover), and (c) the link between a and b—that is, to manage services—medical benefits, worker's compensation, risk management, EAPs, occupational safety—in ways that promote health and productivity. An overview of HPM can be found in Goetzel and Ozminkowski (2000) and Goetzel et al. (2001).

In a benchmark study of 43 organizations, Goetzel et al. (2001) identified 10 best-practice HPM themes: (a) alignment between HPM and the overall business strategy of the organization; (b) an interdisciplinary team focus, where diverse functional areas work together, such as human resources, employee benefits, risk management, employee assistance, safety, legal, work–life, health promotion, and security; (c) a champion or a team of champions with a sense of purpose and passion; (d) senior management and business operations were key members of the team; (e) prevention, health promotion, and wellness staff were heavily engaged; (f) emphasis on quality-of-life improvement, not just cost-cutting; (g) data, measurement, reporting, evaluation, and return on investment studies became increasingly important over time; (h) communication was constant and directed throughout the organization; (i) constant need to improve by learning from others; and (j) the team was having fun.

Behavioral Risk Management

Behavioral risk management has been described by Yandrick (1996). The notion that organizations should have policies and practices that reduce health and safety risks is critical in the fields of occupational nursing (Cameron & Heidel, 2000) and for managed care organizations that seek to reduce risks associated with increased health care use. Yandrick (1996) described nine different behavioral risks: (a) problems resulting from high stress; (b) work–life imbalances; (c) employee negligence or indifference; (d) job-related violence; (e) disgruntlement–litigiousness; (f) sabotage and theft, (g) conflicts resulting from racial or gender disharmony, (h) alcohol and drug abuse, and (i) malingering on disability health insurance or workers' compensation. Effective BRM requires that organizations maintain a close relationship with the service organization that provides behavioral health care, fully understanding provider services, standards of quality, and service–use data that can be useful, and collaborating with those providers or EAPs in managing risk through prevention and health care promotion.

BRM combines a sophisticated needs assessment with customized programming for reducing behavioral risks in five core steps: (a) conduct a behavioral risk audit (using survey, interviews, and organizational records) to determine current level of risks in the nine risk categories; (b) aggregate these data to derive an overall picture of organizational risk; (c) assess both individual and organizational risk and effectiveness of current risk management practices, such as those provided by the EAP and behavioral health care; (d) integrate this information through a management information system to help determine which activities are having an impact on individual–organizational risk and which programs are needed; (e) use information from (a) through (d) to develop a prevention, early intervention, or health promotion strategy. Returning to step a, risk managers examine changes to assess the effectiveness of interventions. Thus, BRM is an on-going integrated process. Yandrick (1996) provided several case examples of organizations that are attempting to control costs through BRM processes, including DuPont, the University of California, U.S. Oil, and the World Bank. Readers interested in other perspectives and cases should consult Wolfe and Parker (1994) and Steinbach (2000).

Healthy Culture Planning

R. Allen and colleagues developed the third practice model in organizational health (J. Allen & Bellingham, 1994; R. Allen & Allen, 1987). Their core premises are that social norms within organizations promote either healthy or unhealthy lifestyles and that the organizational-level interventions can be very effective in developing norms that promote health. This organizational culture change model has evolved over 30 years, and has most recently been labeled "the culture change planner" (Allen, 2001).

There are four phases for building supportive cultural environments. Phase I analyzes the current culture, develops program leaders, and harnesses leadership commitment through allocation of resources to any change project. Phase II creates high-level involvement of all those in the change effort, often centering around an introductory workshop designed to enable participants to visualize the desired culture. The goal of Phase III is to integrate systems through developing processes and programs for individual self-help, peer support, organizational support, and leadership development. Phase IV repeats evaluation of performance, programs, and cultural information to determine the degree to which objectives have been met and to set new objectives.

The healthy culture planning process uses various tools (www.healthy culture.com), including surveys, videos, training curriculum, self-assessments, coaching, and consultation. Healthy culture planning is similar to other large-scale interventions in organizational development but with a special focus on health. The interested reader should consult Holman and Devane (1999) for 18 leading approaches to creating positive cultural change.

The Healthy Company

Rosen (1991, 1996, 1998), through qualitative interviews and consultation, has studied a sample of progressive, people-oriented companies and derived strategies that distinguish those with healthy leadership and cultures from those that are less healthy. The book, *The Healthy Company,*(1991) distinguishing eight principles of healthy companies, is designed as a guide for leaders who wish to create a healthy company. Each principle is described along with practical tips, self-assessment questionnaires, research, company examples, and comments from leaders. The eight principles emphasize respect, nonauthoritarian leadership, flexibility, diversity, and a balance in work and family life, along with investments in health at both the individual and organizational levels. In Rosen's continued analyses (1996) leadership emerged as the single most important part of building healthy cultures. The importance of leadership is also recognized in HPM, BRM, and healthy culture planning (i.e., leadership development is part of implementation strategy).

Awarding Healthy Company Practices

A company may be motivated to adopt any of these healthy practice models to be recognized within their industry as being "a good and healthy place to work." This recognition is increasingly important as companies compete to be the "employer of choice." Several national awards provide such recognition. Perhaps the most prestigious of these is the C. Everett Koop National Health Award that acknowledges companies for comprehensive wellness efforts (Ziegler, 1998; see healthproject.stanford.edu/ koop/work.html for a list of winners since 1994, along with evaluation summaries and critiques). The National Health Award has three sets of criteria: reducing health risks, reducing medical care costs, and documenting effectiveness at reaching these goals.

The Wellness Councils of America has developed seven benchmarks for exemplary wellness initiatives and presents bronze, silver, and gold "well workplace" awards (Hunnicutt, 2000; see www.welcoa.org for a list of winners since 1993, also organized by U.S. state). The seven critical benchmarks are (a) exemplary senior-level support, (b) cohesive wellness teams, (c) data to drive the wellness initiative, (d) crafting an operating/ budgetary plan, (e) choosing appropriate programs, (f) creating supportive environments, and (g) consistently evaluating plans.

Other annual recognitions include the Canadian Healthy Workplace Award (www.nqi.ca), *Workforce Magazine*'s Optimas Award for promoting employee quality of life (www.workforce.com), and *Fortune Magazine*'s Top 100 Companies to Work For (www.fortune.com). The latter entails surveying employees with a Great Place to Work Trust Index (a climate measure assessing trust, pride, and camaraderie), a culture audit, and analysis of supporting materials (employee handbooks, orientation and recruiting materials, employee newsletters and videos, etc.; see Levering & Moskowitz, 1994; also www.greatplacetowork.com).

From a sociological perspective, these awards and recognitions may contribute to the crystallization of a cross-industry social norm, social comparison processes, and an increase in the level of organizational health in the economy. It is possible that companies may look to such awards as a way of determining their own level of health. Occupational health psychologists could conduct research to determine the within- and cross-industry effects of these awards and social comparison processes.

Summary and Application of Practitioner Approaches: Redundancy and Integration

It seems that healthy companies use strategies that integrate elements across four different practices: linking health with productivity, managing risk, building healthy cultures, and leadership development. These practices appear to serve redundant, interdependent, and integrated functions. Each practice entails a range of routines that serve the other practices such that, if there are difficulties or problems in one practice, other practices can take over deficient functions. For example, in the HPM model, cultural elements are in the background but it seems that HPM yields positive outcomes without explicit reference to culture. Similarly, BRM includes leadership development as one possible intervention, but it seems that BRM can yield results without a focus on leadership. Each approach also points to the importance of some integrative function, whether it is the presence of champions and an interdisciplinary HPM team, a BRM staff that "owns the process," or systems integration in healthy culture planning.

Health Promotion and Disease Management: Building the Evidence Base

A core principle in creating healthy organizations is that employers make efforts in health promotion (Theme 4). As this section demonstrates, there is substantial evidence that the workplace can be a very effective vehicle for educating citizens (especially those at high risk) on the powerful role of behavior on health and for promoting health behavior to prevent disease.

Collectively there have been more than 115 studies conducted between 1980 and 2000 that demonstrate the clinical and cost-effectiveness of comprehensive health promotion and disease management programs delivered in worksites. These studies demonstrate such outcomes with a wide variety of populations, size of worksites, and varying degrees of methodological quality. In fact, the most recent studies using more precise methodologies and statistical analyses tend to support rather than refute earlier findings. These scientific studies not only show that workplace health promotion programs prevent disease but that they also result in cost savings. The following sections review studies, point out areas for improvement, and list key insights that have been abstracted from previous reviews.

A Synthesis of Previous Reviews

There have been several reviews of studies on comprehensive health promotion (Goetzel, 2001; Pelletier, 1991, 1993, 1996) and a recent update on 15 studies conducted between 1998 to 2000 (Pelletier, 2001). The reader is encouraged to consult these reviews because this overview highlights only a sample of studies. Comprehensive worksite-based health promotion and disease management programs refer to those programs that provide an ongoing, integrated, program of health promotion and disease prevention that integrates the particular components (i.e. smoking cessation, stress management, lipid reduction, etc.) into a coherent, ongoing program that is consistent with corporate objectives and includes program evaluation (Pelletier, 1991, 1993, 1996).

Single risk-factor interventions, even though they might be reported as clinical and cost-effective, such as smoking cessation and hypertension screening, are not covered in this brief review.

Many programs provide services that can reach high-risk populations. Every program included in an earlier review (Pelletier, 1999) offered individualized risk-reduction counseling to high-risk employees in the context of a worksite risk-education reduction for all employees. That is, high-risk individuals could access services within a *work environment* that was supportive of health promotion across all levels of risk and a variety of health risk factors. The most significant clinical and cost outcomes are likely to be evidenced when an intervention is "selective" or focused on identified individualized risks. Such a disease management intervention needs to provide focused, consistent, sustained behavioral change, plus appropriate medical oversight. A multiple risk-factor intervention model is also applicable to single risk factors, such as smoking and hypertension, as well as to other chronic conditions such as stress, arthritis, musculoskeletal disorders, video display terminal (VDT) disabilities, back injuries or pain, and cancer, which constitute major clinical and cost liabilities to employers.

Among these comprehensive models, cardiovascular programs are perhaps the most well-developed and evaluated. One randomized trial involving 32 worksites focused on weight reduction and smoking cessation as cardiovascular risks (Jones, Bly, & Richardson, 1990). Among program participants, weight loss averaged 4.8 pounds and 43% of the smoking program participants quit. There were no significant treatment effects for the weight loss program. The cost of each smoker quitting was estimated to be $100 to $200.

One of the most rigorous worksite studies assessed multiple risk-factor reduction interventions for the management of cardiovascular disease at General Motors. The initial study by the University of Michigan group addressed weight loss and smoking cessation among 7804 employees in four different GM worksites over a three-year intervention period (e.g., Erfurt, Foote, & Heirich, 1991), and found that more frequent follow-up counseling was associated with greater participation in smoking cessation, weight loss, and greater reduction in blood pressure among hypertensives. More recently, Heirich and Seick (2000) have extended this model to reducing risks for alcohol abuse, finding that individual counseling resulted in reduced alcohol consumption for those at risk.

Pelletier (2001) described three notable methodological trends in the research on health promotion most recently published (1998 to 2000). These trends are (a) a decrease in the number of formal randomized clinical trials (RCT) in worksites; (b) an increase in companies conducting very focused disease-management programs and evaluating such interventions in pre- and postdesigns (Goetzel, Jacobson, Aldana, Vardell, & Yee, 1998; Ozminkowski et al., 2000) but not as formal RCTs; and (c) an increase in companies conducting observational studies to track the pre- and postclinical and cost outcomes of participants versus nonparticipants in comprehensive worksite programs (e.g., Schrammel, Griffiths, & Griffiths, 1998).

In addition to the Pelletier reviews, Aldana (1998) identified 24 studies that assessed the effect of health promotion on medical expenses, 17 studies that assessed effects on absenteeism, and 5 studies on cost-effectiveness. Reductions in medical care cost and absenteeism were significant in most cases, and the average cost–benefit ratio for studied health care costs and calculated cost–benefit ratios was $3.35 for every $1 spent. Aldana and Pronk (2001) concluded that even the most effective health promotion programs can affect only a portion, perhaps 0 to 20%, of all absenteeism.

Methodological Concerns

Unfortunately, although many of the studies reviewed by Pelletier (1999, 2001) have exhibited adequate to strong methodologies, some have been characterized by methodological weaknesses, including weak designs, brief follow-up periods, low participation rates and selection bias, sample attrition, and varying procedures for assessing costs and benefits. Randomized designs are seldom used (especially recently) and too often the worksite has not been appropriately used as the unit of analysis. Because virtually all worksite programs are voluntary, low participation rates (sometimes only 10%) and self-selection plague such studies. Relatively few studies focus appropriately on high-risk employees, where improvements can have the greatest impact.

Key Insights on Effectiveness

Based on a synthesis of the different reviews and the accumulated evidence it is possible to extract some key insights on health promotion. These insights are listed in Table 4.2 and describe the current state of evidence-based knowledge concerning (a) effectiveness of worksite health promotion and (b) what is needed to demonstrate effectiveness. This list may be compared with the list of principles that were derived from the earlier conceptual review (Table 4.1).

It is clear from this list of insights that when health promotion programs are well-integrated into the human resource strategy of an organization and accepted as the "norm" for the organization, they are likely to be

Table 4.2. Key Evidence-Based Insights From Research in
Worksite Health Promotion

Key insight	Description
There is evidence for overall effectiveness.	Comprehensive programs focused on multiple risk factors are likely to reduce employee risks for chronic disease.
It is important to integrate all cost savings in assessing effectiveness.	Current estimates of effectiveness may underestimate the value of health promotion because they lack integration. They are derived from assessing costs in a piecemeal fashion (e.g., combining absenteeism, sick days, sales/revenue losses). Integrated disability management is likely to evidence greater return on investment.
Short-term focus on disease management can yield evidence of effectiveness.	Disease-management interventions are more likely than general programs to generate return on investment because they focus on individuals who typically affect medical or related costs, such as absenteeism and productivity, in the near term.
Follow-up assessment is critical.	A program must be sustained for a minimum of one year to bring about risk reductions among employees and three to five years to demonstrate cost-effectiveness. Extending the length of follow-up is associated with a positive, measurable impact of the intervention.
Continued support from senior management.	Senior management should support worksite health promotion programs so that they can become part of the culture of the organization. Program effects are more likely to be maintained if the employer continues to reinforce employee risk reductions.
Employees must see support at all levels.	Employees need to perceive that senior management, supervisors, and coworkers have positive attitudes toward health because these factors are associated with improved employee health status.
High-risk employees must be served.	For a program to be effective in reducing overall morbidity and mortality, it needs the involvement of high-risk employees.
For high-risk employees, more than organizational-level health is needed.	The general health promotion environment of a worksite appears to be a necessary but not sufficient prerequisite to engender sustained risk reductions among high-risk employees.
When funds permit use programs that provide individual counseling.	The most effective (although more expensive) approach involves sustained, periodic individual counseling and support. Interventions that depend solely on educating the general employee population is relatively inexpensive but less effective.

well-implemented and to be effective. Feeling valued as an employee, having control over job performance to reduce "job strain," and being satisfied with work appear to be significant predictors of employee health and health behaviors. However, this "cultural" health may not be sufficient for addressing employees who are at high-risk for disease. In those cases, employees (as well as their dependents) may need access to programs and technologies that will specifically help them to address and manage those risks. Thus, multilevel or integral organizational health may not be possible solely through organizational-level (cultural) programs or through individual-level (health promotion) programs, but through a strategic combination of both.

The list also points to the importance of considering both the type of outcome and the temporal dimension when assessing effectiveness. To demonstrate some evidence for clinical effectiveness in the short-term it may help to use disability management programs and target high-risk populations. However, sustained programmatic efforts may be necessary to demonstrate long-term cost effectiveness. The list of insights in Table 4.2 may be considered as underlying principles for those involved in designing program evaluations in work settings. They may also be helpful for those who are working within managed care settings and are wishing to coordinate efforts with initiatives in BRM or HPM.

Toward an Integral Model of Organizational Wellness

The previous sections provide persuasive evidence that a variety of comprehensive health promotion and disease management (CHP/DM) programs aimed at the workforce can have a positive impact on worker health and on monetary outcomes. The reviews by Pelletier (1999, 2001) have shown clearly that CHP/DM programs can reduce employees' risk of disease. Most of the accumulated evidence is quite convincing, having been generated through well-designed studies conducted across a wide range of occupations and workplaces. Moreover, these studies and others (e.g., Goetzel, 2001; Goetzel et al., 1998) have demonstrated that CHP/DM programs typically result in a positive return on investment. It also seems clear that even HP programs that are less than comprehensive can have positive effects on participating workers in workplaces that are not especially healthy or supportive, particularly if they have an effective champion. Nonetheless, the evidence-based insights in Table 4.2 suggest that to optimize chances for significant and sustained impact, programs should target high-risk individuals and should exist within a healthy work culture. In other words, promotion efforts (Theme 4) should be internally congruent (Theme 5).

At the organizational level, there is evidence that healthy organizational cultures are associated with the practice of health promotion and the health and productivity of the workforce. Although the causal direction is unclear, because virtually all the data on this issue is observational and correlational in nature. Indeed, as one moves from research on health promotion programs aimed at workers to related writings on healthy work cultures, both the volume of actual studies and the quality of the methodologies drops off sharply. Nonetheless, some intriguing models—"road maps" to the healthy organization—are emerging.

Perhaps the most valid descriptions of a healthy organization are the 10 best practices of HPM studied by Goetzel et al. (2001, p. 13). Among these practices are health promotion and wellness staff who believe in and practice healthy lifestyles, employee empowerment, and self-responsibility. Moreover, they actively advocate the establishment of a "healthy company" culture. The HPM team members in these companies do not view wellness as an end in itself but as a means to support the main business mission of their organization. Indeed, if the primary focus is on improving worker health and building a healthy organization *without specific and continuing reference to how these health states affect business operations,* health promotion activities will be marginalized by senior management—activities they are happy to support (to a point) as long as business is good and costs minimal (slack) but that are seen as unnecessary luxuries when costs need cutting.

Advocates of the healthy organization would do well to consider that organizations, like individuals, need structure and challenge as much as they need flexibility and caring (see Theme 6), and that congruence needs to exist across departments (see Theme 5). The HPM approach seems in part to reflect the need for business "sinew" in the health promotion dynamic—more so, perhaps, than other healthy organization perspectives. For example, Rosen's (1991) eight principles of a healthy company are almost entirely pitched toward the "chaos" end of the spectrum, emphasizing diversity, flexibility, stress reduction, and so forth, over structure, challenge, and (perhaps most important) the importance of making the "business case" for healthy, humanistic organizational practices.

There is no denying that these approaches are appealing to managers and purchasers of programs in healthy culture development, who seem less concerned about the evidence base for effectiveness. This may be a result of the fact that (a) it may be more difficult to demonstrate program impact on culture than on individual-level health; (b) by training and disposition, purchasers generally place less emphasis on scientific effectiveness; and (c) there are no clear, measurable, uniformly accepted standards for organizational-level health as there are for physical illness and medical costs—although award mechanisms are a step in this direction (e.g., the Koop Award). Unfortunately, because of myriad shortfalls in research and monitoring systems, we know too little about which particular elements of a culture foster health and productivity.

The conceptual themes and evidence reviewed in this chapter raise the intriguing possibility that the resources allocated to organizational development (OD)/cultural change efforts (often faddish and ineffective) may have been better invested in improving employee health and well-being. We hypothesize that (a) because investments of the HPM variety have the upstream (cross-level) effect of improving the organizational culture, they may be a better investment than specialized culture change programs; and (b) these health promotion investments, to be optimally effective, must have the same type of leadership and supports that are targeted by culture change programs.

In a similar vein, as occupational health psychologists become more concerned with the potential broader effects of health promotion and disease management on organizational health and functioning, it may help to apply the concept of "readiness to change" from the stages of change theory formulated by Prochaska and DiClemente (1983). Perhaps organizations, like individuals, are located at any given time along a continuum of "readiness to change" (Eby, Adams, Russell, & Gaby, 2000; cf. "community readiness," Edwards, Jumper-Thurman, Plested, Oetting, & Swanson, 2000). We hypothesize that only when the organization is confident can it embark on a significant change toward becoming a healthy company. Other readiness-to-change principles might also apply—for example, that organizations might not be ready to move toward healthier status if they are especially stressed (going through a slump, undergoing personnel turbulence, and so forth); that organizations may fail at initial attempts to become healthier but succeed in moving forward at a later date when the internal and external environments are more supportive.

As mentioned at the outset of this chapter, the authors seek to encourage occupational health psychologists to reach beyond issues of individual worker health to cross discipline and organizational levels in a more dynamic or integrated approach to promoting organizational wellness. To do so, occupational health psychologists must play a more proactive role in assessing relationships and integrating strategies between organizational-, job-, and individual-level health promotion. Occupational health psychologists can begin to build a more systematic and scientific study of healthy organizations by formulating, operationalizing, and testing hypotheses like those proposed previously. Following the sections of this chapter, occupational health psychologists can (a) sharpen, clarify, and operationalize conceptions of a healthy company; (b) identify and distinguish those aspects of systemic interventions or practice models that are most effective, and (c) use key insights from the neighboring field of comprehensive health promotion (see Table 4.2).

In the view of the authors, the HPM approach appears the most promising of the strategies for promoting healthy workforce both at the organizational and the individual-level of analysis, for the reasons stated previously. However, which approach is better—HPM, BRM, and so forth—and under what circumstances is an empirical question. The set of core themes (Figure 4.1 and Table 4.1) may provide occupational health psychologists some tools for understanding these limiting conditions. Under some circumstances (during stages of resiliency or periods of stability), Allen's healthy culture planning might be effective for laying the groundwork and also for sustaining a culture that supports circumscribed health promotion programs. Perhaps Yandrick's BRM model may be more internally congruent within high-risk or safety sensitive worksites.

If we are to shed light on these central questions of organizational health, we must apply more dynamic concepts of organizational health, raise and broaden our sights, sharpen and apply improved systems of measurement at the organizational level, and explore the relationships among intervention strategies, worker health and performance, and organizational performance and wellness.

References

Adams, T. B., Bezner, J. R., Drabbs, M. E., Zambarano, R. J., & Steinhardt, M. A. (2000). The relationship of spiritual and psychological dimensions of wellness to perceived wellness. *Journal of American College Health, 48,* 165–174.

Agor, W. H. (1997). The measurement, use, and development of intellectual capital to increase public sector productivity. *Public Personnel Management, 26*(2), 175–186.

Aldana, S. G. (1998, March/April). Financial impact of worksite health promotion and methodological quality of evidence. *The Art of Health Promotion, 2*(1), 1–8.

Aldana, S. G., & Pronk, N. P. (2001). Health promotion programs, modifiable health risks, and employee absenteeism. *Journal of Occupational and Environmental Medicine, 43*(1), 36–46.

Allen, J. (2001). *Culture change planner.* Retrieved June 1, 2001, from www.healthyculture. com /Articles/CCplanner.html

Allen, J., & Bellingham, R. (1994). Building supportive cultural environments. In M. O'Donnell & J. S. Harris (Eds.), *Health promotion in the workplace* (pp. 204–216). Albany, NY: Delmar.

Allen, R., & Allen, J. (1987). A sense of community and positive culture: Core enabling factors in successful cultural base health promotion programs. *American Journal of Health Promotion, 1*(3), 40–47.

Anderson, P. (1999). Complexity theory and organization science. *Organization Science, 10*(3), 216–232.

Anderson, P., Whitmer, W., Goetzel, R. Ozminkowski, R. J., Wasserman, J., et al. (2000). The relationship between modifiable health risks and group-level health care expenditures. *American Journal of Health Promotion, 15*(1), 45–52.

Barrier, M. (1997, Sept.). Building a healthy company culture. *Nations Business, 85*(9), 57–79.

Bassi, L. J. (1997). Harnessing the power of intellectual capital. *Training & Development, 51*(12), 27–30.

Beckhard, R. (1997). The healthy organization: A profile. In F. Hesselbein, M. Goldsmith, & R. Beckhard (Eds.), *The organization of the future* (pp. 325–328). San Francisco: Jossey-Bass.

Beer, M. (1980). *Organizational change and development: A systems view.* Santa Monica, CA: Goodyear.

Bennett, J. B., & Lehman, W. E. K. (1997). Employee views of organizational wellness and the EAP: Influence on substance use, drinking climates, and policy attitudes. *Employee Assistance Quarterly, 13*(1), 55–72.

Bennett, J. B., & Lehman, W. E. K. (1999). Employee exposure to co-worker substance use and negative consequences: The moderating effects of work group membership. *Journal of Health and Social Behavior, 40*(3), 307–322.

Bennett, J. B., & Lehman, W. E. K. (2001). Team-oriented workplace substance abuse prevention: Experimental assessment of effects on attitudes, peer encouragement, and help-seeking. *Journal of Occupational Health Psychology, 6*(3), 243–254.

Bennis, W. (1993). Beyond bureaucracy; Essays on the development and evolution of human organization. In W. Bennis, *Toward a truly scientific management. The concept of organizational health.* San Francisco: Jossey-Bass. (Originally published 1962)

Bonebright, C. A., Clay, D. L., & Ankenmann, R. D. (2000). The relationship of workaholism with work-life conflict, life satisfaction, and purpose in life. *Journal of Counseling Psychology, 47*(4), 469–477.

Brown S. L., & Eisenhardt, K. M. (1998). Competing on the edge: *Strategy as structured chaos*. Boston: Harvard Business School.

Cameron, K. S., Sutton, R. I., & Whetten, D. A. (Eds.). (1988). *Readings in organizational decline: Frameworks, research, and prescriptions*. New York: Ballinger /Harper and Row.

Cameron, M., & Heidel, S. (2000). Behavioral risk management: A partnership between occupational health nursing and occupational psychiatry. *AAOHN Journal, 48*(11), 533–541.

Caplan, R. D. (1987). Person–environment fit in organizations: Theories, facts, and values. In A. W. Riley & S. J. Zaccaro (Eds.), *Occupational stress and organizational effectiveness* (pp. 103–140). New York: Praeger.

Cheng, J. L. C., & Kesner, I. F., (1997). Organizational slack and response to environmental shifts: The impact of resource allocation patterns. *Journal of Management, 23*(1), 1–18.

Christensen, A. J., Moran, P. J., & Wiebe, J. S. (1999). Assessment of irrational health beliefs: Relation to health practices and medical regimen adherence. *Health-Psychology, 18*(2), 169–176.

Cohen, D., & Prusak, L. (2001). *In good company: How social capital makes organizations work*. Cambridge, MA: Harvard Business School.

Cook, R. F., Back, A. S., & Trudeau, J. (1996). Preventing alcohol use problems among blue-collar workers: A field test of the working people program. *Substance Use and Misuse, 31,* 255–275.

Cooper, C. L. (1999). Can we live with the changing nature of work? *Journal of Managerial Psychology, 14*(7/8), 569–572.

Corrigan, P. W., & Penn, D. L. (1999). Lessons from social psychology on discrediting psychiatric stigma. *American Psychologist, 54*(9), 765–776.

Cunninghman, J. B. (1997). *The stress management sourcebook*. Los Angeles: Lowell House.

Danna, K., & Griffin, R. W. (1999). Health and well-being in the workplace: A review and synthesis of the literature. *Journal of Management, 25*(3), 357–384.

Eby, L. T., Adams, D. M., Russell, J. E. A., & Gaby S. H. (2000). Perceptions of organizational readiness for change: Factors related to employees' reactions to the implementation of team-based selling. *Human Relations, 53*(3), 419–442.

Edwards, R. W., Jumper-Thurman, P., Plested, B. A., Oetting, E. R., & Swanson, L. (2000). Community readiness: Research to practice. *Journal of Community Psychology, 28*(3), 291–307.

Erfurt J. C., Foote, A., Heirich, M. A. (1991). Worksite wellness programs; Incremental comparisons of screening and referral alone, health education, follow-up counseling, and plant organization. *American Journal of Health Promotion, 5,* 438–448.

Erfurt, J. C., & Holtyn, K. (1991). Health promotion in small business: What works and what doesn't work. *Journal of Occupational Medicine, 33*(1), 66–73.

Fleisher, C. S., Brown, W. S., & Fleisher, A. W. (1996). Comprehensive organizational wellness. In M. A. Rahim, R. T. Golembiewski, G. C. C. Lundberg (Eds.), *Current topics in management* (Vol. 1, pp. 167–185). Greenwich, CT: JAI Press.

Ginsberg, M. R., Kilburg, R. R., & Gomes, P. G. (1999). Organizational counseling and the delivery of integrated human services in the workplace: An evolving model for employee assistance theory and practice. In J. M. Oher (Ed.), *The employee assistance handbook* (pp. 439–455). New York: John Wiley & Sons.

Goetzel, R. Z. (2001, May/June). The financial impact of health promotion and disease prevention programs. *American Journal of Health Promotion, 15*(5).

Goetzel, R. Z., Dunn, R. L., Ozminkowski, R. J., Satin, K., Whitehead, D., & Cahill, K. (1998). Differences between descriptive and multivariate estimates of the impact of Chevron corporation's Health Quest Program on medical expenditures. *Journal of Occupational and Environmental Medicine, 40*(6), 538–545.

Goetzel, R. Z., Guindon, A. M., Turshen, I. J., & Ozminkowski, R. J. (2001). Health and productivity management: Establishing key performance measures, benchmarks, and best practices. *Journal of Environmental and Occupational Medicine, 43*(1), 10–17.

Goetzel R. Z., Jacobson B. H., Aldana S. G., Vardell K., & Yee L. (1998). Health care costs of worksite health promotion participants and non-participants. *Journal of Occupational and Environmental Medicine, 40*(4), 341–346.

Goetzel, R. Z., & Ozminkowski, R. J. (2000). Health and productivity management: Emerging opportunities for health promotion professionals for the 21st century. *American Journal of Health Promotion, 14*(4), 211–214.

Golaszweski, T. (2000). Health risks and group-level health care expenditures. *American Journal of Health Promotion, 15*(1), 53–54.

Gowing, M. K., Kraft, J. D., & Quick, J. C. (1998). *The new organizational reality: Downsizing, restructuring, and revitalization.* Washington, DC: American Psychological Association.

Guthrie, J. P., & Olian, J. D. (1990). Using psychological constructs to improve health and safety: The HRM niche. *Research in Personnel and Human Resource Management, 8,* 141–201.

Heany, C. A., & Goetzel, R. Z. (1997). A review of health-related outcomes of multi-components worksite health promotion programs. *American Journal of Health Promotion, 11*(4), 290–308.

Heirich, M., & Sieck, C. J. (2000). Worksite cardiovascular wellness programs as a route to substance abuse prevention. *JOEM, 42*(1), 47–56.

Hochschild, A. (1997). *The time bind: When work becomes home and home becomes work.* New York: Metropolitan Books.

Hock, D. (1999). *Birth of the chaordic age.* San Francisco: Berrett-Koehler.

Holman, P., & Devane, T. (1999). *The change handbook: Group methods for shaping the future.* San Francisco: Berrett-Koehler.

Hoy, W. K., & Woolfolk, A. E. (1993). Teachers' sense of efficacy and the organizational health of schools. *Elementary School Journal, 93*(4), 355–372.

Hunnicutt, D. (2000). America's healthiest companies: Scaling the heights of good health. *Business & Health, 18*(3), 36–38.

Israel, B. A., Parker, E. A., Goldenhar, L. M., & Heaney, C. A. (1996). Occupational stress, safety, and health: Conceptual framework and principles for effective prevention interventions. *Journal of Occupational Health Psychology 1*(3), 261–286.

Jaffe, D. T. (1995). The healthy company: Research paradigms for personal and organizational health. In S. L. Sauter & L. R. Murphy (Eds.), *Organizational risk factors for job stress* (pp. 13–40). Washington, DC: American Psychological Association.

James, K. (1999). Re-thinking organizational stress: The transition to the new employment age. *Journal of Managerial Psychology, 14*(7/8), 545–557.

Jones, R., Bly, J., & Richardson, J.(1990). A study of a worksite health promotion program and absenteeism. *Journal of Occupational Medicine, 32,* 95–99.

Karasek, R. (2001). Toward a psychosocially healthy work environment: Broader roles for psychologists and sociologists. In N. Schneiderman, M. A. Speers, J. M. Silva, J. H. Gentry, & A. Tomes (Eds.), *Integrating behavioral and social sciences with public health* (pp. 267–292). Washington, DC: American Psychological Association.

Karasek, R., Brisson, C., Kawakami N., Houtman, I., Bongers, P., et al. (1998). The Job Content Questionnaire (JCQ): An instrument for internationally comparative assessments of psychosocial job characteristics. *Journal of Occupational Health Psychology, 3*(4), 322–355.

Kelly, S., & Allison, M. A. (1999). *The complexity advantage: How the science of complexity can help your business achieve peak performance.* New York: McGraw-Hill.

Kessler, R., & Underwood, L. (1993). *Understanding stress and depression.* New York: Oxford University Press.

Kidwell, R. E., Jr., Mossholder, K. W., & Bennett, N. (1997). Cohesiveness and organizational citizenship behavior: A multilevel analysis using work groups and individuals. *Journal of Management, 23*(6), 775–793.

Kilburg, R. R., Stokes, E. J., & Kuruvilla, C. (1998). Toward a conceptual model of organizational regression. *Consulting Psychology Journal: Practice and Research, 50*(2), 101–119.

Kozlowski, S. W. J., & Salas, E. (1997). A multilevel organizational systems approach for the implementation and transfer of training. In J. K. Ford (Ed.), *Improving training effectiveness in work organizations* (pp. 247–287). Mahwah, NJ: Erlbaum

Landsbergis, P. A., Cahill, J., & Schnall, P. (1999). The impact of lean production and related new systems of work organization on worker health. *Journal of Occupational Health Psychology, 4*(2), 108–130.

Lau, R. S. M., & May, B. E. (1998). A win–win paradigm for quality of work life and business performance. *Human Resource Development Quarterly, 9*(3), 211–226.

Lawson, M. B. (2001). In praise of slack: Time is of the essence. *Academy of Management Executive, 15*(3), 125–135.

Levering, R., & Moskowitz, M. (1994). *The 100 best companies to work for in America.* New York: Plume Books.

Livingstone, L. P., Nelson, D. L., & Barr, S. H. (1997). Person environment fit and creativity: An examination of supply-value and demand-ability versions of fit. *Journal of Management, 23*(2), 119–146.

Loscocco, K. A., & Spitze, G. (1990). Working conditions, social support, and the well-being of female and male factory workers. *Journal of Health and Social Behavior, 31,* 313–327.

MacDonald, D. A., Friedman, H. L., & Kuentzel, J. G. (1999). A survey of measures of spiritual and transpersonal constructs: Part one research update. *Journal of Transpersonal Psychology, 31*(2), 137–154.

Maslow, A. H. (1998). *Eupsychian management.* Homewood, IL: R. D. Irwin. (Originally published 1965)

Mayo, A. (2000). The role of employee development in the growth of intellectual capital. *Personnel Review, 29*(4), 521–533.

Mayrhofer, W. (1997). Warning: Flexibility can damage your organizational health! *Employee Relations, 19*(6), 519–534.

Megel, M. E., Wade, F., Hawkins, P., Norton, J., & Sandstrom, S. (1994). Health promotion, self-esteem, and weight among female college freshmen. *The Journal of Health-Behavior, Education and Promotion 18*(4), 10–19.

Miles, M. B. (1965). Planned change and organizational health: Figure and ground. In F. D. Carver & T. J. Sergiovvani (Eds.), *Organizations and human behavior* (pp. 375–391). New York: McGraw-Hill.

Mitroff, I. I., & Denton, E. A. (1999). *A spiritual audit of corporate America: A hard look at spirituality, religion, and values in the workplace.* San Francisco: Jossey-Bass.

Morgan, G. (1998). *Images of organization.* San Francisco: Berrett-Koehler.

Murphy, L. R. (1996). Stress management in work settings: A critical review of the health effects. *American Journal of Health Promotion. 11*(2), 112–135.

National Wellness Institute. (2001). *TestWell: An online wellness assessment.* Stevens Point, WI: Author.

O'Donnell. M. (2001). *Health promotion in the workplace* (3rd ed.). Albany, NY: Delmar.

Oldham, G. R., & Gordon, B. I., (1999). Job complexity and employee substance use: The moderating effects of cognitive ability. *Journal of Health and Social Behavior, 40,* 290–306.

Overholt, M. H., Connally, G. E., Harrington, T. C., & Lopez, D. (2000). The strands that connect: An empirical assessment of how organizational design links employees to the organization. *Human Resource Planning, 23*(2), 38–51.

Ozminkowski, R. J., Goetzel, R. Z., Smith, M. W., Cantor, R. I., Shaughnessy, A., & Harrison, M. (2000). The impact of the Citibank, NA, health management program on changes in employee health risks over time. *JOEM, 42*(5), 502–511.

Pascale, R. T., Millemann, M., & Gioja, L. (2000). *Surfing the edge of chaos: The laws of nature and the new laws of business.* New York: Crown Business.

Pelletier, K. R. (1991). A review and analysis of the health and cost-effective outcomes studies of comprehensive health promotion and disease prevention programs. *American Journal of Health Promotion, 5,* 311–315.

Pelletier K. R. (1993). A review and analysis of the health and cost-effective outcome studies of comprehensive health promotion and disease prevention programs at the worksite: 1991–1993 update. *American Journal of Health Promotion, 8,* 43–49.

Pelletier K. R. (1996). A review and analysis of the health and cost-effective outcome studies of comprehensive health promotion and disease prevention programs at the worksite: 1993–1995 update. *American Journal of Health Promotion, 10,* 380–388.

Pelletier, K. R. (1999). A review and analysis of the clinical and cost-effectiveness studies of comprehensive health promotion and disease management programs at the worksite: 1995–1998 Update (IV). *American Journal of Health Promotion, 13*(6), 333–345.

Pelletier, K. R. (2001). A review and analysis of the clinical and cost effectiveness studies of comprehensive health promotion and disease management programs at the worksite: 1998–2000. Update V. *American Journal of Health Promotion, 16*(2), 107–116.

Peterson, M., & Wilson, J. (1998). A culture work health model: A theoretical conceptualization. *American Journal of Health Behavior, 22*(5), 328–390.

Powell, D. R. (1999). Characteristics of successful wellness programs. *Employee Benefits Journal, 24*(3), 15–21.

Powell, G. N. (1998, Winter). Reinforcing and extending today's organizations: The simultaneous pursuit of person-organization fit and diversity. *Organizational Dynamics,* 50–61.

Prochaska, J. O., & DiClemente, C. C. (1983). Stages and processes of self-change of smoking: Toward an integrative model of change. *Journal of Consulting and Clinical Psychology, 51,* 390–395.

Quick, J., & Quick, J. (1984). *Organizational stress and preventive management.* New York: McGraw-Hill.

Quinn, R. E. (2000). *Change the world: How ordinary people can accomplish extraordinary results.* San Francisco: Jossey-Bass.

Rand, T. (1999). Why businesses fail: An organizational perspective. *EMERGENCE, 1*(4), 97–114.

Reflections. (2000). 1(4) [entire issue].

Ribisl, K. M., & Reischl, T. M. (1993). Measuring the climate for health at organizations. *Journal of Occupational Medicine, 35*(8), 812–824

Rosen, R. H. (1991). *The healthy company: Eight strategies to develop people, productivity, and profits.* Los Angeles: Jeremy P. Tarcher.

Rosen, R. H. (1996). *Leading people: Transforming business from the inside out.* New York: Viking.

Rosen, R. (1998). Leadership in the new organization. In M. K Gowing, J. D Kraft, & J. C. Quick (Eds.), *The new organizational reality: Downsizing, restructuring, and revitalization* (pp. 221–238). Washington, DC: American Psychological Association.

Sayce, L. (2000). *From psychiatric patient to citizen: Overcoming discrimination and social exclusion.* New York: St. Martin's Press.

Schein, E. (1965). *Organizational psychology.* Englewood Cliffs, NJ: Prentice-Hall.

Schrammel, P., Griffiths R. I., & Griffiths C. B. (1998). A workplace breast cancer screening program. Costs and components. *AAOHN Journal, 46*(11), 523–529.

Schwartz, P., & Gibb, B. (1999). *When good companies do bad things: Responsibility and risk in an age of globalization.* New York: John Wiley & Sons.

Seybold, K. S., & Hill, P. C. (2001). The role of religion and spirituality in mental and physical health. *Current Directions in Psychological Science, 10*(1), 21–24.

Simone G. E., Barber, C., Birnbaum, H. G., Frank, R. G., Greenberg, P. E., Rose, R. M., Wang, P. S., & Kessler, R. C. (2001). Depression and work productivity: The comparative costs of treatment versus non treatment. *Journal of Occupational and Environmental Medicine, 43*(1), 2–9.

Snow, D. L., & Kline, M. L. (1995). Preventive interventions in the workplace to reduce negative psychiatric consequences of work and family stress. In C. M. Mazure (Ed.), *Does stress cause psychiatric illness?* (pp. 221–270). Washington, DC: American Psychiatric Press.

Soderfeldt B., Soderfeldt M., Jones K., O'Campo P., Muntaner C., Ohlson C. G., & Warg, L. E. (1997). Does organization matter? A multilevel analysis of the demand-control model applied to human services. *Social Science and Medicine, 44*(4), 527–534.

Stacey, R. D., Griffin, D., & Shaw, P. (2001). *Complexity and management: Fad or radical challenge?* London: Routledge.

Stein, S. J., & Skinner, H. A. (1998). Why computerized life-style assessment is good for business. In S. Klarreich (Ed.), *Handbook of organizational health psychology: Programs to make the workplace healthier* (pp. 35–41). Madison, CT: Psychosocial Press/International Universities Press.

Steinbach, T. (2000). Workplace strategies for removing obstacles to employee health. *Employee Benefits Journal, 25*(1), 9–10.

Stokols, D. (1992). Establishing and maintaining healthy environments: Toward a social ecology of health promotion. *American Psychologist, 47*(1), 6–22.

Sturm, R., Zhang, W., & Schoenbaum, M. (1999). How expensive are unlimited substance abuse benefits under managed care? *Journal of Behavioral Health Services and Research, 26*(2), 203–210.

Syvantek, D. J., & Brown, L. L. (2000). A complex-systems approach to organizations. *Current Directions in Psychological Science, 9*(2), 69–74.

Terry, P. (1998). How mature is your organization's prevention effort? *Healthcare Forum Journal, 41*(5), 54–58.

Vagg, P. R., & Spielberger, C. D. (1998). Occupational stress: Measuring job pressure and organizational support in the workplace. *Journal of Occupational Health Psychology, 3*(4), 294–305.

Van-Yperen, N. W., & Snijders, T. A. B. (2000). A multilevel analysis of the demands-control model: Is stress at work determined by factors at the group level or the individual level. *Journal of Occupational Health Psychology 5*(1), 182–190.

Walker, S. N., Sechrist, K., & Pender, N. J. (1987). The health promoting lifestyle profile: Development and psychometric validation. *Nursing Research, 36*(2), 76–81.

Warr, P. (1999). Well-being and the workplace. In D. Kahneman, E. Diener, & N. Schwarz (Eds.), *Well-being: The foundations of hedonic psychology* (pp. 392–412). New York: Russell Sage.

Wech, B. A., Mossholder, K. W., Steel, R. P., & Bennett, N. (1998). Does work group cohesiveness affect individuals' performance and organizational commitment? A cross-level examination. *Small Group Research, 29*(4), 472–494.

Wolfe, R. A., & Parker, D. F. (1994). Employee health management: Challenges and opportunities. *Academy of Management Executive, 8*(2), 22–31.

Yandrick, R. M. (1996). *Behavioral risk management: How to avoid preventable losses from mental health problems in the workplace.* San Francisco: Jossey-Bass.

Ziegler, J. (1998). America's healthiest companies. *Business & Health, 16*(12), 29–31.

5

Health Psychology and Work Stress: A More Positive Approach

Debra L. Nelson and Bret L. Simmons

"I'm stressed out" is the refrain of many workers. They know too well the experience of distress or strain that can accompany work. They also know, however, that there are times when they operate "in the zone" at work. Time is suspended, there is a feeling of engagement, intense task focus, and pleasurable emotions. Yet it seems easier for workers to describe the negative experience of stress than the positive experience of stress. Although many have heard the term *distress,* few are familiar with *eustress.* The purpose of this chapter is to propose a more positive, holistic approach for understanding work stress by incorporating eustress, the positive stress response, along with its positive indicators and associated positive outcomes.

We begin by exploring the definitions of health. Work stress has its roots in occupational health psychology, and our definitions of health have shaped and informed our definitions of stress. We then briefly highlight four prevailing work stress approaches to show that the emphasis has largely been on the negative. Next, we draw on existing stress research to develop a definition of eustress and present the holistic model of work stress, which explicitly incorporates the positive response and positive outcomes of the stress process. Highlighting the role of the positive, we present several indicators of eustress and describe the individual differences that may be related to eustress. Finally, we explore the idea of eustress generation as a complement to distress prevention, in efforts to manage work stress and health.

Conceptions of Health

In examining the prevailing views of what constitutes health, it appears that much lip service is paid to health as the presence of positive states, but operationally our definition of health remains the absence of disease. More than 50 years ago, health was defined by the World Health Organization (1948) as "a state of complete physical, mental, and social well-being and not merely the absence of disease or infirmity." Yet freedom from illness is still the norm in defining health for scientists and many of those in the medical community. Because medicine was long concerned with only the physical body, and with returning that physical body from disease states back to neutral functioning, it followed that the medical conception of health became the absence of negative conditions.

Ryff and Singer (1998) traced the philosophical, rather than the medical, writings on health and noted that many philosophers have argued for models of optimal human functioning. Philosophers as early as Aristotle conceived of such positive conditions as eudaemonia, the realization of one's true potential. Bertrand Russell (1958) wrote about the causes of happiness, concluding that zest (a friendly interest in persons and things) and affection were essential for human well-being. Following the writings of philosophers through to modern times, Ryff and Singer concluded that the key goods in life central to positive human health are having purpose in life, quality connections to others, self-regard, and mastery. They further asserted that human well-being is a multidimensional, dynamic process that involves intellectual, social, emotional, and physical potential. Health, then, is viewed as the presence of the positive in the mind as well as in the body. This view is consistent with the holistic model of health, which posits six dimensions of health–wellness: emotional, intellectual, spiritual, occupational, social, and physical. The Old English root of the word "health" is *hal,* meaning sound or whole, indicating that no part of the individual is separate or independent (Edlin, Golanty, & Brown, 1996).

The philosophical view of health, as opposed to the medical view, thus emphasizes positive human health. Unfortunately, the medical view of health as the absence of disease still prevails. Because our knowledge of work stress has evolved from the medical model, it too emphasizes the prevention of the negative.

Theories of Work Stress

The literature on work stress has blossomed over the past 10 years, and several theories have emerged. Although it is beyond the scope of this chapter to consider all of those theories, it is important to examine some of the more prominent ones to determine their focus (or lack of focus) on the positive aspects of stress. Four theories that have generated considerable attention are the cognitive appraisal approach, the person–environment fit approach, the psychoanalytic approach, and preventive stress management.

The person–environment fit approach, based on the pioneering work of Robert Kahn, emphasized the stressful nature of confusing or conflicting role demands (Kahn, Wolfe, Quinn, Snoek, & Rosenthal (1964). Fit is defined as a match between an individual's skills and abilities and the demands of the job, communicated as clear role expectations. A lack of person–environment fit leads to distress. The bulk of the research on the person–environment fit model has focused on the negative—that is, the relationship between poor fit and distress and actions to take to improve fit. There is little attention to the positive consequences of fit and the individual's response to positive person–environment fit.

The demand–control model (Karasek, 1979; Theorell & Karasek, 1996) identified a high-strain job as one that has a high level of responsibility, without accompanying authority. High-strain jobs are related to symptoms such as depression, job dissatisfaction, and increased numbers of sick days absent from work. The model also suggests that the "best" job is an active job, one in which high demands are balanced by high decision latitude. However, most of the research attention on the demand–control model has focused on ways to redesign high-strain jobs by increasing the worker's control. Comparably little attention has been paid to the positive effects of active jobs.

Richard Lazarus and his colleagues (Lazarus, DeLongis, Folkman, & Gruen, 1985; Lazarus & Folkman, 1984) proposed the cognitive appraisal approach, which emphasized the individual's role in classifying situations as threatening or nonthreatening. Accordingly, positive and negative responses can occur simultaneously, as a result of the same stressor, and should be considered separate but related constructs. Part of the value of this approach is its acknowledgment that the assessment of the positive and negative aspects of stressors differs from individual to individual. Following the initial appraisal, individuals then focus on either the stressor or their response to the stressor in an attempt to manage the stress response. The cognitive appraisal approach highlights the difficulties of separating the stressor, the individual's perception of the stressor, and the response. Although Lazarus acknowledged the existence of positive responses, he, like the majority of stress researchers, focused almost exclusively on negative responses and the associated coping mechanisms intended to alleviate them. In theory, however, the positive stress response is valid and parallel to the rationale of coping, it should be accompanied by mechanisms intended to enhance the pleasurable experience.

The preventive stress management approach developed by Quick and Quick (1984) focused on the joint responsibility of individuals and organizations to manage stress. Grounded in notions of public health, it advocates a three-tiered stress prevention model: Change the cause of stress, manage the individual's response to stress, and obtain professional care to heal symptoms of distress. This tradition pays homage to the notion of eustress, defining it as the healthy, positive, constructive outcome of stressful events and the stress response. However, the bulk of the work on preventive stress management is on the prevention and resolution of distress. Little guidance is given on identifying eustress, creating work conditions that promote eustress, or generating eustress at work.

These four approaches may be considered representative of the research on work stress as a whole. The emphasis, as it has been in medicine and in health psychology, has been on the negative—that is, identifying causes of distress, identifying coping methods for dealing with stressors, and healing the wounds of distress. There is a lamentable lack of attention to identifying causes of eustress, defining eustress, identifying a process (similar to coping) of managing eustress, and finding ways of generating eustress at work.

Accentuating the Positive

There is some good news in the field of psychology. The positive psychology movement has taken issue with psychology's exclusive focus on pathology and repairing damage. Positive psychology is a science of positive subjective experience, positive individual traits, and positive institutions (Seligman & Csikszentmihalyi, 2000). Such subjective experiences include well-being, contentment, happiness, flow, and satisfaction. Positive traits include hope, wisdom, creativity, and courage, among others. Thus, positive psychology is the study of strengths and virtues rather than weakness and suffering. Its focus is on learning how to develop the qualities that allow individuals to flourish.

Extending this movement into the realm of occupational health psychology, and specifically into the study of work stress, entails the examination of positive human emotions—both those that are transitory and those that are long-lasting. It allows us to study the positive aspects of the stress experience. Who stays healthy under stress? Are there benefits to be gained from trauma, and if so, what are they? What does resilience mean, and how does it relate to long-term well being? In keeping with the focus of this chapter, what is positive stress? Is there a positive component of the stress response? What are the positive effects of stress? What individual traits are most likely to engender a positive stress experience? We believe that positive psychology can serve as an impetus for moving the study of stress in a more constructive direction.

The Concept of Eustress

Hans Selye may have been the first to use the term *eustress* in his writings on human stress. Selye postulated that the stress response is nonspecific—that is, both positive and negative stimuli produce an undifferentiated physiological response in the body. From this perspective, cognitive appraisal of stimuli is irrelevant. He described eustress as desirable and associated with positive *effects* of an antecedent response (Selye, 1976). Following Selye's conception of eustress, Quick, Quick, Nelson, and Hurrell (1997) identified eustress as essentially good health and high performance. They also described eustress as the effect of the stress response being channeled into positive and constructive outcomes. Beyond this, little has been accomplished in extending and shaping the concept of eustress or in describing how the positive type of stress experience occurs.

We believe that eustress can be better conceptualized by identifying it as positive aspects of the stress response itself rather than positive effects of the stress response. We further assert that a more complex understanding is needed, one in which the presence–absence of the positive (eustress) as well as the presence–absence of the negative (distress) is included to fully appreciate the stress response. This idea can perhaps best be explained by what we call the "bathtub analogy." Two basic things are necessary to achieve a comfortable bath: the level of water in the tub and the temperature of that water. Two things determine the level of the water in the tub: the flow of water into the bathtub, and the flow of water down the drain over time. Similarly, both hot water and cold water flow into the bathtub simultaneously to determine the water temperature. If we compare the way stress is commonly studied to the bathtub, the current approach is like studying a bathtub with only a cold water faucet (distress). We have identified the sources of this cold water (stressors) and we can tell individuals how to either decrease the incoming flow of cold water or increase the flow of cold water out of their bathtubs (distress prevention). We also know a great deal about the physiological, behavioral, and psychological consequences of sitting in a bath of cold water for long periods of time. Herein lies the problem: A more complete model of stress should acknowledge that there are two faucets (hot and cold) and that managing both are necessary if you want to get the water level and temperature just right for a comfortable bath. Few individuals take a totally cold bath (distress) or a totally hot bath (eustress). Similarly, few, if any stressors, are appraised as purely positive or purely negative. It is usually some combination of the two.

Holistic Model of Stress

We propose a more holistic model of stress, shown in Figure 5.1, that incorporates both positive and negative psychological responses to demands. The model also incorporates a broad range of demands, select individual difference variables that may be especially salient for cognitive appraisal, coping, and outcome variables representing things important to the individual both at work and away from work. We also propose a new concept, savoring, that is the parallel for the positive response of coping for the negative response. The demands, distress response, coping, and outcomes portion of the model are well-known in the occupational stress literature, so they will be discussed only briefly. The unique aspects of this model, the indicators of eustress, the individual differences that may promote eustress, and savoring eustress will be discussed in greater detail.

The physical or psychological stimuli to which the individual responds are commonly referred to as either *stressors* or *demands*. Stressors at work take the form of role demands, interpersonal demands, physical demands, workplace policies, and job conditions (Barnett, 1998; Quick et al., 1997). Some of these demands will not be salient for some individuals, yet may produce significant responses in others. Because our knowledge of these demands is embedded in the pathological perspective of stress and health, these demands will commonly be interpreted as *distressors*. We suggest that to be consistent with the cognitive appraisal approach to stress that

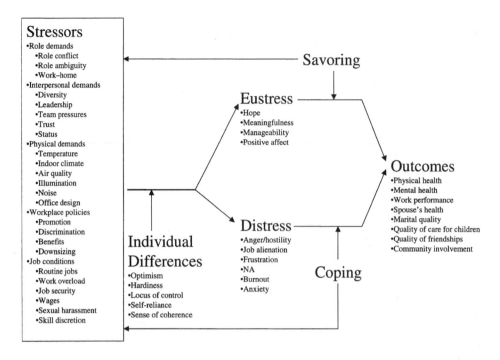

Figure 5.1. A holistic model of stress.

provides the theoretical foundation of this model, the assignment of valence should be reserved for the individual stress response.

Because the stress response is complex, we contend that most if not all of these stressors will elicit *both* a degree of negative and a degree of positive response for any individual. For example, one of the most significant sources of stress for hospital nurses is the death of a patient (Gray-Toft & Anderson, 1981). It is easy to understand how the loss of a patient could result in distress for a nurse. Yet along with the loss, the death of a patient may at the same time be appraised as positive. One study found that contrary to expectations, the variable death–dying had a significant, positive relationship with eustress and a nonsignificant, negative relationship with distress. The interpretation was that when the nurses in the study were faced with the demand of dealing with death–dying in their patients, they apparently became significantly more engaged in their work (Simmons, 2000).

In terms of outcomes, work stress and its associated problems cost organizations an estimated $200 billion or more each year in things such as decreased productivity, absenteeism, turnover, worker conflict, higher health care costs, and more worker's compensation claims of all kinds (DeFrank & Ivancevich, 1998; Farren, 1999). The fact that distress is not healthy is well-established. "Heart attack, stroke, cancer, peptic ulcer, asthma, diabetes, hypertension, headache, back pain, and arthritis are among the many diseases and symptoms that have been found to be caused or worsened by stressful events" (Quick et al., 1997, p. 77). Ganster and Schaubroeck (1991) reviewed the literature on work stress and found that although there is not convincing evidence that stressors associated with the job cause health effects, the indirect evidence strongly suggests a work stress effect. Recent evidence has confirmed that job strain (distress) is associated with increased report of medical symptoms and health-damaging behavior in men (Weidner, Boughal, Connor, Peiper, & Mendell, 1997).

It is not surprising that there is less evidence concerning the relationship between eustress and health. Edwards and Cooper (1988) speculated that eustress may improve health directly through physiological changes or indirectly by reducing existing distress. They reviewed findings from a variety of sources and found that the bulk of the evidence suggests a direct effect of eustress on health. They noted that this evidence is merely suggestive rather than conclusive, and that only one study was able to demonstrate that eustress is associated with an improvement in physiological functioning rather than just a reduction in damage. There was no evidence to suggest that eustress was associated with a deterioration in health.

A recent review of the literature stated that "positive emotional states *may* promote healthy perceptions, beliefs, and physical well-being itself" (Salovey, Rothman, Detweiler, & Steward, 2000, p. 110, emphasis added). Yet several recent empirical studies of hospital nurses operationalized eustress and distress as separate responses indicated by the presence of multivariate positive and negative psychological states (Simmons, 2000; Simmons & Nelson, 2001). These cross-sectional studies hypothesized that in response to the demands of the job, hospital nurses would experience significant levels of both eustress and distress, and each stress response would have a separate effect on the nurses' perceptions of their health. They found that even in the presence of a demanding work environment, the hospital nurses were actively engaged in their work and reported significant levels of eustress, and eustress in turn had a significant positive relationship with their perception of their own health. Hope was the indicator of eustress with the strongest positive relationship with the nurses' perception of health (Simmons & Nelson, 2001). In addition to being healthy and productive themselves, eustressed nurses may have a concrete impact on the health of patients by inspiring positive expectations and raising the patients' levels of hope (Salovey et al., 2000).

Eustressed workers are engaged, meaning that they are enthusiastically involved in and pleasurably occupied by the demands of the work at hand. Workers can be engaged and perceive positive benefits even when confronted with extremely demanding stressors. A study of female and male soldiers participating in the U.S. peacekeeping mission in Bosnia found that soldiers that were engaged in meaningful work during the deployment found it to be a positive experience (Britt, Adler, & Bartone, 2001). It is interesting to note that a factor such as witnessing the destruction caused by warring factions was associated with reporting greater positive benefits. In the context of the mission, the destruction was likely seen as justification for the mission, which added meaning to the soldiers' work.

Female soldiers in this study self-reported more positive benefits as a result of the deployment than men, although the effect size for gender was small.

Research shows that positive aspects of work for women are also positive influences in the home environment (Barnett & Marshall, 1992; Barnett, Marshall, & Sayer, 1992). In a study of licensed practical nurses and social workers, there were no negative spillover effects from job to parenting or from parenting to job, but there were positive spillover effects from job to parenting (Barnett et al., 1992). Women that perceived their jobs as rewarding experienced less of the mental health effects of troubled relationships with their children. Challenge was the specific aspect of a rewarding job that provided the positive-spillover effect (Barnett et al., 1992). When employed mothers enjoyed high rewards from challenge at work, they reported low distress, regardless of their level of disaffection they experienced in their relationship with their children.

Work Attitudes That Indicate Eustress

Each stress response, both positive and negative, will have its associated effect indicators, and can be expected to produce differential effects on the outcome variables (e.g., health). Indicators of the stress response could be physiological, behavioral, as well as psychological. The model presented will focus only on the psychological response. As suggested by Edwards and Cooper (1988), the indicators of the positive response will be positive psychological states (e.g., positive affect, meaningfulness, and hope), and the indicators of the negative response will be negative psychological states (e.g., negative affect). Consistent with this holistic representation of stress, eustress and distress can be operationally defined as follows (Simmons, 2000; Simmons & Nelson, 2001):

- *Eustress:* A positive psychological response to a stressor, as indicated by the presence of positive psychological states.
- *Distress:* A negative psychological response to a stressor, as indicated by the presence of negative psychological states.

Eustress reflects the extent to which cognitive appraisal of a situation or event is seen to either benefit an individual or enhance his or her well-being. We expect that most work situations elicit a mixed bag of both positive and negative responses in individuals. For example, a recently promoted individual should be expected to experience joy and satisfaction associated with the recognition of achievement and excitement about the opportunity to pursue new goals and challenges at work. At the same time, and as a result of the same situation, the individual may also experience a degree of disappointment if the additional compensation associated with the promotion is perceived as inadequate, or may experience the beginnings of the anxiety they anticipate about having to tell friends, family, and colleagues that the new promotion involves relocation to another city. On the other hand, an individual recently downsized out of a job can be expected to experience hostility associated with the loss and anxiety as a result of the uncertainty of having to find a new job. Yet at the same time they may feel relief to be leaving an overworked job in a sinking ship, or may see it as an opportunity to spend more coveted time with family.

Positive and negative responses are separate, distinct, multivariate, and potentially interactive in nature. To assume the presence of the positive by simply observing the absence of the negative, or visa versa, is an unacceptably simplistic approach to understanding the sources, responses, and consequences of stress. The full range of the stress response cannot be appreciated without a strategy to assess eustress and distress concurrently.

When assessing eustress as we have defined it, the indicators of eustress should be positive psychological states, such as attitudes or emotions. Stable dispositional variables are not acceptable indicators of eustress, which must be subject to change according to cognitive appraisals of stressors. Work attitudes are preferable indicators. The work attitudes positive affect (PA), meaningfulness, manageability, and hope may be good indicators of eustress (Simmons, 2000; Simmons & Nelson, 2001; Simmons, Nelson, & Neal, 2001). Although conceptually distinct, these constructs all represent an aspect of *engagement,* one of the primary indicators of the eustress response.

Positive Affect

Positive affect is a state of pleasurable engagement and reflects the extent to which a person feels enthusiastic, active, and alert (Watson, Clark, & Tellegen, 1988). Positive affect can be measured as a state or trait, with state PA capturing how one feels at given points in time, whereas the trait represents stable individual differences in the level of affect generally experienced (George & Brief, 1992; Watson & Pennbaker, 1989). State and trait PA are both conceptually and empirically distinct, and state PA is a separate factor from negative affect (George & Brief, 1992).

People in a positive state process information more heuristically or strategically, and people in a negative state process information more systematically. Positive affect is associated with seeing the opportunity in an issue as well as lower levels of risk taking (Mittal & Ross, 1998). Others have described those in a positive mood as "smarter" at processing information than those in a negative mood (Staw & Barsade, 1993). Positive affect has been shown to be effective in medical contexts, improving decision making among medical students and creative problem solving and diagnostic reasoning processes among practicing physicians (Estrada, Isen, & Young, 1994, 1997; Isen, Rosenzweig, & Young, 1991).

Meaningfulness and Manageability

These two constructs are part of a new scale developed by a nurse to measure situational sense of coherence (Artinian, 1997). Sense of coherence was a term developed to denote factors that promote a healthy response to stressful situations (Antonovsky, 1993). It has traditionally been measured as a trait variable, but was adapted by Artinian (1997) as a situational or state measure. Two of three subscales are appropriate as indicators of eustress.

Meaningfulness is the extent to which one feels that work makes sense emotionally, that problems and demands are worth investing energy in, are worthy of commitment and engagement, and are challenges that are welcome. The literature on psychological empowerment has described meaningfulness as a sense of purpose or personal connection about work (Spreitzer, 1995; Thomas & Velthouse, 1990). A representative item of one of the state indicators of meaningfulness is, "At work, do you have the feeling that you don't really care about what goes on around you (very seldom/very often)" (Simmons, 2000, p. 127).

In their study of peacekeepers in Bosnia, Britt et al. (2001) operationalized meaningful work with indicators of job importance, soldier engagement, and the relevance of peacekeeping to the soldier's identity. The meaningfulness of work was a significant predictor of deriving benefit from the mission. The strongest zero-order correlation in the study was the significant positive relationship between soldier engagement and job importance.

Manageability is the extent to which one perceives that resources are at one's disposal that are adequate to meet the demands posed by the work situation. This is not a common construct in the work stress literature, but it functions somewhat similar to the concept of control. For example, even in a demanding work situation (e.g., a hospital critical care unit), the attitude of manageability will develop as a positive response to the extent that adequate resources (e.g., proper equipment, adequate staffing and training) are available. Items representing indicators of state manageability are, "When you think of the challenges you are facing at work, do you feel that (there is no solution/you can find a solution)" and "People you count on at work often disappoint you (always happens/never happens)" (Simmons, 2000, p. 127).

Hope

Hope has been identified as a positive emotion reflecting a degree of expected benefit resulting from an evaluation of a particular situation (Lazarus, 1993; Smith, Haynes, Lazarus, & Pope, 1993). Hope was defined as a cognitive set that is based on a sense of successful goal-directed determination and planning to meet goals (Snyder et al., 1996). As a belief that one has both the will and the way to accomplish one's goals, hope has also been suggested as an attribute of emotional intelligence (Huy, 1999). The state hope scale thus provides a snapshot of a person's goal-directed thinking and engagement.

Gender differences in state hope did not emerge in any of the studies conducted to develop and validate the scale. The lack of gender differences for hope is consistent with findings of the scale for dispositional hope, which has been administered to thousands of men and women of different backgrounds, education, and occupations (Snyder, 1994). The positive spin on this finding is that men and women are equally hopeful.

Conversely, it may be that the goals toward which hope is applied are different for women and men (Snyder, 1994). Like a glass ceiling effect, some women may have been socially conditioned to expect to have fewer of life's goals, especially those associated with work, open to them. If women perceive that many goals at work are not available to them, they may not even think of certain goals as being attainable. In effect, women may limit their goals to those left open to them. Thus women may report high hope for the goals they perceive they are "allowed" to have.

The positive psychological states meaningfulness, manageability, hope, and positive affect are examples of constructs that may be good indicators of eustress. A study of eustress in hospital nurses found that all of these indicators loaded positively and significantly on a second-order factor of eustress (Simmons, 2000). The indicator with the strongest factor loading on eustress was meaningfulness. In this study, eustress was differentiated from a second-order factor distress. Eustress was significantly and positively related to the nurses' perceptions of their health, and the relationship between distress and health was negative but nonsignificant.

Although we have briefly discussed these four indicators of eustress, they should not be considered the only or even the best indicators of eustress. In theory, any positive psychological state could be a potential indicator of eustress, and much more research is needed on positive psychological states at work. For example, the differences and similarities between the engagement of eustress and familiar concepts such as satisfaction, involvement, and self-efficacy will require empirical examination. Although it is never a requirement to demonstrate that distress is not simply dissatisfaction, it should be anticipated that there might be some who are skeptical that eustress does not differ significantly from job satisfaction. If the variable hope is retained as an indicator of eustress, it would be beneficial to include self-efficacy in the design of the study to differentiate these two goal-directed attitudes. Much more research needs to be done to identify other effective indicators of eustress, as well as potential gender and cultural differences in these indicators.

Individual Differences That Promote Eustress

Because individual differences have been studied in conjunction with the stress process, the focus has been largely on identifying individual factors that predispose individuals to cope less well with stress. Type A behavior, for example, has been implicated as a risk factor for cardiovascular disease, with studies indicating that the hostility–anger component of Type A appears to be the most noxious one (Wright, 1988). Negative affect's role in the stressor–strain connection has also been extensively examined, with the conclusion that individuals with negative affect possess more negative appraisals and perceptions (Watson, Pennebaker, & Folger, 1987). Thus, those individuals with negative affect experience a stronger connection between stressors and strains, either because they are more sensitive to stressors or because they create more stressors because of their negative view of the world (McCrae & Costa, 1994).

In accordance with a more positive emphasis, we believe there is benefit in identifying those individual differences that would promote eustress through their role in generating more positive appraisals (challenge, as opposed to threat) of demands. Alternatively, these characteristics could work to arm individuals with the belief that they are equipped to handle a demand (secondary appraisal), or even encourage the savoring process. Five possible candidates for inclusion in studies of eustress are optimism, locus of control, hardiness, self-reliance, and sense of coherence.

Optimism

As an individual difference variable, optimism has been associated with good mood, perseverance, achievement, health, and longevity. Peterson (2000) recommended distinguishing between "little" and "big" optimism to gain a greater understanding of optimism's benefits. Little optimism encompasses specific expectations about positive outcomes. An example of little optimism would be, "I expect to perform well in my presentation today." This form of optimism is typified by Seligman's (1991) learned optimism construct, which is related to an optimistic explanatory style. Links have been established between attributions for positive events and well-being (Peterson & Seligman, 1987).

In contrast, big optimism involves a larger and more global expectation, for example, "Mankind is on the verge of a great discovery." This type of optimism is more in line with Scheier and Carver's (1992) description of dispositional optimism. Scheier and Carver (1992) define dispositional optimism as the global expectation that good things will be plentiful in the future and that bad things will be scarce. Dispositional optimism's relationship with health has mainly been explored in terms of coping. Optimists engage in more active problem-solving types of coping, as opposed to avoidant coping. Other mechanisms linking optimism and health include enhanced immune function (Segerstrom, Taylor, Kemeny, & Fahey, 1998) and better health habits (Morrill, Ickovics, Golubchikov, Beren, & Rodin, 1996). Peterson (2000) suggested that big optimism could be a biological tendency, and that it is socially encouraged and modeled.

Peterson's argument is that optimism can exist at very different levels of abstraction. Big optimism, according to Peterson, produces a general state of vigor and resilience. Little optimism may be the product of an individual's learning. It is associated with positive outcomes because it produces behaviors that help individuals adapt to specific situations.

Optimism may relate to the eustress process in any of several ways. It may lead individuals to initiate more positive primary appraisals. It could equip individuals with the belief that they can handle a certain situation (as in "little" optimism). Certainly, because the eustress process is heavily dependent on appraisal, optimism is a reasonable individual difference to examine in future studies of eustress. The big versus little distinction is an intriguing one and may be useful in helping to explain optimism's role in promoting eustress.

Locus of Control

Locus of control is a generalized expectancy that is dichotomized into internal and external categories. An individual with an internal locus of control believes that outcomes occur as a result of his or her own actions. In contrast, an individual with an external locus of control believes that outcomes occur as a result of other people's actions, or uncontrollable factors such as fate, chance, or luck (Rotter, 1966). Cohen and Edwards (1988) conducted an extensive review of personality as a moderator in the stress–strain relationship, and concluded that generalized expectancy of control (i.e., locus of control) was a construct with a powerful moderating effect. Thus, locus of control can buffer the sequence of events that links stress with health problems.

Lefcourt and Davidson-Katz (1991) explained that this buffering could occur as part of the primary appraisal process. Externals, with their belief that their actions have little effect over outcomes, are more likely to perceive demands as threats. Locus of control can also come into play in the secondary appraisal phase. During secondary appraisal (the self-assessment appraisal), individuals evaluate their resources for dealing with the demand. Externals, during secondary appraisal, are more likely to feel that they do not have sufficient resources for coping with the demand they are facing.

Stating this within the positive framework, we can conclude that internals are more likely to enjoy the stress-buffering properties of locus of control. Internals are more likely to appraise demands as opportunities rather than threats (primary appraisal) and to believe that they possess the necessary resources for coping with the demand (secondary appraisal). In addition, they are more likely to select problem-solving forms of coping as a first choice, and resort to emotion-focused coping only when they see that their own efforts will not solve the problem. They are more flexible in their choice of coping methods than are externals. As a result of this process, their efforts are associated with vigor, humor, and life satisfaction rather than dysphoria, immune-system dysfunctions, and related illnesses experienced by externals (Lefcourt & Davidson-Katz, 1991).

Hardiness

Hardiness, as originally conceived by Kobasa and Maddi (Kobasa, 1979; Kobasa, Maddi, & Kahn 1982; Ouellette, 1993) is an individual's view of their place in the environment that is simultaneously expressed through commitment, challenge, and control in their actions, thoughts, and feelings. Commitment involves finding persons and situations interesting and meaningful; it refers to engagement in life. People who are committed view their activities as purposeful. Challenge, as a dimension of hardiness, is the view that changes are opportunities for growth rather than threats, and it also reflects the ability to tolerate ambiguity. Control is reflected in the belief that an individual has influence over his or her life. It is the interplay of commitment, challenge, and control that is proposed to promote stress resistance and facilitate psychological and physical health (Ouellette & DiPlacido, 2001).

Hardiness also relates to transformational coping, or reframing a stressor such that is less threatening or is perceived as an opportunity rather than a threat. In addition, it is associated with seeking social support and with engaging in health-promoting behaviors (Maddi, 1998). The early research on hardiness was conducted at a large telephone company, where executives were studied for five years using questionnaires. Hardy executives were less likely to report physical illness than those executives who were low on hardiness (Maddi, 1998). Several additional studies have supported the relationship between hardiness and health (Wiebe & Williams 1992) and between hardiness and performance (e.g., Westman, 1990).

Research on the potential mechanisms whereby hardiness is related to health is helpful in speculating about the potential role of hardiness in the eustress process. For example, hardy individuals are less likely to appraise events pessimistically (Wiebe, 1991); perhaps this would enable them to appraise stressors as challenges or to engage in transformational coping and therefore to respond eustressfully. It may be of benefit to assess the three dimensions of hardiness separately in their relation to eustress. Florian, Mikulincer, and Taubman (1995) found that the three facets of hardiness showed different relationships with cognitive appraisal processes and coping mechanisms. Control was related to reduced threat appraisals and to the increased use of problem-focused coping and support-seeking behaviors. Commitment also was associated with lower threat appraisals, but was associated with the emotion-focused form of coping.

Many questions can arise when considering the relationship between hardiness and eustress. Presumably, a greater sense of control would result in more opportunity appraisals; and the support-seeking behavior associated with hardiness would permit individuals to engage in positive secondary appraisals (i.e., to believe that they could cope with the demand). Commitment, as a sense of engagement, might facilitate the savoring process. Hardy individuals might be committed to enacting and prolonging that sense of flow associated with savoring.

Self-Reliance

As an individual difference, self-reliance is a characteristic pattern of forming relationships with others. Ainsworth and Bowlby (1991) studied infants' attachments with their primary caregivers and concluded that the attachment process is a biological imperative that is related to survival of the human species. In observing the interactions between infants and their mothers, they identified three distinct patterns of attachment: secure (later termed self-reliant), avoidant, and anxious–ambivalent, with the latter two being unhealthy, insecure attachment patterns. Secure infants believe their caregiver will be available and helpful in times of distress, whereas insecure infants believe no one will be available in their times of need. This early history with caregivers forms the basis for individuals' beliefs about the responsiveness of others and for the formation of attachments to others in later life. These beliefs crystallize into internal working models of how one should relate to other people.

Attachment orientations extend into adulthood, and they are related to effectiveness and satisfaction at work (Hazan & Shaver, 1990). The attachment orientations have been labeled in the management literature as self-reliant (secure), counterdependent (avoidant), and overdependent (anxious–ambivalent) (Nelson, Quick, & Joplin, 1991). Self-reliant individuals, possessing a sense of security, form interdependent, flexible relationships with others. Adults who are self-reliant form close and supportive relationships with others both inside and outside the organization. They are comfortable working alone, or asking for assistance from others, as each situation demands. They report fewer symptoms of distress, and are better able to develop the social support necessary for effective performance at work (Nelson, Quick, & Simmons, 2001).

Counterdependent individuals often overinvest in work, and prefer to work alone rather than seek out support and assistance. As a result, they find themselves isolated, and may even refuse support when it is offered. Counterdependence is rooted in the belief that others will not be there when you need them and that it is best to depend only on oneself. Overdependent individuals search out and depend on more support than is appropriate, and often appear clingy and unable to reciprocate by providing support to others. It, like counterdependence, has its roots in the belief that others cannot be counted on for support. As a result, overdependent people may drain their social support sources by exhausting others' resources. Both counterdependent and overdependent individuals report greater distress symptoms and diminished well-being.

Self-reliance holds promise as an individual difference that may impact the eustress process. Self-reliant individuals, with their inherent belief that others are dependable and can be trusted to provide support, may be bolstered to either appraise demands as challenges or to believe that they have access to the resources (social support systems) that will allow them to manage these demands. In addition, their comfort in both working alone or interdependently gives self-reliant individuals security and flexibility in meeting demands that may be related to the confidence of viewing demands as challenging rather than threatening.

Sense of Coherence

Another appealing individual difference that can be studied within the context of eustress is sense of coherence, a view of life as comprehensible, manageable, and meaningful (Antonovsky, 1987, 1993). Having a sense of purpose in life is central to sense of coherence. Ryff and Singer (1998) noted that this is a core feature of positive human health. Part of the appeal of sense of coherence lies in its connection with salutogenesis, the process of successfully resolving stressors and maintaining health, rather than pathogenesis, failures in coping that lead to disease. Sense of coherence is thus a salutogenic strength for adaptively coping with stress.

Central to Antonovsky's theory is the notion that under stress, people with a strong sense of coherence cope more effectively, are better able to use their own resources and those of others, and therefore experience better health and well-being. In reviewing the research on sense of coherence, Ouellette and DiPlacido (2001) noted that the evidence for the salutogenic effects are more strongly supported with regard to psychological health than physical health. They do note that sense of coherence facilitated health and well-being among patients recovering from joint replacement surgery and those living with rheumatoid arthritis.

The mechanisms through which sense of coherence operates to have a salutogenic effect are informative in terms of its potential relationship with eustress. It has been positively related to health-promoting behaviors, social support use, and problem-focused coping (Antonovsky, 1993). We propose that individuals with a strong sense of coherence are more likely to appraise demands as challenges, to believe that they have (or can get from others) the resources they require to manage a demand, and are more likely to engage in effective coping methods for dealing with demands. They may be more likely to enact eustressful, rather than distressful, responses to demands.

A More Holistic Approach to Managing Health at Work

The research literature on work stress has focused strongly on pathology and on healing the wounded. The importance of this venture cannot be denied. We have learned much about stressors (causes of stress), coping, and symptoms of distress. Great strides have been made in assisting both individuals and organizations in managing distress. This, however, is only half the battle. As a complement to healing the wounded, we must also find ways of building and capitalizing on strengths. Distress prevention and eustress generation together provide a more holistic framework for managing occupational health issues.

Distress Prevention

As mentioned earlier in this chapter, one framework that allows for a comprehensive gathering of distress-focused interventions is that of preventive stress management, as originally proposed by Quick and Quick (1984) and as elaborated on by Quick et al. (1997). Central to the preventive stress management philosophy is the idea that stress is inevitable, but distress is not. Rooted in a public health framework, the three levels of preventive stress management are primary prevention, which is intended to reduce, change, or eliminate stressors; secondary prevention, which is focused on modifying the individual's or organization's response to stressors; and tertiary prevention, which attempts to heal individual or organizational symptoms of distress.

Primary prevention includes activities to directly change or eliminate the stressor and would encompass job redesign efforts. Karasek's (1979) job strain model, for example, indicated that it is possible to increase the demand level of a job without making it distressful so long as job discretion is also increased. Time management efforts also focus on eliminating or changing stressors. Also included in primary prevention, however, are efforts to change the individual's perception of the stressor. Cognitive restructuring and learned optimism, which alter the individual's internal self-talk, are primary prevention methods.

Secondary prevention efforts target the individual or organizational response to stress. Exercise, meditation, and other forms of relaxation and nutrition would all fall under the heading of secondary prevention. These techniques focus on lowering the risk of disease. Notable among the secondary prevention efforts is the work of Pennebaker and his colleagues (e.g., Smyth & Pennebaker, 2001), which demonstrates the psychological and somatic health benefits of writing about traumatic events and stressors.

Tertiary prevention is the most direct form of healing the wounds of distress. It consists of getting professional help (counseling, physical therapy, medical treatment, etc.) for symptoms of distress. Organizational efforts at tertiary prevention are often facilitated by employee assistance programs.

Our knowledge of preventing distress has grown. We can tell individuals a lot about how to prevent or resolve distress. Our next task, and a formidable one, is to learn how to help individuals and organizations generate eustress, savor it, and reap the benefits in terms of increased health, well-being, and performance.

Eustress Generation

As a complement to preventing distress, we must learn to generate eustress at work. Accordingly, if we are truly interested in eustress generation, we must measure and assess wellness and positive functioning. A model of eustress generation must go beyond positive coping with distress and distress prevention.

The contrast between the view of positive psychology presented and the more common view is captured in a recent article by Folkman and Moskowitz (2000). They accepted the fact that positive and negative affect can co-occur during a stressful period of time. They suggested that positive and negative responses are produced by different events (stressors). In their study, the effects of the positive response are viewed as a coping strategy, a way to adapt to distress and its negative effects. Several recent studies of the happy–productive worker hypothesis provide additional support for the need to develop a model of eustress generation. One study found that a pleasantness-based measure of dispositional affect predicted rated job performance, although the same was not true of state positive affect in this study (Wright & Staw, 1999). A second set of studies found that psychological well-being was predictive of job performance for 47 human service workers (Wright & Cropanzano, 2000). Unfortunately, psychological well-being was operationalized as the absence of the negative (e.g., how often have you felt depressed or very unhappy), again supporting the prevailing primacy of distress.

A model of eustress generation recognizes that the interpretation of and response to work demands can be positive as well as negative. Managers interested in eustress generation might identify which aspects of the work employees find most engaging, and then more important identify *why* individuals find the work pleasurable and consider what could be done to enhance the positive aspects of the work experience. Similar to the Quick et al. (1997) concept of primary distress prevention, this could be thought of as primary eustress generation via job redesign. Accordingly, we suggest that job redesign efforts must be assessed for their ability to generate the eustress as well as to prevent distress. It is important to note that any assignment of positive valence to work demands must be employee-generated and should not be considered a "one size fits all" solution.

If hopeful employees are healthy employees, then the generation of hope in workers as an indicator of eustress merits additional attention. The ability to generate hope among an organization's members may be particularly important during radical change efforts. When people believe that their actions will lead to positive results, they may be more willing to accept difficult and uncertain challenges. Managers can generate hope by establishing goals that are meaningful to all members, allocating the organizational resources necessary for individuals to excel at their jobs, and maintaining a frequent and inspirational dialogue with their constituents (Huy, 1999). Others have suggested that trust in management and procedural justice may result in primary appraisals that result in more hopeful employees during periods of organizational downsizing by reducing the extent to which downsizing is evaluated as a threat (Mishra & Spreitzer, 1998).

An example of an organizational resource that may be important for generating both manageability and hope is information. Role ambiguity has been shown to have a strong negative impact on hope (Simmons & Nelson, 2001). Role ambiguity is the confusion a person experiences related to not understanding what is expected, not knowing how to perform or change to meet new expectations, or not knowing the consequences of failing to meet expectations (Nelson & Quick, 2000). Relationships between employees and their supervisors that are open and supportive can reduce the role ambiguity and increase satisfaction. Managers who are easily accessible, who actively share information regarding current as well as evolving expectations with their constituents, and who encourage their management staff to do the same should establish a solid foundation for the generation of hope by lessening role ambiguity.

In parallel to the preventive stress management model, secondary eustress generation would target the individual response to work demands. Strategies for identifying and then managing negative responses, or coping, are well-documented (Quick et al., 1997). Similar strategies are needed to help individuals identify and manage, or savor, positive responses.

This will first require the previously mentioned effort to identify valid eustress responses, describe them in terms that clearly differentiate them from distress responses, and link them to health benefits in the same way that distress responses have been linked to health consequences. If the health benefit has significant valence for the individual, and the expectancy that eustress could promote the health benefit is firmly established, then the individual could choose strategies to enhance their exposure to demands that they appraise to be appreciably positive.

The key to eustress generation may be helping individuals develop competencies for recognizing eustress in themselves and others to complement existing competencies for recognizing distress. The challenge for researchers will be to propose, validate, improve, and articulate ways that the presence of the positive can be recognized and understood as more than just the absence of the negative.

In situations in which jobs have a high degree of control, individuals can savor eustress by enhancing their exposure to the demands that they believe precipitated the responses recognized as positive. For example, if an individual identifies a trusting relationship with a supervisor as a source of hope for them at work, then the individual might engage in behaviors that make themselves more trustworthy in the eyes of the supervisor. Having linked trusting relationships with a positive response for themselves at work, individuals may also seek to develop more trusting relationships with others at work, especially with those whom they may have a "stressful" relationship with. In this example of dealing with a stressful relationship, the eustress-generation approach of promoting the positive stands in contrast to the distress prevention approach of avoiding the stressor by avoiding the person (Quick et al., 1997).

In situations where jobs do not have a high degree of control, organizations can facilitate individuals savoring the positive. This may be challenging because as a result of cognitive appraisal, eustress recognition and interest in eustress generation will always be highly individualistic. Yet even in jobs with high demands and low decision latitude, the potential for positive appraisals remains. For example, the previously cited study of soldiers participating in a U.S. peacekeeping mission in Bosnia showed that the soldiers found meaningfulness in the challenge of their mission (Britt et al., 2001). Recall that a factor such as witnessing the destruction caused by warring factions was associated with reporting greater positive benefits, because in the context of the mission the destruction was likely seen as justification for the mission, which added meaning to the soldier's work. The degree of eustress experienced by the soldiers did not result from witnessing the destruction; rather it resulted from the organization providing the opportunity for purposeful engagement by defining a clear mission that was perceived beneficial, and then providing the resources necessary to accomplish the mission (i.e., manageability).

This chapter has proposed a more positive, holistic approach for understanding work stress by incorporating eustress, the positive response to stress. This approach is embedded in a view of health that emphasizes the presence of the positive mental, spiritual, and physical well-being in addition to the absence of disease and dysfunction. A tremendous opportunity exists for researchers to clarify and validate this more holistic approach to stress and health. This is a worthy endeavor, the goal of which is to influence a change in the refrain of many workers from "I'm stressed out" to "I'm engaged."

References

Ainsworth, M. D. S., & Bowlby, J. (1991). An ethological approach to personality. *American Psychologist, 46,* 333–341.

Antonovsky, A. (1987). *Unraveling the mysteries of health.* San Francisco: Jossey-Bass.

Antonovsky, A. (1993). The structure and properties of the sense of coherence scale. *Social Science and Medicine, 36,* 725–733.

Artinian, B. M. (1997). Situational sense of coherence: Development and measurement of the construct. In B. M. Artinian & M. M. Conger (Eds.), *The intersystem model: Integrating theory and practice* (pp. 18–30). Thousand Oaks, CA: Sage.

Barnett, R. C. (1998). Toward a review and reconceptualization of the work/family literature. *Genetic, Social, and General Psychology Monographs, 124,* 125–182.

Barnett, R. C., & Marshall, N. L. (1992). Worker and mother roles, spillover effects, and psychological distress. *Women & Health, 18,* 9–40.

Barnett, R. C., Marshall, N. L., & Sayer, A. (1992). Positive-spillover effects from job to home: A closer look. *Women & Health, 19,* 13–41.

Britt, T. W., Adler, A. B., & Bartone, P. T. (2001). Deriving benefits from stressful events: The role of engagement in meaningful work and hardiness. *Journal of Occupational Health Psychology, 6,* 53–63.

Cohen, S., & Edwards, J. R. (1988). Personality characteristics as moderators of the relationship between stress and disorder. In W. J. Neufeld (Ed.), *Advances in the investigation of psychological stress* (pp. 235–283). New York: Wiley.

DeFrank, R. S., & Ivancevich, J. M. (1998). Stress on the job: An executive update. *Academy of Management Executive, 12,* 55–66.

Edlin, G., Golanty, E., & Brown, K. M. (1996). *Health and wellness* (5th ed.). Sudbury, MA: Jones and Bartlett.

Edwards, J. R., & Cooper, C. L. (1988). The impacts of positive psychological states on physical health: A review and theoretical framework. *Social Science Medicine, 27*(12), 1147–1459.

Estrada, C. A., Isen, A. M., & Young, M. J. (1994). Positive affect improves creative problem solving and influences reported sources of practice satisfaction in physicians. *Motivation and Emotion, 18,* 285–299.

Estrada, C. A., Isen, A. M., & Young, M. J. (1997). Positive affect facilitates integration of information and decreases anchoring in reasoning among physicians. *Organizational Behavior and Human Decision Processes, 72,* 117–135.

Farren, C. (1999). Stress and productivity: What tips the scale? *Strategy and Leadership, 27,* 36–37.

Florian, V., Mikulincer, M., & Taubman, O. (1995). Does hardiness contribute to mental health during a stressful real-life situation? The roles of appraisal and coping. *Journal of Personality and Social Psychology, 68,* 687–695.

Folkman, S., & Moskowitz, J. T. (2000). Positive affect and the other side of coping. *American Psychologist, 55,* 647–654.

Ganster, D. C., & Schaubroeck, J. (1991). Work stress and employee health. *Journal of Management, 17,* 235–271.

George, J. M., & Brief, A. P. (1992). Feeling good-doing good: A conceptual analysis of mood at work-organizational spontaneity relationship. *Psychological Bulletin, 112,* 310–329.

Gray-Toft, P., & Anderson, J. G. (1981). Stress among hospital nursing staff: Its causes and effects. *Social Science Medicine, 15,* 639–647.

Hazan, C., & Shaver, P. R. (1990). Love and work: An attachment theoretical perspective. *Journal of Personality and Social Psychology, 52,* 511–524.

Huy, Q. N. (1999). Emotional capability, emotional intelligence, and radical change. *Academy of Management Review, 24,* 325–345.

Isen, A. M., Rosenzweig, A. S., & Young, M. J. (1991). The influence of positive affect on clinical problem solving. *Medical Decision Making, 11,* 221–227.

Kahn, R. L., Wolfe, R. P., Quinn, R. P., Snoek, J. D., & Rosenthal, R. A. (1964). *Organizational stress: Studies in role conflict and ambiguity.* New York: Wiley.

Karasek, R. A. (1979). Job demands, job decision latitude, and mental strain: Implications for job redesign. *Administrative Science Quarterly, 24,* 285–308.

Kobasa, S. C. (1979). Stressful life events, personality, and health: An inquiry into hardiness. *Journal of Personality and Social Psychology, 37,* 1–11.

Kobasa, S. C., Maddi, S. R., & Kahn, S. (1982). Hardiness and health: A prospective study. *Journal of Personality and Social Psychology, 42,* 168–177.

Lazarus, R. S. (1993). From psychological stress to the emotions: A history of changing outlooks. In L. W. Porter & M. R. Rosenzweig (Eds.), *Annual Review of Psychology* (Vol. 44, pp. 1–21). Palo Alto, CA: Annual Reviews.

Lazarus, R. S., DeLongis, A., Folkman, S., & Gruen, R. (1985). Stress and adaptational outcomes: The problem of confounded measures. *American Psychologist, 40,* 770–779.

Lazarus, R. S., & Folkman, S. (1984). *Stress, appraisal and coping.* New York: Springer.

Lefcourt, H. M., & Davidson-Katz, K. (1991). Locus of control and health. In C. R. Snyder & D. R. Forsyth (Eds.), *Handbook of social and clinical psychology* (pp. 246–266). New York: Pergamon Press.

Maddi, S. (1998). Hardiness in health and effectiveness. In H. S. Friedman (Ed.), *Encyclopaedia of mental health* (Vol. 2, pp. 323–335). San Diego, CA: Academic Press.

McCrae, R. R., & Costa, P. T., Jr. (1994). The stability of personality: Observations and evaluations. *Current Directions in Psychological Science, 3,* 173–175.

Mishra, A. K., & Spreitzer, G. M. (1998). Explaining how survivors respond to downsizing: The roles of trust, empowerment, justice, and work redesign. *Academy of Management Review, 23,* 567–588.

Mittal, V., & Ross, W. T., Jr. (1998). The impact of positive and negative affect and issue framing on issue interpretation and risk taking. *Organizational Behavior and Human Decision Processes, 76,* 298–324.

Morrill, A. C., Ickovics, J. R., Golubchikov, V. V., Berens, S. E., & Rodin, J. (1996). Safer sex: Social and psychological predictors of behavioral maintenance and change among heterosexual women. *Journal of Consulting and Clinical Psychology, 64,* 819–828.

Nelson, D. L., & Quick, J. C. (2000). *Organizational behavior: foundations, realities, and challenges* (3rd ed.). Cincinnati, OH: South-Western.

Nelson, D. L., Quick, J. C., & Joplin, J. (1991). Psychological contracting and newcomer socialization: An attachment theory foundation. *Journal of Social Behavior and Personality, 6,* 55–72.

Nelson, D. L., Quick, J. C., & Simmons, B. L. (2001). Preventive management of work stress: Current themes and future challenges. In A. Baum, T. Revenson, & J. Singer (Eds.), *Handbook of health psychology* (pp. 349–364). Mahwah, NJ: Erlbaum.

Ouellette, S. C. (1993). Inquiries into hardiness. In L. Goldberger & S. Breznitz (Eds.), *Handbook of stress: Theoretical and clinical aspects* (2nd ed.; pp. 202–240). New York: Free Press.

Ouellette, S. C., & DiPlacido, J. (2001). Personality's role in the protection and enhancement of health: Where the research has been, where it is stuck, how it might move. In A.

Baum, T. Revenson, & J. Singer (Eds.), *Handbook of health psychology* (pp. 175–193). Mahwah, NJ: Erlbaum.

Peterson, C. (2000). The future of optimism. *American Psychologist, 55,* 44–55.

Peterson, C., & Seligman, M. E. P. (1987). Explanatory style and illness. *Journal of Personality, 55,* 238–265.

Quick, J. C., & Quick, J. D. (1984). *Organizational stress and preventive management.* New York: McGraw-Hill.

Quick, J. C., Quick, J. D., Nelson, D. L., & Hurrell, J. J. (1997). *Preventive stress management in organizations.* Washington, DC: American Psychological Association.

Rotter, J. B. (1966). Generalized expectancies for internal versus external control of reinforcements. *Psychological Monographs, 80,* 1–28.

Russell, B. (1958). *The conquest of happiness.* New York: Liveright.

Ryff, C. D., & Singer, B. (1998). The contours of positive human health. *Psychological Inquiry, 9,* 1–28.

Salovey, P., Rothman, A. J., Detweiler, J. B., & Steward, W. T. (2000). Emotional states and physical health. *American Psychologist, 55,* 110–121.

Scheier, M. F., & Carver, C. S. (1992). Effects of optimism on psychological and physical well being: Theoretical overview and empirical update. *Cognitive Therapy and Research, 16,* 201–228.

Segerstrom, S. C., Taylor, S. E., Kemeny, M. E., & Fahey, J. L. (1998). Optimism is associated with mood, coping, and immune change in response to stress. *Journal of Personality and Social Psychology, 74,* 1646–1655.

Seligman, M. E. P. (1991). *Learned optimism.* New York: Knopf.

Seligman, M. E. P., & Csikszentmihalyi, M. (2000). Positive psychology. *American Psychologist, 55,* 5–14.

Selye, H. (1976). *Stress in health and disease.* Boston: Butterworths.

Simmons, B. L. (2000). *Eustress at work: Accentuating the positive.* Unpublished doctoral dissertation, Oklahoma State University.

Simmons, B. L., & Nelson, D. L. (2001). Eustress at work: The relationship between hope and health in hospital nurses. *Health Care Management Review, 26,* 7–18.

Simmons, B. L., Nelson, D. L., & Neal, L. J. (2001). A comparison of the positive and negative work attitudes of home healthcare and hospital nurses. *Health Care Management Review, 26,* 63–74.

Smith, C. A., Haynes, K. N., Lazarus, R. S., & Pope, L. K. (1993). In search of the "hot" cognitions: Attributions, appraisals, and their relation to emotion. *Journal of Personality and Social Psychology, 65,* 916–929.

Smyth, J. M., & Pennebaker, J. W. (2001). What are the health effects of disclosure? In A. Baum, T. A. Revenson, & J. E. Singer (Eds.), *Handbook of health psychology* (pp. 339–348). Mahwah, NJ: Erlbaum.

Snyder, C. R. (1994). *The psychology of hope: You can get there from here.* New York: Free Press.

Snyder, C. R., Sympson, S. C., Ybasco, F. C., Borders, T. F., Babyak, M. A., & Higgins, R. L. (1996). Development and validation of the state hope scale. *Journal of Personality and Social Psychology, 70,* 321–335.

Spreitzer, G. M. (1995). Psychological empowerment in the workplace: Dimensions, measurement, and validation. *Academy of Management Journal, 38,* 1442–1465.

Staw, B. M., & Barsade, S. G. (1993). Affect and managerial performance: A test of the sadder-but-wiser vs. happier-and-smarter hypothesis. *Administrative Science Quarterly, 38,* 304–331.

Theorell, T., & Karasek, R. A. (1996). Current issues relating to psychosocial job strain and cardiovascular disease research. *Journal of Occupational Health Psychology, 1,* 9–26.

Thomas, K., & Velthouse, B. (1990). Cognitive elements of empowerment: An "interpretive" model of intrinsic task motivation. *Academy of Management Review, 15,* 666–681.

Watson, D., Clark, L. A., & Tellegen, A. (1988). Development and validation of brief measures of positive and negative affect: The PANAS scale. *Journal of Personality and Social Psychology, 54,* 1063–1070.

Watson, D., & Pennebaker, J. W. (1989). Health complaints, stress and distress: Exploring the central role of negative affectivity. *Psychological Review, 96,* 234–254.

Watson, D., Pennebaker, J. W., & Folger, R. (1987). Beyond negative affectivity: Measuring stress and satisfaction in the workplace. *Journal of Organizational Behavior Management, 8,* 141–152.

Weidner, G., Boughal, T., Connor, S. L., Peiper, C., & Mendell, N. R. (1997). Relationship of job strain to standard coronary risk factors and psychological characteristics in women and men of the family heart study. *Health Psychology, 16,* 239–247.

Westman, M. (1990). The relationship between stress and performance: The moderating effect of hardiness. *Human Performance, 3,* 141–155.

Wiebe, D. J. (1991). Hardiness and stress moderation: A test of proposed mechanisms. *Journal of Personality and Social Psychology, 50,* 89–99.

Wiebe, D. J., & Williams, P. G. (1992). Hardiness and health: A social psychophysiological perspective on stress and adaptation. *Journal of Social and Clinical Psychology, 11,* 238–262.

World Health Organization. (1948). *World Health Organization constitution.* Geneva: Author.

Wright, L. (1988). The Type A behavior pattern and coronary artery disease. *American Psychologist, 43,* 2–14.

Wright, T. A., & Cropanzano, R. (2000). Psychological well-being and job satisfaction as predictors of job performance. *Journal of Occupational Psychology, 5,* 84–94.

Wright, T. A., & Staw, B. M. (1999). Affect and favorable work outcomes: two longitudinal tests of the happy-productive worker thesis. *Journal of Organizational Behavior, 20,* 1–23.

Part II

Causes of and Risks to
Health and Safety

Part II includes a tightly defined set of six chapters that address key causes of health and safety at work as well as key risks to health and safety. These chapters focus on factors both within the specific workplace as well as broader occupational factors, such as technology, and factors from the personal life domain, such as the family. These six chapters again reflect both the interdisciplinary nature of occupational health psychology and its international context, with contributions from Sweden in Europe and Israel in the Middle East as well as contributions from across the United States.

Chapter 6 by Zohar expands Smith et al.'s description of the work environment, work organization and supervision by a presentation of safety climate that includes shared perceptions concerning safety policies, procedures, and practices including management practices. Based on this conceptualization of safety climate, Zohar then presents a multilevel model of safety climate relating safety climate to behavior–outcome expectancies, safety behavior, injury rates, and health problems. The model identifies several contextual factors, leadership, and job and technology characteristics that can influence safety climate. To conclude, Zohar addresses issues in the measurement of safety climate and identifies future research directions to further our understanding of the relations between safety climate, safety behavior, and occupational safety and health.

Frone's chapter 7 provides an overview of the literature on work–family balance, including a discussion of the major causes and outcomes of work–family balance. Although work–family balance has generally focused on the negative aspects of work–family conflict, Frone suggests there also can be work-to-family and family-to-work facilitation. The research that has been done, to date, on work–family facilitation suggests that the processes may be different from those operating under conditions of work–family conflict. Frone ends the chapter with a discussion of personal and organizational initiatives to promote work–family balance.

Hours of work are generally recognized as one possible contributor to work–family conflict. In addition, as Smith, Folkard, and Fuller indicate in chapter 8, working nontraditional hours has been identified as a risk for both physical and psychological impairment. Smith, Folkard, and Fuller provide an overview of the biological basis for some of the reactions to shiftwork and then review the literature on shiftwork and health. In this review they also discuss individual and situational factors that have been found to promote tolerance to shiftwork. Smith et al. conclude their chapter with a presentation of interventions to improve shiftworkers' health and effectiveness.

Chapter 9 by Spielberger, Vagg, and Wasala discusses the problem of occupational stress with primary emphasis on job pressures and lack of organizational support as two key causes of stress and health risks at work. Job stress has been labeled a modern health epidemic by Paul Rosch, president of the American Institute of Stress, based on a variety of indicators such as workers' compensation claims, job losses, and absence days from work because of illness. The authors review the effects of occupational stress on productivity, employee burnout, and health-related problems. They go on to examine conceptual models of stress in the workplace and focus on job pressures and lack of support as two overarching sources of stress and health risk for people at work. The authors consider the role of personality and emotion in the stress process model and discuss the Job Stress Survey as the basis for intervention and action.

Job control has been considered one of the key aspects of the work environment that affects employees' health. Theorell, in chapter 10, describes control as a basic human need. In the work environment, the demand–control model of stress characterizes control as decision latitude—that is, authority over decisions and intellectual discretion. Theorell describes the demand–control model and reviews the evidence linking decision latitude to cardiovascular disease as well as the risk of cardiovascular disease including providing a description of the mechanisms by which this link occurs. Theorell concludes the chapter with a review of ways decision latitude has been improved with the concurrent improvement in health.

In their chapter in Part I, Smith et al.'s chapter included some discussion of technology in their model. However, chapter 11 by Coovert and Thompson provides a more detailed description of technology. Such topics as mobile computing and collaborative support are described. Then Coovert and Thompson present the basis for the connection between technology and health and wellness. Physical concerns primarily focus on musculoskeletal disorders and psychological concerns, although occupational differences may exist, and have tended to indicate that technology can reduce employees' control, increase their sense of isolation, and present concerns about privacy. Suggestions are made for alleviating these negative effects, including a view of the future as might be realized through "cooperative buildings."

6

Safety Climate: Conceptual and Measurement Issues

Dov Zohar

Work accidents cost the American economy an estimated $108.4 billion a year (National Safety Council, 1999), in addition to human suffering and loss of life. A fatal work injury occurs every two hours in the United States, and a disabling injury every 8 seconds (National Safety Council, 1999). Large-scale accidents such as the Chernobyl or Bhopal disasters have provided dramatic evidence of the economic and human cost of industrial accidents. However, despite the economic and social significance of safety issues, they have received only cursory attention by management scholars (Fahlbruch & Wilpert, 1999; Shannon, Mayr, & Haines, 1997). An exception is the growing body of research on safety climate–culture, which has captured increasing attention since the inquiry into the Chernobyl disaster identified inadequate safety culture as a major underlying factor for the accident (IAEA, 1986, 1991). However, this literature is characterized by conceptual ambiguity, evident in the fact that many authors fail to discriminate between safety *climate* and *culture* (Cox & Flin, 1998), in addition to including a host of variables that belong neither to climate nor culture as defined in the organizational behavior literature. This chapter is based on the premise that safety climate and culture must be clearly distinguished on grounds of discriminant validity. Using these constructs interchangeably, or operationalizing culture with climate scales, as is the common practice, results in conceptual slippage damaging to both. However, given the multitude of proposed solutions concerning ways of mapping safety climate onto safety culture it hardly seems worthwhile suggesting yet another solution. A more beneficial strategy would be to increase conceptual clarity for each construct (considered in isolation) before attempting integration. The purpose of this chapter, therefore, is to review the climate literature from an analytical perspective and to offer a model of safety climate that clarifies its nature. To begin with, some basic attributes of organizational climate are considered.

Attributes of Organizational Climate

Organizational climate refers to shared perceptions among members of an organization with regard to its fundamental properties—in other words, policies, procedures, and practices (Reichers & Schneider, 1990; Rentsch, 1990). A multilevel interpretation suggests that policies define strategic goals and means of goal attainment, whereas procedures provide tactical guidelines for action related to these goals and means. Practices, on the other hand, relate to the execution of policies and procedures by managers across the organizational hierarchy (Zohar, 2000a). Because organizations have multiple goals and means of attaining goals, senior managers must develop policies and procedures for each organizational facet (e.g., customer service, product quality, employee safety). To the extent that these policies are sufficiently clear and unequivocal, they allow a consensus among employees concerning their nature. This results in the formation of multiple climates in organizations, with employees focusing concurrently on different organizational facets such as the climates for service (Schneider & Bowen, 1985; Schneider, White, & Paul, 1998), innovation (Abbey & Dickson, 1983; Anderson & West, 1996), and safety (Dedobbeleer & Beland, 1991; Zohar, 1980).

Climate is an emergent property, characterizing groups of individuals. Operationally, it is assessed by aggregating individual perceptions to the required unit of analysis (organization, department, work group), and using the mean to represent the climate for that entity (Reichers & Schneider, 1990). Research to date has identified three validation criteria for aggregated perceptions. The first is within-unit homogeneity, or consensus of perceptions. Without sufficient homogeneity, an aggregate score is not a valid indicator of climate (James, 1982). Because climate, like leadership and cohesion, is a group-level property, it follows that the individual level of analysis must be excluded from models of climate (Glick, 1988; Patterson et al., 1996; Rousseau, 1988). Thus, variables such as personal beliefs concerning why accidents happen or job involvement should not be considered as climate variables. The second criterion is between-unit variability, relating to units of analysis such as different organizations or subunits within an organization. In other words, homogeneity of perceptions within the chosen unit of analysis must coincide with heterogeneity, or variance, between units (Glick, 1985; Patterson et al., 1996; Payne, 1990; Rousseau, 1988). The third validation criterion is that units of analysis should correspond to natural social units such as work groups, departments, or organizations. Although there has been some debate concerning this requirement (Joyce & Slocum, 1984), most authors consider it necessary (Glick, 1988; Patterson et al., 1996; Payne, 1990). This contradicts the psychological climate perspective (James & Jones, 1974) whereby individuals sharing the same views of the organization are clustered by statistical means, although they may never have met or seen each other.

Previous research using indexes of agreement such as intraclass correlation (ICC1, ICC2; James, 1982) and within-group correlation (R_{wg}; James, Demaree, & Wolf, 1984, 1993) indicated that homogeneity of climate perceptions may vary. Because homogeneity statistics offer no test of statistical significance, Glick (1985) provided a heuristic for the R_{wg} coefficient whereby values of 0.70 and higher warrant aggregation of individual responses. Note, however, that this implies that climates may vary appreciably in terms of homogeneity (granted, of course, that a certain threshold value is surpassed). It follows, therefore, that climates can be described in terms of two independent parameters: (a) strength of climate (weak to strong), referring to the internal consistency with which climate perceptions are held; and (b) level of climate (low to high), referring to the relative position of the climate mean on the relevant continuum. Thus, for example, high safety climate relates to supportive policies concerning safety and health, though such a climate may be strong or weak, depending on the extent of agreement among employees in their respective organizations or subunits. This will have important implications for the effect of climate on safety behavior.

The Core Meaning of Safety Climate

As noted previously, organizations have multiple goals and means of attaining those goals, so that senior managers must develop facet-specific policies and procedures to which employees attend, resulting in multiple specific climates. Thus, safety climate relates to shared perceptions with regard to *safety* policies, procedures, and practices. However, assessment of such policies, procedures, and practices can be quite complex, requiring, among other things, establishment of differences between formally declared policies and procedures and their enforced counterparts (i.e., managerial practices). Formal policy is explicit, relating to overt statements and formal procedures, whereas enforced policy or enacted practices are tacit, derived from observing senior, middle, and lower management patterns of action concerning key policy issues. (This distinction is akin to that made by Argyris and Schon (1996) between formally espoused theories of action, or policies, and theories-in-use.) From a functional perspective, climate perceptions should refer only to policies-in-use, or enacted policies, rather than to their formal counterparts, because they inform employees of the probable consequences of safety behavior. Thus, a consensus should occur when management displays an internally consistent pattern of action concerning safety, even if it differs from formally declared policy. For example, site managers might expect workers to bend company safety rules, except in life-threatening situations, whenever production falls behind schedule, despite official claims to the contrary. If this is done consistently, it will promote a low safety climate, as described by Pate-Cornell (1990) and Wright (1986) with regard to managerial practices on offshore oil platforms.

Given that safety issues are inherent to every manufacturing process while competing with other issues such as speed or profitability, it follows that (enforced) safety policies and procedures can be construed in terms of the *relative priorities* of safety and production goals. Because relative priorities provide an economical means of interpreting the pragmatic meaning of enforced policies for company employees, it is proposed that safety climate perceptions refer to those policy attributes that indicate the true priority of safety. This agrees with the constructivist principle of least effort (Zipf, 1965), suggesting that employees will opt for the most economical means to assess enforced policies and procedures. The object of safety climate perceptions is, therefore, the (true) priority of safety, so that climate level reflects its consensual priority, rather than numerous procedures considered individually. In other words, climate perceptions relate to "procedures-as-pattern" rather than to individual procedures. In this respect, safety climate is assumed to be a social construct (Rochlin, 1999), part of an active process of organizational sense-making (Drazin, Glynn, & Kazanjian, 1999; Weick, 1995), as opposed to passive observation of isolated safety procedures. Thus, for example, whenever safety issues are ignored or made contingent on production pressures, workers will infer low safety priority. All that is required for such a policy to become a source of (low) climate perceptions is that it remains unequivocal and stable.

Climate–Behavior Relationships

Apart from precise definitions, a theoretical model of safety climate should also specify the link between climate perceptions and organizational safety records. Although there is empirical evidence concerning relationships between climate level and injury rate (e.g., Hofmann & Stetzer, 1996; Zohar, 2000a), the underlying variables have hardly been explored. I propose, therefore, that climate perceptions affect safety records in the following manner: (a) climate perceptions influence behavior–outcome expectancies; (b) expectancies influence prevalence of safety behavior; and (c) behavioral safety influences company safety records. The first stage—between climate perceptions and behavior–outcome expectancies—is implicit in the definition of climate presented previously. Given that climate perceptions are related to enacted policies that indicate the true priorities of key task facets, it follows that climate perceptions will influence outcome expectancies. In fact, employees pay attention to enacted policies rather than to their formalized counterparts because they indicate probable consequences—in other words, they inform behavior–outcome expectancies. The second stage, relating to the effect of expectancies on behavior, is based on social learning and expected valence–utility constructs (Bandura, 1986; Lawler, 1971; Vroom, 1964), although it can also be explained in terms of other theoretical constructs (James, James, & Ashe, 1990; Schneider & Reichers, 1983). Thus, the higher the perceived likelihood of obtaining a result by certain actions (e.g., stressing speed over safety) and the more valued the result, the greater the motivation to act in a specific manner. This presents the rationale for a positive relationship between safety–climate level and behavioral safety in organizations. Climate strength should be the moderator variable for this relationship, because the less the homogeneity of climate perceptions, the weaker the climate–behavior relationship (Zohar & Luria, 2001). Thus, climate strength should have a significant impact on the

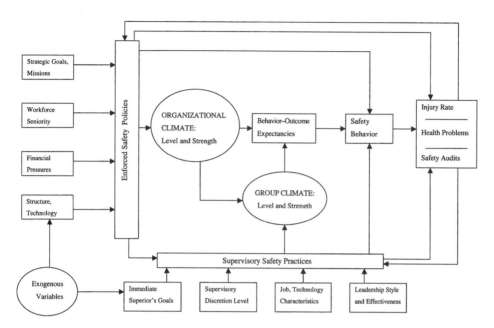

Figure 6.1. A multilevel model of safety climate. The figure includes climate-mediated and unmediated links between safety policies and practices and outcome variables, as well as feedback loops, suggesting that the incidence of injury could induce senior managers or supervisors to modify their emphasis on safety measures.

predictive power of climate level. Finally, the third stage is based on much empirical evidence concerning the significance of human action in industrial accidents. Given that human error accounts for about 85% of accidents across industries (Heinrich, 1931; Reason, 1990, 1997), behavioral safety should be positively related with company safety records. This should result in a global relationship of safety climate and safety records.

This theoretical model is congruent with the operant perspective for organizational climate or culture (Glenn, 1991; Thompson & Luthans, 1990), which also has been applied in the context of safety climate (Cooper, 2000; Hantula, 1999). An important concept is meta-contingencies—in other words, stable organization (wide contingencies for a whole class of role behaviors). When the various procedures are perceived by the workforce as converging on a particular priority for safety, this results in a specific meta-contingency for safety behavior. Based on the law of effect (Skinner, 1974), such meta-contingency should result in increased frequency of safety behavior and thus influence injury rates. Note, however, that this explanation does not preclude traditional, value-based explanations because any safety priority is related to certain values and basic assumptions (Schein, 1992). In other words, values and basic assumptions are antecedents of organizational policies and practices.

The entire path is presented in Figure 6.1. This figure includes climate-mediated and unmediated links between safety policies, unsafe behavior, and injury rate, as well as feedback loops suggesting that the incidence of unsafe behavior or injury could induce senior managers or supervisors to modify their emphasis on safety measures. It remains to be proven, though, that climate perceptions (partially) mediate the effect of policies and procedures on role behavior and provide incremental prediction unaccounted for by direct effects. The *un*mediated effect of managerial action can be accounted for by two factors. First, environmental constraints directly affect behavior. If safety devices are installed, employees must operate machines more safely, regardless of climate perceptions. Second, internal selection and attrition processes are important (Schneider, 1987). Bringing safety violations to the attention of senior managers or making safety a performance criterion will probably result in discrimination against violators when personnel decisions are made. Over time, in companies with appropriate safety procedures, violators are likely to be transferred to less risky jobs or induced to leave the company. This too will affect the incidence of safe behavior, regardless of climate perceptions.

Figure 6.1 also suggests that there may be two types of exogenous variables. One type includes variables likely to influence climate level or strength, although they are not part of this construct. For example, strategic goals and stakeholder pressures can induce higher safety climate, whereas financial pressure and a belief that safety is ultimately the responsibility of individual workers would result in lower climate. At the group level, individual supervisory goals and the technology of particular subunits could also influence climate level and strength. For example, increased technological hazards because of the use of inflammable raw materials might result in greater emphasis on safety in some work groups. The second type includes exogenous variables that have been shown to predict safety outcomes (e.g., workforce seniority, empowerment) though unrelated to safety climate, and these should be included as control variables in statistical models. They clarify the unique meaning of safety climate.

The mediation effect of climate perceptions is based on aspects of the definition of climate as outlined previously—climate perceptions relate to the priority of safety as inferred from the global pattern of executed procedures. As related to this priority, climate perceptions influence action in many situations where there are *no* specific procedures for appropriate role behavior. In other words, because procedures do not cover all work situations and contingencies (except in highly routinized work; see Hall, 1987; Perrow, 1979), there are many situations in which behavior must be guided by internal standards based on assessment of procedures-as-pattern. In such situations, climate perceptions will play an important mediating role, thereby exerting an incremental effect on behavior. In other words, the mediating effect of climate perceptions can be attributed to their potential influence on behavior–outcome expectancies in situations for which no specific procedures have been defined. Accident investigations and models of human error suggest that such situations are especially conducive to injury (Brown, 1991; Rasmussen, 1982, 1990; Reason, 1990, 1997).

In terms of safety behavior, climate perceptions play an additional mediation role, because of employees' bias against safe conduct in regular job conditions. Contrary to the assumption that self-preservation overrides other motives (Maslow, 1970), safety studies indicate that careless behavior prevails during regular job activities. For example, failure to use protective gear provided at the workplace accounts for about 40% of work accidents, a statistic that has not changed for more than 20 years (National Safety Council, 1999). The bias against safe behavior can be explained, in decision-theory terms, as an outcome of assigning greater weight to short-term gains (i.e., melioration), coupled with underestimation of the likelihood of possible "rare" events (Herrnstein, Loewnstein, Prelec, & Vaughan, 1993). Safety precautions often entail a modest but immediate (hence certain) cost. For example, protective gear often causes personal discomfort such as sweating, blurred vision, or restricted manual dexterity. If the likelihood of injury during routine activity is underestimated and becomes infinitely small, the expected utility of *un*safe behavior exceeds that of safe behavior. From the perspective of prospect theory (Kahneman & Tversky, 1979), the value–function for loss associated with safe behavior is much steeper than that of gain. One factor that can modify the value–function for safe behavior is contingent (and immediate, hence certain) reward or punishment from management. This has proven much more effective than pledge- or fear-based interventions, including supplying detailed risk information (Cooper, Phillips, Sutherland, & Makin, 1994), providing the basis for behavioral safety interventions (Krispin & Hantula, 1996). Thus, the incremental effect of safety climate perceptions in situations not covered by specific procedures is likely to be stronger than that of other climates, because of the inherent bias toward unsafe behavior.

Some indirect evidence for the incremental effect of climate perceptions posited in this model is provided in a study by Saari and Nasanen (1989), in which public feedback concerning housekeeping levels in a shipyard was provided over an extended period of time. Over a two-year period, accidents related to housekeeping decreased substantially. However, accidents *not* related to housekeeping also decreased, which suggests that meta-contingencies or climate changes produced an incremental effect unaccounted for by environmental change alone. According to the authors, the incremental effects surpassed the direct effect of improved housekeeping standards. Similar results have been reported in other behavior modification studies (Komaki, Collins, & Penn, 1982; Reber, Wallin, & Chokar, 1984).

A Multilevel Model of Safety Climate

Another aspect of the climate model presented in Figure 6.1 is that climate can be investigated at two hierarchical levels: organizational and subunit or group level (Glick, 1988; Patterson, Payne, & West, 1996; Rousseau, 1988). To date, organization and subunit safety climates have been studied separately, dealing either with one unit of analysis or the other (Zohar, 2000a). The same applies for other fields of organizational behavior research, in which researchers focus either on micro- or macrolevels of analysis (O'Reilly, 1991). Nonetheless, it has been repeatedly argued that organizational processes do take place simultaneously at several levels, and that processes at different levels are linked in some way (Dansereau & Alutto, 1990; House, Rousseau, & Thomas-Hunt, 1995; Klein, Dansereau, & Hall, 1994). In other words, processes that take place at one hierarchical level have an impact on other levels, mostly as a result of interdependence between individuals, and of the need to balance hierarchical exchanges between organizational levels (Katz & Kahn, 1978; March & Simon, 1959). In the context of safety climate, this implies that a theoretical model should identify the differential meaning of climates at different organizational levels, as well as identifying cross-level relationships.

To make climate a multilevel construct, several assumptions are required. These relate to individuals as members both of an organization and of subunits in that organization. The following assumptions require explication: (a) Policies and procedures that are established at the organization level must be implemented or executed by unit managers throughout the organizational hierarchy. That is, top managers are concerned with policy making and establishing procedures to facilitate policy implementation, and supervisors at lower hierarchical levels execute these policies and associated procedures through interaction with subordinates. This creates a potential for discrepancy between formal and executed policy, including a reflexive discrepancy whereby top managers do not implement their own formal policies. (b) Policy execution is affected by personal and technological group-level factors, including levels of work routinization. Low routinization requires greater discretion in policy implementation because procedures cannot cover all possible situations (Hage & Aiken, 1969; Perrow, 1967). Between-group differences relating to different ways of implementing company policies and procedures are, therefore, to be expected in a single organization. For example, unit supervisors may set lenient or severe safety standards within the boundaries set by top management. (c) Individual employees discriminate between procedures instituted by top management and those executed by unit managers, facilitated by two main sources of information. The first is the degree of difference between subunits, detected through social comparisons among employees in different subunits (Schneider & Reichers, 1983). For example, by social comparison, members of one subunit may conclude that their immediate superior is much more lenient regarding protective gear usage than other superiors. Thus, although "typical" or modal supervisory pressures would identify company-level policy regarding use of protective gear, the discrepancy between what most supervisors do and what a specific supervisor does would identify subunit practices. Another source of information concerns assessment of the degree to which supervisory behavior during interaction with group members is backed by company management. For example, if a supervisor initiates disciplinary action in response to a safety violation, this is indicative of supervisory emphasis on safety. The degree to which higher level managers are willing to back up this action is indicative of organization-wide emphasis. Together, this information can help employees to discriminate between company-level and group-level emphasis on safety. (d) Level of analysis simultaneously defines the unit of aggregation and the target or referent of climate perceptions. At the organization level, climate perceptions are aggregated across the company, and company-level emphasis on safety is the referent object. At the group level, perceptions are aggregated within subunits, and supervisory emphasis is the referent object. By adjusting the referent of perceptions and assuming that individuals discriminate between procedural and supervisory emphasis on safety, a theoretical framework for a multilevel model is established.

Together, these assumptions explain the important cross-level phenomenon of group-level variation within a single organization-level climate. The key issue in group-level variation relates to the restraining effect of instituted procedures on supervisory practices. The first assumption listed previously indicates that unit managers must turn company-level procedures into situation-specific action directives. The second assumption indicates that this process requires discretionary decision making, because procedures cannot cover all possible contingencies (except in highly routinized work). Hence, unit managers must continually decide *how* to implement procedures, while taking into account situation-specific factors. It must be emphasized that supervisory roles entail considerable discretion because supervisors manage other people, rather than dealing directly with production technology. This creates interpersonal problems of sufficient complexity to allow us to define supervision as inherently little-routinized (Hage & Aiken, 1969; Perrow, 1967). For example, a supervisor must decide whether to put more or less emphasis on safety in a situation in which increased heat may have made some workers fatigued or irritated (i.e., increased supervisory pressure could induce even greater fatigue or irritation). The discretionary power inherent in supervisory roles is a necessary and sufficient condition for creating group-level variation, resulting in corresponding climate variation. This was supported in a recent study of group-level safety climate, using 53 work groups in a single manufacturing company (Zohar, 2000a). In this study, safety climate perceptions revealed sufficiently high within-group homogeneity and between-group variance to warrant group-level aggregation. Climate levels were also shown to predict minor injury records in work groups for a five-month period following climate measurement, after controlling for departmental risk levels. Similar results were obtained in military field units, using 61 platoons in 3 brigades (Zohar & Luria, 2001).

The corollary of the assumption that supervisory discretion is a necessary and sufficient condition for group-level climate variation is that the greater the supervisory discretion, the greater the expected variation of (group) climate levels in a single organization. This increases the likelihood of discrepancy between formal and executed policy at various levels in the organizational hierarchy. I thus propose a threshold model in which, up to a certain point, group-level variation is assessed as remaining within the boundaries set by company policies, beyond which boundaries employees consider the variation as boundary crossing—in other words, discrepancy. Such discrepancies can occur either within organizational levels ("top management doesn't back up its own policy") or between levels ("some unit managers exceed or fall short of company safety standards"). Organization-level factors influencing supervisory discretion include structure and culture. A relevant structural parameter is formalization (Hage & Aiken, 1969). Supervisors in a formalized organization, where procedures are both highly specific (and thus numerous) and rigid will enjoy little discretion, and policy boundaries will also be narrow and rigid (unless top management does not back them up). Because structure reflects culture, this is likely to be accompanied with considerable power distance between hierarchical levels (Hofstede, 1998). Other group-level factors can also influence supervisory discretion with regard to safety—for example, local hazards, supervisory expert power, and physical distance from headquarters. An experienced supervisor reporting to a passive superior will probably enjoy greater discretion and, as a consequence, greater likelihood of discrepant group-level climate will result.

Assessing instituted procedures at company level and their execution at the group level as distinctively different assessment targets is similar to the distinction between procedural and interactional justice. In the organizational justice literature, procedural justice refers to employees' assessment of fairness in formal procedures, based on criteria such as consistency, bias suppression, and correctability (Skarlicki & Folger, 1997; Thibaut & Walker, 1975). Interactional justice, on the other hand, refers to employees' assessment of the quality of interpersonal treatment during enactment of formal procedures by their superiors. Supervisors' behavior is judged on such criteria as exhibiting respect, listening to concerns, providing explanations, and being truthful (Bies & Moag, 1986; Moorman, 1991). Studies of organizational justice have repeatedly indicated that both kinds of justice are assessed independently by employees, who are able to discriminate between them (Ball, Trevino, & Sims, 1994; Tyler & Lind, 1992). Similarly, it is suggested that procedures as instituted by upper level managers and their implementation by lower level managers are distinctive attributes of the workplace to which workers attend when forming climate perceptions.

Implications for Safety Climate Measurement

Reviews of the literature indicate that authors of climate measures use management (upper or lower) commitment to the safety and health of employees as a primary target of climate perceptions (i.e., high commitment is functionally equivalent with a priority for safety over production). In a thematic analysis of available measurement scales, Flin, Mearns, O'Connor, and Bryden (2000) concluded that management commitment was the prime theme, appearing in 13 out of the 18 safety–climate scales under review. Similar results were reported in another review of 15 partially overlapping measurement scales (Guldenmund, 2000). Examination of the measures covered in both reviews indicates that, in addition to direct assessment of (perceived) management commitment, they include other subscales concerning procedural features of the safety system (e.g., training, audits, compliance, communication). This is often presented as an empirically derived list, based on findings suggesting that they predict important safety outcomes such as accident rate (e.g., Niskanen, 1994; Ostrom, Wilhelmsen, & Kaplan, 1993). To enhance discriminant validity, I propose that measures of safety climate should only include those procedural features indicative of managerial commitments, hence serving as concrete indicators of the true priority of safety (in addition to direct, unmediated assessment of managerial commitments or priorities). This is akin to the use of artifacts, stories, and ceremonies in identifying basic assumptions and values (Schein, 1992), except that here I suggest retaining a single focus relating to the overriding priority of safety.

Climate indicators can be subdivided into universal versus industry-specific items. Some indicators of safety priority refer to universal features in that they are applicable to all industries where safety is a relevant issue. These include procedural features such as the (real) status of safety officer, effect of safe conduct on personnel decisions, investment in safety devices and safety training, and timely communication of safety information (e.g., Dedobbeleer & Beland, 1991; Glennon, 1982; Zohar, 1980). Other indicators relate to industry-specific features—for example, efficacy of the permit-to-work system in nuclear plants (Lee, 1996), appropriateness of safety procedures under changing conditions aboard offshore oil installations (Mearns, Flin, Gordon, & Fleming, 1998), and insistence on universal precautions against bloodborne pathogens in health care clinics (DeJoy, Murphy, & Gershon, 1995). This means that safety-climate measures may include three item classes: unmediated perceptions of (real) managerial commitment or direct assessment of relative priorities, mediated assessment through universal indicators, and assessment based on industry-specific indicators. The first two classes allow unlimited, between-unit comparisons, but the third increases measurement sensitivity for within-unit and within-industry comparisons. A subset of items in each class may relate to situations in which safety and production come into overt conflict, identified here as "acid-test indicators." That is, it is assumed that employees will pay particular attention to managerial action in such situations, thus providing the clearest indication of true priorities. Management action when there is strong pressure to meet production deadlines, or when the required safety devices cost more than a few hundred dollars, will be assigned greater weight by employees in assessing true priorities.

Another classification of climate items concerns levels of analysis. A climate survey may include company-level and group-level items relating to commitments and resultant indicators of upper- and lower level managerial practices. This agrees with the idea that referent objects of climate perceptions should be adjusted to the level of analysis. Thus, organization-level climate indicators should refer to issues such as financial expenditure on safety devices, reducing production speed in favor of safety, and personnel decisions based on safety criteria. Group-level indicators, however, should refer to issues such as supervisory monitoring and rewarding practices, individualized coaching of group members, and willingness to interrupt production to correct safety hazards. Therefore, although content of some items may vary considerably between different climate measures, depending on the work environment of the employees and level of analysis, subscales should retain the single underlying theme of true safety priority. By default, this means that other variables known to influence safety outcomes should be included as independent variables in theoretical and measurement models.

Boundary Stipulations for Safety Climate

This exposition of the safety climate construct can clarify relevant boundaries and explain consequences of inadvertently crossing them. When subscales refer to features of safety systems that are *not* related to safety priority or any other designated issue, conceptual ambiguity will arise. For example, when climate subscales relate to supervisory satisfaction, knowledge, and support (Safety Research Unit, 1993); workers' skills, abilities, and motivation (Niskanen, 1994); or optimism, self-esteem, and risk-taking (Geller, Roberts, & Gilmore, 1996) conceptual ambiguity will result, because they are not connected to any focal issue, including assessment of safety priority (apart from being individual-level variables). Such variables can be included in safety models in which climate is only one variable, among others that are equally independent. This distinction is especially relevant for risk-perception items, often used in climate measures (Flin et al., 2000). Risk assessment should be included in measures of safety climate where subscale items relate to risk *resulting from management action or inaction*—in other words, as an indicator of relative priorities rather than technological hazards (which vary between subunits regardless of climate levels). Otherwise, it should be an independent variable in safety models. Similarly, items asking for assessment of the overall likelihood of being injured on the job over a period of 12 months (e.g., Dedobbeleer & Beland, 1991) should be avoided in samples where likelihood of injury might be markedly influenced by factors over which management has little control.

Second, if climate is an emergent property related to organization-level or group-level properties, then individual-level variables should not be included in measurement instruments because this would create conceptual ambiguity, especially if used by many authors as in safety climate measurement. (For discussions of levels issues see Dansereau & Alutto, 1990; Glick & Roberts, 1984; House et al., 1995; Klein et al., 1994; Rousseau, 1985). For example, Williamson, Feyer, Cairns, and Biancotti (1997) devised a 62-item safety climate questionnaire designed to represent the different measures of safety climate published over the years. Though half the items in this scale refer to top-management commitment and company-level procedures, the other half includes individual-level items referring to personal beliefs (e.g., "Accidents will happen no matter what I do") and safety attributions (e.g., "When I have worked unsafely it has been because I was not trained properly"). Although the latter may have important safety implications, they ought to be independent (individual-level) variables rather than components of safety climate. This has important implications for statistical analysis, requiring hierarchical linear models instead of single-level regression models (Hofmann & Stetzer, 1996; Zohar, 2000a).

Another boundary stipulation concerns the fact that meaningful aggregation requires homogeneity of perceptions within the chosen unit of analysis. Otherwise, the calculated mean scores might be thought to reflect climate level when, in fact, there is no climate at all (i.e., no consensus). This may be true of companies or installations in which management is inconsistent with regard to safety issues, resulting in little agreement among employees. For example, management might emphasize safety under normal operating conditions but deemphasize it when production of key products falls behind schedule. Such wavering will result in reduced agreement among employees. Disregarding this criterion, as in most published research, reinforces the use of variables for which there is little reason to expect consensus to begin with (e.g., perceived risk in a technologically diverse organization). (For exceptions see Hofmann & Stetzer, 1996; Zohar, 2000a.) If homogeneity statistics are included, it should be possible to assess which climate variables warrant aggregation and proceed accordingly. For example, in a study designed to improve supervisory safety practices, it turned out that (contrary to expectations) safety climate factors failed to meet criteria of homogeneity, hence the resulting perceptions were not considered as group-climate variables (Zohar, 2000c). This highlights the importance of considering both climate parameters—in other words, level and strength.

Conclusion

The ideas presented in this chapter have conceptual and methodological implications. Methodologically, climate-measurement research should include the ongoing search for perceptual cues or indicators used by workers to assess the relative priority of safety. As noted, such indicators may be either universal or industry-specific and relate to different hierarchical levels. It is probable that some will provide more sensitive or reliable assessment of climate level, and that certain combinations will result in better measurement instruments. Research designed to identify new, potentially better climate indicators might require several research strategies.

One strategy involves organization- and group-level comparisons between high- and low-accident companies. A recent review of the literature identified a heterogeneous list of procedural variables associated with lower accident rates (Shannon, Mayr, & Haines, 1997), some of which have not been incorporated in the available scales. They include speed of hazard correction, completeness of accident investigation, monitoring unsafe behavior, composition and scope of duties of joint safety committees, and regularity of safety retraining. Other variables identified in this review should be excluded, however, despite their demonstrated discriminatory power (e.g., empowerment of workforce, good labor relations, and workforce seniority).

Another strategy involves qualitative data collection techniques such as focus-group discussions. This was used, for example, in the development of an offshore oil-platform climate scale (Cox & Cheyne, 2000) in which employees were asked to discuss what they understood by the terms "safety" and "safety culture." Subscales were based on issues identified in the focus groups, together with themes highlighted in other offshore and generic climate measures. This resulted in identification of various safety-climate indicators such as: "There is a good communication here about safety issues which affect me', 'I do not receive praise for working safely," and "Sometimes I am not given enough time to get the job done safely." Note that these markers are universal, since they do not relate safety to unique attributes of offshore installations.

An additional strategy for uncovering relevant indicators is derived from the often-encountered discrepancy between formally espoused and enforced safety policies. Employees at various organizational levels are asked to recall incidents where it became clear to them that management action diverged from formally espoused policies (Zohar & Luria, 2001). This strategy is based on the assumption that employees recall personally meaningful episodes and that their descriptions of these episodes reveal perceptual cues to which they attend in assessing true priorities. For example, a foreman in a metal processing plant reported that it took several days and repeated appeals to replace a worker's worn-out safety gloves because of management concern that gloves were being replaced too often. This contradicted management's formally declared drive to improve safety records. A worker in another work group in the same company reported that metal debris was left around an electric jig-saw (a safety hazard) until a safety audit by government inspectors was due, at which time it was removed. The contrast between ongoing tardiness and sudden activity revealed the managerial hypocrisy to this worker. These incidents suggest that ease of replacing protective equipment, or whether housekeeping is genuine or forced, could be safety-climate indicators in some industries. This methodology could also help to identify acid-test indicators, because policy discrepancies often arise when safety and production are in direct conflict. For example, a foreman in a food processing plant reported that, during the week before a major holiday, when demand was at its peak, he was pressured to clear clogged pipes in an oven in which temperature exceeded the safety level for such an operation by 30°C. This was contrary to the company's own rules. Bending safety rules because of work pressure might thus be an acid-test indicator. This could be refined with situation-anchored rating scales of levels of work pressure to assess perceived relationships between work pressure and management willingness to bend safety rules (i.e., how much work pressure is encountered before management is willing to bend rules?). Assuming that safety rules can also be ordered along a continuum of risk, this should result in a refined assessment of real priorities (i.e., how much risk would management be willing to take at each level of work pressure?). The various strategies should make it possible to identify an increasing number of safety-climate indicators, which could then be subjected to further psychometric testing.

Another direction for methodological research concerns psychometric comparisons of available scales. As noted, there are more than 20 climate measures that meet minimal criteria (Flin et al., 2000; Guldenmund, 2000) and new ones are continually being published (Cox & Flin, 1998). Because measurement scales provide operationalization of a construct, it is important to conduct evaluative research to converge on mutually agreed measures. Mueller, DaSilva, Townsend, and Tetrick (1999) conducted one such study, comparing four compatible safety climate measures to identify the best measurement model (Brown & Holmes, 1986; Coyle, Sleeman, & Adams, 1995; Dedobbeleer & Beland, 1991; Zohar, 1980). This was done by asking 500 working students to fill all four climate scales, followed by confirmatory factor analysis. The final model was a four-factor model that retained a high degree of overlap with Zohar's (1980) eight-factor model. The four factors were management commitment to safety, rewards for working safely, effect of safe behavior on social standing, and effect of required work pace on safety. (Note that the first two factors are more in line with the suggested focus on safety priority.) There was also evidence for a single higher order factor of safety climate that could be useful in global comparisons of organizations. (This supports the use of universal climate indicators for global comparisons and specific ones for within-industry or within-company comparisons.) Studies of this sort should help to evaluate measurement models.

Theoretically and conceptually, there is a need for research into the hypothesized path leading from climate to behavior to injuries (Figure 6.1). Although many authors consider the climate–behavior relationship well-founded, there is surprisingly little empirical evidence in this regard. Furthermore, much of the available evidence is tainted by single-source bias relating to self-report of behavior safety and injury data. However, several authors have recently supported the predictive validity of safety climate (including proxy measures) with objective minor-injury data (Hofmann & Morgeson, 1999; Zohar, 2000a; Zohar & Luria, 2001). The potential benefit of pursuing this line of work is evident from a study in which it was found that subscales (i.e., climate indicators) associated with open, rewarding supervisory safety practices were more predictive of subunit injuries than corrective, punitive practices (Zohar, 2000b).

Finally, if safety climate is to be used as a bridge to the larger organizational behavior literature, other important relationships, notably between climate and leadership and motivation must be established. Recent attempts at integrating leadership and safety climate suggest a mediation model whereby, in contexts where job performance has direct safety implications, the quality of leader–member interaction influences leader commitment to members' welfare, in turn influencing safety-climate perceptions in the group and, ultimately, safety behavior of group members. This means that leadership style is an antecedent of safety-climate level. The model is based on evidence suggesting that closer, higher quality relationships increase leaders' commitment to members' welfare (Bass, 1990). In situations involving heightened risk of injury, welfare also covers members' physical well-being, as reported by Hofmann and Morgeson (1999). Commitment to subordinates' safety, and the practices with which it is being expressed, provide the targets for climate perceptions, establishing the link between leadership style and safety climate. The mediating role of safety climate has been supported in two recent studies (Barling, Loughlin, & Kelloway, 2000; Zohar, 2000b). They demonstrated that transformational and constructive leadership (but not corrective leadership—in other words, management-by-exception) predicted injury rate, with safety climate as mediator. This suggests that relationships between leadership dimensions and safety climate should be further explored, including investigation of moderator variables likely to influence this relationship (e.g., consistency of managerial practice, which is likely to influence climate strength).

The relationship between safety climate and motivation also presents research opportunities. As noted previously, safety behavior of employees poses a managerial challenge because of employees' bias against safe conduct under regular job conditions. The negative value function for safe behavior can be modified by introducing short-term rewards that outweigh immediate costs, for which one readily available resource is leader–member exchange. An effective supervisor who is also committed to safety will observe whether work is performed properly, including the use of protective gear, and express approval or disapproval immediately afterward (Komaki, 1998). If this is done uniformly and consistently to all group members and in all situations, subordinates will infer a high safety priority, resulting in high (and strong) safety climate and as a consequence high safety motivation. Because supervisory contingencies are known to influence members' motivation and behavior (Komaki, 1998), this obviates the need to include external contingencies characteristic of most behavior-based safety interventions (see reviews in Krispin & Hantula, 1996; McAfee & Winn, 1989; O'Hara, Johnson, & Beehr, 1985). Hence, interventions that improve supervisory safety practices might offer a new strategy whose distinctive feature is that supervisory practice is modified to introduce change in safety climate and motivation on the shop floor. The viability of this approach, identified as supervision-based safety, was tested recently by Zohar (2002c), who provided evidence indicating that improved supervisory safety practices resulted in significant and stable changes in safety climate scores, minor injury rates, and earplug use. Future research should identify additional ways for inducing such change, taking advantage of the robust motivational and behavioral outcomes afforded by the law of effect. Given the human and economic cost of occupational accidents, this and other lines of research suggested previously should be considered not only as an intellectual but also as a societal challenge.

References

Abbey, A., & Dickson, J. W. (1983). R&D work climate and innovation in semiconductors. *Academy of Management Journal, 26,* 362–368.

Anderson, N., & West, M. A. (1996). The team climate inventory: Development of the TCI and its applications in team-building for innovation. *European Journal of Work and Organizational Psychology, 5,* 53–66.

Argyris, C., & Schon, D. A. (1996). *Organizational learning II: Theory, method, and practice.* Reading, MA: Addison-Wesley.

Ball, G. A., Trevino, L. K., & Sims, H. P. (1994). Just and unjust punishment: Influences on subordinate performance and citizenship. *Academy of Management Journal, 37,* 299–322.

Bandura, A. (1986). *Social foundations of thought and action.* Englewood Cliffs, NJ: Prentice Hall.

Barling, J., Loughlin, C., & Kelloway, K. (2000, April 15–19). *Development and test of a model linking transformational leadership and occupational safety.* Paper presented at the annual conference of the Society for Industrial and Organizational Psychology, New Orleans.

Bass, B. M. (1990). From transactional to transformational leadership: Learning to share the vision. *Organizational Dynamics, 18,* 19–31.

Bies, R. J., & Moag, J. S. (1986). Interactional justice: Communication criteria of fairness. In R. J. Lewicki, B. H. Sheppard, & M. H. Bazerman (Eds.), *Research on negotiations in organizations* (Vol. 1, pp. 43–55). Greenwich, CT: JAI Press.

Brown, I. D. (1991). Accident reporting and analysis. In J. R. Wilson & E. N. Corlett (Eds.), *Evaluation of human work* (pp. 755–778). New York: Taylor and Francis.

Brown, R. L., & Holmes, H. (1986). The use of a factor-analytic procedure for assessing the validity of an employee safety climate model. *Accident Analysis and Prevention, 18,* 455–470.

Cooper, M. D. (2000). Towards a model of safety culture. *Safety Science, 36,* 111–136.

Cooper, M. D., Phillips, R. A., Sutherland, V. J., & Makin, P. J. (1994). Reducing accidents using goal setting and feedback: A field study. *Journal of Occupational and Organizational Psychology, 67,* 219–240.

Cox, S. J., & Cheyne, A. J. (2000). Assessing safety culture in offshore environments. *Safety Science, 34,* 111–129.

Cox, S. J., & Flin, R. (1998). Safety culture: Philosopher's stone or man of straw? *Work & Stress, 12,* 189–201.

Coyle, I. R., Sleeman, S. D., & Adams, N. (1995). Safety climate. *Journal of Safety Research, 26,* 247–254.

Dansereau, F., & Alutto, J. A. (1990). Level of analysis issues in climate and culture research. In B. Schneider (Ed.), *Organizational climate and culture* (pp. 193–236). San Francisco: Jossey-Bass.

Dedobbeleer, N., & Beland, F. (1991). A safety climate measure for construction sites. *Journal of Safety Research, 22,* 97–103.

DeJoy, D. M., Murphy, L. R., & Gershon, R. M. (1995). Safety climate in health care settings. In A. C. Bittner & P. C. Champney (Eds.), *Advances in industrial ergonomics and safety* (Vol. 7, pp. 923–929). London: Taylor and Francis.

Drazin, R., Glynn, M. A., & Kazanjian, R. K. (1999). Multilevel theorizing about creativity in organizations: A sensemaking perspective. *Academy of Management Review, 24,* 286–307.

Fahlbruch, B., & Wilpert, B. (1999). System safety: An emerging field for I/O psychology. In C. L. Cooper & I. T. Robertson (Eds.), *International review of industrial and organizational psychology* (Vol. 14, pp. 55–93). New York: Wiley.

Flin, R., Mearns, P., O'Connor, R., & Bryden, R. (2000). Measuring safety climate: Identifying the common features. *Safety Science, 34,* 177–192.

Geller, E. S., Roberts, D. S., & Gilmore, M. R. (1996). Predicting propensity to actively care for occupational safety. *Journal of Safety Research, 27,* 1–8.

Glenn, S. S. (1991). Contingencies and meta-contingencies: Relations among behavioral, cultural, and biological evolution. In P. A. Lamal (Ed.), *Behavioral analysis of societies and cultural practices* (pp. 39–73). Washington, DC: Hemisphere.

Glennon, D. P. (1982). Safety climate in organizations. In *Proceedings of the 19th annual conference of the ergonomics society of Australia-NZ* (pp. 17–31). Sydney: APS.

Glick, W. H. (1985). Conceptualizing and measuring organizational and psychological climate: Pitfalls in multi-level research. *Academy of Management Review, 10,* 601–616.

Glick, W. H. (1988). Organizations are not central tendencies: Shadowboxing in the dark, Round 2. *Academy of Management Review, 13,* 133–137.

Glick, W. H., & Roberts, K. (1984). Hypothesized interdependence, assumed independence. *Academy of Management Review, 9,* 722–735.

Guldenmund, F. W. (2000). The nature of safety culture: A review of theory and research. *Safety Science, 34,* 215–257.

Hage, J., & Aiken, M. (1969). Routine technology, social structure, and organizational goals. *Administrative Science Quarterly, 14,* 366–378.

Hall, R. H. (1987). *Organizations: Structures, processes, and outcomes* (4th ed.). Englewood Cliffs, NJ: Prentice Hall.

Hantula, D. (1999). Safety culture and behavioral safety: From contingencies to meta-contingencies. *Proceedings of the ASSE symposium on best practices in safety management* (pp. 190–206). Philadelphia, PA: ASSE.

Heinrich, H. W. (1931). *Industrial accident prevention: A scientific approach.* New York: McGraw-Hill.

Herrnstein, R. J., Loewnstein, G. F., Prelec, D., & Vaughan, W. (1993). Utility maximization and melioration: Internalities in individual choice. *Journal of Behavior & Decision Making, 6,* 149–185.

Hofmann, D. A., & Morgeson, F. P. (1999). Safety-related behavior as a social exchange: The role of perceived organizational support and leader-member exchange. *Journal of Applied Psychology, 84,* 286–296.

Hofmann, D. A., & Stetzer, A. (1996). A cross-level investigation of factors influencing unsafe behaviors and accidents. *Personnel Psychology, 49,* 307–339.

Hofstede, G. (1998). Attitudes, values and organizational culture: Disentangling the concepts. *Organization Studies, 19,* 477–492.

House, R. J., Rousseau, D. M., & Thomas-Hunt, M. (1995). The meso paradigm: A framework for the integration of micro and macro organizational behavior. *Research in Organizational Behavior, 17,* 71–114.

International Atomic Energy Agency (IAEA). (1986). *Summary report on the post-accident review meeting on the Chernobyl accident* (International Atomic Energy Agency Safety Series 75-INSAG-1). Vienna: Author.

International Atomic Energy Agency (IAEA). (1991). *Safety culture* (International Atomic Energy Agency Safety Series 75-INSAG-4). Vienna: Author.

James, L. R. (1982). Aggregation bias in estimates of perceptual agreement. *Journal of Applied Psychology, 67,* 219–229.

James, L. R., Demaree, R. G., & Wolf, G. (1984). Estimating within-group inter-rater reliability with and without response bias. *Journal of Applied Psychology, 69,* 85–98.

James, L. R., Demaree, R. G., & Wolf, G. (1993). Rwg: An assessment of within-group inter-rater agreement. *Journal of Applied Psychology, 78,* 306–309.

James, L. R., James, L. A., & Ashe, D. K. (1990). The meaning of organizations: The role of cognition and values. In B. Schneider (Ed.), *Organizational climate and culture* (pp. 40–84). San Francisco: Jossey-Bass.

James, L. R., & Jones, A. P. (1974). Organizational climate: A review of theory and research. *Psychological Bulletin, 81,* 1096–1112.

Joyce, W. G., & Slocum, J. W. (1984). Collective climate: Agreement as a basis for defining aggregate climates in organizations. *Academy of Management Journal, 27,* 721–742.

Kahneman, D., & Tversky, A. (1979). Prospect theory: An analysis of decision under risk. *Econometrica, 47,* 263–291.

Katz, D., & Kahn, R. L. (1978). *The social psychology of organizations* (2nd ed.). New York: Wiley.

Klein, K. J., Dansereau, F., & Hall, R. J. (1994). Levels issues in theory development, data collection, and analysis. *Academy of Management Review, 19,* 195–229.

Komaki, J. L. (1998). *Leadership from an operant perspective.* New York: Routledge.

Komaki, J. L., Collins, R. L., & Penn, P. (1982). The role of performance antecedents and consequences in work motivation. *Journal of Applied Psychology, 67,* 334–340.

Krispin, J., & Hantula, D. (1996, Oct. 12–14). *A meta-analysis of behavioral safety interventions in organizations.* Paper presented at the 1996 annual meeting of the Eastern Academy of Management, Philadelphia, PA.

Lawler, E. E. (1971). *Pay and organizational effectiveness: A psychological view.* New York: McGraw Hill.

March, J. G., & Simon, H. A. (1959). *Organizations.* New York: Wiley.

Maslow. A. (1970). *Motivation and personality* (2nd ed.). New York: Harper and Row.

McAfee, R. B., & Winn, A. R. (1989). The use of incentives and feedback to enhance work place safety: A critique of the literature. *Journal of Safety Research, 20,* 7–19.

Mearns, K., Flin, R., Gordon, R., & Fleming, M. (1998). Measuring safety climate on offshore installations. *Work & Stress, 12,* 238–254.

Moorman, R. H. (1991). Relationship between organizational justice and organizational citizenship behaviors: Do fairness perceptions influence employee citizenship. *Journal of Applied Psychology, 76,* 845–855.

Mueller, L., DaSilva, N., Townsend, J., & Tetrick, L. (1999, April 19–24). *An empirical evaluation of competing safety climate measurement models.* Paper presented at the 1999 annual meeting of the Society for Industrial and Organizational Psychology, Atlanta, Georgia.

National Safety Council. (1999). *Injury facts.* Itasca, IL: National Safety Council.

Niskanen, T. (1994). Safety climate in the road administration. *Safety Science, 17,* 237–255.

O'Hara, K., Johnson, C. M., & Beehr, T. A. (1985). Organizational behavior management in the private sector: A review of empirical research. *Academy of Management Review, 10,* 848–864.

O'Reilly, C. A. (1991). Organizational behavior: Where we've been, where we're going. *Annual Review of Psychology, 42,* 427–458.

Ostrom, L., Wilhelmsen, C., & Kaplan, B. (1993). Assessing safety culture. *Nuclear Safety, 34,* 163–172.

Pate-Cornell, M. E. (1990). Organizational aspects of engineering system safety: The case of offshore platforms. *Science, 250,* 1210–1217.

Patterson, M., Payne, R., & West, M. (1996). Collective climates: A test of their socio-psychological significance. *Academy of Management Journal, 39,* 1675–1691.

Payne, R. (1990). Madness in our method: A comment on Jakofsky and Slocum's paper A longitudinal analysis of climates. *Journal of Organizational Behavior, 11,* 77–80.

Perrow, C. (1967). A framework for the comparative analysis of organizations. *American Sociological Review, 32,* 194–208.

Perrow, C. (1979). *Complex organizations: A critical essay* (2nd ed.). Glenview, IL: Scott, Foresman.

Rasmussen, J. (1982). Human errors: A taxonomy for describing human malfunction in industrial installations. *Journal of Occupational Accidents, 4,* 311–333.

Rasmussen, J. (1990). The role of error in organizing behavior. *Ergonomics, 33,* 1185–1199.

Reason, J. (1990). *Human error.* New York: Cambridge University Press.

Reason, J. T. (1997). *Managing the risks of organizational accidents.* Aldershot, UK: Ashgate.

Reber, R. A., Wallin, J. A., & Chokar, J. S. (1984). Reducing industrial accidents: A behavioral experiment. *Industrial Relations, 23,* 119–125.

Reichers, A. E., & Schneider, B. (1990). Climate and culture: An evolution of constructs. In B. Schneider (Ed.), *Organizational climate and culture* (pp. 5–39). San Francisco: Jossey-Bass.

Rentsch, J. R. (1990). Climate and culture: Interaction and qualitative differences in organizational meanings. *Journal of Applied Psychology, 75,* 668–681.

Rochlin, G. I. (1999). Safe operations as a social construct. *Ergonomics, 42,* 1549–1560.

Rousseau, D. M. (1985). Issues of level in organizational research: Multilevel and cross-level perspectives. In L. L. Cummings & B. M. Staw (Eds.), *Research in organizational behavior* (Vol. 7, pp. 1–37). Greenwich, CT: JAI Press.

Rousseau, D. M. (1988). The construction of climate in organizational research. In C. L. Cooper & I. T. Robertson (Eds.), *International review of industrial and organizational psychology* (Vol. 3, pp. 139–158). New York: Wiley.

Saari, J., & Nasanen, M. (1989). The effect of positive feedback on industrial housekeeping and accidents. *International Journal of Industrial Ergonomics, 4,* 201–211.

Safety Research Unit. (1993). *The contribution of attitudinal and management factors to risk in the chemical industry.* Final Report to the Health and Safety Executive. Guilford, UK: Surry University.

Schein, E. H. (1992). *Organizational culture and leadership* (2nd ed.). San Francisco: Jossey-Bass.

Schneider, B. (1987). The people make the place. *Personnel Psychology, 40,* 437–453.

Schneider, B., & Bowen, D. E. (1985). Employee and customer perceptions of service in banks: Replication and extension. *Journal of Applied Psychology, 70,* 423–433.

Schneider, B., & Reichers, A. E. (1983). On the etiology of climates. *Personnel Psychology, 36,* 19–39.

Schneider, B., White, S., & Paul, M. C. (1998). Linking service climate and customer perceptions of service quality: Test of a causal model. *Journal of Applied Psychology, 83,* 150–163.

Shannon, H. S., Mayr, J., & Haines, T. (1997). Overview of the relationship between organizational and workplace factors and injury rates. *Safety Science, 26,* 201–217.

Skarlicki, D. P., & Folger, R. (1997). Retaliation in the workplace: The roles of distributive, procedural, and interactional justice. *Journal of Applied Psychology, 82,* 434–443.

Skinner, B. F. (1974). *About behaviorism.* New York: Vintage.

Thibaut, J., & Walker, L. (1975). *Procedural justice: A psychological analysis.* Hillsdale, NJ: Erlbaum.

Thompson, K. R., & Luthans, F. (1990). Organizational culture: A behavioral perspective. In B. Schneider (Ed.), *Organizational climate and culture* (pp. 319–344). San Francisco: Jossey-Bass.

Tyler, T. R., & Lind, E. A. (1992). A relational model of authority in groups. *Advances in Experimental Social Psychology, 25,* 115–191.

Vroom, V. H. (1964). *Work and motivation.* New York: Wiley.

Weick, K. E. (1995). *Sensemaking in organizations.* Thousand Oaks, CA: Sage.

Williamson, A. M., Feyer, A. M., Cairns, D., & Biancotti, D. (1997). The development of safety climate: The role of safety perceptions and attitudes. *Safety Science, 25,* 15–27.

Wright, C. (1986). Routine deaths: Fatal accidents in the oil industry. *Sociological Review, 4,* 265–289.

Zipf, G. K. (1965). *Human behavior and the principle of least effort.* New York: Hafner.

Zohar, D. (1980). Safety climate in industrial organizations: Theoretical and applied implications. *Journal of Applied Psychology, 65,* 96–102.

Zohar, D. (2000a). A group-level model of safety climate: Testing the effect of group climate on micro-accidents in manufacturing jobs. *Journal of Applied Psychology, 85,* 587–596.

Zohar, D. (2000b, Aug. 4–9). *Safety climate and leadership factors as predictors of injury records in work groups.* Paper presented at the annual meeting of the Academy of Management, Toronto.

Zohar, D. (2000c). Modifying supervisory practices to improve sub-unit safety: A leadership-based intervention model. *Journal of Applied Psychology, 87,* 156–163.

Zohar, D., & Luria, G. (2001, April 27–29). *Climate strength: Identifying boundary conditions for organizational climate.* Paper presented at the 16th annual conference of the Society for Industrial and Organizational Psychology, San Diego.

7

Work–Family Balance

Michael R. Frone

Social roles play important functions in the lives of all individuals (e.g., Ashforth, Kreiner, & Fugate, 2000; Clark, 2000). They help to define who we are—imposing self-definitional boundaries. They influence what we do—imposing behavioral boundaries. They influence how and with whom we interact—imposing relational boundaries. They influence what we think about—imposing cognitive boundaries. They influence how we feel about things—imposing affective boundaries. They structure our use of time—imposing temporal boundaries. Finally, they structure our physical location—imposing spatial boundaries. The primary social roles that make up the lives of most adults are depicted in Figure 7.1. As shown in this figure, one can make a broad distinction between work and nonwork domains of life (e.g., Rice, McFarlin, Hunt, & Near, 1985). Within the nonwork domain, several subdomains of social roles exist—family, religious, community, leisure, and student. Because social roles provide meaning and structure in people's lives, researchers from many disciplines are interested in the notion of balance between social roles. This interest partly derives from the understanding that despite the various types of boundaries fostered by social roles, these boundaries differ in permeability and flexibility, and transitions across boundaries occur often (e.g., Ashforth et al., 2000; Clark, 2000). It also derives from the expectation that imbalance between social roles may be an important stressor that can influence outcomes in the affected life domains and can influence the overall health and well-being of individuals exposed to the imbalance.

The overall goal of this chapter, therefore, is to provide an overview of the literature on work–family balance. Toward this end, I will (a) define work–family balance, (b) review early and contemporary models of work–family balance, (c) review the major causes and outcomes of work–family balance, and (d) explore strategies for promoting work–family balance. Because of the extensive work–family literature that has developed, I cannot provide an exhaustive review of each of these issues in a short chapter. Nonetheless, while being selective, I will try to provide a broad overview.

The focus of this review is on the relationship between work and family roles for three reasons. First, in contrast to other nonwork roles, conceptual interest in the relationship between work and family has been much stronger, with a research history that dates back to at least the 1930s

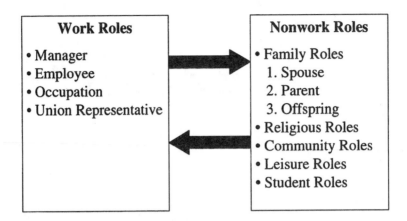

Figure 7.1. Work and nonwork social roles. The term *nonwork* is not meant to imply that social roles such as parent or student do not entail work. In an effort to circumvent this problem, some researchers refer to "work" and "life" roles. However, this creates the opposite problem in that the distinction implies that work is not a life role. It would be more precise to label the two broad life domains employment and nonemployment. However, I maintain the work and nonwork distinction to be consistent with the majority of previous research.

(for reviews, see Marshall, 1992; Marshall, Chadwick, & Marshall, 1992). Second, a number of widely documented demographic changes and structural changes in the family—increased proportion of women working, increases in the divorce rate, increased life expectancy, more dual-earner and single-earner families, and more families with the simultaneous demands of child care and eldercare—have affected both work and family roles and their interrelation (e.g., Bond, Galinsky, & Swanberg, 1998; Ferber, O'Farrell, & Allen, 1991). These changes have further stimulated a large and growing literature devoted to understanding the dynamic relationship between work and family life. Third, although some researchers have written more generally about the nexus between work and "nonwork" roles (e.g., Hart, 1999; Rice et al., 1985), the term "nonwork" is often used synonymously for "family." In addition, little empirical research exists on the nexus between work and *specific* nonwork roles other than family. For example, researchers often use measures of nonwork role characteristics that confound all nonfamily and family roles (e.g., work–nonwork conflict or nonwork satisfaction). Although I will review this research when relevant, it is impossible to draw specific conclusions about the relationship between work and a nonwork role other than family (see Hammer, Grigsby, & Woods, 1998; Markel & Frone, 1998; Rice, Frone & McFarlin, 1992, for exceptions).

What Is Work–Family Balance?

Although there is no shortage of reference to the phrase "work–family balance," most writers act as though its meaning is self-evident. That is, one would be hard-pressed to find an explicit definition of the phrase "work–family balance" or an explanation of what it means for work and family life to be "in balance." For many writers, work–family balance represents a vague notion that work and family life are somehow integrated or harmonious. Close examination of empirical research, however, suggests two more precise meanings for work–family balance. The first, and most widely held, meaning of work–family balance is a lack of conflict or interference between work and family roles. As will be summarized later, a large literature exists devoted to exploring the prevalence, predictors, and outcomes of work–family conflict (also referred to as work–family interference, work–family tension, and negative work–family spillover). The most widely cited definition of work–family conflict states that it is

> a form of interrole conflict in which the role pressures from the work and family domains are mutually incompatible in some respect. That is, participation in the work (family) role is made more difficult by virtue of participation in the family (work) role. (Greenhaus & Beutell, 1985, p. 77).

Work–family researchers also have pointed out that this definition implies a bidirectional dimension to work–family conflict (e.g., Frone, Russell, & Cooper, 1992a, 1992b; Frone, Yardley, & Markel, 1997). In other words, work can interfere with family (work-to-family conflict) and family can interfere with work (family-to-work conflict).

But does work–family balance mean something more than a lack of interrole conflict or interference? Recent research suggests that work–family facilitation (also referred to as work–family enhancement and positive work–family spillover) may be a second component of work–family balance (e.g., Grzywacz & Marks, 2000; Kirchmeyer, 1992). Work–family facilitation represents the extent to which participation at work (or home) is made easier by virtue of the experiences, skills, and opportunities gained or developed at home (or work). As with work–family conflict, work–family facilitation has a bidirectional dimension, where work can facilitate family life (work-to-family facilitation) and where family can facilitate work life (family-to-work facilitation). However, in contrast to work–family conflict, much less research has focused on the prevalence, predictors, and outcomes of work–family facilitation.

Based on the literature just reviewed, Figure 7.2 presents a four-fold taxonomy of work–family balance. The two primary dimensions are the direction of influence between work and family roles (work-to-family versus family-to-work) and the type of effect (conflict versus facilitation). The arrows in Figure 7.2 indicate that low levels of interrole conflict and high levels of interrole facilitation represent work–family balance. Several earlier studies have provided factor analytic support for the distinction between work-to-family conflict and family-to-work conflict (e.g., Frone et al., 1992b; Netemeyer, Boles, & McMurrian, 1996). More recently, Grzywacz and Marks (2000) reported factor-analytic results supporting the full four-fold taxonomy of work–family balance.

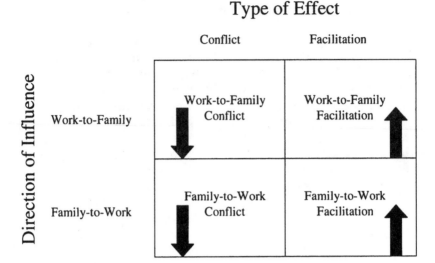

Figure 7.2.   Dimensions of work–family balance.

Models of Work–Family Balance

A number of attempts have been made to represent the relationship between work and family roles. These attempts can be divided into an earlier body of research that tried to uncover the basic types of relationships between work and family roles, and a more recent body of research that tries to explore the relationship between work and family from a more integrative and dynamic vantage point. Next I will summarize both early and more contemporary approaches to conceptualizing the work–family interface.

Early Conceptions of the Work–Family Interface

Early research on work and family life resulted in several taxonomies of models to describe the relationship between work and family life (for reviews, see Edwards & Rothbard, 2000; Morf, 1989). However, six basic models or linking mechanisms (Edwards & Rothbard, 2000) can be identified in past research. Morf (1989) further classified these models as being either noncausal or causal. The three noncausal models posit that even if work and family variables are interrelated, no causal relationship exists between work and family life. The *segmentation model* postulates that work and family life represent independent domains that do not influence one another. The *congruence model* postulates that although work and family variables may exhibit either a positive or negative correlation, the relationship is spurious because both the work and family variables share a common cause. For example, the positive correlation between job and family satisfaction may be spurious because both variables are the outcome of stable personality dispositions, such as negative affectivity or positive affectivity (Frone, Russell, & Cooper, 1994). The *identity or integrative model* postulates that work and family roles are so closely interweaved that they are indistinguishable, such as among ministers or rabbis, or what might be found in family-owned and operated businesses.

In contrast, the three causal models posit that what happens in one domain of life (e.g., work) can have a causal impact on what happens in another domain of life (e.g., family). The *spillover model* postulates a positive relationship between work and family. In other words, a change in one domain leads to a parallel change in another domain, such as suggested by a positive correlation between job and family values. The *compensation model* postulates a negative relationship between work and family. Increasing dissatisfaction in one life domain (e.g., family) leads to a reduction of time and energy to that role, which then leads to an increase in time and energy devoted to a second life domain (e.g., work) in an effort to compensate for the lack of rewards or for undesirable experiences in the first life domain (e.g., family). The *resource drain model* also postulates a negative relationship between work and family. Specifically, the use of finite resources (time, energy, or attention) in one life domain (e.g., work) reduces the availability of these same resources for use in another life domain (e.g., family).

A limitation of early research on work and family life was that these models were derived posthoc with the intent to uncover *the* mechanism that best described the relation between work and family (e.g., Lambert, 1990). However, empirical evidence suggests that all of these linking mechanisms exist and that many may operate simultaneously (e.g., Lambert, 1990). When considered individually, none of these linking mechanisms provide a useful conceptual basis for understanding the dynamics of work–family balance. Rather, they all need to be brought together, along with other processes, to develop an integrative and dynamic understanding of work–family balance.

Contemporary Conceptions of the Work–Family Interface

Compared to early research on the relationship between work and family life, recent work takes a more integrative and dynamic view of the work–family interface. Although this work is too complex to summarize in detail, I will describe briefly two areas of research that will improve understanding of work–family balance. The first area of research is the development of integrative models of work–family balance (e.g., Edwards & Rothbard, 2000; Frone et al., 1992a; Frone, Yardley, et al., 1997). For example, Frone, Yardley, et al.'s (1997) model of the work–family interface extends early research on work–family balance in several ways. First, it represents several linking mechanisms simultaneously. Second, an explicit attempt is made to portray reciprocal relationships between work and family life. Third, a distinction is made between work-to-family and family-to-work conflict. Fourth, a distinction is drawn between proximal and distal predictors of work–family conflict. Fifth, each dimension of work–family conflict has a unique relation to domain-specific antecedents and outcomes. For example, it is hypothesized that the domain-specific antecedents of work-to-family conflict reside in the work domain and its domain-specific outcomes reside in the family domain. Sixth, the relationships between work–family conflict and role-related affect (e.g., job and family satisfaction) are differentiated into predictive and outcome relations. Because of these conceptual enhancements, Frone, Yardley, et al.'s (1997) model may be considered more integrative than earlier models of work–family balance. However, it is by no means a complete model of work–family balance. For example, the model does not incorporate work–family facilitation. The number of empirical studies testing integrative models of work–family balance has grown over the past decade. Nonetheless, additional efforts are required to extend current integrative models of work–family balance.

The second area of research that can broaden our understanding of work–family balance is represented by recent theoretical models of role boundaries and the dynamic process of role transitions (e.g., Ashforth et al., 2000; Clark, 2000). For example, Ashforth et al. (2000) postulated that role boundaries differ in their level of flexibility and permeability. The flexibility of role boundaries represents the extent to which a role can be "enacted in various settings and at various times" (Ashforth et al., 2000, p. 474). The permeability of role boundaries represents the extent to which one can be "physically located in the role's domain but psychologically and/or behaviorally involved in another role" (Ashforth et al., 2000, p. 474). In addition, Ashforth et al. (2000) posited that individuals maintain multiple role identities that can differ in contrast. Contrast represents the extent to which two role identities differ in terms of the defining features of the identities.

Based on the notion of role boundaries (flexibility and permeability) and role identities (contrast), Ashforth et al. (2000) proposed that any pair of roles can be placed along a continuum ranging from high segmentation to high integration. Two roles are segmented when the role identities exhibit high contrast and the role boundaries are inflexible and impermeable. In contrast, two roles are integrated when the role identities exhibit low contrast and the role boundaries are flexible and permeable. Both segmentation and integration have benefits and costs regarding work–family balance. The benefits of segmentation are clarity regarding when a role should be salient, low chance of cross-role distractions, and ease of psychologically compartmentalizing role identities. The cost of segmentation is that the transition between the roles becomes more difficult. In contrast, the benefit of integration is that the transition between roles is simplified. However, the costs of integration are little clarity regarding when a role should be salient, high chance of cross-role distractions, and difficulty in psychologically compartmentalizing role identities. Theoretical models of role transitions (Ashforth et al., 2000; Clark, 2000) have much potential to help define the conditions that minimize and maximize work–family balance. Nonetheless, to date little systematic empirical research has tested the propositions emanating from these models.

Level of Work–Family Balance

Having defined work–family balance in terms of conflict and facilitation, what do we know about the level of work–family balance in the lives of employees? Many studies have reported mean levels for the frequency or amount of work–family balance. Unfortunately, because all of these studies have used response scales with vague qualifiers (e.g., never, rarely, sometimes, often, very often), little can be concluded about the absolute frequency or amount of work–family balance (e.g., Schwarz, 1999). Thus, most research attention has been paid to two types of relative comparisons.

The first type of comparison has been to examine the relative frequency or amount of work-to-family conflict versus family-to-work conflict (Frone et al., 1992b). Despite the variety of samples used in past research—ranging from convenience samples of employees in one or more organizations (e.g., Bernas & Major, 2000; Eagle, Miles, & Icenogle, 1997; Frone, Yardley, et al., 1997; Grandey & Cropanzano, 1999) to regional probability samples (e.g., Frone et al., 1992b; Marks, 1998) to national probability samples (e.g., Frone, 2000; Grzywacz & Marks, 2000)—the results consistently show that work-to-family conflict is reported to occur more frequently than family-to-work conflict. Thus, it appears that work has a more deleterious impact on family life than family life has on work. Only one study has explored the relative frequency of work-to-family facilitation versus family-to-work facilitation. In contrast to the pattern of results for work–family conflict, Grzywacz and Marks's (2000) findings showed the opposite pattern— family-to-work facilitation was reported to occur more frequently than work-to-family facilitation. Thus, it appears that family has a more beneficial impact on work life than work life has on family. When we consider interrole conflict and interrole facilitation simultaneously, work and family roles exhibit a pattern of asymmetry that favors work roles. In other words, compared to family roles, work roles encounter lower levels of cross-role interference or conflict and higher levels of cross-role facilitation.

The second type of relative comparison is the examination of gender differences in the extent of work–family balance (Frone et al., 1992a). Across a variety of samples—ranging from convenience samples of employees from a single organization (e.g., Eagle et al., 1997; Grandey & Cropanzano, 1999) to regional probability samples (e.g., Frone et al., 1992b; Marks, 1998) to national probability samples (e.g., Frone, 2000; Grzywacz & Marks, 2000), men and women report similar levels of work-to-family conflict and family-to-work conflict. Moreover, Grzywacz and Marks (2000) recently found that this lack of gender difference also extends to reports of work-to-family facilitation and family-to-work facilitation. Although some studies with large samples may report statistically significant gender differences, the absolute size of these differences is typically not large enough to be of practical importance, and they often disappear after controlling for gender differences in age and family demographic characteristics (marital status, parental status).

Causes of Work–Family Balance

Work–Family Conflict

A large body of research exists exploring the predictors of work–family conflict. Much of this research used measures that only assess work-to-family conflict or used global measures that confound the measurement of work-to-family conflict and family-to-work conflict. However, recent conceptual models and empirical research suggest that work-to-family conflict and family-to-work conflict have unique role-related causes (Frone et al., 1992b; Frone, Yardley, et al., 1997). Specifically, the role-related causes of work-to-family conflict and family-to-work conflict reside in the work and family domains, respectively. Therefore, the present review will focus on past research that assessed separately both dimensions of work–family conflict. This focus also is useful when exploring potential common causes of both types of conflict. The various predictors of work–family conflict that have been examined can be grouped into two general categories—role environment and personality—that are discussed in turn.

Role environment. Previous research has examined several types of role-related predictors of work–family conflict: behavioral involvement, psychological involvement, role-related stressors and affect, and role-related resources. Behavioral involvement represents the amount of time devoted to work and family roles. As more time is devoted to one role, it would be expected that less time would be available to meet the demands of another role. Consistent with this notion, a number of studies have found that the number of weekly hours devoted to family activities and chores is positively related to levels of family-to-work conflict, whereas the number of weekly hours devoted to work is positively related to levels of work-to-family conflict (e.g., Frone, Yardley, et al., 1997; Grzywacz & Marks, 2000; Gutek, Searle, & Klepa, 1991; Netemeyer et al. 1996; O'Driscoll, Ilgen, & Hildreth, 1992).

Psychological involvement represents the degree to which individuals identify with a social role and see it as important to their self-concept. High levels of psychological involvement in a given role (e.g., work) may cause one to be mentally preoccupied with that role while in the physical role space of a second role (e.g., family). This may make it difficult to become engaged in the activities required by the second role. Consistent with this notion, a number of studies have found that psychological family involvement is positively related to family-to-work conflict, whereas psychological job involvement is positively related to work-to-family conflict (e.g., Adams, King, & King, 1996; Carlson & Kacmar, 2000; Frone et al., 1992a).

Work and family stressors, dissatisfaction, and distress have been examined as potential causes of work–family conflict. It is generally hypothesized that role characteristics can produce role-related dissatisfaction or distress, which may lead to cognitive preoccupation with the source of the distress or to reduced levels of psychological and physical energy. The resulting increase in cognitive preoccupation or reduction in energy can undermine an individual's ability or willingness to meet the obligations of other roles (Frone, Yardley, et al., 1997). Consistent with this line of reasoning, past research has found that work demands, work-role conflict, work-role ambiguity, and job distress or dissatisfaction are positively related to reports of work-to-family conflict (e.g., Bernas & Major, 2000; Carlson & Kacmar, 2000; Frone et al., 1992a; Frone, Yardley, et al., 1997; Grandey & Cropanzano, 1999; Grzywacz & Marks, 2000). Similarly, family demands, family-role conflict, family-role ambiguity, and family distress or dissatisfaction are positively related to reports of family-to-work conflict (e.g., Bernas & Major, 2000; Carlson & Kacmar, 2000; Frone et al., 1992a; Frone, Yardley, et al., 1997; Grandey & Cropanzano, 1999; Grzywacz & Marks, 2000; Marks, 1998).

Work and family social support have been explored as potential resources that reduced work–family conflict. For example, a supportive supervisor may not make excessive demands that would cause an employee to work at home. Likewise, a supportive spouse or other family member may provide direct assistance with demands at home, thereby reducing the likelihood that an individual is preoccupied with these problems at work. Past research has found that higher levels of social support at work are related to lower levels of work-to-family conflict, whereas higher levels of social support at home are related to lower levels of family-to-work conflict (e.g., Adams et al., 1996; Bernas & Major, 2000; Frone, Yardley, et al., 1997; Grzywacz & Marks, 2000).

Personality. Although most research has explored role characteristics as potential causes of work–family conflict, a few studies have begun to examine personality dispositions as causes of work–family conflict. Various personality characteristics, such as mastery, hardiness, positive affectivity, and extraversion may be conceived of as individual resources in that they capture a tendency to actively cope with problems at work and home, thereby reducing the likelihood of work–family conflict. Other personality variables, such as negative affectivity and neuroticism, may be conceived of as individual deficits in that they capture a tendency to avoid problems at work and home, thereby increasing the likelihood of work–family conflict. Several recent studies have found that high levels of hardiness, extraversion, and self-esteem were associated with lower levels of both work-to-family and family-to-work conflict (Bernas & Major, 2000; Grandey & Cropanzano, 1999; Grzywacz & Marks, 2000). One study reported that high levels of neuroticism were associated with higher levels of both work-to-family and family-to-work conflict (Grzywacz & Marks, 2000).

Summary. Past research examining the role-related predictors of work–family conflict supports three general conclusions. First, consistent with the conceptual models developed by Frone and colleagues (1992a; Frone, Yardley, et al., 1997), past research suggests that it is important to distinguish between the two types of work–family conflict because the role-related antecedents of work-to-family conflict reside in the work domain, whereas the role-related antecedents of family-to-work conflict reside in the family domain. Second, both dimensions of work–family conflict are affected by similar types of role characteristics, such as behavioral involvement, psychological involvement, stressors, and resources. Third, despite their unique role-related antecedents, the two types of work–family conflict share common causes in personality dispositions.

Work–Family Facilitation

Only one study has explored the predictors of both work-to-family facilitation and family-to-work facilitation (Grzywacz & Marks, 2000). Because little conceptual development exists regarding the putative causal antecedents of work–family facilitation, an overall conceptual model of work–family facilitation did not guide the selection of predictor variables in this study. Nonetheless, Grzywacz and Marks's (2000) study was based on the implicit assumption that the predictors of work–family conflict and work–family facilitation are similar, though parallel work and family predictors were not always assessed. These researchers found that behavioral involvement at work, work demands, family demands, and family conflict were unrelated to both work-to-family facilitation and family-to-work facilitation. Although work-related social support and decision latitude were positively related to *both* types of work–family facilitation, family-related social support was positively related to only family-to-work facilitation. Finally, high levels of extraversion were associated with high levels of both work-to-family and family-to-work facilitation, whereas neuroticism was unrelated to both types of work–family facilitation.

In summary, because little conceptual and empirical attention has been devoted to understanding the putative causal antecedents of work–family facilitation, no reasonable conclusions can be drawn at this time. Nonetheless, the results of Grzywacz and Marks's (2000) study suggest that the processes underlying work–family conflict may not generalize to work–family facilitation. This suggests that it may not be useful to take an integrative model of work–family conflict and simply substitute in work–family facilitation. Rather, new models need to be developed to elucidate the causal antecedents of work–family facilitation.

Outcomes of Work–Family Balance

Work–Family Conflict

A growing body of research has explored the potential outcomes of work–family conflict. As with research on the antecedents of work–family conflict, past studies of the outcomes of work–family conflict often used measures that only assess work-to-family conflict or used global measures that confound the measurement of work-to-family conflict and family-to-work conflict. This is an important limitation because recent conceptual models and empirical research suggest that work-to-family conflict and family-to-work conflict have unique role-related outcomes (Frone et al., 1992a; Frone, Yardley, et al., 1997). Specifically, the role-related outcomes of work-to-family conflict and family-to-work conflict reside in the family and work domains, respectively. Therefore, the present review will focus on past research that *assessed separately and simultaneously modeled* both dimensions of work–family conflict. Because both types of work–family conflict are positively correlated, studies that merely report zero-order correlations can lead to biased conclusions regarding the role-related outcomes of work–family conflict. This focus also is essential when exploring whether both types of work–family conflict have an independent effect on employee health (Frone, 2000; Frone, Russell, & Barnes, 1996). The various outcomes of work–family conflict that have been examined can be roughly grouped into two general categories—role-related outcomes and general health outcomes—which are discussed in turn.

Role-related outcomes. Previous research has examined affective and behavioral role-related outcomes. Consistent with the directional dimension of work–family conflict, a number of studies have shown collectively that work-to-family conflict is predictive of family dissatisfaction or distress, whereas family-to-work conflict is predictive of work dissatisfaction or distress (Carlson & Kacmar, 2000; Frone et al., 1992a; Frone, Barnes, & Farrell, 1994; Frone, Yardley, et al., 1997; O'Driscoll et al., 1992). Turning to behavioral outcomes, research shows that work-to-family conflict is predictive of family-related absenteeism and tardiness and poor family-related role performance, whereas family-to-work conflict is predictive of work-related absenteeism and tardiness and poor work-related role performance (Frone, Yardley, et al., 1997; Howson & O'Driscoll, 1996; MacEwen & Barling, 1994).

Regarding the work-related behavioral outcomes, Frone et al. (1992a) speculated that one outcome—turnover—might not be related to family-to-work conflict. Specifically, Frone et al. (1992a) hypothesized that family-to-work conflict would result in work-related absenteeism, tardiness, and poor performance, whereas work-to-family conflict would result in work-related turnover and intentions to quit. Work-related absenteeism, tardiness, and poor performance are the direct outcomes of family demands that keep an individual from coming to work, from leaving home on time, and from concentrating on and devoting effort to task performance. Thus, only family-to-work conflict is expected to predict work-related absenteeism, tardiness, and poor performance. In contrast, family-to-work conflict is not expected to predict work-related turnover or intentions to quit. The reason is that quitting one's job may not be viewed as a viable way of reducing family-to-work conflict because its root causes are demands and constraints in the family domain. In other words, even if one changed jobs, family-to-work conflict is likely to remain because one's family situation has not changed. On the contrary, because the root causes of work-to-family conflict are in the work domain, changing jobs may reduce work-to-family conflict. Thus, severe work-to-family conflict may predict intentions to quit a job and actual turnover because leaving a job may be viewed as a plausible coping mechanism. The research summarized earlier supports the hypothesis that only family-to-work conflict predicts work-related absenteeism, tardiness, and performance (Frone, Yardley, et al., 1997; Howson & O'Driscoll, 1996; MacEwen & Barling, 1994). Moreover, three studies support Frone et al.'s (1992a) speculation that only work-to-family conflict is predictive of intentions to quit one's job and actual turnover (Greenhaus, Parasuraman, & Collins, 2001; Howson & O'Driscoll, 1996; Kirchmeyer & Cohen, 1999).

General health outcomes. Past research has explored the relation of work–family conflict to the mental health, physical health, and health-related behaviors of employees. Frone et al. (1996) used identity theory to hypothesize that work-to-family conflict and family-to-work conflict would each have an independent relation to employee health outcomes. Past research provides strong support for this hypothesis. Work-to-family conflict and family-to-work conflict are independently and positively related to psychological distress (Frone et al., 1996; Hughes & Galinsky, 1994; Kirchmeyer & Cohen, 1999; MacEwen & Barling; 1994; Marks, 1998; O'Driscoll et al., 1992), self-reported poor physical health (Frone et al., 1996; Grzywacz, 2000; Marks, 1998), and heavy alcohol use (Frone et al., 1996). Nonetheless, these studies suffer from two important limitations. First, past research on psychological distress has used measures that capture subclinical levels of distress. Using data from the National Comorbidity Survey, Frone (2000) reported that both types of work–family conflict were independently and positively related to having clinically significant mood, anxiety, and substance dependence disorders. Second, past research has used cross-sectional data and self-reported outcome measures. In an effort to address this limitation, Frone, Russell, and Cooper (1997) tested the relation of work–family conflict to several self-reported and objective health outcomes in a four-year longitudinal study. The results showed that after controlling for baseline assessments of the outcomes, the baseline assessment of work-to-family conflict was related to higher levels of heavy alcohol use at follow-up. In addition, the baseline assessment of family-to-work conflict was positively related to depressive symptoms, poorer self-reported physical health, and to an objective assessment of hypertension status at follow-up. This study provides support for a causal effect of work–family conflict on employee health. However, the failure to find both types of work–family conflict related to each outcome variable is likely to be a function of the extended time lag of four years, which results in a very conservative test of these relations.

Based on identity theory and research on gender-role socialization, Frone et al. (1996) hypothesized that gender would moderate the relationship between work–family conflict and health but that the direction of gender's moderating influence would differ across the two types of work–family conflict. Specifically, Frone et al. (1996) hypothesized that the relation between work-to-family conflict and health would be stronger among women, whereas the relationship between family-to-work conflict and health would be stronger among men. However, research using both cross-sectional and longitudinal data and both regional and national probability samples has failed to support the moderating effect of gender (Frone, 2000; Frone et al., 1996; Frone, Russell, et al., 1997; Grzywacz, 2000; Marks, 1998). In other words, the deleterious effect of both types of work–family conflict on employee health is similar for men and women.

Summary. Based on past research, three general conclusions can be drawn. First, consistent with the conceptual models developed by Frone and colleagues (1992a; Frone, Yardley, et al., 1997), past research suggests that it is important to distinguish between the two types of work–family conflict because the role-related outcomes of work-to-family conflict reside in the family domain, whereas the role-related outcomes of family-to-work conflict reside in the work domain. One exception is that although work-related absenteeism, tardiness, and performance may be an outcome of family-to-work conflict, intentions to quit a job and turnover may be an outcome of work-to-family conflict. Second, both dimensions of work–family conflict are related to the mental health, physical health, and health-related behaviors of employees. Third, no compelling evidence exists that the strength of the relations of work–family conflict to role-related and overall health outcomes differ for males and females.

Work–Family Facilitation

No research has examined the relation of both work-to-family facilitation and family-to-work facilitation to role-related outcomes. Only one study has explored the relationship of both types of work–family facilitation to employee health outcomes (Grzywacz, 2000). In contrast to findings described earlier for work–family conflict, Grzywacz (2000) failed to find strong evidence that either type of work–family facilitation was related to physical health. However, consistent with research on work–family conflict, Grzywacz (2000) found that both types of work–family facilitation were negatively related to poor mental health and that gender did not moderate the relationships between work–family facilitation and both physical and mental health.

In summary, because little conceptual and empirical attention has been devoted to understanding the putative outcomes of work–family facilitation, no reasonable conclusions can be drawn at this time. Additional research needs to determine whether the types of processes and outcomes related to work–family conflict apply to work–family facilitation. It may be that work–family conflict and work–family facilitation have a set of common and a set of unique outcomes.

Promoting Work–Family Balance

When considering the promotion of work–family balance, a number of important, and sometimes contentious, issues exist that cannot be addressed in this chapter. For example, how is responsibility for the promotion of work–family balance apportioned across relevant stakeholders (employees, employers, government, and society)? What types of initiatives and costs can each relevant stakeholder be expected to assume? Which organizational and workforce characteristics are related to the provision of work–family initiatives by employers and their use by employees? Although a discussion of these issues is beyond the scope of this review, the research summarized earlier consistently shows that work–family conflict is related to a number of deleterious outcomes in the work domain (job dissatisfaction, job withdrawal, poor job performance), in the family domain (family dissatisfaction, family withdrawal, poor family performance), and in the personal domain (poor mental and physical health and unhealthy behaviors). Therefore, some attention needs to be devoted to identifying and evaluating the initiatives that are already in place to promote work–family balance. In addition to decreasing work–family conflict, work–family balance can be improved by increasing work–family facilitation. However, consistent with the paucity of research exploring the prevalence, predictors, and outcomes of work–family facilitation, no research has explored strategies to augment work–family facilitation. Therefore, the research reviewed next focuses on currently used strategies to reduce the occurrence of or manage the impact of work–family conflict. The literature that exists can be grouped according to whether work–family conflict is managed through personal initiatives or organizational initiatives.

Personal Initiatives

The findings reported earlier on the predictors of work–family conflict suggest a number of things that individual employees might do to reduce both types of work–family conflict. They can seek out and develop appropriate social support at work or at home, reduce or reorganize the time devoted to work or family demands, reduce the psychological importance of work or family roles, and find ways to reduce or better cope with stressors and distress at work and home. Many of these suggestions support recommendations of past researchers who have looked at how employees cope with work–family conflict. Hall (1972) proposed three types of coping behavior in response to work–family conflict. *Structural role redefinition* refers to attempts to alter external, structurally imposed expectations. Examples include eliminating role activities, negotiating a reduction in or modification of work hours, reallocating or sharing role tasks, and seeking out and fostering sources of social support. *Personal role redefinition* refers to attempts to alter one's internal conception of role demands. Examples include establishing priorities among role demands, ignoring role demands, changing one's attitude toward roles, and eliminating a role. Finally, reactive role behavior refers to attempts to meet all role demands. Examples include more efficient planning and scheduling and working harder and longer within each role.

Based on interviews with 9 men and 15 women, Wiersma (1994) reported 14 strategies used to manage conflict, such as hiring outside help, setting priorities, cognitive reappraisal, avoidance, and mutual sharing. Becker and Moen (1999) found that the strategies used by 100 middle-class dual-earner couples to manage work–family conflict fell into three broad categories. *Placing limits* is a strategy that limits the encroachment of work on family time by limiting hours worked, refusing overtime, turning down jobs with travel, and turning down promotions that require relocation. *Job versus career* is a strategy where one person pursues a "career" and the other person holds a "job." The person holding the job is the primary caregiver, moves to follow his or her spouse's career, and reduces work time while children are young. *Trading off* is a sequential version of the job versus career strategy, where the person pursuing the career versus holding a job changes over time because of changing career opportunities or family stage.

Relative to the amount of research devoted to studying the prevalence, predictors, and outcomes of work–family conflict, very little research has been devoted to understanding the personal initiatives that individuals and couples use to manage work–family conflict. The research conducted to date has merely attempted to catalog the strategies used by individuals to cope with work–family conflict. However, this work is limited in several ways. First, the taxonomies of coping that have been described are based on very small and very narrow samples. Developing a comprehensive taxonomy of coping strategies will require samples that are much larger and more representative of the employed population struggling to cope with conflict between work and family life. Second, no research has explicitly attempted to evaluate whether the coping strategies that have been documented actually reduce work–family conflict (i.e., improve work–family balance). Third, no research has looked at the conditions under which certain strategies might be more effective. For example, in developing taxonomies of coping behavior, past research has failed to entertain the idea that the types of coping strategies used and that are effective may differ for work-to-family conflict versus family-to-work conflict.

Organizational Initiatives

The organizational initiatives being promoted to help employees balance work and family life tend to be discussed under the general rubric of family-friendly organizational policies or benefits. Approximately 30 to 40 organizational work–family initiatives have been identified in the literature (e.g., Frankel, 1998; Galinsky & Bond, 1998). These initiatives fall into several categories that include flexible work arrangements (e.g., flextime, compressed work week, reduced work hours, work at home), leaves (e.g., maternal leave, paternal leave, leave to care for seriously ill family members), dependent-care assistance (e.g., on-site day care for children, voucher or direct subsidies for child care, elder care, and child care referral services), and general resource services (e.g., employee assistance programs, work–family seminars, programs for teenage children of employees).

Despite the number of organizational work–family initiatives being promoted, very few studies have explicitly set out to answer the following question: Do organizational work–family initiatives reduce work–family conflict or enhance work–family facilitation? Four studies have examined work–family conflict and none have addressed work–family facilitation. Goff, Mount, and Jamison (1990) found that use of an on-site day care center was unrelated to an overall measure of work–family conflict that confounded items assessing work-to-family and family-to-work conflict. Judge, Boudreau, and Bretz (1994) found that the availability of work–family policies was negatively related to work-to-family conflict and was unrelated to family-to-work conflict among male executives. Thomas and Ganster (1995) found that, in a sample of health care professionals, the availability of information and referral services, flexible work schedules, and dependent care were unrelated to an overall measure of work–family conflict that confounded items assessing work-to-family and family-to-work conflict. Thompson, Beauvais, and Lyness (1999) reported that the availability of work–family benefits was negatively related to work-to-family conflict. Thompson et al. (1999) did not assess family-to-work conflict.

Overall, the research to date on the relationship of organizational work–family initiatives to work–family balance is meager and inconsistent. A number of improvements should be incorporated into future research. For example, although it appears that the availability of work–family benefits is related to lower levels of work-to-family conflict, only one study separately assessed both types of work–family conflict. The failure to explore the relationship between work–family benefits and family-to-work conflict is surprising in light of past research findings. First, research shows that family-to-work conflict is the primary predictor of negative work behaviors. Second, employers offer many work–family benefits to improve employee performance and productivity by reducing family-to-work conflict. Third, family-to-work conflict—not work-to-family conflict—is positively related to employed parents' desire for organizational work–family initiatives (Frone & Yardley, 1996). Thus, one would expect that organizational work–family initiatives are related to lower levels of family-to-work conflict. In fact, Frone and Yardley (1996) argued that past failures to document a relationship between the availability of work–family benefits and reductions in work–family conflict may be the joint outcome of (a) failing to distinguish between the two types of conflict and (b) failing to consider baseline measures of work–family conflict within an experimental design. Researchers also should assess the extent to which employees use work–family benefits rather than the mere availability of such benefits. Why should the availability of work–family benefits exhibit a strong relation to lower levels of work–family conflict if employees feel uncomfortable using the benefits? Finally, research should begin to explore the relationship of organizational work–family initiatives to work–family facilitation.

Conclusion

This review suggests that work–family balance may be a multidimensional construct that needs to be defined in terms of both the direction of influence between work and family roles (work-to-family versus family-to-work) and the type of effect (conflict versus facilitation). When examining the level, predictors, or outcomes of work–family balance, it is important first to distinguish between conflict and facilitation, and then within each of these categories it is important to distinguish between the directions of influence. The more recent and integrative research on work–family conflict clearly shows that it is important to distinguish between and to model simultaneously work-to-family conflict and family-to-work conflict. Because of the unique role-related predictors and outcomes of both types of work–family conflict, efforts to improve functioning in the work role need to focus on ways (personal coping initiatives or organizational work–family initiatives) to reduce family-to-work conflict. In contrast, efforts to improve functioning in the family role need to focus on ways (personal coping initiatives or organizational work–family initiatives) to reduce work-to-family conflict. Because both types of conflict may influence employee health, strategies are needed to reduce both types of conflict. As the research on the predictors of work–family conflict suggests, each type of work–family conflict may be reduced by seeking out and developing appropriate social support, attempting to reduce or reorganize time investments, reducing psychological investments, and finding ways to reduce or better cope with stressors and distress in the relevant work or family role. However, equally clear from past research is the conclusion that we do not really know which personal initiatives and organizational work–family initiatives reduce the two types of work–family conflict. Much more research needs to focus on identifying personal and organizational initiatives that reduce work–family conflict and on documenting the cost-effectiveness of these work–family initiatives.

In terms of understanding the dynamics of work–family balance, the preponderance of research has been and continues to be devoted to work–family conflict. As noted earlier, a broad conceptualization of work–family balance would not merely define it in terms of reducing work–family conflict. It would embrace the notion that work–family balance also is defined in terms of promoting work–family facilitation, which is in keeping with the growing interest in "positive psychology" (Seligman & Csikszentmihalyi, 2000). However, a compelling case for including work–family facilitation as a viable component of work–family balance awaits the same level of research interest devoted to work–family conflict. The small amount of research reviewed earlier on work–family facilitation suggests that different processes may be at work compared to work–family conflict. To understand the predictors, outcomes, and promotion of work–family facilitation, researchers may need to develop new conceptual models. It is likely a mistake to take established models of work–family conflict and simply substitute in work–family facilitation.

Research should move beyond work–family balance to explore the balance between work and the other nonwork or life roles depicted in Figure 7.1 (see Hammer et al., 1998; Markel & Frone, 1998; Rice et al., 1992, for examples). However, it is important to assess the characteristics of each role separately. The current tendency among many researchers to use measures that confound all nonwork roles (e.g., work–nonwork conflict, nonwork distress) is based on the faulty, or at least unsubstantiated, premise that the processes underlying the relationship between work and all other nonwork roles are the same. To the extent that the processes underlying the relationship between work and other nonwork roles (family, student, leisure) might differ, the use of such general measures will undermine a complete understanding of how life at work relates to life outside work. In fact, it may be useful for future work–family research to begin looking separately at the various family roles (spouse, parent, offspring). Such an approach also would argue for moving from research with a predominate focus on the individual as the unit of analysis to more research in which the family is the unit of analysis. One might even argue for research that explores the work group as the unit of analysis because the family-to-work conflict or family-to-work facilitation of one employee may affect not only his or her own work performance but the performance of coworkers and the work group as well.

Research on work–family balance has progressed substantially over the past decade. Nonetheless, plenty of work remains to develop a comprehensive understanding of the complex relationship between work and family and between work and other nonwork roles. In keeping with recent conceptual developments, our knowledge will continue to develop only through the use of integrative, multivariate models of balance between work and nonwork roles. Studies that rely on zero-order correlations and measures that do not assess all relevant dimensions of balance (e.g., both work-to-family and family-to-work conflict) will likely lead to inaccurate conclusions and less useful policy recommendations.

References

Adams, G. A., King, L. A., & King, D. W. (1996). Relationships of job and family involvement, family social support, and work–family conflict with job and life satisfaction. *Journal of Applied Psychology, 81,* 411–420.

Ashforth, B. E., Kreiner, G. E., & Fugate, M. (2000). All in a day's work: Boundaries and micro role transitions. *Academy of Management Review, 25,* 472–491.

Becker, P. E., & Moen, P. (1999). Scaling back: Dual-earner couples' work-family strategies. *Journal of Marriage and the Family, 61,* 995–1007.

Bernas, K. H., & Major, D. A. (2000). Contributors to stress resistance: Testing a model of women's work-family conflict. *Psychology of Women Quarterly, 24,* 170–178.

Bond, J. T., Galinsky, E., & Swanberg, J. E. (1998). *The 1997 national study of the changing workforce.* New York: Families and Work Institute.

Carlson, D. S., & Kacmar, K. M. (2000). Work–family conflict in the organization: Do life role values make a difference? *Journal of Management, 26,* 1031–1054.

Clark, S. C. (2000). Work/family border theory: A new theory of work/family balance. *Human Relations, 53,* 747–770.

Eagle, B. W., Miles, E. W., & Icenogle, M. L. (1997). Interrole conflicts and the permeability of work and family domains: Are there gender differences? *Journal of Vocational Behavior, 50,* 168–184.

Edwards, J. R., & Rothbard, N. P. (2000). Mechanisms linking work and family: Clarifying the relationship between work and family constructs. *Academy of Management Review, 25,* 178–199.

Ferber, M. A., O'Farrell, B., & Allen, L. R. (Eds.). (1991). *Work and family: Policies for a changing work force.* Washington, DC: National Academy Press.

Frankel. M. (1998). Creating the family friendly workplace: Barriers and solutions. In S. Klarreich (Ed.), *Handbook of organizational health psychology: Programs to make the workplace healthier* (pp. 79–100). Madison, CT: Psychosocial Press.

Frone, M. R. (2000). Work–family conflict and employee psychiatric disorders: The national comorbidity survey. *Journal of Applied Psychology, 85,* 888–895.

Frone, M. R., Barnes, G. M., & Farrell, M. P. (1994). Relationship of work–family conflict to substance use among employed mothers: The role of negative affect. *Journal of Marriage and the Family, 56,* 1019–1030.

Frone, M. R., Russell, M., & Barnes, G. M. (1996). Work–family conflict, gender, and health-related outcomes: A study of employed parents in two community samples. *Journal of Occupational Health Psychology, 1,* 57–69.

Frone, M. R., Russell, M., & Cooper, M. L. (1992a). Antecedents and outcomes of work-family conflict: Testing a model of the work-family interface. *Journal of Applied Psychology, 77,* 65–78.

Frone, M. R., Russell, M., & Cooper, M. L. (1992b). Prevalence of work–family conflict: Are work and family boundaries asymmetrically permeable? *Journal of Organizational Behavior, 13,* 723–729.

Frone, M. R., Russell, M., & Cooper, M. L. (1994). Relationship between job and family satisfaction: Causal or noncausal covariation? *Journal of Management, 20,* 565–579.

Frone, M. R., Russell, M., & Cooper, M. L. (1997). Relation of work-family conflict to health outcomes: A four-year longitudinal study of employed parents. *Journal of Occupational and Organizational Psychology, 70,* 325–336.

Frone, M. R., & Yardley, J. K. (1996). Workplace family-supportive programmes: Predictors of employed parents' importance ratings. *Journal of Occupational and Organizational Psychology, 69,* 351–366.

Frone, M. R., Yardley, J. K., & Markel, K. (1997). Developing and testing an integrative model of the work-family interface. *Journal of Vocational Behavior, 50,* 145–167.

Galinsky, E., & Bond, J. T. (1998). *The 1998 business work-life study: A sourcebook.* New York: Families and Work Institute.

Goff, S. J., Mount, M. K., & Jamison, R. L. (1990). Employer supported child care, work/family conflict, and absenteeism: A field study. *Personnel Psychology, 43,* 793–809.

Grandey, A. A., & Cropanzano, R. (1999). The conservation of resources model applied to work–family conflict and strain. *Journal of Vocational Behavior, 54,* 350–370.

Greenhaus, J. H., & Beutell, N. J. (1985). Sources of conflict between work and family roles. *Academy of Management Review, 10,* 76–88.

Greenhaus, J. H., Parasuraman, S., & Collins, K. M. (2001). Career involvement and family involvement as moderators of relationships between work–family conflict and withdrawal from a profession. *Journal of Occupational Health Psychology, 6,* 91–100.

Grzywacz, J. G. (2000). Work–family spillover and health during midlife: Is managing conflict everything. *American Journal of Health Promotion, 14,* 236–243.

Grzywacz, J. G., & Marks, N. F. (2000). Reconceptualizing the work–family interface: An ecological perspective on the correlates of positive and negative spillover between work and family. *Journal of Occupational Health Psychology, 5,* 111–126.

Gutek, B. A., Searle, S., & Klepa, L. (1991). Rational versus gender role explanations for work-family conflict. *Journal of Applied Psychology, 76,* 560–568.

Hall, D. T. (1972). A model of coping with role conflict: The role behavior of college educated women. *Administrative Science Quarterly, 17,* 471–486.

Hammer, L. B., Grigsby, T. D., & Woods, S. (1998). The conflicting demands of work, family, and school among students at an urban university. *Journal of Psychology, 132,* 220–226.

Hart, P. M. (1999). Predicting employee life satisfaction: A coherent model of personality, work and nonwork experiences, and domain satisfactions. *Journal of Applied Psychology, 84,* 564–584.

Howson, M., & O'Driscoll, M. P. (1996). *Satisfaction with childcare and job–family conflict: Implications for absenteeism, lateness, and turnover intentions.* Unpublished manuscript, University of Waikato, Hamilton, New Zealand.

Hughes, D. L., & Galinsky, E. (1994). Gender, job and family conflicts, and psychological symptoms. *Psychology of Women Quarterly, 18,* 251–270.

Judge, T. A., Boudreau, J. W., & Bretz, R. D. (1994). Job and life attitudes of male executive. *Journal of Applied Psychology, 79,* 767–782.

Kirchmeyer, C. (1992). Perceptions of nonwork-to-work spillover: Challenging the common view of conflict-ridden domain relationships. *Basic and Applied Social Psychology, 13,* 231–249.

Kirchmeyer, C., & Cohen, A. (1999). Different strategies for managing the work/non-work interface: A test for unique pathways to outcomes. *Work and Stress, 13,* 59–73.

Lambert, S. J. (1990). Processes linking work and family: A critical review and research agenda. *Human Relations, 43,* 239–257.

MacEwen, K. E., & Barling, J. (1994). Daily consequences of work interference with family and family interference with work. *Work and Stress, 8,* 244–254.

Markel, K. S., & Frone, M. R. (1998). Job characteristics, work-school conflict, and school outcomes among adolescents: Testing a structural model. *Journal of Applied Psychology, 83,* 277–287.

Marks, N. F. (1998). Does it hurt to care? Caregiving, work-family conflict, and midlife well-being. *Journal of Marriage and the Family, 60,* 951–966.

Marshall, C. M. (1992). Family influences on work. In S. J. Bahr (Ed.), *Family research: A sixty-year review, 1930–1990* (pp. 115–166). New York: Lexington.

Marshall, C. M., Chadwick, B. A., & Marshall, B. C. (1992). The influence of employment on family interaction, well-being, and happiness. In S. J. Bahr (Ed.), *Family research: A sixty-year review, 1930–1990* (pp. 167–229). New York: Lexington.

Morf, M. (1989). *The work/life dichotomy: Prospects for reintegrating people and jobs.* New York: Quorum.

Netemeyer, R. G., Boles, J. S., & McMurrian, R. (1996). Development and validation of work–family conflict and family–work conflict scales. *Journal of Applied Psychology, 81,* 400–410.

O'Driscoll, M. P., Ilgen, D. R., & Hildreth, K. (1992). Time devoted to job and off-job activities, interrole conflict, and affective experiences. *Journal of Applied Psychology, 77,* 272–279.

Rice, R. W., Frone, M. R., & McFarlin, D. B. (1992). Work–nonwork conflict and the perceived quality of life. *Journal of Organizational Behavior, 13,* 155–168.

Rice, R. W., McFarlin, D. B., Hunt, R. G., & Near, J. P. (1985). Organizational work and the perceived quality of life: Toward a conceptual model. *Academy of Management Review, 10,* 296–310.

Schwarz, N. (1999). Self-reports: How the questions shape the answers. *American Psychologist, 54,* 93–105.

Seligman, M. E. P., & Csikszentmihalyi, M. (2000). Positive psychology: an introduction. *American Psychologist, 55,* 5–14.

Thomas, L. T., & Ganster, D. C. (1995). Impact of family supportive work variables on work–family conflict and strain: A control perspective. *Journal of Applied Psychology, 80,* 6–15.

Thompson, C. A., Beauvais, L. L., & Lyness, K. S. (1999). When work–family benefits are not enough: The influence of work–family culture on benefit utilization, organizational attachment, and work–family conflict. *Journal of Vocational Behavior, 54,* 392–415.

Wiersma, U. J. (1994). A taxonomy of behavioral strategies for coping with work–home role conflict. *Human Relations, 47,* 211–221.

8

Shiftwork and Working Hours

Carlla S. Smith, Simon Folkard, and Julie A. Fuller

The advent of modern industrial processes, the globalization of the economy, and the proliferation of information technology, among other factors, have contributed to the creation of a 24-hour society in recent times. As the demand for 24-hour availability of goods and services has risen over the past few decades, the prevalence of shiftwork has likewise increased. In the United States, approximately 20% of all nonagricultural workers experience some type of shiftwork, and 25% of these shiftworkers work at night (U.S. Congress, Office of Technology Assessment, 1991). Estimates for European workers are similar (Wedderburn, 1996).

Shiftwork is defined as any arrangement of daily working hours that differs from the standard daylight hours. Organizations that adopt shiftwork systems extend their hours of work past eight hours by using successive teams of workers. The nature of shift systems can vary widely along several dimensions, including the number and length of shifts, the presence or absence of night work, the direction and speed of the shift rotation (or whether the shift rotates or not), the length of the shift cycles, the start and stop times of each shift, and the number and placement of days off.

The scientific community has long maintained that individuals who regularly work atypical hours (i.e., shiftwork of some type) are at greater risk for physical and psychological impairment or disease than typical day workers (e.g., Costa, 1996; Costa, Folkard, & Harrington, 2000). This risk is assumed to originate from the physical and psychological stress that develops from work schedule-related disruptions of their biological functions, sleep, and social and family life. The risk is further exacerbated by extended hours of work beyond the standard 40-hour week, a trend that has also been increasing over the past several years (Costa et al., 2000).

In this chapter, we explore the relationships between shiftwork and health. We do not attempt to be comprehensive, but rather representative, in our review of the published research literature. First, we provide general background information on circadian rhythms to prepare the reader for the balance of the chapter. Second, we review the empirical literature on shiftwork and various types of health-related strains or outcomes. Third, we examine some of the factors (e.g., age, personality) that have been investigated in the search for the "shiftwork tolerant" individual. Fourth, we explore the various types of interventions that have been attempted to enhance shiftwork effectiveness. Fifth, in light of our review, we summarize the research findings and then discuss implications for future research.

Theoretical Framework

Life on earth has evolved in an environment subject to regular and pronounced changes produced by planetary movements. The rotation of the earth on its own axis results in the 24-hour light/dark cycle, whereas its rotation around the sun gives rise to seasonal changes in light and temperature. During the process of evolution, these periodic changes have become internalized, and it is now widely accepted that living organisms possess a "body clock," such that organisms do not merely respond to environmental changes but actually anticipate them.

Circadian Rhythms and the Internal Body Clock

The anticipation of environmental events is mediated by regular cyclic changes in body processes. In humans, the most pronounced of these are the approximately 24-hour "circadian" ("around a day") rhythms that occur in almost all physiological measures (Minors & Waterhouse, 1981).

Evidence that these circadian rhythms are at least partially controlled by an internal, or "endogenous," body clock comes from studies in which people have been isolated from their normal environmental time cues, or *zeitgebers* (from the German for "time givers"). In their pioneering studies, Aschoff and Wever (1962) isolated individuals from all environmental time cues in a temporal isolation unit for up to 19 days, and Siffre (1964) lived in an underground cave for two months. In both studies, people continued to wake up and go to sleep on a regular basis, but instead of doing so every 24 hours, they did so about every 25 hours. The circadian rhythms of other physiological measures, including body temperature and urinary electrolytes, typically showed an identical period to that of their sleep–wake cycle.

Approximately a third of the people who have subsequently been studied in this way, however, have spontaneously shown a rather different pattern of results. In these cases, the sleep–wake cycle and body temperature rhythms have become "internally desynchronized," meaning that the temperature rhythm continues to run with an average period of about 25 hours, the sleep–wake cycle shows either a much shorter or a much longer period than either 25 or 24 hours (Wever, 1979). It is interesting to note that this phenomenon of "spontaneous internal desynchronization" occurs more frequently in older people and in those with higher neuroticism scores (Lund, 1974), topics we discuss later in this chapter.

Endogenous and Exogenous Components

At a more theoretical level, the fact that the temperature rhythm and sleep–wake cycle can run with distinctly different periods from one another suggests that the human "circadian system" comprises two, or perhaps more, underlying processes. The first of these is a relatively strong endogenous body clock that is dominant in controlling the circadian rhythm of body temperature (and of other measures, such as urinary potassium and plasma cortisol) and is relatively unaffected by external factors. The second is a weaker process that is more exogenous in nature (i.e., it is more prone to external influences) and is dominant in controlling the sleep–wake cycle (and other circadian rhythms, such as those in plasma growth hormone and urinary calcium). Some debate exists regarding whether this second process truly has a clock-like nature, but there seems to be general agreement that some circadian rhythms are dominantly controlled by the endogenous body clock, and others are more influenced by external factors.

These two processes are thought to be asymmetrically coupled, such that the endogenous clock exerts a considerably greater influence on the weaker process than vice versa. For example, internally desynchronized individuals show such a strong tendency to wake up at a particular point of the temperature rhythm, regardless of when they fell asleep, that their sleep periods can vary in duration from 4 to 16 hours (Czeisler, Weitzman, Moore-Ede, Zimmerman, & Kronauer, 1980). Therefore, sleep is likely to be disrupted unless the temperature rhythm has adjusted to any changes in the sleep–wake cycle.

Adjustment to Shiftwork

Under normal circumstances, both the endogenous body clock and the weaker exogenous process are entrained to a 24-hour period by strong natural *zeitgebers,* including the light–dark cycle. As a result, all circadian rhythms normally show a fixed-phase relationship to one another. For example, urinary adrenaline reaches a maximum around midday, and body temperature peaks at about 8.00 PM. Similarly, all other circadian rhythms reach their maxima at their appointed time, allowing us to fall asleep at night and wake up in the morning. The occasional late night may affect those rhythms controlled by the weaker process, but are less likely to upset the strong oscillator and, hence, our body temperature rhythm and the time at which we spontaneously wake up.

This inherent stability in the human circadian system, however, can pose problems if a mismatch arises between the internal timing system and external time cues. The simplest example of this occurs when people fly across time zones, because all the *zeitgebers* change. A flight from Europe to the United States involves crossing several time zones, so that on arrival the timing system is 5 to 9 hours too early for the local *zeitgebers.* Body temperature rhythms usually take more than a week to delay their timing by the appropriate amount (Wegmann & Klein, 1985). For the first few nights, this often results in people waking up in the early hours of the morning and being unable to resume sleep. The rhythms in other processes adjust at different rates, presumably depending on the degree to which they are controlled by the endogenous clock or the weaker exogenous process. As a result, the normal phase relationship between rhythms breaks down and is only slowly reestablished as the various rhythms adjust to the new time zone. This internal dissociation between rhythms is thought to be responsible for the disorientation and general malaise typical of "jet lag."

These feelings of jet lag are normally worse following an eastward flight, which requires an advancing of the body's timing system, than following a westward one, which requires a delay. This "directional asymmetry" effect is related to the fact that the endogenous period of the circadian system is somewhat greater than 24 hours. Thus, in the absence of any *zeitgebers,* rhythms tend to delay rather than to advance, assisting adjustment to westward flights but inhibiting adjustment to eastward ones.

This directional asymmetry has implications for the design of shift systems. When shiftworkers go on the night shift, most environmental *zeitgebers* remain constant and discourage adjustment of the circadian system. The natural light–dark cycle, the clock time, and most social cues do not change while the timing of shiftworkers' work can be delayed by up to 16 hours and that of their sleep by up to 12 hours. From what we know so far, it is clear that the adjustment of a shiftworker's body clock to these changes is likely to be very slow, if indeed it occurs at all.

Review of Empirical Literature on Shiftwork and Health

In the previous section, we discuss how the experience of shiftwork, especially night work, provokes circadian disharmony, resulting in decreases in sleep quality and quantity. In the short-term, the effects of these deficits are quite obvious (e.g., increased fatigue, sleepiness), and, if unabated, they can presumably lead to more serious medical conditions. In this section, we discuss these short-term and chronic health effects of working shifts.

Sleep and Fatigue

Sleep is the primary human function disrupted by shiftwork. Many bodily processes, such as temperature, blood pressure, and heart rate, are at their lowest ebb at night; so it is not surprising that people who try to work at night and sleep during the day often report that they cannot do either very well. Shiftworkers who need to sleep during the day may have difficulty in falling asleep and remaining asleep because they are attempting sleep when they are at odds with their circadian rhythms. And because of work and personal demands, shiftworkers rarely achieve full adjustment to their shiftwork schedules.

The unfortunate outcome of shiftwork is that both the quality and quantity of shiftworkers' sleep suffers (Costa, 1996). One almost immediate result is fatigue (Luna, French, & Mitcha, 1997; Tepas & Carvalhais, 1990). Severe sleep disturbances may develop over time and result in the development of chronic fatigue, anxiety, nervousness, and depression, any or all of which frequently demand medical intervention (Costa et al., 2000). Such effects are aggravated by long working hours, which accompany extended (e.g., 12-hour) shifts or multiple jobs or roles (e.g., the working mother). However, the primary concern with disrupted sleep and resultant fatigue is that it will culminate in the development of more serious conditions, such as serious injury or disease.

Accidents and Injuries

As we discussed in the previous section, shiftwork and the resulting biological dysfunction that often accompany it may culminate in serious errors and injury, especially on the night shift (Costa, 1996). Although some researchers have not found the expected increase in night-shift accidents (e.g., Barreto, Swerdlow, Smith, & Higgins, 1997), Folkard and his colleagues have demonstrated conclusively that when a priori risk is constant (i.e., work conditions are identical) across shifts, accidents and injuries occur more frequently at night (Folkard, Åkerstedt, Macdonald, Tucker, & Spencer, 2000; Smith, Folkard, & Poole, 1994). Similarly, the accidents and injuries that occur on the night shift are often more serious than those on the day shift (i.e., requiring prompt medical attention rather than first aid; Smith et al., 1994). Another related finding is that, relative to day workers, night workers are more frequently involved in automotive accidents while driving home after work (Monk, Folkard, & Wedderburn, 1996). Sleep deprivation, fatigue, and circadian malaise are the obvious culprits in most of these unfortunate incidents.

Research has also shown that accident and injury rates can vary according to the type of shift system (i.e., rotating or fixed or different hybrid [mixed] systems), although the nature and extent of these differences vary (e.g., Barreto et al., 1997; Barton, Smith, Totterdell, Spelten, & Folkard, 1993). Selection of the best type of shift system is a complex issue, which has been debated by shiftwork researchers (Folkard, 1992; Wedderburn, 1992; Wilkinson, 1992). This topic will be discussed in some detail later in this chapter.

Shift-related differences in error or accident rates may reflect methodological confounds, such as the type of work performed and the workers' experience. Studies such as Smith et al. (1994) are rare in that these researchers were able to make comparisons across shifts that were identical in a priori risk. In contrast, supervision is usually decreased at night, and night shift workers tend to be less experienced than day workers (especially in the United States). True shift differences may also be masked by the fact that the day shift typically has the heaviest workload, whereas maintenance and repair activities are often reserved for the night shift (Costa et al., 2000; Smith et al., 1997); the type of work performed may also vary across different types of shift systems (Smith et al., 1997). Regardless of these issues, however, the potential risk for serious error and injuries on the night shift should not be underestimated. The infamous industrial mishaps in the nuclear facilities at Three Mile Island and Chernobyl, as well as the *Challenger* space shuttle disaster, all occurred during the night shift. Shift schedules and fatigue were cited as major contributing factors to each incident (Price & Holley, 1990).

Psychological–Emotional Disorders

A common finding in shiftwork research is that psychological and emotional distress frequently accompanies shiftwork (e.g., Barton et al., 1993; Williamson, Gower, & Clarke, 1994), although the magnitude of the effects is sometimes low (e.g., Barton, 1994; Tucker, Barton, & Folkard, 1996). These findings are consistent with the psychological effects of shifting schedules and the resulting sleep disruption discussed previously.

Shiftworkers' psychological and emotional states are frequently assessed in empirical studies, although the physical disorders (e.g., gastrointestinal, cardiovascular) appear to have attracted the most attention. However, the psychological distress that often accompanies shiftwork from its onset may be the primary factor that provokes many (approximately 20 to 50%, depending on the data source) to leave shiftwork (Costa, 1996).

Gastrointestinal Disorders

Gastrointestinal disorders are the most prevalent health complaint associated with shift and night work (e.g., Angersbach et al., 1980; Vener, Szabo, & Moore, 1989). According to Costa et al. (2000), 20 to 75% of shift and night workers, compared to 10 to 25% of day workers, complain of irregular bowel movements and constipation, heartburn, gas, and appetite disturbances. Gastrointestinal complaints are commonly assessed in shiftwork studies, and most researchers report reliable effects, although the size of these effects is sometimes small (e.g., Barton et al., 1993). In many cases, these complaints eventually develop into chronic diseases, such as chronic gastritis and peptic ulcers (Costa, 1996).

Night work, not just shiftwork, appears to be the critical factor in the development of gastrointestinal disease (Angersbach et al., 1980). A review of 36 epidemiological studies, covering 50 years of data and 98,000 workers, indicated that disorders of the digestive tract were two to five times more common among shiftworkers who experienced night work than among day workers or shiftworkers who did not work at night (Costa, 1996). Tucker, Smith, Macdonald, and Folkard (2000) also reported that the development of digestive problems was associated with working longer shifts (i.e., 12 hours versus 8 hours) and relatively early shift changeovers (i.e., 6 AM vs. 7 AM).

Researchers have often speculated that gastrointestinal problems may be greater for shiftworkers because they have less access to healthy food than day workers (i.e., restaurants and stores are often closed between 12 and 6 AM), and their irregular hours encourage inconsistent dietary habits. However, the scant research that has addressed this issue (e.g., Lennernas, Hambraeus, & Åkerstedt, 1994) found no differences in nutritional intake between day and shiftworkers. Other factors, such as circadian disruption and sleep deficit, may be the culprits (Vener et al., 1989).

Cardiovascular Disorders

Despite years of debate, most researchers now acknowledge that a relationship between shiftwork and cardiovascular disease exists (e.g., Tucker et al., 1996). In an impressive longitudinal study spanning 15 years, Knutsson, Åkerstedt, Jonsson, and Orth-Gomer (1986) reported an increased risk of cardiovascular disease in shiftworkers. Specifically, as a group, shiftworkers demonstrated increased cardiovascular risk factors (e.g., smoking) and increased morbidity from cardiovascular disease as years in shiftwork increased. Occupations with a high percentage of shiftworkers are also associated with a greater risk of heart disease (Costa et al., 2000). In a recent meta-analysis of the epidemiological literature on shiftwork and heart disease, Bøggild and Knutsson (1999) reported that shiftworkers have a 40% greater risk for cardiovascular mortality or morbidity than day workers.

Similar to our discussion on the origin of gastrointestinal disorders in shiftworkers, the etiology of cardiovascular disorders is unknown (Åkerstedt & Knutsson, 1997). The risk factors for cardiovascular disease are consistent with many of the problems associated with shiftwork, such as gastrointestinal symptoms, sleeping dysfunction, smoking, and poor working conditions (i.e., those found in many industrial environments). Shiftwork can also function as a stressor, thus exacerbating the stress response over time and resulting in increased blood pressure, heart rate, cholesterol, and alterations in glucose and lipid metabolism (Costa, 1996).

In a study of more than 2,000 Swedish men, Peter, Alfredsson, Knutsson, Siegrist, and Westerholm (1999) reported that, in addition to the direct effects of shiftwork on cardiovascular risk, psychosocial work factors in the form of effort–reward imbalance mediated the effects of shiftwork on cardiovascular risk. Therefore, the evidence to date strongly suggests that shiftwork is a contributing factor in the development of cardiovascular disease, but the specific etiology is complex and multifaceted.

Women's Reproductive Disorders

The influence of night and shiftwork on women's reproductive functions has been empirically investigated in several studies (Costa, 1996). Given that shiftwork disrupts periodic or cyclic functions, such as sleep and digestion, its negative effects on the female menstrual cycle are not surprising. In female shiftworkers, these effects include irregularities in cycle length or pattern (Hatch, Figa-Talamanca, & Salerno, 1999; Uehata & Sasakawa, 1982), spontaneous abortions, and lower rates of pregnancies and deliveries (Nurminen, 1989). Shiftwork has also been associated with premature delivery and low birthweight (Nurminen, 1989).

In addition to coping with shiftwork, women frequently experience additional stress from domestic and childcare responsibilities. Female shiftworkers with children appear to be especially at risk, because research has shown that they have shorter and more frequently interrupted daytime sleep periods (Dekker & Tepas, 1990) and report greater tiredness than other groups of shiftworkers (Uehata & Sasakawa, 1982). However, some research has not found gender differences (Härmä, 1993).

Review of Empirical Literature on Shiftwork Tolerance

In the previous section, we discussed the manner in which shiftwork directly affects women's reproductive health. Another way of expressing this idea is to say that gender moderates the shiftwork–strain relationship, such that shiftwork adversely influences reproductive functions. Other individual (e.g., age, personality), as well as situational (e.g., type of shift system) variables also moderate the shiftwork–health strain relationship. Often, however, these variables are treated analytically as predictors (main effects) rather than moderators (interactive effects). The criterion is generally operationalized as "shiftwork tolerance," which is defined as the absence of the most common health-related complaints of shiftwork, such as sleep disturbances and gastrointestinal complaints (Härmä, 1993). We examine each characteristic in turn as it relates to health or shiftwork tolerance.

Individual Factors

Researchers have investigated the relationhips between several personal-level factors and the experience of shiftwork. We examine only those variables that have demonstrated the most consistent relationships.

Age. Over the age of 45 to 50, shiftworkers increasingly encounter difficulties in altering their sleep–wake cycles (Härmä, 1993; Nachreiner, 1998). Specifically, with aging, people experience a decrease in slow wave (deep) sleep, an increase in stage 1 (light) sleep, and an increase in the number and length of arousals during sleep (Miles & Dement, 1980). The physiological effects of aging are also associated with a reduction in amplitude and a tendency toward internal desynchronization of circadian rhythms (Costa et al., 2000; Härmä, 1993, 1996). Aging is also related to morning orientation, or the expressed preference for morning or early day activity (see next section), such that the circadian activity peak occurs almost two hours earlier in elderly relative to younger people (Lieberman, Wurtman, & Teicher, 1989). All of these changes in circadian functioning imply that shift changes and night work are inadvisable for shiftworkers over 50.

In addition, health problems increase with advancing age, and the effect of shiftwork generally is to increase that health risk or decrease shiftwork tolerance (Nachreiner, 1998; Tepas, Duchon, & Gersten, 1993) by further disrupting circadian functions and sleep. An interesting finding reported by Oginska, Pokorski, and Oginski (1993) is that female shiftworkers' reports of subjective health improved after age 50, whereas the opposite was true for males. This gender difference may reflect the decreased child-care and domestic responsibilities of older women. Another study cited similar reasons for the increased alertness and decreased sleep difficulties reported by older female shiftworkers compared to their younger counterparts (Spelten, Totterdell, Barton, & Folkard, 1995).

Morningness and circadian type. Morningness (morning–evening orientation) is defined as the expressed preference for morning or evening activities; the guiding assumption is that people who express preferences for activities at the extremes of the 24-hour day (i.e., early morning or late evening), when feasible, behave in accord with those preferences (Horne & Östberg, 1976; C. Smith, Reilly, & Midkiff, 1989).

Research has demonstrated that preference for early morning activity is related to phase advances (i.e., earlier circadian peaks), whereas preference for late evening activity is related to phase delays (i.e., later circadian peaks). Morning types are therefore thought to be especially suited to morning or early day shifts and evening types to evening or late-night shifts (see Tankova, Adan, & Buela-Casal, 1994). Morningness is also related to rigidity in sleep habits, or the inability to change sleep schedules, which is especially true for extreme morning types (Hildebrandt & Stratmann, 1979). However, empirical evidence indicates that morningness is only weakly to moderately related to health strains or shiftwork tolerance (e.g., Bohle & Tilley, 1989; Steele, Ma, Watson, & Thomas, 2000), but several conflicting studies do exist (e.g., Costa, Lievore, Casaletti, Gaffuri, & Folkard, 1989; Kaliterna, Vidacek, Prizmic, & Radosevic-Vidacek, 1995).

The notion of circadian type was created by Folkard, Monk, and Lobban (1979) to address other characteristics of circadian rhythms than phase (morningness). The construct rigidity–flexibility was developed to assess the stability of circadian rhythms, and the construct vigor–languidity, the amplitude of the rhythms. Folkard et al. (1979) hypothesized that flexibility–rigidity, or the flexibility of one's sleeping habits, and vigor–languidity, or one's ability to overcome drowsiness, are important contributors to adjustment to shiftwork; specifically, people with flexible- and low-amplitude rhythms should better adjust to the demand of shiftwork. Both the flexibility and vigor dimensions have been reported to relate to long-term tolerance to shiftwork (Costa et al., 1989; Vidacek, Kaliterna, & Radosevic-Vidacek, 1987). In fact, in Vidacek et al.'s (1987) prospective study, vigor was the best predictor of shiftwork tolerance after three years. More recent studies have also supported the relationship between flexibility and vigor and shiftwork tolerance (e.g., Steele et al., 2000).

These individual differences in circadian rhythms have helped researchers to understand why some people prefer, and presumably adapt better to, different shift schedules. However, the use of morningness or circadian-type measures as selection or placement instruments for night workers and shiftworkers would be premature because relevant validation data are lacking, although they may be helpful in shiftwork counseling and education programs.

Personality. Researchers have investigated other individual differences as they relate to shiftwork tolerance. Introversion–extroversion is a well-known personality variable that, similar to morningness, has demonstrated relationships with circadian phase. Specifically, introverts have a somewhat earlier circadian phase (i.e., are more morning-oriented) than extroverts (Blake, 1967; Vidacek et al., 1987). Circadian adjustment to shift schedules also seems to occur faster in extroverts than introverts (Colquhoun & Condon, 1980).

Likewise, researchers have reported a relationship between neuroticism and shiftwork tolerance across several studies, such that shiftworkers who are very neurotic are less tolerant to shiftwork (e.g., Iskra-Golec, Marek, & Noworol, 1995). However, neuroticism does not appear to predict shiftwork tolerance (Kaliterna et al., 1995). Some evidence even suggests that neuroticism increases with exposure to shiftwork, and hence, behaves more like an outcome or strain measure than a moderator variable (Bohle & Tilley, 1989).

Situational Factors: Shift System Characteristics

The relative merits of different types of shift systems (i.e., Is there one best type of shift system?) have probably been debated more than any other issue in shiftwork research. The debate has often focused on the advantages and disadvantages of fixed versus rotating systems or different types of rotating systems (e.g., Folkard, 1992; Wedderburn, 1992; Wilkinson, 1992). Although the general consensus is that no best shift system exists, shiftwork researchers agree that some systems are definitely worse than others. To simplify this discussion, we examine each of the major components of shift systems (fixed versus rotating, length of rotation, direction of rotation, number of days off, number of night shifts, length of shift, weekly hours, annual hours, and overtime).

Regarding health effects, fixed shifts are certainly preferable for day or afternoon shifts because workers can easily maintain their diurnal orientation. However, shiftworkers on permanent night shifts rarely achieve adaptation to their hours of work because, on their rest days, they typically revert back to a diurnal (day) orientation to engage in social or family activities. So, in effect, permanent night workers create their own rotating shift because they must physiologically readapt to night work and day sleep after every rest period (Folkard, 1992).

Rotating shifts present a wide array of options. One of the most common rotating shifts is the weekly rotation, in which shiftworkers change their shift schedule every week. Unfortunately, the weekly rotating shift is also one of the worst from a circadian perspective: Just as the shiftworker's body is beginning to adapt (i.e., the circadian rhythms are only partially inverted), the shift changes, and adaptation must begin again. (Adaptation to an 8-hour change usually requires 10 to 14 days, if it occurs at all.) Very slowly rotating shifts (e.g., every 3 to 4 weeks) are acceptable, providing shiftworkers adapt to and maintain their current schedule (again, an unlikely assumption). When primarily considering circadian effects, most shiftwork researchers advocate the rapidly rotating shift (i.e., every 2 to 3 days). Such a rapid rotation limits the number of consecutive night shifts, thus permitting shiftworkers to retain a diurnal orientation. Therefore, no readaptation to a new shift is required, and night work must be endured for only a few days, thus circumventing chronic sleep deprivation (Folkard, 1992; Knauth, 1993).

The direction of the rotation is another shift characteristic that may influence the physiological adaptation to the shift schedule (see Knauth, 1993, for a review; Totterdell & Folkard, 1990). A shift system that progresses from morning to evening to night shift is a forward-rotating system because it rotates in a clockwise fashion (phase delay); a shift system that progresses from night to evening to morning shifts is a backward-rotating system because it rotates in a counterclockwise system (phase advance). The forward-rotating system is preferable physiologically because it complements the body's endogenous circadian rhythms, which have a cycle of slightly more than 24 hours. In other words, a forward-rotating system is equivalent to flying west, thus gaining time. The existing data favor the forward-rotating system's hypothesized superiority, especially in terms of less fatigue, higher alertness, and fewer sleep disturbances (e.g., Barton & Folkard, 1993; Tucker, Smith, Macdonald, & Folkard, 2000). However, too few studies have compared forward and backward rotating systems to permit any generalization (Tucker et al., 2000).

When designing shift schedules, the number of days off between shifts and the number of night shifts must be considered (Knauth, 1993). Sufficient time off between shifts is necessary to reduce sleep debt and fatigue and maintain well-being. After more than two to three days on the night shift, several days of leisure time may be needed to recuperate before the next shift (e.g., Tepas & Mahan, 1989; Totterdell, Spelten, Smith, Barton, & Folkard, 1995).

The effects of shift length, usually 8 versus 12 hours, have been debated without resolution. The 12-hour shift or compressed work week has been very popular in industry and health care because this type of compressed schedule permits longer blocks of free or leisure time. However, in 12-hour shifts, increased fatigue, particularly toward the end of the shift, is a major concern; if the shift involves night work, these effects can be exacerbated. Shiftwork researchers therefore recommend that 12-hour night shifts be limited to one or two consecutive nights. Longer shifts also permit longer exposure to environmental toxins, such as industrial by-products; most threshold values are based on an 8-hour working day, and the risk for a 12-hour day (longer exposure) is rarely unknown (Knauth, 1993).

Despite these limitations, empirical comparisons of the health- and sleep-related effects of 12-hour shift systems have generally been positive (e.g., Johnson & Sharit, 2001; Mitchell & Williamson, 2000; Williamson et al., 1994), with a few exceptions (e.g., Bourdouxhe et al., 1999). In a recent review of the research evaluating shift length, Smith, Folkard, Tucker, and Macdonald (1998) also concluded that shiftworkers on 12-hour shifts, compared to those on 8-hour shifts, do not experience greater difficulties with sleep, health, and well-being, and may even show improvements. They cautioned, however, that several factors need to be taken into account in each case before adopting 12-hour systems. Specifically, older shiftworkers may be at greater risk for excessive fatigue and medical complaints. Shiftworkers who must perform physically demanding tasks, endure exposure to toxic substances, or cope with an accumulation of job-related stressors (e.g., noise) may also be at greater risk.

Excessive weekly hours, annual hours, and overtime are critical factors to consider in the workplace, especially for shiftworkers (Spurgeon, Harrington, & Cooper, 1997). In their meta-analyses on the effects of hours of work on health, Sparks, Cooper, Fried, and Shirom (1997) reported small, but significant, positive mean correlations between health symptoms, physiological and psychological health symptoms, and hours of work. The authors cautioned, however, that these correlations may be underestimates because of the degree of aggregation necessary to conduct the meta-analyses. For example, the physiological measures included mild (e.g., headaches) to serious health symptoms (e.g., myocardial infarction), some of which showed stronger relationships with hours of work than others. This issue has become especially salient with the popularity of 12-hour shifts, which afford shiftworkers sufficient free time to "moonlight" or obtain alternate employment; their schedule also permits them to "double-shift," or work two shifts if needed. The problems of excessive fatigue, sleep deficits, and overexposure to workplace toxins may become very serious in these situations, and the shiftworkers in question should be closely monitored.

Interventions to Improve Shiftworkers' Health and Effectiveness

The most common shiftwork intervention, manipulations or changes in shift system characteristics, has been discussed in some depth in a previous section and therefore is only briefly discussed here. Other attempts to improve the shiftworker's adaptation include the ingestion of pharmaceutical agents, exposure to bright lights, and education and counseling programs.

Manipulations of Shift System Characteristics

Because of the ongoing controversy regarding the optimal combination of shift system characteristics for health and well-being, shiftwork experts have explored this issue in some depth. Much of the research we discussed in the section on shift-system characteristics attempted to manipulate some aspect of a shift system to determine the effects of those changes. For many of these shift characteristic comparisons, researchers collected cross-sectional data at one point in time and compared these data, assuming that any health-related differences could be attributed to the different shift characteristics (e.g., Barton & Folkard, 1993). Few longitudinal studies have been published, although longitudinal research, with appropriate pre- and postassessments, has increased with the recent interest in the relative merits of 12-hour shift systems (e.g., Lowden, Kecklund, Axelsson, & Åkerstedt, 1998; Mitchell & Williamson, 2000).

Melatonin

Probably the most widely publicized shiftwork intervention involves the introduction of sleep aids to enhance on-shift adaptation. For decades, shiftworkers have used pharmacological aids to improve sleep, diminish fatigue, and enhance alertness, although long-term use of many of these drugs is not advisable because of potential side-effects (Walsh, 1990). Melatonin, the latest pharmacological sleep aid, seems to avoid the pitfalls of the earlier hypnotics. Melatonin is a pineal hormone that is present in humans and other species, and its purpose in the body is to initiate sleep. Because melatonin is a substance normally found in the body, administering it to control the onset of sleep does not introduce some of the negative effects experienced with other drugs. Numerous controlled clinical studies have demonstrated the efficacy and safety of melatonin in enhancing sleep and adaptation to new shift schedules or time zones (Arendt & Deacon, 1997).

The use of melatonin, however, is not without problems. For example, if taken at the wrong time of day, it may actually impair sleep and adaptation. Melatonin is not a controlled drug, so the purity (and therefore safety) of the various over-the-counter preparations is unknown. Interactions between melatonin and other drugs have also not been explored. Therefore, shiftworkers, who may need long-term use of melatonin, are advised to take it only under medical supervision (Arendt & Deacon, 1997).

Bright Lights

Another modern intervention to aid adaptation to shift changes is the administration of bright lights. More than 20 years ago, researchers discovered that exposure to very bright light (2500 lux; indoor illumination is about 500 lux) could suppress the normal nocturnal secretion of melatonin and therefore delay sleep and entrain human circadian rhythms (see Eastman, 1990, for a review of the early research). These effects have also been demonstrated in field settings with shiftworkers (e.g., Stewart, Hayes, & Eastman, 1995). Some results, however, have been mixed and inconsistent (e.g., Budnick, Lerman, & Nicolich, 1995). To achieve the desired effects, shiftworkers must follow, and their employing organizations must support, a strict schedule of exposure to bright light over time. The allocation of resources to achieve this outcome can be considerable, and therefore bright

light exposure has not achieved the popularity of over-the-counter melatonin to enhance adaptation to shift changes and night work.

Education and Counseling Programs

Education and counseling programs have been used to impart information
that can aid adaptation to shiftwork. Programs or workshops that deliver
mostly general information about shiftwork and its effects on human functioning, as well as recommendations for coping with these issues, have
been reported, for example, for emergency room physicians (Smith-Coggins,
Rosekind, Buccino, Dinges, & Moser, 1997). Smith-Coggins and colleagues
devised a well-controlled study using both objective and subjective criteria
to assess the effectiveness of the workshop they presented to a group of
physicians. However, their results indicated that, although the physicians
in the experimental group used the strategies they learned 85% of the time
according to their log book entries, the intervention did not significantly
improve the criteria (performance and mood).

The disappointing results in this well-controlled study support Tepas's
(1993) argument that educational information alone is often not particularly helpful, and in some cases may actually be misleading or confusing.
The workshop content usually has face validity but questionable criterion-
related validity, or the assessment of the workshop material relative to its
ability to change important criteria (e.g., sleep, mood; see Smith-Coggins
et al., 1997). Tepas maintained that educational workshops are best used
in the context of a larger effort to improve the existing shift schedule. Such
a process was used by Sakai, Watanabe, and Kogi (1993); they used an
educational program to aid them in analyzing, planning, and implementing
an improved shift rotation schedule in a disabled persons' facility.

In a similar vein, Wedderburn and Scholarios (1993) collected shiftworkers' opinions on guidelines for shiftworkers that were developed by a
team of European shiftwork experts and published as the *Bulletin of Shiftwork Topics No. 3.* Six of the 24 guidelines focused at the personal level
were supported by a majority of the shiftworkers (e.g., on shiftwork, "I
avoid taking sleeping pills," "I avoid alcohol before sleeping") and six were
opposed by a majority (e.g., when working nights, "I use earplugs in bed",
"I avoid eating fatty foods"). These types of guidelines often have been, in
some form, incorporated into shiftwork legislation, which we discuss next.

Shiftwork Legislation

Shiftwork legislation has been developed by the European community to
guard the health and safety of shiftworkers. For example, the International
Labour Organisation (ILO) Night Work Convention (No. 171) and Recommendation (No. 178) concerning Night Work (1990) and the European Directive 93/104 deals with "certain aspects of the organisation of working time."
This document discusses specific measures for nightworkers, such as health

assessments before assignment to night work, reassessments at regular intervals, and reassessments in case of health complaints. Other issues include transferring workers out of night work and into day work for health reasons, limiting the average hours worked per week to 48, including overtime, and providing a minimum rest period of 11 hours per day and 24 hours per week. Several European countries (France, Germany, Austria, Portugal, the United Kingdom, and the Netherlands) have already passed laws that conform to this directive (Costa et al., 2000).

International regulations have also dealt with equality of treatment for female shiftworkers, consideration of job design factors, expanded health and safety measures, and participatory practices for introducing change in the workplace (Kogi, 1998; Kogi & Thurman, 1993). When treated as law, these directives and regulations should have a profound influence on the health of night and shiftworkers by limiting some of the most dangerous practices. Unfortunately, beyond the Occupational Health and Safety Act (OSHA) of 1971, which requires employers to provide a workplace "free from recognized hazards likely to cause death or serious physical harm to [their] employees," no legislation has been specifically targeted toward night or shiftworkers in the United States.

Conclusion

Our goal in this chapter was to explore the relationships between shiftwork and health. The research evidence clearly indicates that the experience of shiftwork adversely affects sleep, promotes fatigue, and is associated with the occurrence of accidents and injuries. Shiftwork is also related to the development of psychological, gastrointestinal, cardiovascular, and women's reproductive disorders. Although the data are largely not causal, the convergence of the evidence is strongly suggestive. To further complicate this issue, a number of individual (e.g., age, personality) and situational (e.g., amount of night work) characteristics may influence shiftworkers' health. For example, a shiftworker over 50 who is on a fixed night shift is at greater health risk than younger shiftworkers who are on day or evening shifts. The most destructive component is the amount of night work, not simply shiftwork, and the impact of night work increases over time. A number of interventions, with varying degrees of success, have also been developed to ease the plight of shiftworkers (e.g., melatonin ingestion, educational and counseling programs).

The final report is distinctly negative: Shiftwork, and especially night work, which disrupts the human circadian system, is associated with increased health risk for minor and life-threatening disorders. Regardless of its impact on health, however, shiftwork will remain as a necessary way of structuring work because of the current and future demands of society. On a positive note, we have considerable knowledge at our disposal to address these issues. Therefore, our task as researchers and practitioners is to improve research and the tools (e.g., interventions) we develop from that research. Toward that end, we offer a few suggestions.

Because most shiftwork research is cross-sectional, researchers sample from a workforce in which an unknown number of shiftworkers have already transferred out of shiftwork for health or personal reasons. As a consequence, only the "successful" shiftworkers remain in shiftwork. The result is that researchers may greatly underestimate the negative impact of shiftwork (a sobering thought!); conversely, studies of former shiftworkers may overestimate the negative impact of shiftwork (Costa et al., 2000). This fact is important to recall when interpreting effect sizes in shiftwork research.

Another problem has been the lack of standardized measures to use in shiftwork research, which often makes comparisons across studies difficult. To address this issue, Barton et al., (1995) proposed a battery of self-report instruments, the Standard Shiftwork Index (SSI), to be used in shiftwork research. Some of the measures in this battery have been widely used in other areas of research (e.g., personality inventories) and some are fairly specific to shiftwork research (e.g., morningness scales). The authors considered such issues as scale length, ease of administration, and scale psychometric properties when developing the SSI. The scales fall into three areas: (a) general, contextual variables (e.g., timing and duration of shifts, workload); (b) outcomes or criteria (e.g., digestive symptoms, job satisfaction); (c) and modifiers or moderators (e.g., morningness, coping strategies).

Barton and her colleagues tested the SSI in large samples of nurses and industrial workers. Their results were used to generate a normative database, validity coefficients based on hypothesized relationships among the variables, and other psychometric data, such as scale-factor analyses. Over the past five years, various parts of the SSI have been used by shiftwork researchers (e.g., Tucker et al., 1996), and we strongly suggest that researchers consider using the battery in their future investigations.[1]

Personal control is yet another important issue in shiftwork research and practice. Psychologists have long known that personal control and choice are critical to maintain psychological and physical health and well-being (e.g., Folkman, 1984). It is not surprising that shiftwork researchers have discovered that the opportunity to exert individual control over the selection of the hours or shift one works is important in achieving shiftwork tolerance (e.g., Barton, 1994; Barton et al., 1993). Therefore, individual choice or participation in the design of actual shift schedules should increase acceptance and positive attitudes toward the shift system (e.g., Sakai et al., 1993).

Knauth (1997) stated that "a 'tailor-made' shift system should be a compromise between the employer's goals, the wishes of the employee, and ergonomic recommendations for the design of the shift systems." According to Knauth, only management's goals and ergonomic features have traditionally been considered when designing shift systems. However, if the new system is to achieve a high acceptance among shiftworkers, then a participatory process (i.e., their input) in the design and implementation of the new system is as necessary as the ergonomic features of the shift system. In

---

[1]The SSI can be obtained by contacting Simon Folkard.

fact, shiftwork experts consider worker participation in the design and implementation of shift systems to be so universally appropriate that it has been incorporated into international shiftwork regulations and directives (Kogi, 1998).

Perhaps the most neglected topic, however, is the role extraorganizational factors play in shiftworkers' mental and physical health. Although the importance of domestic and social factors has been discussed in previous reviews of shiftwork and health and shiftwork tolerance (e.g., Costa et al., 2000; Härmä, 1996), studies on such topics are rare (e.g., Smith & Folkard, 1993). This dearth of research is surprising, given that the most frequent complaint of shiftworkers is that shiftwork interferes with their personal lives (e.g., Bohle & Tilley, 1998; Monk, 1989). On a more sobering note, Tepas et al. (1985) reported that divorces and separations were 50% more frequent in night workers than in other groups of workers.

In conclusion, decades of research indicate that shiftworkers are at greater health risk than comparable day workers. Using that knowledge, researchers have designed interventions to alleviate the risk. In the twenty-first century, our goals as applied researchers should be to improve and augment our research and the interventions developed from it.

References

Åkerstedt, T., & Knutsson, A. (1997). Cardiovascular disease and shift work. *Scandinavian Journal of Work, Environment and Health, 23*, 241–242.

Angersbach, D., Knauth, P., Loskant, H., Karvonen, M. J., Undeutsch, K., & Rutenfranz, J. (1980). A retrospective cohort study comparing complaints and diseases in day and shift workers. *International Archives of Occupational and Environmental Health, 45*, 127–140.

Arendt, J., & Deacon, S. (1997). Treatment of circadian rhythm disorders—melatonin. *Chronobiology International, 14*, 185–204.

Aschoff, J., & Wever, R. A. (1962). Spontanperiodik des Menschen bei Ausschluss aller Zeitgeber. *Naturwissenschaften, 49*, 337–342.

Barreto, S. M., Swerdlow, A. J., Smith, P. G., & Higgins, C. D. (1997). Risk of death from motor-vehicle injury in Brazilian steelworkers: A nested case-control study. *International Journal of Epidemiology 26*, 814–821.

Barton, J. (1994). Choosing to work at night: A moderating influence on individual tolerance to shift work. *Journal of Applied Psychology, 79*, 449–454.

Barton, J., & Folkard, S. (1993). Advanced versus delaying shift systems. *Ergonomics, 36*, 59–64.

Barton, J., Smith, L., Totterdell, P., Spelten, E., & Folkard, S. (1993). Does individual choice determine shift system acceptability? *Ergonomics, 36*, 93–99.

Barton, J., Spelten, E., Totterdell, P., Smith, L., Folkard, S., & Costa, G. (1995). The Standard Shiftwork Index—A battery of questionnaires for assessing shiftwork-related problems. *Work and Stress, 9*, 4–30.

Blake, M. J. (1967). Relationship between circadian rhythm of body temperature and introversion–extraversion. *Nature, 215*, 896–897.

Bøggild, H., & Knutsson, A. (1999). Shift work, risk factors and cardiovascular disease. *Scandinavian Journal of Work, Environment and Health, 25*, 85–99.

Bohle, P., & Tilley, A. J. (1989). The impact of night work on psychological well-being. *Ergonomics, 32*, 1089–1099.

Bohle, P., & Tilley, A. J. (1998). Early experience of shiftwork: Influences on attitudes. *Journal of Occupational and Organizational Psychology, 71*, 61–79.

Bourdouxhe, M. A., Queinnec, Y., Granger, D., Baril, R. H., Guertin, S. C., Massicotte, P. R., Levy, M., & Lemay, F. L. (1999). Aging and shiftwork: The effects of 20 years of rotating 12-hour shifts among petroleum refinery operators. *Experimental Aging Research, 25,* 323–329.

Budnick, L. D., Lerman, S. E., & Nicolich, M. J. (1995). An evaluation of scheduled bright light and darkness on rotating shiftworkers: trial and limitations. *Journal of Industrial Medicine, 27,* 71–82.

Colquhoun, W. P., & Condon, R. (1980). Introversion–extroversion and the adaptation of the body-temperature rhythm to night work. *Chronobiologia, 7,* 428.

Costa, G. (1996). The impact of shift and night work on health. *Applied Ergonomics, 27,* 9–16.

Costa, G., Folkard, S., & Harrington, J. M. (2000). Shift work and extended hours of work. In P. Baxter, P. H. Adams, T-C. Aw, A. Cockcroft, & J. M. Harrington (Eds.), *Hunter's diseases of occupations* (9th ed., pp. 581–589). London: Arnold.

Costa, G., Lievore, F., Casaletti, G., Gaffuri, E., & Folkard, S. (1989). Circadian characteristics influencing interindividual differences in tolerance and adjustment to shiftwork. *Ergonomics, 32,* 373–385.

Czeisler, C. A., Weitzman, E. D., Moore-Ede, M. C., Zimmerman, J. C., & Kronauer, R. S. (1980). Human sleep: Its duration and organization depend on its circadian phase. *Science, 210,* 1264–1267.

Dekker, D. K., & Tepas, D. I. (1990). Gender differences in permanent shiftworker sleep behavior. In G. Costa, G. Cesana, K. Kogi, & A. Wedderburn (Eds.), *Shiftwork: Health, sleep, and performance* (pp. 77–82). Frankfurt: Peter Lang.

Eastman, C. I. (1990). Circadian rhythms and bright light: Recommendations for shift work. *Work and Stress, 4,* 245–260.

Folkard, S. (1992). Is There A 'Best Compromise' Shift System? *Ergonomics, 35,* 1453–1463.

Folkard, S., Åkerstedt, T., Macdonald, I., Tucker, P., & Spencer, M. (2000). Refinement of the three-process model of alertness to account for trends in accident risk. In S. Hornberger, P. Knauth, G. Costa, & S. Folkard (Eds.), *Shiftwork in the 21st century: Challenge for research and practice* (pp. 49–54). Frankfurt am Main: Peter Lang.

Folkard, S., Monk, T. H., & Lobban, M. (1979). Towards a predictive test of adjustment to shiftwork. *Ergonomics, 22,* 79–91.

Folkman, S. (1984). Personal control and stress and coping processes: A theoretical analysis. *Journal of Personality and Social Psychology, 46,* 839–852.

Härmä, M. (1993). Individual differences in tolerance to shiftwork: A review. *Ergonomics, 36,* 101–109.

Härmä, M. (1996). Aging, physical fitness, and shiftwork tolerance. *Applied Ergonomics, 27,* 25–29.

Hatch, M. C., Figa-Talamanca, I., & Salerno, S. (1999). Work stress and menstrual patterns among American and Italian nurses. *Scandinavian Journal of Work, Environment and Health, 25,* 144–150.

Hildebrandt, G., & Stratmann, I. (1979). Circadian system response to night work in relation to the individual circadian phase position. *International Archives of Occupational and Environmental Health, 43,* 73–83.

Horne, J. A., & Östberg, O. (1976). A self-assessment questionnaire to determine morningness-eveningness in human circadian rhythms. *International Journal of Chronobiology, 4,* 97–110.

Iskra-Golec, I., Marek, T., & Noworol, C. (1995). Interactive effect of individual factors on nurses; health and sleep. *Work and Stress, 9,* 256–261.

Johnson, M. D., & Sharit, J. (2001). Impact of a change from an 8-h to a 12-h shift schedule on workers and occupational injury rates. *International Journal of Industrial Ergonomics, 27,* 303–319.

Kaliterna, L., Vidacek, S., Prizmic, Z., & Radosevic-Vidacek, B. (1995). Is tolerance to shiftwork predictable from individual difference measures? *Work and Stress, 9,* 140–147.

Knauth, P. (1993). The design of shift systems. *Ergonomics, 36,* 15–28.

Knauth, P. (1997). *Changing schedules: shiftwork. Chronobiology International, 14,* 159–171.

Knutsson, A., Åkerstedt, T., Jonsson, B. G., & Orth-Gomer, K. (1986). Increased risk of ischemic heart disease in shift workers. *Lancet, 2,* 89–92.

Kogi, K. (1998). International regulations on the organization of shift work. *Scandinavian Journal of Work, Environment and Health, 24,* 7–12.

Kogi, K., & Thurman, J. E. (1993). Trends in approaches to night and shiftwork and new international standards. *Ergonomics, 36,* 3–13.

Lennernäs, M., Hambraeus, L., & Åkerstedt, T. (1994). Nutrient intake in day workers and shift works. *Work & Stress, 8,* 332–342.

Lieberman, H. R., Wurtman, J. J., & Teicher, M. H. (1989). Aging, nutrient choice, activity, and behavioral responses to nutrients. *Annals of the New York Academy of Sciences, 561,* 196–208.

Lowden, A., Kecklund, G., Axelsson, J., & Åkerstedt, T. (1998). Change from an 8-hour shift to a 12-hour shift, attitudes, sleep, sleepiness and performance. *Scandinavian Journal of Work Environment and Health, 24,* 69–75.

Luna, T. D., French, J., & Mitcha, J. L. (1997). A study of USAF air traffic controller shiftwork: sleep, fatigue, activity, and mood analyses. *Aviation Space and Environmental Medicine, 68,* 18–23.

Lund, R. (1974). Personality factors and desynchronization of circadian rhythms. *Psychosomatic Medicine, 36,* 224–228.

Miles, L. E., & Dement, W. C. (1980). Sleep and aging. *Sleep, 3,* 1–220.

Minors, D. S., & Waterhouse, J. M. (1981). *Circadian Rhythms and the Human.* Bristol: Wright PSG.

Mitchell, R. J., & Williamson, A. M. (2000). Evaluation of an 8 hour versus a 12 hour shift roster on employees at a power station. *Applied Ergonomics, 31,* 83–93.

Monk, T. H. (1989). Human factors implications of shiftwork. *International Review of Ergonomics, 3,* 111–128.

Monk, T. H., Folkard, S., & Wedderburn, A. I. (1996). Maintaining safety and high performance on shiftwork. *Applied Ergonomics, 27,* 17–23.

Nachreiner, F. (1998). Individual and social determinants of shiftwork tolerance. *Scandinavian Journal of Work, Environment and Health, 24,* 35–42.

Nurminen, T. (1989). Shift work, fetal development and course of pregnancy. *Scandinavian Journal of Work, Environment and Health, 15,* 395–403.

Oginska, H., Pokorski, J., & Oginski, A. (1993). Gender, aging, and shiftwork intolerance. *Ergonomics, 36,* 161–168.

Peter, R., Alfredsson, L., Knutsson, A., Siegrist, J., & Westerholm, P. (1999). Does a stressful psychosocial work environment mediate the effects of shift work on cardiovascular risk factors? *Scandinavian Journal of Work, Environment and Health, 25,* 376–381.

Price, W. J., & Holley, D. C. (1990). Shiftwork and safety in aviation. *Occupational Medicine, 5,* 343–377.

Sakai, K., Watanabe, A., & Kogi, K. (1993). Educational and intervention strategies for improving a shift system: An experience in a disabled persons' facility. *Ergonomics, 36,* 219–225.

Siffre, M. (1964). *Beyond time.* (H. Briffault, Ed. and Trans.). New York: McGraw Hill.

Smith, C. S., Reilly, C., & Midkiff, K. (1989). Evaluation of three circadian rhythm questionnaires with suggestions for an improved measure of morningness. *Journal of Applied Psychology, 74,* 728–738.

Smith, C. S., Silverman, G. S., Heckert, T. M., Brodke, M. H., Hayes, B. E., Silverman, M. K., & Mattimore, L. K. (1997). Shift-related differences in industrial injuries: Application of a new research method in fixed-shift and rotating-shift systems. *International Journal of Occupational and Environmental Health, 3,* 46–52.

Smith, L., & Folkard, S. (1993). The perceptions and feelings of shiftworkers' partners. *Ergonomics, 35,* 299–305.

Smith, L., Folkard, S., & Poole, C. J. (1994). Increased injuries on night shift. *The Lancet, 244,* 1137–1139.

Smith, L., Folkard, S., Tucker, P., & Macdonald, I. (1998). Work shift duration: A review comparing eight hour and twelve hour shift systems. *Occupational and Environmental Medicine, 55,* 217–229.

Smith-Coggins, R., Rosekind, M. R., Buccino, K. R., Dinges, D. F., & Moser, R. P. (1997). Rotating shiftwork schedules: Can we enhance physician adaptation to night shifts? *Academic Emergency Medicine, 4,* 951–961.

Sparks, K., Cooper, C., Fried, Y., & Shirom, A. (1997). The effects of hours of work on health: A meta-analytic review. *Journal of Occupational and Organizational Psychology, 70,* 391–408.

Spelten, E., Totterdell, P., Barton, J., & Folkard, S. (1995). Effects of age and domestic commitment on the sleep and alertness of female shiftworkers. *Work and Stress, 9,* 165–175.

Spurgeon, A., Harrington, J. M., & Cooper, C. L. (1997). Health and safety problems associated with long working hours: A review of the current position. *Occupational and Environmental Medicine, 54,* 367–375.

Steele M. T., Ma, O. J., Watson, W. A., & Thomas, H. A. (2000). Emergency medicine residents' shiftwork tolerance and preference. *Academic Emergency Medicine, 7,* 670–673.

Stewart, K. T., Hayes, B. C., Eastman, C. I. (1995). Light treatment for NASA shiftworkers. *Chronobiology International, 12,* 141–151.

Tankova, I., Adan, A., & Buela-Casal, G. (1994). Circadian typology and individual differences—A review. *Personality and Individual Differences, 16,* 671–684.

Tepas, D. I. (1993). Educational programmes for shiftworkers, their families, and prospective shiftworkers. *Ergonomics, 36,* 199–209.

Tepas, D. I., Armstrong, D. R., Carlson, M. L., Duchon, J. C., Gersten, A., et al. (1985). Changing industry to continuous operations: Different strokes for different plants. *Behavior Research Methods, Instruments, and Computers, 17,* 670–676.

Tepas, D. I., & Carvalhais, A. B. (1990). Sleep patterns of shiftworkers. *Occupational Medicine: State of Art Review, 5,* 199–208.

Tepas, D. I., Duchon, J. C., & Gersten, A. H. (1993). Shiftwork and the older worker. *Experimental Aging Research, 19,* 295–320.

Tepas, D. I., & Mahan, R. P. (1989). The many meanings of sleep. *Work and Stress, 3,* 93–102.

Totterdell, P., & Folkard, S. (1990). The effects of changing from weekly rotating to a rapidly rotating shift schedule. In G. Costa, G. Cesana, K. Kogi, & A. Wedderburn (Eds.), *Shiftwork: Health, sleep, and performance* (pp. 646–650). Frankfurt: Peter Lang.

Totterdell, P., Spelten, E., Smith, L., Barton, J., & Folkard, S. (1995). Recovery from work shifts: How long does it take? *Journal of Applied Psychology, 80,* 43–57.

Tucker, P., Barton, J., & Folkard, S. (1996). Comparison of eight and twelve hour shifts: Impacts on health, well-being, and alertness during the shift. *Occupational Environmental Medicine, 53,* 767–772.

Tucker, P., Smith, L., Macdonald, I., & Folkard, S. (2000). Effects of direction of rotation in continuous and discontinuous eight hour shift systems. *Occupational and Environmental Medicine, 57,* 678–684.

U.S. Congress, Office of Technology Assessment. (1991). *Biological rhythms: Implications for the worker* (OTA-BA-463). Washington, DC: U.S. Government Printing Office.

Uehata, T., & Sasakawa, N. (1982). The fatigue and maternity disturbances of night workwomen. *Journal of Human Ergology, 11,* 465–474.

Vener, K. J., Szabo, S., & Moore, J. G. (1989). The effect of shift work on gastrointestinal (GI) function: A review. *Chronobiologia, 16,* 421–439.

Vidacek, S., Kaliterna, L., & Radosevic-Vidacek, B. (1987). Predictive validity of individual differences measures for health problems in shiftworkers: Preliminary results. In A. Oginski, J. Pokorski, & J. Rutenfranz (Eds.), *Contemporary advances in shiftwork research* (pp. 99–106). Krakow: Medical Academy.

Walsh, J. K. (1990). Using pharmacological aids to improve waking function and sleep while working at night. *Work and Stress, 4,* 237–243.

Wedderburn, A. I. (1992). How fast should the night shift rotate? A rejoinder. *Ergonomics 35,* 1447–1451.

Wedderburn, A. I. (1996). Statistics and news. *Bulletin of European Studies on Time No. 9. Dublin: European Foundation for the Improvement of Living and Working Conditions,* 1–72.

Wedderburn, A. I., & Scholarios, D. (1993). Guidelines for shiftworkers: Trials and errors? *Ergonomics, 36,* 211–217.

Wegmann, H-M., & Klein, K. E. (1985). Jet-lag and aircrew scheduling. In S. Folkard & T. H. Monk (Eds.), *Hours of work: Temporal factors in work scheduling* (pp. 263–276). Chichester, UK: Wiley.

Wever, R. A. (1979). *The circadian system of man: Results of experiments under temporal isolation.* New York: Springer.

Wilkinson, R. T. (1992). How fast should the night shift rotate? *Ergonomics, 35,* 1425–1446.

Williamson, A. M., Gower, C. G. I., & Clarke, B. C. (1994). Changing the hours of shiftwork: A comparison of 8- and 12-hour shift rosters in a group of computer operators. *Ergonomics, 37,* 287–298.

9

Occupational Stress: Job Pressures and Lack of Support

Charles D. Spielberger, Peter R. Vagg, and Carol F. Wasala

The effects of occupational stress on productivity, employee burnout, and health-related problems have received increasing attention during the past decade (e.g., Cooper & Cartwright, 1994; Karasek & Theorell, 1990; Quick, Quick, Nelson, & Hurrell, 1997; Spielberger & Reheiser, 1994; Turnage & Spielberger, 1991). In this research, the costs and consequences of job stress for both employees and organizations have been clearly demonstrated. Stress in the workplace has been linked to "the use of drugs and alcohol on the job, and counter productive behaviors such as . . . doing inferior work on purpose, stealing from employers, purposely damaging property . . . and various kinds of white collar crimes" (Ryland & Greenfeld, 1991, p. 43). The costs of occupational stress to U.S. business and industry is now more than $150 billion a year, according to Wright and Smye (1996).

Interest in and concerns about occupational stress have continued to increase during the 1990s. A study of American workers by the Northwestern National Life Insurance Company (1991) found that the proportion of employees who reported "feeling highly stressed" more than doubled between 1985 and 1990; two thirds of those surveyed reported significantly reduced productivity. In a follow-up study, 40% of the 1200 respondents reported that their jobs were so stressful that they experienced burnout (Northwestern National Life, 1992). Highly stressed employees were also more than twice as likely to suffer from stress-related medical problems. As a consequence, many organizations now recognize that overworked employees who are stressed out do not perform as well as those who enjoy their jobs and have time to relax (Fraser, 2001).

Increased concerns about job stress have stimulated numerous studies and helped to identify important sources of stress in the workplace (Quick et al., 1997). However, this research has been guided by theories that are often conflicting and that differ from study to study, resulting in diverse goals of investigation, conceptual confusion, and inconsistent research findings (Kasl, 1978; Schuler, 1980). Kahn and Byosiere (1992) have reviewed and evaluated the most influential models of occupational stress and summarized empirical findings relating to these models. Some investigators

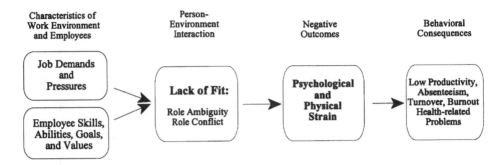

Figure 9.1. Person–Environment Fit (PE-Fit) Model for the study of occupational stress.

have focused on the pressures of a particular job, and others have been concerned primarily with the behavioral and health consequences of work-related stress (Schuler, 1991). The diverse models of occupational stress have also stimulated the construction of a variety of job stress measures. Therefore, to clarify and comprehend research on occupational stress, it is essential to understand both the conceptual models that have guided this research and the measures that have been developed to assess stress and strain in the workplace.

Conceptual Models of Stress in the Workplace

Kurt Lewin (1951) observed, more than a half century ago, that the characteristics of a person interact with environmental stressors to determine how much strain is experienced by an individual and the effects of strain on behavior and health. French, Kahn and their colleagues (French & Caplan, 1972; French, Caplan, & Harrison, 1982; French & Kahn, 1962; Kahn, Wolfe, Quinn, Snoeck, & Rosenthal, 1964) subsequently incorporated Lewin's concepts of stress and strain in their Person–Environment Fit (PE-Fit) theory, which became widely accepted as the major conceptual framework for research on occupational stress (Chemers, Hays, Rhodewalt, & Wysocki, 1985; Edwards & Cooper, 1990). In the context of PE-Fit theory, job stress results from an incompatible person–environment fit that produces psychological strain and stress-related medical and mental health problems (French et al., 1982).

Guided by PE-Fit theory, research on occupational stress has investigated organizational demands, job duties and requirements, job pressures, employee skills and abilities, job satisfaction, and individual differences in attitudes, personality traits, and health status (e.g., Beehr & Newman, 1978; Cooper, Kirkcaldy, & Brown, 1994; Cooper & Marshall, 1976; Marshall & Cooper, 1979). The PE-Fit model (French et al., 1982; Kahn & Byosiere, 1992), as it applies to the study of occupational stress, is outlined in Figure 9.1. When job demands and pressures in the work environment exceed the skills and abilities of an employee, or when these demands conflict with the employee's goals and values, this lack of fit contributes to work overload, role ambiguity, and conflicting role demands. The resulting psychological and physical strain may then lead to adverse behavioral consequences, such as lower productivity, absenteeism, turnover, employee burnout, and health-related problems.

PE-Fit concepts, especially role ambiguity and role conflict (Caplan, 1987; French et al., 1982; Kahn et al., 1964), have been investigated in numerous studies (e.g., Fisher & Gitelson, 1983; Hamner & Tosi, 1974; Keenan & Newton, 1984). Although the PE-Fit model appropriately emphasizes the interaction of the skills and abilities of the worker with the pressures and demands of the work environment, this model has been criticized because it lacks specificity, gives insufficient attention to specific sources of stress in the workplace (Edwards & Cooper, 1990), and "has not yielded a highly focused approach" (Chemers et al., 1985, p. 628). The adequacy of the PE-Fit model has also been questioned because it fails to identify important person and environmental variables (Schuler, 1980), and does not distinguish between different forms and types of fit (Eulberg, Weekley, & Bhagat, 1988; Ganster, Fusilier, & Mayes, 1986).

The Stress at Work model developed by Cooper and Marshall (1976; Marshall & Cooper, 1979) contributes to improving PE-Fit theory by identifying five major categories of occupational stress: (a) pressures intrinsic to the job itself; (b) the employee's role in the organization; (c) interpersonal relationships at work; (d) limitations in career development; and (e) organizational structure and climate. Pressures intrinsic to the job include difficult working conditions such as time pressures and work overload. Lack of clarity regarding the employee's organizational responsibilities contributes to role conflict and ambiguity. Stressful interpersonal relationships at work result from difficulties with supervisors, coworkers, and subordinates. Limitations in career development lead to concerns about job security and opportunity for advancement. Failure to recognize an employee's contributions and lack of participation in decision making are examples of stressors related to organizational structure and climate. The Stress at Work model also takes into account the personal characteristics of employees and the effects on occupational stress of life crises and family problems.

Karasek's (1979) Demand–Control model focuses on interactions between the objective demands of the work environment and the decision latitude of employees in meeting these demands (Karasek & Theorell, 1990). The combination of high job demands with relatively little control contributes to lowered productivity and a greater risk of health-related problems (Theorell & Karasek, 1996). The Demand–Control model also recognizes the importance of support from supervisors and coworkers (Karasek, Triantis, & Chaudhry, 1982). According to Karasek et al. (1998, p. 325), "Jobs which are high in demand, low in control, and also low in social support at work carry the highest risk of illness." However, control latitude is very difficult to measure, as was noted by Sauter and Hurrell (1989, p. xvi), who observed that "fundamental questions remain concerning the conceptualization and operationalization of the [control] construct." Similarly, Fletcher and Jones (1993) concluded that the Demand–Control model, "despite its popularity and intuitive appeal, has proved difficult to validate in the workplace" (p. 320).

The PE-Fit, Stress at Work, and Demand–Control models of occupational stress focus on the interactions of job pressures with the skills, abilities, and decision latitude of workers. While recognizing the importance of identifying specific sources of stress in the workplace, Kahn and Byosiere (1992) noted that these models do not give adequate consideration to the critical role of cognitive appraisal in mediating the effects of stressful working conditions on the emotional reactions of the worker. Edwards and Rothbard (1999) have also noted that the PE-Fit model needs to give greater attention to how employees' values, goals, and desires influence their appraisal of specific sources of job-related stress.

Lazarus's (1966) general model of psychological stress and coping conceptualizes stress as a process that involves a complex transaction between a person and her or his environment (Lazarus & Folkman, 1984). In applying his Transactional Process model to occupational stress, Lazarus (1991) emphasized the distinction between sources of stress in the workplace ("stressors") and the emotional reactions that are evoked when a particular stressor is cognitively appraised as threatening. Three types of appraisal mediate the effects of stressors on emotional reactions. (a) Primary appraisal occurs when a stressor is evaluated in terms of its immediate impact on a person's well-being. (b) Secondary appraisal takes into account the resources of the employee for coping with the stressor. (c) Reappraisal incorporates new information resulting from the worker's appraisal of the effectiveness of her or his efforts to cope with a particular stressor.

Spielberger's State–Trait Process (STP) model of occupational stress focuses on the perceived severity and frequency of occurrence of two major categories of stressor events, job pressures and lack of support. The STP model endeavors to integrate Lazarus's Transactional Process model with Spielberger's (1972) state–trait conception of anxiety and anger (Spielberger, Jacobs, Russell, & Crane, 1983; Spielberger, Krasner, & Solomon, 1988). The STP model also recognizes the importance of individual differences in personality traits in determining how workplace stressors are perceived and appraised. Consistent with Quick et al.'s (1997, p. 10) definition of occupational stress as "the mind body arousal resulting from the physical and/or psychological demands associated with the job," the appraisal of a stressor as threatening leads to the emotional arousal of anxiety and anger and the associated activation of the autonomic nervous system. If severe and persistent, the resulting psychological and physical strain may cause adverse behavioral consequences, such as employee burnout and health-related problems (Spielberger & Vagg, 1999; Vagg & Spielberger, 1998).

The PE-Fit, Stress at Work, Demand–Control, Transactional Process, and STP models are overlapping and complementary conceptualizations of stress in the workplace. These models have stimulated and guided the construction of a number of measures of occupational stress, which have been reviewed and evaluated by Murphy (1995), Quick et al. (1997), and Hurrell, Nelson, and Simmons (1998). Eight of the most widely used job stress measures are briefly described in the approximate chronological order of their publication. Each measure is considered within the context of the model(s) of occupational stress that guided its development.

Measurement of Occupational Stress

PE-Fit theory guided the development of the Work Environment Scale (WES), which was designed by Insel and Moos (1974) to measure organizational climate. The WES includes subscales that assess work pressures, interpersonal relationships among employees, and supervisory support (Moos, 1981). PE-Fit and Kahn et al.'s (1964) role stress theory contributed to the construction of the Stress Diagnostic Survey (SDS; Ivancevich & Matteson, 1976, 1980), an empirically developed comprehensive self-report inventory. The revised and expanded SDS (Ivancevich, Matteson, & Dorin, 1990) has been used to assess the frequency that specific sources of stress are experienced in a variety of occupations (e.g., flight attendants, computer operators, professional and managerial personnel).

Karasek's (1979) Demand–Control model provides the conceptual framework for the Job Content Questionnaire (JCQ), which was initially constructed to measure work-related social and psychological factors that contributed to cardiovascular disorders (Karasek, Schwartz, & Peiper, 1983). Widely used in research on job demands, decision latitude, skill use, and job dissatisfaction (Karasek et al., 1998; Karasek, Hulbert, & Simmerman, 1995), the JCQ also assesses supervisor and coworker support, depression, and sleeping problems (Hurrell et al., 1998). According to Theorell and Karasek (1996, p. 23), research with the JCQ has established a " . . . clear relationship between adverse job conditions (particularly low decision latitude) and coronary heart disease."

The Occupational Stress Inventory (OSInv) was developed by Osipow and his colleagues (Osipow, 1998; Osipow & Davis, 1988; Osipow, Doty, & Spokane, 1985; Osipow & Spokane, 1980, 1987) as a generic measure for the assessment of three major categories of PE-Fit variables: occupational role stress; psychological and physical strain; and coping resources. The OSInv includes scales for assessing role overload, role ambiguity, vocational strain, interpersonal strain, physical strain, self-care, and social support. This inventory has been widely used to compare the stress levels of a number of different occupational groups (Forney, 1982; Pelletier, 1983; Rayburn, Richmond, & Rogers, 1982) and to evaluate the effectiveness of stress management programs for reducing occupational stress and strain (Higgins, 1986).

The construction and validation of the Occupational Stress Indicator (OSInd; Cooper, Sloan, & Williams, 1988) was guided by Cooper and Marshall's (1976) Stress at Work model, which incorporates aspects of the PE-Fit, Demand–Control, and Transactional Process models. The six major dimensions of occupational stress assessed by the OSInd are job pressures, control over job pressures, job satisfaction, type-A personality, coping strategies, and physical and mental health problems. Recently revised and shortened by Williams and Cooper (1998), the OSInd has been renamed the

Pressure Management Indicator (PMI). Profiles based on PMI scores provide information on specific job pressures, differences in employee characteristics, and the effects of occupational stress on employee physical and mental health.

The STP model was applied by Spielberger and his colleagues in the development of measures to assess work-related stressors experienced by law enforcement officers and high school teachers (Grier, 1982; Spielberger, Grier, & Pate, 1980; Spielberger, Westberry, Grier, & Greenfield, 1981). Sixty stressor events were selected for the Police Stress Survey (PSS) on the basis of focused discussion groups with police officers. Of these stessors, 39 were found to be equally appropriate for teachers by simply substituting "teacher" and "school" for "police officer" and "department." Additional research demonstrated that 30 of the 39 stressors described generic, job-related events experienced by managerial, professional, and clerical employees in a wide range of business, industrial, and educational settings (Spielberger, 1991). In keeping with Murphy and Hurrell's (1987) recommendation that measures of occupational stress include a core set of stressors, these 30 items were selected for the Job Stress Survey (JSS; Spielberger, 1991; Spielberger & Vagg, 1999). The empirically based procedures that were used to identify the generic sources of stress assessed by the JSS were considered by Kasl (1998, p. 393) to be "phenomenologically faithful to the experience of workers."

The JSS assesses the perceived severity ("intensity") of 30 specific sources of occupational stress and how often each of these stressors was experienced in the work environment during the previous six months. A self-report questionnaire that assesses the intensity and frequency of stressful work events was also developed by Motowidlo, Packard, and Manning (1986). In a study of nurses working in a hospital setting, they found that ratings of perceived intensity and frequency of occurrence were associated with decrements in job performance. The Work Stress Inventory (WSI; Barone, 1994; Barone, Caddy, Katell, Roselione, & Hamilton, 1988) has separate scales for measuring the intensity and frequency of occurrence of organizational stress and job risk. The Organizational Stress scale of the WSI assesses job pressures and lack of support but does not distinguish between these concepts. The WSI Job Risk scale consists of items that are concerned primarily with aspects of the work environment that involve safety, physical exertion, and hazardous physical conditions.

The Generic Job Stress Questionnaire (GJSQ) was developed by researchers at the U.S. National Institute for Occupational Safety and Health (NIOSH) on the basis of a comprehensive review of the job stress literature (Hurrell & McLaney, 1988). The 13 GJSQ scales were either adapted from other job stress measures with demonstrated reliability and validity or constructed to assess job stress dimensions for which no valid measures were available (Hurrell et al., 1998). Influenced primarily by PE-Fit and Demand–Control theory, the GJSQ evaluates role conflict and ambiguity, job responsibilities, work load, skill use, and job demands and control. Job dissatisfaction, somatic problems, depression, and other sources of distress in the workplace are also assessed by the GJSQ.

In summary, measures of occupational stress provide information about a number of factors that influence stress in the workplace, which include physical and psychological strain, social support, and individual differences in ability, personality, and coping skills. Although all of these dimensions contribute to our understanding of the nature and impact of occupational stress, the omnibus nature of most job stress measures are both sources of strength and significant concern (Hurrell et al., 1998; Kasl, 1998). The items included in several of the most widely used measures of occupational stress are also lengthy and multidimensional in content and inquire about group reactions rather than the stress experienced by a particular respondent (Williams & Cooper, 1998). The use of Likert-type scales to assess the extent of agreement or disagreement with an item statement also seems more appropriate for measuring attitudes, values, or personality characteristics than for evaluating sources of stress in the workplace. Interpreting the findings obtained with most measures of occupational stress is further complicated because the perceived severity of a particular stressor tends to be confounded with how often the stressor was experienced (Hurrell et al., 1998). As Dewe (1989, p. 993) has observed, "When measuring work stressors, more attention should be given to such facets as intensity, frequency and the meaning individuals attribute to events."

Measuring Job Pressures and Lack of Support

Many employees evaluate their work environment in terms of the perceived severity and frequency of occurrence of specific job demands and pressures and the level of support provided by supervisors, coworkers, and organizational policies and procedures (Cox & Ferguson, 1994; Hurrell et al., 1998). Failing to take the frequency of occurrence of a particular stressor into account may contribute to overestimating the effects of highly stressful events that rarely occur in a particular work setting, while underestimating the impact of moderately stressful events that are frequently experienced. In responding to the JSS, employees rate the perceived severity of 30 generic sources of stress and report how often each of these stressors was experienced during the previous six months. Factor analyses of JSS severity and frequency ratings for a large heterogeneous sample of corporate, industrial, military, and university employees ($N = 2173$) identified two strong factors for both males and females. The content of the items with strong loadings on these factors for both sexes clearly described job pressures and lack of support, giving clear meaning to these factors (Spielberger & Vagg, 1999; Vagg & Spielberger, 1998).

Although perceived severity and frequency of occurrence of generic sources of stress were emphasized in the construction and validation of the JSS, little attention was given to examining relationships between the JSS Job Pressure and Lack of Support scales and the sources of stress that are generally studied in the organizational research literature. Organizational researchers have traditionally focused on two work-related types of job pressure: (a) conditions and requirements of a job; and (b) duties and responsibilities of the employee. In contrast, factor analyses of the JSS have consistently identified only a single job pressure factor (Spielberger & Reheiser, 1994; Spielberger & Vagg, 1999). However, the content of a number of JSS job pressure items is clearly related to job conditions and requirements—for example, excessive paperwork, time pressures, deadlines, and working overtime—whereas other job pressure items describe employee duties and responsibilities—for example, the assignment of disagreeable or unfamiliar duties or assuming increased responsibility.

In factor analyses of the JSS, lack of support items defined a second major source of occupational stress (Spielberger & Reheiser, 1994; Spielberger & Vagg, 1999; Vagg & Spielberger, 1998), whereas organizational researchers have identified and conceptualized two support categories: Perceived organizational support and social support. In the organizational research literature, these two categories are assumed either to have beneficial effects on employees or to protect (buffer) the employee from the potentially negative effects of stressful events. Perceived organizational support is generally defined as the degree to which employees believe the organization is committed to rewarding their work effort and meeting their need for approval (Eisenberger, Fasolo, & Davis-LaMastro, 1990; Eisenberger, Huntington, Hutchison, & Sowa, 1986). Examples of this type of support include salary increases, promotions, and recognition of good performance, which have been found to be inversely related to job tension and employee burnout (Cropanzano, Howes, Grandey, & Toth, 1997).

In the organizational research literature, social support is defined as the availability and quality of an employee's relationships with supervisors, coworkers, family, and friends and the amount of positive consideration and task assistance received from them (Cohen & Wills, 1985; Fusilier, Ganster, & Mayes, 1986; Kottke & Sharafinski, 1988). Social support, especially from supervisors, has a beneficial effect on worker performance and well-being (Ganster et al., 1986; Karasek et al., 1982) and "buffers the effect of stressors on ill health" (Frese, 1999, p. 187), thereby contributing to lower health care costs (Manning, Jackson, & Fusilier, 1996). In a recent meta-analysis study, the availability of social support was found to moderate the stressor–strain relationship, mitigate the influence of perceived stressors, or reduce levels of strain (Viswesvaran, Sanchez, & Fisher, 1999).

The capability of the JSS to assess the four major sources of occupational stress identified in the organizational research literature was investigated in a recent study by Wasala (2001), who used confirmatory factor analysis and structural equation modeling to examine frequency ratings of the 30 JSS items given by a large sample of managers and professionals. The best fitting model identified five first-order factors; job pressure and lack of support emerged as higher order factors. The higher order job pressure factor was associated with two first-order factors, which were defined by JSS items with content that described work-related conditions and requirements and duties and responsibilities. The higher order lack of support factor was associated with three first-order factors, which were defined by JSS items with content related to *lack* of perceived organizational

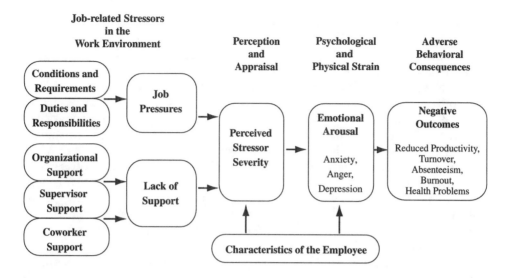

Figure 9.2. Expanded state–trait process model for the study of organizational stressors and work-related stress.

support, *lack* of support from supervisors, and *lack* of support from co-workers.

The first-order occupational stress factors identified by Wasala (2001) encompassed essentially the same stressor categories that have been traditionally investigated by organizational researchers. Including these five factors in the STP model, as shown in Figure 9.2, emphasizes the importance of examining each of these categories of stressors as components of the higher order job pressure and lack of support factors. Two of Wasala's first-order factors, defined by items describing social support from supervisors or coworkers, were consistent with previous research (e.g., Cooper et al., 1988; Karasek et al., 1982), demonstrating the need to differentiate between these two types of social support. Wasala's results also provide evidence of the importance of distinguishing between *lack* of support from supervisors and coworkers as major sources of stress, and the beneficial or buffering effects of *available* support that protect employees from job-related stressors.

Effects of Organizational Level and Gender on Occupational Stress

Of the numerous variables that influence occupational stress, organizational level and gender are especially important (Spielberger & Reheiser, 1994; Spielberger & Vagg, 1999; Vagg & Spielberger, 1998, 1999). As might be expected, employees at lower organizational levels reported feeling more alienated and experiencing less satisfaction with their jobs than those with higher positions in a particular organization (Judge, Boudreau, & Brenz,

1996; Karasek, 1979; Kasl, 1978; Long, 1998; Petty, McCarthy, & Catano, 1992; Seegers & van Elderen, 1996; Theorell & Karasek, 1996). They also take more sick days (Vahterra, Pentti, & Uutela, 1996) and have a greater risk for developing coronary heart disease (Marmot, 1994).

The effects of gender on occupational stress have been investigated in a number of studies (Jick & Payne, 1980; Quick & Quick, 1984; Quick et al., 1997; Spielberger & Reheiser, 1994; Turnage & Spielberger, 1991). Women tended to report experiencing more work-related psychological stress, whereas men reported more severe physical distress (Jick & Mitz, 1985). Interpersonal conflict also appeared to cause more job stress for women than for men (Narayanan, Menon, & Spector, 1999). However, Martocchio and O'Leary (1989), in a meta-analysis of 15 studies, found relatively few gender differences in the occupational stress reported by men and women. Similarly, Guppy and Rick (1996) also failed to find gender differences in occupational stress.

The JSS has been used extensively to evaluate the impact of organizational level on occupational stress (Spielberger & Reheiser, 1994; Vagg & Spielberger, 1998; Vagg, Spielberger, & Wasala, in press). Spielberger and Vagg (1999) found that the higher stress scores of employees at higher organizational levels were a result primarily to their more frequent experience of job pressures. They also found that women, especially those at lower organizational levels, reported experiencing job pressures more frequently than men. However, in a recent study of organizational level and gender effects for 1791 working adults, Vagg et al. (in press) found relatively few significant main or interaction effects for the nine JSS scales and subscales, whereas significant differences attributable to these variables were found for 29 of the 30 individual JSS items.

In the Vagg et al. (in press) study, differences resulting from organizational level were more numerous and were larger in magnitude than those resulting from gender. Employees at higher organizational levels reported that they experienced stress more often in "making critical decisions" and "dealing with crisis situations" than did employees at lower levels, who reported that "inadequate salary" and "lack of opportunity for advancement" were more stressful. Women reported that "insufficient personal time" was perceived as more stressful and occurred more often, and men indicated that "lack of participation in policy decisions" and "conflicts with other departments" were both more stressful and occurred more frequently. These gender effects appear to reflect traditional male–female role differences, with men reporting being more concerned about their role in the organization and women being more stressed by conflict between job requirements and their desire to take care of themselves and others.

Conclusion

Increased concerns about the reduced productivity, adverse health consequences, and rising costs that result from stress in the workplace are reflected in a 20-fold increase in the number of studies of occupational stress that have been reported in the psychological and medical literature during the past quarter century (Spielberger & Vagg, 1999). Much of this research was stimulated by Person–Environment Fit theory, described in Figure 9.1, which conceptualizes occupational stress as resulting from an incompatible fit between the job demands and pressures of the work environment and the skills, abilities, and values of the employee (French & Kahn, 1962; Kahn et. al., 1964). PE-Fit concepts, especially role ambiguity and role conflict (French, et al., 1982), have been investigated in numerous studies, encompassing a wide range of content such as job duties and responsibilities, organizational and social support, employee skills and abilities, job satisfaction, and health-related problems.

As research on occupational stress has proliferated, the PE-Fit model has been increasingly criticized as lacking in specificity and failing to identify and quantify the impact on employees of specific sources of stress in the workplace (Chemers, Hays, Rhodewalt, & Wysocki, 1985; Edwards & Cooper, 1990; Fletcher & Jones, 1993; Ganster et al., 1986). These limitations have given rise to the development of models that incorporated, expanded, and modified the concepts of PE-Fit theory, while also stimulating the construction and validation of numerous measures of occupational stress. Cooper and Marshall's (1976; Marshall & Cooper, 1979) Stress at Work model, which identified five major categories of occupational stress, guided the development of the OSInd and, more recently, the PMI. Karasek's (1979) Demand–Control model, which focuses on the demands of the work environment and the decision latitude of the worker in fulfilling job requirements, provided the conceptual framework for the JCQ that has been used extensively in occupational stress research (Karasek et al., 1995, 1998; Theorell & Karasek, 1996).

Elements of PE-Fit and Demand–Control theory are incorporated in Lazarus's (1966, 1991) Transactional Process model (Lazarus & Folkman, 1984), and in the State–Trait Process model developed by Spielberger (1972; Spielberger & Vagg, 1999). These models conceptualize stress as a complex process that consists of three major components: (a) sources of stress (stressors) that are encountered in the work environment; (b) perception and appraisal of a particular stressor by an employee; and (c) the emotional reactions that are evoked when a stressor is appraised as threatening. In addition, Lazarus's theory recognizes the importance of taking the employee's coping resources into account, and Spielberger's STP model emphasizes the need to assess the effects of individual differences in personality on both cognitive appraisal and the level of intensity of the emotional reactions that are evoked when a stressor is appraised as more or less threatening. When the resulting emotional strain is severe, occurs frequently, and persists over time, both models predict that this will lead to adverse behavioral and health outcomes such as reduced productivity, absenteeism, employee burnout, and health-related problems.

In a recent study of the factor structure of the JSS, using confirmatory factor analysis and structural equation modeling, Wasala (2001) identified five first-order factors and found that job pressure and lack of support emerged as higher order factors, which have been described by Quick (1998, p. 292) as representing "key dimensions of occupational stress." The expanded STP model, presented in Figure 9.2, incorporates the five first-order stressor categories identified by Wasala (2001), which are similar to those previously identified by organizational researchers. Three of these first-order factors were essentially the same as the stressor categories that have been investigated by organizational researchers. However, rather then the single social support factor reported in the organizational research literature, Wasala (2001) found two factors that were defined by JSS items with content related to *lack of support* from supervisors or coworkers. These results also highlight the importance of distinguishing between the adverse consequences of *lack of support* and the potentially beneficial or buffering effects of *available* social support.

Recent research with the JSS provides strong evidence that occupational stress is substantially influenced by organizational level and gender. Significant organizational level or gender differences were found by Vagg et al. (in press) in the mean scores for 29 of the 30 JSS items, indicating that it is essential to take into account the unique sources of stress described by each JSS item when evaluating the determinants of occupational stress. It should also be noted that organizational level had a substantially stronger influence on occupational stress than gender and that employees at higher organizational levels reported that they experienced job pressures more frequently than did those at lower levels (Spielberger & Reheiser, 1994; Spielberger & Vagg, 1999). Lack of support was rated as highly stressful by both male and female employees at all organizational levels, especially lack of support by supervisors.

To understand and assess the occupational stress experienced by individual employees or groups of workers, it is essential to evaluate both the perceived severity and how often a stressor event is experienced in the workplace during a specified time period. Although both the perceived severity and frequency of a particular stressor influence the amount of strain experienced by a worker, frequency of occurrence seems to have more adverse behavioral and health-related consequences. Stressor events that occur with moderate to high frequency should be especially targeted by management for needed changes in the work environment. Sources of stress that are perceived by employees as more severe should be given special attention in employee assistance and stress management programs. Reducing the perceived severity and frequency of occurrence of work-related stressors, and helping employees to adapt and cope with the inherent demands, responsibilities, and requirements of their jobs will contribute to increased productivity and job satisfaction and reduced absenteeism, burnout, and health-related problems.

References

Barone, D. F. (Ed.). (1994). *Developing a transactional psychology of work stress.* New York: Taylor and Francis.

Barone, D. F., Caddy, G. R., Katell, A. D., Roselione, F. B., & Hamilton, R. A. (1988). The Work Stress Inventory: Organizational stress and job risk. *Educational and Psychological Measurement, 48,* 141–154.

Beehr, T. A., & Newman, J. E. (1978). Job stress, employee health, and organizational effectiveness: A facet analysis, model and literature review. *Personnel Psychology, 31,* 665–699.

Caplan, R. D. (1987). Person–environment fit theory and organizations: Commensurate dimensions, time perspectives, and mechanisms. *Journal of Vocational Behavior, 31,* 248–267.

Chemers, M. M., Hays, R. B., Rhodewalt, F., & Wysocki, J. (1985). A person–environment analysis of job stress: A contingency model explanation. *Journal of Personality and Social Psychology, 49,* 628–635.

Cohen, S., & Wills, T. A. (1985). Stress, social support, and the buffering hypothesis. *Psychological Bulletin, 98*(2), 310–357.

Cooper, C. L., & Cartwright, S. (1994). Healthy mind: Healthy organization—A proactive approach to occupational stress. *Human Relations, 47,* 455–470.

Cooper, C. L., Kirkcaldy, B. D., & Brown, J. (1994). A model of job stress and physical health: The role of individual differences. *Personality Individual Differences, 16,* 653–655.

Cooper, C. L., & Marshall, J. (1976). Occupational sources of stress: A review of the literature relating to coronary heart disease and mental ill health. *Journal of Occupational Psychology, 49,* 11–28.

Cooper, C. L., Sloan, S. J., & Williams, S. (1988). *The Occupational Stress Indicator (OSI).* Windsor, UK: NFER Nelson.

Cox, T., & Ferguson, E. (1994). Measurement of the subjective work environment. *Work & Stress, 8,* 98–109.

Cropanzano, R., Howes, J. C., Grandey, A. A., & Toth, P. (1997). The relationship of organizational politics and support to work behaviors, attitudes and stress. *Journal of Organizational Behavior, 18*(2), 159–180.

Dewe, P. J. (1989). Examining the nature of work stress: Individual evaluations of stressful experiences and coping. *Human Relations, 42*(11), 993–1013.

Edwards, J. R., & Cooper, C. L. (1990). The person–environment fit approach to stress: Recurring problems and some suggested solutions. *Journal of Organizational Behavior, 11,* 293–307.

Edwards, J. R., & Rothbard, N. P. (1999). Work and family stress and well-being: An examination of person–environment fit in the work and family domains. *Organizational Behavior and Human Decision Processes, 77*(2), 85–129.

Eisenberger, R., Fasolo, P., & Davis-LaMastro, V. (1990). Perceived organizational support and employee diligence, commitment and innovation. *Journal of Applied Psychology, 75*(1), 51–59.

Eisenberger, R., Huntington, R., Hutchison, S., & Sowa, D. (1986). Perceived organizational support. *Journal of Applied Psychology, 71,* 500–507.

Eulberg, J. R., Weekley, J. A., & Bhagat, R. S. (1988). Models of stress in organizational research: A metatheoretical perspective. *Human Relations, 41,* 331–350.

Fisher, C. D., & Gitelson, R. (1983). A meta-analysis of the correlates of role conflict and ambiguity. *Journal of Applied Psychology, 68,* 320–333.

Fletcher, B. C., & Jones, F. (1993). A refutation of Karasek's demand–discretion model of occupational stress with a range of dependent measures. *Journal of Organizational Behavior, 14,* 319–330.

Forney, D. S. (1982). *Sex and age and the incidence of reported stress, strain, and burnout among career development professionals.* Unpublished master's thesis, University of Maryland, College Park.

Fraser, J. A. (2001). *White-collar sweatshop: The deterioration of work and its rewards in corporate America.* New York: W. W. Norton.

French, J. R. P., Jr., & Caplan, R. D. (1972). Occupational stress and individual strain. In A. J. Marrow (Ed.), *The failure of success* (pp. 30–66). New York: Amacom.

French, J. R. P., Jr., Caplan, R. D., & Harrison, R. V. (1982). *The mechanisms of job stress and strain.* London: Wiley.

French, J. R. P., Jr., & Kahn, R. L. (1962). A programmatic approach to studying the industrial environment and mental health. *Journal of Social Issues, 18*(3), 1–47.

Frese, M. (1999). Social support as a moderator of the relationship between work stressors and psychological dysfunctioning: A longitudinal study with objective measures. *Journal of Occupational Health Psychology, 4*(3), 179–192.

Fusilier, M., Ganster, D. C., & Mayes, B. T. (1986). The social support and health relationship: Is there a gender difference? *Journal of Occupational Psychology, 59,* 145–153.

Ganster, D., Fusilier, M. R., & Mayes, B. T. (1986). Role of social support in the experience of stress at work. *Journal of Applied Psychology, 71*(1), 102–110.

Grier, K. S. (1982). A comparison of job stress in law enforcement and teaching. *Dissertation Abstracts International, 43,* 870B.

Guppy, A., & Rick, J. R. (1996). The influences of gender and grade on perceived work stress and job satisfaction in white collar employees. *Work & Stress, 10*(2), 154–164.

Hamner, W. C., & Tosi, H. L. (1974). Relationship of role conflict and role ambiguity to job involvement measures. *Journal of Applied Psychology, 59,* 497–499.

Higgins, N. (1986). Occupational stress and working women: The effectiveness of two stress-reduction programs. *Journal of Vocational Behavior, 29,* 66–78.

Hurrell, J. J., & McLaney, A. M. (1988). Exposure to job stress: A new psychometric instrument. *Scandinavian Journal of Work Environment and Health, 14*(Suppl. 1), 27–28.

Hurrell, J. J., Nelson, D. L., & Simmons, B. L. (1998). Measuring job stressors and strains: Where we have been, where we are, and where we need to go. *Journal of Occupational Health Psychology, 3*(4), 368–389.

Insel, P. M., & Moos, R. H. (1974). *Work Environment Scale, Form R.* Palo Alto, CA: Consulting Psychologists Press.

Ivancevich, J. M., & Matteson, M. T. (1976). *Stress Diagnostic Survey (SDS): Comments and psychometric properties of a multidimensional self-report inventory.* Houston, TX: FD Associates.

Ivancevich, J. M., & Matteson, M. T. (1980). *Stress and work, A managerial perspective.* Glenview, IL: Scott, Foresman.

Ivancevich, J. M., Matteson, M. T., & Dorin, F. P. (1990). *Stress Diagnostic Survey (SDS).* Houston, TX: FD Associates.

Jick, T. D., & Mitz, L. E. (1985). Sex differences in work stress. *Academy of Management Review, 10,* 408–420.

Jick, T. D., & Payne, R. (1980). Stress at work. *Exchange, 5*(3), 50–56.

Judge, T. A., Boudreau, J. W., & Brentz, R. D. (1996). Job and life attitudes of male executives. *Journal of Applied Psychology, 79*(5), 767–782.

Kahn, R. L., & Byosiere, P. (1992). Stress in organizations. In M. D. Dunnette & L. M. Hough (Eds.), *Handbook of industrial and organizational psychology* (Vol. 3, pp. 571–650). Palo Alto, CA: Consulting Psychologists Press.

Kahn, R. L., Wolfe, D. M., Quinn, R. P., Snoeck, J. D., & Rosenthal, R. A. (1964). *Organizational stress: Studies in role conflict and ambiguity.* New York: Wiley.

Karasek, R. A. (1979). Job demands, job decision latitude, and mental strain: Implications for job redesign. *Administrative Science Quarterly, 24,* 285–307.

Karasek, R. A., Brisson, C., Kawakami, N., Hourman, I., Bongers, P., & Amick, B. (1998). The Job Content Questionnaire (JCQ): An instrument for internationally comparative assessments of psychosocial job characteristics. *Journal of Occupational Health Psychology, 3,* 322–355.

Karasek, R. A., Hulbert, K., & Simmerman, B. (1995). *JCQ user's project summary: 10 years of job content questionnaire use.* Unpublished manuscript, University of Massachusetts, Lowell.

Karasek, R. A., Schwartz, J., & Peiper, C. (1983). *Validation of a survey instrument for job-related cardiovascular illness.* New York: Columbia University.

Karasek, R. A., & Theorell, T. (1990). *Healthy work: Stress, productivity, and the reconstruction of working life.* New York: Basic Books.

Karasek, R. A., Triantis, K. P., & Chaudhry, S. S. (1982). Coworker and supervisor support as moderators of associations between task characteristics and mental strain. *Journal of Occupational Behaviour, 3*(2), 181–200.

Kasl, S. V. (1978). Epidemiological contributions to the study of work stress. In C. L. Cooper & R. L. Payne (Eds.), *Stress at work* (pp. 3–38). New York: Wiley.

Kasl, S. (1998). Measuring job stressors and studying the health impact of the work environment: An epidemiologic commentary. *Journal of Occupational Health Psychology, 3*(4), 390–401.

Keenan, A., & Newton, T. J. (1984). Frustration in organizations: Relationships to role stress, climate, and psychological strain. *Journal of Occupational Psychology, 57,* 57–65.

Kottke, J. L., & Sharafinski, C. E. (1988). Measuring perceived supervisory and organizational support. *Educational and Psychological Measurement, 48,* 1975–1079.

Lazarus, R. S. (1966). *Psychological stress and the coping process.* New York: McGraw-Hill.

Lazarus, R. S. (1991). Psychological stress in the workplace. *Journal of Social Behavior and Personality, 6,* 1–13.

Lazarus, R. S., & Folkman, S. (1984). *Stress, appraisal, and coping.* New York: Springer.

Lewin, K. (1951). *Field theory in social science.* New York: Harper.

Long, B. C. (1998). Coping with workplace stress: A multiple-group comparison of female managers and clerical workers. *Journal of Counseling Psychology, 45*(1), 65–78.

Manning, M. R., Jackson, C. N., & Fusilier, M. R. (1996). Occupational stress, social support and the costs of health care. *Academy of Management Journal, 39*(3), 738–750.

Marmot, M. (1994). Work and other factors influencing coronary health and sickness absence. *Journal of Applied Psychology, 74,* 495–501.

Marshall, J., & Cooper, C. (1979). Work experiences of middle and senior managers: The pressure and satisfaction. *International Management Review, 19,* 81–96.

Martocchio, J. J., & O'Leary, A. M. (1989). Sex differences in occupational stress: A meta-analytic review. *Journal of Applied Psychology, 74,* 495–501.

Moos, R. H. (1981). *Work Environment Scale manual.* Palo Alto, CA: Consulting Psychologists Press.

Motowidlo, S. J., Packard, J. S., & Manning, M. R. (1986). Occupational stress: Its causes and consequences for job performance. *Journal of Applied Psychology, 71*(4), 618–629.

Murphy, J. R. (1995). Occupational stress management: Current status and future directions. In C. L. Cooper & D. M. Rousseau (Eds.), *Trends in Organizational Behavior* (Vol. 2, pp. 1–14). Chichester, UK: John Wiley & Sons.

Murphy, J. R., & Hurrell, J. J. (Eds.). (1987). *Stress measurement and management in organizations: Development and current status.* New York: Praiger.

Narayanan, L., Menon, S., & Spector, P. E. (1999). Stress in the workplace: A comparison of gender and occupation. *Journal of Organizational Behavior, 20*(1), 63–73.

Northwestern National Life. (1991). *Employee burnout: America's newest epidemic.* Minneapolis, MN: Author.

Northwestern National Life. (1992). *Employee burnout: Causes and cures.* Minneapolis, MN: Author.

Osipow, S. H. (1998). *Occupational Stress Inventory—Revised: Professional manual.* Odessa, Fl: Psychological Assessment Resources.

Osipow, S. H., & Davis, A. S. (1988). The relationship of coping resources to occupational stress and strain. *Journal of Vocational Behavior, 32,* 1–15.

Osipow, S. H., Doty, R. E., & Spokane, A. R. (1985). Occupational stress, strain, and coping across the life span. *Journal of Vocational Behavior, 27,* 98–108.

Osipow, S. H., & Spokane, A. R. (1980). *The Occupational Environment Scales, Personal Strain Questionnaire and Personal Resources Questionnaire, Form E-1.* Columbus, OH: Marathon Consulting & Press.

Osipow, S. H., & Spokane, A. R. (1987). *Occupational Stress Inventory.* Odessa, FL: Psychological Assessment Resources.

Pelletier, D. M. (1983). Career officers pass stress tests. *College Placement Council Spotlight, 6*(1–2), 98–108.

Petty, G. M. H., McCarthy, M. E., & Catano, V. M. (1992). Psychological environments and burnout: Gender considerations within the corporation. *Journal of Organizational Behavior, 13,* 701–711.

Quick, J. C. (1998). Introduction to the measurement of stress at work. *Journal of Occupational Health Psychology, 3*(4), 291–292.

Quick, J. C., & Quick, J. D. (1984). *Organizational Stress and Preventive Management.* New York: McGraw-Hill.

Quick, J. C., Quick, J. D., Nelson, D. L., & Hurrell, J. J. J. (1997). *Preventive Stress Management in Organizations*. Washington, DC: American Psychological Association.

Rayburn, C. A., Richmond, L. J., & Rogers, L. (1982). Women, men, and religion: Stress within sanctuary walls. *Journal of Pastoral Counseling, 17,* 75–83.

Ryland, E., & Greenfeld, S. (1991). Work stress and well-being: An investigation of Antonovsky's sense of coherence model. *Journal of Social Behavior and Personality, 6*(7), 39–54.

Sauter, S. L., & Hurrell, J. J., Jr. (Eds.). (1989). Introduction. In S. L. Sauter, J. J. Hurrell, & C. L. Cooper (Eds.), *Job control and worker health* (pp. xiii–xx). Chichester, UK: Wiley.

Schuler, R. S. (1980). Definition and conceptualization of stress in organizations. *Organizational Behavior and Human Performance, 25,* 184–215.

Schuler, R. S. (Ed.). (1991). Foreword. In P. L. Parrewe (Ed.), *Handbook on job stress*. Corte Madera, CA: Select Press.

Seegers, G., & van Elderen, T. (1996). Examining the model of stress reactions of bank directors. *European Journal of Psychological Assessment, 12*(3), 212–223.

Spielberger, C. D. (Ed.). (1972). *Anxiety as an Emotional State* (Vol. 1). New York: Academic Press.

Spielberger, C. D. (1991). *Preliminary test manual for the Job Stress Survey (JSS)*. Odessa, FL: Psychological Assessment Resources.

Spielberger, C. D., Grier, K. S., & Pate, J. M. (1980). The Florida Police Stress survey. *Florida Fraternal Order of Police Journal* (Winter), 66–67.

Spielberger, C. D., Jacobs, G., Russsell, S., & Crane, R. S. (Eds.). (1983). *Assessment of anger: The State–Trait Anger scale* (Vol. 2). Hillsdale, New Jersey: Erlbaum.

Spielberger, C. D., Krasner, S. S., & Solomon, E. P. (Eds.). (1988). *The Experience, expression, and control of anger*. New York: Springer.

Spielberger, C. D., & Reheiser, E. C. (1994). Job stress in university, corporate, and military personnel. *International Journal of Stress Management, 1,* 19–31.

Spielberger, C. D., & Vagg, P. R. (1999). *Job Stress Survey–Professional manual*. Odessa, FL: Psychological Assessment Resources.

Spielberger, C. D., Westberry, L. G., Grier, K. S., & Greenfield, G. (1981). The Police Stress survey: Sources of stress in law enforcement. *Human Resources Institute Monograph Series, University of South Florida, 3*(6).

Theorell, T., & Karasek, R. A. (1996). Current issues relating to psychosocial job strain and cardiovascular disease research. *Journal of Occupational Health Psychology, 1,* 9–26.

Turnage, J. J., & Spielberger, C. D. (1991). Job stress in managers, professionals, and clerical workers. *Work & Stress, 5,* 165–176.

Vagg, P. R., & Spielberger, C. D. (1998). Occupational stress: Measuring job pressure and organizational support in the workplace. *Journal of Occupational Health Psychology, 3*(4), 294–305.

Vagg, P. R., & Spielberger, C. D. (1999). The Job Stress survey: Assessing perceived severity and frequency of occurrence of generic sources of stress in the workplace. *Journal of Occupational Health Psychology, 4*(3), 1–5.

Vagg, P. R., Spielberger, C. D., & Wasala, C. F. (in press). Effects of organizational level and gender on stress in the workplace. *International Journal of Stress Management*.

Vahterra, J., Pentti, J., & Uutela, A., (1996). The effect of objective job demands on registered sickness absence spells: Do personal, social, and job-related resources act as moderators? *Work & Stress, 10*(4), 286–308.

Viswesvaran, C., Sanchez, J. I., & Fisher, J. (1999). The role of social support in the process of work stress: A meta-analysis. *Journal of Vocational Behavior, 54,* 314–334.

Wasala, C. F. (2001). *Organizational stressors and work-related stress*. Unpublished master's thesis, University of South Florida, Tampa.

Williams, S., & Cooper, C. L. (1998). *Pressure Management Indicator (PMI)*. Harrogate, UK: RAD.

Wright, L. A., & Smye, M. D. (1996). *Corporate Abuse: How Lean and Mean Robs People and Profits*. New York: Macmillan.

10

To Be Able to Exert Control Over One's Own Situation: A Necessary Condition for Coping With Stressors

Töres Theorell

To be able to exert control over one's own situation has been viewed as an effective stress management and coping strategy for job stress for several decades. My own early work in this area dates back into the 1970s. Since then, Sutton and Kahn (1987) specifically examined control along with prediction and understanding as three antidotes to organizational stress. Ganster (1989; Ganster & Fusilier, 1989) provided excellent broad reviews of the research on the control construct, though mostly a U.S. perspective. Terry and Jimmieson (1999) conducted an even more extensive review of the research on work control and employee well-being over the intervening decade, from a more international perspective and with a well-structured focus on the demand–control model. This chapter does not re-review these earlier works but does present a unique, more detailed look at the issue of control and the ability to exert control as a central construct in occupational health psychology.

First, I present some definitions of concepts that are relevant to the exertion of control when an individual is making efforts to cope with stressors, namely stress (according to Selye's physiological perspective), fighting for and losing control, interaction between genes and environment, open and covert coping, locus of control, and finally decision latitude and its components intellectual discretion and authority over decisions. Second I discuss the assessment of decision latitude that represent the possibility that the organization gives the individuals to exert control. There are more "objective" and more "subjective" assessment methods, and I discuss the relationship between them. Third I discuss the associations between control (decision latitude) and health. During the recent decades the scientific literature on this topic has been growing rapidly. Health effects of both long-lasting exposure to low levels of decision latitude and sudden losses of control at work are discussed. I also discuss health effects of the classical combination of high demands and low decision latitude (job strain), according to Karasek. Fourth, I discuss part physiological and other mechanisms linking control to health. Fifth I discuss possible organizational interventions that may improve control and health.

Definitions

To make the message in this chapter clear I have to start by defining "stress" and "exerting control." Hans Selye (1950) has introduced the most widely used definition of stress in physiological research. According to Selye, stress is a nonspecific arousal reaction in response to all situations that require mobilization of energy. The arousal aims at the facilitation of the body's attempts to make a physical effort. The bodily reactions aim at the avoidance of disturbing signals from the body. This physiological stress definition implies first of all that stress is a reaction—what triggers the reaction is labeled a stressor. It also implies that stress is a neutral concept. According to this way of defining stress it is not negative in itself, although it may become negative during certain conditions. Finally, it implies that stress is a natural and healthy reaction in all situations that require increased energy.

The possibility to exert control over one's own situation probably represents a fundamental need. It has also been occupying the minds of some of our most important philosophers. The most obvious example of this is the existential philosophers. In different ways they all express the importance for the individuals of not allowing the environment to take over the individual's life (Cannon, 1999; Heidegger, 1972). In a corresponding way it could be said that Freud's psychoanalytical theory deals with the ego fight for keeping control over significant forces—both the primitive "id" and the more sophisticated "super-ego" (Freud, 1963).

To have the possibility of exerting control over one's own life means that one is able to take command over everyday situations—even most of the somewhat unexpected situations that one may face. A person who is able to exert a reasonable amount of control over his or her situation does not run the risk of being humiliated in many everyday situations. To exert control is of course related to power; those who have power are also able to issue control (Syme, 1989).

Stress and the issue of control have a close relationship in the sense that stress is triggered mainly when we run the risk of losing control over a situation and keep fighting to keep it. Once we have lost control it is no longer of interest to continue fighting. In that situation it is more relevant to save energy. This induces a bodily state of passiveness. A physiologist emphasizing this aspect was J. P. Henry, who differentiated the fight for the retention of control from the reactions associated with loss of control (Henry & Stephens, 1977).

Control and Stress in Relation to the Individual: Genes and Environment

How to exert control over a situation is a function partly of coping, our individual way of handling situations that require the mobilization of energy. There is a constant interplay between our individual way of handling such situations and the environment despite the fact that coping is partly determined by genetic factors and partly by childhood experiences. In twin research it has been shown that the majority of the variance in the component of coping labeled locus of control is determined by experiences in adult life—that is to say, by working life and adult family life experiences (Pedersen et al., 1989). An external locus of control implies that the individual does not believe that he or she can do anything about a problem: The environment has to act. An internal locus of control means that the person has to act him- or herself. This aspect of coping is of fundamental importance in many situations—for instance, in chronic diseases.

During long-lasting illness the individual becomes particularly dependent and thus shows more external locus of control. The less dependent (showing more internal locus of control) the patient becomes the better the rehabilitation has been. One of the aims of good rehabilitation is accordingly to move locus of control to a more internal orientation.

Another important aspect of exerting control is the exploration of whether the coping pattern is open or covert. We have studied this aspect of coping at work by asking employees what they do when they are exposed to a humiliating situation at work—for example, a supervisor or a work mate has treated them in an unfair way. There are basically two kinds of answers. In the first group of answers there are those implying that the employee is facing the person who treated him or her badly with this fact, either directly or some day later. This is the open coping pattern.

In the second group of answers—the covert coping pattern—action is avoided and the person who treated him or her may never know about the humilated feeling of the employee. One implication of this is that persons with the covert coping pattern are more frequently humiliated in "normal life" situations. In a study of 6000 working men and women in Stockholm, patterns of coping in such humiliating situations were explored by means of a standardized questionnaire. They were asked to describe what they normally do when they are treated in an unfair way by either a supervisor or a workmate. Those who reported that they had small possibilities to influence their work situation in general were more likely to report a covert coping situation than others. In the same study a higher prevalence of elevated blood pressure was found in individuals with a less open or a more covert coping pattern. This was particularly true among the male participants (Theorell, Alfredsson, Westerholm, & Falck, 2000). This association between the work environment and the coping pattern may imply that a work environment in which the employees feel that they have good possibilities to influence their work environment is also a worksite where it is possible to speak up when somebody is being treated badly. In environments with a small possibility for the employees to influence the situation, they may suffer and not report to others when they are humiliated. The basic dimension is of course possibility to exert control. If it does not make any difference what one says, one gradually stops telling others about one's thoughts.

With regard to locus of control and open–covert coping, one of the conclusions may be that the psychosocial environment that is created around us may influence the way in which we cope with stressful situations. When human beings are aided in their search for solutions they may be able to develop more active coping patterns. The coping pattern that we have developed in a given situation will subsequently influence our way of acting in similar future situations (Parkes, 1991; Ursin, 1997). Obviously the supervisors are very important in the creation of these climatic factors. Supervisors could facilitate for the employees to exert control but they could also concentrate all power to themselves. Decision latitude of employees is different from decision latitude of supervisors. The organization sets the larger context and the supervisor is the primary attachment of the employee to the organization.

The Basic Components in Decision Latitude

Exerting control in the work situation may be regarded from two points of view: the supervisor's and the employee's. We analyze it from the point of view of the employee in this instance. Using this point of departure, decision latitude is used to label the possibility that the employee has to make decisions about his or her own work (Karasek, 1979; Karasek & Theorell, 1990). One other limitation in the present overview is that possibility to influence the employee's decisions about the work process refers to the possibility that the organization gives the employees. There are also other components in possibility to influence decisions, several of them related to the individual's experiences and capacity. They will not be discussed. With these limitations in the definition of decision latitude, two basic components can be discerned: authority over decisions and intellectual discretion.

Authority over decisions refers to the democracy aspect of the work organization. Good influence over what should be done and how it should be done is labeled good authority over decisions. This could also be labeled good task control (Karasek & Theorell, 1990). The second aspect, *intellectual discretion or skill discretion*, refers to the possibility for the employees to decide how their knowledge is used and developed—in other words, knowledge control. Good possibility to influence the development of the employees' competence (for instance, by means of continuous education or job rotation) is labeled a high intellectual discretion. If the employees have a high intellectual discretion they have a relatively good possibility to exert control in unexpected situations that may arise.

The two basic components of decision latitude are mostly added to one another. There is ground for this both because in most working populations they are correlated and because they are interconnected in the history of industrialism and Taylorism (Taylor, 1911/1967). Taylor introduced scientific principles for labor division in industry, an important step in the

intensification of industrialism. When division of labor was originally introduced in the late 1800s, the workers lost their possibility to influence the
working process (authority over decisions) because somebody else decided
the speed of the process and the execution of the different parts. But they
also lost overview over the work process. This meant that their knowledge
was not used and that it was not developed (Karasek & Theorell, 1990). But
in many circumstances it is now also necessary to study the two components
separately. The experience during interventions in the worksite has also
been that they could be influenced quite differently during change processes. They could also have separate effects on health outcomes.

Psychological demands and decision latitude are the two basic elements
in the demand–control model (Karasek, 1979; Karasek & Theorell, 1990),
which has been used extensively in efforts to explore the psychosocial work
environment in relation to health. Low demands and high decision latitude
is the ideal situation (*relaxed*), whereas high demands and low decision
latitude is associated with the worst health consequences (*strain*). Job
situations with low demands and low decision latitude are labeled *passive*.
Jobs with high demands and high decision latitude correspond to *active*
situations. Despite the high demand level in the active situation, adverse
health consequences are not as likely as in the strain situation because
the high decision latitude increases the possibility for the individual to
handle the demands.

Assessment

It is important to separate the theoretical concept of control from the
assessment of it in practice. The organizational aspect of decision latitude
is mostly measured by means of questionnaires that are answered by the
workers themselves. In this case individual experiences and characteristics
of course flavor the responses. Another strategy is to ask experts to make
more "objective" or at least "external" judgments of "authority over decisions" and "intellectual discretion." Experts could be either from the occupational health care teams (Hasselhorn et al., 2001) or external experts of
the working process (North, Syme, Feeney, Shipley, & Marmot, 1996).
There are also special standardized techniques for observing these kinds
of parameters (Volpert, 1982). A third principle that has been used extensively in the assessment of decision latitude has been to use national surveys of working populations. For each psychosocial dimension (for instance,
physical demands, psychological demands, intellectual discretion, authority
over decisions, and social support) a mean score is calculated for each
occupational group according to international classification systems and
also for subgroups defined according to gender, age, and duration of employment in the occupation. By means of such a classification it is possible to
record what the likely score for an individual would be given his or her
occupation, gender, age, and duration of employment. Several such systems
for imputation of psychsocial conditions have been published in the United
States and in Sweden (Alfredsson, Karasek, & Theorell, 1982; Alfredsson,

Spetz, & Theorell, 1985; Fredlund, Hallqvist, & Diderichsen, 2000; Johnson, Stewart, Fredlund, Hall, & Theorell, 1990; Schwartz, Pieper, & Karasek, 1988). Such scores are imprecise because they do not take into account true variations between worksites in an occupation.

What is the relationship between different kinds of psychosocial scores? For decision latitude and its components authority over decisions and intellectual discretion, a good agreement has been found between expert scores and self-rated conditions (Hasselhorn et al., 2001; Karasek & Theorell, 1990)—despite the fact that they are different in nature. In a recent epidemiological study of 2275 working men in Stockholm, the correlation between expert assessments performed by occupational health care teams and self-ratings was 0.56. This means that 31% of the variance was common to both methods—which is one way of stating that approximately one third of the variation in ratings was common to the individuals' and the experts' opinions. The agreement between self-ratings and expert assessments was particularly good for blue collar workers. An even better correlation in the general male Swedish working population—0.65—was found between imputed scores derived from the most recent Swedish classification system based on national surveys (Fredlund et al., 2000) and self-ratings. These agreements for decision latitude are much better than the agreement between psychological demands according to self-ratings and according to expert ratings respectively. It should be emphasised that neither expert ratings nor self-ratings necessarily represent the truth—they are simply different aspects of decision latitude.

Systematic observations of different aspects of decision latitude at work—the possibility to develop mental skills and prevalence of hindrances—have also been standardized and published (Härenstam, Rydbäck, Karlqvist, & Wiklund, 2000; Waldenström, Josephson, Persson, & Theorell, 1998). A summary of the characteristics of questionnaires, imputation systems, expert ratings, and systematic observations has been published recently (Landsbergis & Theorell, 2000).

Control Over and Control at Work

One final aspect of decision latitude is that a distinction could be made between control over and control at work (Aronsson, 1985; Karasek & Theorell, 1990). Control over work represents aspects of work that are clearly related to power over the whole working process. It is accordingly related to market aspects of planning of the production and to democracy aspects of work in society. Control at work is more clearly related to the work tasks and is closer to the worker. Most of the published studies in this field deal with control at work, whereas control over work has been less extensively studied and is more difficult to study. It is quite conceivable that those who work in information technology have a view of their job as allowing a high decision latitude when they analyze their tasks. On the other hand, the processes governing the market do not allow these workers a lot of control over the work process. In future research we need more indirect reliable methods for the assessment of control over work.

Associations Between Decision Latitude and Health

There are many situations in which we react physiologically because we fear that we are losing control. This may be an important reason for the consistent and strong relationships between loss of control and illness onset. Such situations arise, for instance, in job loss. There are several studies indicating that illness risk increases when there is threat of unemployment and when employees lose their jobs (Janlert, 1997; Hammarström & Olofsson, 1998), although there is also a discussion regarding the direction of this relationship. There is agreement that both forwards and backwards associations exist together. Thus, there is both an increased risk among employees with illness of becoming unemployed and an increased risk of becoming ill after the onset of unemployment (Hallsten, 1998; Isaksson, Hellgren & Pettersson, 2000).

Loss of Control at Work

Even when individuals have a job, they may lose possibilities to exert control at work. This could also be of significance to illness risk. This has recently been explored in two different epidemiological studies on the risk of coronary heart disease. One was a prospective examination of state employees in England (Bosma et al., 1997). Health was measured by means of registers and self-reported data. Biological data such as serum lipids and blood pressure were also measured. All these measurements were performed at approximately two-year intervals. Among other things the participants were asked how much decision latitude they had at work. It could be shown that individuals who had lost a significant amount of decision latitude at work between two examinations had a significantly greater risk of developing new coronary heart disease (without having had symptoms previously) during follow-up. The risk was approximately doubled even after adjustment for accepted biological risk factors such as smoking habits, serum lipids, and blood pressure.

The other study was a case control study of first myocardial infarctions in Stockholm, the so-called SHEEP (Stockholm Heart Epidemiology Program). All men and women between the ages of 45 to 65 who had suffered a first myocardial infarction (Theorellet al., 1998) in the greater Stockholm region were invited. A matched group of men and women without coronary heart disease were invited as referents. The myocardial infarction patients were examined within three months after the infarction. The same medical and psychosocial examinations were performed on all participants. Occupation was recorded for every year during the whole working career. This made it possible to impute a measure of decision latitude for each year and participant (specified with regard to occupation, gender, age, and duration of employment in the occupation) from the Swedish classification system (Johnson et al., 1990).

The hypothesis was that participants who had lost decision latitude during the 10 years preceding the examination would have a greater likelihood of belonging to the myocardial infarction group than others. There was support for this hypothesis in men and particularly so in the age group between 45 to 54. Significantly lowered decision latitude was operationally defined to have occurred among the 25% who had had the least favorable development (lowered) of decision latitude during the period. After adjustment for accepted biological risk factors the odds ratio of belonging to the myocardial infarction in this group was 1.8. Thus there was almost a doubled risk of having a first myocardial infarction in this group. Among men between 55 and 65 there was no such excess risk associated with lost decision latitude at work. This difference between the middle aged and the older men could be a result of expectations—after the age of 55 men in the modern working world could expect decreasing decision latitude rather than increased. Accordingly, a decreased level of decision latitude may not be perceived as such a negative event as it could be in men younger than age 55. Another explanation could be that a large proportion of men between the age of 55 and 65 have stopped working and thus those remaining in the working population may be a selected group. Nor was there any relationship between loss of decision latitude and risk of myocardial infarction in women. It should be pointed out that the number of women was smaller, however.

That loss of decision latitude may have importance also for the risk of developing acute neck–shoulder pain has been illustrated in a case control study of low back pain and neck–shoulder pain (Fredriksson, 2000). In this study physical as well as psychosocial conditions were examined at work as well as outside work. During an interview the participants described their situation at the time of the examination. Afterward they were asked to assess whether the situation had changed with regard to decision latitude at work during the past five years. Those who reported that they had experienced decreased decision latitude had an increased likelihood of belonging to the neck–shoulder pain group even after adjustment for a number of possible confounders such as previous neck–shoulder pain episodes, socioeconomic status, and age. In this particular study the associations between loss of decision latitude and illness risk were stronger than the one between a low level of decision latitude and illness risk.

That loss of decision latitude may induce increased illness risk is something to consider when jobs are reorganized. If many persons go through work changes that mean less decision latitude, lower status, and less possibility for development of competence there is obviously an increased risk that the prevalence of certain illnesses will arise. Accordingly there is reason to contact those who are in these risk situations and try to help them find new meaningful and dignified tasks.

Long-Term Exposure to Low Decision Latitude

Another possibility is to explore whether a low level of decision latitude per se is associated with increased risk of developing illness—without any loss of decision latitude. In the longitudinal study of state employees in England one has tried in a systematic way to illuminate this question

(Bosma et al., 1997). There were several questions about the work environment on several occasions approximately biannually. On these occasions a medical examination was performed and blood samples were drawn for the assessment of serum lipids and other relevant biological parameters. The part of decision latitude that has been studied in this examination has been authority over decisions. In men as well as in women a significant relationship was found between a small degree of authority over decisions and increased risk of developing new coronary heart disease during the follow-up period. The analyses were adjusted for accepted biological risk factors. Socioeconomic factors (education and social class) and a number of individual psychological characteristics could also be adjusted for. The most important psychological trait was "negative affectivity," which is the tendency to complain about conditions in general.

The excess risk associated with a small authority over decisions was in the order of 50%. It is interesting to note that the corresponding excess risk associated with authority over decisions according to expert assessments was of the same order of magnitude (40%) as the one associated with self-rated authority over decisions.

In a study of the long-term effects of exposure to low decision latitude (Johnson, Stewart, Hall, Fredlund, & Theorell, 1996) the working career in a large number of Swedes was related to risk of dying a cardiovascular death during follow-up. The individuals had participated in the Surveys of Living Conditions, ULF. They had responded to a question regarding what occupation that they had during each year of their working career. By means of the classification system (Johnson et al., 1990), decision latitude was imputed for each individual for each year. The results indicated that there may have been a cumulated beneficial effect from high decision latitude, which was evident up to a period of 15 to 20 years. After 20 years there was no additional cumulative effect.

Thus, in the British study of the state employees as well as in the Swedish study of cardiovascular deaths in the general working population there was evidence of a protective effect of high decision latitude on the risk of developing cardiovascular disease.

Job Strain: The Combination of High Demands and Low Decision Latitude

Most studies of the association between low decision latitude have been focused on the combination of a small decision latitude and a high level of psychological demands (job strain). The demand–control model (Karasek, 1979; Karasek & Theorell, 1990) stipulates that this combination is particularly dangerous in relation to illness risk. The results of these studies have been summarized recently by Belkić and others (Belkić, Schnall, & Ugljesic, 2000). Several of these studies show no association between psychological demands and the risk of cardiovascular disease. But in most of the studies the precision of the predictions increases when psychological demands and decision latitude are combined compared to when decision latitude is studied separately. The excess risk associated with job strain is between 40 and 150% in most of the studies that are based on self-ratings. In studies based on imputed scores—when the only information available has been occupation—the excess risk has been lower: between 20 and 100%. The strongest explanatory factor has been decision latitude.

Three different studies in the Nordic countries have shown similar results with regard to etiologic fraction (Alfredsson, Spetz, & Theorell, 1984; Olsen & Søndergaard-Kristensen, 1988; Theorell et al., 1998). In the SHEEP study, the proportion of myocardial infarctions due to job strain that could be prevented in the working population was computed. The assumption was that the strain of those 25% with the most pronounced job strain could be improved to the level of the remaining 75%. This proportion (etiological fraction) was 7% for men and 13% for women. This calculation was performed after adjustment for accepted biological risk factors and social class. In men younger than age 55, the etiological fraction was 11%.

Job strain has been more consistently associated with heart disease risk in studies of blue collar workers than among white collar workers. There are more studies of men than of women, and the associations are less clear for women than for men (Belkić et al., 2000).

The relationship between low decision latitude and the risk of developing musculoskeletal disorders has not been as strong and consistent as the one between decision latitude and cardiovascular disease risk. The relationship seems to vary between different study populations and may vary also between men and women as well as between social groups and occupational groups (Anonymus, 1996). There may also be differences in the relationship between different types of musculoskeletal disorders (neck–shoulder pain or low back pain are the largest groups). In some studies psychological demands are more important and in others one of the two basic aspects of decision latitude. In a recent study (Vingård et al., 2000) lack of decision latitude (in particular the intellectual discretion component according to a systematic interview) was associated with low back pain in men and also with elevated interleukin-6 concentration in serum (Theorell et al., 2000). Interleukin-6 is related to inflammatory activity in tissues and also to stress reactions. In women, on the other hand, the patterns of associations were different. There were also different patterns of associations for neck–shoulder pain than for low back pain in this large case-control study. An interesting observation in this examination was that particularly in women the most powerful predictions were made when there were both physical and psychosocial adverse working conditions. The likelihood of having consulted for low back pain, for instance, was three-fold among women who reported both job strain and physical load compared to women without this combination. Women with the combination of low decision latitude and physical load had a doubled risk compared to those without these joint loads. Lack of decision latitude may thus be significant in combination with other factors in the etiology of low back pain.

Functional gastrointestinal disorders such as dyspepsia or irritable bowel syndrome have also been related to low decision latitude at work (Nyrén, 1995; Westerberg & Theorell, 1997). The findings in these studies indicate that both in men and women the likelihood of having such gastrointestinal symptoms increase when self-reported job decision latitude is low and particularly so if psychological demands at work are reported to be high. Epigastric pain and acid regurgitation correspond to dyspepsia, whereas constipation and diarrhea as well as pain in the lower part of the abdomen belong to symptoms that are frequent in irritable bowel syndrome.

In summary, lack of decision latitude has been related to the risk of developing cardiovascular disease and functional gastrointestinal disorders. It may also have importance to the development of musculoskeletal disorders. Conversely, a high level of decision latitude may be protective. But how do these relationships arise? The relative risks associated with a low decision latitude may not be very great, but because low decision latitude is a widespread phenomenon at work, the association does have considerable impact on public health.

What Are the Mechanisms?

In principle there are two ways in which decision latitude can influence illness risk. The first is related to lifestyle factors, such as smoking and dietary habits as well as use of alcohol and drugs. Such lifestyle factors could be influenced by psychosocial factors at work as well as by factors outside work. The second path is related to direct effects of psychosocial factors on endocrine systems and metabolism. There are divided opinions regarding the relative importance of these paths among researchers. Israeli studies of a large cohort of industrial workers have indicated that there are significant effects of decision latitude on smoking habits (Melamed, 1995) and there are similar findings in a study in Sweden (Jonsson, Rosengren, Dotevall, Lappas, & Wilhelmsen, 1999). Other studies have shown that there are such relationships between lack of physical exercise and low decision latitude (Johansson, Johnson, & Hall, 1991). Despite these results there are many studies that have shown that the relationship between low decision latitude and cardiovascular illness risk remains after adjustment for lifestyle factors (Bosma et al., 1997; Theorell et al., 1998), and there are even studies that indicate a strengthened relationship after adjustment for such factors (Haynes, 1991). This indicates that the second pathway may be important.

Fighting for Control: Mobilization of Energy

Fighting for control should be reflected in physiological reactions. There is considerable support for this notion (Belkić et al., 2000; Theorell, 1997). Lack of decision latitude makes it necessary to mobilize energy to restore control in many situations. In such situations those systems are activated that supply us with fuel in the threatening situation. At the same time those systems are activated that facilitate our adaptation to a physically demanding situation. Sensitivity to pain is diminished, coagulation of blood is facilitated, and water and salt are retained to keep the blood volume intake during the fighting stage. In this situation mobilization of energy and adaptation to physical effort are given the highest priority at the expense of anabolism—the body's processes aiming at restoration and re-pairing of worn out cell functions. There is a continuous breakdown of bodily tissues. The muscles and the skeleton are being constantly rebuilt to be adapted to the needs created by our pattern of bodily movements. Muscle cells are worn out and have to be replaced. There are corresponding processes going on in the white blood cells, for instance. If the anabolism is neglected the condition of these organ systems will deteriorate and the risk of injury will increase. Anabolism is stimulated by deep sleep (stage IV) in particular. Therefore deep sleep is essential to the anabolism. In the long run this is very important to our protection against damage in periods of crisis. Furthermore, there is a relationship between anabolism and repro-duction. Partly the same hormones are responsible for these functions. The most obvious example is the sex hormones in men and women. It has been shown that the serum concentration of testosterone decreases in white collar workers when their level of job strain (demands in relation to decision latitude) increases (Theorell, Karasek, & Eneroth, 1990). Police superinten-dents who lost their jobs had a lowered serum testosterone concentration when this happened. Their concentration was normalized three years later when most of them had new similar jobs (Grossi, Theorell, Jürisoo, & Setterlind, 1999). In a corresponding way female caring personnel had a lowered oestradiol one year after that had been subjected to downsizing and reorganization in a large regional hospital in Sweden (Hertting & Theorell, 2001)—a situation in which they lost control over part of the caring process.

The mobilization of energy is mirrored in many ways in the body (Theorell, 2000). The acute mobilization could be assessed as elevated heart rate and blood pressure but also in increased electromyographic activity in the muscles. There is elevated excretion of adrenalin and noradrenalin in blood and urine. As soon as the activation has been going on for some minutes the HPA (hypothalamo pituitary adrenocortical) axis is activated. This can be measured as an elevation of the concentration of cortisol in blood and saliva. If the mobilization of energy is pronounced and repeated frequently during a long period of at least several months other changes may arise, so called disturbances of regulation. This could be summarized under the umbrella term allostasis (McEwen, 1998). Some examples with particular relevance to the exertion of control include

1. The normal regulation of the serum concentration of cortisol is disturbed. Under normal conditions the cortisol concentration is high in the morning and low in the evening. Under normal condi-tions there is also an elevation of the excretion of cortisol in situa-tions that require mobilization of energy. When there is a distur-bance of regulation this does not function in the normal way. One such disturbance is common in individuals who suffer from a classi-cal psychiatric depression—the concentration of cortisol is high in

saliva and blood both in the morning and the evening, as if the inhibition mechanism is not functioning (Rubin, Poland, Lesser, Winston & Blodgett, 1987). The opposite pattern—low concentration both in the morning and the evening with small variations in relation to stressful situations—is frequently observed in the chronic fatigue syndrome (Demitrack et al., 1991). In the latter case the accelerator function seems to be disturbed.

2. Effects on coagulation. Two different epidemiological studies have shown that the concentration of fibrinogen in blood plasma is elevated in individuals with a low level of decision latitude at work. This seems to be particularly true when indirect assessment (imputation of scores from national surveys or expert assessments) is used (Brunner et al., 1996; Tsutsumi, Theorell, Hallqvist, & Reuterwall, 1999).

There seems to be direct relationships between lack of decision latitude and the activities in the immune system as well. Higher serum concentrations of interleukin-6 were found in men who reported a low decision latitude than in other men in a Swedish study (Theorell, Hasselhorn, Vingård, Andersson, & the MUSIC Norrtälje Study Group, et al., 2000). A longitudinal study of spontaneous variations in the relationship between psychological demands and decision latitude showed that such variations were associated with variations in the serum concentration of immunoglobulin G—when job strain increased a concomitant elevation of immunoglobulin G concentration was observed (Theorell, Orth-Gomér, & Eneroth, 1990).

The most extensive studies on a physiological function in relation to decision latitude have been the studies of blood pressure. Blood pressure elevation during daily activities—recorded by means of fully automated equipment—has been shown to be related to a combination of high demands and low decision latitude in several studies both of men and women (Schnall, Landsbergis, & Baker, 1994). In such studies the combination of high demands and low decision latitude has turned out to be crucial. There has been no consistent relationship between job strain or decision latitude on one hand and blood pressure measured in the conventional way (in the supine position in the doctor's office) on the other hand.

Conclusion

The demand–control model has turned out to be educationally useful in efforts to improve the psychosocial work environment. Several attempts have been made to increase the authority over decision making at work. Evaluations of such attempts have been made. These studies investigated if there is any relationship between change in the experience of control at work and improved health of the employees. For example, in one study (Jackson, 1983) hospital outpatient facilities were randomly allocated to an experimental and a control population. To increase decision latitude for the employees the frequency of staff meetings was substantially increased to two per month. To improve social support, the staff were trained in participatory group problem techniques. Follow-up data in the two populations after six months showed that there was a significant drop in role ambiguity and role conflict in the experimental population but not in the control population. As a result the staff in the experimental population experienced significantly reduced emotional strain, job dissatisfaction, absenteeism, and intentions to leave the job.

In another study that represents a less conclusive but useful kind of evaluation (Edling & Wahlstedt, 1997; Theorell & Wahlstedt, 1999), mail deliverers were offered the possibility to move to a new postal office in the same region—an adaptation to a marked increase in the size of the population in the area. The employees in both stations were subjected to a follow-up study. When the new station started a number of psychosocial work environment changes were instituted aiming at increased decision latitude and improved social climate for the employees—for instance, more responsibility for a particular area for the working group aiming at increased cohesiveness. The results indicated that the development of physical ergonomic conditions did not differ between the groups during the year of follow-up but that social climate improved more in the new station. Possibly as a consequence the prevalence of symptoms from the neck–shoulder region decreased in the new station but not in the old one. In a third study (Orth-Gomér, Eriksson, Moser, Theorell, & Fredlund, 1994), the occupational health care team offered a two-day course in psychosocial stress for the employees in offices and also explored the psychosocial work environment as well as individual conditions by means of standardized questionnaires. On the basis of the findings a number of *changes* involving the employees were started, all aiming at improved decision latitude and social support. The findings after eight months indicated significantly improved autonomy and intellectual discretion as well as significantly improved social climate in the experimental group and no changes in the control group. No significant changes in personal habits (such as smoking and diet) were found. Despite this a significantly improved serum lipid pattern was found, indicative of reduced coronary heart disease risk, in the experimental group but not in the control group. There are several other experiences in the field (Karasek & Theorell, 1990; Kompier & Cooper, 1999), which indicate that psychosocial improvements of this kind take time, usually several months, and that collective feedback and *support* belong to the necessary conditions for successful organizational changes.

Usually, simple organizational solutions constitute the framework of the changes. One example would be an attempt to change the role of a foreman to become more of a coordinator rather than a supervisor, or (as in the first example described earlier) introducing regular structured meetings for organized information exchange

There have been attempts to increase cohesiveness in a work team by allowing the group to take responsibility over a large number of diverse tasks in the working process—accordingly less specialization—as in the second example. A common result with such an approach is an improvement in perceived authority over decisions as well as improved social support.

Thus, whereas several studies have evaluated the health effects of psychosocial interventions involving the whole staff and also interventions focusing on foremen, no studies have evaluated the employee health effects of interventions specifically focused on higher level managers.

In a study of an insurance company there was an anxiety-provoking social situation at the company during spring 1998. The whole company was affected by a thorough discussion about the basic conditions. A program for the improvement of the managers' psychosocial competence was started. It lasted from August 1998 until May 1999. Participation in the program was mandatory for the managers, who had to attend 30-minute lectures every second week. The lectures were followed by group discussions based on the themes discussed by the seminar leaders. The two-week intervals were intended to be periods of practical application of the knowledge in the organization. Psychosocial processes always take time to develop. The program was evaluated by means of a follow-up of managers and their employees in the experimental division as well as in a comparison sample in the same company (where no similar program was ongoing). There were 300 participants in the evaluation. The results indicated that compared to the levels preceding the experimental period, authority over decisions had improved after one year in the experimental group (in managers as well as in other employees). During the same period the serum cortisol concentration had decreased in the experimental group—not among the managers themselves but among the other employees. No similar changes had taken place in the comparison group. Because the work demands and the tempo in this organization was high the interpretation was that the lowered cortisol level in the experimental group reflected a lowered physiological arousal level (Theorell, Emdad, Arnetz, & Weingarten, 2001).

The examples that I have described illustrate that it is possible to improve decision latitude. Social climate and support may change at the same time, and it is often very difficult to disentangle these effects from one another because they are interwoven. In addition it may be very difficult to know whether it is the organizational effects that are important or whether effects on individual coping pattern are responsible for the beneficial effects.

When such improvement efforts are planned it is important to be systematic. If there are problems in a worksite one has to discuss how to do the initial exploration, and all parties have to be sympathetic to it. After this the use of the results of the exploration should be actively planned. There must be resources and time for follow-up (not only weeks and months but actually years) and possible redesign efforts. The results of the exploration should be fed back to the worksites both to the managers and to the employees. After this, those responsible should be aware that there will always be discussions and conflicts regarding the solution of practical problems. One has to work with the redesign in a structured way—groups have to be selected for formulating solutions. The planning includes deadlines and feedback to managers. The feedback should be thoroughly planned.

Attention both to individual and organizational aspects of the psychosocial working conditions seems to be important in improvement efforts. This always makes it more difficult to evaluate which components are beneficial. On the other hand, practical experiences have indicated that the likelihood of success increases when individual and organization attention is combined (Karasek & Theorell, 1990).

This chapter has discussed the basic aspects of control. There has been a short review of possibilities to record decision latitude for employees. Research has shown that a low decision latitude is associated with increased illness risks and vice versa. Low control seems to be particularly dangerous to health if it is combined with high demands. Recent research illustrates some of the physiological mechanisms that may link low control to bad health, and evaluation of interventions shows that it is often possible and meaningful to make efforts to improve control for employees.

References

Alfredsson, L., Karasek, R., & Theorell, T. (1982). Myocardial infarction risk and psychosocial environment: An analysis of the male Swedish working force. *Social Science and Medicine, 3,* 463–467.

Alfredsson, L., Spetz, C-L., & Theorell, T. (1984). *I huvudbilaga 1-3, Hälsopolitiska mål och behovsbaserad planering* (Goals of health policy and planning based upon needs). Stockholm: Ministry of Health, SUO.

Alfredsson, L., Spetz C-L., & Theorell, T. (1985). Type of occupation and near-future hospitalization for myocardial infarction and some other diagnoses. *International Journal of Epidemiology, 14,* 378–388.

Anonymus. (1996). Musculoskeletal disorders: Work-related risk factors and prevention—Scientific committee for musculoskeletal disorders of the international commission on occupational health (ICOH). *International Journal of Occupational and Environmental Health, 2,* 239–246.

Aronsson, G. (1985). Arbetsinnehåll—handledningsutrymme—stressreaktioner Teorier och fältstudier del 1 (Work contents—decision latitude—stress reactions. Theories and field studies part I). Stockholm: Department of Psychology, University of Stockholm.

Belkić, K., Schnall, P., & Ugljesic, M. (2000). Cardiovascular evaluation of the worker and workplace: A practical guide for clinicians. In P. Schnall, K. Belkić, P. Landsbergis, & D. Baker (Eds.), *The workplace and cardiovascular disease* (pp. 163–188). Philadelphia: Hanley & Belfus.

Bosma, H., Marmot, M., Hemingway, H., Nicholson, A., Brunner, E., & Stansfeld, S. (1997). Low job control and risk of coronary heart disease in Whitehall II study. *British Medical Journal, 314,* 558–565.

Brunner, E., Davey Smith G., Marmot, M., Canner, R., Beksinska, M., & O'Brien, J. (1996). Childhood social circumstances and psychosocial and behavioural factors as determinates of plasma fibrinogen. *Lancet, 347,* 1008–1013.

Cannon, B. (1999). Sartre and existential psychoanalysis. *Humanistic Psychologist, 27*(1), 23–50.

Demitrack, M. A., Dale, J. K., Straus, S. E., Lune, I., Listwak, S. J., Kruesi, M. J., Chrousos, G. P., & Gold, P. W. (1991). Evidence for impaired activation of the hypothalamic-pituitary-adrenal axis in patients with chronic fatigue syndrome. *Journal of Clinical Endocrinology and Metabolism, 73,* 1224–1234.

Edling, C., & Wahlstedt, K. (1997). Organizational changes at a postal sorting terminal: Their effects upon work satisfaction, psychosomatic complaints and sick leave. *Work & Stress, 11*(3), 279–291.

Fredlund, P., Hallqvist, J., & Diderichsen, F. (2000). *Psykosocial yrkesexponering—en uppdatering av ett klassifikationssystem för yrkesrelaterade psykosociala exponeringar* (Psychosocial occupational exposure—an update of a classification system for psychosocial exposure). *Arbete och hälsa 2000*, 11.

Fredriksson, K. (2000). On causes of neck and shoulder pain in the general population. *Arbete och hälsa 2000*, 14.

Freud, S. (1963). Anxiety. In *The complete psychological works of Sigmund Freud: Introductory lectures on psycho-analysis* (J. Strachey (ed. and trans.)). London: Hogarth Press. (Originally published 1916–1917).

Ganster, D. C. (1989). Worker control and well-being: A review of research in the workplace. In S. L. Sauter, J. J. Hurrell, Jr., & C. L. Cooper (Eds.), *Job control and worker health* (pp. 3–23). Chichester, UK: John Wiley & Sons.

Ganster, D. C., & Fusilier, M. R. (1989). Control in the workplace. In C. L. Cooper & I. T. Robertson (Eds.), *International Review of Industrial and Organizational Psychology* (Vol. 4, pp. 235–280). Chichester, UK: Wiley.

Grossi, G., Theorell, T., Jürisoo, M., & Setterlind, S. (1999). Psychophysiological correlates of organizational change and threat of unemployment among police inspectors. *Integrative Physiological and Behavioral Science, 1*, 30–42.

Hallsten L. (1998), Mental health and unemployment. Mental health selection to the labour market. *Arbete och hälsa, 7*, 1–224.

Hammarström, A., & Olofsson, B-L. (1998). Health and drug use—Relations to unemployment and labour market position. In *Young and unemployed in Scandinavia—A Nordic comparative study*. In I. Julkunen & J. Carle (Eds.), *Nord 14* (pp. 93–114). Copenhagen: Nordic Council of Ministers.

Härenstam, A., Rydbäck, A., Karlqvist, M., & Wiklund, P. (2000). Work life and organizational changes and how they are perceived by the employees. In K. Isaksson, C. Hogstedt, C. Eriksson, & T. Theorell (Eds.), *Health effects of the new labour market* (pp. 105–117). New York: Kluwer Academic/Plenum Press.

Hasselhorn, H-M., Theorell, T., Hammar, N., Alfredsson, L., Westerholm, P., & the WOLF Study Group. (2001). Occupational health care team ratings and self reports of demands decision latitude—Results from the Swedish WOLF study.

Haynes, S. G. (1991). The effect of job demands, job control, and new technologies on the health of employed women: A review. In M. Frankenhaeuser & U. Lundberg (Eds.), *Women, work, and health: Stress and opportunities. The Plenum series on stress and coping* (pp. 157–169). New York: Plenum Press.

Heidegger, M. (1972). *Being and time*. Oxford: Basil Blackwell.

Henry, J. P., & Stephens, P. M. (1977). Stress, health, and the social environment: *A sociologic approach to medicine*. New York: Springer.

Hertting, A., & Theorell, T. (2001). Physiological changes associated with downsizing of personnel and reorganisation in the health care sector. *Psychotherapy and Psychosomatics, 71*, 117–122.

Isaksson, K., Hellgren, J., & Pettersson, P. (2000). Repeated downsizing: Attitudes and well-being for surviving personnel in a Swedish retail company. In K. Isaksson, C. Hogstedt, C. Ericksson, & T. Theorell (Eds.), *Health effects of the new labor market* (pp. 85–101). New York: Kluwer Academic/Plenum Press.

Jackson, S. (1983). Participation in decision making as a strategy for reducing job related strain. *Journal of Applied Psychology, 68*, 3–19.

Janlert, U. (1997). Unemployment as a disease and diseases of the unemployed. *Scandinavian Journal of Work, Environment and Health, 3*, 79–83.

Johansson, G., Johnson, J. V., & Hall, E. M. (1991). Smoking and sedentary behaviour as related to work organization. *Social Science Medicine, 32*, 837–846.

Johnson, J. V., Stewart, W., Fredlund, F., Hall, E. M., & Theorell, T. (1990). *Psychosocial job exposure matrix: An occupationally aggregated attribution system for work environment exposure characteristics. Stress Research Reports, 221*. Stockholm: National Institute for Psychosocial Factors and Health.

Johnson, J., Stewart, W., Hall, E., Fredlund, P., & Theorell, T. (1996). Long-term psychosocial work environment and cardiovascular mortality among Swedish men. *American Journal of Public Health, 86*, 324–331.

Jonsson, D., Rosengren, A., Dotevall, A., Lappas, G., och Wilhelmsen, L. (1999). Job control, job demands and social support at work in relation to cardiovascular risk factors in MONICA 1995, Göteborg. *Journal of Cardiovascular Risk, 6*(6), 379–385.

Karasek, R. A. (1979). Job demands, job decision latitude, and mental strain: Implications for job redesign. *Administrative Science Quarterly, 24,* 285–307.

Karasek, R. A., & Theorell, T. (1990). *Healthy Work.* New York: Basic Books.

Kompier, M., & Cooper, C. (Eds.). (1999). *Preventing stress, improving productivity. European case studies in the workplace.* London: Routledge.

Landsbergis, P., & Theorell, T. (2000). Measurement of psychosocial exposure variables. In P. Schnall, K. Belkić, P. Landsbergis, & D. Baker (Eds.), *The workplace and cardiovascular disease* (pp. 163–188). Philadelphia: Hanley & Belfus.

McEwen, B. S. (1998). Protective and damaging effects of stress mediators. *Seminars in Medicine of the Beth Israel Deaconess Medical Centre, 338*(3), 171–179.

Melamed, S. (1995). Repetitive work, work underload and coronary heart disease risk factors among blue-collar workers: The Cordis study. *Journal of Psychosomatic Research, 39*(1), 19–29.

North, F. M., Syme, S. L., Feeney, A., Shipley, M., & Marmot, M. (1996). Psychosocial environment and sickness absence among British civil servants: The Whitehall II study. *American Journal of Public Health, 86*(3), 332–340.

Nyrén, O. (1995). Non-ulcer dyspepsia—Studies in epidemiology, pathophysiology, and therapy. Doctoral thesis, Uppsala University, Sweden.

Olsen, O., & Sondergaard-Kristensen, T. (1988). *Cardiovascular illness and work environment. Part 3. What relative importance has the work environment to cardiovascular illness in Denmark?* Copenhagen: Arbejdsmiljofondet.

Orth-Gomér, K., Eriksson, I., Moser, V., Theorell, T., & Fredlund, P. (1994). Lipid lowering through work stress reduction. *International Journal of Behavioral Medicine, 1*(3), 204–214.

Parkes, K. (1991). Locus of control as moderator: An explanation for additive versus interactive findings in the demand-discretion model of work stress? *British Journal of Psychology, 82*(3), 291–312.

Pedersen, N. L., Gatz, M., Plomin, R., Nesselrode, J. R., McClearn, G. E. (1989). Individual differences in locus of control during the second half of the life span for identical and fraternal twins reared apart and reared together. *Journal of Gerontology, 44*(4), 100–105.

Rubin, R. T., Poland, R. E., Lesser, I. M., Winston, R. A., & Blodgett, A. L. (1987). Neuroendocrine aspects of primary endogenous depression. I. Cortisol secretory dynamics in patients and matched controls. *Archives of General Psychiatry, 44,* 328–336.

Schnall, P. L., Landsbergis, P. A., & Baker, D. (1994). Job strain and cardiovascular disease. *Annual Review of Public Health, 15,* 381–411.

Schwartz, J., Pieper, C., & Karasek, R. (1988). A procedure for linking job characteristics to health surveys. *American Journal of Public Health, 78,* 904–909.

Selye, H. (1950). *The physiology and pathology of exposure to stress.* Montreal, Canada: Medical Publishers, Acta.

Sutton, R. I., & Kahn, R. L. (1987). Prediction, understanding, and control as antidotes to organizational stress. In J. W. Lorsch (Ed.), *Handbook of organizational behavior* (pp. 272–285). Englewood Cliffs, NJ: Prentice-Hall.

Syme, L. (1989). Control and health. In A. Steptoe & A. Appels (Eds.), *Stress, personal control and health* (pp. 3–18). Chichester, UK: John Wiley & Sons.

Taylor, F. (1967). *The principles of scientific management.* New York: Norton. (Originally published 1911)

Terry, D. J., & Jimmieson, N. L. (1999). Work control and employee well-being: A decade review. In C. L. Cooper & I. T. Robertson (Eds.), *International review of industrial and organizational psychology* (Vol. 14, pp. 95–148). Chichester, UK: John Wiley & Sons.

Theorell, T. (1997). Fighting for and losing or gaining control in life. In B. Folkow, T. Schmidt, & K. Uvnäs-Moberg (Eds.), *Stress, health and the social environment. Henry's Ethologic Approach to Medicine, Reflected by Recent Research in Animals and Man. Acta Physiologica Scandinavica* (Suppl. 640), 107–111.

Theorell, T. (2000). Neuroendocrine mechanisms. In P. L. Schnall, K. Belkić, P. Landsbergis, & D. Baker (Eds.), *The workplace and cardiovascular disease* (pp. 139–146). Philadelphia: Hanley & Belfus.

Theorell, T., Alfredsson, L., Westerholm, P., & Falck, B. (2000). Coping with unfair treatment at work—What is the relationship between coping and hypertension in middle-aged men and women? *Psychotherapy and Psychosomatics, 69,* 86–94.

Theorell, T., Emdad, R., Arnetz, B., & Weingarten, A-M. (in press). Employee effects of an educational program for managers at an insurance company. *Psychosomatic Medicine, 63,* 724–733.

Theorell, T., Hasselhorn, H-M., Vingård, E., Andersson, B., & the MUSIC-Norrtälje Study Group. (2000). Interleukin 6 and cortisol in acute musculoskeletal disorders: Results from at case-referent study in Sweden. *Stress Medicine, 16,* 27-35.

Theorell, T., Karasek, R. A., & Eneroth, P. (1990). Job strain variations in relation to plasma testosterone fluctuations in working men—A longitudinal study. *Journal of International Medicine, 227,* 31–36.

Theorell, T., Orth-Gomér, K., & Eneroth, P. (1990). Slow-reacting immunoglobulin in relation to social support and changes in job strain. *Psychosomatic Medicine, 52*(5), 511–516.

Theorell, T., Tsutsumi, A., Hallquist, J., Reuterwall, C., Hogstedt, C., Fredlund, P., Emlund, N., Johnson, V. J., & the SHEEP Study Group. (1998). Decision latitude, job strain, and myocardial infarction: A study of working men in Stockholm. *American Journal of Public Health, 88*(3), 382–388.

Theorell, T., & Wahlstedt, K. (1999). In M. Kompier & C. Cooper (Eds.), *Preventing stress, improving productivity* (pp. 195–221). London: Routledge.

Tsutsumi, A., Theorell, T., Hallqvist, J., & Reuterwall, C. (1999). Association between job characteristics and plasma fibrinogen in a normal working population: A cross sectional analysis in referents of the SHEEP study. *Journal of Epidemiology & Community Health, 53*(6), 348–354.

Ursin, H. (1997). Sensitization, somatization, and subjective health complaints. *International Journal of Behavioral Medicine, 4*(2), 105–116.

Vingård, E., Alfredsson, L., Hagberg, M., Kilbom, Å., Theorell, T., Waldenström, M., Wigaeus Hjelm, E., Wiktorin, C., Hogstedt, C., & the MUSIC-Norrtälje Study Group. (2000). To what extent do current and past physical and psychosocial occupational factors explain care-seeking for low back pain in a working population? Results from the Musculoskeletal Intervention Center-Norrtälje Study. *Spine, 25*(4), 493–500.

Volpert, W. (1982). The model of the hierarchical–sequential organization of action. In W. Hacker, W. Volpert, M. von Cranach (Eds.), *Cognitive and motivational aspects of action* (pp. 35–51). Amsterdam: North-Holland.

Waldenström, M., Josephson, M., Persson, C., & Theorell, T. (1998). Interview reliability for assessing mental work demands. *Journal of Occupational Health Psychology, 3*(3), 209–216.

Westerberg, L., & Theorell, T. (1997). Working conditions and family situation in relation to functional gastrointestinal disorders. The Swedish Dyspepsia Project. *Scandinavian Journal of Primary Health Care, 15*(2), 76–81.

11

Technology and Workplace Health

Michael D. Coovert and Lori Foster Thompson

It is nearly impossible to reflect on occupational health and well-being without considering the implications of technology in the workplace. Recent technological advances have transformed the way people interact with their jobs and their colleagues, and all signs indicate that contemporary changes merely reflect the tip of a much larger, more technically sophisticated iceberg. This chapter addresses the impact of technology on the health and wellness of office workers. We begin our discussion by describing the technological climate in which contemporary office workers operate. Next, we address various health concerns, which stem from human interactions with computer technology. Finally, we focus on the future of organizational computing and discuss the notion of wellness amid radical new configurations of workplace technology.

The Technological Climate of Modern-Day Office Work

Before considering the computer boom's impact on workplace health and wellness, it is important to recognize the technological climate in which contemporary organizations function. Personal computers are currently commonplace, and there is a movement toward increasingly interconnected technology that supports natural, mobile, autonomous, and collaborative electronic activities. Such technologies, as discussed next, correspond to trends in workplace computing, which are now at various stages of development and implementation.

Connectivity and Natural Interaction

The 1960s marked the beginning of an era characterized by a growing reliance on sophisticated office technology such as photocopy machines and increasingly capable typewriters. The desktop personal computer (PC) was introduced by IBM in 1981, and by the 1990s organizations had these machines networked together. Today, electronic information is more available than ever before. Office workers' machines are connected—to each other and to vast sources of information. Organizations are posting growing amounts of data on Intranets, which operate like the World Wide Web but have access that is restricted to particular people (*Merriam-Webster's Collegiate Dictionary,* 1998). Similarly, the volume of information available via the widely accessible Internet is rising rapidly. In short, office workers have grown progressively connected; their networked computers facilitate rapid communication within and across companies and countries.

The term "user friendly" originated in 1977 and became a popular buzzword in the 1980s (*Merriam-Webster's Collegiate Dictionary,* 1998). Both the designers and consumers of computer technology continue to focus on this concept. Stemming from the premise that technology should adapt to humans rather than the other way around, user-friendly computing environments permit natural human–computer interactions. Certain movements, postures, and communication styles (e.g., hand gestures) are familiar to humans, who have spent a lifetime using them to interact with other entities. Technology should exploit these natural skills. People should not be required to learn radically new movements and interaction styles to communicate by, with, and through computers.

Both interfaces and human–computer interaction strategies have evolved in recent years, generating technology that is increasingly user-friendly. First, there were simple interfaces operating at the command-line level and requiring keyboard input devices. Significant advances were made with GUI (graphical user interface) and associated WIMP (Windows, Icons, Menu, Pointer; such as Microsoft Windows®) environments. GUI programs allow computer users to interact easily with computers by using a mouse to make choices from menus or groups of icons (*Merriam-Webster's Collegiate Dictionary,* 1998). This environment was first seen on the Xerox® Star business computer. Today, there is a movement toward technology that is omnipresent yet unobtrusive. Titled "ubiquitous" or "quiet" computing, this concept abandons the currently awkward route to electronic information and maintains that workers should not be required to constantly access and generate information through a single piece of equipment sitting on a desktop. As an alternative, proponents suggest that computers should be located everywhere in the environment surrounding the worker. Though abundant, such computers should be virtually invisible to the user. That is, computers themselves should no longer be the focal point—something workers have to deal with to accomplish a task. Rather, they should disappear as they become more and more prevalent and as workers take them for granted. Telephones (and recently mobile cellular phones) provide an example of a now-ubiquitous device that has blended into the environment. Most people do not notice telephones when they walk into a room, yet they assume that these devices will be available when needed. Furthermore, people are generally able to use new telephones easily without expending thought and effort on how to do so. Communication (the task or goal) is the focal point; the telephone (the device) is not.

Mobile Computing

Modern-day workers have been likened to nomads, who constantly carry their work between office, home, hotel, car, and so on (Berggren, Montán, Nord, & Östergren, 2000). As a consequence, there is a recent trend toward mobile computing technology, which allows workers to journey with their equipment. For example, a cellular telephone paired with voicemail allows one to send, retrieve, and edit voice data from any location. Recent advances in wireless technologies and the current downsizing of computers to laptops, notebooks, and palmtops have facilitated the transition toward mobile computing. This movement is therefore likely to continue, expanding the definitions of "office" and "office worker," and leading to true nomadic computing. The driving philosophy is that workers need to be connected to computers continually—not just when they are at some home base, such as an office or a home computer. This connectivity is achieved through body-worn computers, which are always on and always providing information to the user. Most body-worn computers are battery operated and connected to a network via small wireless devices. Some are observable, and others are disguised and look like pieces of clothing or accessories (Mann, 1996).

Autonomous Adaptive Assistance

The advancement of intelligent-agent technology represents yet another important trend in workplace computing. Broadly defined, an intelligent agent is a computer program that performs tasks autonomously, without direct human supervision. Conventional electronic tools operate under the "direct manipulation" human–computer interaction metaphor, requiring users to explicitly initiate all tasks and monitor all events (Maes, 1994). Intelligent agents are considered the opposite of direct manipulation technology because they are able to autonomously infer the demands of a situation and adapt to these demands, initiating tasks without being told to do so. In this regard, an intelligent agent has been likened to an English butler that performs tasks with a keen ability to perceive and attend to user needs (Negroponte, as cited in Selker, 1994). An example of an early, simple agent is the Office Assistant available to workers using Microsoft Word® and Excel®. This "assistant" performs a number of tasks, such as correcting typos, capitalizing words, and automatically numbering itemized lists. The worker does not "ask" the Office Assistant for this help; rather, the program monitors workers' activities and initiates assistance when it seems most appropriate (Coovert & Thompson, 2001).

Most organizations currently use computer programs that incorporate basic forms of intelligent-agent technology. At best, these commonplace programs provide assistance with very simple tasks. At worst, they annoy people by incorrectly inferring their preferences and intruding on their work. Significant advances in intelligent-agent technology are expected during the coming years. Thus, agent-based assistance and agent–human collaborations will become much more frequent, sophisticated, and useful in the future.

Recognizing the benefits of collaboration, many organizations now assign work to groups and teams. Like individuals, groups and teams have been affected by the computer revolution; indeed, many collaborative efforts now occur electronically. Groups and teams need different types and levels of computer support, which are distinct from the technological requirements of individuals working alone. Computer supported cooperative work (CSCW; see Coovert & Thompson, 2001) is an area that focuses on technology in collaborative work settings. Supportive technology, labeled "groupware" and "teamware," can include hardware, software, services, and / or interpersonal process support (Coovert & Thompson, 2001).

Collaborative Support

In sum, workplace computing trends involve increasingly interconnected computer technology that supports natural, mobile, autonomous, and collaborative electronic activities. These trends are not mutually exclusive (e.g., intelligent agents and sophisticated connectivity facilitate the development of nomadic and ubiquitous computing); together they depict the environment in which modern-day office work and technology progress. Although strides are being made in the development and implementation of workplace technologies, the most advanced computational devices are not always available to office workers. Thus, many modern-day professionals struggle to use their computers efficiently and comfortably.

Health and Wellness in the Modern-Day Office

The technological evolution of the office environment has produced many benefits, yet it has also brought with it some concomitant negative outcomes. In many instances, technology has adversely affected the health of office workers. The following pages describe some of these effects, first in terms of office workers' physical health and then in terms of their psychological well-being. This discussion is followed by a consideration of various factors (e.g., correct ergonomic design), which may mitigate technology's negative impact on workplace health.

Physical Health Concerns in Today's Technological Office

To date, most organizations are nowhere near the ubiquitous, natural, and seamless technological environment promoted by visionaries. Rather, the typical organization requires workers to spend large portions of their day in offices or cubicles, facing glowing computer screens, and operating keyboard and input devices (often in a repetitive fashion) to generate and access the information necessary for their work. Literally hundreds of studies have examined the perception of harmful factors in the workplace caused by computerization. As an example, Rasanen, Notkola, and Husman (1997) surveyed several thousand salaried employees in the Finnish workforce and asked about perceived harmful work conditions. More than 94 percent of all respondents reported at least one harmful work condition, and more than half recounted three such conditions. The most commonly reported concerns involved factors that are often viewed as byproducts of increasing levels of technological sophistication: increased work pace, noise, mental demands, and repetitive movements. The latter of these concerns, repetitive movement, is largely implicated in the development and exacerbation of musculoskeletal disorders.

Musculoskeletal Disorders and Their Consequences

As currently configured, the modern-day office environment can lead to a host of technology-related musculoskeletal disorders (MSDs). MSDs are injuries and disorders of the soft tissues (including muscles, tendons, ligaments, joints, and cartilage) as well as the nervous system. Example MSDs include carpal tunnel syndrome, tendinitis, and tenosynovitis. Carpal tunnel syndrome is the compression and entrapment of the median nerve, where it passes through the wrist into the hand, in the carpal tunnel. The median nerve is the main nerve that extends down the arm to the hand and provides a sense of touch in the forearm, index, and middle fingers, and half of the ring finger. Tendinitis refers to tendon inflammation, which occurs when a muscle or tendon is repeatedly tensed from overuse or unaccustomed use. Finally, tenosynovitis is the inflammation or injury of the synovial sheath surrounding the tendon. This condition usually results from repetitive stress or excessive repetitive motion (such as that which is often attributed to keyboard use).

The effects of musculoskeletal disorders are costly and long-term. According to the U.S. Department of Labor, MSD costs total more than $50 billion a year. The expense to employers ranges between $15 and $18 billion in worker's compensation claims with one out of every three dollars going for MSD-related claims. MSDs are also costly to an individual's quality of life. The parts of a body affected by MSDs include a worker's arms, hands, fingers, neck, shoulders, legs, wrists, and back. MSDs cause a number of debilitating conditions including pain, numbness, stiff joints, muscle loss, difficulty in moving, tingling, and sometimes paralysis. Employees are often forced to take disability leave or early retirement to recover. In fact, MSDs are reportedly the third most frequent reason for disability and early retirement (Brenner & Ahern, 2000).

Sadly, some individuals afflicted with MSDs never regain full health. In a study examining carpal tunnel syndrome and other upper extremity cumulative trauma disorders, Keogh, Nuwayhid, Gordon, and Gucer (2000) investigated 537 worker compensation claimants for a variety of symptoms. Four-year postclaim follow-ups indicated that most individuals still suffered persistent symptoms that were severe enough to interfere with daily life. These symptoms included job loss, depression, and family disruption, indicating that certain MSDs are not easily recovered from, and they tend to disrupt life long after the point of initial diagnosis.

The Occurrence and Antecedents of Musculoskeletal Disorders

MSDs are indeed a prevalent problem, and the occurrence in the United States alone is quite startling. According to the U.S. Department of Labor, approximately 1.8 million people report work-related musculoskeletal disorders (such as carpal tunnel syndrome, tendinitis, or back injury) each year. In response to the frequency and severity of these disorders, recent research has offered an increased focus on the antecedents of MSDs. Particular MSDs, such as carpal tunnel syndrome, are long thought to be a byproduct of computer use; however, Stevens, Witt, Smith, and Weaver (2001) recently presented data indicating that the incidence of carpal tunnel syndrome is no more prevalent among computer users than it is in the general population. Other studies indicate that MSDs result from *multiple* risk factors (e.g., repetitive motion, age, gender, stress, tension, etc.), which can cause the disorder or exacerbate an existing predisposition. For instance, research has shown that certain types of computer users with particular stressors may be especially prone to MSDs. Ekman, Andersson, Hagberg, and Hjelm (2000) investigated musculoskeletal health symptoms reported by computer and mouse users in the Swedish workforce. These authors studied both gender and psychosocial factors in different occupational groups across several thousand longtime computer users. Certain responses on questionnaire items differentiated men and women in terms of reported musculoskeletal health symptoms. For example, age seemed to be a stronger health risk factor for men than for women. For female computer users, role overload and loss of control (in terms of work planning) were especially related to musculoskeletal health and well-being.

A recent survey, which examined work-related health complaints among a large population of Finnish employees, found that the most common complaints involved musculoskeletal system symptoms. Moreover, respondents largely believed that these work-related musculoskeletal complaints were associated with harmful ergonomic work designs (Rasanen et al., 1997). Indeed, attention to ergonomics can substantially alter the relationship between technology and workplace health. The field of ergonomics emphasizes the value of fitting the design of the job to the worker (rather than forcing the worker to fit the job) and focuses on adapting job tasks, tools, work stations, and other equipment to reduce the stress exerted on the worker's body. (It is also important to consider cognitive ergonomics—that is, matching the job in terms of its cognitive demands to the employee's mental representation of work.)

A wealth of research investigates the relationships between ergonomics and musculoskeletal health. As an exemplar, Gilad and Harel (2000) have linked keyboard shapes to work–health issues. Their findings demonstrated that using a specific keyboard design (a "negative" design—the keyboard tilts in a downward direction) caused the worker to exert less effort, stress the flexor muscle less, and increase overall typing quality when compared to alternative keyboard designs. In a related initiative, Lincoln et al. (2000) integrated the results of 24 different studies focusing on ergonomics and work-related carpal tunnel syndrome. The studies came from a variety of disciplines and each had used ergonomic interventions that attempted to reduce or eliminate carpal tunnel syndrome. The intervention strategies included keyboard support systems, computer mouse designs, wrist supports, alternative keyboards, and tool redesign. Also reviewed were personnel interventions, such as ergonomic awareness programs, on-the-job exercise programs, splint wearing, and ergonomic training. A careful examination of the studies failed to conclusively demonstrate that the interventions prevent carpal tunnel syndrome in the working population (Lincoln et al., 2000). Clearly, more research needs to be done to elucidate the antecedents of carpal tunnel syndrome.

Although issues related to keyboards and other input devices have dominated much of the ergonomic research, the position of the computer monitor is also of critical importance in determining the amount of stress and strain placed on workers' bodies. Several investigations have looked at the optimal angle and height of a computer monitor. Straker and Mekhora (2000) placed a monitor at two different heights, one in a high position and the second in a low position. (Position was relative to the straightforward gaze of an individual whose head is level.) Two thirds of the study participants preferred the high monitor position, which also led to a reduction in cervical and spinal muscle activity and a less-flexed head, neck, and trunk posture. The high monitor position may, however, compromise the visual acuity for the workers. Thus, there is a trade-off between the optimal viewing height and the height at which the monitor will produce the least amount of musculoskeletal stress and strain.

Gomzi, Bobic, Ugrenovic, and Goldoni (1999) examined the relationship between the ergonomic design features of video display terminals and the psychological characteristics that typify the operators of those terminals. Using a questionnaire study, health problems of various types (including psychological disturbances) were assessed and correlated with ergonomic characteristics of the work station. The results showed that complaints over health status are significantly related to the Neuroticism dimension on the Eysenck Personality Questionnaire. Psychological characteristics and job tasks relative to the ergonomic condition of the environment were all related to perceived levels of job stress and physical health complaints.

In short, technology-related pains and syndromes can be quite serious, and they are often linked to office ergonomics. Although research focusing on the antecedents of MSDs has recently received increased emphasis, much more work is needed to clarify inconclusive and inconsistent findings. Research has yet to establish the exact manner in which proposed antecedents interact, and we have not yet pinpointed the processes by which these variables and disorders affect office workers. In the future, we must begin building an ecological model of workers interacting with technology, as it may be that the technology in-and-of itself is only a piece of a much larger puzzle pertaining to negative physical health factors in the workplace.

Psychological Health Concerns in Today's Technological Office

In many cases, technology adversely affects office workers' psychological health, in addition to their physical well-being. Negative psychological effects stem from a variety of factors, including office noise, changing work demands, a lack of control on the job, isolation from others, and reductions in privacy. Research has linked most of these technology-related variables to psychological stress. Stress, in turn, can lead to a host of undesirable outcomes, including psychological strains, negative attitudes, low job satisfaction, and mood disturbances.

Job-Specific Effects

Research suggests that technological change does not influence all professions equally. Subsequent to a technological change, some professions will react according to a stress reaction model (workers initially react with increased levels of stress to the introduction of the technology, but once the implementation is complete, workers return to stasis), whereas others will follow a stress accumulation model (stress is more lasting and may even build up over time). Jarvenpaa (1997) described a three-year study that followed the implementation of technological change within three different job groups (office workers, judges, and clerks). The new technology immediately affected each of the three different groups. The negative stress initially experienced by office workers diminished over time; however, the other two groups did not show similar reductions in stress.

Control

Modern-day office technology is far from perfect, and its failures are often a source of stress and frustration for human operators who are unable to control technological breakdowns (such as a computer crashing), malfunctions (such as the inability to log onto an e-mail account), and deficiencies (such as an intelligent agent whose unwelcome "help" will not go away). A worker's lack of control is a key component of the stress and anxiety produced by technological issues. Research has shown that for the first few years following the introduction of new technology, the main predictor of job dissatisfaction is lack of control (Lindstrom, Leino, Seitsamo, & Torstila, 1997). Fenster and colleagues (1999) actually defined stressful work as "high demand in combination with low control"; their research indicates that such a combination can affect people physically as well as psychologically, as has been discussed in previous chapters. Specifically, these authors examined the relationship between high work demand, low control, and menstrual functioning among women. Results indicated that women in stressful jobs demonstrated more than twice the risk for short-cycle length compared to women who were not working in stressful jobs. Thus it appears that the lack of control experienced by workers who are required to deal with technological failures, inadequacies, and changes generate psychological stress and concomitant physical effects.

Isolation

The notion of workplace carries with it not just an environment in which work gets done (thereby achieving the organization's goals), but it also involves a fulfillment of social needs. Social needs are satisfied, in part, by individual interactions with others in the work environment. Ample evidence supports this perspective (cf., Timpka & Sjoberg, 1998; Viller & Sommerville, 2000). Nevertheless, until ubiquitous and mobile computing become commonplace, office workers will continue the currently awkward route to electronic information, which requires them to constantly access and generate data through a single piece of equipment sitting on a desktop. This requirement ties employees to their desks and limits opportunities for social interaction among coworkers. Although the Internet (e.g., e-mail) provides a new outlet for social interaction, there is some debate concerning whether this medium improves or actually harms participation in community life and social relationships (Kraut et al., 1998).

The ability to meet employees' social needs at work becomes an additional challenge when considering the area of telework. It is well known that many organizations have been moving toward increased use of workers who occupy space that is not in the traditional or central office but rather at their own homes. The notion of telework is often mentioned in conjunction with the desire to allow workers to achieve a better balance between the demands of their work and home lives. This increased balance is thought to be achieved through several mechanisms, including the ability to maintain a more flexible and adaptable schedule; an avoidance of the daily commute between home and the workplace; a decrease in the amount of time children need to be in child care; a decrease in the likelihood of the "latchkey child" problem by allowing the parent to be at home; and sometimes a positive impact on the family budget by not having to pay for parking and associated commuting expenses. A final advantage touted by proponents of telework involves the benefits of exposing children to their parents' work, thereby giving them a fuller appreciation of adult responsibility.

Does the ability to work at home really increase the quality of workers' lives? One of the primary downsides of telework is that employees often report feeling isolated. Furthermore, some people insist that working at home can have a detrimental impact, not only in terms of opportunities to interact with colleagues but also in terms of career progression. Because teleworkers are infrequently at the office, they are left out of conversations and critical decision-making circles; this diminished visibility in turn leads to reduced chances for promotion.

In short, telework does not always increase the quality of work life, and it sometimes increases isolation and the psychological stress associated with jobs. Recent research investigating men and women who do professional work at home provide some interesting leads concerning the aspects of telework that seem to generate stress. The literature (cf., Mirchandani, 2000) cites three key reasons why teleworkers are especially prone to psychological stress. The first is that the proximity between home and work may increase the likelihood that an employee's occupational and family roles will run together. Unless they keep work and family roles separate, teleworkers will constantly need to choose between which demands to fulfill at any point in time throughout the day. This role conflict leads to increased stress. (This principle is noteworthy in that the integration of work and family life is often touted as one of the advantages of telework.) A second reason why individuals who work at home experience stress is that they do not have a clear and separate boundary between the work and nonwork day, and they will often work longer hours throughout the day (or weekend) than those who operate in a central office location. Therefore, separation from the office can lead to workaholic tendencies that, in turn, can have a negative impact on one's psychological health. A third reason teleworkers need to maintain a distinction between home and work is to protect the professionalism of their work lives and the quality of their family lives. It is interesting to note that it appears that an intervention as straightforward as quality circles (i.e., groups of workers who meet regularly to discuss and propose solutions to problems) can significantly reduce the stress associated with telework (Konradt, Schmook, Wilm, & Hertel, 2000).

Privacy

As previously indicated, office computers are becoming increasingly interconnected—to each other and to the larger organization. The technological infrastructure of the organization is not always viewed as a positive force, especially when the workplace is monitored electronically. Technological advances enable an increased variety of watchdog technologies that track workers' behaviors. Various types of surveillance methods are currently being used, including the number of keystrokes per unit of time, the length of telephone calls, the amount of time between telephone calls, and the length of time in which employees are away from their desks. Issues that have been raised with respect to electronic monitoring include privacy, fairness, quality of work life, and a host of stress-related illnesses (Rosenberg, 1999).

Computer monitoring is attractive to many managers because it allows them to keep close tabs on their employees. Although electronic surveillance often seems like a good idea to organizations that want to ensure that workers are staying on-task, there are some important side-effects to consider. In 1987, the Office of Technology Assessment released a report titled, "The Electronic Supervisor: New Technology, New Tensions" (U.S. Congress, Office of Technology Assessment, 1987). The report described several of the benefits of electronic technology, such as the ability to impart timely feedback on performance and the opportunity to provide an objective basis for evaluation. The report goes on to address the possible disadvantages related to computer-based monitoring. In particular, disadvantages exist when privacy is invaded, thereby causing psychological stress. As Fairweather (1999) has pointed out, a basic tenet of the psychological contract between workers and organizations mandates that employees should not have to reveal their entire selves to the employer. In many cases, electronic monitoring violates this tenet, causing tension among office workers. This type of stress has been linked to psychological illnesses such as anxiety, depression, and nervous breakdowns (Howard, 1985). At a minimum, continual employee monitoring leads to very low morale (Fairweather, 1999). In a nutshell, the appropriateness of computer monitoring depends on how it is used. It can either be administered in an unfair sense or it can be used reasonably, to provide an objective basis for employee evaluations.

Recently, the courts have addressed the issue of workplace surveillance (Rosenberg, 1999). One key case, *Smyth v. Pillsbury,* seems to have set a precedent. In this case, Smyth sued the Pillsbury Co. for wrongful discharge after the company read (and disapproved of) some of his e-mail. The electronic communications privacy act of 1986, which specifically "prohibits the unauthorized interception and disclosure of the content of electronic communication," was at the center of this case. The court ultimately decided that employees have very few rights with respect to workplace privacy, even when management consistently assures workers that e-mail will not be monitored. The court seemingly considered the familiar recommendation that employees should treat e-mail as they would a postcard: anyone who comes across it can read it, and workers should not anticipate any level of privacy associated with this form of communication. Thus, the legal trend clearly indicates that there is no legal protection afforded to employees' privacy in the workplace. In the days to come, it will be important to consider the degree to which this philosophy extends to invasions of privacy that occur via video systems, telephone monitoring, computer conferencing, and so forth.

Improving Office Health and Wellness: Contemporary Solutions

Although modern-day technology is capable of adversely affecting office workers' physical and psychological health, a number of strategies can be implemented to mitigate the computer revolution's negative effect. Consider an office undergoing technological transformations, for instance. Loss of control (and the concomitant resistance to change) can produce negative emotions, yet strategies for increasing user acceptance can reduce resistance and ease the transition. Many approaches exist for increasing the acceptability of new computer systems to users. A number of these strategies come directly from the field of industrial–organizational psychology, and they include approaches such as participative management. Participation is the process whereby end-users become involved in designing the systems that they will later use in their work (increasing the amount of control they have over the technology). Carayon and Karsh (2000) reported on their successful attempt at a participative design strategy. Employees who were involved in the implementation of the new system reported higher levels of job satisfaction and rated the system as performing better than did those end-users who did not participate in the implementation of the system. Thus, participative design and implementation is one of the numerous strategies that can reduce technology's negative effect on workplace health.

Improving Workplace Ergonomics

Unlike participative design techniques, other strategies require a careful focus on ergonomics. Sometimes, ergonomic solutions to workplace problems are simple, inexpensive, and even commonsense. Workers trained to detect ergonomic concerns in their offices can often take preventive measures to remove, eliminate, or decrease the likelihood of injury. Some simple changes can be made by merely adjusting the height of working surfaces, providing telephone handsets, offering fatigue breaks, changing the order in which tasks are performed, providing ergonomic chairs or stools, putting supplies and equipment within easy reach, and reducing the weight or size of items workers must lift.

One straightforward approach that can be easily implemented by most organizations is a training program designed to promote ergonomic awareness. Such programs teach employees the correct way to perform tasks as well as how to properly use the equipment and tools associated with their work to prevent forces that stress workers' joints. Key training components provide the opportunity to develop methods to keep joints in neutral, non-load bearing positions such as using adjustments provided on chairs and other work equipment. Sometimes merely rearranging the position of a telephone, printer, or keyboard can result in better working postures. In short, some of the debilitating stressors associated with office work can be removed via training programs that focus on physical and psychological stressors, the proper use and adjustment of equipment, and the value of small rest breaks used to exercise and stretch body joints. As suggested by Dov Zohar's discussion of safety climates (chapter 6, this volume), supervisory practices may influence the degree to which employees carry out ergonomic safety procedures taught in training programs. Future research should examine whether the leaders' safety policies moderate the relationship between ergonomic training programs and various health problems.

Ergonomic solutions to workplace problems are also moving beyond simple fixes and training programs. One of the most extensive efforts stems from the work of the U.S. Department of Labor, which proposed specific legislation promoting ergonomic standards across industries. The proposal called for ergonomics programs for individual jobs. It is believed that such programs would significantly reduce the number and severity of musculo-skeletal disorders caused by risk factors in the workplace. (For the reader interested in additional detail, there is quite a lot of readily accessible information regarding the field of ergonomics available from the U.S. Department of Labor's Occupational Safety and Health Administration.)

The Occupational Safety and Health Administration (OSHA) standards outline several actions that employers must take if workers develop MSD signs or symptoms. The complete set of employer behaviors is documented in the standards. One critical responsibility involves determining whether workplace incidents meet the definition of an "action trigger" (an event that should trigger an action on the part of the employer). Action triggers are risk factors that have come into play for one or more employees. One action trigger involves repetition, which is defined as the act of repeating the same motion every few seconds for two hours at a time while using a device (such as a keyboard or mouse) steadily for more than four hours per day. Six other action triggers are described in the standards.

OSHA recommends several courses of action that an employer can take if employees have work-related MSDs or are at risk for developing them as indicated by the action triggers. These recommendations include the following programs. (a) Management leadership–employee participation: This program emphasizes the importance of assigning responsibilities for setting up and managing ergonomics programs within the workplace. By ensuring that specific individuals are targeted with responsibility for maintaining resources and information, this program encourages employee participation and it promotes commitment to company policies and effective ergonomic practices. (b) Training: Each employee is trained in setting up and managing an ergonomics program. Training focuses on recognizing the signs of MSD hazards and symptoms, and it should demonstrate how to implement and evaluate controls that are used to address job hazards. (c) Job hazard analysis and control: This program focuses on the need to monitor all employees who perform jobs where MSDs exists. By using a set of tools that can assess relevant MSD risk factors (these tools are available from OSHA), employers can take preemptive actions (such as fixing problems and reducing or eliminating errors) early on. (d) MSD management: This program provides recommendations for handling employees with an incidence of MSD. Access to health care professionals should be provided as well as a follow-up evaluation. MSD management includes any temporary work restrictions determined to be necessary. (e) Program evaluation: The ergonomics program that is put in place should be evaluated on a routine basis. This evaluation should allow employee input and include any corrective actions targeted toward deficiencies found in the program.

Although the U.S. Congress failed to enact the standards into law, the OSHA program is the most comprehensive current ergonomics effort of its kind, and its implementation would produce significant payoffs. The anticipated benefits include the prevention of 4.6 million MSDs within the first 10 years of program implementation; the protection of 102 million workers at more than 6 million worksites; $9.1 billion in savings, which would accrue annually; and a $27,700 savings in direct costs, which would occur for each MSD prevented. The cost to employers is anticipated to be $4.5 billion annually, and the anticipated cost for bringing an individual's work station into compliance averages nearly $250 per year. In short, organizations can greatly benefit by following the OSHA recommendations, even though the program has yet to be enacted as law.

The Future of Technology and Workplace Health

The health concerns and solutions discussed thus far are largely based on the present-day mode of human–computer interaction: a worker, a telephone, a desktop computer, voicemail, e-mail, and associated paraphernalia. Technology is progressing rapidly, however, and major innovations are on the horizon. Because innovations invariably lead to new problems and solutions, we conclude our consideration of technology and employee health by offering a glimpse of the future workplace and speculating on the health-related implications surrounding new work arrangements.

The Technological Climate of Future Office Work: Cooperative Buildings

The technological trends discussed at the beginning of this chapter (ubiquitous computing, intelligent agents, etc.) have not been fully realized. These anticipated technologies require further research, development, and integration, which is well underway. Although these innovations have value on their own, their full benefits are only available via the comprehensive integration and combined use of the technologies (Streitz et al., 1999). It is predicted that the amalgamation of these new creations will occur in the form of the dynamic, user-friendly, technically rich "cooperative building" of the future. These buildings include a number of fascinating features, such as smart rooms, dynamic and adaptive electronic assistance, and support for informal interactions and collaboration among on- and off-site workers.

Smart Rooms

Smart rooms within cooperative buildings are partially predicated on the principles of augmented reality. In a basic sense, augmented reality systems give electronic properties to workplace objects. These properties augment the objects, affording them previously unrealized functionality while allowing them to serve their original purposes. Smart rooms also rely on the concept of ubiquitous computing. Whereas modern office buildings include one computer per office or desk, smart rooms contain computers virtually everywhere. Rather than invading the workplace, these computers reside in or on everyday objects, such as walls, chairs, and desks. For instance, an ordinary swivel chair can be retrofitted with a sensor that gives it functionality beyond comfortable seating. With the proper add-on technology, the chair can serve as an input device, in lieu of a mouse for instance. The chair is linked to a chair-like icon on a computer screen. Swiveling in a particular direction enables the user to communicate his or her attention to specific participants during virtual meetings in electronic chat rooms represented on the computer screen (Cohen, 1999). Similarly, recently developed armchairs equipped with built-in computers allow people to compute privately or project their electronic documents onto a shared wall space, where other workers can directly modify documents (Streitz et al., 1999). A pen can be equipped with a scanner, which allows workers to scan documents, in addition to writing on them (Weiser, 1991). The use of pens and chairs as input devices exemplifies the fact that cooperative buildings allow input from a wide variety of sources (e.g., hand gestures, voice commands, scanners, etc.), which are much more natural than keyboard and mouse entry. Moreover, the technology in cooperative buildings is designed to be used effortlessly, with little or no previous training (Berggren et al., 2000).

Enhanced Electronic Assistance

The advantages of cooperative buildings extend beyond smart input devices. Cooperative buildings themselves assist and collaborate with workers. Augmented items are easily found when buildings and objects assist with the hunt. For example, an everyday book fitted with a small, inexpensive computer "tab" will beep on command. By tracking the beeping noise, a worker can easily locate the desired book (Weiser, 1991). Moreover, a voice command, such as "Send Don Ridel the paper I presented at last year's APA conference," will prompt a series of actions. Various technologies will recognize the identity of the person issuing the command, determine the title and location of the paper, identify the address of the recipient, and transmit the document (Berggren et al., 2000). A multitude of inconspicuous computers cooperate with each other and the worker, who is no longer required to walk to his or her office and manually complete this sequence of steps through a single machine sitting atop his or her desk. Indeed, human–computer interaction in the cooperative building has been relabeled "human–information interaction," because the worker deals with information through the computer, rather than spending large portions of the day struggling with the computer itself.

Dynamic and Adaptive

Cooperative buildings are dynamic and adaptive in that they are able to adjust themselves to the preferences and requirements of their inhabitants.

Smart floors can determine the identity and location of a worker based solely on his or her footsteps (Kidd et al., 1999), and other technologies, such as active electronic identity badges, can serve the same purpose. Thus, the building is able to track who is in each room at every moment in time. Moreover, intelligent agent-based systems can infer the preferences of all workers, based on their past choices and behaviors, and the building is thus able to adjust itself to accommodate the predilections of its inhabitants. In presentations, for example, the size of text on the overhead slides, the volume of the speaker's amplified voice, and the amount of ambient light can be automatically adapted to suit the desires of the particular audience attending the meeting. Similarly, an electronically augmented bulletin board can adjust itself to display only the information that is of interest to the particular person viewing it (Weiser, 1991).

Supporting Informal Interaction

Proponents of cooperative buildings argue that desktop computers and virtual reality systems impair health and wellness by isolating workers. In contrast, cooperative buildings are designed to promote chance encounters and social interactions. This is accomplished via augmented dwelling spaces for the workforce. Such spaces can be as simple as a computer-enhanced commons area (similar to a hotel lobby) or they can be as innovative as wilderness areas and caves or domes within the building specifically designed to allow workers the opportunity to experience the mysterious and exploratory environment. Open spaces, such as playgrounds and gardens, also allow people to gather and interact. These common areas are designed to provide an open office, thereby preventing isolation and promoting inspiration, wellness, creativity, and productivity (Moltke & Andersen, 1998).

Cooperative buildings counter isolation in other ways too. "Ambient media" allow a person working alone in an office to sense activity in other parts of the organization. For instance, the amount of traffic in the commons area may be represented by a series of moving spotlights on a worker's office wall. When many people are moving about the common space, the lights will shift quickly. Slow moving lights indicate little activity. Similarly, water ripples reflected in the ceiling may represent the distant activity of a teammate (Berggren et al., 2000). Such subtle, ambient media reside at the periphery of workers' senses. Although they connect people to others in the organization, these technologies do not dominate workers' attention and distract them from their tasks.

Supporting Teleworkers

Finally, it is important to note that cooperative buildings support off-site work and interactions by intimately linking the organization's physical and digital worlds. The physical world exists in the form of the building, and various computer technologies make the digital world possible. Sophisticated teamware, videoconferencing, and nomadic computing technologies, for example, can capitalize on Internet capabilities and on-site structures to blend the physical and digital aspects of the organization, allowing on- and off-site workers to collaborate almost as if they were sitting together inside the cooperative building. Ambient media and Web cameras can allow nomadic telecommuters to "log in" and experience the traffic flow of the physical building. Similar technology could enable on-site workers to sense the number of people remotely logged into some aspect of the organization. In short, cooperative buildings take steps to prevent the isolation of nomadic and teleworkers. The physical space gives a sense of place and community and acts as a forum for face-to-face interaction, and the digital world integrates into the physical space to allow the building to reach far beyond its physical structure (Huang, Waldvogel, & Lertsithichai, 1999).

Health and Wellness in the Cooperative Building

Cooperative buildings appear quite plausible, especially in light of the current research and development efforts geared toward this technology (Streitz & Halkia, 2001). If they become a reality, these digitally enhanced buildings will radically change human–computer interaction, with implications for workplace health. We conclude by speculating on the manner in which the cooperative building of the future may alter health and wellness among office workers.

Musculoskeletal Health

If managed appropriately, future work in the cooperative building may be free from many of the technology-driven health problems discussed earlier. As previously indicated, musculoskeletal disorders are currently a major concern, and they can be mitigated by careful attention to ergonomics. In essence, cooperative buildings provide the ultimate ergonomic fix. Smart rooms support multiple input modes, such as hand gestures, voice commands, and swivel chairs. In the cooperative building, human–information interaction will be virtually effortless, thereby reducing repetitive motions and the associated musculoskeletal disorders that result from unnatural human–computer interaction. Room settings that adjust to individual preferences (e.g., overheads with adaptable font sizes) can reduce physical strain as well.

Cooperative buildings may affect psychological wellness, in addition to physical health. Adaptive assistance (e.g., computers that assume certain tasks, such as finding a requested conference paper and sending it to a colleague) can help reduce the anxiety associated with work and information overload. Rooms or caves that permit exploration can promote relaxation and ease psychological tensions. Depending on how they are managed, cooperative buildings may also affect control, isolation, and privacy for better or for worse. As previously discussed, these three variables are all related to psychological wellness.

Control

In some ways, cooperative buildings can promote feelings of control. In today's world, feelings of low control, helplessness, and stress occur when familiar technology fails unpredictably and when new technology is forced on ill-prepared workers. In the cooperative building of the future, advances in hardware and networking technologies will lessen the frequency of system incompatibilities, unforeseen technical problems, and connection errors, thereby minimizing the occurrence of these uncontrollable stressors. In addition, future workers are less likely to be stressed by frequently changing technology. Adaptive, electronic technologies can be used effortlessly, with little or no previous training (Berggren et al., 2000). Future workers will interact with information, not technology; therefore, most will not even notice upgrades and technical changes.

At the same time, cooperative buildings may impede feelings of control, especially if the influx of intelligent-agent technology is not managed carefully. As previously indicated, intelligent-agent technology is advancing steadily, and agents will be able to provide sophisticated assistance to humans in the future (e.g., setting up appointments on a worker's behalf, or adjusting a room to the preferences of a worker). To the extent that humans remain in control, this relationship will ease many workplace burdens. To the extent that workers are unable to stop their agents' activities, this relationship will cause frustration, stress, and other health concerns. As previously suggested, role overload and loss of control have been empirically linked to health and well-being. Thus, it will be important to give workers the power to override electronic systems.

Isolation

The structural components of cooperative buildings (e.g., electronically enhanced commons areas, ambient media, etc.) ensure that both on-site workers and telecommuters have opportunities to informally socialize and experience the presence of their colleagues. These interactions may moderate the feelings of loneliness and isolation experienced by many modern-day workers. On the other hand, excessive opportunities for interaction may cause workers to feel as though their colleagues are always present, thereby blurring the distinction between work and leisure. As chapter 7, this volume, discusses in detail, work–nonwork balance is a very important health issue. Already, many people are informally expected to check their professional voice-mail and e-mail accounts after they have left the office. As previously discussed, this amalgamation of work and family roles can increase stress and anxiety. Further obscuring the distinctions between work and home, advances in cooperative buildings could threaten the precious balance between people's personal and professional lives. This issue will require careful attention to prevent work from diminishing the future employee's nonwork existence.

Privacy

One of the most serious future issues concerns privacy within cooperative buildings. Most contemporary electronic monitoring systems track only the activities that occur via desktop computers (e.g., e-mail messages, Internet usage, etc.). In contrast, cooperative building features depend on the technology's ability to track people as they move throughout the entire building and beyond. Thus, workers are followed via electronic badges, smart floors, and similar devices, and privacy is reduced. The personal data generated by future tracking devices could be very dangerous in the wrong hands. Fortunately, cryptographic technologies are being developed, which secure messages from one ubiquitous computer to another and safeguard private information stored in networked systems (Weiser, 1991). It will be important for computer scientists to design these features into cooperative buildings from the outset. Finally, organizations should allow workers the freedom to turn tracking devices off at will, thereby increasing control and privacy while decreasing feelings of psychological stress.

References

Berggren, M., Montán, S., Nord, H., & Östergren, M. (2000). *Smart spaces*. Retrieved March 12, 2001, from http://www.docs.uu.se/~cmb/smart-spaces.pdf

Brenner, H., & Ahern, W. (2000). Sickness absence and early retirement on health grounds in the construction industry in Ireland. *Occupational and Environmental Medicine, 57,* 615–620.

Carayon, P., & Karsh, B. T. (2000). Sociotechnical issues in the implementation of imaging technology. *Behaviour & Information Technology, 19,* 247–262.

Cohen, M. (1999). A swivel chair as an input device. In N. A. Streitz, J. Siegel, V. Hartkopf, & S. Konomi (Eds.), *Cooperative buildings: Integrating information, organizations, and architecture* (pp. 208–209). New York: Springer.

Coovert, M. D., & Thompson, L. F. (2001). *Computer supported cooperative work: Issues and implications for workers, organizations, and human resource management.* Thousand Oaks, CA: Sage.

Ekman, A., Andersson, A., Hagberg, M., & Hjelm, E. W. (2000). Gender differences in musculoskeletal health of computer and mouse users in the Swedish workforce. *Occupational Medicine-Oxford, 50,* 608–613.

Fairweather, N. B. (1999). Surveillance in employment: The case of teleworking. *Journal of Business Ethics, 22,* 39–49.

Fenster, L., Waller, K., Chen, J., Hubbard, E. E., Windham, G. C., Elkin, E., & Swan, S. (1999). Psychological stress in the workplace and menstrual function. *American Journal of Epidemiology, 149,* 127–134.

Gilad, I., & Harel, S. (2000). Muscular effort in four keyboard designs. *International Journal of Industrial Ergonomics, 26,* 1–7.

Gomzi, M., Bobic, J., Ugrenovic, Z., & Goldoni, J. (1999). Personality characteristics of VDT operators and computer-related work conditions. *Studia Psychologica, 41,* 15–21.

Howard, R. (1985). *Brave new workplace.* New York: Viking Books.

Huang, J., Waldvogel, M., & Lertsithichai, S. (1999). Design of Swisshouse: A physical/virtual cooperative workspace. In N. A. Streitz, J. Siegel, V. Hartkopf, & S. Konomi (Eds.), *Cooperative buildings: Integrating information, organization, and architecture* (pp. 215–220). New York: Springer.

Jarvenpaa, E. (1997). Implementation of office automation and its effects on job characteristics and strain in a district court. *International Journal of Human-Computer Interaction, 9,* 425–442.

Keogh, J. P., Nuwayhid, I., Gordon, J. L., & Gucer, P. (2000). The impact of occupational injury on injured worker and family: Outcomes of upper extremity cumulative trauma disorders in Maryland workers. *American Journal of Industrial Medicine, 38,* 498–506.

Kidd, C. D., Orr, R., Abowd, G. D., Atkeson, C. G., Essa, I. A., MacIntyre, B., Mynatt, E., Starner, T. E., & Newstetter, W. (1999). The aware home: A living laboratory for ubiquitous computing research. In N. A. Streitz, J. Siegel, V. Hartkopf, & S. Konomi (Eds.), *Cooperative buildings: Integrating information, organizations, and architecture* (pp. 191–198). New York: Springer.

Konradt, U., Schmook, R., Wilm, A., & Hertel, G. (2000). Health circles for teleworkers: Selective results on stress, strain, and coping styles. *Health Education Research, 15,* 327–338.

Kraut, R., Patterson, M., Lundmark, V., Kiesler, S., Mukophadhyay, T., & Scherlis, W. (1998). Internet paradox: A social technology that reduces social involvement and psychological well-being? *American Psychologist, 53,* 1017–1031.

Lincoln, A., Vernick, J., Ogaitis, S., Smith, G., Mitchell, C., & Agnew, M. (2000). Interventions for the prevention of work-related carpal tunnel syndrome. *American Journal of Preventive Medicine, 18,* 37–50.

Lindstrom, K., Leino, T., Seitsamo, J., & Torstila, I. (1997). A longitudinal study of work characteristics and health complaints among insurance employees in VDT work. *International Journal of Human-Computer Interaction, 9,* 343–368.

Maes, P. (1994). Agents that reduce work and information overload. *Communications of the ACM, 37,* 31–40.

Mann, S. (1996). "Smart clothing": Wearable multimedia and "personal imaging" to restore the balance between people and their intelligent environments. *Proceedings of the ACM 96 Multimedia,* 18–22.

Merriam-Webster's collegiate dictionary. (1998). (10th ed.). Springfield, MA: Merriam-Webster.

Mirchandani, K. (2000). "The best of both worlds" and "Cutting my own throat": Contradictory images of home-based work. *Qualitative Sociology, 23,* 159–182.

Moltke, I., & Andersen, H. H. K. (1998). Cooperative buildings—The case of office VISION. In N. A. Streitz, S. Konomi, & H. Burkhardt (Eds.), *Cooperative buildings: Integrating information, organization, and architecture* (pp. 163–176). New York: Springer-Verlag.

Rasanen, K., Notkola, V., & Husman, K. (1997). Perceived work conditions and work-related symptoms among employed Finns. *Social Science & Medicine, 45,* 1099–1110.

Rosenberg, R. (1999). The workplace on the verge of the 21st century. *Journal of Business Ethics, 22,* 3–14.

Selker, T. (1994). COACH: A teaching agent that learns. *Communications of the ACM, 37,* 92–99.

Stevens, J. C., Witt, J. C., Smith, B. E., & Weaver, A. L. (2001). The frequency of carpal tunnel syndrome in computer users at a medical facility. *Neurology, 56,* 1431–1432.

Straker, L., & Mekhora, K. (2000). An evaluation of visual display unit placement by electromyography, posture, discomfort and preference. *International Journal of Industrial Ergonomics, 26,* 389–398.

Streitz, N. A., Geißler, J., Holmer, T., Konomi, S., Müller-Tomfelde, C., Reischl, W., Rexroth, P., Seitz, P., & Steinmetz, R. (1999). i-LAND: An interactive landscape for creativity and innovation. *Proceedings of the CHI 1999 Conference on Human Factors in Computing Systems,* 120–127.

Streitz, N., & Halkia, M. (2001). *Three dimensions of situated computing in cooperative buildings.* Retrieved March 22, 2001, from   http://www.daimi.au.dk/~mbl/chi2000-sitcomp/pdf/Streitz.pdf

Timpka, T., & Sjoberg, C. (1998). Development of systems for support of collaboration in health care: The design arenas. *Artificial Intelligence in Medicine, 12,* 125–136.

U.S. Congress, Office of Technology Assessment. (1987). *The electronic supervisor: New technology, new tensions* (OTA-CIT-333). Washington, DC: U.S. Government Printing Office.

Viller, S., & Sommerville, I. (2000). Ethnographically informed analysis for software engineers. *International Journal of Human Computer Studies, 53,* 169–196.

Weiser, M. (1991). The computer for the 21st century. *Scientific American, 265,* 94–104.

Part III

Symptoms, Disorders, and Interventions

Regardless of how effectively organizations design prevention and public health programs to protect the health and safety of people at work, some individuals experience symptoms and health disorders. Primary and secondary interventions aim to help those without symptoms or health disorders to maintain their health, and tertiary interventions aim to help those with symptoms and health disorders to restore their health and well-being. The first two chapters in this part focus on two key symptoms or health disorders, and the remaining four chapters address specific primary, secondary, or tertiary interventions for health and safety.

Chapter 12 by Shirom addresses the chronic occupational health problem of burnout, beginning with an examination of the Maslach Burnout Inventory, the Pines' Burnout Measure, and the Shirom-Melamed Burnout Measure. Shirom conducts a critical review of the various approaches to burnout. The central part of the chapter is a review of the research literature, with emphasis placed on longitudinal studies as well as the antecedents, symptoms, and consequences of burnout. In addition, the chapter addresses personality traits associated with burnout, burnout and job performance, burnout and health, burnout at the organizational level of analysis, and approaches to reduce burnout in work organizations.

Chapter 13 by Landsbergis, Schnall, Belkić, Baker, Schwartz, and Pickering focuses on cardiovascular disease, which continues to be the leading cause of death for men and women in all the industrialized nations. The authors note that the mortality rates have dropped over the past 40 years, yet the incidence rates have shown little or no decline over the past 20 years. The chapter emphasizes the link between workplace stressors and cardiovascular disease, with emphasis on the epidemiological data, and explores the mechanism by which work stressors lead to cardiovascular outcomes. The chapter closes with a discussion of the prevention and management of work-related hypertension and cardiovascular disease.

Chapter 14 by Cooper, Dewe, and O'Driscoll briefly discusses the changing nature of work and the increasing need in the United States and Europe for preventive interventions for employees. The authors discuss the context of employee assistance programs (EAP). Although these counseling programs may be in-house, they are usually delivered through an expert external agency or contractor. Normally funded by the employer as an employee benefit, EAPs provide counseling, information, and referral to appropriate internal or external counseling treatment and support services for troubled employees. The chapter traces the somewhat different historical evolution of EAPs in the United States and in Europe, though EAPs are often used in similar ways as globalization has progressed.

Heaney, in chapter 15, presents a conceptual framework that includes factors in the work environment and personal factors that influence stress and health. Drawing on this conceptual model, she identifies potential points for interventions. These include reducing exposure to stressors, enhancing individual and social resources, and identifying and treating symptoms of short-term strain. Therefore, the model incorporates primary, secondary, and even tertiary interventions, although the focus of the chapter is on primary prevention. In addition to identifying the potential targets for intervention, Heaney presents the criteria used in public health for selecting the targets of interventions. A discussion of strategies for change are categorized as either individual level strategies focusing on employee beliefs, attitudes, and behaviors or organizational-level change strategies such as changes to organizational structures, policies, priorities, and procedures, although she acknowledges that some intervention efforts may include both strategies.

In chapter 16, Semmer focuses on changes to the work environment for improving employee health, reviews the literature on how task and technical interventions, role clarity, and social relationships influence employees' health, and examines interventions implementing multiple changes in the work environment. Although he concludes that the results are encouraging with many positive outcomes, not all studies have been supportive of the effectiveness of changing jobs or social relationships in promoting health or preventing distress. He concludes the chapter with some alternative approaches that should be considered in developing and evaluating prevention programs.

Part III concludes with chapter 17 by Quillian-Wolever and Wolever on the preventive stress management skills individuals may use for health protection and health enhancement in the workplace. Their chapter categorizes stress responses into four domains: physical, cognitive, emotional, and behavioral stress responses. The remainder of the chapter then discusses stress management skills and coping strategies that map onto these four domains, considering the evidence for the efficacy and effectiveness of these various stress management strategies.

12

Job-Related Burnout: A Review

Arie Shirom

This review focuses on the conceptual meaning of burnout and on some of the major antecedents, symptoms, and consequences of burnout in work organizations. Burnout is viewed as an affective reaction to ongoing stress whose core content is the gradual depletion over time of individuals' intrinsic energetic resources, including the expression of emotional exhaustion, physical fatigue, and cognitive weariness (Shirom, 1989). The review starts with a critical analysis of the major conceptual approaches to burnout. Given the complexity of this construct and the controversy over its operational definition (Maslach, Schaufeli, & Leiter, 2001), this conceptual analysis is essential for understanding the phenomenon of burnout. Because in this field of research there are few attempts to theoretically posit burnout's relationships with other variables (Moore, 2000), I proceed in the next section to theoretically interrelate stress at work and burnout. The following sections cover the empirical literature on burnout. Typically, empirical studies on burnout are based on a cross-sectional study design and measure burnout by asking respondents to complete a self-report questionnaire. In this review, preference is given to longitudinal studies on burnout because they provide more credence to cause and effect statements. To summarize the empirical evidence available on burnout, I shall rely on the few meta-analytic studies of burnout and on the narrative, mostly occupation-specific literature reviews. The sections that follow deal with personality traits associated with burnout, burnout and job performance, burnout and health, burnout at the organizational level of analysis, and approaches to reduce burnout in work organizations.

This review focuses on burnout of employees in work organizations, excluding research that deals exclusively with nonemployment settings (e.g., athletes' burnout; Dale & Weinberg, 1990). In the same vein, I shall not cover research that deals with burnout in life domains other than work, like crossover of burnout among marital partners (e.g., Pines, 1996; Westman & Etzion, 1995). This review gives preference to research that investigated work-related antecedents of burnout rather than to studies in which burnout has been associated with stresses in other life spheres (e.g., Farber, 1991, 2000; Jackson, Schwab, & Schuler, 1986). In several advanced market economies, such as the United States, Netherlands, and United Kingdom, the incidence of stress-related workers' compensation claims, and the frequency of mental health claims for every 1000 employees covered by the relevant workers' compensation laws, have risen sharply in recent years (cf. Schaufeli & Enzmann, 1998). Therefore, burnout at work can be regarded as a major public health problem and a cause for concern for policy makers.

The Conceptual Basis of Burnout

During the 1980s and early 1990s, research on burnout, regardless of the conceptual approach used, dealt almost exclusively with people-oriented professionals (e.g., teachers, nurses, doctors, social workers, and police officers). Professionals in these occupational groups tend to be employed in the public sector. In most of today's advanced market economies, the public sector has to adjust to consumers' growing demands for quality service, downsizing, and budgetary retrenchments. People-oriented professionals often enter their profession with service-oriented idealistic goals. They typically work under norms that expect them to continuously invest emotional, cognitive, and physical energy in service recipients. In this context, the previously stated changes are likely to create a process of emotional exhaustion, mental weariness, and physical fatigue. One of the early pioneers in scientifically investigating this phenomenon, Freudenberger (Freudenberger, 1974, 1980) labeled it as burnout.

Freudenberger's pioneering work inspired the three conceptual approaches toward the construct of burnout reviewed in this chapter. These three conceptualizations were proposed by Maslach and her colleagues (Maslach, 1982; Maslach & Leiter, 1997), by Pines and her colleagues (Pines & Aronson, 1988; Pines, Aronson, & Kafry, 1981) and by Shirom and Melamed (Shirom, 1989; Hobfoll & Shirom, 1993, 2000; Melamed, Kushnir, & Shirom, 1992). I shall focus on the validity of the first conceptual approach toward burnout, including the measurement instrument constructed by Maslach and her colleagues, the Maslach Burnout Inventory (MBI; Maslach, Jackson, & Leiter, 1996). The reason for this focus is that the MBI was one of the very first scientifically validated burnout measurement instruments, and it has been the most widely used in scholarly research (Schaufeli & Enzmann, 1998). The first version of the MBI reflected the field's preoccupation with professionals in people-oriented occupations. Subsequently, the construction of newer versions of the popular MBI, applicable to other occupational groups (Maslach et al., 1996), extended the study of burnout to other categories of employees.

The Maslach Burnout Model and Inventory

According to this conceptualization (Maslach, 1982; Maslach & Jackson, 1981; Maslach & Leiter, 1997), burnout is viewed as a syndrome that consists of three dimensions: emotional exhaustion, depersonalization, and reduced personal accomplishment. Emotional exhaustion refers to feelings of being depleted of one's emotional resources. This dimension was regarded as the basic individual stress component of the syndrome (Maslach et al., 2001). Depersonalization, referring to negative, cynical, or excessively detached response to other people at work, represents the interpersonal component of burnout. Reduced personal accomplishment, referring to feelings of decline in one's competence and productivity and to one's lowered sense of self-efficacy, represents the self-evaluation component of burnout (Maslach, 1998, p. 69). The three dimensions were not deducted theoretically but resulted from labeling exploratory factor-analyzed items initially collected to reflect the range of experiences associated with the phenomenon of burnout (Maslach, 1998, p. 68; Schaufeli & Enzmann, 1998, p. 51).

Subsequently, Maslach and her colleagues modified the original definition of the latter two dimensions (cf., Maslach, Schaufeli, & Leiter, 2001, p. 399). Depersonalization was replaced by cynicism, referring to the same cluster of symptoms. The new label for this dimension of the syndrome poses new problems. Cynicism is an emerging concept in psychology and organizational behavior, used to refer to negative attitudes involving frustration from, disillusionment and distrust of organizations, persons, groups, or objects (Andersson & Bateman, 1997; Dean, Brandes, & Dharwadkar, 1998). Abraham (2000) has suggested that work cynicism, one of the forms of cynicism that she had identified in her research, tends to be closely related to burnout. Garden (1987) has argued that this dimension of the syndrome of burnout gauges several distinct attitudes, including distancing, hostility, rejection, and unconcern. It follows that the discriminant validity of this component of burnout relative to the current conceptualizations of employee or work cynicism has yet to be established.

The third dimension was relabeled as reduced efficacy or ineffectiveness, depicted to include the self-assessments of low self-efficacy, lack of accomplishment, lack of productivity, and incompetence (Leiter & Maslach, 2001). Each of these concepts—self-efficacy, accomplishment or achievement, personal productivity or performance, and personal competence— represent well-known and distinct fields of research in the behavioral sciences. The authors of the MBI have yet to clarify on what theoretical grounds these concepts should be grouped together in the same cluster of symptoms. Such diverse cluster of symptoms related to effectiveness may obscure the meaning of the third dimension underlying the MBI. To illustrate, does reduced efficacy refer to one's personal judgment of how well one can execute courses of action required to deal with prospective situations, as self-efficacy is customarily defined (e.g., C. Lee & Bobko, 1994; Stajkovic & Luthans, 1998)? Alternatively, does this dimension of burnout reflect one's belief in one's knowledge and skills, as competence is often conceptualized (Foschi, 2000; Sandberg, 2000)? Or does it relate to self-assessed job performance or performance expectations (e.g., Stajkovic & Luthans, 1998)? It appears that the second and third dimensions of the MBI, as currently defined, probably represent several multifaceted constructs, each having different implications with regard to the emotional exhaustion component of burnout suggested by the authors of the MBI (cf., Moore, 2000, p. 341).

Clearly, the conceptualization of burnout as measured by the MBI relates to it as a multidimensional construct. A construct is multidimensional when it refers to several distinct but related dimensions that are viewed as a single theoretical construct (Law, Wong, & Mobley, 1998). The proponents of this multidimensional view of burnout (e.g., Maslach, 1998) argue that it provides a holistic representation of a complex phenomenon, broadly conceived as referring to the process of wear and tear or continuous encroachment on employees' resources. However, they have yet to provide convincing theoretical arguments about why the three different clusters of symptoms that make up their conceptualization of burnout should "hang together" (Maslach et al., 2001). They argue in addition that their conceptualization allows researchers to use broadly conceived types of stress in both the work and the family domains as potential antecedents of burnout, thus increasing its explained variance. However, there is a paucity of evidence that there are specific antecedent variables or mechanisms leading to all three clusters of symptoms included in the syndrome of burnout (Collins, 1999; R. Lee & Ashforth, 1996; Schaufeli & Enzmann, 1998). A case in point is the phase model of burnout, developed by Golembiewski and his colleagues and tested in a series of studies (see, for example, Golembiewski & Boss, 1992; Golembiewski, Munzenrider, & Stevenson, 1986; Golembiewski & Munzenrider, 1988). It was constructed on the basis of the theoretical assumption that individuals experiencing burnout on the dimension of emotional exhaustion do not necessarily experience either of the other two clusters of symptoms. Indeed, Golembiewski and his colleagues (cf. Golembiewski & Boss, 1992; Golembiewski et al., 1986, 1988) have provided in their books considerable amount of evidence that supports this theoretical proposition.

Maslach (1998, p. 70) has argued that the addition of the dimensions of cynicism and reduced personal efficacy to the core dimension of emotional exhaustion was justified in that the former two dimensions add the interpersonal aspect of burnout to the conceptualization of the phenomenon. However, items that tap interpersonal aspects of work appear in the emotional exhaustion scale, like "working with people all day is really a strain for me," and "Working with people directly puts too much stress on me" (Maslach & Jackson, 1981). Conceptually, therefore, the view of burnout as a syndrome that includes three clusters of symptoms lacks theoretical underpinnings, has not been supported by evidence demonstrating common etiology for the three dimensions, and includes two clusters of symptoms, cynicism and reduced personal effectiveness that appear to be too heterogeneous for advancing our knowledge on burnout.

The MBI, the measurement scale whose process of construction has led inductively to the previously discussed conceptualization, has been the most popular instrument for measuring burnout in empirical research (for a review of studies using it, see Collins, 1999; R. Lee & Ashforth, 1996; Schaufeli & Enzmann, 1998). It contained items purportedly assessing each of the three clusters of symptoms included in the syndrome view of burnout, which is emotional exhaustion, cynicism or depersonalization, and reduced effectiveness or lowered professional efficacy. It asks respondents to indicate the frequency over the work year with which they have experienced each feeling on a 7-point scale ranging from 0 (never) to 6 (every day). Three subscales are usually constructed, referring to each of the dimensions discussed (for a recent psychometric critique, see Barnett, Brennan, & Careis, 1999). The factorial validity of the MBI has been extensively studied (Byrne, 1994; Handy, 1988; R. Lee & Ashforth, 1996; Schaufeli & Dieren-donck, 1993; Schaufeli & Buunk, 1996). Most of the researchers examining this aspect of MBI validity have reported that a three-factor solution better fits their data than does a two-dimensional or a one-dimensional structure (for recent examples, see Boles, Dean, Ricks, Short, & Wang, 2000; Schutte, Toppinen, Kalimo, & Schaufeli, 2000). Researchers using the MBI have most often constructed three different scales corresponding to the three dimensions of emotional exhaustion, cynicism, and reduced personal effec-tiveness. Several studies have argued, on both theoretical and psychometric grounds, that the use of a total score to represent total burnout should be avoided (e.g., Kalliath, O'Driscoll, Gillespie & Bluedorn, 2000; Koeske & Koeske, 1989; Moore, 2000;). The emotional exhaustion dimension has been consistently viewed as the core component of the MBI (e.g., Burke & Green-glass, 1995; Cordes, Dougherty & Blum, 1997; Moore, 2000). Most studies have shown it to be the most internally consistent and stable relative to the other two components (Schaufeli & Enzmann, 1998). In meta-analytic reviews, it has been shown to be the most responsive to the nature and intensity of work-related stress (R. Lee & Ashforth, 1996; Schaufeli & Enzmann, 1998).

Pines's Burnout Model and Measure

Pines and her colleagues defined burnout as the state of physical, emotional, and mental exhaustion caused by long–term involvement in emotionally demanding situations (Pines & Aronson, 1988, p. 9). This view does not restrict the application of the term burnout to the helping professions, as was initially the case with the first version of the MBI (Winnubst, 1993). A possible drawback is that this approach does not view burnout in a work context. Indeed, it was applied not only to employment relationships (Pines, Aronson & Kafry, 1981) and organizational careers (Pines & Aronson, 1988) but also to marital relationships (Pines, 1988, 1996) and to the aftermath of political conflicts (Pines, 1993).

Much like the MBI, the conceptualization of burnout emerged from clinical experiences and case studies. In the process of actually constructing a measure that purported to assess burnout, dubbed the burnout measure (BM), Pines and her colleagues have moved away from the definition offered previously. In the BM, Pines and her colleagues viewed burnout as a syn-drome of co-occurring symptoms that include helplessness, hopelessness, entrapment, decreased enthusiasm, irritability, and a sense of lowered self-esteem (cf. Pines, 1993). None of these symptoms is anchored in the context of work or employment relationships. The BM is considered a one-dimen-sional measure yielding a single-composite burnout score. Evidently, the overlap between the conceptual definition and the operational definition is minimal (cf. Schaufeli & Enzmann, 1998, p. 48). In addition, the discriminant validity of burnout, as assessed by the BM, relative to depression, anxiety, and self-esteem, is impaired (cf. Shirom & Ezrachi, 2001). This has led researchers to describe the BM as an index of psychological strain that encompasses physical fatigue, emotional exhaustion, depression, anxiety, and reduced self-esteem (e.g., Schaufeli & Dierendonck, 1993, p. 645).

Shirom–Melamed Burnout Model and Measure

The conceptualization of burnout that underlies the Shirom–Melamed Burnout Measure (S-MBM) was inspired by the work of Maslach and her colleagues and Pines and her colleagues, as described earlier. Burnout is viewed as an affective state characterized by one's feelings of being depleted of one's physical, emotional, and cognitive energies. Theoretically, the S-MBM was based on Hobfoll's (1989, 1998) Conservation of Resources (COR) theory. The basic tenets of COR theory are that people are motivated to obtain, retain, and protect that which they value. The things that people value are called resources, of which there are several types, including material, social, and energetic resources. The conceptualization of burnout formulated by Shirom (1989) on the basis of COR theory (Hobfoll & Shirom, 1993, 2000) relates to energetic resources only, and covers physical, emotional, and cognitive energies. Burnout thus represents a combination of physical fatigue, emotional exhaustion, and cognitive weariness.

According to COR theory (Hobfoll, 1989, 1998) stress at work occurs when individuals are either threatened with resource loss, lose resources, or fail to regain resources following resource investment. One of the corollaries of COR theory is that stress does not occur as a single event but rather represents an unfolding process, wherein those who lack a strong resource pool are more likely to experience cycles of resource loss. The affective state of burnout is likely to exist when individuals experience a cycle of resource loss over a period of time at work (Hobfoll & Freedy, 1993). For example, a reference librarian who comes to work every morning to face yet another line of students impatiently awaiting her help, lacking opportunities to replenish her resources, is likely to cycle into a forceful spiral of resource loss and as a result feel burned out at work.

There are three reasons for the focus on the combination of physical fatigue, emotional exhaustion and cognitive weariness in the conceptualization of burnout that has led to the construction of the S-MBM. First, these forms of energy are individually possessed, and theoretically are expected to be closely interrelated. COR theory postulates that personal resources affect each other and exist as a resource pool and that lacking one is often associated with lacking the other (Lerman et al., 1999). Empirical research conducted with the S-MBM has supported the linkage among physical fatigue, emotional exhaustion, and cognitive weariness (e.g., Melamed et al., 1999; Shirom, Westman, Shamai, & Carel, 1997). Second, the three forms of individually possessed energy included in the S-MBM represent a coherent set that does not overlap any other established behavioral science concept, like depression and anxiety or like aspects of the self-concept such as self-esteem and self-efficacy. Third, the conceptualization of the S-MBM clearly differentiates burnout from stress appraisals anteceding burnout, from coping behaviors that individuals may engage in to ameliorate the negative aspects of burnout like distancing themselves from client recipients and from probable consequences of burnout like performance decrements. This stands in contrast to the two other conceptualizations of burnout outlined previously.

A series of studies that confirmed expected relationships between the S-MBM and physiological variables have lent support to its construct validity. In these studies, respondents' total score on the S-MBM was used to predict risk factors for cardiovascular disease (Melamed et al., 1992; Shirom et al., 1997), quasi-inflammatory factors in the blood (Lerman et al., 1999), salivary cortisol levels (Melamed et al., 1999) and upper respiratory infections (Kushnir & Melamed, 1992). However, the convergent validity of the S-MBM relative to the MBI and the BM has yet to be established, as has its discriminant validity relative to other types of possible emotional reactions to chronic stress at work, like anger, hostility, anxiety, and depressive symtomatology. The factorial validity of the S-MBM needs to be investigated in additional occupational categories. Also, there is a paucity of evidence with regard to the possibility that different types of stress may have varying effects on physical fatigue, emotional exhaustion, and cognitive weariness, thus casting doubt on the use of a single composite score of the S-MBM to represent burnout. There is some indirect evidence suggesting that each of the three components of the S-MBM may be related to a different coping style (Vingerhoets, 1985).

Models of Stress at Work and Burnout

Past reviews of the burnout literature (i.e., Burke & Richardson, 2000; Cordes & Dougherty, 1993; Moore, 2000; Schaufeli & Enzmann, 1998; Hobfoll & Shirom, 2000; Shirom, 1989) view it as a consequence of one's exposure to chronic job stress. The chronic stresses that may lead to burnout include qualitative and quantitative overload, role conflict and ambiguity, lack of participation, and lack of social support. Burnout has been shown to be more job-related and situation-specific relative to emotional distress such as depression (Maslach, Schaufeli, & Leiter, 2001). Among the major theoretical approaches to work-related stress and its outcomes reviewed in Cooper (1998), those that have been applied to investigate stress–burnout relationships are the demand–control–support model, the effort–reward imbalance perspective, and the person–environment fit model. It should be noted that these theoretical perspectives differ in their conceptualization of stress and place different emphasis on individual personality differences and on situational variables that may moderate stress–burnout relations. In addition, the different models have not been systematically compared with regard to their predictive validity of burnout.

This review argues that the most robust theoretical view of stress and burnout relationships is that based on Hobfoll's COR theory (Hobfoll & Shirom, 1993, 2000). According to COR theory (Hobfoll, 1989, 1998), when individuals experience loss of resources, they respond by attempting to limit the loss and maximize the gain of resources. To achieve this, they usually use other resources. When circumstances at work or otherwise threaten people's obtaining or maintaining resources, stress ensues. COR theory postulates that stress occurs under one of three conditions: (a) when resources are threatened, (b) when resources are lost, and (c) when individuals invest resources and do not reap the anticipated rate of return. COR theory (Hobfoll, 1988, 1998) further postulates that because individuals strive to protect themselves from resource loss, loss is more salient than gain, and therefore employees are more sensitive to workplace stresses that threaten their resources. For example, for teachers, the demand to discipline students and facing negative feedback from their supervisors will be more salient than rewards that they might receive. The stress of interpersonal conflict has been shown to be particularly salient in the burnout phenomenon (Leiter & Maslach, 1988).

A recent meta-analysis (R. Lee & Ashforth, 1996) examined how demand-and-resource correlates and behavioral and attitudinal correlates were related to each of the three scales that make up the MBI. In agreement with the COR theory-based view of stress and burnout outlined earlier, these authors found that both the demand and the resource correlates were more strongly related to emotional exhaustion than to either depersonalization or personal accomplishment. These investigators also found that consistent with COR theory of stress, emotional exhaustion was more strongly related to the demand correlates than to the resource correlates, suggesting that workers might have been sensitive to the possibility of resource loss. These meta-analytic results were subsequently reconfirmed by additional studies, like Demerouti and colleagues (Demerouti, Bakker, Nachreiner, & Schaufeli, 2000), who used a burnout scale that focused on energy depletion.

Applying these notions to burnout, we argue that individuals feel burned out when they perceive a continuous net loss, which cannot be replenished, of physical, emotional, or cognitive energy that they possess. This feeling of ongoing net loss of any combination of individuals' physical vigorousness, emotional robustness, and cognitive agility represents an emotional response to the experienced stresses. The net loss, in turn, cannot be compensated for by expanding other resources, or borrowing, or gaining additional resources by investing extant ones. Burned-out individuals may exacerbate their losses by entering an escalating spiral of losses (Hobfoll & Shirom, 2000). Then, they may reach an advanced stage of burnout, wherein their symptoms of depression may become the predominant emotions, or may reach advanced stages of burnout that manifest themselves in symptoms of psychological withdrawal, like acting with cynicism toward and dehumanizing their customers or clients. As noted by Schaufeli and Enzmann (1998), longitudinal studies to date have not supported the notion that there is a time lag between the stress experience and the feelings of burnout. It could be that stress and burnout change simultaneously, and therefore the failure of the eight longitudinal studies examined by Schaufeli and Enzmann (1998) to reproduce the effects of stress on burnout found in most cross-sectional studies.

This theoretical perspective has direct implications with regard to phase or process theories of burnout (e.g., Golembiewski & Boss, 1992; Golembiewski, Boudreau, Munzenrider, & Lou, 1996; Leiter & Maslach, 2001). These phase or process theories of burnout have been reviewed by Burke and Richardson (2000), who noted that such theories should include the consequences of burnout salient to individuals and organizations. Thus COR theory implies that during the early stages of burnout, it will be characterized by a process of depletion of energy resources directed at coping with the threatening demands, that is with work-related stresses. During this stage of coping, burnout may occur concomitantly with a high level of anxiety, because of the direct and active coping behaviors that usually entail a high level of arousal. When and if these coping behaviors prove ineffective, the individual may give up, and engage in emotional detachment and defensive behaviors that may lead to depressive symptoms (cf. Shirom & Ezrahi, 2001). Cherniss (1980a, 1980b) found that in the later stages of burnout individuals behave defensively and hence display cynicism toward clients, withdrawal, and emotional detachment (for empirical support, see Burke & Greenglass, 1989, 1995). These attempts at coping have limited effectiveness and often cycle to heighten burnout and problems for both the individuals and the organizations in which they work. The unique core of burnout, as posited earlier, is distinctive in content and nomological network from either depression or anxiety, as demonstrated by Corrigan et al. (1994) and by Leiter and Durum (1994). Measures of depression, such as the Beck Depression Inventory (Beck, Ward, Mendelson, Mock, & Enbaugh, 1961) include items whose contents gauge passivity and relative incapacity for purposeful action. In addition, as proposed previously, later phases of burnout may be accompanied by depressive symptomatology. The two considerations may explain the often reported high positive correlation between burnout and measures of depression (e.g., Meier, 1984; Schaufeli & Enzmann, 1998). It follows that burnout is conceptually distinct from depression. Depressive symptomatology is affectively complex, and includes lack of pleasurable experience, anger, guilt, apprehension, and physiological symptoms of distress. Moreover, cognitive views of depression regard it as related primarily to pessimism about the self, capabilities, and the future (Fisher, 1984).

This theoretical position may be exemplified by burnout among people-oriented professionals, such as teachers, social workers, and nurses. When faced with overload and interpersonal stress on the job on an ongoing basis, the key issue for them is the amount of emotional energy they need to meet these job demands. When they feel emotionally exhausted, direct or problem-focused coping, which invariably requires that they invest emotional energy, is no longer a viable option. Presumably, they use emotion-focused coping to ameliorate their feelings of emotional exhaustion and attempt to distance themselves from their service recipients, psychologically withdraw from their job tasks, or limit their exposure to their clients.

This may explain the often-found linkage between emotional exhaustion and cynicism (R. Lee & Ashforth, 1996). In a recent study of the process of burnout among general practitioners, a study that used a five-year longitudinal design, Bakker and his colleagues (Bakker et al., 2000) found that repeated confrontation with demanding patients over a long period of time depleted the GPs' emotional resources, with perceptions of inequity or lack of reciprocity mediating the process. This study (Bakker et al., 2000) also reported that emotional exhaustion evoked a cynical attitude toward patients. However, this linkage of emotional exhaustion and cynicism does not mean that emotional exhaustion is necessarily followed by cynical attitudes or indirect coping styles like distancing. It does not necessarily follow from this linkage that burnout's core meaning and ways of coping with advanced stages of it belong to the same conceptual space (cf. Maslach et al., 2001, p. 403).

Individual Traits Predisposing Employees to Burnout

In this section and those that follow, I shall refer to the empirical research that has been published on burnout. This voluminous research was already covered in part by meta-analytic studies (Collins, 1999; R. Lee & Ashforth, 1996; Schaufeli & Enzmann, 1998). The reference to empirical studies in this review is rather selective. Most of this research has measured burnout by the MBI. In references made to this body of studies, I shall focus on results reported for the emotional exhaustion scale. Adverse organizational conditions have been shown to be more significant in the etiology of burnout than personality factors (Schaufeli & Enzmann, 1998). The lesson to burnout researchers is that it is plausible that individual traits predisposing employees to burnout interact with organizational features that are conductive to the development of burnout. As an example, when a major economic slump moves management to require that all employees increase their input of available personal energy and time to ensure the organization's survival, those employees who possess high self-esteem are less likely to experience burnout as a result (Cordes & Dougherty, 1993).

One of the predictions of COR theory is that individuals who lack strong resources are more likely to experience cycles of resource losses. When not replenished, such cycles are likely to result in chronic depletion of energy, namely progressive burnout. Cherniss (1995) posited that the advance of burnout is contingent on individuals' level of self-efficacy, and there is some support for this contention (Brouwers & Tomic, 2000). Lower levels of burnout would be expected in work situations that allow employees to experience success and thus feel efficacious, namely under job and organizational conditions that provide opportunities to experience challenge, control, feedback of results, and support from supervisors and coworkers (cf. Brouwers & Tomic, 2000; Schaufeli & Buunk, 1996). Thus Chang and his colleagues (Chang, Rand, & Strunk, 2000) found, in a study of working college students, that optimism was a potent predictor of the emotional exhaustion scale of the BMI even after the effects of stress were controlled. Chang et al. (2000) concluded that concrete affirmation of job accomplishments, such as by merit awards, and increasing employees' optimistic expectancies may lower their risk for job burnout.

The role of personality factors in the etiology of burnout is complex and multifaceted and probably hardly explored (Kahill, 1988). Garden (1989, 1991) concluded that certain personality types self-select individuals into specific occupations and that subsequently the same individuals interact with stressful occupational environments that are conducive to the experience of burnout. Other possible paths of influence of personality characteristics on burnout may exist. Several studies have reported a postive association of Type A behavior pattern and emotional exhaustion (Schaufeli & Enzmann, 1998). Neuroticism may lead people to report higher levels of burnout regardless of the situation (cf. Watson & Clark, 1984). Hardiness, as a personality trait, has also been found to buffer the effects of stress on burnout. In a study of nurses, Zellars, Perrewé, and Hochwarter (2000) found that among the big five personality factors, only neuroticism predicted the MBI's emotional exhaustion scale, after controlling for the effects of sociodemographic and stress variables.

Burnout may exacerbate certain personality traits. It appears that the complex interactions between personality traits and burnout have yet to be described and understood. As noted, there is some evidence that personality factors explain additional variance in job burnout even after considering the effects of types of stress considered to be the most potent predictors of this phenomenon.

The Consequences of Burnout: Performance in Organizations

Burnout has been linked to several negative organizational outcomes, including increased turnover and absenteeism (e.g., Jackson, Schwab, & Schuler, 1986; Parker & Kulik, 1995), lower organizational commitment (Maslach & Leiter, 1997), and the self-reported use of violence by police officers against civilians (Kop, Euwema, & Schaufeli, 1999). I shall focus on burnout–job performance relationships. Although the available evidence is still meager, it supports the argument that burnout is differentially related to self-assessed, supervisor-assessed, and objectively measured job performance. In general, burnout was found to be negatively related to subjectively assessed performance but not significantly associated with objectively assessed performance. Based on six studies, Schaufeli and Enzmann (1998) concluded that self-rated performance correlated weakly with the MBI emotional exhaustion scale, with only about 5% of the variance shared. In comparison, other-rated performance or objectively assessed performance, in seven studies, was found to share only 1% of the variance with the MBI emotional exhaustion scale, and the expected negative correlations were found in only four out of the seven studies. To illustrate, Parker and Kulik (1995) reported that, after controlling for negative affectivity, performance of nurses who were higher in their feeling of emotional exhaustion was rated lower both by the nurses themselves and independently by their supervisors.

Wright and Cropanzano (1999), using the emotional exhaustion scale (EE) of the MBI in a longitudinal design, reported finding a correlation of -.27 between this scale and a one-item measure of global performance as assessed by the supervisors of 52 social workers over a three-year period. In a similar vein, Wright and Bonnett (1997) found that the EE scale negatively predicted Time 2 performance (supervisor assessed, one item tapping global performance), after controlling for Time 1 performance, age and gender, among 44 human- service personnel. These studies (including Parker & Kulik, 1995) failed to find relationships among performance and the two other MBI-derived scales, depersonalization and reduced personal accomplishment, thus lending support to the pivotal importance of emotional exhaustion in the burnout experience.

The evidence described previously lends credence to the major propositions of COR theory regarding the possible reasons for burnout's negative impact on job performance. The negative correlation between burnout and job performance is likely to be explained by burned-out individuals' impaired coping ability and their reduced level of motivation to perform.

Organizational-Level Burnout

The literature on burnout has dealt almost exclusively with the individual level of analysis. With few exceptions (e.g., Leiter & Maslach, 1988; Leiter & Meachem, 1986; O'Driscoll & Schubert, 1988), the potentialities of investigating group or organizational burnout have not been systematically explored. It is plausible that burnout on the individual level of analysis has its organizational counterpart. There may be parallel processes operating at the individual and organizational levels of analysis. The open-systems approach postulates that there is dynamic interplay and interconnectedness among elements of any system, its subsystems, and within the more inclusive system. Focusing on organizational burnout may entail a much higher system complexity than the extant focus on individual burnout (cf. Staw, Sandelands, & Dutton, 1981).

A process of depletion of organizational resources may be self-imposed by those at the helm of the organization, like setting unrealistic production targets that overload and overuse the employees' available energetic resources, eventually also exacerbating their level of burnout. This process may be externally imposed by stakeholders' excessive demands for product or service quality that continuously deplete the organization's energetic resources. Kramer (1990, 1991) has summarized the literature on the effects of resource scarcity on group and intergroup conflict and cooperation. Organizational behavior has imported the resource-based model of the firm from economics as a major theoretical framework. Within this resource-based view of organizations, issues like resource mobility and heterogeneity have been applied to explain firms' competitive advantage (Barney, 1991).

There is indirect evidence from several studies that there exist a phenomenon of concentration of burned-out employees in certain work groups. Rountree (1984) studied task groups in organizations and found out that almost 90% of those high on burnout were members of work groups having at least 50% of all their members suffering from advanced burnout. Bakker and Schaufeli (2000) found evidence for burnout contagion processes among teachers. Still, the evidence is largely indirect and does not clarify if the concentration of burned-out employees in certain work groups is a result of common exposure to stress, contagion processes that operate in these work groups, or other possible alternative explanations. Organizational burnout may lead to organizational decline and death. Organizational decline and downsizing (Mone, McKinley, & Barker, 1998) may be likened to the chronic fatigue stage of burnout.

Approaches to Reducing Burnout

In this section, I review studies that evaluated interventions designed to reduce burnout. It has been argued that workplace-based interventions aimed at reducing stress and modifying some of the maladaptive responses to stress often have little or no effect (Briner & Reynolds, 1999). Is this conclusion relevant to interventions designed to ameliorate burnout? Most of the burnout interventions reported in the literature are individual-oriented and provide treatment, not prevention, much like other stress interventions (Nelson, Quick, & Simmons, 2001). There are hardly any reports on interventions that were based on a systematic audit of the structural sources of workplace burnout with the objectives of alleviating or eliminating the stresses leading to burnout.

An intervention frequently used by organizations attempting to ameliorate burnout among their employees is peer support groups. The theoretical perspective offered in this chapter may explain the focus of many interventions on enriching and strengthening the social support available to or used by burned-out employees. According to the predictions of COR theory, the depletion of one's energetic resources and impoverished social support are closely related (Hobfoll, 1989, 1998). Those lacking a strong resource pool, including those with impoverished social support, are more likely to become burned-out or to go through cycles of resource loss when they cope with work-related stress. In addition, people with depleted energetic resources who complain of physical fatigue, emotional exhaustion, and cognitive weariness may appear to their significant others at work as less attractive and therefore less likely to have access to social support. There is considerable support for these arguments. In a review of the area of social support and stress, Curtona and Russell (1990) integrated four studies that had investigated the effects of social support on burnout among public school teachers, hospital nurses, therapists, and critical care nurses, respectively. In all four studies, negative associations between social support and burnout were found. For reasons explained earlier, these negative relationships may be reciprocal.

The peer social support intervention is particularly popular in educational institutions (e.g., Cooley & Yavanoff, 1996; Travers & Cooper, 1996; Vandenberghe & Huberman, 1999). Such peer-based support groups provide their members with informational and emotional support, and in some cases instrumental support too (Burke & Richardson, 2000). Because social support is a major potential route to resources that are beyond those that individuals possess directly, it is a critical resource in many employment-related stressful situations (Hobfoll & Shirom, 2000) and may help them to replenish their depleted energetic resources. However, how social support is actually used depends on several factors, including one's sense of mastery and environmental control.

In a longitudinal research of burnout among teachers, Brouwers and Tomic (2000) found that emotional exhaustion had a negative effect on self-efficacy beliefs and that this effect occurred simultaneously rather than over time. They (Brouwers & Tomic, 2000) reasoned that interventions that incorporate enactive mastery experiences, the most important source of self-efficacy beliefs, were likely to have an ameliorative effect on teachers' emotional exhaustion. An example would be having teachers learn and experiment with skills to cope with disruptive student behaviors. In the same vein, the environmental sense of control is an important stress management resource (cf., Fisher, 1984). Those with a high sense of control tend to use their resources judiciously, relying on themselves when this is deemed most appropriate and using available social support when this is the more effective coping route (Hobfoll & Shirom, 2000). Therefore, interventions that combine both social support and bolstering of control may be more efficacious in reducing burnout in organizations. For example, a multifaceted intervention that combined peer social support and bolstering of professional self-efficacy was found to reduce burnout (measured by the S-MBM) relative to a control group of nonparticipants (Rabin et al., 2000). Yet another example is the study of Freedy and Hobfoll (1994), who enhanced nurses' coping skills by teaching them how to use their social support and individual mastery resources and found a significant reduction in emotional exhaustion in the experimental group relative to the non-treated control group.

Senior management has a role to play in instituting preventive measures, including steps to ameliorate chronic work-related stress, particularly overload; training programs designed to promote effective stress management techniques and on-site recreational facilities. Organizational interventions to reduce burnout have great potential but are complex to implement and costly in terms of resources required. The changing nature of employment relationships, including the transient and dynamic nature of employee–employer psychological contract, entails putting more emphasis on individual-oriented approaches to combat burnout. The role of individual coping resources, including self-efficacy, hardiness, and social support from friends and family, may become more important in future interventions.

Future Research

An important area for future research is the discriminating validity of burnout, according to either of its different operational definitions, and other types of emotional distress, particularly anxiety and depression. I have argued that burnout, anxiety, and depression are conceptually distinct emotional reactions to stress. Studies that support this contention were cited earlier (e.g., Schaufeli & Dierendonck, 1993). Still, the overlap found in several studies (Cherniss, 1995; Schaufeli & Enzmann, 1998) between depression and the emotional exhaustion scale of the MBI, the most robust and reliable out of the three scales that make up the MBI, is a cause for concern. The propositions that early stages of individuals' burnout are more likely to be accompanied by heightened anxiety and more progressive stages of burnout may be linked to depressive symptomatology need to be tested in longitudinal research.

The plausibility of the proposition that burnout, as conceptualized in terms of its core meaning, will overlap to some extent with the disease state of chronic fatigue syndrome (CFS) or with its immediate precursor, chronic fatigue, has yet to be tested. In future investigations, individuals who score highest on burnout measures should be followed up for possible development of CFS.

Yet another important area of research concerns burnout as a possible precursor of cardiovascular disease. Early in the 1960s and 1970s, prospective studies found that being tired on awakening or being exhausted at the end of the day were possible antecedents of cardiovascular heart disease (Appels & Mulder, 1988, 1989). Appels and Mulder (1988, 1989) found out that those initially high on their measure of vital exhaustion (a combination of burnout, anxiety, and depression) were significantly more at risk to develop myocardial infarction within four years, after controlling for known risk factors such as blood pressure, smoking, cholesterol, and age (cf. Appels & Schouten, 1991). In cross-sectional studies that tested the associations among cardiovascular risk factors and burnout, Melamed et al. (1992, 1999) found evidence linking the two entities. In a semilongitudinal study, Shirom and his colleagues (Shirom et al., 1997) were able to show that burnout predicts elevated levels of cholesterol and triglycerides among male and female blue-collar employees. Longitudinal studies of fairly large and occupationally representative samples should be conducted to cross-validate these findings.

Conclusion

Given the data provided on the prevalence of burnout in advanced market economies, improving our understanding of the complex relationships between stress and burnout is critical for informing prevention, intervention, and public policy efforts. Advances in our knowledge are unlikely to results from research using fuzzy concepts and relying on instruments whose construct validity is in doubt. For this reason, in this review I have selectively focused on theoretical and conceptual issues in burnout research.

Burnout research still has to uncover the specific contexts in which stress exerts it effects on burnout. A recent meta-analysis of the literature (Collins, 1999) suggested that when the effects of different types of stress on burnout are compared across studies, larger effect sizes are obtained with job-specific stress measures relative to generic chronic stress measures like role conflict and ambiguity. The effects of stress on burnout were shown in this review and its predecessors to vary across situational factors, available coping resources such as social support and control, and enduring personal factors such as neuroticism and hardiness. It follows that future research should look for moderators and mediators of stress–burnout relationships.

Burnout is likely to represent a pressing social problem in the years to come. Competitive pressures in the manufacturing industry that originate in the global market, the continuing process of consumer empowerment in service industries, and the rise and decline of the high-tech industry are among the factors likely to affect employees' levels of burnout in different industries. In addition, employees in many advanced market economies experience heightened job insecurity, demands for excessive work hours, the need for continuous retraining in the wake of the accelerating pace of change in informational technologies, and the blurring of the line separating work and home life. In many European countries, employers are enjoined by governmental regulations on occupational health to implement preventive interventions that concern job stress and burnout. This review is an attempt to steer future research on burnout along the line suggested earlier to make future preventive interventions more effective.

References

Abraham, R. (2000). Organizational cynicism: Bases and consequences. *Genetic, Social, and General Psychology Monographs, 126,* 269–292.

Andersson, L. M., & Bateman, T. S. (1997). Cynicism in the workplace: Some causes and effects. *Journal of Organizational Behavior, 18,* 449–465.

Appels, A., & Mulder, P. (1988). Excess fatigue as a precursor of myocardial infarction. *European Heart Journal, 9,* 758–764.

Appels, A., & Mulder, P. (1989). Fatigue and heart disease: The association between "vital exhaustion" and past, present and future coronary heart disease. *Journal of Psychosomatic Research, 33,* 727–738.

Appels, A., & Schouten, M. (1991). Burnout as a risk factor for coronary heart disease. *Behavioral Medicine, 17,* 53–59.

Bakker, A. B., & Schaufeli, W. B. (2000). Burnout contagion processes among teachers. *Journal of Applied Social Psychology, 30,* 2289–2308.

Bakker, A. B., Shaufeli, W. B., Sixma, H. J., Bosveld, W., & Van Dierendonck, D. (2000). Patient demands, lack of reciprocity, and burnout: A five-year longitudinal study among general practitioners. *Journal of Organizational Behavior, 21,* 425–441.

Barnett, R. C., Brennan, R. T., & Careis, K. C. (1999). A closer look at the measurement of burnout. *Journal of Applied Biobehavioral Research, 4,* 65–78.

Barney, J. (1991). Special theory forum on the resource-based model of the firm: origins, implications, and prospects. *Journal of Management, 17,* 97–98.

Beck, A. T., Ward, C. H., Mendelson, M., Mock, J., & Erbaugh, J. (1961). An inventory for measuring depression. *Archives of General Psychiatry, 4,* 561–571.

Boles, J. S., Dean, D. H., Ricks, J. M., Short, J. C., & Wang, G. P. (2000). The dimensionality of the Maslach Burnout Inventory across small business owners and educators. *Journal of Vocational Behavior, 56,* 12–34.

Briner, R. B., & Reynolds, S. (1999). The costs, benefits, and limitations of organizational level stress interventions. *Journal of Organizational Behavior, 20,* 647–664.

Brouwers, A., & Tomic, W. (2000). A longitudinal study of teacher burnout and perceived self-efficacy in classroom management. *Teaching and Teacher Education, 16,* 239–253.

Burke, R. J., & Greenglass, E. R. (1989). Psychological burnout among men and women in teaching: An examination of the Cherniss model. *Human Relations, 42,* 261–273.

Burke, R. J., & Greenglass, E. (1995). A longitudinal study of psychological burnout in teachers. *Human Relations, 48,* 187–203.

Burke, R. J., & Richardson, A. M. (2000). Psychological burnout in organizations. In R. T. Golembiewski (Ed.), *Handbook of organizational behavior.* (2nd ed.; pp. 327–368). New York: Marcel Dekker.

Byrne, B. M. (1994). Burnout: Testing for validity, replication, and invariance of causal structure across elementary, intermediate, and secondary teachers. *American Educational Research Journal, 31,* 645–673.

Chang, E., Rand, K. L., & Strunk, D. R. (2000). Optimism and risk for job burnout among working college students. *Personality and Individual Differences, 29,* 255–263.

Cherniss, C. (1980a). *Professional burnout in human service organizations.* New York: Praeger.

Cherniss, C. (1980b). *Staff burnout: Job stress in the Human Services.* Beverly Hills, CA: Sage.

Cherniss, C. (1995). *Beyond burnout.* New York and London: Routledge.

Collins, V. A. (1999). *A meta-analysis of burnout and occupational stress.* Unpublished doctoral dissertation, University of North Texas, Texas. University Microfilm Accession Number: AAT 9945794.

Cooley, E., & Yavanoff, P. (1996). Supporting professionals-at-risk: Interventions to reduce burnout and improve retention of special educators. *Exceptional Children, 62,* 336–355.

Cooper, C. L. (Ed.). (1998). *Theories of organizational stress.* New York: Oxford University Press.

Cordes, C. L., & Dougherty, T. W. (1993). A review and integration of research on job burnout. *Academy of Management Review, 18,* 621–656.

Cordes, C. L., Dougherty, T. W., & Blum, M. (1997). Patterns of burnout among managers and professionals: A comparison of models. *Journal of Organizational Behavior, 18,* 685–701.

Corrigan, P. W., Holmes, E. P., Luchins, D., Buican, B., Basit, A., & Parkes, J. J. (1994). Staff burnout in a psychiatric hospital: A cross-lagged panel design. *Journal of Organizational Behavior, 15,* 65–74.

Curtona, C. E., & Russell, D. W. (1990). Type of social support and specific stress: Toward a theory of optimal matching. In B. R. Sarason, I. G. Sarason, & G. R. Pierce (Eds.), *Social support: An interactional view* (pp. 319–361). New York: Wiley.

Dale, J., & Weinberg, R. (1990). Burnout in sport: A review and critique. *Applied Sport Psychology, 2,* 67–83.

Dean, J. W., Brandes, P., & Dharwadkar, R. (1998). Organizational cynicism. *Academy of Management Review, 23,* 341–352.

Demerouti, E., Bakker, A. B., Nachreiner, F., & Schaufeli, W. B. (2000). A model of burnout and life satisfaction amongst nurses. *Journal of Advanced Nursing, 32,* 454–464.

Farber, B. A. (1991). *Crisis in education: Stress and burnout in the American teacher.* San Francisco: Jossey-Bass.

Farber, B. A. (2000). Introduction: Understanding and treating burnout in a changing culture. *Psychotherapy in Practice, 56,* 589–594.

Fisher, S. (1984). *Stress and the perception of control.* London: Erlbaum.

Foschi, M. (2000). Double standards for competence: Theory and research. *Annual Review of Sociology, 26,* 21–42.

Freedy, J. R., & Hobfoll, S. E. (1994). Stress inoculation for reduction of burnout: A conservation of resources approach. *Anxiety, Stress and Coping, 6,* 311–325.

Freudenberger, H. J. (1974). Staff burnout. *Journal of Social Issues, 30,* 159–164.

Freudenberger, H. J. (1980). *Burnout: The high costs of high achievement.* New York: Anchor Press.

Garden, A. M. (1987). Depersonalization: A valid dimension of burnout? *Human Relations, 40,* 545–560.

Garden, A. M. (1989). Burnout: The effects of psychological types on research findings. *Journal of Occupational Psychology, 62,* 223–234.

Garden, A. M. (1991). The purpose of burnout: A Jungian interpretation. *Journal of Social Behavior and Personality, 6,* 73–93.

Golembiewski, R. T., & Boss, W. (1992). Phases of burnout in diagnosis and intervention. *Research in Organizational Change and Development, 6,* 115–152.

Golembiewski, R. T., Boudreau, G. T., Munzenrider, R. F., & Lou, H. (1996). *Global burnout: A worldwide panepidemic by the phase model.* Greenwich, CT: JAI Press.

Golembiewski, R. T., & Munzenrider, R. (1988). *Phases of burnout: Developments in concepts and applications.* New York, New York: Praeger.

Golembiewski, R. T., Munzenrider, R., & Stevenson, J. (1986). *Stress in Organizations.* New York: Praeger.

Handy, J. A., (1988). Theoretical and methodological problems within occupational stress and burnout research. *Human Relations, 41,* 351–365.

Hobfoll, S. E. (1988). *The ecology of stress.* Washington, DC: Hemisphere.

Hobfoll, S. E. (1989). Conservation of resources: A new attempt at conceptualizing stress. *American Psychologist, 44,* 513–524.

Hobfoll, S. E. (1998). *The psychology and philosophy of stress, culture, and community.* New York: Plenum Press.

Hobfoll, S. E., & Freedy, J. (1993). Conservation of resources: A general theory applied to burnout. In W. B. Schaufeli, C. Maslach, & T. Marek (Eds.) *Professional burnout: Recent developments in theory and research* (pp. 115–135). New York: Taylor & Francis.

Hobfoll, S. E., & Shirom, A. (1993). Stress and burnout in work organizations. In R. T. Golembiewski (Ed.), *Handbook of organization behavior* (pp. 41–61). New York: Dekker.

Hobfoll, S. E., & Shirom, A. (2000). Conservation of resources theory: Applications to stress and management in the workplace. In R. T. Golembiewski (Ed.), *Handbook of organization behavior* (2nd rev. ed., pp. 57–81). New York: Dekker.

Jackson, S. E., Schwab, R. L., & Schuler, R. S. (1986). Toward an understanding of the burnout phenomenon. *Journal of Applied Psychology, 71,* 630–640.

Kahill, S. (1988). Symptoms of professional burnout: A review of the empirical evidence. *Canadian Psychology, 29,* 284–297.

Kalliath, T. J., O'Driscoll, M. P., Gillespie, D. F. & Bluedorn, A. G. (2000). A test of the Maslach Burnout Inventory in three samples of healthcare professionals. *Work & Stress, 14,* 35–50.

Koeske, C. F., & Koeske, R. D. (1989). Construct validity of the Maslach Burnout Inventory: A critical review. *Journal of Applied Behavioral Science, 25,* 131–144.

Kop, N., Euwema, M., & Schaufeli, W. (1999). Burnout, job stress, and violent behaviour among Dutch police officers. *Work & Stress, 13,* 326–340.

Kramer, R. M. (1990). The effects of resource scarcity on group conflict and cooperation. In E. Lawler (Ed.), *Advances in group processes* (Vol. 7, pp. 151–177). Greenwich, CT: JAI Press.

Kramer, R. M. (1991). Intergroup relations and organizational dilemmas: The role of categorization processes. *Research in Organization Behavior, 13,* 191–228.

Kushnir, T., & Melamed, S. (1992). The Gulf War and burnout. *Psychological Medicine, 22,* 987–995.

Law, K. S., Wong, C. S., & Mobley, W. H. (1998). Toward a taxonomy of multidimensional constructs. *Academy of Management Review, 23,* 741–745.

Lee, C., & Bobko, P. (1994). Self-efficacy beliefs: Comparison of five measures. *Journal of Applied Psychology, 79,* 364–369.

Lee, R., & Ashforth, B. E. (1996). A meta-analytic examination of the correlates of the three dimensions of job burnout. *Journal of Applied Psychology, 81,* 123–133.

Leiter, M. P., & Durum, J. (1994). The discriminant validity of burnout and depression: A confirmatory factor analytic study. *Anxiety, Stress, and Coping, 7,* 357–373.

Leiter, M. P., & Maslach, C. (1988). The impact of interpersonal environment on burnout and organizational commitment. *Journal of Organizational Behavior, 9,* 297–308.

Leiter, M. P., & Maslach, C. (2001). Burnout and health. In A. Baum, T. A. Revenson, & J. E. Singer (Eds.), *Handbook of health psychology* (pp. 415–422). New Jersey: Erlbaum.

Leiter, M. P., & Meachem, K. A. (1986). Role structure and burnout in the field of human services. *Journal of Applied Behavioral Science, 22,* 47–52.

Lerman, Y., Melamed, S., Shargin, Y., Kushnir, T., Rotgoltz, Y., Shirom, A., & Aronoson, M. (1999). The association between burnout at work and leukocyte adhesiveness/aggregation. *Psychosomatic Medicine, 61,* 828–833.

Maslach, C. (1982). *Burnout: The cost of caring.* Englewood Cliffs, NJ: Prentice Hall.

Maslach, C. (1998). A multidimensional theory of burnout. In C. L. Cooper (Ed.), *Theories of organizational stress* (pp. 68–85). Oxford: Oxford University Press.

Maslach, D., & Jackson, S. (1981). The measurement of experienced burnout. *Journal of Occupational Behavior, 2,* 99–115.

Maslach, C., Jackson, S. E., & Leiter, M. P. (1996). *Maslach Burnout Inventory Manual.* 3rd ed. Palo Alto, CA: Consulting Psychologists Press.

Maslach, C., & Leiter, M. P. (1997). *The truth about burnout.* San Francisco: Jossey-Bass.

Maslach, C., Schaufeli, W. B., & Leiter, M. P. (2001). Job burnout. *Annual Review of Psychology, 52,* 397–422.

Meier, S. T. (1984). The construct validity of burnout. *Journal of Occupational Psychology, 57,* 211–219.

Melamed, S., Kushnir, T., & Shirom, A. (1992). Burnout and risk factors for cardiovascular disease. *Behavioral Medicine, 18,* 53–61.

Melamed, S., Ugarten, U., Shirom, A., Kahana, L., Lerman, Y., & Froom, P. (1999). Chronic burnout, somatic arousal and elevated cortisol levels. *Journal of Psychosomatic Research, 46,* 591–598.

Mone, M. A., McKinley, W., & Barker, V. L. (1998). Organizational decline and innovation: A contingency framework. *Academy of Management Review, 23,* 115–132.

Moore, J. E. (2000). Why is this happening? A causal attribution approach to work exhaustion consequences. *Academy of Management Review, 25,* 335–349.

Nelson, D. L., Quick, J. C., & Simmons, B. L. (2001). Preventive management of work stress: Current themes and future challenges. In A. Baum, T. A. Revenson, & J. E. Singer (Eds.), *Handbook of health psychology* (pp. 349–364). Mahwah, NJ: Erlbaum.

O'Driscoll, M. P., & Schubert, T. (1988). Organizational climate and burnout in a New Zealand social service agency. *Work & Stress, 2,* 199–204.

Parker, P. A., & Kulik, J. A. (1995). Burnout, self- and supervisor-related job performance, and absenteeism among nurses. *Journal of Behavioral Medicine, 18,* 581–599.

Pines, A. (1988). *Keeping the spark alive: Preventing burnout in love and marriage.* New York: St. Martin Press.

Pines, A. (1993). Burnout. In L. Goldberger & S. Breznitz (Eds.), *Handbook of stress* (2nd ed., pp. 386–403). New York: Free Press.

Pines, A. (1996). *Couple burnout.* New York and London: Routledge.

Pines, A., & Aronson, E. (1988). *Career burnout: Causes and cures.* New York: Free Press.

Pines, A., Aronson, E., & Kafry D. (1981). *Burnout: From tedium to personal growth.* New York: Free Press.

Rabin, S., Saffer, M., Weisberg, E., Kornitzer-Enav, T., Peled, I., & Ribak, J. (2000). A multifaceted mental health training program in reducing burnout among occupational social workers. *Israel Journal of Psychiatry and Related Science, 37,* 12–19.

Rountree, B. H. (1984). Psychological burnout in task groups: Examining the proposition that some task groups of workers have an affinity for burnout, while others do not. *Journal of Health and Human Resource Administration, 7,* 235–249.

Sandberg, J. (2000). Understanding human competence at work: An integrative approach. *Academy of Management Journal, 43,* 9–25.

Schaufeli, W. B., & Buunk, B. P. (1996). Professional burnout. In M. J. Schabracq, J. A. M.Winnust, & C. L. Cooper (Eds.), *Handbook of work and health psychology* (pp. 311–346). New York: Wiley.

Schaufeli, W. B., & Dierendonck, D. Van (1993). The construct validity of two burnout measures. *Journal of Organizational Behavior, 14,* 631–647.

Schaufeli, W. B., & Enzmann, D. (1998). *The burnout companion to study and practice: A critical analysis.* Washington, DC: Taylor & Francis.

Schaufeli, W. B., Maslach, C., & Marek, T. (Eds.). (1993). *Professional burnout.* Washington, DC: Taylor & Francis.

Schutte, N., Toppinen, S., Kalimo, R., & Schaufeli, W. (2000). The factorial validity of the Maslach Burnout Inventory-General Survey (MBI-GS) across occupational groups and nations. *Journal of Occupational and Organizational Psychology, 73,* 53–66.

Shirom, A. (1989). Burnout in work organizations. In C. L. Cooper & I. Robertson (Eds.), *International review of industrial and organizational psychology* (pp. 26–48). New York: Wiley.

Shirom, A., & Ezrachi, J. (2001). *On the discriminant validity of burnout, depression and anxiety.* Submitted for publication.

Shirom, A., Westman, M., Shamai, O., & Carel, R. S. (1997). The effects of work overload and burnout on cholesterol and triglycerides levels: The moderating effects of emotional reactivity among male and female employees. *Journal of Occupational Health Psychology, 2,* 275–288.

Stajkovic, A. D., & Luthans, F. (1998). Self-efficacy and work-related performance: A meta-analysis. *Psychological Bulletin, 124,* 240–261.

Staw, B. M., Sandelands, L. E., & Dutton J. E. (1981). Threat-rigidity effects in organizational behavior: A multilevel analysis. *Administrative Science Quarterly, 28,* 501–524.

Travers, C., & Cooper, C. (Eds.). (1996). *Teachers under pressure: Stress in the teaching profession.* London: Routledge.

Vandenberghe, R., & Huberman, A. M. (Eds.). (1999). *Understanding and preventing teacher burnout: A sourcebook of international research and practice.* New York: Cambridge University Press.

Vingerhoets, A. J. J. M. (1985). *Psychosocial Stress: An Experimental Approach.* Lisse, Switzerland: Swets & Zeitlinger.

Watson, D., & Clark, L. A. (1984). Negative effectivity: The disposition to experience aversive emotional states. *Psychological Bulletin, 96,* 465–490.

Westman, M., & Etzion, D. (1995). Crossover of stress, strain and resources from one spouse to another. *Journal of Organizational Behavior, 16,* 169–181.

Winnubst, J. (1993). Organizational structure, social support, and burnout. In W. Schaufeli, C. Maslach, & T. Marek (Eds.), *Professional burnout: Recent developments in theory and research* (pp. 151–162). Washington, DC: Taylor & Francis.

Wright, T. A., & Bonnett, D. G. (1997). The contribution of burnout to work performance. *Journal of Organizational Behavior, 18,* 491–499.

Wright, T. A., & Cropanzano, R. (1999). Emotional exhaustion as a predictor of job performance and voluntary turnover. *Journal of Applied Psychology, 83,* 486–493.

Zellars, K. L., Perrewé, P. L., & Hochwarter, W. A. (2000). Burnout in health care: The role of the five factors of personality. *Journal of Applied Social Psychology, 30,* 1570–1598.

13 ⸻⸻⸻⸻⸻⸻⸻⸻⸻⸻⸻⸻⸻⸻

The Workplace and Cardiovascular Disease: Relevance and Potential Role for Occupational Health Psychology

Paul A. Landsbergis, Peter L. Schnall, Karen L. Belkić, Dean Baker, Joseph E. Schwartz, and Thomas G. Pickering

Cardiovascular disease (CVD) is the major cause of morbidity and mortality in the industrialized world. It is projected that CVD will become the most common cause of death worldwide by 2020, causing more than 36% of all deaths (Braunwald, 1997, p. 1364). However, based primarily on studies of nonindustrialized populations (Carvalho et al., 1989; Cooper, Rotimi, & Ward, 1999), CVD and hypertension appear to be of relatively recent historical origin (Schnall & Kern, 1981). A major cross-cultural study found virtually no rise in blood pressure (BP) with age and no hypertension among hunter–gatherers, herders, or traditional family farmers (Waldron et al., 1982). In contrast, men and women in urban industrial societies have steady rises of BP with age and hypertension is common (Schnall & Kern, 1981; Waldron et al., 1982). This study also found substantial ($r = 0.46$–0.67) and significant associations between BP and involvement in a money economy even after controlling for salt consumption and, for men, after controlling for body mass index (Waldron et al., 1982).

A number of individual risk factors for CVD have been identified, including cigarette smoking, total (and low density lipoprotein) cholesterol, hypertension, fibrinogen, overweight, diabetes, and sedentary behavior (Kannel, 1992). However, many cases do not occur in "high-risk" individuals (Whelton, He, & Klag, 1994)—for example, in the multiple risk factor intervention trial, more than 30% of the CHD deaths resulting from systolic

Some of the research findings in this chapter were supported in part by grants HL18232, HL30605, HL55165 and HL47540 from the National Heart, Lung and Blood Institute, Bethesda, MD.

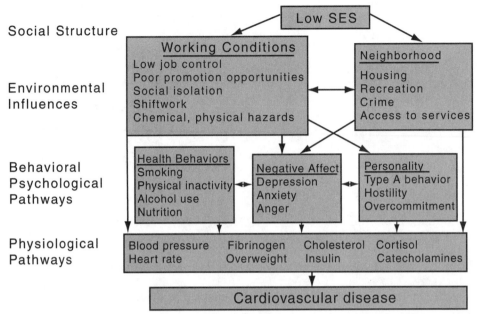

Figure 13.1.   Levels of causation of CVD. Adapted with permission from McKinlay and Marceau (1999).

BP > 110 mm Hg were in the group with "normal" systolic BP (110–139 mm Hg; Stamler, 1991).

Over the past 20 years, an extensive body of evidence has documented that lower socioeconomic status (Kaplan & Keil, 1993) and work stressors (Karasek & Theorell, 1990; Schnall, Belkić, Landsbergis, & Baker, 2000) are important risk factors for hypertension and CVD. Job control was "the biggest factor contributing to the socioeconomic gradient in CHD risk across civil service employment grade" in the Whitehall study (Kawachi & Marmot, 1998; Marmot, Bosma, Hemingway, Brunner, & Stansfeld, 1997). A model of the impact of social structure and environment on behavior, psychological characteristics, physiology, and CVD is depicted in Figure 13.1. For example, sedentary behavior and smoking "often arise in the context of individuals trapped in low-control work environments" (Kawachi & Marmot, 1998, p. 162). More advantaged communities and individuals have greater resources for the promotion of "hygienic" life-styles and the "reduction of alienating living and working conditions which are conducive to initiating and maintaining unhealthful behaviors" (Wing, Casper, Riggan, Hayes, & Tyroler, 1988, p. 925).

Current Economic and Workplace Trends

Current economic and workplace trends, resulting from economic globalization, may be having dramatic effects on the health of lower socioeconomic groups (Cooper, 1996; Tuchsen, 1993). These trends include stagnant or falling real income, downsizing, contingent and temporary work, and new management systems such as "lean production" that intensify work (Landsbergis, Cahill, & Schnall, 1999). Income inequality in the United States is at the highest level over the past 60 years (Wolff, 1995), and the United States "is the most unequal among developed countries" (U.S. Departments of Labor and Commerce, 1994, p. 19). Concurrently, substantial changes in job characteristics have been occurring. In Europe, "time constraints" (i.e., workload demands) increased between 1977 to 1996 (European Foundation, 1997), and in the United States, increases between 1977 to 1997 were reported for "never enough time to get everything done on my job" (from 40 to 60%) (Bond, Galinsky, & Swanberg, 1998). U.S. workers' average weekly work hours are now the longest in the developed world (International Labour Office, 1999). The proportion of "high strain" (high demand–low control) jobs in Europe increased from 25% to 30% between 1991 to 1996 (European Foundation, 1997).

Trends in CVD

Although CVD *mortality* in industrialized countries has fallen over the past 40 years (Liao & Cooper, 1995), CVD *incidence* in the United States has shown little or no decline over the past 20 years (Rosamond et al., 1998; Wilson et al., 1991). The gap between higher and lower socioeconomic status in CVD mortality (Gonzalez, Artalejo, & Calero, 1998; Marmot & Theorell, 1991) and incidence (Hallqvist, Lundberg, Diderichsen, & Ahlbom, 1998; Tuchsen & Endahl, 1999) is *increasing*. Increases in work stressors produced by economic globalization may be playing an important role in maintaining incidence rates for CVD.

Work Stressors and CVD: Epidemiological Data

Various models of work stressors have been investigated. The most highly studied construct is *job strain*—in other words, work that combines high psychological work demands with low job decision latitude, or job control (Karasek & Theorell, 1990). More recently, the *effort–reward* model defines deleterious job conditions as a "mismatch between high workload (high demand) and low control over long-term rewards" (Siegrist, Peter, Junge, Cremer, & Seidel, 1990, p. 1128). Low reward includes concepts such as low "esteem reward" (e.g., respect, support), low income, and low "status control" (e.g., poor promotion prospects, job insecurity, status inconsistency). A number of studies have examined *threat-avoidant vigilant work*—in other words, work that involves continuously maintaining a high level of vigilance to avoid disaster, such as loss of human life (Belkić, Landsbergis, et al., 2000). This is a feature of a number of occupations at high risk for CVD—for example, urban mass transit operators, truck drivers, air traffic controllers, and sea pilots. Long work hours (Falger & Schouten, 1992; Sokejima & Kagamimori, 1998) and shift work (Steenland, 2000) have also been investigated (see chapter 11, this volume). Prolonged exposure to stressful working conditions appears to be particularly deleterious (Belkić, Schnall, Savic, & Landsbergis, 2000).

Several reviews have been published on the association between these psychosocial work stressors and CVD (Belkić, Landsbergis, et al., 2000; Kristensen, Kronitzer, & Alfedsson, 1998; Schnall, Landsbergis, & Baker, 1994). As of 2000, there have been 24 studies of job strain and CVD (primarily CHD) among men (Belkić, Landsbergis, et al., 2000), and 6 studies among women (Brisson, 2000), most with significant positive associations. Four CVD studies have tested the moderating effect of job control on job demands and two of these found significant interactions (Hallqvist, Diderichsen, et al., 1998; Johnson & Hall, 1988). Among men, the impact of job strain on CVD is more consistent and stronger among blue-collar workers (e.g., Johnson & Hall, 1988; Theorell et al., 1998), with risk ratios as high as 10.0 (Hallqvist, Diderichsen, et al., 1998), than among men in jobs with higher socioeconomic status.

Of five studies of effort–reward imbalance among men (Bosma, Peter, Siegrist, & Marmot, 1998; Lynch, Krause, Kaplan, Salonen, & Salonen, 1997; Lynch, Krause, Kaplan, Tuomilehto, & Salonen, 1997; Peter et al., 1999b; Siegrist, 1996; Siegrist et al., 1990), all found significant positive associations between exposure and CVD. No studies of effort–reward and CVD in women have been published to date.

Significant associations with death as a result of heart attacks were found for "economic and financial implications of decisions taken at work, as well as the relevance of possible damage and hazards both economic and for human life as a consequence of possible mistakes made at work" among Italian male railroad workers (Menotti & Seccareccia, 1985). In the United States, cardiovascular disability was associated with the job dimensions "alert to changing conditions" and "hazardous job situation" (Murphy, 1991). Swedish men whose jobs entailed risk of explosion had an increased risk of hospitalization for myocardial infarction (MI; Alfredsson, Spetz, & Theorell, 1985). However, only a few epidemiologic studies have specifically examined aspects of threat-avoidant vigilant activity and CVD outcomes. The strongest evidence for this risk factor comes from studies of single occupations, where professional drivers, particularly urban transport operators, emerge as the occupation with the most consistent evidence of elevated risk of CHD and hypertension (Belkić et al., 1998).

Among women, in the Framingham Heart Study, 8-year heart disease incidence for *clerical* workers was double the rate for white-collar workers (Haynes & Feinleib, 1980) and 14-year incidence among *blue-collar* women was more than triple the rate for white-collar women (Eaker, Packard, & Thom, 1989). Twenty-year risk of MI or coronary death showed little difference between these occupational categories. However, other measures of socioeconomic status, such as low education or having a husband with a clerical or blue-collar occupation (versus white-collar), were associated with increased 20-year risk (Eaker, 1992). The association between job strain and CHD among Framingham clerical women was odds ratio = 5.2, substantially higher than the OR = 2.9 for all women (LaCroix, 1984). The combination of work and home stressors may help to explain increased CHD risk in lower socioeconomic-status women (Haynes & Feinleib, 1980).

Work Stressors and Hypertension

A number of studies have explored whether the increased risk of CVD because of job strain is mediated by high BP.

Effect of blood pressure measurement techniques and where measurements are taken. Few studies of job strain and casual clinic BP have shown significant associations (Schnall et al., 1994); however, strong evidence of an association is found in studies where BP is measured by an ambulatory (portable) monitor (Belkić, Landsbergis, et al., 2000). This difference in findings may be explained, in part, by the imprecision and possible bias of taking "casual" BP measurements. For example, relaxation can occur when people are away from work, resulting in lower BP. There are also various atypical psychosocial stimuli present in a clinic that can affect BP, such as anxiety as a result of seeing a doctor. An alternative method of measuring BP is ambulatory monitoring, in which a person wears an automatic monitor on his or her arm throughout the work day (Pickering, 1991). Compared to casual BP measurements, ambulatory monitoring provides a more reliable measure of BP, because there is no observer bias and the number of readings is increased. It is also a more valid measure of average BP, because BP is measured during a person's normal daily activities and exposure to the daily stressors that influence persistent increases in BP. Ambulatory BP is a better predictor of target organ damage, such as increases in the size of the heart's left ventricle, and CVD, than are casual clinic BP readings (Verdecchia, Clement, Fagard, Palatini, & Parati, 1999).

Occult (hidden) work-related hypertension. The widespread application of ambulatory BP (AmBP) monitoring has focused attention on "white coat" hypertension (elevated casual clinic BP with normal AmBP), an entity of low predictive value with respect to hypertensive sequelae. Meanwhile, occult work-related hypertension, which is often characterized by the *opposite* pattern (normal casual clinic BP and elevated work AmBP), remains underdetected despite its potential clinical importance. In the Work Site BP Study (Schnall et al., 1990), 86 men with elevated casual clinic BP and 181 with normal casual clinic BP underwent AmBP on a working day. Twenty-seven men had "white coat" hypertension, and 36 had occult workplace hypertension. Thus, among working populations, the problem of occult workplace hypertension could be of even greater magnitude than that of "white coat" hypertension (Belkić et al., 2001).

Epidemiological data. Of 10 cross-sectional studies of job strain (or its components) and AmBP among men, many indicate significant positive associations with work BP (Belkić, Landbergis, et al., 2000). In the five studies in which measurements were also made outside of work, job strain was associated with leisure time systolic BP. Both cohort studies of ambulatory BP among men found significant associations with job strain (Schnall, Landsbergis, Schwartz, Warren, & Pickering, 1998; Theorell et al., 1988). Of the six cross-sectional studies of job strain and AmBP among women, four indicate a significant positive association with work systolic BP (Brisson, 2000). Work systolic BP in men facing job strain is typically 4 to 8 mm Hg higher than those without job strain. In studies of women, estimates of the magnitude of effect have been even higher. One AmBP study tested the moderating effect of job control on job demands and found a significant interaction (Landsbergis, Schnall, Warren, Pickering, & Schwartz, 1994). Studies of high effort–low reward at work have shown significant positive associations with hypertension in men (Peter & Siegrist, 1997), in men and women (Peter et al., 1998), and with a comanifestation of hypertension and high LDL-cholesterol in men (Siegrist, Peter, Georg, Cremer, & Seidel, 1991).

The Work Site Blood Pressure (BP) Study, a longitudinal study of psychosocial factors and ambulatory BP, was begun at Cornell Medical College in 1985 in New York City. At the first round of data collection (Time 1), men employed in "high strain" jobs were at increased risk of hypertension ($OR = 2.7$), had increased left ventricular mass index (7.3 g/ m^2; Schnall et al., 1990), and had higher levels of work (6.7 mm Hg systolic, 2.7 mm Hg diastolic), home and sleep ambulatory BP (AmBP), controlling for potential risk factors (Landsbergis et al., 1994; Schnall, Schwartz, Landsbergis, Warren, & Pickering, 1992).

Examining data from Time 1 and a second round of data collection 3 years later (Time 2), it was possible to construct a measure of repeated or cumulative exposure to job strain, which exhibited a consistent pattern of associations with work, home, and sleep AmBP . The chronically exposed group exhibited an 11 to 12 mm Hg higher systolic and 6 to 9 mm Hg higher diastolic work AmBP than the group unexposed at both times. These effect sizes are substantial, more than twice the difference between Black and White individuals in this sample and more than the estimated effect of aging 25 years or gaining 50 pounds in weight (Schnall et al., 1998).

Examining the 3-year change in AmBP between Time 1 and Time 2, those reporting job strain at Time 1 but no job strain at Time 2 exhibited a decrease in systolic AmBP of 5.3 mm Hg at work and 4.7 mm Hg at home ($p < .05$; Schnall et al., 1998). The decrease in AmBP associated with a decrease in job strain over time suggests that early detection and prevention strategies should be effective. The cross-sectional association between job strain and AmBP in men was also substantially greater for men with lower socioeconomic status (Landsbergis, Schnall, Warren, Pickering, & Schwartz, 1999), implying that increased efforts at early detection and prevention are required in this group.

Population Attributable Risk of Psychosocial Work Factors

The population attributable risk (PAR%) of CVD as a result of psychosocial work factors may be substantial. Karasek and Theorell estimated a prevalence of exposure of 15 to 25% in Sweden and a resulting PAR% of 7 to

16% for men (Karasek & Theorell, 1990). A relative risk of 2.0 and a prevalence estimate for job strain of 15 to 25% (a conservative estimate given current economic trends and current European surveys) produces a PAR% of 13 to 20%. In Denmark, the PAR% for monotonous high-paced work (a conservative proxy measure for job strain) was estimated at 6% for men and 14% for women (Kristensen et al., 1998). However, few studies have examined the combined or synergistic effect of workplace stressors, which would increase estimates of the proportion of CVD as a result of work. One Swedish study (Peter et al., 1999) did find that the combined effects of exposure to job strain and to effort–reward imbalance on CVD were much stronger than the separate effects of each model.

Mechanisms by Which Work Stressors Can Lead to CVD Outcomes

There are "intimate connections between the social environment and the central nervous system (CNS), and the CNS and the cardiovascular system via the autonomic and neuroendocrine systems" (Schnall, Belkić, Landsbergis, & Baker, 2000b, p. 2). This interrelation has been conceptualized as "econeurocardiology," the biological paradigm by which social factors, such as work stressors, are perceived and processed by the CNS, resulting in pathophysiological changes that increase risk of cardiovascular disease (Belkić, Schnall, Landsbergis, & Baker, 2000; Wolf, 2000). Although the mechanisms remain to be fully elucidated, at least four possible pathways exist by which job stressors may influence CVD risk (Schnall et al., 1994). The first three pathways, reviewed in this section, involve known cardiac risk factors, increased risk of cardiac events among vulnerable individuals, and atherosclerosis. Possible social psychological pathways are reviewed in the next section.

Known CVD Risk Factors

We review the evidence on the association between work stressors and known CVD risk factors, such as hypertension, serum cholesterol, cigarette smoking, sedentary behavior, and atheroschlerosis in this section.

Hypertension. The strongest empirical evidence for a role for job stressors in the promotion of known CVD risk factors is for hypertension (Belkić, Schnall, Landsbergis, et al., 2000). Sympathetic nervous system overactivity (associated with job stressors) is also implicated in the clustering of hypertension and various atherogenic biochemical abnormalities, together known as the cardiovascular metabolic syndrome (CVM). The CVM includes hypertension, increased total cholesterol, triglycerides and insulin; decreased high-density lipoprotein (HDL) cholesterol; central obesity; insulin resistance and glucose intolerance; and hypercoagulability and reduced fibrinolysis (Fossum, Hoieggen, Moan, Rostrup, & Kjeldsen, 2000).

Building on the work of Henry and Stephens (Henry, 1992), Frankenhauser and colleagues confirmed the involvement of two neuroendocrine systems in the stress response—the *sympathoadrenal medullary* system (which secretes the catecholamines, epinephrine, and norepinephrine), and the *hypothalamic-pituitary-adrenal cortical* system (which secretes corticosteroids such as cortisol). Under demanding conditions in which organisms can exert control, epinephrine levels increase, and some studies suggest that cortisol levels may decline (Frankenhaeuser & Johansson, 1986). However, in demanding but low-control situations (analogous to "job strain"), both epinephrine and cortisol are elevated (Frankenhaeuser, 1989; Schwartz, Belkić, Schnall, & Pickering, 2000). Elevated levels of both catecholamines and cortisol have severe consequences for myocardial pathology (Fredriksson, Sundin, & Frankenhaeuser, 1985; Steptoe, 1981). Cortisol enhances and prolongs the effect of epinephrine (Theorell, 2000). The combination of these hormones appears to promote BP elevation (Schwartz et al., 2000), dyslipidemia (Theorell, 2000), and the CVM (Fossum et al., 2000). The physiology of the stress response contradicts the standard advice given in stress management programs—that stress depends only on a person's *perception* of environmental *demands*. In fact, levels of *control* available to individuals in the environment is key to the type of stress response elicited.

These simple models may not capture the complexity of the stress response, and profound regulatory cortisol disturbances resulting from chronic arousal (Theorell, 2000). Short-term cortisol and adrenalin elevation has been associated with healthier coping in stressful situations (Karasek & Theorell, 1990). However, chronic elevation of cortisol appears in clinical depression, an apparent risk factor for CHD (Rozanski, Blumenthal, & Kaplan, 1999), and low cortisol levels reflect exhausted function, which has also been associated with cardiac death (Appels & Otten, 1992).

Personal control may reduce the duration of the stress response (Frankenhaeuser, 1989). Repetitive and machine-paced jobs and excessive overtime tend to prolong "unwinding," the return of neuroendocrine levels to baseline (Frankenhaeuser & Johansson, 1986). AmBP studies indicate a "carryover" effect in which the work, home, and sleep BP of "high strain" workers is elevated above levels of other workers (Belkić, Landsbergis, et al., 2000). Another obstacle to "unwinding" may be the dual role (the additional responsibility for household and children) that many workers (particularly women) face when they return home (Hall, 1992). A Canadian study found evidence of synergism between family responsibilities and job strain in their effect on BP among college-educated women (Brisson et al., 1999).

Known risk factors other than hypertension. Research on the association of work stressors with serum cholesterol and behavioral CVD risk factors has produced inconsistent results. Effort–reward imbalance was associated with LDL/HDL cholesterol ratio in several studies (Peter et al., 1998; Siegrist, Matschinger, Cremer, & Seidel, 1988) and with the combined occurrence of hypertension and hyperlipidemia (Siegrist et al., 1991). Some evidence exists for an association of job strain with smoking intensity and cessation (Green & Johnson, 1990; Hellerstedt & Jeffery, 1997; Kawakami, Haratani, & Araki, 1998) although null studies have also been reported. In the Work Site BP Study, among men, an increase in job decision latitude over 3 years was associated with quitting smoking (Landsbergis et al., 1998). Job strain has been associated with BMI (Netterstrom, Kristensen, Damsgaard, Olsen, & Sjol, 1991) and skinfold thickness (Georges, Wear, & Mueller, 1992), but other studies of job strain and other job stressors have found no association with overweight. Several studies found sedentary behavior to be associated with low latitude for men and women (Hellerstedt & Jeffery, 1997; Johansson, Johnson, & Hall, 1991) and high job demands for women (Johansson et al., 1991), however, null studies also exist.

Risk of cardiac events in vulnerable persons. The influence of sympatho-adrenal activity on cardiovascular function includes increased myocardial oxygen demand and decreased myocardial oxygen supply that can lead in vulnerable individuals to myocardial ischemia (Belkić, 2000b), destabilization of the cardiac electrical substrate (Belkić, 2000a), as well as increased risk of clot formation and disruption of unstable plaques (Steptoe & Marmot, 2000). Platelet activation and the concentration of fibrinogen also play a role in acute thrombosis (Steptoe & Marmot, 2000). Job strain may inhibit anabolic (regenerative) processes, which may contribute to an adverse, atherogenic metabolic profile (Theorell, 2000). Environmental stressors may act as potential triggers of life-threatening arrhythmias and sudden cardiac death (see Belkić, 2000a; Willich, Maclure, Mittleman, Arntz, & Muller, 1993). Young men who have suffered a heart attack and return to high strain jobs may be particularly at risk for CHD-related mortality (Theorell, Perski, Orth-Gomer, Hamsten, & de Faire, 1991). However, the evidence to date is not as clear with respect to women who return to high strain jobs after cardiac events (Orth-Gomer et al., 2000).

Atherosclerosis. Hypertension contributes to atherosclerosis (Steptoe & Marmot, 2000). In addition, low decision latitude is associated with high plasma fibrinogen, suggesting a link with coagulation and, thus, atherosclerosis (Brunner et al., 1996; Markowe et al., 1985). This pathway is consistent with the association between epinephrine levels and coagulation (Gertler & White, 1976; Haft, 1974), for example, the stimulation of platelet adhesiveness by epinephrine. Progression of coronary atherosclerosis over time has been associated with low job decision latitude (Langosch, Brodner, & Borcherding, 1983) and with high demands and low economic rewards at work (Lynch, Krause, Kaplan, Tuomilehto, et al., 1997).

Insights From Behavioral Medicine–Social Psychological Mechanisms

Although much research has focused on negative affect as a CVD risk factor, there has been a tendency to view behavioral–psychological factors in isolation, without conceptualizing them in relation to objective stressors, in the work environment and elsewhere. Figure 13.1 presented a model of affect, behavior, and personality as outcomes of social conditions and as mediators of the effects of social stressors on CVD risk. Behavioral–psychological factors may also interact with social stressors in increasing CVD risk.

Role of Job Characteristics

Additional research is needed on the hypothesis that job stressors may increase the risk of hypertension and CVD, in part by shaping personality or increasing negative affect. Karasek's job demands–control model describes the adult socialization of personality traits and behavior patterns that occur at work. Chronic adaptation to low control–low demand situations ("passive" jobs) can result in reduced self-efficacy, greater external locus of control, reduced ability to solve problems or tackle challenges (Karasek & Theorell, 1990), and feelings of depression (Karasek, 1979) or "learned helplessness"—yet these jobs are not associated with increases in BP. Conversely, when high (but not overwhelming) job demands are matched with greater authority and skill, more active learning and greater internal locus of control develop. This can enable individuals to develop a broader range of coping strategies. For example, in Sweden, workers whose jobs became more "passive" over six years reported less participation in political and leisure activities. In contrast, workers in jobs that became more "active" participated more in these activities (Karasek & Theorell, 1990, p. 53). In a U.S. study, evidence was seen for increased intellectual flexibility, nonauthoritarianism, capacity to take responsibility for one's actions, and intellectually demanding leisure time after 10 years among those with greater occupational self-direction, a concept similar to decision latitude (Kohn & Schooler, 1982). This research points to the organization of work not only as a potential source of stress and increased disease risk, but also potentially as a key factor in the promotion of physical and mental health and the development of one's creative potential, effective coping, and social involvement outside work.

Role of Personality–Negative Affect

The precise role played by personality traits (e.g., Type A behavior, overcommitment, or hostility) or negative affect (e.g., anxiety, anger, or depression) in the development of hypertension and CVD remains unclear. Current evidence is more consistent for an association with CVD than with hypertension.

Hypertension. Empirical support for the concept of the "hypertensive personality" remains equivocal (Shapiro, 1988). Hypertension has been associated with internalized aggression (Perini et al., 1990) and with anxiety (Jonas, Franks, & Ingram, 1997; Markovitz, Matthews, Kannel, Cobb,

& D'Agostino, 1993), although other studies have failed to find these associations (Jonas et al., 1997; Markovitz et al., 1993; Sparrow, Garvey, Rosner, & Thomas, 1982). However, methodological problems have plagued studies of this association (see Friedman et al., 2001). Another limitation is the lack of a model that predicts *specific* interactions or mediation between work stressors and personality characteristics in the development of hypertension. For example, in one study, suppressed anger was associated with the prevalence of hypertension in male hourly workers only among those reporting job stress (Cottington, Matthews, Talbott, & Kuller, 1986). Other studies have shown that asymptomatic participants with hypertension (Knox, Svensson, Waller, & Theorell, 1988), as well as those with normal BP with a family history of hypertension (Theorell, 1990), seem to express fewer emotions and have a noncomplaining attitude (Karasek & Theorell, 1990). Theorell hypothesizes that such personality characteristics may result in part from a stressful work environment that "enforces a noncomplaining attitude and prevents development of active emotional coping" (Theorell, 1990). Thus, he observed an association between *underreporting* of stress and an *increased* physiologic response. Data among urban transport operators corroborates these premises: Operators with borderline or definite hypertension were distinguished from those with normal BP by having a low admitted fear during driving, while showing increased BP rise together with heightened selective attention during laboratory paradigms that mimicked stressful aspects of the traffic environment (Belkić et al., 1996; Emdad et al., 1997)

CVD. Job stressors may also increase the risk of CVD, in part by influencing personality characteristics or negative affect. Many emotions "are responses to power and status differentials embedded within social situations" (Kubzansky, Kawachi, Weiss, & Sparrow, 1998, p. 55). Positive associations have been found between anxiety and job stressors in a number of studies (Bourbonnais, Brisson, Moisan, & Vezina, 1996; Bourbonnais, Comeau, & Vezina, 1999; Stansfeld, North, White, & Marmot, 1995). Depression has also been associated prospectively with CVD (Anda et al., 1993; Aromaa et al., 1994), and linked with stressful job characteristics (Karasek, 1979; Lennon, 1987; Mausner-Dorsch & Eaton, 2000; Stansfeld et al., 1995).

Type A behavior has been described as a stable personality trait, however, Matthews and Haynes pointed out that

> this behavior pattern is thought to be encouraged by Western society because it appears to offer special rewards and opportunities to those who can think, perform, and even play more rapidly and aggressively than their peers. . . . it is seen as the outcome of a set of predispositions interacting with specific types of eliciting situations, including those that are stressful or challenging. (1986, p. 924)

However, the assumption that Type A is a stable personality characteristic contributed to researchers measuring it only once at baseline, resulting in significant misclassification and bias in many studies. Evidence exists that the hostility component of Type A is a risk factor for CHD (Smith, 1992), and some studies have found associations between hostility and job stressors (Bosma, Stansfeld, & Marmot, 1998; Landsbergis, Schnall, Deitz, Friedman, & Pickering, 1992). "Overcommitment" in the effort–reward imbalance model (reminiscent of the work overinvolvement component of Type A behavior) is considered to be "a personal characteristic which is rather stable over time" (Siegrist et al., 1990, p. 1128), however, it has been associated with job strain (Peter, 1997).

Finally, negative affectivity (NA) has been proposed as a confounder of the stress–illness association (McCrae, 1990). However, it has not been associated with MI (Costa & McCrae, 1985) or BP (Landsbergis et al., 1992), and, in the Whitehall study, controlling for NA barely affected the association between low job control and CHD (Bosma, Peter, et al., 1998). In short, contrary to widely held beliefs, there is currently little evidence supporting an etiologic role for psychological or personality factors in essential hypertension (Friedman et al., 2001) and limited evidence for a role in CVD.

Occupational Health Psychology in the Prevention and Management of Work-Related Hypertension and CVD

The occupational health psychologist can play a key role in preventing and managing work-related hypertension and CVD. As part of a public health strategy, we recommend a team approach in which occupational health psychologists work together with clinicians, health educators, ergonomists, epidemiologists, and other health professionals to identify high-risk workplaces and occupations, facilitate the provision of clinical care, and design and implement workplace interventions (as in Herbert et al., 1997).

Risk Assessment

The first step in this process is *worksite surveillance*. Experts in Japan, Europe, and the United States have called for a program of surveillance at individual workplaces and monitoring at national and regional levels to identify the extent of work-stress related health problems and to provide baselines against which to evaluate efforts at amelioration. They recommended that workplaces assess both workplace stressors and health outcomes known to result from such exposures ("The Tokyo Declaration," 1998). First, the surveillance team needs to ascertain whether the current occupation is high-risk; whether workers are exposed to any physical, chemical, work schedule, or psychosocial CVD risk factors at work; and if any of these been increasing over time (Belkić, Schnall, & Ugljesic, 2000). Questionnaires, such as the Job Content Questionnaire (Karasek et al., 1985), the Effort-Reward Imbalance Questionnaire (Siegrist & Peter, 1996), and the Occupational Stress Index (Belkić, Savic, Theorell, & Cizinsky, 1995) can help assess job characteristics and job stressors. Second, workplace screening should be conducted for biomedical CVD risk factors, including worksite point estimates of BP (Schnall & Belkić, 2000). Such surveillance can help to identify clusters of work-related hypertension and help target worksites for primary and secondary prevention programs.

Another modality of risk assessment is *an occupational history* of individual workers. The occupational health psychologist would have the expertise to identify those workplace exposures that may affect cardiovascular well-being and could prepare a succinct narrative to become part of the clinical record. We have developed hands-on tools that effectively trained graduate students to acquire this practical skill (Schnall, Belkić, Landsbergis, & Baker, 2001).

Preventing CVD and Improving the Cardiovascular Health of Working People

Both individual health promotion and workplace protection–prevention programs are needed to combat the epidemic of CVC. However, because of the limitation of health promotion programs, primary prevention strategies, namely job redesign, are fundamental. The occupational health psychologist can also play an important role in secondary and tertiary prevention by working together with clinicians.

Health promotion. One important role for the occupational health psychologist is counseling patients to reduce their levels of unhealthy behaviors, such as smoking. However, cardiac risk factor counseling in isolation may have poor efficacy, particularly among occupational groups with a heavy burden of exposure to occupational stressors. For example, Fisher and Belkić stated,

> Despite devotion of substantial time and the use of state-of-the-art methods . . . our efforts applied systematically among professional drivers were, at best, only minimally effective, unless there was a concomitant amelioration in stressful working conditions. (Fisher & Belkić, 2000)

Although stress management interventions may have positive effects, if employees return to an unchanged work environment and high levels of job stressors, those beneficial effects are likely to be eroded (Nowack, 2000).

Worksite health promotion. Few health promotion programs have "focused on the physical, psychosocial or policy work environment," including job strain. Many "programs have emphasized risk-factor reduction strategies . . . but have not integrated disease prevention and safety programs with organizational policies to enhance the physical and social quality of the workplace" (Stokols, Pelletier, & Fielding, 1995, p. 1137). Another limitation is the tendency for less participation by higher risk—for example, lower socioeconomic status employees (Lewis, Huebner, & Yarborough, 1996).

A number of researchers have recommended integrating workplace health promotion and occupational health, to develop complementary behavioral and environmental interventions (Dejoy & Southern, 1993; Heaney & Goetzel, 1997). One example of such a program is the WellWorks Project conducted in 24 worksites in Massachusetts. A "significant association was observed between participation in nutrition and [environmental] exposure-related activities, suggesting that participation in programs to reduce exposures to occupational hazards might contribute to blue-collar workers' participation in health promotion activities." In addition, "when workers were aware of change their employer had made to reduce exposures to occupational hazards, they were more likely to participate in both smoking control and nutrition activities" (Sorensen, Stoddard, Ockene, Hunt, & Youngstrom, 1996, p. 191). Barriers to participation, such as blue-collar workers' time constraints and job responsibilities, were addressed, for example, through negotiation of time-off for participation in health promotion activities (Sorensen et al., 1995).

Tertiary prevention: return to work after cardiac events. Cardiologists are called on to judge the cardiovascular work fitness of patients who have suffered cardiac events. Complicating the issue is that jobs in which public safety could be compromised with the occurrence of an acute cardiac event (deGaudemaris, 2000) are often those with high exposure to potentially cardio-deleterious factors (e.g., urban transit operators, air traffic controllers; Fisher & Belkić, 2000). On the other hand, advances in cardiovascular therapy permit the cardiovascular function of many patients to be restored to make returning to work *potentially* possible (deGaudemaris, 2000). In the study of Theorell et al. (Theorell et al., 1991), among men who had suffered a first MI below age 45, the predictive strength for five-year CHD mortality of returning to a high strain job was of similar magnitude to the degree of coronary atherosclerosis and more powerful than left ventricular ejection fraction. The expertise of the occupational health psychologist could be indispensable in helping clinicians to tackle this most delicate issue: "Should heart attack patients return to stressful jobs?" Namely, the occupational health psychologist could identify potentially modifiable cardionoxious stressors in the patient's work environment, and then together with the clinician formulate and implement a plan to provide a safer return to work after cardiac events.

Promoting Healthy Work: Job Redesign and Cardiovascular Health

The effectiveness of a limited number of interventions to improve work organization and job design, reduce job stressors, and create a more healthy work organization have been documented (International Labor Office, 1992;

Landsbergis et al., 1993; Murphy, Hurrell, Sauter, & Keita, 1995). For example, an intervention among Swedish civil servants included worker committees that developed and carried out action plans to reduce work stressors. A significant decrease in apolipoprotein B/AI ratio occurred in the intervention group, but not in the control group. Stimulation from and autonomy over work significantly increased in the intervention group but remained the same in the control group (Orth-Gomer, Eriksson, Moser, Theorell, & Fredlund, 1994). An intervention on an inner-city bus line in Stockholm was designed to diminish time pressure and promote traffic flow. There was a significant decline in systolic BP (−10.7 mm Hg) in the intervention group that was greater than in the comparison group (−4.3; Rydstedt, Johansson, & Evans, 1998). A Swedish field study also showed that systolic BP, heart rate, epinephrine, and self-reported tiredness increased significantly from the start to the end of a day shift at a traditional auto assembly line, but not at a more flexible work organization with small autonomous groups having greater opportunities to influence the pace and content of their work (Melin, Lundberg, Soderlund, & Granqvist, 1999).

There have been no published job redesign studies in the United States that have examined CVD outcomes per se. However, a number of job redesign programs in the United States have been conducted that have examined other stress-related health outcomes and that provide valuable guidance for current efforts. These programs have included efforts to reduce symptoms of "burnout" among employees of a state child protection agency through a labor–management committee and new technology (Cahill & Feldman, 1993), increase participation in decision making through labor–management committees at an automobile manufacturer (Israel, Schurman, & House, 1989), and reduce work-related musculoskeletal disorders through job redesign at a meat-packing plant (Smith & Zehel, 1992).

In addition to job redesign, legislative or regulatory approaches have been used. However, efforts to regulate (Warren, 2000) or collectively bargain (Landsbergis, 2000) over work organization and psychosocial stressors such as job strain have met with limited success in the United States. A promising development in this area is recent legislation in states such as California and New Jersey, which provide minimum staffing levels and limits on mandatory overtime for health care workers. Valuable models for the United States include legislation in Scandinavia, the European Union (Levi, 2000), and Japan (Shimomitsu & Odagiri, 2000) that regulate work organization and job stressors as health hazards.

Occupational health psychologists can also work with labor–management committees and other health professionals to develop and evaluate the impact of job redesign programs, help convince employers of the long-term benefits of such programs, involve employees in such programs, and help develop appropriate legislation and regulations. In short, the occupational health psychologist can potentially play a pivotal, multi-faceted role in helping to create and promote a "heart healthy" work environment.

References

Alfredsson, L., Spetz, C., & Theorell, T. (1985). Type of occupation and near-future hospitalization for myocardial infarction and some other diagnoses. *International Journal of Epidemiology, 14,* 378–388.

Anda, R., Williamson, D., Jones, D., Macera, C., Eaker, E., Glassman, A., & Marks, J. (1993). Depressed affect, hopelessness, and the risk of ischemic heart disease in a cohort of U.S. adults. *Epidemiology, 4*(4), 285–293.

Appels, A., & Otten, F. (1992). Exhaustion as precursor of cardiac death. *British Journal of Clinical Psychology, 31,* 351–356.

Aromaa, A., Raitasalo, R., Reunanen, A., Impivaara, O., Heliovaara, M., Knekt, P., Lehtinen, V., Joukamaa, M., & Maatela, J. (1994). Depression and cardiovascular disease. *Acta Psychiatrica Scandinavica* (Suppl. 377), 77–82.

Belkić, K. (2000a). Cardiac electrical stability and environmental stress. *Occupational Medicine: State of the Art Reviews, 15*(1), 117–120.

Belkić, K. (2000b). Myocardial oxygen supply and demand: Environmental triggers of imbalance. *Occupational Medicine: State of the Art Reviews, 15*(1), 132–136.

Belkić, K., Emdad, R., & Theorell, T. (1998). Occupational profile and cardiac risk: Possible mechanisms and implications for professional drivers. *International Journal of Occupational Medicine and Environmental Health, 11,* 37–57.

Belkić, K., Emdad, R., Theorell, T., Cizinsky, S., Wennberg, A., Hagman, M., Johnasson, L., Savic, C., & Olsson, K. (1996). *Neurocardiac mechanisms of heart disease risk among professional drivers.* Final report. Stockholm: Swedish Fund for Working Life.

Belkić, K., Landsbergis, P. A., Schnall, P., Baker, D., Theorell, T., Siegrist, J., Peter, R., & Karasek, R. (2000). Psychosocial factors: Review of the empirical data among men. *Occupational Medicine: State of the Art Reviews, 15*(1), 24–46.

Belkić, K., Savic, C., Theorell, T., & Cizinsky, S. (1995). *Work Stressors and Cardiovascular Risk: Assessment for Clinical Practice.* Part I (256). Stockholm: National Institute for Psychosocial Factors and Health. Section for Stress Research, Karolinska Institute, WHO Psychosocial Center.

Belkić, K., Schnall, P., Landsbergis, P., & Baker, D. (2000). The workplace and CV health: Conclusions and thoughts for a future agenda. *Occupational Medicine: State of the Art Reviews, 15*(1), 307–322.

Belkić, K. B., Schnall, P. L., Landsbergis, P. A., Schwartz, J. E., Gerber, L., Baker, D., & Pickering, T. G. (2001). Hypertension at the workplace—An occult disease? The need for work site surveillance. *Advances in Psychosomatic Medicine, 22,* 116–138.

Belkić, K., Schnall, P., Savic, C., & Landsbergis, P. A. (2000). Multiple exposures: Toward a model of total occupational burden. *Occupational Medicine: State-of-the-Art Reviews, 15*(1), 94–98.

Belkić, K., Schnall, P., & Ugljesic, M. (2000a). Cardiovascular evaluation of the worker and workplace: A practical guide for clinicians. *Occupational Medicine: State of the Art Reviews, 15*(1), 213–222.

Bond, J. T., Galinsky, E., & Swanberg, J. E. (1998). *The 1997 National Study of the Changing Workforce.* New York: Families and Work Institute.

Bosma, H., Peter, R., Siegrist, J., & Marmot, M. (1998). Two alternative job stress models and the risk of coronary heart disease. *American Journal of Public Health, 88,* 68–74.

Bosma, H., Stansfeld, S. A., & Marmot, M. G. (1998). Job control, personal characteristics, and heart disease. *Journal of Occupational Health Psychology, 3*(4), 402–409.

Bourbonnais, R., Brisson, C., Moisan, J., & Vezina, M. (1996). Job strain and psychological distress in white-collar workers. *Scandinavian Journal of Work, Environment and Health, 22,* 139–145.

Bourbonnais, R., Comeau, M., & Vezina, M. (1999). Job strain and evolution of mental health among nurses. *Journal of Occupational Health Psychology, 4,* 95–107.

Braunwald, E. (1997). Cardiovascular medicine at the turn of the millennium: Triumphs, concerns and opportunities. *New England Journal of Medicine, 337,* 1360–1369.

Brisson, C. (2000). Women, work and cardiovascular disease. *Occupational Medicine: State of the Art Reviews, 15*(1), 49–57.

Brisson, C., Laflamme, N., Moisan, J., Milot, A., Masse, B., & Vezina, M. (1999). Effect of family responsibilities and job strain on ambulatory blood pressure among white-collar women. *Psychosomatic Medicine, 61*(2), 205–213.

Brunner, E. J., Smith, G. D., Marmot, M. G., Canner, R., Beksinska, M., & O'Brien, J. (1996). Childhood social circumstances and psychosocial and behavioral factors as determinants of plasma fibrinogen. *Lancet, 347,* 1008–1013.

Cahill, J., & Feldman, L. H. (1993). Computers in child welfare: Planning for a more serviceable work environment. *Child Welfare, 72,* 3–12.

Carvalho, J. J. M., Baruzzi, R. G., Howard, P. F., Poulter, N., Alpers, M. P., Franco, L. J., Marcopito, L. F., Spooner, V. J., Dyer, A. R., Elliott, P., Stamler, J., & Stamler, R. (1989). Blood pressure in four remote populations in the INTERSALT study. *Hypertension, 14,* 238–246.

Cooper, C. (1996). Working hours and health. *Work & Stress, 10,* 1–4.

Cooper, R. S., Rotimi, C. N., & Ward, R. (1999, Feb.). The puzzle of hypertension in African-Americans. *Scientific American,* 56–63.

Costa, P. T., & McCrae, R. R. (1985). Hypochondriasis, neuroticism, and aging: When are somatic complaints unfounded? *American Psychologist, 40,* 19–28.

Cottington, E. M., Matthews, K. A., Talbott, E., & Kuller, L. H. (1986). Occupational stress, suppressed anger, and hypertension. *Psychosomatic Medicine, 48,* 249–260.

deGaudemaris, R. (2000). Clinical issues: Return to work and public safety. *Occupational Medicine: State of the Art Reviews, 15*(1), 223–230.

Dejoy, D. M., & Southern, D. J. (1993). An integrative perspective on work site health promotion. *Journal of Occupational Medicine, 35*(12), 1221–1230.

Eaker, E. D. (1992). Myocardial infarction and coronary death among women: Psychosocial predictors from a 20-year follow-up of women in the Framingham study. *American Journal of Epidemiology, 135*(8), 854–864.

Eaker, E. D., Packard, B., & Thom, T. H. (1989). Epidemiology and risk factors for coronary heart disease in women. In P. S. Douglas (Ed.), *Heart disease in women* (pp. 129–145). Philadelphia: FA Davis.

Emdad, R., Belkić, K., Theorell, T., Cizinsky, S., Savic, C., & Olsson, K. (1997). Work environment, neurophysiologic and psychophysiologic models among professional drivers with and without cardiovascular disease: Seeking an integrative neurocariologic approach. *Stress Medicine, 13,* 7–21.

European Foundation. (1997). *Time constraints and autonomy at work in the European Union.* Dublin: European Foundation for the Improvement of Living and Working Conditions.

Falger, P. R. J., & Schouten, E. G. W. (1992). Exhaustion, psychologic stress in the work environment and acute myocardial infarction in adult men. *Journal of Psychosomatic Research, 36,* 777–786.

Fisher, J., & Belkić, K. (2000). A public health approach in clinical practice. In P. Schnall, K. Belkić, P. A. Landsbergis, & D. Baker (Eds.), *The workplace and cardiovascular disease. Occupational medicine: State of the art reviews* (Vol. 15, pp. 245–256). Philadelphia: Hanley and Belfus.

Fossum, E., Hoieggen, A., Moan, A., Rostrup, M., & Kjeldsen, S. E. (2000). The cardiovascular metabolic syndrome. *Occupational Medicine: State of the Art Reviews, 15*(1), 146–150.

Frankenhaeuser, M. (1989). A biopsychosocial approach to work life issues. *International Journal of Health Services, 19*(4), 747–758.

Frankenhaeuser, M., & Johansson, G. (1986). Stress at work: Psychobiological and psychosocial aspects. *International Review of Applied Psychology, 35,* 287–299.

Fredriksson, M., Sundin, O., & Frankenhaeuser, M. (1985). Cortisol excretion during the defence reaction in humans. *Psychosomatic Medicine, 47,* 313–319.

Friedman, R., Landsbergis, P. A., Schnall, P. L., Pieper, C., Gerin, W., Pickering, T. G., & Schwartz, J. E. (2001). Psychological variables in hypertension: Relationship to casual or ambulatory blood pressure in men. *Psychosomatic Medicine, 63,* 19–31.

Georges, E., Wear, M. L., & Mueller, W. H. (1992). Body fat distribution and job stress in Mexican-American men of the Hispanic Health and Nutrition Examination Survey. *American Journal of Human Biology, 4,* 657–667.

Gertler, M. M., & White, P. D. (1976). *Coagulation factors and coronary heart disease: a 25-year study in retrospect.* Oradell, NJ: Medical Economics.

Gonzalez, M. A., Artalejo, F. R., & Calero, J. R. (1998). Relationship between socioeconomic status and ischaemic heart disease in cohort and case-control studies: 1960–1993. *International Journal of Epidemiology, 27*(3), 350–358.

Green, K. L., & Johnson, J. V. (1990). The effects of psychosocial work organization on patterns of cigarette smoking among male chemical plant employees. *American Journal of Public Health, 80,* 1368–1371.

Haft, J. J. (1974). Cardiovascular injury induced by sympathetic catecholamines. *Progress in Cardiovascular Disease, 17,* 73–86.

Hall, E. M. (1992). Double exposure: The combined impact of the home and work environments on psychosomatic strain in Swedish women and men. *International Journal of Health Services, 22*(2), 239–260.

Hallqvist, J., Diderichsen, F., Theorell, T., Reuterwall, C., Ahlbom, A., & the SHEEP Study Group. (1998). Is the effect of job strain on myocardial infarction due to interaction between high psychological demands and low decision latitude? Results from Stockholm Heart Epidemiology Program (SHEEP). *Social Science and Medicine, 46*(11), 1405–1415.

Hallqvist, J., Lundberg, M., Diderichsen, F., & Ahlbom, A. (1998). Socioeconomic differences in risk of myocardial infarction 1971–1994 in Sweden: Time trends, relative risks and population attributable risks. *International Journal of Epidemiology, 27,* 410–415.

Haynes, S. G., & Feinleib, M. (1980). Women, work and coronary heart disease: Prospective findings from the Framingham Heart Study. *American Journal of Public Health, 70*(2), 133–141.

Heaney, C. A., & Goetzel, R. Z. (1997). A review of health-related outcomes of multi-component worksite health promotion programs. *American Journal of Health Promotion, 11,* 290–308.

Hellerstedt, W. L., & Jeffery, R. W. (1997). The association of job strain and health behaviors in men and women. *International Journal of Epidemiology, 26*(3), 575–583.

Henry, J. P. (1992). Biological basis of the stress response. *Integrative Physiological and Behavioral Science, 27,* 66–83.

Herbert, R., Plattus, B., Kellogg, L., Luo, J., Marcus, M., Mascolo, A., & Landrigan, P. J. (1997). The union health center: A working model of clinical care linked to preventive occupational health services. *American Journal of Industrial Medicine, 31,* 263–273.

International Labour Office. (1992). *Conditions of Work Digest: Preventing Stress at Work.* Geneva: International Labour Office.

International Labour Office. (1999). *Key Indicators of the Labour Market 1999.* Geneva: International Labour Office.

Israel, B. A., Schurman, S. J., & House, J. S. (1989). Action research on occupational stress: Involving workers as researchers. *International Journal of Health Services, 19,* 135–155.

Johansson, G., Johnson, J. V., & Hall, E. M. (1991). Smoking and sedentary behavior as related to work organization. *Social Science and Medicine, 32,* 837–846.

Johnson, J. V., & Hall, E. M. (1988). Job strain, workplace social support, and cardiovascular disease: A cross-sectional study of a random sample of the Swedish working population. *American Journal of Public Health, 78*(10), 1336–1342.

Jonas, B. S., Franks, P., & Ingram, D. D. (1997). Are symptoms of anxiety and depression risk factors for hypertension? Longitudinal evidence from the National Health and Nutrition Examination Survey I Epidemiologic Follow-Up Study. *Archives of Family Medicine, 6,* 43–51.

Kannel, W. B. (1992). The Framingham experience. In M. Marmot & P. Elliott (Eds.), *Coronary heart disease epidemiology* (pp. 67–82). Oxford: Oxford University Press.

Kaplan, G. A., & Keil, J. E. (1993). Socioeconomic factors and cardiovascular disease: A review of the literature. *Circulation, 88*(4 Pt. 1), 1973–1998.

Karasek, R. A. (1979). Job demands, job decision latitude and mental strain: Implications for job redesign. *Administrative Science Quarterly, 24,* 285–308.

Karasek, R. A., Gordon, G., Pietroskovsky, C., Frese, M., Pieper, C., Schwartz, J., Fry, L., & Schirer, D. (1985). *Job content instrument: Questionnaire and user's guide.* Los Angeles/ Lowell, MA: University of Southern California/University of Massachusetts, Lowell.

Karasek, R., & Theorell, T. (1990). *Healthy work: Stress, productivity, and the reconstruction of working life.* New York: Basic Books.

Kawachi, I., & Marmot, M. (1998). What can we learn from studies of occupational class and cardiovascular disease? *American Journal of Epidemiology, 148,* 160–163.

Kawakami, N., Haratani, T., & Araki, S. (1998). Job strain and arterial blood pressure, serum cholesterol, and smoking as risk factors for coronary heart disease in Japan. *International Archives of Occupational and Environmental Health, 71*(6), 429–432.

Knox, S., Svensson, J., Waller, D., & Theorell, T. (1988). Emotional coping and the psychophysiological substrates of elevated blood pressure. *Behavioral Medicine, 2,* 52–58.

Kohn, M. L., & Schooler, C. (1982). Job conditions and personality: A longitudinal assessment of their reciprocal effects. *American Journal of Sociology, 87,* 1257–1286.

Kristensen, T. S., Kronitzer, M., & Alfedsson, L. (1998). *Social factors, work, stress and cardiovascular disease prevention.* Brussels: European Heart Network.

Kubzansky, L. D., Kawachi, I., Weiss, S., & Sparrow, D. (1998). Anxiety and coronary heart disease: A synthesis of epdemiological, psychological, and experimental evidence. *Annals of Behavioral Medicine, 20*(2), 47–58.

LaCroix, A. Z. (1984). *High demands/low control work and the incidence of CHD in the Framingham cohort.* Unpublished doctoral dissertation, University of North Carolina, Chapel Hill.

Landsbergis, P. (2000). Collective bargaining to reduce CVD risk factors in the work environment. *Occupational Medicine: State-of-the-Art Reviews, 15*(1), 287–292.

Landsbergis, P. A., Cahill, J., & Schnall, P. (1999). The impact of lean production and related new systems of work organization on worker health. *Journal of Occupational Health Psychology, 4*(2), 108–130.

Landsbergis, P. A., Schnall, P. L., Deitz, D., Friedman, R., & Pickering, T. (1992). The patterning of psychological attributes and distress by "job strain" and social support in a sample of working men. *Journal of Behavioral Medicine, 15*(4), 379–405.

Landsbergis, P. A., Schnall, P. L., Deitz, D. K., Warren, K., Pickering, T. G., & Schwartz, J. E. (1998). Job strain and health behaviors: Results of a prospective study. *American Journal of Health Promotion, 12*(4), 237–245.

Landsbergis, P. A., Schnall, P. L., Warren, K., Pickering, T. G., & Schwartz, J. E. (1994). Association between ambulatory blood pressure and alternative formulations of job strain. *Scandinavian Journal of Work, Environment and Health, 20*(5), 349–363.

Landsbergis, P. A., Schnall, P. L., Warren, K., Pickering, T. G., & Schwartz, J. E. (1999). The effect of job strain on ambulatory blood pressure in men: Does it vary by socioeconomic status? In N. E. Adler, M. Marmot, B. S. McEwen, J. Stewart (Eds.), *Socioeconomic status and health in industrial nations* (pp. 414–416). New York: Academy of Sciences.

Landsbergis, P. A., Schurman, S. J., Israel, B. A., Schnall, P. L., Hugentobler, M. K., Cahill, J., & Baker, D. (1993, Summer). Job stress and heart disease: Evidence and strategies for prevention. *New Solutions,* 42–58.

Langosch, W., Brodner, B., & Borcherding, M. (1983). Psychosocial and vocational longterm outcomes of cardiac rehabilitation with postinfarction patients under the age of forty. *Psychosomatic Medicine, 40,* 115–128.

Lennon, M. C. (1987). Sex differences in distress: The impact of gender and work roles. *Journal of Health and Social Behavior, 28,* 290–305.

Levi, L. (2000). Legislation to protect worker CV health in Europe. *Occupational Medicine: State-of-the-Art Reviews, 15*(1), 269–273.

Lewis, R. J., Huebner, W. H., & Yarborough, C. M. (1996). Characteristics of participants and nonparticipants in worksite health promotion. *American Journal of Health Promotion, 11,* 99–106.

Liao, Y., & Cooper, R. S. (1995). Continued adverse trends in coronary heart disease mortality among blacks, 1980–91. *Public Health Reports, 110,* 572–579.

Lynch, J., Krause, N., Kaplan, G. A., Salonen, R., & Salonen, J. T. (1997). Workplace demands, economic reward and progression of carotid atherosclerosis. *Circulation, 96*(1), 302–307.

Lynch, J., Krause, N., Kaplan, G. A., Tuomilehto, J., & Salonen, J. T. (1997). Work place conditions, socioeconomic status, and the risk of mortality and acute myocardial infarction: The Kuopio Ischemic Heart Disease Risk Factor Study. *American Journal of Public Health, 87,* 617–622.

Markovitz, J., Matthews, K. A., Kannel, W. B., Cobb, J. L., & D'Agostino, J. B. (1993). Psychological predictors of hypertension in the Framingham Study: Is there tension in hypertension? *Journal of the American Medical Association, 270*(20), 2439–2443.

Markowe, H. L., Marmot, M. G., Shipley, M. J., Bulpitt, C. H., Meade, T. W., Stirling, Y., Vickers, M. V., & Semmence, A. (1985). Fibrinogen: A possible link between social class and coronary heart disease. *British Medical Journal, 291,* 1312–1314.

Marmot, M. G., Bosma, H., Hemingway, H., Brunner, E., & Stansfeld, S. (1997). Contribution of job control and other risk factors to social variations in coronary heart disease incidence. *Lancet, 350,* 235–239.

Marmot, M., & Theorell, T. (1991). Social class and cardiovascular disease: The contribution of work. In J. V. Johnson & G. Johansson (Eds.), *The psychosocial work environment: Work organization, democratization and health* (pp. 33–48). Amityville, NY: Baywood.

Matthews, K. A., & Haynes, S. G. (1986). Type A behavior pattern and coronary disease risk: Update and critical evaluation. *American Journal of Epidemiology, 123*(6), 923–960.

Mausner-Dorsch, H., & Eaton, W. (2000). Psychosocial work environment and depression: Epidemiologic assessment of the demand-control model. *American Journal of Public Health, 90,* 1765–1770.

McCrae, R. R. (1990). Controlling neuroticism in the measurement of stress. *Stress Medicine, 6,* 237–241.

McKinlay, J. B., & Marceau, L. D. (1999). A tale of three tails. *American Journal of Public Health, 89,* 295–298.

Melin, B., Lundberg, U., Soderlund, J., & Granqvist, M. (1999). Psychophysiological stress reactions of male and female assembly workers: A comparison between two different forms of work organization. *Journal of Organizational Behavior, 20,* 47–61.

Menotti, A., & Seccareccia, F. (1985). Physical activity at work and job responsibility as risk factors for fatal coronary heart disease and other causes of death. *Journal of Epidemiology and Community Health, 39,* 325–329.

Murphy, L. R. (1991). Job dimensions associated with severe disability due to cardiovascular disease. *Journal of Clinical Epidemiology, 44*(2), 155–166.

Murphy, L., Hurrell, J., Sauter, S., & Keita, G. E. (1995). *Job stress interventions.* Washington, DC: American Psychological Association.

Netterstrom, B., Kristensen, T. S., Damsgaard, M. T., Olsen, O., & Sjol, A. (1991). Job strain and cardiovascular risk factors: A cross-sectional study of employed Danish men and women. *British Journal of Industrial Medicine, 48*(10), 684–689.

Nowack, K. (2000). Screening and management of the workplace in relation to cardiovascular disease risk. *Occupational Medicine: State-of-the-Art Reviews, 15*(1), 231–233.

Orth-Gomer, K., Eriksson, I., Moser, V., Theorell, T., & Fredlund, P. (1994). Lipid lowering through work stress reduction. *International Journal of Behavioral Medicine, 1*(3), 204–214.

Orth-Gomer, K., Wamala, S. P., Horsten, M., Schenck-Gustafsson, K., Schneiderman, N., & Mittleman, M. A. (2000). Marital stress worsens prognosis in women with coronary heart disease. *Journal of the American Medical Association, 284*(23), 3008–3014.

Perini, C., Muller, F. B., Rauchfleisch, U., Battegay, R., Hobi, V., & Buhler, F. R. (1990). Psychosomatic factors in borderline hypertensive subjects and offspring of hypertensive parents. *Hypertension, 16,* 627–634.

Peter, R. (1997). Comparative analysis of the effort-reward imbalance model and the job strain model: Preliminary results from a Swedish case-control study. In *Socio-economic variations in cardiovascular disease in Europe: The impact of the work environment and lifestyle* (The Heart at Work Network; pp. 102–104). London: University College London, Department of Epidemiology and Public Health.

Peter, R., Alfredsson, L., Hammar, N., Siegrist, J., Theorell, T., & Westerholm, P. (1998). High effort, low reward and cardiovascular risk factors in employed Swedish men and women: baseline results from the WOLF study. *Journal of Epidemiology and Community Health, 52,* 540–547.

Peter, R., Hallqvist, J., Reuterwall, C., Siegrist, J., Theorell, T., & the SHEEP Study Group. (1999). Psychosocial work environment and myocardial infarction: improving risk prediction by combining two complementary job stress models. (Submitted).

Peter, R., & Siegrist, J. (1997). Chronic work stress, sickness absence, and hypertension in middle managers: General or specific sociological explanations? *Social Science & Medicine, 45,* 1111–1120.

Pickering, T. G. (1991). *Ambulatory monitoring and blood pressure variability.* London: Science Press.

Rosamond, W. D., Chanbless, L. E., Folsom, A. R., Cooper, L. S., Conwill, D. E., Clegg, L., Wang, C.-H., & Heiss, G. (1998). Trends in the incidence of myocardial infarction and in mortality due to coronary heart disease, 1987 to 1994 [abstract]. *The New England Journal of Medicine, 339,* 863.

Rozanski, A., Blumenthal, J. A., & Kaplan, J. (1999). Impact of psychological factors on the pathogenesis of cardiovascular disease and implications for therapy. *Circulation, 99,* 2192–2217.

Rydstedt, L. W., Johansson, G., & Evans, G. W. (1998). The human side of the road: Improving the working conditions of urban bus drivers. *Journal of Occupational Health Psychology, 3,* 161–171.

Schnall, P., & Belkić, K. (2000). Point estimates of blood pressure at the worksite. *Occupational Medicine: State-of-the-Art Reviews, 15*(1), 203–208.

Schnall, P., Belkić, K., Landsbergis, P., & Baker, D. (2001). *Occupational health psychology: Work organization and health.* http://www.workhealth.org/UCLA%20OHP%20class/UCLA%20OHP%20home%20page.html

Schnall, P., Belkić, K., Landsbergis, P. A., & Baker, D. e. (2000a). The workplace and cardiovascular disease. *Occupational Medicine: State-of-the-Art Reviews, 15*(1).

Schnall, P., Belkić, K., Landsbergis, P. A., & Baker, D. (2000b). Why the workplace and cardiovascular disease? *Occupational Medicine: State-of-the-Art Reviews, 15*(1), 1–5.

Schnall, P. L., & Kern, R. (1981). Hypertension in American society: An introduction to historical materialist epidemiology. In P. Conrad & R. Kern (Eds.), *The sociology of health and illness: Critical perspectives* (pp. 97–122). New York: St. Martin's Press.

Schnall, P. L., Landsbergis, P. A., & Baker, D. (1994). Job strain and cardiovascular disease. *Annual Review of Public Health, 15,* 381–411.

Schnall, P. L., Landsbergis, P. A., Schwartz, J., Warren, K., & Pickering, T. G. (1998). A longitudinal study of job strain and ambulatory blood pressure: Results from a three-year follow-up. *Psychosomatic Medicine, 60,* 697–706.

Schnall, P. L., Pieper, C., Schwartz, J. E., Karasek, R. A., Schlussel, Y., Devereux, R. B., Ganau, A., Alderman, M., Warren, K., & Pickering, T. G. (1990). The relationship between "job strain," workplace diastolic blood pressure, and left ventricular mass index. Results of a case-control study [published erratum appears in JAMA 1992 Mar 4 267(9):1209]. *Journal of the American Medical Association, 263*(14), 1929–1935.

Schnall, P. L., Schwartz, J. E., Landsbergis, P. A., Warren, K., & Pickering, T. G. (1992). Relation between job strain, alcohol, and ambulatory blood pressure. *Hypertension, 19,* 488–494.

Schwartz, J., Belkić, K., Schnall, P., & Pickering, T. (2000). Mechanisms leading to hypertension and CV morbidity. *Occupational Medicine: State of the Art Reviews, 15*(1), 121–132.

Shapiro, A. P. (1988). Psychological factors in hypertension: An overview. *American Heart Journal, 116,* 632–637.

Shimomitsu, T., & Odagiri, Y. (2000). Working life in Japan. *Occupational Medicine: State of the Art Reviews, 15*(1), 280–281.

Siegrist, J. (1996). Adverse health effects of high-effort/low-reward conditions. *Journal of Occupational Health Psychology, 1,* 27–41.

Siegrist, J., Matschinger, H., Cremer, P., & Seidel, D. (1988). Atherogenic risk in men suffering from occupational stress. *Atherosclerosis, 69,* 211–218.

Siegrist, J., & Peter, R. (1996). *Measuring effort-reward imbalance at work: Guidelines.* Dusseldorf: University of Dusseldorf.

Siegrist, J., Peter, R., Georg, W., Cremer, P., & Seidel, D. (1991). Psychosocial and biobehavioral characteristics of hypertensive men with elevated atherogenic lipids. *Atherosclerosis, 86,* 211–218.

Siegrist, J., Peter, R., Junge, A., Cremer, P., & Seidel, D. (1990). Low status control, high effort at work and ischaemic heart disease: Prospective evidence from blue collar men. *Social Science and Medicine, 31,* 1127–1134.

Smith, M., & Zehel, D. (1992). A stress reduction intervention programme for meat processors emphasizing job design and work organization. *Conditions of Work Digest, 11*(2), 204–213.

Smith, T. W. (1992). Hostility and health: Current status of a psychosomatic hypothesis. *Health Psychology, 11,* 139–150.

Sokejima, S., & Kagamimori, S. (1998). Working hours as a risk factor for acute myocardial infarction in Japan: Case-control study. *British Medical Journal, 317,* 775–780.

Sorensen, G., Himmelstein, J. S., Hunt, M. K., Youngstrom, R., Hebert, J. R., Hammond, S. K., Palombo, R., Stoddard, A., & Ockene, J. K. (1995). A model for worksite cancer prevention: integration of health protection and health promotion in the WellWorks Project. *American Journal of Health Promotion, 10*(1), 55–62.

Sorensen, G., Stoddard, A., Ockene, J. K., Hunt, M. K., & Youngstrom, R. (1996). Worker participation in an integrated health promotion/health protection program: Results from the WellWorks Project. *Health Education Quarterly, 23,* 191–203.

Sparrow, D., Garvey, A. J., Rosner, B., & Thomas, H. E. (1982). Factors in predicting blood pressure change. *Circulation, 65,* 789–794.

Stamler, J. (1991). Blood pressure and high blood pressure: Aspects of risk. *Hypertension, 18*(Suppl. 1), 95–107.

Stansfeld, S. A., North, F. M., White, I., & Marmot, M. G. (1995). Work characteristics and psychiatric disorder in civil servants in London. *Journal of Epidemiology and Community Health, 49,* 48–53.

Steenland, K. (2000). Shift work, long hours, and CVD: A review. *Occupational Medicine: State-of-the-Art Reviews, 15*(1), 7–17.

Steptoe, A. (1981). *Psychological factors in cardiovascular disorders.* London: Academic Press.

Steptoe, A., & Marmot, M. (2000). Atherogenesis, coagulation and stress mechanisms. *Occupational Medicine: State of the Art Reviews, 15*(1), 136–138.

Stokols, D., Pelletier, K. R., & Fielding, J. E. (1995). Integration of medical care and worksite health promotion. *Journal of the American Medical Association, 273*(14), 1136–1142.

Theorell, T. (1990). Family history of hypertension—An individual trait interacting with spontaneously occurring job stressors. *Scandinavian Journal of Work, Environment and Health, 16*(Suppl. 1), 74–79.

Theorell, T. (2000). Neuroendocrine mechanisms. *Occupational Medicine: State of the Art Reviews, 15*(1), 139–146.

Theorell, T., Perski, A., Akerstedt, T., Sigala, F., Ahlberg-Hulten, G., Svensson, J., & Eneroth, P. (1988). Changes in job strain in relation to changes in physiological states—A longitudinal study. *Scandinavian Journal of Work, Environment and Health, 14,* 189–196.

Theorell, T., Perski, A., Orth-Gomer, K., Hamsten, A., & de Faire, U. (1991). The effects of the strain of returning to work on the risk of cardiac death after a first myocardial infarction before age 45. *International Journal of Cardiology, 30,* 61–67.

Theorell, T., Tsutsumi, A., Hallqvist, J., Reuterwall, C., Hogstedt, C., Fredlund, P., Emlund, N., Johnson, J., & the SHEEP Study Group. (1998). Decision latitude, job strain and myocardical infarction: A study of working men in Stockholm. *American Journal of Public Health, 88,* 382–388.

The Tokyo Declaration. (1998). *Journal of the Tokyo Medical University, 56*(6), 760–767.

Tuchsen, F. (1993). Working hours and ischaemic heart disease in Danish men: A 4-year cohort study of hospitalization. *International Journal of Epidemiology, 22,* 215–221.

Tuchsen, F., & Endahl, L. A. (1999). Increasing inequality in ischaemic heart disease morbidity among employed men in Denmark 1981–1993: The need for a new preventive policy. *International Journal of Epidemiology, 28,* 640–644.

U.S. Departments of Labor and Commerce. (1994). *Fact Finding Report. Commission on the Future of Worker-Management Relations.* Washington, DC: Author.

Verdecchia, P., Clement, D., Fagard, R., Palatini, P., & Parati, G. (1999). Task force III: Target-organ damage, morbidity and mortality. *Blood Pressure Monitoring, 4,* 303–317.

Waldron, I., Nowatarski, M., Freimer, M., Henry, J. P., Post, N., & Witten, C. (1982). Cross-cultural variation in blood pressure: A qualitative analysis of the relationship of blood pressure to cultural characteristics, salt consumption and body weight. *Social Science and Medicine, 16,* 419–430.

Warren, N. (2000). U.S. regulations for work organization. *Occupational Medicine: State-of-the-Art Reviews, 15*(1), 275–280.

Whelton, P. K., He, J., & Klag, M. J. (1994). *Blood pressure in Westernized populations.* In J. D. Swales (Ed.), *Textbook of hypertension* (pp. 11–21). London: Blackwell Scientific.

Willich, S. N., Maclure, M., Mittleman, M., Arntz, H. R., & Muller, J. E. (1993). Sudden cardiac death support for a role of triggering in causation. *Circulation, 87,* 1442–1450.

Wilson, P. W. F., D'Aostino, R. B., Levy, D., Castelli, W. P., Belanger, A. J., Sytkowski, P. A., & Kannel, W. B. (1991, Nov. 11–14). *Trends in coronary heart disease: A comparison of the original (1956–1968) and offspring Framingham study cohorts.* Paper presented at the American Heart Association, Anaheim, CA.

Wing, S., Casper, M., Riggan, W., Hayes, C. G., & Tyroler, H. A. (1988). Socioenvironmental characteristics associated with the onset of decline of IHD mortality in US. *American Journal of Public Health, 78,* 923–926.

Wolf, S. (2000). The environment-brain-heart connection. *Occupational Medicine: State of the Art Reviews, 15*(1), 107–109.

Wolff, E. (1995). *Top heavy: A study of wealth inequality in America.* New York: Twentieth Century Fund Press.

14

Employee Assistance Programs

Cary L. Cooper, Philip Dewe, and
Michael O'Driscoll

There is some concern about a potential backlash in the United States against the impact of globalization in terms of a shift in employment practices. The argument has been made that globalization is leading to higher mobility between employers, to more intrinsic job insecurity, to a short-term contract culture of employment and ultimately to substantial employee stress. From our perspective, the U.S. workplace has always had substantial elements of all of these characteristics, with the process of globalization only marginally moving it faster and further along the continuum toward a completely "contingent" workforce. The issue for the leaders of the business community in the rest of the world is whether they should also be traveling in this direction. The developed world has moved toward Americanization of work, as more and more companies are outsourcing, delayering, using "interim management" and the like, with many more employees in effect selling their services to organizations on a freelance or short-term basis.

This has led to what employers now refer to euphemistically as "the flexible workforce," although in family-friendly terms it is anything but flexible. The psychological contract between employer and employee in terms of reasonably permanent employment for work well done is truly being undermined, as more and more employees no longer regard their employment as secure and many more engage in short-term contract or part-time working. Indeed, in an International Survey Research survey of 400 companies in 17 countries, employing more than 8 million workers throughout Europe, the "employment security" of workers significantly declined between the mid- to late 1980s to the late 1990s: the United Kingdom from 48 to 70%, Germany from 55 to 83%, France from 50 to 64%, the Netherlands from 61 to 73%, Belgium from 54 to 60% and Italy from 57 to 62%. In addition, in the United Kingdom, for example, from the early 1980s to the end of the 1990s, the number of individuals working part-time has doubled, with the number of people employed in firms of more than 500 employees having slumped to about a third of the employed population and with nearly 1 in 10 workers now self-employed. The future of work seems to be in small- to medium-sized businesses or self-employed portfolio careers or outsourced workers in virtual organizations. Cooper and Jackson have predicted,

> Most organizations will have only a small core of full time permanent employees, working from a conventional office. They will buy most of the skills they need on a contract basis, either from individuals working at home and linked to the company by computers and modems, or by hiring people on short terms contracts to do specific jobs or carry out specific projects. In this way, companies will be able to maintain the flexibility they need to cope with a rapidly changing world. (1997, p. 2)

These changes and those that are anticipated in the future are leading to increases in workplace stress. The big-picture issue is how we deal with or manage stress at work. There are a number of options to consider in looking at the management and prevention of stress, which can be termed as primary, secondary, and tertiary levels of intervention.

Levels of Intervention

Primary prevention is concerned with taking action to reduce or eliminate stressors (i.e., sources of stress) and to promote positively a supportive and healthy work environment. As the type of action required by an organization will vary according to the kinds of stressors operating, any intervention needs to be guided by some earlier diagnosis or stress audit to identify what these stressors are and whom they are affecting. Stress audits typically take the form of a self-report questionnaire administered to employees on an organization-wide, site, or departmental basis. A widely validated example of such a diagnostic instrument is the Occupational Stress Indicator (OSI; Cooper, Sloan, & Williams, 1988).

Secondary prevention is concerned with the prompt detection and management of mental concerns such as depression and anxiety by increasing individual and collective awareness of stress and improving stress management skills. Initiatives that fall into this category are generally focused on training and education, and involve awareness-raising activities and skills training programs. Stress education and stress management courses can, for example, serve a useful function in helping individuals to recognize the symptoms of stress in themselves and others, and to extend or develop their coping skills and stress resilience

Tertiary prevention is concerned with the rehabilitation and recovery process of those individuals who have suffered, or are suffering from, mental or physical ill health as a result of stress (Cooper & Cartwright, 1986). One of the main approaches that organizations can consider to assist in the recovery and rehabilitation of stressed employees is workplace counseling. An example of workplace-based professional counseling is the employee assistance program (EAP). Workplace counseling and EAPs are the most common form of stress management, because they can be introduced quickly and provide a resource for dealing immediately with employee distress.

Defining and Describing an EAP

In their book *Employee Assistance and Workplace Counseling,* Berridge, Cooper, and Highley defined an EAP as a systematic, organized and continuing provision of counseling, advice and assistance, provided or funded by the employer, designed to help employees and (in most cases) their families with problems arising from work-related and external sources (1997).

The authors go on to say that there are many definitions of EAPs, reflecting the wide range of participants in such programs, the varying interest groups as providers or purchasers, and the differing views of professional commentators. The UK Employee Assistance Professionals Association (EAPA) defines an EAP as

> A mechanism for making counseling and other forms of assistance available to a designated workforce on a systematic and uniform basis, and to recognise standards. (EAPA, 1994)

This definition highlights certain requisite characteristics of any EAP—its clear extent of coverage of all or selected employees and their dependants, its systematic provision of counseling as a right rather than by privilege or patronage, and its adherence to levels of service quality on an independent verified basis. It also emphasizes the drive for professionalism, necessary to confer occupational status and social recognition of an expert personal service in a confidential and fiduciary relationship.

A definition that brings out the EAP provider's viewpoint is

> A confidential and professional service provided as an employee benefit which complements and extends in-company resources in the constructive and supportive management of people impacted by concerns in their personal and work lives. (Megranahan, 1995)

The focus is on the EAPs' compatibility and integration with corporate goals and culture and with managerial practices in the motivation and development of staff members. The provider contractor accepts working within the framework of the organization's structures and processes, while retaining professional standards of service.

This definition tends to mirror U.S. practice from which it draws its essence. This is succinctly expressed in a recent formulation:

> a program that provides direct service to an organization's workers who are experiencing many different types of problems in their personal or work lives. (Cunningham, 1994, p. 5).

A more recent comprehensive definition was developed by Berridge and Cooper:

> a programmatic intervention associated with the work context, usually at the level of the individual employee, using behavioural science knowledge and methods for the control of certain work-related problems (nota-

> bly alcoholism, drug abuse and mental health) that adversely affect job
> performance, with the objective of enabling the individual to return to
> making her or his full job contribution and re-attaining fully functioning
> in personal life. (1993, p. 89)

Such as definition attempts to reconcile the two potentially conflicting
foci of attention of an EAP: the client and the employing organization.

In Britain and Europe more widely, EAPs tend to have two primary objectives:

- To help the employees of organizations distracted by a range of
  personal concerns, including (but not limited to) emotional, stress,
  relationship, family, alcohol, drug, financial, legal, and other problems to cope with such concerns and learn themselves to control
  the stresses produced (EAPA, 1994).
- To assist the organization also in the identification and amelioration
  of productivity issues in employees whose job performance is adversely affected by such personal concerns (EAPA, 1994).

The intended beneficiaries of the EAP hence are both the individuals
(the primary focus in European practice) and her or his employing organization (less directly in Europe, but more emphasized in U.S. practice). At
the personal level, the objective of employee counseling is not personal
restructuring (i.e., psychotherapy), but the effect on individual coping and
adjustment to work and nonwork life can be considerable. At corporate
levels, equally, the outcomes are intended as a corporate consultancy intervention, but being

> more or less deeply embedded into the organizational processes of the
> firm, it becomes part of organizational discourse, it reflects and nour-
> ishes the organizational culture, and it becomes part of the organiza-
> tional learning, problem-solving and adaptation mechanisms. (Berridge
> & Cooper, 1994, p. 5)

The variability of objectives for EAPs can result in many differing
modes of program delivery. The modus operandi of external contractor–
providers is often the main factor, because standardization of the mode of
delivery is a key to their provision of a high-quality service with economical
use of internal production factors. The choice of contractor–provider may
be central in determining whether the employer–organizational adopts an
EAP with a suitable delivery method. The main dimensions of delivery
methods are shown in Figure 14.1.

In the United States, in-house, on-site provision is still widely found,
especially among large employers and in government service. In Britain and
Europe, the later developments of EAPs in a different and more stringent
economic climate has predisposed delivery methods to be by external contractor–providers, who use a network of counselors to provide services for
a variety of large and smaller employer clients alike.

	In-house provision of EAP and Counseling services	External contractor provision of EAP and counseling services
On-site EAP and counseling services	1. Often relatively direct control by Occupational Health (OH) or Human Resources Management (HRM) departments.	2. Unusual, but may be found where many functions/services are subcontracted, or have been "floated off" from former in-house services.
Externally located EAP and counseling services	3. Unusual but may occur for reasons of confidentiality, using an adjacent location, or as part of a "mixed model" provision, as a partnership with a contractor.	4. Customary delivery model in Britain, using provider company's offices, or affiliate counselors' consulting rooms or home premises

Figure 14.1. Delivery methods for EAP and counseling services.

Source: Berridge, Cooper, & Highley (1997).

The essential components of an EAP should reflect the provider's and the employer's preferred practice model, the resources available to the organization, the needs of its employees, and the size and the configuration of the organization (Davis & Gibson, 1994; Lee & Gray, 1994). Berridge et al. provided the following list that covers many of the essential elements that distinguish the EAP by its integrated approach and its systematic design, meshing with the administrative and social systems of the organization and its environment:

1. A systematic survey of the organization to determine the nature, causes, and extent of problems perceived by individuals, taking into account the viewpoints of all the stakeholders and functional specialists in the organization.
2. A continuing commitment on the part of the employing organization at the top level to provide counseling, advisory and assistance services to troubled employees on a no-blame and no-cost confidential basis.
3. An effective program of promotion and publicity of the EAP to all employees as potential clients, emphasizing in particular its confidentiality, access, and scope in issues covered.
4. A linked program of education and training on the goals and methods of the EAP for all staff members, focusing on the definition of "troubled" employee; the individual's responsibility for well-being; the roles of managers, supervisors, and shop stewards within the design and implementation of the EAP; and the duties and capabilities of counselors, including any limitations on their activities.
5. A procedure for contact with the EAP and referral to counseling, details of procedures for self-referral, and (if appropriate) manage-

rial referral. In cases of managerial referral, employee consent for referral needs to be obtained.

6. A definition of problem assessment procedures, including diagnosis routes, confidentiality guarantees, timeliness, scope of counselors' training, and their accreditation, competencies, and organizational knowledge.
7. A protocol outlining the extent of short-term counseling and longer term treatment and assistance.
8. A statement of the macro and micro linkages with other services in the community or with specialist resources or support mechanisms.
9. A procedure for the follow-up and monitoring of employees subsequent to their use of the EAP service, with the necessary provisions for their appropriate use and deployment.
10. An administrative channel for the feedback of aggregated statistics on the age and short and longer term outcomes of the EAP, generated by the provider.
11. An evaluation procedure of individual and corporate benefits of the EAP, on the most impartial basis that is practical (EAPA, 1994, 1997).

These are the key activities that make EAPs as an entity distinct from other forms of workplace counseling services, whether internal or external. Although desirable, these elements are not all to be found as part of most EAPs (Berridge et al., 1997).

Assessment of the Effectiveness of EAPS

Although EAPs have been in existence, in different forms, for about 40 years and have been implemented in a wide variety of organizations (Arthur, 2000; Highley & Cooper, 1994), less attention has been given to evaluating their impact than to developing and conducting the programs. Given the amount of time, energy, and funding invested in mounting and implementing EAPs, the relative inattention to assessing their effectiveness is somewhat surprising. Reasons vary but include a lack of clearly defined success criteria (Arthur, 2000; Berridge & Cooper, 1994), resistance on the part of EAP providers toward having their efforts evaluated (Davis & Gibson, 1994), concerns over confidentiality of information on clients (Highley & Cooper, 1994), unavailability of information in a usable form for evaluation research (Davis & Gibson, 1994), and methodological difficulties associated with conducting valid assessments of EAP effectiveness (Arthur, 2000).

Highley and Cooper (1994) elaborated on some of the more critical issues in EAP evaluations. One problem that confronts research in this area, as well as assessments of all organizational interventions, is the definition of what the program is intended to achieve. As noted earlier in this chapter, EAPs frequently have multiple goals, including enhancement of employee morale and motivation, promoting an image of the organization as caring for the welfare of its employees, productivity improvements (for example, by reducing absenteeism and tardiness, as well as more direct effects on job performance per se), and reduction of disciplinary problems. In addition, EAPs may be adopted by an organization to reduce the financial costs of medical and disability claims (Every & Leong, 1994). Given the range of intended benefits, and that achieving significant improvements in all of these areas is unlikely, the assessment of whether or not a particular intervention has been effective poses considerable challenges for the evaluator.

Several different assessment criteria have been applied in evaluations of EAP effectiveness. French, Zarkin, and Bray (1995) summarized four major components that need to be incorporated into research on EAPs:

1. *Process evaluation,* which documents the nature of the EAP, the manner in which it is delivered, and the intensity of service delivery. Such evaluation assesses whether implementation of the EAP has been optimal, hence maximizing the likelihood of positive benefits.
2. *Cost analysis* focuses on collecting data concerning the financial, and perhaps other (e.g., time, human resources) costs associated with the intervention.
3. *Outcome analysis* examines the consequences of the EAP intervention, such as those itemized above.
4. *Cost-effectiveness* is predominantly an assessment of the outcomes of the program in relation to the financial costs of implementing it.

Although French and his colleagues concentrated primarily on the financial aspects of EAPs, other commentators have reviewed different evaluation criteria. For instance, Becker, Hall, Fisher, and Miller (2000) noted that it is important to assess both quantitative (e.g., financial) and qualitative effectiveness criteria. The latter include possible improvements in employees' work-related motivation, better management–employee relations, enhanced organizational climate, and reduced psychological strain among employees. These criteria are as important as the more strictly quantitative benefits that organizations hope to achieve by adopting EAPs.

It is also important to consider the criteria required for effectiveness research to generate valid conclusions about the relative benefits of an EAP. Arthur noted that evaluation research

> should include the collection of uniform and standardised data that would allow comparison with other studies, a true experimental research design, the inclusion of employees who use other kinds of mental health services, linking the mental health status of individuals with their counselling utilisation rates, the use of adequate control groups, collection of data at least 3 years prior to and 3 years following the EAP intervention, random assignment of employees to different treatment and non-treatment conditions, the employment of work-performance indicators and a cost-benefit or economic analysis. (2000, p. 553)

Few, if any, EAP effectiveness studies incorporate all of these criteria, and Arthur (2000) commented that more has been written about how to do such research than actual reports of EAP evaluations. In addition, because of several factors, which we outline later in the chapter, evidence for the effectiveness of EAPs is inconsistent at best.

Despite the difficulties of conducting evaluation research in this field, recent investigations have demonstrated both the benefits and the limitations of EAPs. A full review of this literature is not intended; rather, we will summarize findings from a sample of studies that illustrate some general themes emerging from this line of research. For example, Westhuis, Hayashi, Hart, Cousert, and Spinks (1998) evaluated a drug and alcohol treatment program with 12,000 military personnel in the United States. Their research incorporated several of the features outlined by Arthur (2000) as necessary for a valid evaluation of effectiveness, including a quasi-experimental design that collected measures pre- and postintervention and two data sources (the participants' commanding officer and the drug and alcohol counselor responsible for the EAP intervention). Comparison of "treatment combinations" suggested that a combined-treatment approach, which entailed individual counseling and group therapy, along with increasing educational awareness, led to the most successful rehabilitation outcomes. Success in this context was defined broadly in terms of return to service.

In their assessment of EAP effectiveness relating to substance abuse and work performance problems, Hiatt, Hargrave, and Palmertree (1999) also collected data from employees' supervisors and EAP counselors. This research was conducted on what the authors referred to as a "broad brush" EAP, but did not provide a detailed explanation of the specific elements of the intervention. Nevertheless, improvements in performance-related criteria were observed, especially job attendance.

Effectiveness studies frequently include satisfaction as a criterion variable (Arthur, 2000). Typically, employee satisfaction with EAP interventions has been found to be quite high, and counselor satisfaction is (perhaps not surprisingly) also high (Harlow, 1998). For example, MacDonald and his colleagues reported that more than 90% of employees in a Canadian transportation company indicated high levels of satisfaction with the EAP services provided, and 69% said that these services had a positive effect on their overall quality of life. In respect to job performance, 46% of employees reported some or great improvement in their own job performance. Reports from counselors in the program also suggested a favorable reaction to the outcomes of the program (MacDonald, Lothian, & Wells, 1997; MacDonald, Wells, Lothian, & Shain, 2000).

In contrast to these positive evaluations of EAPs, some studies have reported little or no systematic advantages over other forms of treatment or counseling. For instance, in a well-controlled investigation of the effects of an EAP on Australian government employees, Blaze-Temple and Howat (1997) found that, although EAP counseling was effective, there was no substantial advantage in terms of cost-effectiveness of EAP-based counseling over self-arranged counseling. Similarly, in a comprehensive study of the effects of various stress-management training interventions on both employee mental health and organizational variables (such as absenteeism), Whatmore, Cartwright, and Cooper (1999) found that most of the gains that had been observed at three months postintervention had virtually dissipated by six months following completion of the intervention, suggesting that positive benefits may not be sustained, particularly if there is no systematic follow-up.

In summary, this brief overview of EAP evaluations illustrates that findings on the outcomes of EAPs are mixed (see Arthur, 2000) and that it is simply not possible to draw general conclusions about the effectiveness of these interventions. As noted previously, one reason for this lack of conclusiveness lies in the design of EAP evaluations, which are often suboptimal and do not include longitudinal pre- and postintervention assessments, comparative data with other forms of intervention, multiple sources of information (such as managers and organizational clients, as well as counselors and employees), and the variety of types of information needed to ensure that benefits are not limited to self-reports of satisfaction levels or financial outcomes.

There is no doubt that program evaluations, in the field of EAPs as in other areas of evaluation, are challenging and fraught with potential pitfalls. Some of these have been noted earlier. An additional "problem" is that the term *employee assistance program* encompasses a wide range of different types and foci of intervention, ranging from substance abuse programs through to stress management training and even more global wellness programs. The multidimensionality of EAPs means that it may not be possible to derive general conclusions that reflect all intervention types and formats. Rather, it may be more appropriate to examine the specific goals of a particular program and the extent to which those goals have been achieved. Nevertheless, it is evident that evaluations of EAPs need to be more systematic and rigorous than has often been the case until now, and must examine a range of outcomes that demonstrate benefits to a variety of stakeholders.

Theoretical Issues and EAPs

It is clear from the earlier sections of this chapter that there is a "considerable amount of activity" (Kompier & Cooper, 1999, p. 1) in the field of stress management through the use of EAPs, although this activity may be confined to large organizations (Whatmore et al., 1999). There is, however, a belief that organizations may not benefit from the marketing claims made about EAPs in terms of improved productivity, morale, and performance (Arthur, 2000). Evidence that the effectiveness of such programs is mixed can be partly explained in terms of the difficulties associated with evaluation, the fact that symptom relief is at times separated out from performance measures, because little work has been carried out on the long-term effects of such programs and because the primary responsibility for stress management is, more often than not, left to the individual (see Arthur, 2000; Cooper

& Cartwright, 1994; Reynolds & Briner, 1994). Even so, those making use of EAPs generally appear satisfied with the interventions they receive (Arthur, 2000), and difficulties associated with gauging EAP effectiveness may be more the result of the ad hoc way in which they are applied (Bull, 1997) and the fact that their purpose and objectives are not always clearly expressed (Health and Safety Commission, 1999).

Although there is no standardized model of EAP practice (Arthur, 2000), this in itself cannot be responsible for the debate surrounding the use and effectiveness of EAPs. When considering the application of such programs it may first be necessary to take a step back and reflect on the importance of theory, the issue of ethics, the question of organizational context, and the concerns of managers. Turning first to the importance of theory a number of authors (Arthur, 2000; Briner & Reynolds, 1999; Dewe, 1994; Murphy, 1995) have pointed to the need to make more explicit use of theory when considering the relevance and utility of EAPs and the issues they are expected to resolve. The view expressed is that traditional cause and effect assertions linking, for example, stress to performance are "no longer good enough" (Briner & Reynolds, 1999, p. 658) and that such approaches may no longer be "serviceable" (Lazarus, 1991, p. 1) or even support a workable theory when dealing with those suffering from stress at work. This is not to challenge the historical importance of interactional (cause and effect) models of stress nor the information they have provided. It is simply to draw attention to the fact that "treating everyone as though they were alike, and work environments as though they have common effects on everyone" (Lazarus, 1991, p. 10) may now be too superficial an approach to EAP intervention (Arthur, 2000).

Moving forward now requires that stress be thought of in transactional terms (Lazarus, 1999), where stress is viewed as relational in nature. In this way stress does not reside solely in the individual or solely in the environment but in the transaction between the two. Even more important is that thinking of stress in transactional terms points to the processes of appraisal as the link between the individual and the environment. In this way attention shifts to the process of stress and away from seeing individuals and environments as "separate causal antecedents of stress" (Lazarus, 1991, p. 11). This transactional view offers, as Lazarus (1999) makes clear, a very different perspective on work stress and therefore a more cognitive–individual-process oriented approach to stress management and EAPs. In summary, the emphasis from a transactional perspective when considering stress interventions is on recognizing the individual and the environment as a *single analytic unit,* rather than as separate sets of variables to be manipulated independently" (Lazarus, 1991, p. 10).

There is considerable debate about the application of the transactional model to a work setting (Brief & George, 1991; Dewe, 1991, 1992; Frese & Zapf, 1999; Harris, 1991; Perrewé & Zellars, 1999; Schaubroeck, 1999). The issue that is relevant concerns its individual-level focus. Although there is agreement that stress is essentially an individual-level phenomenon, the significance of work in people's lives leads some to suggest that what is more important is to identify those work conditions that "adversely affect *most* worker exposed to them" (Brief & George, 1991, p. 16) rather than to focus on interindividual processes. The argument that the transactional models interindividual level of analysis limits the directions that can be given to those involved in stress management and "does not necessarily provide ... insight into ways of correcting the stressful circumstances" (Harris, 1991, p. 27) still needs to be tested empirically because whether it is possible to produce favorable environmental changes for all is in itself a moot point (Briner & Reynolds, 1999; Lazarus, 1991).

Others issues are also debated when the transactional approach to stress is the focus of attention. These include, for example, whether objective rather than subjective measurement of stress holds more promise for stress intervention strategies (Frese & Zapf, 1999), the utility of problem-focused versus emotion-focused coping (Cooper, Dewe, & O'Driscoll, 2001) in managing stressful encounters, and the importance of primary appraisal—the meanings individuals give to events—and how such meanings should be treated when considering different stress interventions. Accepting that it is the transactional encounter itself that should now become the unit of analysis (Lazarus, 1991) does offer those responsible for EAPs a theoretical framework and a set of conceptual pathways that emphasize that such interventions "must be part of holistic strategies" (Arthur, 2000, p. 557) and reinforces that programs targeting only one level of intervention are not, in comparison with those combining multiple-level interventions as successful (Cooper & Sadri, 1991). Even more important is that unless EAPs, and other stress management programs as well, are set within some theoretical framework, then attempts to help those whose working lives we study may "be simple and clear—but also hopelessly wrong" (Briner & Reynolds, 1999, p. 661).

The transactional approach to stress also draws attention to the issues of power and control. From this perspective the issue becomes one of the resources available to individuals to cope with the demands of work. It draws attention to the influence that organizational structures and culture can have in constraining and directing individuals to think and act in particular ways (Dewe, 1994; Handy, 1988), raising questions about how far individuals can actually act on their own behalf (Thoits, 1995). The transactional approach offers as a framework a more "sophisticated matching of the person and the environment" (Lazarus, 1991, p. 10). Each is bound to the other through the adaptational encounter and "forces a more comprehensive strategy to evolve" (Dewe, 1994, p. 30) when considering the role of EAPs.

Two other issues are important when considering the use of EAPs or any stress management program. The first draws attention to the fact that although many organizations are concerned enough about the demands of work to put in place EAPs, little attempt has been made to find out what managers understand by stress (Westman & Eden, 1991), the extent to which they think their organization has a responsibility to address such problems, what motives lie behind the introduction of such programs (Reynolds & Briner, 1994), and whether they actually regard stress to be a problem (Daniels, 1996).

The second issue concerns the ethical considerations surrounding the use of EAPs. At the very heart of the matter is the concept of informed consent. The individual has a right to information, so that an agreement to participate in an intervention is an informed one. A number of issues must be confronted to ensure informed consent. They would include, for example, information on what the program involves and its duration; the nature of the individuals' involvement; why they are being asked to participate and on what basis they are being invited; a clear description of potential risks and benefits to the individual; how issues such as privacy, confidentiality, and anonymity are to be respected; how the information gathered is going to be used; who has access to that information and how it is to be stored and the rights of participants to decline to take part, to withdraw from the program, to refuse to answer any particular question, and to continue to ask questions so that informed consent is maintained. When considered in these terms then the manager's right to manage may need to be reviewed so that the individual's right to make an informed judgment is protected.

Future Role of EAPs

Three areas appear to be consistently referred to when considering the future development of EAPs. These include (a) agreeing on a clear understanding of the role of EAPs, and whether contemporary theory supports them in such a role, (b) establishing methods for evaluating their role, and (c) considering the nature of the problems EAPs will be required to address in the future.

There is in most reviews of EAPs (Geurts & Grundemann, 1999) agreement that one of the challenges facing most organizations is to increase awareness to work stress in general and stress prevention in particular. But this challenge is not simply to get people to agree that stress prevention—or in this case EAPs—are mutually beneficial but to seriously consider questions such as, "Why do organizations introduce stress management intervention?" (Briner, 1997, p. 65), "For whom and to what ends?" (Reynolds & Briner, 1994, p. 73), and what role in this process of increasing awareness and establishing programs has management (Daniels, 1996), primary care groups (Arthur, 2000), outside experts, and employees (Sutherland & Cooper, 2000).

The other theme allied to this issue of awareness is that of theory and theory-based program development. It is clear from this chapter that theory has been noticeably absent in the rush to establish some sort of stress management intervention. This has led to definitional and conceptual confusion and "too many baseless assumptions" (Briner, 2000, p. 6) about the relationship between work and stress and therefore the extent to which stress interventions can reasonably be expected to be successful (Briner & Reynolds, 1999). It is now time to redirect attention toward "the goal of answering some basic theoretical and empirical questions concerning organizational stress" (Briner & Reynolds 1999, p. 661) that take us way from

separating out the work environment and individual to applying the principles of transaction "requiring a very different perspective on work stress"
(Lazarus, 1991, p. 6). The significance of the transactional process for EAPs
is that it forces a more comprehensive strategy to evolve (Dewe, 1994), one
that recognizes that EAPs in themselves are not sufficient to counter the
effects of stress (Arthur, 2000), it is more closely related to the way in
which individuals see their job and requires as much attention to be given
to process as has been given to structure (Lazarus, 1999), and it establishes
a link between theory and practice emphasizing as a result a subject-
centers or collaborative approach rather than an expert-centered approach
that "remains at some distance from the problems and individuals" (Shipley
& Orlans, 1988, p. 111).

A second challenge facing the development of EAPs is their evaluation.
Evaluation is inexplicably linked with theory. If little attention is paid to
the nature of stress then "at best measurement of effectiveness is partial"
(Liukkonen, Cartwright, & Cooper, 1999, p. 49). Although it may be possible
through analyzing examples of best practice to establish those factors that
may contribute to a successful approach (Geurts & Grundemann, 1999)
noting that the "success of stress prevention depends on a subtle combination of two approaches, that is, 'bottom-up' (participation) and 'top-down'
(top management support)" (Kompier & Cooper, 1999, p. 335), this provides
more of a general approach than what specific indexes need to be measured
for evaluative purposes. The latter may now require that more attention
be given to evidence-based approaches (Briner, 2000), requiring that the
difficulties of establishing a link between outcomes and intervention be
given more focused attention (Kompier & Cooper, 1999), the identification
of costs and benefits associated with programs such as EAPs accepting that
this may only be achieved by adopting "a wider and more holistic approach"
(Liukkonen et al., 1999, p. 49) that requires both quantitative and qualitative measurement and a more systematic approach to EAP design and
implementation.

What of the role of EAPs in the future? If legislation and litigation
begin to establish a picture of what the courts think the organizations'
responsibility for the general health and well-being of their employees
should be, this will change the role of EAPs from reactive to proactive
procedures. They will be required to adopt some sort of audit function and
have to juggle the need to comply with health and safety legislation on the
one hand and individual rights to privacy, confidentiality, and informed
consent on the other—not to mention human resource issues such as selection, assessment, promotion, and training, and employment issues such as
employment agreements and grievances and issues of equity, fairness, and
trust in terms of the psychological contract. All of this will require an
even greater emphasis on evaluation; evaluative techniques; processes and
procedures, including an audit trail of what a systematic intervention strategy involves. In the future EAPs will also be responsible or required to
deal with issues of work–life balance and the conflicts that may emerge
from home–work interactions. They will become part of a wider social
responsibility of organizations that involves issues of family-friendly poli-

cies, issues of diversity including gender, ethnicity, ageism, and discrimination. Such programs will also be part of a move toward human resource accounting where organizations attempt to report on their investment in people and the value they place on a healthy workforce. The changes mentioned at the beginning of this chapter coupled with the demands on organizations to meet social and legislative goals also require those who study work stress to become far more rigorous in the way EAPs are researched and evaluated so that this research can contribute to those whose working lives we study.

References

Arthur, A. R. (2000). Employee assistance programmes: The emperor's new clothes of stress management? *British Journal of Guidance and Counseling, 28,* 549–559.

Becker, L., Hall, M., Fisher, D., & Miller, T. (2000). Methods for evaluating a mature substance abuse prevention/early intervention program. *Journal of Behavioral Health Services and Research, 27,* 166–177.

Berridge, J., & Cooper, C. L. (1993). Stress and coping in US organizations: The role of the employee assistance programme. *Work and Stress, 7,* 89–102.

Berridge, J., & Cooper, C. L. (1994). The employee assistance programme: Its role in organizational coping and excellence. *Personnel Review, 23,* 4–20.

Berridge, J., Cooper, C., & Highley C. (1997). *Employee assistance programmes and workplace counselling.* Chichester, UK: John Wiley.

Blaze-Temple, D., & Howat, P. (1997). Cost benefit of an Australian EAP. *Employee Assistance Quarterly, 12,* 1–24.

Brief, A. P., & George, J. M. (1991). Psychological stress and the workplace: A brief comment on Lazarus' outlook. In P. L. Perrewé (Ed.), *Handbook on job stress* [Special Issue]. *Journal of Social Behavior and Personality, 6,* 15–20.

Briner, R. B. (1997). Improving stress assessment: Toward an evidence-based approach to organizational stress interventions. *Journal of Psychosomatic Research, 43,* 61–71.

Briner, R. B. (2000). Stress management 2: Effectiveness of interventions. *Employee Health Bulletin, 18,* 2–7.

Briner, R. B., & Reynolds, S. (1999). The costs, and limitations of organizational level stress interventions. *Journal of Organizational Behavior, 20,* 647–664.

Bull, A. (1997) Organizational stress: Sources and responses. In C. Feltham (Ed.), *The gains of listening: Perspectives on counseling at work* (pp. 28–46). Buckingham, UK: Open University Press.

Cooper, C. L., & Cartwright, S. (1994). Healthy mind; Healthy organization—A proactive approach to occupational stress. *Human Relations, 47,* 455–471.

Cooper, C. L., & Cartwright, S. (1986) *Mental health and stress in the workplace. A guide for employers.* London: Her Majesty's Stationary Office.

Cooper, C. L., & Jackson, S. E. (1997) *Creating tomorrows' organizations: A handbook for future research in organizational behaviour.* Chichester, UK: John Wiley.

Cooper, C. L., Dewe, P. J., & O'Driscoll, M. P. (2001). *Organizational stress: A review and critique of theory, research, and applications.* London: Sage.

Cooper, C. L., & Sadri, G. (1991). The impact of stress counselling at work. In P. L. Perrewé (Ed.), *Handbook on job stress* [Special Issue]. *Journal of Social Behavior and Personality, 6,* 411–424

Cooper, C., Sloan, S. J., & Williams, S. (1988). *Occupational stress indicator.* London: NFER-Nelson.

Cunningham, G. (1994). *Effective employee assistance programs: A guide for EAP counselors and managers.* Thousand Oaks, CA: Sage.

Daniels, K. (1996). Why aren't managers concerned about occupational stress? *Work and Stress, 10,* 352–366.

Davis, A., & Gibson, L. (1994). Designing employee welfare provisions. *Personnel Review, 23,* 33–45.

Dewe, P. J. (1991). Primary appraisal, secondary appraisal and coping: Their role in stressful work encounters. *Journal of Occupational Psychology, 64,* 331–351.

Dewe, P. J. (1992). Applying the concept of appraisal to work stressors: Some exploratory analysis. *Human Relations, 45,* 143–164.

Dewe, P. J. (1994) EAPs and stress management: From theory to practice to comprehensiveness. *Personnel Review, 23,* 21–32.

Employee Assistance Professionals Association (EAPA). (1994). *Standards of practice and professional guidelines for employee assistance programs.* London: Author.

Employee Assistance Professionals Association (EAPA). (1997). *UK EAPA guidelines for the audit and evaluation of workplace counselling programmes,* London: Author.

Every, D., & Leong, D. (1994). Exploring EAP cost-effectiveness: Profile of a nuclear power plant internal EAP. *Employee Assistance Quarterly, 10,* 1–12.

Frese, M., & Zapf, D. (1999). On the importance of the objective environment in stress and attribution theory. Counterpoint to Perrewé and Zellars. *Journal of Organizational Behavior, 20,* 761–765.

French, M., Zarkin, G., & Bray, J. (1995). A methodology for evaluating the costs and benefits of employee assistance programs. *Journal of Drug Issues, 25,* 451–470.

Geurts, S., & Grundemann, R. (1999). Workplace stress and stress prevention in Europe. In M. Kompier & C. Cooper (Eds.), *Preventing stress, improving productivity: European case studies in the workplace* (pp. 9–32). London: Routledge.

Handy, J. A. (1988). Theoretical and methodological problems within occupational stress and burnout research. *Human Relations, 41,* 351–369.

Harlow, K. (1998). Employee attitudes toward an internal employee assistance program. *Journal of Employment Counseling, 35,* 141–150.

Harris, J. R. (1991). The utility of the transactional approach for occupational stress research. In P. L. Perrewé, (Ed.), *Handbook on job stress* [Special Issue]. *Journal of Social Behavior and Personality, 6,* 21–29.

Health and Safety Commission. (1999). *Managing stress at work: A discussion document.* London: Health and Safety Executive.

Hiatt, D., Hargrave, G., & Palmertree, M. (1999). Effectiveness of job performance referrals. *Employee Assistance Quarterly, 14,* 33–43.

Highley, J., & Cooper, C. (1994). Evaluating EAP's. *Personnel Review, 23,* 46–59.

Kompier, M., & Cooper, C. (1999). Improving work, health and productivity through stress prevention. In M. Kompier & C. Cooper (Eds.), *Preventing stress, improving productivity: European case studies in the workplace* (pp. 1–8). London: Routledge.

Lazarus, R. S. (1991). Psychological stress in the workplace. In P. L. Perrewé (Ed.), *Handbook on job stress* [Special Issue]. *Journal of Social Behavior and Personality, 6,* 1–13.

Lazarus, R. S. (1999). *Stress and emotion: A new synthesis.* London: Free Association Books

Lee, C., & Gray, J. A. (1994). The role of employee assistance programmes. In C. L. Cooper & S. Williams (Eds.), *Creating healthy work organizations* (pp. 215–242). Chichester, UK: John Wiley.

Liukkonen, P., Cartwright, S., & Cooper, C. (1999). Costs and benefits of stress prevention in organizations: Review and new methodology. In M. Kompier & C. Cooper (Eds.), *Preventing stress, improving productivity: European case studies in the workplace* (pp. 33–51). London: Routledge.

MacDonald, S., Lothian, S., & Wells, S. (1997). Evaluation of an employee assistance program at a transportation company. *Evaluation and Program Planning, 20,* 495–505.

MacDonald, S., Wells, S., Lothian, S., & Shain, M. (2000). Absenteeism and other workplace indicators of employee assistance program clients and matched controls. *Employee Assistance Quarterly, 15,* 41–57.

Megranahan, M. (1995, Nov. 29). *The impact of employee assistance programmes.* Paper presented to postgraduate course in organizational psychology, Manchester School of Management, Manchester, UK.

Murphy, L. R. (1995). Occupational stress management: Current status and future directions. In C. Cooper & D.M. Rousseau (Eds.), *Trends in organizational behavior* (pp. 1–14). Chichester, UK: John Wiley.

Perrewé, P. L., & Zellars, K. L. (1999). An examination of attributions and emotions in the transactional approach to the organizational stress process. *Journal of Organizational Behavior, 20,* 739–752.

Reynolds, S., & Briner, R. (1994). Stress management at work: With whom, for whom and to what ends? *British Journal of Guidance and Counselling, 22,* 75–89.

Schaubroeck, J. (1999). Should the subjective be the objective? On studying mental processes, coping behavior, and actual exposures in organizational stress research. *Journal of Organizational Behavior, 20,* 753–760.

Shipley, P., & Orlans, V. (1988). Stress research: An interventionist perspective. In J. J. Hurrell, L. R. Murphy, & S. L. Sauter (Eds.), *Occupational stress: Issues and developments in research* (pp. 110–122). New York: Taylor & Francis.

Sutherland, V., & Cooper, C. L. (2000). *Strategic stress management.* London: Macmillan Books.

Thoits, P. A. (1995). Stress, coping, and social support processes: Where are we? What next? *Journal of Health and Social Behavior* (Extra Issue), 53–79.

Westhuis, D., Hayashi, R., Hart, L., Cousert, D., & Spinks, M. (1998). Evaluating treatment issues in a military drug and alcohol treatment program. *Research on Social Work Practice, 8,* 501–519.

Westman, M., & Eden, D. (1991). Implicit stress theory: The spurious effects of stress on performance ratings. In P. L. Perrewé (Ed.), *Handbook on job stress* [Special Issue]. *Journal of Social Behavior and Personality, 6,* 127–140

Whatmore, L., Cartwright, S., & Cooper, C. (1999). United Kingdom: Evaluation of a stress management programme in the public sector. In M. Kompier & C. Cooper (Eds.), *Preventing stress, improving productivity: European case studies in the workplace* (pp. 149–174). London: Routledge.

15

Worksite Health Interventions: Targets for Change and Strategies for Attaining Them

Catherine A. Heaney

During the past 50 years, the field of occupational safety and health has benefited from a dramatic growth in the understanding of causes of occupational injuries and illnesses (Levy & Wegman, 2000). One consequence of this increased understanding is an expansion of the scope of the occupational risk factors being addressed. Although continuing to investigate the physical and chemical hazards in the workplace that have been the traditional focus of occupational safety and health efforts, occupational safety and health professionals have also recognized the role of work organization factors and their potential effects on health (National Institute for Occupational Safety and Health, 1999). During this same time period, the area of worksite health promotion has also burgeoned (O'Donnell, 2001). Worksite health promotion efforts have traditionally focused on employee behavior change of personal lifestyle risk factors. For these efforts, the worksite serves as a convenient venue for health programs, providing access to adult populations that might otherwise be hard to reach and providing organizational structures and norms that can facilitate successful individual behavior change (e.g., employer-provided incentives and the social influence of coworkers).

Although knowledge about worksite hazards and individual risk factors for ill health has been accumulating, our ability to develop and implement effective worksite-based interventions to address these hazards and risk factors has lagged. For example, some carefully developed and meticulously implemented worksite health promotion programs have failed to bring about substantial, meaningful changes in employee health behaviors (see the set of systematic reviews edited by Wilson, Holman, & Hammock, 1996). There have been similarly disappointing results for some occupational health and safety interventions (see the state-of-the-art reviews edited by Rivara & Thompson, 2000). This chapter will describe and critique our current approaches to worksite-based interventions. More specifically, targets for intervention will be examined and the processes or strategies for change that are incorporated into worksite-based interventions will be addressed. Finally, two particularly important areas for future research and practice will be discussed: employee participation in the design of worksite health programs and diffusion of effective worksite health programs across organizations.

Conceptual Model

An integrative conceptual framework for examining the relationship between work and health is based on a comprehensive model of stress and health, initially developed by researchers at the University of Michigan (French & Kahn, 1962; Katz & Kahn, 1978) and recently updated (Baker, Israel, & Schurman, 1996; Israel, Baker, Goldenhar, Heaney, & Schurman, 1996). This conceptual framework (depicted in Figure 15.1) presents the interplay of environmental, social, organizational, and individual factors as they influence employee health. Individuals experience conditions in the physical, social, and organizational environments. These conditions are referred to as stressors if they are likely to be perceived as harmful or threatening (Lazarus & Folkman, 1984) or if they place a demand on employees that results in a physiological adaptational response (Selye, 1993). Exposure to stressors may have a direct effect on health (e.g., when an equipment breakdown directly causes injury) or effects on health may be mediated through individual employees' perceptions and responses (e.g., when an equipment breakdown causes an employee to worry). The intensity and duration of the stressor, in combination with an employee's response to the stressor, influence the likelihood that exposure to the stressor will result in adverse physiological, psychological, or behavioral consequences. Each step of the process outlined in Figure 15.1 is influenced by, among other things, employees' individual resources and the social resources provided within the organizational context. Thus, this model reflects a complex and dynamic process.

Targets and Strategies for Intervention

The major constructs depicted in Figure 15.1 represent important influences on employee health, and thus are potentially important targets for change for worksite health programs. Table 15.1 summarizes the potential points of intervention suggested by Figure 15.1, providing examples of specific targets for change. Organizational and engineering changes can be made to reduce exposure to physical and chemical hazards or problematic work organization factors. Individual employee resources can be enhanced to facilitate stressor reduction (e.g., solve problems) or to strengthen employee well-being and reduce vulnerability to stress symptoms. Social resources can be enhanced through social network interventions (Gottlieb, 2000) and through changes in organizational problem solving and decision making (Klein, Ralls, Smith-Major, & Douglas, 2000). Finally, short-term

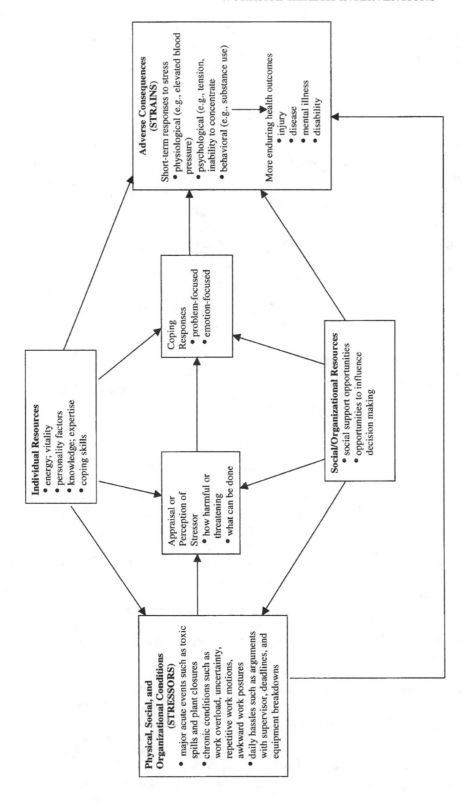

Figure 15.1.   Conceptual framework for work, stress, and health.

Table 15.1. Targets of Change for Worksite Interventions

Type of intervention	Examples of targets of change
Reduce exposure to stressors	• Work tasks • Work schedules • Ambient environment (e.g., noise, lighting)
Enhance individual resources to reduce exposure to or appraisal of stressors	• Employee knowledge and skills relevant to the stressor (e.g., personal protective equipment use, time management, conflict resolution)
Enhance individual resources to strengthen overall well-being and to reduce vulnerability to stress symptoms	• Employee health behaviors • Employee knowledge and skills relevant to emotion-focused coping (e.g., skills in relaxation or meditation)
Enhance social resources to reduce exposure to or appraisal of stressors	• Structures and processes for organizational problem solving • Social support networks
Identify and treat symptoms of short-term strain	• Availability and acceptability of health care services • Screening for early identification of illness

consequences of stress can be identified and treated to reduce long-term health problems.

The need to change organizational structures, policies, procedures, and priorities is ubiquitous across many of the targets for change outlined in Table 15.1. Organizational-level change is needed to reinforce adaptive employee norms and facilitate healthy behaviors, to reduce environmental risk factors, and to enhance social resources within the organization. And although there has been a strong endorsement among worksite health researchers and practitioners of the proposition that organizational change is crucial, there has been much less implementation of it. Some worksite health interventions continue to fall prey to "the psychological fallacy" (Katz & Kahn, 1978) or belief that organizations can be changed simply by targeting individual organization members for change. Research clearly indicates that organizations constrain employee behaviors and coping efforts (Heaney, House, Israel, & Mero, 1995; Menaghan & Merves, 1984; Parkes, 1990), and that individual-level interventions are not very effective at bringing about organizational change (Macy & Izumi, 1993).

To date, the choice of change target for most worksite health programs has been determined more by philosophy, disciplinary assumptions, and perceived feasibility than by critical assessment of empirical criteria. Several planning frameworks in public health intervention development suggest that targets of intervention be chosen based on the following criteria: (a) importance and prevalence of the health problem; (b) prevalence of the risk factor; (c) strength of association between the risk factor and the health problem; and (d) modifiability of the risk factor (Bartholomew, Parcel, & Kok, 1998; Green & Kreuter, 1999; Jeffery, 1989). When these public health criteria are applied to the conceptual model presented in Figure 15.1, they translate into the following questions (Heaney & van Ryn, 1990):

1. What strains are being experienced by employees?
2. What are the various physical, social, and organizational conditions that are potential stressors in this workplace?
3. Who is experiencing these stressors and perceiving them as stressful (e.g., a few idiosyncratic individuals or an identifiable subgroup)? How widespread is the perception of stress?
4. To what extent are these perceptions of stress linked to short-term and long-term adverse outcomes?
5. How modifiable is the stressor? Can exposure to the stressor be reduced?

Answers to these questions can then guide the choice of intervention targets. To answer these questions, an extensive needs assessment must be conducted. Because the process in Figure 15.1 is highly dependent on organizational context and employee characteristics, it is difficult to directly apply findings from one organization to the intervention development process in another. However, the availability of easily accessed, valid, and reliable measures of many of the major concepts in the framework makes it feasible for even smaller organizations to implement comprehensive assessments (see Cohen, Kessler, & Gordon, 1997; Hurrell, Nelson, & Simmons, 1998).

It is important to note that the various available targets of intervention are not mutually exclusive; interventions may incorporate several targets of change. For example, the introduction of flexible scheduling for employees may be complemented by an employee training program in time management skills. A social ecological perspective suggests that multiple targets of change at multiple levels (e.g., individual, work team, organization) will be most likely to effectively reduce health problems (Stokols, 1996). Social ecology also emphasizes the dynamic interplay among physical environment, social environment, and personal factors. The dynamic nature of ecosystems not only implies the importance of "fit" between employee, work unit, organization, and larger economic environment but also implies that changes at one level bring about changes in another. For example, research has shown that levels of exposure to physical hazards and psychosocial conditions at work can be related to employees' intentions to modify their own behavioral risk factors (e.g., smoking and diet) (Chan & Heaney, 1997; Sorensen et al., 1996; Walsh, Jennings, Mangione, & Merrigan, 1991). The investigation of the nature and magnitude of these cross-level linkages will provide useful guidance to interventionists as they try to determine the most appropriate and effective points of intervention.

Another consideration in choosing targets for intervention is the identification of "high impact leverage points" (Stokols, 1996, p. 290). These
leverage points are people, behaviors, roles, and environmental conditions
that exert a disproportionately large influence on employee health and
well-being. For example, House (1981) has suggested that the front-line
supervisor is such a leverage point. If front-line supervisors increase their
supportive exchanges with coworkers and subordinates, many employees
stand to benefit in terms of enhanced well-being. Another example of a
high-impact leverage role within the organization might be the person
responsible for ensuring compliance with health and safety regulations.
Changes in that person's behavior might have far-reaching repercussions
for large groups of employees. Finally, opinion leaders may serve as high-
impact leverage points because of their ability to bring about changes in
others' attitudes and behaviors (Lam & Schaubroeck, 2000; Rogers, 1995).

Although the conceptual framework in Figure 15.1 suggests a plethora
of potential targets for change, it provides little guidance in terms of identifying strategies for change. Strategies for change are the activities that
change agents engage in or implement to bring about the desired intervention outcomes. Types of strategies include training, counseling, consulting,
use of the media, facilitating group process, policy advocacy, and others.
Once a target for change has been identified, how does one go about effecting
that change in as timely, appropriate, and cost-effective a manner as possible? What tactics should be used to reduce the likelihood of undesirable
outcomes while optimizing desired change?

Most planning frameworks suggest that social science theories, intervention effectiveness research, program evaluation results, and knowledge
gained from local needs and resource assessments should inform choices
of tactics and strategies (Bartholomew et al., 1998; Green & Kreuter, 1999).
In the following discussion, strategies for change are categorized as follows:
(a) individual-level change strategies that focus on changing employees'
beliefs, attitudes, and behaviors; and (b) organizational-level change strategies that focus on changing organizational structures, policies, priorities,
and procedures.

Individual-Level Change

When attempting to change employee beliefs, attitudes, and behaviors,
theories of social influence and social learning have been used to guide
intervention development. The most commonly used theories include social
cognitive theory (Bandura, 1986), the health belief model (Janz & Becker,
1984), the transtheoretical model of change (Prochaska, DiClemente, &
Norcross, 1992), the theory of reasoned action (Fishbein & Ajzen, 1980), and
information-processing models (McGuire, 1973). Although these various
theories place differing amounts of emphasis on cognitive, affective, and
behavioral processes, they all aid in identifying the major explanatory
factors that influence the target of change and, in some cases, they also
identify strategies for modifying the explanatory factors. For example, so-

cial cognitive theory (Bandura, 1986) places great emphasis on efficacy expectations (beliefs regarding one's ability to successfully carry out a course of action or perform a behavior) and outcome expectations (beliefs that the performance of a behavior will have desired effects or consequences) as explanatory factors for behavior. The theory further posits that both types of expectations can be influenced through observational and experiential learning (Bandura, 1986). Thus, to increase health care employees' compliance with universal precautions, an intervention might incorporate learning activities that allow employees to hear about or observe others' successful use of the desired procedures and to practice the procedures themselves. Theories that have undergone rigorous testing and have been applied in many different settings and with various target populations are the most useful for developing intervention strategies.

Although psychological theories of learning and social influence have been well-integrated into health promotion interventions in other settings (Glanz, Lewis, & Rimer, 1997), worksite health programs (and particularly occupational safety and health programs) have not been adequately informed by social science theory (Goldenhar & Schulte, 1994). However, a few studies serve as useful examples of how worksite intervention strategies that are attempting individual level change can be well-guided by theory. For example, Sinclair, Gershon, Murphy, and Goldenhar (1996) used protection motivation theory to guide their development of an intervention to change employee behavior to reduce needlestick injuries among workers in the health care industry.

As another example, Witte et al. (1992) used fear-arousal theories to guide formative research to facilitate development of effective safety messages to reduce tractor-related injuries among farmers. In the worksite health promotion arena, Glasgow, Terborg, Hollis, Severson, and Boles (1995) based their heart disease prevention program on the transtheoretical model of change, providing intervention activities matched to employees' levels of motivational readiness.

Organizational-Level Change

Worksite health researchers and practitioners have made less use of organizational change theory and its associated voluminous body of research than they have of theories describing individual-level change. Several factors may inhibit application of organizational change theory and research to worksite health programs. One such factor is that the outcomes of interest for most published organizational change interventions revolve around the health of the organization (productivity, efficiency, profits) rather than the health of the employee. And although several conceptualizations of healthy organizations include the well-being of employees (Lawler, 1992; Pfeffer, 1998), most of the research does not examine health outcomes. Indeed, although there is some evidence that taking care of employee health issues is correlated with productivity and corporate profits (Pfeffer, 1998), there is also evidence suggesting that the two are not always complementary

(Kaminski, 2001; Landsbergis, Cahill, & Schnall, 1999). Thus, the process of translating results from the organizational change literature to the field of worksite health is not straightforward.

A second factor that may inhibit the application of organizational change theories is that they tend to emphasize the influence of the organizational context on the change process (Molinsky, 1999). Such contextualizing limits the ability of the program developer to apply the findings from one organization to another and strongly suggests that "off the shelf" programs are not likely to be effective if adopted without modification (Argyris, 1993; Colarelli, 1998). Perhaps because of the contextual nature of the conceptual frameworks, organizational change research tends to be more idiographic than nomothetic (see Quick, 1997). In other words, much of the research is oriented toward understanding change processes within a particular organization rather than examining change processes across organizations. Methodologies focus on case studies and include more ethnographic approaches rather than experimental or epidemiological methods. Thus, the application of the findings in the literature tends to be in terms of "lessons learned" from diverse cases rather than empirically derived generalizations about effective change processes. Although these "lessons learned" can be instructive, they may be less compelling to intervention developers who have been steeped in positivist, experimental research traditions.

A last factor that may inhibit use of the organizational change literature is the state of the knowledge base in this literature. Rosabeth Kanter, who has been examining organizational change processes for several decades, wrote, "Despite volumes of literature on planned change, legions of consultants, and the best efforts of corporate leaders, organizational change still appears to be a chaotic process" (Kanter, Stein, & Jick, 1992, p. 370). For every prescription or proposed guideline for effective organizational change, there are qualifications, exceptions, and contradictory evidence. For example, almost every review of organizational change processes concludes that support from top management is essential for success (Kanter et al., 1992; Kotter, 1996; Nadler, 1998). However, a recent analysis by Molinsky (1999) suggested that top management support can actually undermine a change effort if it is operationalized in ways that inadvertently diminish the perceived credibility of the change effort. The inconsistencies in the research evidence make it difficult for a worksite health researcher or practitioner to use the literature to inform intervention development.

In spite of these complexities and inconsistencies, various organization change scholars have culled from the literature suggested strategies for maximizing the success of planned change efforts (Kanter et al., 1992; Kotter, 1996; Porras & Robertson, 1992; Schein, 1987). There are striking similarities among the guidelines put forth by different authors. Their intellectual roots are firmly entrenched in Lewin's (1951) influential model for conceptualizing change. Lewin posited three stages to the process: unfreezing the old behavior, moving to a new behavior, and then refreezing or stabilizing the new behavior. Thus, change was conceptualized as moving from one equilibrium point to another. Building on this framework, organizational change theorists linked the stages to action steps that change agents should take to facilitate progress through the stages. These steps typically include analyzing or diagnosing the current situation, creating the perception of a need for change, creating a shared vision for change, providing leadership and assigning responsibility for change, communicating the change to all stakeholders; providing necessary education and training, modifying organizational structures, and policies to support the change effort; involving employees in local innovations; and evaluating the change effort to provide feedback for additional change (Kanter et al., 1992; Kotter, 1996; Schein, 1987).

Summary: Targets and Strategies for Intervention

The worksite health intervention literature has provided a fair amount of attention to the issue of targets of change but relatively little attention to issues of strategy. In part, this is because published accounts of interventions rarely provide detailed descriptions of the program activities and change processes, nor do they explicate the basis for decisions about strategies for change. It is even more rare for intervention research to formally compare the effectiveness of various strategies for bringing about targeted changes. The example of smoking control efforts at the workplace is illustrative. In a recent review, Eriksen and Gottlieb (1998) concluded that there is consistent evidence that smoking control policies reduce cigarette consumption at work among smokers and reduce environmental tobacco smoke exposure for all employees. However, the results across studies differ markedly, and few studies have examined the degree of management support for smoking control programs, the extent to which the organizational climate was consistent with smoking control efforts, and how the programs were designed, communicated, and implemented. There continues to be little discussion of intervention strategy and little accumulation of empirical guidance for strategic and tactical choices in worksite health interventions.

Strategies: Participation and Dissemination

This section will address issues of strategy within two important areas of worksite intervention research: employee participation in the design and conduct of worksite health interventions and the diffusion of effective worksite health interventions among organizations.

Employee Participation

Employee participation has been an important component of long-standing traditions in organizational change theory and research. For example, it is a central component of organizational development (Porras & Robertson,

1992), action research (Argyris, 1993), and popular quality-improvement programs such as Total Quality Management (Hackman & Wageman, 1995; Klein et al., 2000). More recently, practitioners and researchers have embraced employee participation in the planning, development, implementation, and evaluation of worksite health programs (Goldenhar, LaMontagne, Katz, Heaney, & Landsbergis, in press). Sometimes employee participation is used as a strategy for bringing about a desired targeted change and sometimes employee participation is a desired target of change in and of itself. Worksite health promotion programs have incorporated employee participation in a variety of ways, including seeking employee input into the assessment of employee health needs (e.g., through employee surveys or focus groups), having employee advisory boards guide the planning process, and having employee groups take full responsibility for the implementation of health promotion efforts. In occupational safety and health, participatory ergonomics, defined as "the involvement of people in planning and controlling a significant amount of their own work activities, with sufficient knowledge and power to influence both processes and outcomes in order to achieve desirable goals" (Wilson & Haines, 1997, pp. 492–493), best exemplifies programs that emphasize employee participation both as a means to effecting ergonomic innovation and as an important outcome in itself. Participatory strategies have also been a central component of some worksite-stressor reduction interventions (see, e.g., Israel, Schurman, & House, 1989; Landsbergis & Vivona-Vaughan, 1995).

Although participatory strategies have gained in popularity, the nature of those strategies has varied greatly. The word *participation* has been used to indicate strategies ranging from the provision of information to employees by management (e.g., company newsletters, "state-of the-company" presentations), to opportunities for employees to voice concerns or suggestions (e.g., suggestion boxes, open forums), to joint labor–management problem-solving groups with unequal influence in decision making, and finally to initiatives with joint control of resources and influence (Cotton, Vollrath, Froggatt, Lengnick-Hall, & Jennings, 1988; Robertson & Minkler, 1994). Several authors have provided classification schemes for participatory strategies, identifying the important decision points in designing these types of strategies (Cotton et al., 1988; Eklund, 2000; Klein et al., 2000). These classification schemes have been synthesized in Table 15.2.

A few worksite health programs that have used participatory strategies illustrate some of the different choices that have been made. For programs that have used representative participation, representatives have been elected by their peers (Landsbergis & Vivona-Vaughan, 1995), chosen by labor and management leaders (Israel et al., 1989), and self-selected through expressions of employee interest (Bohr, Evanoff, & Wolf, 1997). The scope of the issues addressed has ranged from one health behavior issue (Eriksen & Gottlieb, 1998), to a set of ergonomic issues relevant to a work unit (Bohr et al., 1997), to more system-wide changes (Cahill & Feldman, 1993). The duration and intensity of the participatory processes varied from five meetings held over the course of seven months (Landsbergis

Table 15.2. Strategy Choice Points for Employee Participation Initiatives

Category	Choice point
Scope of initiative	• What range of issues will be addressed? • To what extent will decisions be made relevant to personal job performance, work teams, and/or larger organizational units? • Is the participatory process anticipated to continue indefinitely or for a discrete time period? • Will the program be initiated in a small number of organizational units or instituted organization-wide?
Group composition and process	• Will participation be mandatory or voluntary? • To what extent will all employees be provided opportunities for participation versus participation of employee representatives? If the latter, how will representatives be chosen? • To what extent will decisions made by the group be reviewed (and potentially modified) by others in the organization? • Will participation occur through formal and/or informal processes?
Organizational support for initiative	• How much and what types of training will be provided to employees so that they can participate effectively? • To what extent will employees be allowed to participate on work time (e.g., released from other job duties, allocated time outside of meetings to perform follow-up)? • To what extent will organizational structures and processes be modified to reinforce participation (e.g., reward system, hiring practices)?

Note. Adapted from Cotton et al. (1988), Eklund (2000), Klein et al. (2000), and Wilson and Haines (1997).

& Vivona-Vaughan, 1995) to weekly meetings over the course of two years (Evanoff, Bohr, & Wolf, 1999).

Most of the research examining employee-participation strategies has been focused on the outcomes of employee satisfaction and performance (see Cotton et al., 1988; Klein et al., 2000; Lawler, 1992, for reviews). Reviewers have concluded that the use of participatory strategies has had mixed results. Cotton et al. (1988) suggested that these mixed results may be a result of the great variety of ways in which participation has been operationalized and that the most effective participatory strategies are those that are ongoing, direct, and that provide employees with significant influence in decision making relevant to how they perform their jobs. However, subsequent reviews have questioned the methodology used by Cotton et al. (1988) and have not successfully replicated their results (Leana, Locke, & Schweiger, 1990; Wagner, 1994). Although the empirical literature addressing participatory strategies is extensive, it offers little guidance about how best to optimize effectiveness through the choice points listed in Table 15.2. This remains a critical priority for future worksite health intervention research.

Published accounts of worksite health programs that incorporated participatory strategies (Bohr et al., 1997; Haims & Carayon, 1998; Israel et al., 1989; Landsbergis & Vivona-Vaughan, 1995), as well as reviews of employee-participation strategies more broadly (Klein et al., 2000; Lawler, 1992; Neuman, 1989), suggest that barriers to successful implementation of such strategies include factors leading to both managerial and employee resistance. Front-line supervisors may fear an erosion of their power and influence; they may resent a perceived increase in workload as they are assigned to guide the participatory efforts and instructed to release other employees from their usual duties; and they may infer a lack of top management support for the effort if organizational structures and processes are not modified to complement the participatory initiative. In terms of the employees, they may experience frustration with their inability to implement their chosen solutions within the existing organizational structure, either because of a lack of access to needed resources or because the real decisions of the organization are made outside of the participatory process. Employees may also become frustrated with participatory strategies if they feel that they are not provided with the information that they need to make informed choices and not given enough time during their work days to participate effectively. Finally, if the organization has a history of distrust between labor and management, employees may perceive the purpose of the participatory strategies to be more manipulative (e.g., to enhance employee morale) than productive (e.g., to improve quality of work life). Approaches that reduce these barriers by providing real opportunities for employee influence in identifying, prioritizing, and implementing solutions and by maximizing the extent to which organizational structures and practices facilitate and reinforce the participatory strategies may have the greatest likelihood of success.

Diffusion of Interventions

The impact of any preventive intervention is dependent on both its efficacy in bringing about the targeted change and its "reach," or the extent to which members of the target population have access to and participate in the program (Glasgow, Vogt, & Boles, 1999). Once a program has proven successful in demonstration projects and efficacy trials, it is imperative that the program be adopted and implemented by new organizations. For example, VDT operators will not benefit from an effective ergonomics innovation if that innovation is not introduced in a large proportion of worksites that employ VDT operators. Unfortunately, diffusion of preventive interventions to new organizations often proceeds at a very slow rate (Parcel, Perry, & Taylor, 1990).

A staged process has been suggested to underlie optimal diffusion of preventive interventions to new organizations. Although different researchers have offered a variety of number and types of stages, there is general consensus on the importance of at least four stages: (a) the dissemination stage during which organizations are made aware of the programs and their benefits; (b) the adoption stage during which the organization commits to initiating the program; (c) the implementation stage during which the organization offers the program or services; and (d) the maintenance or institutionalization stage during which the organization makes the program part of the organization's routines and standard offerings. At each of these stages, the structures, norms, and resources of the adopting organization will influence the choice of strategies for enhancing diffusion (Goodman, Steckler, & Kegler, 1997).

Diffusion efforts are most likely to be successful when informed by diffusion theory and diffusion research. To the best of my knowledge, no published studies have examined the diffusion of employee health interventions among organizations. Although there have been investigations of the extent to which worksite health promotion programs have been implemented by organizations (U.S. DHHS, 1993), occupational safety and health regulations have been acted on and complied with by organizations (U.S. GAO, 1991), and employee involvement practices have been adopted by organizations (Lawler, Mohrman, & Ledford, 1995), there have been no studies of the diffusion process itself. However, a few studies have investigated organizational adoption of health programs that are intended to serve the clients of organizations rather than the employees. For example, randomized trials testing strategies for enhancing the diffusion of prevention curricula among schools (Rohrbach, D'Onofrio, Backer, & Montgomery, 1997; Smith, Steckler, McCormick, & McLeroy, 1995) and the diffusion of preventive health services among medical care practices (Solberg, Kottke, Brekke, Conn, et al., 1998) have been conducted.

The results of research in these two areas have suggested that additional reliance on organizational change theory might enhance our ability to diffuse programs more rapidly and thoroughly. Although initial or traditional efforts to enhance diffusion focused on the characteristics of the innovation (Rogers, 1995), focus has shifted to the strategies of the change process itself. For example, Rohrbach et al. (1997) suggested that "change agents and school personnel should work as a team to diagnose any problems that may impede program implementation and develop action plans to address them" and that "change agents need to promote the involvement of teachers, as well as that of key administrators, in decisions about program adoption and implementation" (p. 927–928). Goodman et al. (1997) suggested that a diffusion intervention in North Carolina schools might have been more effective if it had included more participative problem diagnosis and action planning and if the consultation provided had been less directive and more oriented toward increasing the fit between the host organization and the program.

Solberg, Kottke, Brekke, Conn, et al. (1998) reviewed studies of the diffusion of preventive health services and suggested that the major barriers to more rapid and effective diffusion are clearly "systems problems," with medical practices not having the structures and processes in place to facilitate successful provision of preventive health care services. The nature of the "systems problems" (and thus the nature of the appropriate solutions) differs across potential adopting organizations, and thus a major part of the solution is to build local capacity for diffusion within the organization (e.g., continuous quality improvement teams). Building on these findings, Solberg, Kottke, and Brekke (1998) developed the IMPROVE (Improving Prevention Through Organization, Vision, and Empowerment) program. They used a 7-step improvement process that draws from the participative problem-solving approaches of action research (Argyris, 1993) and from process-consultation strategies (Schein, 1987).

Summary: Participation and Dissemination

The large literature on employee participation and the much smaller literature on diffusion of interventions among organizations are quite different but offer similar conclusions. Both literatures indicate that there has been little theoretical or empirical guidance for making decisions about strategies for change. Both literatures also point to the importance of strategies that allow for local adaptation of programmatic initiatives. Research that tests the effects of different strategies for change in various organizational settings will provide much needed guidance for worksite health intervention designers.

Conclusion

Often in public health, our knowledge about how to change identified risk or protective factors does not keep pace with epidemiological breakthroughs and other basic science research findings. For example, smoking has long been identified as the major preventable cause of premature mortality in the United States, yet health professionals are still struggling to devise effective strategies for helping people choose to be nonsmokers. Social support has been identified as an important protective factor, but strategies for increasing the social support available to those who need it have been only modestly successful at best. Although the basics of healthy nutrition have been well-understood for decades, Americans are currently experiencing an epidemic of obesity and obesity-related diseases.

Such is also the state of affairs in the occupational health arena. Our understanding of occupational hazards (or potential stressors, to use the language of Figure 15.1) continues to grow, but our ability to mount interventions that effectively reduce the negative impact of these stressors on employee health lags behind. To strengthen our ability to intervene effectively, this chapter provides two broad suggestions: (a) increase the scope of our targets of change, by using a clear, empirically-guided process for selecting the most appropriate targets; and (b) strengthen our change strategies by making better use of well-tested change theories and their associated research. These suggestions are likely to translate into an increased emphasis on work organization factors and organizational change strategies. The complexities and constraints inherent in organizational change efforts may be daunting (Kristensen, 2000), but they are not reason enough for continuing to underuse organizational approaches to worksite health.

To act on the broad suggestions stated earlier, several smaller propositions should be considered. First, for interventions to be driven by a systematic, comprehensive, and data-oriented process rather than by disciplinary boundaries, it is important that multidisciplinary teams address the design and conduct of worksite health interventions. The use of such teams also ensures access to expertise in a wide range of areas (industrial hygiene, health psychology, organizational change, health promotion, biostatistics, ergonomics, etc.) that might be necessary for effective intervention (Goldenhar & Schulte, 1994; Israel et al., 1996).

Second, the effectiveness of any worksite health intervention is likely to be affected by the fit (or lack thereof) between the programmatic change effort, on the one hand, and the organizational context and extraorganizational factors (e.g., market forces, labor availability) on the other. Thus, it is important that the intervention design process blend social science theory and evidence with local preferences, experiences, and needs. Intervention development necessitates an ongoing dialogue not only among experts from different disciplines but between researchers and organization members. A flexible process that allows for local adaptation and local experimentation is likely to be advantageous (Colarelli, 1998; Kanter et al., 1992).

Third, intervention researchers need to critically reflect on how existing research findings can be better used to inform intervention. Given the diversity of relevant research, this is likely to entail drawing from the strengths of various research paradigms (Quick, 1997). For example, rich descriptions of organizational change programs pervade the organizational change literature. How can these case studies be better used? Alternatively, several large randomized controlled trials of worksite cancer prevention programs have been conducted. What can be learned from these trials that would be relevant to worksite interventions more broadly? Gaps in our knowledge about intervention targets and strategies can then be identified and addressed.

Intervention research is fast becoming a high priority in the occupational safety and health arena. The National Occupational Research Agenda identified intervention effectiveness research as a priority area, and funding for this research has doubled between 1996 and 1998 (National Institute for Occupational Safety and Health, 1999). Thus, the time is ripe for setting an intervention research agenda that systematically answers questions about how to choose targets for change and implement the most effective strategies for enhancing employee health.

References

Argyris, C. (1993). *Knowledge for action.* San Francisco: Jossey-Bass.

Baker, E. A., Israel, B. A., & Schurman, S. J. (1996). The integrated model: Implications for worksite health promotion and occupational safety and health practice. *Health Education Quarterly, 23*(2), 175–190.

Bandura, A. (1986). *Social foundations of thought and action.* Englewood Cliffs, NJ: Prentice-Hall.

Bartholomew, L. K., Parcel, G. S., & Kok, G. (1998). Intervention mapping: A process for developing theory- and evidence-based health education programs. *Health Education & Behavior, 25*(5), 545–563.

Bohr, P. C., Evanoff, B. A., & Wolf, L. D. (1997). Implementing participatory ergonomics teams among health care workers. *American Journal of Industrial Medicine, 32,* 190–196.

Cahill, J., & Feldman, L. H. (1993). Computers in child welfare: Planning for a more serviceable work environment. *Child Welfare, 72,* 3–12.

Chan, W. F., & Heaney, C. A. (1997). Employee stress levels and the intention to participate in a worksite smoking cessation program. *Journal of Behavioral Medicine, 20*(4), 351–364.

Cohen, S., Kessler, R. C., & Gordon, L. U. (Eds.). (1997). *Measuring stress: A guide for health and social scientists.* New York: Oxford University Press.

Colarelli, S. M. (1998). Psychological interventions in organizations: An evolutionary perspective. *American Psychologist, 53*(9), 1044–1056.

Cotton, J. L., Vollrath, D. A., Froggatt, K. L., Lengnick-Hall, M. L., & Jennings, K. R. (1988). Employee participation: Diverse forms and different outcomes. *Academy of Management Review, 13,* 8–22.

Eklund, J. (2000). Development work for quality and ergonomics. *Applied Ergonomics, 31,* 641–648.

Eriksen, M. P., & Gottlieb, N. H. (1998). A review of the health impact of smoking control policies at the workplace. *American Journal of Health Promotion, 13,* 83–105.

Evanoff, B. A., Bohr, P. C., & Wolf, L. D. (1999). Effects of a participatory ergonomics team among hospital orderlies. *American Journal of Industrial Medicine, 35,* 358–365.

Fishbein, M., & Ajzen, I. (1980). *Belief, attitude, intention, and behavior: An introduction to theory and research.* Reading, MA: Addison-Wesley.

French, J. R. P., & Kahn, R. (1962). A programmatic approach to studying the industrial environment and mental health. *Journal of Social Issues, 18,* 1–48.

Glanz, K., Lewis, F. M., & Rimer, B. K. (Eds.). (1997). *Health behavior and health education: Theory, research, and practice* (2nd ed.). San Francisco: Jossey-Bass.

Glasgow, R. E., Terborg, J. R., Hollis, J. F., Severson, H. H., & Boles, S. M. (1995). Take heart: Results from the initial phase of a work-site wellness program. *American Journal of Public Health, 85,* 209–216.

Glasgow, R. E., Vogt, T. M., & Boles, S. M. (1999). Evaluating the public health impact of health promotion interventions: The RE-AIM framework. *American Journal of Public Health, 89,* 1322–1327.

Goldenhar, L. M., LaMontagne, A. D., Katz, T., Heaney, C. A., & Landsbergis, P. (in press). The intervention research process in occupational safety and health: An overview from the nora intervention effectiveness research team. *Journal of Occupational and Environmental Medicine.*

Goldenhar, L. M., & Schulte, P. A. (1994). Intervention research in occupational health and safety. *Journal of Occupational Medicine, 36,* 763–775.

Goodman, R. M., Steckler, A., & Kegler, M. C. (1997). Mobilizing organizations for health enhancement: Theories of organizational change. In K. Glanz, F. M. Lewis, & B. K. Rimer (Eds.), *Health behavior and health education* (2nd ed., pp. 287–312). San Francisco: Jossey-Bass.

Gottlieb, B. H. (2000). Selecting and planning support interventions. In S. Cohen, L. G. Underwood, & B. H. Gottlieb (Eds.), *Social support measurement and intervention* (pp. 195–220). New York: Oxford University Press.

Green, L. W., & Kreuter, M. W. (1999). *Health promotion planning: An educational and ecological approach* (3rd ed.). Mountain View, CA: Mayfield.

Hackman, J. R., & Wageman, R. (1995). Total quality management: Empirical, conceptual, and practical issues. *Administrative Science Quarterly, 40,* 309–342.

Haims, M. C., & Carayon, P. (1998). Theory and practice for the implementation of "in-house," continuous improvement participatory ergonomic programs. *Applied Ergonomics, 29*(6), 461–472.

Heaney, C. A., House, J., S. , Israel, B. A., & Mero, R. P. (1995). The relationship of organizational and social coping resources to employee coping behavior: A longitudinal analysis. *Work & Stress, 9*(4), 416–431.

Heaney, C. A., & van Ryn, M. (1990). Broadening the scope of worksite stress programs: A guiding framework. *American Journal of Health Promotion, 4*(6), 413–420.

House, J. S. (1981). *Work stress and social support.* Reading, MA: Addison-Wesley.

Hurrell, J. J., Nelson, D. L., & Simmons, B. L. (1998). Measuring job stressors and strains: Where have we been, where we are, and where we need to go. *Journal of Occupational Health Psychology, 3*(4), 368–389.

Israel, B. A., Baker, E. A., Goldenhar, L. M., Heaney, C. H., & Schurman, S. J. (1996). Occupational stress, safety, and health: Conceptual framework and principles for effective prevention interventions. *Journal of Occupational Health Psychology, 1*(3), 261–286.

Israel, B. A., Schurman, S. J., & House, J. S. (1989). Action research on occupational stress: Involving workers as researchers. *International Journal of Health Services, 19*(1), 135–155.

Janz, N., & Becker, M. (1984). The Health Belief Model: A decade later. *Health Education Quarterly, 11,* 1–47.

Jeffery, R. W. (1989). Risk behaviors and health: Contrasting individual and population perspectives. *American Psychologist, 44*(9), 1194–1202.

Kaminski, M. (2001). Unintended consequences: Organizational practices and their impact on workplace safety and productivity. *Journal of Occupational Health Psychology, 6*(2), 127–138.

Kanter, R. M., Stein, B. A., & Jick, T. D. (Eds.). (1992). *The challenge of organizational change: How companies experience it and leaders guide it.* New York: Free Press.

Katz, D., & Kahn, R. (1978). *The social psychology of organizations.* New York: Wiley.

Klein, K. J., Ralls, R. S., Smith-Major, V., & Douglas, C. (2000). Power and participation in the workplace. In J. Rappaport & E. Seidman (Eds.), *Handbook of community psychology* (pp. 273–295). New York: Kluwer Academic/Plenum.

Kotter, J. P. (1996). *Leading change.* Boston: Harvard Business School Press.

Kristensen, T. S. (2000). Workplace intervention studies. *Occupational Medicine: State of the Art Reviews, 15*(1), 293–305.

Lam, S. S. K., & Schaubroeck, J. (2000). A field experiment testing frontline opinion leaders as change agents. *Journal of Applied Psychology, 85*(6), 987–995.

Landsbergis, P. A., Cahill, J., & Schnall, P. (1999). The impact of lean production and related new systems of work organization on worker health. *Journal of Occupational Health Psychology, 4*(2), 108–130.

Landsbergis, P. A., & Vivona-Vaughan, E. (1995). Evaluation of an occupational stress intervention in a public agency. *Journal of Organizational Behavior, 16,* 29–48.

Lawler, E. E. (1992). *The ultimate advantage: Creating the high involvement organization.* San Francisco: Jossey-Bass.

Lawler, E. E. I., Mohrman, S. A., & Ledford, G. E., Jr. (1995). *Creating high performance organizations.* San Francisco: Jossey-Bass.

Lazarus, R., & Folkman, S. (1984). *Stress, appraisal, and coping.* New York: Springer.

Leana, C. R., Locke, E. A., & Schweiger, D. M. (1990). Fact and fiction in analyzing research on participative decision making: A critique of Cotton, Vollrath, Froggatt, Lengnick-Hall, and Jennings. *Academy of Management Review, 15*(1), 137–146.

Levy, B. S., & Wegman, D. H. (Eds.). (2000). *Occupational health: Recognizing and preventing work-related disease and injury* (4th ed.). Philadelphia: Lippincott, Williams, & Wilkins.

Lewin, K. (1951). Field theory and learning. In D. Cartwright (Ed.), *Field theory in social science: Select theoretical papers* (pp. 60–86). New York: Harper-Collins.

Macy, B. A., & Izumi, H. (1993). Organizational change, design, and work innovation: A meta-analysis of 131 North American field studies—1961–1991. In R. W. a. P. Woodman (Ed.), *Research in organizational change and development* (Vol. 7, pp. 235–313). Greenwich CT: JAI.

McGuire, W. (1973). Persuasion, resistance, and attitude change. In I. deSola Pool & W. Schramm (Eds.), *Handbook of communication*. Chicago: Rand-McNally.

Menaghan, E., & Merves, E. (1984). Coping with occupational problems: The limits of individual efforts. *Journal of Health and Social Behavior, 25*(4), 406–423.

Molinsky, A. L. (1999). Sanding down the edges: Paradoxical impediments to organizational change. *Journal of Applied Behavioral Science, 35*(1), 8–24.

Nadler, D. A. (1998). *Champions of change: How CEOs and their companies are mastering the skills of radical change.* San Francisco: Jossey-Bass.

National Institute for Occupational Safety and Health. (1999). *National Occupational Research Agenda Update, 21 Priorities for the 21st Century* (DHHS Publication #99-124). Washington, DC: Author.

Neuman, J. E. (1989). Why people don't participate in organizational change. *Research in Organizational Change and Development, 3,* 181–212.

O'Donnell, M. P. (Ed.). (2001). *Health promotion in the workplace* (3rd ed.). Albany, NY: Delmar.

Parcel, G. S., Perry, C. L., & Taylor, W. C. (1990). Beyond demonstration: Diffusion of health promotion innovations. In N. Bracht (Ed.), *Health promotion at the community level.* Thousand Oaks, CA: Sage.

Parkes, K. (1990). Coping, negative affectivity, and the work environment: Additive and interactive predictors of mental health. *Journal of Applied Psychology, 75*(4), 399–409.

Pfeffer, J. (1998). *The human equation: Building profits by putting people first.* Boston: Harvard Business School Press.

Porras, J. I., & Robertson, P. J. (1992). Organizational development: Theory, practice, and research. In M. D. Dunnette & L. M. Hough (Eds.), *Handbook of industrial and organizational psychology* (2nd ed., Vol. 3, pp. 719–822). Palo Alto, CA: Consulting Psychologist Press.

Prochaska, J. O., DiClemente, C. C., & Norcross, J. C. (1992). In search of how people change: Applications to the addictive behaviors. *American Psychologist, 47*(9), 1102–1114.

Quick, J. C. (1997). Idiographic research in organizational behavior. In C. L. a. K. Cooper (Ed.), *Creating tomorrow's organizations: A handbook for future research in organizational behavior* (pp. 475–492). Chichester, UK: John Wiley & Sons.

Rivara, F., & Thompson, D. C. (2000). Systematic reviews of injury-prevention strategies for occupational injuries: An overview. *American Journal of Preventive Medicine, 18*(4S), 1–3.

Robertson, A., & Minkler, M. (1994). New health promotion movement: A critical examination. *Health Education Quarterly, 21,* 295–313.

Rogers, E. M. (1995). *Diffusion of innovation* (4th ed.). New York: Free Press.

Rohrbach, L. A., D'Onofrio, C., Backer, T., & Montgomery, S. (1997). Diffusion of school-based substance abuse prevention programs. *American Behavioral Scientist, 39,* 919–934.

Schein, E. H. (1987). *Process consulting.* Reading, MA: Addison-Wesley.

Selye, H. (1993). History of the stress concept. In L. Goldberger & S. Breznitz (Eds.), *Handbook of stress: Theoretical and clinical aspects* (2nd ed., pp. 1–20). New York: Free Press.

Sinclair, R. C., Gershon, R. M., Murphy, L. R., & Goldenhar, L. M. (1996). Operationalizing theoretical constructs in bloodborne pathogens training curriculum. *Health Education Quarterly, 23*(2), 238–255.

Smith, D. W., Steckler, A., McCormick, L. K., & McLeroy, K. R. (1995). Lessons learned about disseminating health curricula to schools. *Journal of Health Education, 26,* 37–43.

Solberg, L. I., Kottke, T. E., & Brekke, M. L. (1998). Will primary care clinics organize themselves to improve the delivery of preventive services? A randomized controlled trial. *Preventive Medicine, 27,* 623–631.

Solberg, L. I., Kottke, T. E., Brekke, M. L., Conn, S. A., Calomeni, C. A., & Conboy, K. S. (1998). Delivering clinical preventive services is a systems problem. *Annals of Behavioral Medicine, 19,* 271–278.

Sorensen, G., Stoddard, A., Hammond, S. K., Hebert, J. R., Avrunin, J. S., & Oskene, J. K. (1996). Double jeopardy: Workplace hazards and behavioral risks for craftspersons and laborers. *American Journal of Health Promotion, 10*(5), 355–363.

Stokols, D. (1996). Translating social ecological theory into guidelines for community health promotion. *American Journal of Health Promotion, 10*(4), 282–298.

U.S. Department of Health and Human Services (U.S. DHHS). (1993). 1992 national survey of worksite health promotion activities: Summary. *American Journal of Health Promotion, 7,* 452–464.

U.S. General Accounting Office (GAO). (1991). *OSHA action needed to improve compliance with hazard communication standard.* Washington DC: Author.

Wagner, J. A. I. (1994). Participation's effects on performance and satisfaction: A reconsideration of research evidence. *Academy of Management Review, 19,* 312–330.

Walsh, D. C., Jennings, S. E., Mangione, T., & Merrigan, D. M. (1991). Health promotion versus health protection? Employees' perceptions and concerns. *Journal of Public Health Policy, 12,* 148–164.

Wilson, J. R., & Haines, H. M. (1997). Participatory ergonomics. In G. Salvendy (Ed.), *Handbook of human factors and ergonomics* (2nd ed., pp. 490–513). New York: Wiley.

Wilson, M. G., Holman, P., B., & Hammock, A. (1996). A comprehensive review of the effects of worksite health promotion on health-related outcomes. *American Journal of Health Promotion, 10*(6), 429–435.

Witte, K., Peterson, T. R., Vallabhan, S., Stephenson, M. T., Plugge, C. D., Givens, V. K., Todd, J. D., Becktold, M. G., Hyde, M. K., & Jarrett, R. (1992). Preventing tractor-related injuries and deaths in rural populations: Using a persuasive health message framework in formative evaluation research. *International Quarterly of Community Health Education, 13*(3), 219–251.

16

Job Stress Interventions and Organization of Work

Norbert K. Semmer

Most attempts to prevent stress at the worksite are directed toward the individual (Ganster, 1995; Ganster & Murphy, 2000; Ivancevich, Matteson, Freedman, & Philips, 1990; Kompier & Cooper, 1999b; Kompier & Kristensen, 2000; Murphy, 1996; Quick, Quick, Nelson, & Hurrell, 1997). Often, it is suggested that more emphasis be placed on changing aspects of the work itself, which, after all, are the supposed causes of stress and of the symptoms resulting from prolonged experience of stress.

The emphasis on changing people and their behaviors is understandable. Changing organizations implies changing a complex social system. This is not easy to do, meets much resistance, and often has unintended side-effects. Compared to this, teaching coping skills to people is an activity that is much less disruptive to the daily routine of an organization. Furthermore, the emphasis on people's behavior reflects the domain of psychology. Finally, many people, including managers, tend to attribute people's stress symptoms to their alleged inability to cope, rather than to characteristics of the work environment (see Kompier & Kristensen, 2000). Nevertheless, this concentration on individuals and their behavior is one-sided, and it seems reasonable to suggest the work environment as a target for change as well. I emphasize "as well" rather than "instead." One sometimes hears the claim that all one needs to do is "remove the causes" of stress. This greatly underestimates the complex interplay between the environment, with its options and restrictions, on the one hand, and people, with their ways of dealing with these options and restrictions, on the other. It also underestimates the extent to which any work environment will have stressful aspects to it, and these often are connected to aspects that are stimulating and challenging.

Changes related to the work itself may imply either primary prevention—that is, creating working conditions that are not conducive to the development of stress symptoms for the healthy—or secondary preven-

I would like to thank Joe McGrath for his helpful comments on an earlier version of this manuscript.

325

tion—that is, preventing existing, but minor, stress symptoms from becoming chronic by altering aspects of the work environment that are responsible for them (see Quick et al., 1997, or Kompier & Kristensen, 2000). Many interventions are both primary and secondary in nature, being directed at a large number of people, some of whom may have problems and some not.

The Rationale for Change: Influences of Work Organization on Health and Well-Being

Despite many ambiguities and conflicting findings, it does seem fair to say that there now is sufficient evidence to conclude that stress at work can have an impact on people's health and well-being (e.g., Beehr, 1995; Ganster & Murphy, 2000; Kahn & Byosiere, 1992; Karasek & Theorell, 1990; Marmot, Siegrist, Theorell, & Feeney, 1999; Quick et al., 1997; Siegrist, 1998; Sonnentag & Frese, in press; Warr, 1999). Authors vary in how they characterize, classify, and model stress factors and resources at work. Despite differences in detail, however, there also seems to be considerable common ground on which most experts in the field would agree.

On a very general level, one can distinguish between (a) features of tasks (such as complexity, variety, and level of stimulation involved); (b) the conditions under which tasks have to be performed (such as working time, ergonomic conditions, speed); (c) role requirements, especially when ambiguous or conflicting; (d) social conditions (such as conflicts, social support, appreciation, and fairness); and (e) wider organizational conditions (such as prospects for development, job security, and the like; Quick et al., 1997). Across all of these, control and influence play a major role (Karasek & Theorell, 1990; Spector, 1998), as do conditions that create impediments to successful task performance (Sonnentag & Frese, in press; Spector & Jex, 1998) and the rewards offered by organizations to people who have to deal with stressful situations (Siegrist, 1998).

Theory and research on stress imply that work should be challenging but not overdemanding. It should provide variability but also control. Role expectations should be reasonably clear and not overly conflicting. Work should not be overly demanding in terms of time, speed, or environmental and ergonomic conditions. It should be embedded in supportive social relationships as well as demanding but supportive leadership. It should be subject to a reasonable psychological contract that offers rewards and security. Most of these desiderata will be found again as features of attempts to prevent stress through changes in the organization of work.

Research on Attempts to Create Healthy Work

Attempts to create a healthy work may focus on ergonomic changes, job content, and work organization. Quick et al. (1997) referred to these as "task and physical demands." Many authors who emphasize changing the objective environment seem to imply this focus. Somewhat less attention has been given to the social environment, or what Quick et al. (1997) referred to as "role and interpersonal demands." Unclear and conflicting expectations have long been recognized as central aspects of stress (Kahn & Byosiere, 1992). Such features as conflicting relationships with others have been shown to constitute important "social stressors," whereas social support has been established as a possible source of relief (Beehr, 1995; Dormann & Zapf, 1999; Frese, 1999; Kahn & Byosiere, 1992; Spector & Jex, 1998). Interventions that reduce interpersonal tension and conflict, strengthen social ties, and clarify goals and expectations—for instance, by training supervisors—therefore may be expected to decrease unnecessary stress and to increase employee health (see McLeroy, Gottlieb, & Heaney, 2002). Such an approach is person-oriented with regard to supervisors but environment-oriented from the perspective of their subordinates.

The following sections concentrate, first, on attempted changes in technical and task demands and then on changes in the social environment. This discussion is followed by an account of comprehensive interventions that cannot be assigned to any one approach. Of course, there is hardly any intervention that does not target multiple aspects. Here, I have tried to categorize interventions according to their dominant focus.

Task and Technical Interventions

Some interventions concentrate on the characteristics of tasks themselves; others focus on working conditions.

Task characteristics. Many attempts to alter job design are not primarily rooted in stress research but rather in more general considerations about what constitutes "good" job design, with special emphasis on the damaging nature of simplified jobs (Parker & Wall, 1998). Potential remedies, such as job rotation and job enlargement, have been developed (Herzberg, Mausner, & Snyderman, 1959). These overlap considerably with the concept of "sociotechnical design" (Cherns, 1987; Trist & Bamforth, 1951), except that the latter focuses more on group work rather than individual job enrichment. Within this tradition, Hackman and Oldham's (e.g., 1980) Job Characteristics Model (JCM) probably had the greatest impact. Well-being is important in these concepts, but the focus often is more on motivation and satisfaction, which is why this approach has been labeled "motivational" (Campion & McClelland, 1993; Campion & Thayer, 1985). These concepts have stimulated attempts at job redesign both in the United Sates (Davis & Cherns, 1975) and in Europe (Parker & Wall, 1998; Ulich, 2001). This research cannot be summarized in this chapter, however. I will concentrate on studies that explicitly include measures of psychological (e.g., depression, anxiety), physical, or psychosomatic health and well-being, or measures that are indirectly related to these concepts such as absenteeism.

One of best-known studies in this area concerns an intervention in a department of a confectionery company (Wall & Clegg, 1981). It was prompted by problems such as "low morale," poor relationships between management and shopfloor, and concomitant problems such as high turnover. Changes concentrated on two aspects of the JCM: task identity (removing barriers in the production hall to make the whole process visible) and autonomy (the group decides on allocation of tasks, rest breaks, production speed, etc.). Measures were taken five months after the project started but before changes took effect, and then again 18 and 28 months later. Changes were observed in those aspects of the model that were targeted (perceived identity, autonomy), but not in skill variety and significance, making a Hawthorne effect unlikely. Intrinsic motivation, job satisfaction, performance, and mental health (assessed by the widely used General Health Questionnaire; GHQ; Goldberg, 1972, 1978) improved. These latter effects were observed for all three intervals ($t1–t2$, $t2–t3$, and $t1–t3$) but the long-term effects were strongest.

Despite the lack of a control group, the study demonstrates convincingly that the effects were specific to the attempted changes, thus lending credibility to attributing the effects on well-being to the increase in autonomy and identity. However, a later study that had a similar approach failed to replicate the findings with regard to mental health (Wall, Kemp, Jackson, & Clegg, 1986). That study investigated the implementation of autonomous working groups at a new site, using a quasi-experimental design. The groups were multiskilled (each member was expected to be able to carry out all tasks), they were responsible for task allocation, reaching production targets, ordering raw material, and training new recruits, and they participated in selecting new members. Results were favorable for job satisfaction, especially for intrinsic job satisfaction, and for productivity, in that the same level of performance was achieved with less personnel—that is, without a supervisor. Intrinsic motivation, organizational commitment, or mental health did not improve, however. The latter even declined for one experimental group, although this group's scores still compared favorably with the general population. Turnover actually increased. The authors attributed this to pressure for production and to a reluctance of team members to react to disciplinary problems. As a result of the latter, such problems were dealt with only at later stages, when problems had already become quite intense.

The Sheffield group has continued work in this area. A number of studies are summarized in Parker, Jackson, Sprigg, and Whybrow (1998). Some of them have also been published separately. Parker, Chmiel, and Wall (1997; Case Study No. 1 in Parker et al., 1998) investigated "strategic" (as opposed to "reactive") downsizing (see Kozlowski, Chao, Smith, & Hedlund, 1993). In particular, HR-policies were adopted to counter potentially negative effects. They included priority for naturally occurring turnover and assistance for those that had to leave. For the "survivors," an empowerment strategy was followed. After four years, cognitive job demands had increased, yet there was no change in strain. Evidently, the potentially negative effects of increased demands were offset by control and participation, which also had increased. Intrinsic satisfaction even improved. This study offers "indirect" evidence for control and participation interventions in that negative effects of downsizing did not occur when counteracted by these aspects.

Another piece of indirect evidence (Study No. 2 in Parker et al., 1998) relates to the introduction of a moving belt that reduced, rather than increased, autonomy, skill variety, and problem-solving demands. As expected, mental health deteriorated significantly. No such effect was observed for two (nonequivalent) control groups.

Case studies 3 and 4 demonstrate how more flexible work structures led to higher job satisfaction, a greater sense of fairness, and improved mental health, as well as reduced absenteeism, over an interval of 16 months. The approach in case 3 was participative, focusing on improvements in communication, broadening job scope, and changes in the appraisal and pay system. In case 4, similar attempts were not followed through stringently and were not embedded within a strategy of participation, and this intervention did not lead to such changes. It is noteworthy, however, that employee concern for those particular aspects of work for which they were given more responsibility did increase.

Several cases deal with teamwork. Sprigg, Jackson, and Parker (2000; case no. 7 in Parker et al., 1998) reported that introducing teamwork led to perceptions of better work characteristics, especially communication, influence over work, and cooperation. Job satisfaction and strain showed positive changes. These effects were, however, confined to a domain in which interdependence was high but did not occur in another domain where interdependence was low. This points to an important boundary condition. Two other cases (5 and 6) show that teamwork did result in more enriched jobs, but mainly for those who were strongly involved in its development—that is, the team leaders. In case number 5, team leaders displayed better mental health than "ordinary" team members seven months after the introduction of teamwork. This effect was linked to their enriched working conditions and occurred despite higher workload and role conflict. Similarly, in case number 6, the benefits of teamwork were stronger for team leaders than for "ordinary" members, except for one group in which the members were highly involved in decision making. These cases, therefore, point to another prerequisite for positive effects—that is, not just nominal participation but active involvement.

The Sheffield studies are noteworthy in several respects. First, they all contain data on important job characteristics (e.g., control, variety, demands, role conflict), on the General Health Questionnaire (GHQ), on job-related strain, and on job satisfaction, using standardized instruments. Second, data are analyzed by appropriate statistical methods. Third, the studies typically have a strong design. Where this was not possible, available data are analyzed carefully to check on the conclusions reached. Thus, Wall and Clegg (1981) can argue against a Hawthorne effect in spite of the lack of a control group, because the effects on perceived work characteristics concern very specifically only those aspects that were, indeed, changed. Also, group differences that can be linked to specific process variables strengthen conclusions in cases 5 and 6 of Parker et al. (1998), even though they are based on retrospective accounts. Fourth, these studies shed light on some important moderating mechanisms, such as interdependence for teamwork, or active participation for job design.

Most other studies in this area have more methodological limitations. Nevertheless, there are some reports that do contain valuable information despite problems in design or analysis. Terra (1995) reported an intervention aiming at autonomy, task identity, improved contact and cooperation, and responsibility for organizational tasks such as quality control, or scheduling of work hours. Supported by management and consultants, experienced employees ("design teams") described existing jobs and developed proposals for combining fragmented tasks, forming self-regulating groups, and establishing cross-functional training. Results are not described clearly, and statistical analyses are lacking. Nevertheless, it is worth noting that, over five years, productivity increased by 66%, and the sickness rate dropped by 50%. Also, absenteeism because of psychological health problems did not change in the target company but rose significantly in comparable plants during the same time period.

Smith and Zehel's (1992) study concerns wrappers, meat processors, and cutters in a meat processing company. Its original focus on upper extremity cumulative trauma disorders was broadened to more general aspects of stressful working conditions, such as machine pacing, short cycles, harsh physical environment, and the potential for job loss. "Focus groups" recommended job rotation, which was introduced. After one year, the wrappers showed reduced musculoskeletal problems and psychosomatic complaints and improved appraisal of working conditions (e.g., concerning pressure to work fast). Meat processors showed a tendency toward deterioration. The cutters profited somewhat in terms of musculoskeletal complaints, psychosomatic symptoms, and pressure to work hard, but reported less job control, and lower job satisfaction. The cutters, who originally had the most skilled and prestigious jobs, evidently resented the skill devaluation resulting from rotating to the other tasks more than they enjoyed the increase in variety. Again, the evaluation is reported rather globally; no statistical details are given.

Musculoskeletal problems that were believed to be responsible for high sickness and turnover rates triggered an intervention aiming at broadening the scope of activities for a group of 20 females workers in Sweden (Kvarnström, 1992). They were trained so that they could rotate among all tasks. Additional training was offered for quality management and for planning and coordinating production. Again, the information given is rather sparse, and no statistical analyses are reported. However, the effects reported are impressive, including a drop in turnover from 39% per year to 0, a reduction in absence because of sickness from 14% to about 5% for those who did not already have chronic musculoskeletal complaints at the outset, and an increase of delivery of output on time from 10 to 98%!

Kompier, Aust, van den Berg, and Siegrist (2000) reported data from a number of studies involving bus drivers. Of the three cases (3, 7, and 13) that have a strong emphasis on work organization, two reported a reduction in absence because of illness, although in one case (3) no numbers are given, and the effect in the other one (from 15 to 6 work days after two years in case 13) is not tested statistically. The third case (7) had no baseline because the company was new, but illness absence numbers are reported to be low for that branch. Subjective health or well-being measures are reported for one case (3), and there was no change. Work satisfaction improved in both cases where it was assessed (3 and 13). In case 13 (reported in more detail in Netterstrøm, 1999), significantly better values for perceived work content, work load, control, leadership climate, and physical work environment were found after nine months. However, only a relatively small number of the drivers participated in this survey.

Landsbergis and Vivona-Vaughan (1995) reported the establishment of "problem-solving committees" in two matched pairs of departments in a public health agency. One member of each pair was randomly assigned to intervention and to waiting status. Department 1 decided to develop a policy and procedures manual, so that procedural uncertainties would be reduced, to introduce a new phone answering system, develop a more equal distribution of work, and increase task variety. Department 2 opted for regular staff meetings, improved filing procedures, and "quiet hours" without phone calls. For Department 1, the effects were negligible for most variables, including strain, and were even negative regarding perceptions of work variables (e.g., goal clarity, skill use, decision latitude), and job satisfaction. For Department 2, results are less clear but also mostly in a negative direction. Depression and sleeping problems were unchanged. From the reasons given by the authors for these results, it seems that implementation was less than optimal. A later project that used a similar approach (Mikkelsen, Saksvik, & Landsbergis, 2000) did show positive effects in the intervention group as compared to the control group, concerning perceptions of most work-related variables (e.g., job demands, decision authority, social support). There also was a significant improvement in work-related stress but not in health complaints.

Summarizing these results, the Sheffield studies (with the exception of Wall et al., 1986) provide evidence for a positive effect on mental health of increases in autonomy, variety, skill use, and so forth. This conclusion is qualified by the fact that the effects are sometimes indirect (e.g., preventing effects of downsizing, demonstrating a deterioration after work simplification and deskilling). One study (Wall et al., 1986) reported an increase in turnover.

In the other studies, sickness rates seem to have been positively affected in four cases (two cases in Kompier et al., 2000; Kvarnström, 1992; and Terra 1995). The results by Mikkelsen et al. (2000) and by Smith and Zehel (1992) are somewhat ambivalent. Concerning health, there are some null findings in these studies (case 3 in Kompier et al., 2000, Landsbergis et al., 1995; Mikkelsen et al., 2000), but only one study that included some negative effects (Smith & Zehel, 1992). There are two negative effects for job satisfaction, one (Smith & Zehel, 1992) related to status problems, the other (Landsbergis & Vivona-Vaughan, 1995) to poor implementation.

Altogether, despite some ambiguities, these studies do indicate quite clearly that enriching tasks carries potential for ameliorating problems of health, well-being, and dissatisfaction. Meta-analyses by Fried and Ferris (1987) and Beekun (1989) support this conclusion for job satisfaction and absenteeism, respectively. However, "beneficial effects" sometimes relate to directly measured health variables, sometimes to absenteeism, and sometimes to job satisfaction, but typically not to all of these.

Changes in Working Conditions: Ergonomics, Time, and Workload. A number of projects are primarily concerned with ergonomic improvements with regard to, for instance, office furniture, drivers' seats, noise reduction, interior climate, and the like. Some are concerned with usability of computer programs. In addition, studies reported here deal with reducing workload or with flexible working time. These approaches would be labeled as "biological" or "perceptual–motor" by Campion and Thayer (1985).

Evans, Johansson, and Rydstedt (1999; Rydstedt, Johansson, & Evans, 1998) reported a study on improving working conditions for Stockholm bus drivers. Changes included (a) improved street maintenance, (b) broadening of road segments, (c) route reconfigurations, (d) improvements in separate bus lines, (e) more even spacing of and better access to bus stops, (f) traffic signal priority for buses, and (g) an automatic passenger information system. A three-wave survey showed a reduction in perceived workload after 1½ years, whereas perceived workload changes in a control group were not significant. No other differences were significant. In addition, a field study was concerned with the concrete driving experiences and included (a) questionnaires, (b) observation data by investigators riding on the bus, and (c) physiological measurements. This study yielded a significant decrease in observer-reported hassles, heart rate at work, and distress after work in the intervention group ($n = 10$) but not in the control group ($n = 31$). Furthermore, physiological changes and perceived stress correlated with driver experimental status (intervention–control). These latter correlations became nonsignificant when controlling for the hassle change score. Thus, the intervention had a positive impact on immediate reactions throughout the workday, but not with regard to long-term changes.

Two studies, both relating to driving examiners, report interventions concerning workload. Meijman, Mulder, van Dormolen, and Cremer (1992) investigated schedules of 9, 10, or 11 driving examinations per day, with each condition lasting a week. A number of effects were reported for the 11-exams condition: Tension at the end of the working day was higher, as were adrenalin levels. A mental task revealed reduced efficiency. Observers riding along in the cars noted that the examiners issued more warnings and rebukes concerning violation of rules. In addition, the failure rate for the two last exams of the day was drastically higher in this condition. Parkes (1986, cited in Parkes and Sparkes, 1998, case 3.8) also compared different numbers of exams per day. Perceived demands and anxiety were reduced, and cognitive performance and job satisfaction increased with reduced load. Exams were reduced from 9 to 8 per day as a result of the study, and perceived demands were still lower five years after the first assessment. Anxiety levels had increased marginally but were lower than could have been expected without the intervention (covariance analysis). So both of these studies document positive short-term effects, and Parkes's study yields indications of a positive long-term effect.

A project in a pharmaceutical company (Poelmans, Compernolle, De Neve, Buelens, & Rombouts, 1999) focused on ergonomic improvements, such as clear criteria for the purchase of furniture and adjusting posture and furniture. The program also involved stress management and supervisor training. It resulted in a significant reduction in absence because of sickness after one year.

In a "participatory ergonomic experiment" (Vink & Kompier, 1997), 45 employees working with visual display units (VDU) were provided with improved furniture and were trained as to its optimal adjustment. Musculoskeletal problems improved. Absenteeism dropped, but not significantly. A similar result was found in case 6 reported by Kompier, Geurts, Gründemann, Vink, and Smulders (1998). It involved mainly ergonomic changes and advice for brick layers and, in addition, focused on better preparation and planning of work. Again, there was a drop in absenteeism, but it was not statistically significant.

Cahill (1992) reported a case study in a child protective agency. Employees complained about high workload, poor information flow, and difficulties in retrieving information from the computer for local use. Changes based on recommendations by a labor–management stress committee were introduced, including quick local data access and the development of computer applications (e.g., for caseload trend analysis) to aid people in working. After six months, people reported more skill discretion, decision latitude, and job satisfaction. Strain did not change, however. Unfortunately, no numbers are given, and statistical analyses are not reported in detail. The lack of change in strain was interpreted in a positive way, because it had been expected that an ongoing reorganization would have created more strain.

Working time has been investigated in several studies. Flexible working time significantly decreased absenteeism in two experimental studies (Kim & Campagna, 1981; Narayanan & Nath, 1982), with the latter also reporting improvements in perceived flexibility and in social relations. In an experimental study by Dunham, Pierce, and Castaneda, 1987, study II), satisfaction and stress each showed nonsignificant improvements. These were not significant after a Bonferoni correction, however, and a sign test indicated a significant improvement overall. There were indications that, especially in the beginning, the flextime arrangement was associated with some problems of coordination and interference with activities. Effects on family and social life were perceived to be positive.

Two of the cases involving bus drivers described in Kompier, Aust, et al. (2000, cases 1 and 2) have an emphasis on working time, such as reduced hours for older or disabled drivers, and report health-related data. Both absences because of sickness and work disability improved after five years in case 1, but there was no statistical testing. Case 2 showed improvements in low back and neck pain as well as in subjective health and well-being after one year, plus a nonsignificant drop in a risk score for cardiovascular disease (CVD). Results for the second case are convincing.

Summarizing these results for the seven workload and ergonomic studies, we find clear short-term benefits in strain in three studies (Evans et al., 1999; Meijman et al., 1992; Parkes, 1986, cited in Parkes & Sparks, 1998), two of which (Evans et al., 1999; Meijman et al., 1992) involve physiological measures.

Long-term results for strain are less clear. Of the four studies that report on it, a positive effect may be accepted, although cautiously, for the Parkes study (Parkes & Sparkes, 1998), and musculoskeletal complaints clearly drop in the Vink and Kompier (1997) study. Evans et al. (1999) and Cahill (1992) report no long-term effect, although in the Cahill study this might be interpreted positively in light of an ongoing reorganization. Absenteeism is reduced in all three cases where it is reported (Kompier et al., 1998, case 6; Poelmans et al., 1999; Vink & Kompier, 1997) but significantly so only in the Poelmans study. Finally, perception of working conditions improved in the Stockholm bus driver study (Evans et al., 1999; Rydstedt et al., 1998) and in Cahill (1992). This latter study also reports an increase in job satisfaction, as do Parkes and Sparkes (1998).

In the five time studies, absence because of sickness dropped in all three studies that measured it, in two of them significantly (Kim & Campagna, 1981; Narayanan & Nath, 1982). Likewise, strain and health data improved in all three studies that assessed it (Dunham et al., 1987; Kompier, Aust, et al., 2000, cases 1 and 2), but significantly so only in the last of these. Job satisfaction and perceptions of working conditions were measured in two studies, and each found an improvement in one of them (Dunham et al., 1987: job satisfaction; Narayana & Nath, 1982: working conditions). Dunham et al. also found perceived improvements in family and social life.

Thus, for all 12 studies, there are clear short-term health and strain effects in all three studies that measured them. There are indications for effects in the longer term in six out of seven studies that report on them, but only three of those are significant. Of the seven studies that report long-term effects, only one clearly yields no effect at all. Three of them report positive and significant changes, two yield positive but nonsignificant changes, and one (Cahill, 1992) reports no change where a higher level of strain might have been expected. Thus, six out of these seven studies show some indication of a positive effect. Absence because of illness is reduced in all six studies that measure it, although significantly so in only three. Finally, job satisfaction increases in all three studies that report on it, significantly so in two of them. Four studies report data on perception of working (or, in one case, living) conditions, and all were positive.

Overall, results refer to different measures of variables and to different time frames. Some results are clearly positive, some are not, and the different measures do not always converge. It is worth noting, though, that in no case was there significant deterioration. So, again, a cautiously positive evaluation seems justified, in the sense that these interventions do show potential for positive effects, although they do not guarantee them, and do not show much potential for negative effects. It seems difficult to predict which outcome variables will be affected.

Improving Role Clarity and Social Relationships

As argued earlier, interventions that reduce interpersonal conflict, strengthen social ties, and clarify goals and expectations might decrease unnecessary stress and increase health. However, although concepts and methods to implement them have been developed for team and leadership training (Tannenbaum & Yukl, 1992) and for organizational development (Porras & Robertson, 1992), these areas have not been strongly linked to stress research (see, however, Golembiewski, Hilles, & Daly, 1987; Numeroff, 1987). One finds only a few studies concerned with stress that focus on this type of intervention (see Quick et al., 1997).

In a study by Quick (1979), goal setting by supervisor–employee interaction significantly reduced role conflict and role ambiguity. A reduction in absenteeism was demonstrated after five months but not maintained after eight months. Quick, Kulisch, Jones, O'Connor, and Peters (1981, cited in Quick et al., 1997) could not replicate the positive effects on role problems, and absenteeism actually increased. It seems likely that positive effects of this kind of intervention depend strongly on a participatory approach, which was more characteristic of the first than of the second study (see Quick et al., 1997).

In a field experiment by Schaubroeck, Ganster, Sime, and Dittman (1993), managers clarified roles among themselves and engaged in dyadic role clarification with subordinates. After three months, role ambiguity was reduced, and satisfaction with supervisors had increased. There were no effects on absenteeism, physical symptoms, and strain. The extent to which employees perceived role clarification behaviors by their superiors was related to psychological health. Moreover, there were indications that those with higher levels of role conflict and ambiguity were benefiting more. Role conflict was reduced in the control group as well, which the authors attributed to the initial responsibility-charting among managers.

Golembiewski et al. (1987) used an organizational development (OD) intervention that concentrated on increasing possibilities for internal promotion and clarifying career-progression paths. Perceptions of working conditions (feeling controlled, work pressure, peer cohesion, supervisor support, and clarity) improved, burnout was reduced, and turnover dropped substantially. The intervention was confounded with an ongoing reorganization, but one would expect this to weaken rather than strengthen the effects of the OD intervention.

Two of the cases reported by Kompier, Aust, et al. (2000) focused on improving communication (4) and performance appraisal and feedback (5). Both reported a significant reduction in absenteeism. Other measures showed no effects, except for improved well-being for those in case 5 who also had received stress-management training.

Cecil and Forman (1990) compared stress-inoculation training to co-worker support groups and controls, and found only stress-inoculation training effective in reducing perceived stress.

Bagnara, Baldasseroni, Parlangei, Tadei, and Tartaglia (1999) reported the establishment of groups in which student nurses could share experiences and had experts as mentors. Group meetings were over and above normal working activity. Such normal working activity characterized the control condition. Results show improvements in anxiety, GHQ, and self-esteem, but with the exception of the GHQ these were found in the control group as well. There are indications that those who initially had high GHQ scores improved more when exposed to the experimental condition, but the statistical analyses reported are not sophisticated enough to be sure about this.

Heaney, Price, and Rafferty (1995) presented an experimental intervention that aimed at increasing the competence and propensity of participants to recognize and mobilize social support and to use problem-solving techniques in groups. Participants were employees who were providing care for mentally ill or disabled people. Participants were expected to train their peers. After three months, significant improvements were found for the participants concerning supervisor support and feedback, self-appraisal of coping, team functioning, and depressive and psychosomatic symptoms. Effects were weaker when peers were included. Additional analyses identified characteristics of people who were at risk for deterioration in important variables, such as well-being. This high-risk subgroup did show a decline in well-being in the control group but not in the intervention group.

Jackson (1983, 1984) varied participation in decision making experimentally, increasing meetings from once to twice per month. This was combined with training for supervisors to enhance the quality of the meetings. The experimental manipulation increased employees' perceived influence and reduced both role conflict and role ambiguity. The two role strains were, in turn, related to general strain (tension), and both tension and perceived influence were related to job satisfaction and turnover intention. Strain was negatively related to absenteeism, which was interpreted by Jackson to indicate that absenteeism was used as a way of preventing strain from escalating (see Hackett & Bycio, 1996).

Schweiger and DeNisi (1991) reported on the effects of communication about an imminent merger in two companies. One company made efforts to disseminate honest information—for example, by a telephone hot line and regular meetings. Uncertainty, stress, job satisfaction, and the perception of the company as trustworthy and caring all got *worse* in both plants. These developments continued, however, in the control plant but stabilized in the experimental plant. There is no information on the effects of the merger itself, but the study does indicate that honest information can buffer the negative effects of anticipating threatening developments. The authors stress the symbolic value of the effort undertaken, communicating to employees the company's caring and concern, and thus increasing perceptions of fairness.

Summarizing these studies, it appears that interventions aiming at role clarification and feedback have a good chance of affecting role ambiguity and, perhaps, role conflict. There are some, but not very consistent, effects on absenteeism. Effects on strain and health are only reported by Golembiewski et al. (1987). The Schaubroeck et al. (1993) study contains some hints on moderating variables, such as perceived strength of intervention.

Interventions that focus on social support were effective in only one of three cases (Heaney et al., 1995). This study demonstrated effects on a rather wide array of outcomes.

The Jackson study shows that increasing people's sense of influence can improve strain, as well as job satisfaction and turnover intentions. Finally, Schweiger and DeNisi (1991) showed the potential of providing honest and open communication in times of anticipated crisis.

Overall, results imply that social interventions do have the potential for positive effects. These effects, however, are by no means certain, and, again, it is difficult to predict which outcome will be influenced by which interventions. Effects seem most likely for those variables that are directly targeted but more difficult to attain for strain and strain-related variables. Of the latter, effects on job satisfaction appear to be most likely. The strength of the intervention and active participation may be modifying variables.

Multiple Changes

Of course, many of the studies discussed so far had several targets. Nevertheless, it seemed easier to identify a major focus in them than in the five studies that follow.

Theorell and Wahlstedt (1999) and Wahlstedt and Edling (1997) reported changes in a postal-sorting terminal, including (a) the forming of new production areas, each with its own budget, and with a smaller number of supervisors, so that staff influence on the work situation was increased; (b) a new status for "senior postmen"; (c) hiring new people; (d) introducing work groups; (e) the possibility of obtaining hot meals; and (f) a change in the shift system. After one year, perceived skill discretion and authority in decision making had increased. Sick leave was reduced, but sleep problems increased. Gastrointestinal complaints did not change on average. Perceived amount of change in working conditions did, however, correlate with reduced sleep problems and gastrointestinal complaints.

An intervention in a mail delivery office (Theorell & Wahlstedt, 1999) included (a) more control and social support, (b) clarification of management roles, (c) better information, (d) more staff, and (e) a new sorter table (to reduce musculoskeletal problems). Changes were implemented in two stations, more so in one of them, and employees could choose at which station they wanted to work. After a year, perceived ergonomic conditions (e.g., repetitive arm movements) had not changed, social support had improved in the more modern station, and decision authority had improved in the more traditional site. Psychological demands had decreased in both stations. Musculoskeletal problems decreased, although significantly only at the more modern site. These changes were related to improvements in social support by superiors and were largely confined to those under the age of 35.

Kawakami, Araki, Kawashima, Masumoto, and Hayashi (1997) reported an attempt to reduce stressors by (a) improving machine speed and performance, (b) reducing the number of checks required, (c) increasing training, (d) standardizing procedures, and (e) enhancing social support by supervisors. After one year, perception of working conditions had not changed. There were no effects for blood pressure. Depressive symptoms decreased significantly in the intervention group but not in the control group. The group × time interaction was significant. A similar effect was found for sick leave.

One case that is reported by Kompier, Aust, et al. (2000, case 8) included (a) reorganization of work, (b) establishment of group work (including own coordination of shift schedules), (c) more free weekends, (d) regular meetings, (e) ergonomic improvements, and (f) health education. Both absenteeism and turnover decreased, and job satisfaction increased.

One of a number of cases reported by Kompier et al. (1998, case 3) reported an improvement in social climate and work atmosphere following the introduction of semiautonomous groups, along with ergonomic improvements and better management of absenteeism. This study also reports a significant decrease in absenteeism.[1]

A project in the Finish forest industry (Kalimo & Toppinen, 1999) included (a) work reorganization (e.g., by integrating production, maintenance, and support), (b) training (e.g., concerning leadership), and (c) improved cooperation and communication. After two years, and then again after ten years, more respondents reported improvements than deteriorations, most notably for communication with superiors, challenging work, and autonomy. However, perceived time pressure had increased. Health indicators did not change.

A Dutch hospital introduced (a) job enrichment and improved work organization; (b) ergonomic and technical changes; (c) improved work–rest schedules; (d) supervisor training; and (e) health promotion activities, such as stress management (Lourijsen, Houtman, Kompier, & Gründemann, 1999). After three years, perceived job content, emotional stress, and appreciation had improved but work pace was perceived to have increased. Emotional exhaustion and health complaints were unchanged. Moreover, at postmeasurement, a control hospital, which also was very active, had improved organization of work and work pace and had fewer complaints

---

[1] These authors report a number of other cases, which used some kind of management of absenteeism. Even though employees may positively evaluate absenteeism consultancy, it seems doubtful if it can be regarded as stress prevention. The fact that most of these studies succeeded in reducing absenteeism might reflect normative changes ("absence culture") rather than changes in the stressfulness of work (see Spector, 1997). Reduced absenteeism can therefore be attributed to changes in working conditions only in the study reported.

about work characteristics than did the intervention hospital. However, the significant drop in absenteeism at the intervention hospital is impressive, starting out higher than both the comparison hospital and the national average but ending lowest.

In Europe, particularly in Germany, "health circles" have become popular (Beermann, Kuhn, & Kompier, 1999). They are similar to quality circles, and topics often overlap, because the problems that cause stress often are the same as those that impair quality (Schurman & Israel, 1995). Typically, groups meet for a number of sessions, usually with an external moderator. Risks and complaints are assessed (by interview, questionnaire, or analysis of company data) and discussed in the circle, and suggestions are handed over to management. Topics concern, for example, ergonomic changes, improvement of communication and training, and work reorganization (Beermann et al., 1999; Ducki, Jenewein, & Knoblich, 1998; Slesina, Beuels, & Sochert, 1998).[2] "Evaluations" generally are rather positive, but they typically relate to satisfaction with the circle, sometimes to the number of suggestions implemented (estimated to be about one third by Slesina et al., 1998) but hardly ever to perceived improvements in working conditions or to health parameters. Friczewski (1994) reported significant improvement in social relations and in physical and psychological well-being. Ducki et al. (1998) reported that absenteeism decreased in that part of a company where a health circle was implemented but increased in the others. Pfaff and Bentz (2000) report a perceived increase in the quality of supervision and social relationships following a one-day health workshop. A health circle in a transport company resulted in changes in ergonomics, shift systems, teamwork structure, more open communication, and the institution of behavior change programs. Absenteeism dropped from 13.5 to less than 10% (Marstedt & Mergner, 1995). Kornadt, Schmook, Wilm, and Hertel (2000) found significant improvements regarding ergonomics, time management, and communication among teleworkers. Thus, there are promising signs but few hard data to support clear conclusions.

The health circle concept has much in common with the participatory action research (PAR) concept (Israel, Baker, Goldenhar, Heaney, & Schurman, 1996; Parkes & Sparkes, 1998; Schurman & Israel, 1995). Both advocate active participation and the development of proposals based on the assessment of local circumstances rather than on premanufactured packages. Reports about the PAR approach are often informative, especially with regard to process evaluation and identification of crucial principles and pitfalls but not very stringent with regard to outcome evaluation.

The studies discussed in this section are quite diverse. What seems striking is the drop in absenteeism in many cases—sometimes occurring in conjunction with improved perceptions of working conditions but in other

---

[2]Health circles might seem similar to health committees in U.S. health promotion projects, such as EAPs. These latter programs, however, typically focus on behavior change, and the environmental component (e.g., fitness facilities, smoking bans, healthy food, or support groups) typically refers to an environment that supports specific health behaviors, not to job design or work organization (Gebhardt & Crump, 1990; O'Donnell, 2002).

cases accompanied by both positive and negative changes. Those negative changes often involve increases in time pressure. Changes in health are mixed, with many null findings and findings that differ for various indicators. For health circles, there are a few promising signs but too little research to allow clear conclusions.

Plausible Approaches, Mixed Results: Problems, Conclusions, Recommendations

Altogether, the studies reported convey the impression that work-related interventions do have potential for positive effects. It is, however, hard to predict specifically which changes are likely to occur, and this prediction becomes more difficult the more distant the variables in question are from the immediate intervention. Thus, many studies report changes in the perception of the work variables they targeted (e.g., autonomy and variety, role ambiguity, and supervisor support). Sometimes, these changes affect stress, well-being, and health variables, sometimes they do not, sometimes they affect some but not others. The outcomes that seem to have the greatest chance of improvement are job satisfaction and absenteeism. However, absenteeism sometimes is reduced without concomitant changes in perceived working characteristics. Finally, workload and, to some degree, turnover, seem to be especially prone to deteriorate, even when other features improve.

Some authors draw very pessimistic conclusions from this state of affairs (e.g., Briner & Reynolds, 1999). Should we, however, expect an unequivocal "yes" to a question as general as "does organizational stress intervention attain its objectives?" The answer to that broad question must inevitably be, "sometimes, and on some measures," and the main issue then becomes determining what can be expected when. We are far from answering that question; but some answers and, in some cases, some refinements of the question, can be suggested. I will first consider issues of outcome measures and discuss whether uniform outcomes across outcome measures ought to be expected. This will be followed by suggestions concerning process variables and by more general methodological remarks. The chapter will close with a short discussion of prerequisites and pitfalls for interventions.

Outcome Measures

The interventions discussed have as their immediate targets a change in working conditions (in a broad sense). Measures such as perceived autonomy in the case of job enrichment, impediments in ergonomic interventions, or role ambiguity in role clarification studies therefore seem especially important. They are, in a sense, a "manipulation check." If these variables do not change, the intervention did not reach its proximal goal. It therefore cannot be expected to attain more distal goals (although this is not impossible).

The next step in the chain concerns measures of health and well-being. Here we find measures of depression, anxiety, and psychosomatic complaints, back and neck pain, medically diagnosed illness, or physiological risk factors. Unfortunately, formulations on stress at work yield rather few indications of specific relationships between stress factors and indicators of well-being that could guide us in choosing among the many measures possible. The meaning of different indicators of well-being is not widely discussed in that literature, and the choice of measures often does not seem to be based on such considerations.

Warr (1990, 1999) suggested three dimensions of well-being, based on the circumplex model of emotion: displeasure versus pleasure (usually equated with satisfaction), anxiety versus comfort, and enthusiasm versus depression. This model could be used to choose measures and to make sure that each dimension is represented. The dimensions are correlated, and they can be combined into a meta-construct of subjective well-being (Diener, 1994). They are, however, not identical, and it is perfectly possible to find effects on one dimension but not the other. The same applies to physiological measures. Arousal, when looked at closely, is not a unitary phenomenon (Meijman & Mulder, 1998), and its various indicators (which are likely to have different temporal characteristics) cannot be expected to all go up or down at the same time.

There are indications that various dimensions of work have specific relations to aspects of well-being. Thus, content variables (e.g., autonomy) seem to have stronger relations to satisfaction, whereas demand variables (e.g., workload) correlate more with high-arousal negative affect, such as anxiety, or psychosomatic symptoms (Warr, 1990; see also Campion, 1988; Houkes, Janssen, de Jonge, & Nijhuis, 2001). Divergent effects are possible, as when people in high-level jobs are more satisfied but at the same time report more anxiety (Warr, 1999). Similarly, Smith and Zehel (1992) reported that cutters who rotated between tasks of different status showed an improvement in health parameters but deterioration in job satisfaction, which seems to be more sensitive to the status component.

All this implies that it is not very reasonable to expect all indicators of well-being and health to show changes in means after a specific time following intervention. There may be differential impact, and there are different time frames (Dormann & Zapf, 2002; McGrath & Beehr, 1990). Improvement on *some* measures might be a perfectly reasonable result. And even if some other measures deteriorate, one might consider looking at a balance of positive and negative effects, because in many cases, trade-offs will be involved.

Two outcome measures that are often used deserve a special comment. *Job satisfaction* is sometimes regarded with skepticism (Sonnentag, 1996), mainly because it might be the consequence of lowered standards (resulting in what has been called "resigned job satisfaction"—Bruggemann, 1974, see also Büssing, Bissels, Fuchs, & Perrar, 1999; Semmer, 1996). Nevertheless, global job satisfaction seems to be quite a sensitive indicator of a general evaluation of the work situation, which is related to variables such as life satisfaction and general well-being (Diener, 1994), turnover (Baillod & Semmer, 1994), a number of job-related behaviors (Roznowski & Hulin, 1992), and—contrary to common belief—performance (Judge, Thoresen, Bono, & Patton, 2001). *Absenteeism,* if assessed by company records, has the advantage of being independent of self-report and of being especially convincing to employers. It is, however, affected by many factors, such as normative considerations (Spector, 1997). In light of this, the impressive reductions in absenteeism sometimes found are rather surprising. They are likely to be connected to the fact that an intervention is taking place, and that the organization is therefore perceived as showing concern about and doing something for its employees. This is akin to a Hawthorne effect.

Creating "Good" Working Conditions Versus Trade-Offs

I argued earlier that a uniform effect on outcome measures might not be a reasonable expectation. A similar argument can be made about working conditions. Most good things come with a price, and that applies to improvements in working conditions as well.

An illustrative example is a study concerning police officers (Orth-Gomér, 1983). Changing a shift system from counterclockwise to clockwise rotation had led to improvements on a number of health-related parameters. Nevertheless, the officers went back to their old schedule, because it gave them larger blocks of free time. Thus, the new system was "healthier," but at the same time interfered more with private life. (It is interesting to note that after the study was finished, the police officers reversed their decision and opted for the "healthy" variant, but the point is that there are trade-offs involved.)

Campion and Thayer (Campion, 1988; Campion & Thayer, 1985) argued that changes that correspond to the motivational model (i.e., work content variables, as in job enrichment) increase satisfaction but often also workload, because mental demands increase. And indeed, higher workload does seem to be a common side-effect of job enrichment and teamwork interventions (e.g., Antoni, 1997; Gerst, Hardwig, Kuhlmann, & Schumann, 1994). Some of this may be inherent in enrichment concepts, because these imply more parameters to be accounted for, more coordination and planning efforts, and so forth. Some of it may be a result of implementation problems, such as increased task assignments going along with enriched jobs. In any case, however, there are trade-offs to consider, and it may often be naïve to expect *only* positive effects. Other aspects to be considered are loss of status (e.g., for superiors or specialists) and increased group conflicts as a result of group autonomy (because groups cannot "delegate" conflict-prone decisions to their superiors any more). Furthermore, the potential "status" aspect of stress factors deserves more attention. Sometimes people take pride in dealing with harsh conditions (Meara, 1974). Older train drivers sometimes opt for straining night rides on intercity long distance trains because these also carry the most prestige. Workers may resist removing some stressful aspects of their work, arguing that "this is a steel plant and not a girls' boarding school" (Slesina et al., 1998, p. 201). A good implementation policy might avoid, or attenuate, some of these effects, but probably not all of them. The question then may be whether a change has more advantages than disadvantages rather than whether it is "good" or not. Incidentally, from this perspective job satisfaction seems a particularly good measure, because it also implies weighting positive and negative aspects of one's work.

Process Considerations

Although quantitative analyses tell us about success or failure, process accounts may lead to more insight about the mechanisms involved (Griffiths, 1999; Kompier & Kristensen, 2000; Kristensen, 2000; Nytrø, Saksvik, Mikkelsen, Bohle, & Quinlan, 2000). Carefully documented qualitative accounts can be extremely informative about the dangers and pitfalls of worksite interventions (e.g., Schurman & Israel, 1995), and we should avoid a one-sided emphasis on quantitative accounts only.

Often, for instance, we do not learn much at all about the quality of the implementation. For example, how were facilitators trained, what mistakes did they make (e.g., in terms of "taking over," in terms of forming coalitions within an organization)? This makes it hard to know if failures were a result of poor concepts, poor implementation, obstruction by people inside the organization, or other factors. Also, we often learn little about the stress introduced by the change process itself. After all, most projects are run while everything else is going on, implying lack of time and resources for the project (Kompier, Cooper & Geurts, 2000) and many temptations to go back to old routines when faced with difficulties (Frei, Hugentobler, Schurmann, & Alioth, 1993). Kompier and coworkers (Kompier, Aust, et al., 2000; Kompier, Cooper, et al., 2000; Kompier & Cooper, 1999a; Kompier et al., 1998) provided good examples by including a section on "obstructing" and "stimulating" factors.

It is deplorable that the link between this area and other attempts to alter organizations is so weak. Thus, the literature on OD (Porras & Robertson, 1992), on Productivity Measurement and Enhancement System (ProMES; e.g., Pritchard, 1995), or on quality circles (e.g., Cordery, 1996) conveys many messages similar to those found in accounts of organizational stress interventions. The training literature suggests that the "posttraining environment" (such as support from supervisors in trying out new skills) is no less important than the training itself (Ford, Kozlowski, Kraiger, Salas, & Teachout, 1997). By contrast, much of the stress intervention literature seems to assume that a "good" intervention "maintains itself," so to speak.

Methodological Considerations

The poor methodological quality of many studies is often deplored (e.g., Beehr & O'Hara, 1987; Briner & Reynolds, 1999; Burke & Richardsen, 2000; Ivancevich & Matteson, 1987; Kompier & Kristensen, 2000). I will not discuss the more general of these issues (see Cook, Campbell, & Peracchio, 1990) nor the counterarguments regarding the difficulties of doing rigorous research in organizations (Griffiths, 1999; Kompier & Kristensen, 2000), because most readers undoubtedly are familiar with both. Rather, I will discuss a few more specific points.

One point concerns samples containing people with different characteristics and different status with regard to the target of the intervention. There often are differences between improvement for those who already have developed symptoms of stress and prevention for those who have not (see Bunce & Stephenson, 2000; Kompier & Kristensen, 2000). Many studies will contain participants from both populations. There is no reason to assume, however, that the effects will be equal for the two groups. Some symptoms may prevail even when the stress factors that caused them have been removed (Frese & Zapf, 1988), as when former shift workers are found to have more health problems than current shift workers (Frese & Semmer, 1986). For those without symptoms, on the other hand, there will not be much room for improvement (floor effect).

Another topic concerns attrition. The analyses reported by Heaney et al. (1995) are good examples for modeling the characteristics of those who have a high probability of not participating or of leaving their job. Analyses like these should be conducted more often.

With regard to long-term effects, it often is argued that evaluation lags are too short. Given the little we know about onset and disappearance of stress symptoms (Dormann & Zapf, in press; McGrath & Beehr, 1990), this is plausible. What is less plausible, however, is the underlying assumption that an intervention that has been well-implemented will be effective forever. Work environments are continuously changing. A new supervisor may change the whole working climate, may restrict or enhance people's autonomy; new colleagues have not gone through the original change process; new technology may be introduced, and so on. In my view, there is no way out of this dilemma. The longer the time frame, the less likely can effects be attributed to the original intervention. The only thing one could try to do is assess working conditions and possible health outcomes continuously. This might profitably be combined with a periodic review of the status of the project (see Pritchard, 1990, for a similar approach). Such reviews might uncover erosions of changes that were implemented, negative side-effects, discontinuities because of new demands, new technology, new people, and so forth, and suggest efforts to revive the project.

The question of trade-offs, already mentioned, applies also to "good designs." Indeed, some aspects of good designs are a threat to others. Thus, many measurement points over extended periods of time will improve the design in theory but may also increase reactivity of measures and the risk of attrition, and thus lead to biased samples and measures (Kompier &

Kristensen, 2000). Shorter measures may be a way out, but this will decrease their reliability. Again, a trade-off is necessary rather than seeking a solution without flaws.

There is reason to believe that statistical significance is being overemphasized (as in psychology in general; Smith, 1996). In most studies, samples will not be very large, which increases the danger of statistical Type II errors. It seems advisable to publish exact data on all effects, regardless of the statistical significance of the individual effect, so that they can be used in meta-analyses. Practical, rather than statistical, significance, should receive more attention, and methods for this have been developed (e.g., Jacobson & Revenstorf, 1988; cf., Bunce & Stephenson, 2000).

Also, we should be much more concerned with changing standards during interventions. A project may raise expectations that go well beyond what is finally implemented, and this might make changes that did occur look much smaller. Sometimes the meaning of a concept (e.g., autonomy) may change during a project, as participants talk and think about possibilities they might never have considered as being realistic for them before. Thus, beta and gamma changes (Golembiewski, Billinsley, & Yeager, 1976; Schaubroeck & Green, 1989; Thompson & Hunt, 1996) may occur, which, if undetected, lead to erroneous conclusions.

Finally, as many authors have stated, the value of case studies should be recognized more, and their role as a complement to (quasi-) experimental studies should be acknowledged (Griffiths, 1999; Kompier & Kristensen, 2000). This should not be taken to mean that no methodological rigor is required or that subjective impressions of change agents can be substituted for well-documented accounts of events. Rather than deploring poor designs on the one side, and the difficulties of implementing rigorous designs on the other, researchers should present the maximum information possible. As Kazdin (1981) pointed out, the real issue is whether we have good reasons to render alternative interpretations implausible. Case studies sometimes have unique possibilities for doing this—for instance, by temporally aligning (objectively recorded) effects with (objectively recorded) events. What types of data are recorded, therefore, may be of equal or greater importance than the overall design, and case studies with well-documented data can be extremely valuable.

Conclusion

In light of the problems just discussed, and in light of the many problems involved in changing organizations, the state of affairs seems less pessimistic than it appears at first—at least if one accepts that the issue is not one of attaining uniformly positive effects but rather one of a balance of effects. There are many positive findings, many null effects, but not very many negative ones—although intervening in a complex system will always run the risk of negative effects. Moreover, quality of studies seems to be improving, and we can expect to have a much better database in the years to come.

It also is important not to pit "person-oriented" and "work-oriented" approaches against each other. If anything, the evidence is stronger for person-oriented than for work-oriented interventions (Bamberg & Busch, 1996; Murphy, 1996; van der Klink, Blonk, Schene, & van Dijk, 2001), although the time effects are not so clear. Also, an increasing number of studies suggest that personal resources (e.g., self-efficacy) may be necessary for taking advantage of opportunities such as increased autonomy (De Rijk, Le Blanc, & Schaufeli, 1998; Jimmieson, 2000; Parker & Sprigg, 1999; Schaubroeck & Merritt, 1997). One effect of stress may be that it undermines the very resources needed to deal with it effectively (Semmer, 1996). Unless personal resources are strengthened by person-oriented approaches, changes in working conditions may not live up to their potential, or may even be resisted by those who need them most but who also have the greatest anxieties with regard to anticipated changes. The strong emphasis on active participation in practically all approaches (Aust, Peter, & Siegrist, 1997; Karasek & Theorell, 1990; Kompier & Cooper, 1999c; Kompier et al., 1998; Quick et al., 1997; Schurman & Israel, 1995; Slesina et al., 1998) reflects this concern. All this argues for a collaboration of person-oriented and work-oriented strategies.

Two additional remarks concern the role of experts and of management. Experts have a delicate role to play. They must provide information, advice, and facilitation but avoid becoming responsible for producing the changes. And they must avoid putting their own theories above client's concerns. Unless proposals are rooted in a diagnosis of problems in the specific context, they might reflect the experts' approach more than the problems of the organization. Especially, many problems do not involve the "big" issues suggested by theory, but rather seemingly trivial problems such as eliminating sources of draft, improving lighting, or having access to spare parts (Ducki et al., 1998; Slesina et al., 1998).

It is often noted that management support is crucial and difficult to achieve, but there is little information on how it can be achieved and maintained. Sometimes it is suggested that the cost-saving potential of interventions might convince management (see Cascio, 2000). However, the fact that many organizations are reluctant to conduct a careful evaluation suggests that cost savings may not be that important—or if they are, it is the *conviction* about cost savings that counts, and not hard data. Furthermore, managers themselves often indicate that other considerations are more important to them, and many rank health-related outcomes higher than cost saving (U.S. Department of Health and Human Services, 1992). It is my hunch that it is important *not* to "sell" projects to managers too hard. Rather, consultants should refrain from getting involved in projects in which management commitment is not assured, and they should make this clear from the outset. If commitment can be gained, it needs to entail time and effort allocated to the project, not just lip service.

My final remark concerns the "Hawthorne" effect. It is often labeled "unspecific"—that is, not directly related to the specifics of the intervention, sometimes with the connotation of being somehow artificial. If it is true, however, that stress at work has much to do with "daily humiliations"

(Cooper, Schabracq, & Winnubst, 1996), and that many problems result from lack of respect, fairness, and appreciation (Rutte & Messick, 1995), then sensing these elements both in one's interpersonal encounters and in one's tasks and working conditions may be at the heart of the problem rather than being "unspecific." If this is true, we should not avoid Hawthorne effects. Rather, we should try to achieve them.

References

Antoni, C. H. (1997). Soziale und ökonomische Effekte der Einführung teilautonomer Arbeitsgruppen—eine quasi-experimentelle Längsschnittstudie (Social and economic effects of introducing partially autonomous teams—A quasi-experimental longitudinal study). *Zeitschrift für Arbeits- und Organisationspsychologie, 41,* 131–142.

Aust, B. Peter, R., & Siegrist, J. (1997). Stress management in bus drivers: A pilot study based on the model of effort-reward imbalance. *International Journal of Stress Management, 4,* 297–305.

Bagnara, S., Baldasseroni, A., Parlangeli, O., Taddei, S., & Tartaglia, R. (1999). Italy: A school of nursing. In M. Kompier & C. Cooper (Eds.), *Preventing stress, improving productivity. European case studies in the workplace* (pp. 297–311). London: Routledge.

Baillod, J., & Semmer, N. (1994). Fluktuation und Berufsverläufe bei Computerfachleuten (Turnover and career paths of computer specialists). *Zeitschrift für Arbeits- und Organisationspsychologie, 38,* 152–163.

Bamberg, E., & Busch, C. (1996). Betriebliche Gesundheitsförderung durch Stressmanagementtraining: Eine Metaanalyse (quasi-)experimenteller Studien (Health promotion at the work site by stress management training: A meta-analysis of (quasi-) experimental studies). *Zeitschrift für Arbeits- und Organisationspsychologie, 40,* 127–137.

Beehr, T. A. (1995). *Psychological stress in the workplace.* London: Routledge.

Beehr, T. A., & O'Hara, L. (1987). Methodological designs for the evaluation of occupational stress interventions. In S. V. Kasl & C. L. Cooper (Eds.), *Research methods in stress and health psychology* (pp. 79–112). Chichester, UK: Wiley.

Beekun, R. I. (1989). Assessing the effectiveness of sociotechnical interventions: Antidote or fad? *Human Relations, 10,* 877–897.

Beermann, B., Kuhn, K., & Kompier, M. (1999). Germany: Reduction of stress by health circles. In M. Kompier & C. Cooper (Eds.), *Preventing stress, improving productivity. European case studies in the workplace* (pp. 222–241). London: Routledge.

Briner, T. B., & Reynolds, S. (1999). The costs, benefits, and limitations of organizational level stress interventions. *Journal of Organizational Behavior, 20,* 647–664.

Bruggemann, A. (1974). Zur Unterscheidung verschiedener Formen von "Arbeitszufriedenheit" (On different forms of "job satisfaction"). *Arbeit und Leistung, 28,* 281–284.

Bunce, D., & Stephenson, K. (2000). Statistical considerations in the interpretation of research on occupational stress management interventions. *Work & Stress, 14,* 197–212.

Burke, R. J., & Richardsen, A. M. (2000). Organizational-level interventions designed to reduce occupational stressors. In P. Dewe, M. Leiter, & T. Cox (Eds.), *Coping, health and organizations* (pp. 191–209). London: Taylor & Francis.

Büssing, A., Bissels, T., Fuchs, V., & Perrar, K.-M. (1999). A dynamic model of work satisfaction: qualitative approaches. *Human Relations, 52,* 999–1028.

Cahill, J. (1992). Computers and stress reduction in social service workers in New Jersey. In V. Di Martino (Ed.) *Preventing stress at work* (Conditions of work digest, 11 (2), pp. 197–203). Geneva: International Labour Office.

Campion, M. A. (1988). Interdisciplinary approaches to job design: A constructive replication with extensions. *Journal of Applied Psychology, 73,* 467–481.

Campion, M. A., & McClelland, C. L. (1993). Follow-up and extension of the interdisciplinary costs and benefits of enlarged jobs. *Journal of Applied Psychology, 78,* 339–351.

Campion, M. A. & Thayer, P. W. (1985). Development and field evaluation of an interdisciplinary measure of job design. *Journal of Applied Psychology, 70,* 29–43.

Cascio, W. F. (2000). *Costing human resources* (4th ed.). Cincinnati, OH: Southwestern College.

Cecil, M. A., & Forman, S. G. (1990). Effects of stress inoculation training and coworker support groups on teachers' stress. *Journal of School Psychology, 28,* 105–118.

Cherns, A. B. (1987). The principles of socio-technical design revisited. *Human Relations, 40,* 153–162.

Cook, T. D., Campbell, D. T., & Peracchio, L. (1990). Quasi experimentation. In M. D. Dunnette & L. M. Hough (Eds.), *Handbook of industrial and organizational psychology* (2nd ed., Vol. 1, pp. 491–576). Palo Alto, CA: Consulting Psychologists Press.

Cooper, C. L., Schabracq, M. J., & J. A. M. Winnubst (1996). Preface. In M. J. Schabracq, J. A. Winnubst, & C. L. Cooper (Eds.), *Handbook of work and health psychology* (pp. xiii–xv). Chichester, UK: Wiley.

Cordery, J. L. (1996). Autonomous work groups and quality circles. In M. A. West (Ed.), *Handbook of work group psychology* (pp. 225–246). Chichester, UK: Wiley.

Davis, L. E. & Cherns, A. B. (1975). *The quality of working life.* New York: Free Press.

De Rijk, A. E., Le Blanc, P. M., & Schaufeli, W. B. (1998). Active coping and need for control as moderators of the job demand–control model: Effects on burnout. *Journal of Occupational and Organizational Psychology, 71,* 1–18.

Diener, E. (1994). Assessing subjective well-being: Progress and opportunities. *Social Indicators Research, 31,* 103–157.

Dormann, C., & Zapf, D. (1999). Social support, social stressors at work, and depressive symptoms: Testing for main and moderating effects with structural equation in a three-wave longitudinal study. *Journal of Applied Psychology, 84,* 874–884.

Dormann, C. & Zapf, D. (2002). Social stressors at work, irritation, and depressive symptoms: Accounting for unmeasured third variables in a multi-wave study. *Journal of Occupational and Organizational Psychology, 75,* 33–58.

Ducki, A., Jenewein, R., & Knoblich, H. -J. (1998). Gesundheitszirkel—Ein Instrument der Organisationsentwicklung (Health circles—An OD instrument). In E. Bamberg, A. Ducki, & A. Metz (Eds.), *Betriebliche Gesundheitsförderung (Health promotion at the workplace;* pp. 267–281). Göttingen, Germany: Hogrefe.

Dunham, R. B., Pierce, J. L., & Castaneda, M. B. (1987). Alternative work schedules: Two field quasi-experiments. *Personnel Psychology, 40,* 215–242.

Evans, G. W., Johansson, G., & Rydstedt, L. (1999). Hassles on the job: A study of a job intervention with urban bus drivers. *Journal of Organizational Behavior, 20,* 199–208.

Ford, J. K., Kozlowski, S. W. J., Kraiger, K., Salas, E., & Teachout, M. (Eds.). (1997). *Improving training effectiveness in work organizations.* Mahwah, NJ: Erlbaum.

Frei, F., Hugentobler, M., Schurman, S., & Alioth, A. (1993). *Work design for the competent organization.* New York: Quorum Books.

Frese, M. (1999). Social support as a moderator of the relationship between work stressors and psychological dysfunctioning: A longitudinal study with objective measures. *Journal of Occupational Health Psychology, 4,* 179–192.

Frese, M., & Semmer, N. (1986). Shiftwork, stress and psychosomatic complaints: A comparison between workers in different shift work schedules. *Ergonomics, 29,* 99–114.

Frese, M., & Zapf, D. (1988). Methodological issues in the study of work stress: Objective vs. subjective measurement and the question of longitudinal studies. In C. L. Cooper & R. Payne (Eds.), *Causes, coping, and consequences of stress at work* (pp. 375–411). Chichester, UK: Wiley.

Friczewski, F. (1994). Das Volkswagen-Gesundheitszirkelprojekt (The Volkswagen health circle project). In G. Westermayer & B. Bähr (Eds.), *Betriebliche Gesundheitszirkel* (Health circles at the workplace; pp. 123–127). Göttingen, Germany: Verlag für Angewandte Psychologie.

Fried, Y., & Ferris, G. R. (1987). The validity of the job characteristics model: A review and meta-analysis. *Personnel Psychology, 40,* 287–322.

Ganster, D. C. (1995). Interventions for building healthy organizations: Suggestions from the stress research literature. In L. R. Murphy, J. J. Hurrell, S. L. Sauter, & G. P. Keita

(Eds.), *Job stress interventions* (pp. 323–336). Washington, DC: American Psychological Association.

Ganster, D. C., & Murphy, L. (2000). Workplace interventions to prevent stress-related illness: Lessons from research and practice. In C. L. Cooper and E. A. Locke (Eds.), *Industrial and organizational psychology: Linking theory with practice* (pp. 34–51). Oxford: Blackwell.

Gebhardt, D. L., & Crump, C. E. (1990). Employee fitness and wellness programs in the workplace. *American Psychologist, 45,* 262–272.

Gerst, D., Hardwig, T., Kuhlmann, M., & Schumann, M. (1994). Gruppenarbeit in der betrieblichen Erprobung (Group work put to test in industry). *Angewandte Arbeitswissenschaft, 142,* 5–30.

Goldberg, D. P. (1972). *The detection of psychiatric illness by questionnaire.* Oxford, UK: Oxford University Press.

Goldberg, D. P. (1978). *Manual for the General Health Questionnaire.* Windsor, UK: National Foundation of Educational Research.

Golembiewski, R. T., Billinsley, K., & Yeager, S. (1976). Measuring change persistency in human affairs: Types of change generated by OD designs. *Journal of Applied Behavioral Science, 12,* 133–157

Golembiewski, R. T., Hilles, R., & Daly, R. (1987). Some effects of multiple OD interventions on burnout and work site features. *The Journal of Applied Behavioral Science, 23,* 295–313.

Griffiths, A. (1999). Organizational interventions: Facing the limits of the natural science paradigm. *Scandinavian Journal of Work, Environment, and Health, 25,* 589–596.

Hackett, R. D., & Bycio, P. (1996). An evaluation of employee absenteeism as a coping mechanism among hospital nurses. *Journal of Occupational and Organizational Psychology, 69,* 327–338.

Hackman, J. R. & Oldham, G. R. (1980). *Work redesign.* Reading, MA: Addison-Wesley.

Heaney, C. A., Price, F. H., & Rafferty, J. (1995). Increasing coping resources at work: A field experiment to increase social support, improve work team functioning, and enhance employee mental health. *Journal of Organizational Behavior, 16,* 335–352.

Herzberg, F., Mausner, B., & Snyderman, B. B. (1959). *The motivation to work* (2nd ed.). New York: Wiley.

Houkes, I., Janssen, P. P. M., de Jonge, J., & Nijhuis, F. J. N. (2001). Specific relationships between work characteristics and intrinsic work motivation, burnout and turnover intention: A multi-sample analysis. *European Journal of Work and Organizational Psychology, 10,* 1–23

Israel, B. A., Baker, E. A., Goldenhar, L. M., Heaney, C. A., & Schurman, S. J. (1996). Occupational stress, safety, and health: Conceptual framework and principles for effective prevention interventions. *Journal of Occupational Health Psychology, 1,* 261–286.

Ivancevich, J. M., & Matteson, M. T. (1987). Organizational level stress management interventions: A review and recommendations. In J. M. Ivancevich & D. C. Ganster (Eds.), *Job stress: From theory to suggestions* (pp. 229–248). New York: Haworth Press.

Ivancevich, J. M., Matteson, M. T., Freedman, S. M., & Philips, J. S. (1990). Worksite stress management interventions. *American Psychologist, 45,* 252–261.

Jackson, S. E. (1983). Participation in decision making as a strategy for reducing job-related strain. *Journal of Applied Psychology, 68,* 3–19.

Jackson, S. E. (1984). Correction to "Participation in decision making as a strategy for reducing job-related strain." *Journal of Applied Psychology, 69,* 546–547.

Jacobson, N. S., & Revenstorf, D. (1988). Statistics for assessing the clinical significance of psychotherapy techniques: Issues, problems and new developments. *Behavioral Assessment, 10,* 133–145.

Jimmieson, N. L. (2000). Employee reactions to behavioural control under conditions of stress: The moderating role of self-efficacy. *Work & Stress, 14,* 262–280.

Judge, T. A., Thoresen, C. J., Bono, J. E., & Patton, G. K. (2001). The job satisfaction-job performance relationship: A qualitative and quantitative review. *Psychological Bulletin, 127,* 376–407.

Kahn, R. L., & Byosiere, P. (1992). Stress in organizations. In M. D. Dunnette & L. M. Hough (Eds.), *Handbook of industrial and organizational psychology* (Vol. 3, pp. 571–650). Palo Alto, CA: Consulting Psychologists Press.

Kalimo, R., & Toppinen, S. (1999). Finland: Organizational well-being. Ten years of research and development in a forest industry corporation. In M. Kompier & C. Cooper (Eds.), *Preventing stress, improving productivity. European case studies in the workplace* (pp. 52–85). London: Routledge.

Karasek,, R., & Theorell, T. (1990). *Healthy work.* New York: Basic Books.

Kawakami, N., Araki, S., Kawashima, M., Masumoto, T., & Hayashi, T. (1997). Effects of work-related stress reduction on depressive symptoms among Japanese blue-collar workers. *Scandinavian Journal of Work, Environment, and Health, 23,* 54–59.

Kazdin, A. E. (1981). Drawing valid inference from case studies. *Journal of Consulting and Clinical Psychology, 49,* 183–192.

Kim, J. S., & Campagna, A. F. (1981). Effects of flexitime on employee attendance and performance: A field experiment. *Academy of Management Journal, 24,* 729–741.

Kompier, M. A. J., Aust, B., van den Berg, A. M., & Siegrist, J. (2000). Stress prevention in bus drivers: Evaluation of 13 national experiments. *Journal of Occupational Health Psychology, 5,* 11–31.

Kompier, M. & Cooper, C. (Eds.). (1999a). *Preventing stress, improving productivity. European case studies in the workplace.* London: Routledge.

Kompier, M., & Cooper, C. (1999b). Introduction: Improving work, health and productivity through stress prevention. In M. Kompier & C. Cooper (Eds.), *Preventing stress, improving productivity. European case studies in the workplace* (pp. 1–8). London: Routledge.

Kompier, M., & Cooper, C. (1999c). Stress prevention: European countries and European cases compared. In M. Kompier & C. Cooper (Eds.), *Preventing stress, improving productivity. European case studies in the workplace* (pp. 312–336). London: Routledge.

Kompier, M. A. J., Cooper, C. L., & Geurts, S. A. E. (2000). A multiple case study approach to work stress prevention in Europe. *European Journal of Work and Organizational Psychology, 9,* 371–400.

Kompier, M. A. J., Geurts, S. A. E., Gründemann, R. W. M., Vink, P & Smulders, P. G. W. (1998). Cases in stress prevention: The success of a participative and stepwise approach. *Stress Medicine, 14,* 144–168.

Kompier, M. A. J., & Kristensen, T. S. (2000). Organizational work stress interventions in a theoretical, methodological and practical context. In J. Dunham (Ed.), *Stress in the workplace: Past, present and future* (pp. 164–190). London: Whurr.

Kornadt, U., Schmook, R., Wilm, A., & Hertel, G. (2000). Health circles for teleworkers: Selective results on stress, strain and coping styles. *Health Education Research, 15,* 327–338.

Kozlowski, S. W. J., Chao, G. T., Smith, E. M., & Hedlund, J. (1993). Organizational downsizing: Strategies, interventions, and research implication. *International Review of Industrial and Organizational Psychology 8,* 263–332.

Kristensen, T. S. (2000). Workplace intervention studies. *Occupational Medicine: State of the Art Reviews, 15,* 293–305.

Kvarnström, S. (1992). Organizational approaches to reducing stress and health problems in an industrial setting in Sweden. In V. Di Martino (Ed.) *Preventing stress at work* (Conditions of work digest, 11 (2), pp. 227–232). Geneva: International Labour Organization.

Landsbergis, P. A., & Vivona-Vaughan, E. (1995). Evaluation of an occupational stress intervention in a public agency. *Journal of Organizational Behavior, 16,* 29–48.

Lourijsen, E., Houtman, I., Kompier, M., & Gründemann, R. (1999). The Netherlands: A hospital, "Healthy working for health." In M. Kompier & C. Cooper (Eds.), *Preventing stress, improving productivity. European case studies in the workplace* (pp. 86–120). London: Routledge.

Marmot, M., Siegrist, J., Theorell, T., & Feeney, A. (1999). Health and the psychosocial environment at work. In M. Marmot & R. G. Wilkinson (Eds.), *Social determinants of health* (pp. 105–131). Oxford: Oxford University Press.

Marstedt, G., & Mergner, U. (1995) *Gesundheit als produktives Potential* (Health as productive potential.). Berlin: Sigma.

McGrath, J. E., & Beehr, T. A. (1990). Time and the stress process: Some temporal issues in the conceptualization and measurement of stress. *Stress Medicine, 6,* 93–104.

McLeroy, K. R., Gottlieb, N. H., & Heaney, C. A. (2002). Social health in the workplace. In M. P. O'Donnell (Ed.), *Health promotion in the workplace* (3rd ed., pp. 459–492). Albany, NY: Delmar.

Meara, H. (1974). Honor in dirty work: The case of American meat cutters and Turkish butchers. *Sociology of Work and Occupations, 1,* 259–283.

Meijman, T. F., & Mulder, G. (1998). Psychological aspects of workload. In P. J. D. Drenth, H. Thierry, & C. J. de Wolff (Eds.), *Handbook of work and organizational psychology* (2nd ed., vol. 2: Work Psychology, pp. 5–33). Hove, UK: Psychology Press.

Meijman, T. F., Mulder, G., van Dormolen, M., & Cremer, R. (1992). Workload of driving examiners: A psychophysiological field study. In H. Kragt (Ed.), *Enhancing industrial performance* (pp. 245–258). London: Taylor & Francis.

Mikkelsen, A., Saksvik, P. Ø., & Landsbergis, P. (2000). The impact of a participatory organizational intervention on job stress in community health care institutions. *Work & Stress, 14,* 156–170.

Murphy, L. R. (1996). Stress management in work settings: A critical review of the health effects. *American Journal of Health Promotion, 11,* 112–135.

Narayanan, V. K., & Nath, R. (1982). A field test of some attitudinal and behavioral consequences of flexitime. *Journal of Applied Psychology, 67,* 214–218.

Netterstrøm, B. (1999). Denmark: Self-rule on Route 166. An intervention study among bus drivers. In M. Kompier & C. Cooper (Eds.), *Preventing stress, improving productivity. European case studies in the workplace* (pp. 175–194). London: Routledge.

Numeroff, R. E. (1987). Team-building interventions: An organizational stress moderator. In J. C. Quick, R. S. Bhagat, J. E. Dalton, & J. D. Quick (Eds.), *Work stress: Health care systems in the workplace* (pp. 171–194). New York: Praeger.

Nytrø, K. Saksvik, P. Ø., Mikkelsen, A., Bohle, P., & Quinlan, M. (2000). An appraisal of key factors in the implementation of occupational stress intervention. *Work & Stress, 14,* 213–225.

O'Donnell, M. P. (Ed.). (2002). *Health promotion in the workplace* (3rd ed.). Albany, NY: Delmar.

Orth-Gomér, K. (1983). Intervention on coronary risk factors by adapting a shift work schedule to biological rhythmicity. *Psychosomatic Medicine, 34,* 407–415.

Parker, S. K., Chmiel, N,. & Wall, T. (1997). Work characteristics and employee well-being within a context of strategic downsizing. *Journal of Occupational Health Psychology, 2,* 289–303.

Parker, S. K., Jackson, P. R., Sprigg, C. A., & Whybrow, A. C. (1998). *Organisational interventions to reduce the impact of poor work design* (HSE Contract Research Report 196/1998). Colegate, UK: Her Majesty's Stationery Office.

Parker, S. K., & Sprigg, C. A. (1999). Minimizing strain and maximizing learning: The role of job demands, job control and proactive personality. *Journal of Applied Psychology, 84,* 925–939.

Parker, S. & Wall, T. (1998). *Job and work design.* Thousand Oaks, CA: Sage.

Parkes, K. R., & Sparkes, T. I. (1998). *Organizational interventions to reduce work stress: Are they effective?* (HSE Contract Research Report 193/1998). Colegate, UK: Her Majesty's Stationery Office.

Pfaff, H., & Bentz, J. (2000). Intervention und Evaluation im DaimlerChrysler Werk Berlin. (Intervention and evaluation at DaimlerChrysler Berlin). In B. Badura, M. Litsch, & C. Vetter (Eds.), *Fehlzeiten-Report 2000* (Absenteeism report; pp. 176–190). Berlin: Springer.

Poelmans, S., Compernolle, T., De Neve, H., Buelens, M., & Rombouts, J. (1999). Belgium: A pharmaceutical company. In M. Kompier & C. Cooper (Eds.), *Preventing stress, improving productivity. European case studies in the workplace* (pp. 121–148). London: Routledge.

Porras, J. I., & Robertson, P. J. (1992). Organizational development. In M. D. Dunnette & L. M. Hough (Eds.), *Handbook of industrial and organizational psychology, vol. 3* (pp. 719–822). Palo Alto, CA: Consulting Psychologists Press.

Pritchard, R. D. (1990). *Measuring and improving organizational productivity.* New York: Praeger.

Pritchard, R. D. (Ed.). (1995). *Productivity measurement and improvement: Organizational case studies.* Westport, CN: Praeger.

Quick, J. C. (1979). Dyadic goal setting and role stress: A field study. *Academy of Management Journal, 22,* 241–252.

Quick, J. C., Quick, J. D., Nelson, D. L., & Hurrell, J. (1997). *Preventive stress management in organizations.* Washington, DC: American Psychological Association.

Roznowski, M., & Hulin, C. (1992). The scientific merit of valid measures of general constructs with special reference to job satisfaction and job withdrawal. In C. J. Cranny, S. C. Smith, & E. F. Stone (Eds.), *Job satisfaction: How people feel about their jobs and how it affects their performance* (pp. 123–163). New York: Lexington.

Rutte, C. G., & Messick, D. M. (1995). An integrated model of perceived unfairness in organizations. *Social Justice Research,* 239–261.

Rydstedt, L. W., Johansson, G., & Evans, G. W. (1998). The human side of the road: Improving the working conditions of urban bus drivers. *Journal of Occupational Health Psychology, 3,* 161–171.

Schaubroeck, J., Ganster, D. C., Sime, W. E., & Ditman, D. (1993). A field experiment testing supervisory role clarification. *Personnel Psychology, 46,* 1–25.

Schaubroeck, J., & Green, S. G. (1989). Confirmatory factor analytic procedures for assessing change during organizational entry. *Journal of Applied Psychology, 74,* 892–900.

Schaubroeck, J., & Merritt, D. E. (1997). Divergent effects of job control on coping with work stressors: The key role of self-efficacy. *Academy of Management Journal, 40,* 738–754.

Schurman, S. J., & Israel, B. A. (1995). Redesigning work systems to reduce stress: A participatory action research approach to creating change. In L. R. Murphy, J. J. Hurrell, S. L. Sauter, & G. P. Keita (Eds.), *Job stress interventions* (pp. 235–263). Washington, DC: American Psychological Association.

Schweiger, D. M., & DeNisi, A. S (1991). Communication with employees following a merger: A longitudinal field experiment. *Academy of Management Journal, 34,* 110–135.

Semmer, N. (1996). Individual differences, work stress, and health. In M. J. Schabracq, J. A. Winnubst, & C. L. Cooper (Eds.), *Handbook of work and health psychology* (pp. 51–86). Chichester, UK: Wiley.

Siegrist, J. (1998). Adverse health effects of effort–reward imbalance at work. In C. L. Cooper (Ed.), *Theories of organizational stress* (pp. 190–204). Oxford: Oxford University Press.

Slesina, W., Beuels, F. -R., & Sochert, R. (1998). *Betriebliche Gesundheitsförderung: Entwicklung und Evaluation von Gesundheitszirkeln zur Prävention arbeitsbedingter Erkrankungen* (Health promotion at the worksite: Development and evaluation of health circles to prevent work related illness). Weinheim: Juventa.

Smith, F. L. (1996). Statistical significance testing and cumulative knowledge in psychology: Implications for training of researchers. *Psychological Methods, 1,* 115–129.

Smith, M. J., & Zehel, D. (1992). A stress reduction intervention programme for meat processors emphasizing job design and work organization (United States). In V. Di Martino (Ed.) *Preventing stress at work* (Conditions of work digest, 11 (2), pp. 204–213). Geneva: International Labour Office.

Sonnentag, S. (1996). Work group factors and individual well-being. In M. A. West (Ed.), *Handbook of work group psychology* (pp. 345–367). Chichester, UK: Wiley.

Sonnentag, S., & Frese, M. (in press). Stress in organizations. In W. C. Bormann, D. R. Ilgen, & R. J. Klimoski (Eds.), *Comprehensive handbook of psychology, Vol. 12: Industrial and Organizational Psychology.* New York: Wiley

Spector, P. E. (1997). *Job satisfaction: Application, assessment, causes, and consequences.* Thousand Oaks, CA: Sage.

Spector, P. E. (1998). A control theory of the job stress process. In C. L. Cooper (Ed.), *Theories of organizational stress* (pp. 153–169). Oxford: Oxford University Press.

Spector, P. E., & Jex, S. M. (1998). Development of four self-report measures of job stressors and strain: Interpersonal Conflict at Work Scale, Organizational Constraints Scale, Quantitative Workload Inventory, and Physical Symptoms Inventory. *Journal of Occupational Health Psychology, 3,* 356–367.

Sprigg, C. A., Jackson, P. R., & Parker, S. K. (2000). Production teamworking: The importance of interdependence and autonomy for employee strain and satisfaction. *Human Relations, 53,* 1519–1543.

Tannenbaum, S. I., & Yukl, G. (1992). Training and development in work organizations. *Annual Review of Psychology, 43,* 399–441.

Terra, N. (1995). The prevention of job stress by redesigning jobs and implementing self-regulating teams. In L. R. Murphy, J. J. Hurrell, S. L. Sauter, & G. P. Keita (Eds.), *Job stress interventions* (pp. 235–263). Washington, DC: American Psychological Association.

Theorell, T., & Wahlstedt, K. (1999). Sweden: Mail processing. In M. Kompier & C. Cooper (Eds.), *Preventing stress, improving productivity. European case studies in the workplace* (pp. 195–221). London: Routledge.

Thompson, R. C., & Hunt, J. G. (1996). Inside the black box of alpha, beta, and gamma change: Using a cognitive-processing model to assess attitude structure. *Academy of Management Review, 21,* 655–690.

Trist, E. L., & Bamforth, K. W. (1951). Some social and psychological consequences of the long-wall method of coal-getting. *Human Relations, 4,* 3–38.

Ulich, E. (2001). *Arbeitspsychologie* (Work psychology, 5th ed.). Zurich: Verlag der Fachvereine.

U.S. Department of Health and Human Services (1992). 1992 National survey of worksite health promotion activities: Summary. *American Journal of Health Promotion, 7,* 452–464.

Van der Klink, J. J. L., Blonk, R. W. B., Schene, A. H., & van Dijk, F. J. H. (2001). The benefits of interventions for work-related stress. *American Journal of Public Health, 91,* 270–276.

Vink, P., & Kompier, M. A. J. (1997). Improving office work: A participatory ergonomic experiment in a naturalistic setting. *Ergonomics, 40,* 435–449.

Wahlstedt, K. G. I., & Edling, C. (1997). Organizational changes at a postal sorting terminal— Their effects upon work satisfaction, psychosomatic complaints and sick leave. *Work & Stress, 11,* 279–291.

Wall, T. D., & Clegg, C. W. (1981). A longitudinal field study of group work redesign. *Journal of Occupational Behaviour, 2,* 31–49.

Wall, T. D., Kemp, N. J., Jackson, P. R., & Clegg, C. W. (1986). An outcome evaluation of autonomous work groups: A long-term field experiment. *Academy of Management Journal, 29,* 280–304.

Warr, P. B. (1990). Decision latitude, job demands, and employee well-being. *Work and Stress, 4,* 285–294.

Warr, P. B. (1999). *Well-being and the workplace.* In D. Kahnemann, E. Diener, & N. Schwarz (Eds.), *Well-being: The foundations of hedonic psychology.* (pp. 392–412). New York: Russell Sage Foundation.

17

Stress Management at Work

Ruth E. Quillian-Wolever and Mark E. Wolever

As we set course into the twenty-first century, the landscape of the work environment is changing at breakneck speed. For many, technology has eliminated the physical boundaries between work and home and removed the temporal boundaries as well. The concept of working "24/7" has become the buzz-phrase, and being "connected" seems essential. With this technological backdrop, business and industry have exhibited significant shifts in operating. Companies are downsizing, right-sizing, and outsourcing. There are hostile takeovers, leveraged buyouts, and globalization. Layoffs, unemployment, employee retraining, and job sharing have become more familiar threats and considerations in the workforce.

These factors have greatly affected approaches to work, perceptions, and expectations of what defines a "good" employee. Furthermore, stress and work strain have become common topics in the popular press, on the nightly news, and in break rooms. When studying stress in the workplace, researchers frequently identify the importance of the person–environment interaction. Conceptually, individual coping styles, vulnerabilities, and resilience are viewed as interacting with external circumstances to yield personal strain (Newman & Beehr, 1979; Rodin & Salovey, 1989).

Job Stress and Health Risks

It is impossible to determine the number of workers experiencing symptoms from work-related stress. Hafen, Karren, Frandsen, and Smith (1996) reviewed studies indicating that 34% of all American employees considered quitting their jobs in 1990 because of job stress, and 46% reported their jobs to be highly stressful. Results of a 1990 Gallop poll indicated that nearly 50% of all Americans say that job stress affects their health, personal relationships, or job performance. Health researchers have confirmed this, showing that psychological stress can have a deleterious influence on an

We wish to acknowledge and thank James L. Spiva, PhD, for his contributions to the early development of these ideas.

individual's health status and may also interfere with the performance of health behaviors. Specifically, recent research with cardiac patients has indicated that mental stress can result in insufficient blood flow to the heart and is associated with significantly higher rates of cardiac events (Blumenthal et al., 1997, 1999; Jiang et al., 1996). High stress is also a risk factor for development of heart disease in population-based studies (Eaker, 1998; Hemingway & Marmot, 1999; Russek, King, Russek, & Russek, 1990). In addition to increasing risk for heart disease, high levels of stress place individuals at risk for diminished health status and other physical illnesses because of compromised immune functioning (Cohen, Tyrrell & Smith, 1991; Herbert & Cohen, 1993; Kiecolt-Glaser et al., 1986; McKinnon, Weisse, Reynolds, Bowles, & Baum, 1989). Moreover, stress levels are related to multiple behaviors that affect health, including sleep (Morin & Kwentus, 1988; Perlis & Youngstedt, 2000), eating behaviors (Alexander & Walker, 1994), levels of exercise (Goldwater & Collis, 1985; LaPerriere et al., 1990; Morgan, 1984; Simons & Birkimer, 1988), as well as alcohol and tobacco consumption (Alexander & Walker, 1994; McLeroy, Green, Mullen, & Foshee, 1984; Seamonds, 1983). Furthermore, elevated stress levels adversely affect quality of life and mental health. It is well-established that chronic levels of elevated stress can contribute to the development of depression (Gold, Goodwin, & Chrousos, 1988; Post, 1992; Sapolsky, 1998). Moreover, depression appears to be predictive of early mortality from all causes (Barefoot & Schroll, 1996; Booth-Kewley & Friedman, 1987). Paul J. Rosch, New York Medical College psychiatrist and past president of the American Institute of Stress summed up the situation by saying, "Work stress may be America's number one health problem" (as cited in Hafen et al., 1996, p. 82).

Job Stress and Cost

The cost of stress is staggering. The California Department of Mental Health and Kaiser-Permanente health organization conducted large-scale, long-term studies that demonstrated that 60% to 90% of all visits to health care providers (Cummings & VandenBos, 1981; Pelletier & Lutz, 1988) and 60% of work absenteeism are caused by stress-related disorders (Cooper & Payne, 1988). In the executive ranks alone it is estimated that 10 to 20 billion dollars are lost annually to absenteeism, hospitalization, and early death, much of it a result of stress (Kiev, 1987). According to the National Council on Compensation Insurance, stress-related claims account for nearly one fifth of all occupational diseases (Brodsky, 1989). In sum, it is estimated that stress-related symptoms and illness are costing industry 150 billion dollars a year in absenteeism, company medical expenses, and lost productivity (Brodsky, 1989). Although it is generally agreed that occupational stress is a significant and growing problem that can be destructive for individuals and organizations (Sauter, Murphy, & Hurrell, 1990), it is unclear how best to approach the reduction of work-related stress.

Primary Versus Secondary Prevention

Organizational theorists have suggested a three-tiered prevention model, previously the domain of epidemiologists and preventive medicine experts, as a framework to use in tackling work stress (Cooper & Cartwright, 1997; Quick & Quick 1984; Quick, Quick, & Horn, 1986). Thus far, much attention has centered on primary prevention as the fundamental and preferred approach to the problem of work stress (Quick, Murphy, Hurrell, & Orman, 1992). The goal of primary prevention is to alter or reduce the nature or source of stress at work. Examples of primary prevention strategies include job redesign, organizational structure modification, and job enlargement. (For a more in-depth discussion on primary and secondary prevention, see chapter 1, this volume.)

Secondary prevention methods are aimed at changing the way that individuals respond to the stressors associated with work to prevent negative health consequences and to improve quality of life. These methods attempt to increase awareness concerning the causes and consequences of stress and to help employees develop more healthful and adaptive response styles. Secondary prevention programs typically include some method of muscle-relaxation training, cognitive–behavioral skills training, meditation, or a combination of these.

Secondary Prevention: Methodological Issues

Murphy (1996) identified multiple challenges inherent in examining the research on secondary prevention programs. Foremost, he noted that a wide range of methodological issues makes it difficult to interpret the literature. There exist significant differences between studies, including different target populations (e.g., all employees offered the intervention versus high-risk employees only), time courses for treatment (varying from a single stress management lecture to long-term programs with multiple meetings), operationalization of dependent measures, and most important different research designs. Valid interpretations of the literature necessitates the appropriate use of comparison groups, as nonspecific effects have been frequently found in intervention studies for stress (Murphy, 1996). Taking all of these methodological concerns into account, there is solid evidence for the effectiveness of work-site stress management programs in reducing the negative effects of stress in individuals; however, the benefits to employers in terms of such measures as absenteeism and worker satisfaction are equivocal (Kolbell, 1995; Murphy, 1996).

Secondary Prevention: Critical Factors

There are several critical factors that need to be addressed when developing a secondary prevention program. To maximize effectiveness, interventions should be based on the nature of the stressors (e.g., organizational versus individual stressors, external versus internal) and the target symptoms of distress (physical versus psychological). Thus, programs should include a careful evaluation of both to ensure success (Kolbell, 1995; Murphy, 1996). Such an evaluation may reveal that a specific stress management intervention would be warranted for a particular workforce or a subset of a larger workforce. Alternatively, the evaluation may indicate that a comprehensive stress management program that includes primary and secondary prevention will best meet the needs of the employees and employer alike. Other critical factors include the availability of financial and human resources, administrative support, skilled trainers, and employee participation (Munz, Huelsman, & Craft, 1995). Pelletier and Lutz (1989) identified specific elements necessary for the "packaged" worksite stress management program. They recommend programs should meet for 45 minutes, once a week, for four to eight weeks. Group size should be between 12 to 15 participants and the groups can be led by either a professional facilitator or a trained peer. Programs should teach one or more stress management techniques. Finally, they noted that ongoing program evaluation is needed to maintain effectiveness.

The next section will review components of successful stress management strategies that have evolved from the scientific literature in occupational health, behavioral medicine, and health psychology. We will review representative examples of secondary stress management models and present a model that combines key features of secondary prevention.

Sample Secondary Prevention Models for Managing Work Stress

One generalizable and comprehensive model is reviewed by Munz et al. (1995), who described a worksite stress management program first used by the Veteran Health Administration in 1981, and subsequently offered by more than 65 Veterans Affairs medical centers. Munz and his colleagues included components of organizational stress reduction as well as an employee assistance program (EAP), emphasizing the importance of the person–organization (transactional) interaction. Within the secondary prevention component of this transactional model, the participants are taught to recognize their responsibility for the program's success. The model helps participants understand the interaction between environmental demands (stressors) and individual characteristics (e.g., personality, perceptions), and the resulting consequences of the stress response on various physical and psychological systems. The importance of self-management of these physical and psychological systems is underlined, and multiple strategies for self-management are aimed at countering the mental, physical, and emotional reactions to stressors. As is common in the field of stress management, the skills include cognitive strategies, physical movement, and relaxation strategies for managing stress.

More specific programs are also successful in targeting more specific goals. Examples include the development of anger management training for law enforcement officers (Abernathy, 1995; Novaco, 1977) and stress inoculation training for staff working with persons with mental retardation (Keyes, 1995). Described as a specialized component of stress management training, Abernathy helped design a program for the Rochester Police Department with the expressed goals of increasing officers' awareness of their anger and improving anger management skills. The six-hour training included an overview of stress; instruction on how to recognize the physical, psychological, and behavioral consequences of anger, relaxation, and meditation exercises; dysfunctional styles of coping; exercising choice in managing anger; and the process of anger resolution.

Keyes (1995) developed a stress inoculation training program for staff working with persons with mental retardation and developmental disabilities that is based on Meichenbaum's (1985) treatment paradigm. The three phases—(a) conceptualization; (b) skills acquisition and rehearsal; and (c) application and follow-through—are presented in a one-day workshop. The purpose of the conceptualization phase is to help staff increase their awareness and understanding of the emotional and behavioral impact of stress and anger. This phase is intended to help staff realize the transactional nature of stress and that they have a degree of control over the stress response by virtue of their thoughts and interpretations of environmental cues. The skills acquisition and rehearsal phase includes training in relaxation (e.g., muscle relaxation, breathing), cognitive strategies (e.g., cognitive restructuring, cognitive errors), problem-solving training (e.g., assessment, generation of alternatives, decision making), and self-instructional training (i.e., guided self-dialogue) used for preparation and confrontation of stress and coping with arousal. The application and follow-through phase uses role play to practice the techniques learned in the two previous phases of training. Staffers are given an opportunity to practice their skills in exercises of graduated intensity, while remaining in a controlled setting.

Proposed Secondary Prevention Model

H. L. Mencken noted that "there is always a well-known solution to every human problem—neat, plausible, and wrong" (1920, pp. 80–81). Nevertheless, to simplify the complicated interactions involved in secondary prevention, we propose a model in Figure 17.1 to aid in understanding coping options available for individuals. Similar to the conceptualization of others (e.g., Keyes, 1995; Lazarus, 1966; Munz et al., 1995), the model presented is a transactional model that recognizes the person–organization interaction, while emphasizing individual cognitive appraisal. Stress is defined as a natural interaction between a perceived challenge, obstacle, or threat to one's goals, health, or happiness (known as the stressor) and the coping responses available to the individual. It is an individual's appraisal that an environmental demand or event is a challenge, obstacle, or threat (Folkman & Lazarus, 1991, Munz et al., 1995). Stress occurs when the individual perceives a challenge and judges that his or her coping resources may not be sufficient to manage the challenge. This appraisal begins a complex

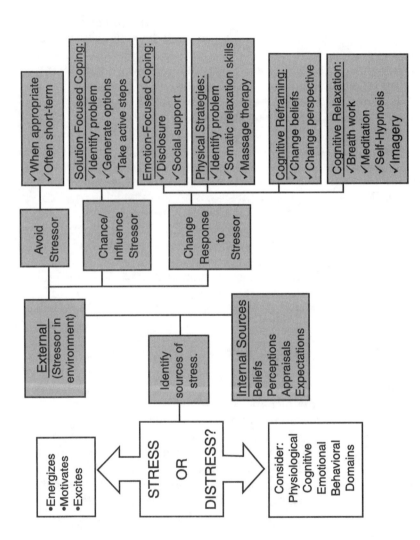

Figure 17.1.   Secondary prevention model: Stress management at work.

stress cascade that affects the physiology, cognitions, emotions, and behavior of the individual. There is an immediate effort to reduce the disturbance by using coping strategies to change the situation, the individual's reaction, or both. Coping resources available to an individual can halt or reverse the cascade at any point. Such resources include skills, talents, knowledge, and support networks, all of which should be included in an effective stress management program.

Self-Awareness

The successful secondary stress management program will help individuals to assess target symptoms. Individuals must first learn to identify their personal phenomenology of stress, as well as indications of stress levels that are too high. Awareness of the physical, mental, emotional, and behavioral reactions to stress ultimately helps define the counter measures used to manage stress. This is essential because distinct interventions tend to affect distinct variables (Murphy, 1996). The second step, then, is to make an informed choice on how to intervene based on the target symptoms, the nature of the stressor, and the available coping skills.

Domains of Response

The key to understanding personal stress symptoms is to divide the experience of stress into four domains of response: physical, cognitive, emotional, and behavioral. Stress is manifest in each domain differently.

Physical stress responses. The body is designed for balance. Individuals develop work, health, and quality of life problems when they chronically invoke the "fight or flight" stress response without allowing for sufficient recuperation. The key is to maintain balance between the sympathetic and parasympathetic branches of the nervous system, between crisis and day-to-day functioning. Part of the issue stems from the fact that human anatomy and physiology have not changed much over the past 10,000 years, yet we live in a vastly different world. The stressors encountered today are quite distinct from those that our ancestors faced. Stressors in twenty-first century Western cultures are more psychological in nature, and rarely are linked with immediate physical threat. The natural ways our ancestors handled the stressors of those days enhanced their survival; increased heart rate, blood pressure, and mobilization of energy sources like glucose and free fatty acids were useful responses when being chased by a predator. The energy sources became quickly available and were transported rapidly through the quickly moving blood to the muscles that needed them to help escape danger. By contrast, these same physiological responses, when repeated frequently, can actually create some diseases (e.g., heart disease) and exacerbate others (e.g., diabetes, many types of cancer, some autoimmune illnesses); frequent worry about making deadlines, frustration when

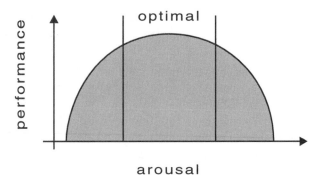

Figure 17.2. Yerkes-Dodson law: The association between arousal and performance.

stuck in traffic, or fuming inside about being discounted in a meeting are not necessarily helped by mobilized physical energy sources and increased blood pressure.

Stress management participants with physical target symptoms indicative of chronic or acute stress should be guided toward skills training on physical relaxation. Chronic health concerns such as hypertension, conditions related to immune suppression, fatigue, and insomnia are strong indicators that stress levels are too high. In addition, more acute indicators that stress levels are too high include temporary fatigue, racing heart rate, shortness of breath, exacerbation of pain (particularly headaches), and muscle tension. These signals can help to focus individuals on coping tools that target physical responses such as exercise, progressive muscle relaxation, deep-breathing, and massage therapy (discussed later).

Cognitive Stress Responses

Just as individuals are taught to monitor physical symptoms, they are also urged to monitor cognitive signs of stress. Multiple aspects of attention, concentration, information-processing speed, short-term memory, awareness–insight, decision making, and judgment all change in response to stress. The usefulness of these changes is a function of the intensity of the change. For example, rapid information processing can be helpful in many situations; racing thoughts are not. Focused attention may be helpful; obsessive thinking is usually not. As illustrated in Figure 17.2, the intensity of sympathetic arousal levels can have a major impact on performance. There is an optimal (moderate) level of arousal at which performance is maximal. If arousal is too low or too high, performance suffers. This optimal stress level can be energizing, motivating, and exciting. Several authors make a distinction between stress and distress (Levi, 1981; Quick & Quick, 1984; Selye, 1976). Distress occurs when the individual experiences stress beyond the optimal zone.

Individuals can increase awareness of cognitive distress by tracking certain mental phenomenon including; racing thoughts, obsessive or perseverative thinking, scattered attention, loss of perspective, tendency to focus on the negative aspects while discounting the positive, difficulty with short-term memory (as a result of attentional problems that impede encoding), and more rigid thinking patterns (less tolerance and lower levels of cognitive flexibility). Coping strategies targeted at cognitive symptoms of stress include mindfulness meditation and cognitive behavioral training.

Emotional Stress Responses

Emotions are a vital part of the human experience. They can point toward pleasure and they can signal danger or threat. Research suggests that people have emotions at all times, even though the emotions may be out of awareness (Diener & Lucas, 2000; Williams & Williams, 1997). Bringing them into awareness and understanding the impact of emotions on health and well-being is an important aspect of stress management. Emotional signs of distress include increased frequency or intensity of anger, impatience, anxiety, or any indication of depression. The emotional response to stress initiates in the lower areas of the brain, and can be influenced by the cortex. Thus, emotional responses are influenced through changing behaviors and thought processes, rather than the emotions being directly changed. In this regard, meditation and cognitive–behavioral training are effective in targeting emotional signals of distress.

Behavioral Stress Responses

The behavioral domain is the domain in which individuals can obtain the most control. Individuals can gain control over behaviors elicited by stress more easily than they can over thoughts, emotions, and physiology. Common behavioral responses to stress that can serve as personal signals that stress levels are too high include increases in alcohol intake; nicotine use; eating when not hungry; increase in prescription and street drug use; sleep disturbances (which can be physical or behavioral in nature), and worsening of communication behaviors. Regarding communication behaviors, people generally demonstrate worse listening skills, withdraw interpersonally, or become aggressive in communication style as stress levels increase. More established, habitual behaviors increase and behaviors that are relatively new tend to decrease. This may be especially true with respect to health behaviors. An individual trying to begin an exercise routine is likely to struggle even more with that when stress levels are high compared to an individual who has been exercising for most of his or her life; the latter individual is more likely to hit the gym when stress increases. Habitual behaviors also include "nervous habits" such as finger-tapping, foot-flicking, head-scratching, pen-chewing, and so forth.

Individuals have four domains in which they experience responses to stressors. Each domain can provide information on whether stress levels are too high, from a performance, quality of life, and health standpoint. It is recommended that individuals identify personal signals to use as target symptoms that can guide selection of the most effective stress management intervention. In general, peer-reviewed studies indicate that physical stress symptoms appear to respond better to muscle relaxation strategies and emotional and cognitive symptoms respond more consistently to cognitive–behavioral strategies (Murphy, 1996). Behavioral signals of distress have not served as frequently as outcomes measures, but in our clinical experience respond to cognitive–behavioral strategies as well.

Behavioral Coping Strategies

The proposed model guides selection of the most effective interventions by distinguishing between internal and external sources of stress. External sources of stress in the workplace originate outside of the individual; in other words, they are not the product of that individual's cognition, behavior, or physical reactions. In the realm of work-site stress, changing external stressors falls into the domain of primary prevention. Such interventions are necessary to target organizational sources of stress at a systems level to affect organizational-relevant variables such as job satisfaction, absenteeism, morale, and productivity (Murphy, 1996). Nonetheless, it is useful to enhance an individual employee's limited options when faced with external stressors in the workplace. There are basically two behavioral approaches to coping with external stressors: Avoid the stressor, or change–influence the stressor.

Avoid the Stressor

The initial coping strategy takes the form of avoidance behavior. An individual should consider this option if it is possible to avoid the threat or obstacle without great cost. The worse the stressor, the more cost one may be willing to pay to avoid it. For example, consider taking a different road to avoid construction on the commute to work, or declining a promotion that would be more stressful to self and family than it is worth. The avoidance strategy is useful in many situations, but there are many stressors one can not avoid (e.g., the behavior of one's immediate supervisor, organizational policy and procedures). In that case, avoidance may provide an occasional break if the stressor is chronic, but avoidance as a primary strategy is not an effective strategy over time.

Change the Stressor: Solution-Focused Coping

Although primary prevention strategies are designed to minimize external stressors, it is essential to consider the ways in which individuals interact with their environments to fully allow for stress management possibilities. A key component in this process is the notion of controllability. Research shows that those individuals who cope with stress most effectively are able to realistically determine what they have control over, and what they do not, and then choose coping strategies accordingly (Sapolsky, 1998). When it is possible to influence the stressor, it is best to use solution-focused approaches involving problem-solving skills and assertion (Williams & Williams, 1994, 1997). When there is little or no control over the stressor, it is best to use emotion-focused approaches (Folkman & Lazarus, 1991), such as use of social support and self-expression of emotion, combined with physical relaxation approaches. Explanation of the emotion-focused techniques leads us into the third coping option. When one can not avoid the stressor or influence–change the stressor, the final option is to change one's response to the stressor.

Learning to use this third behavioral alternative, changing one's response to the stressor, is the main purpose of secondary prevention. This alternative coping approach includes multiple strategies and can be used for dealing with external sources of stress that are out of an individual's control as well as internal sources.

Change Response to the Stressor: Emotional, Physical and Cognitive Coping Strategies

When the stressor is truly out of one's control, or the personal cost of trying to change it outweighs the benefits of such, one still has the option of changing his or her personal response in each of the four domains: physical, cognitive, emotional, and behavioral. Although avoiding the stressor and changing–influencing the stressor are mainly behavioral coping techniques, changing one's personal response to the stressor relies more heavily on emotion-focused techniques and physical relaxation.

Emotion-Focused Techniques

Two emotion-focused approaches have strong empirical evidence backing their efficacy. These are social support and self-disclosure of emotions.

Social support. Research has provided compelling evidence that social connection improves both quality of life and physical health. Four decades of prospective research have consistently demonstrated the importance of this emotion-focused approach to coping. People with lower levels of social connection have been shown to be three to five times more likely to die prematurely from multiple causes of death, including heart attacks, stroke, some cancers, infectious diseases, autoimmune diseases, substance abuse, and suicide (Berkman & Syme, 1979; Blumenthal et al., 1987; Cohen & Wills, 1985; Ornish, 1998; Orth-Gomer & Unden, 1990). Low social support has also been prospectively linked to later incidence of heart disease

Table 17.1. Autonomic Nervous System: Summary of Effects

Function	Sympathetic arousal	Parasympathetic arousal
Skeletal muscles	Tense, in use	Relaxed
Blood	Shunted to skeletal muscles, heart, and lungs	Shunted to central organs
Heart-rate	Increases	Decreases
Respiration	Increases	Decreases
Blood pressure	Increases	Decreases
Stress hormones	Increases	Decreases
Blood sugar	Increases	Decreases
Release of fats into circulation	Increases	Decreases
Sexual functioning	Decreases	Increases
Digestion/peristalsis	Decreases	Increases
Immune functioning	Decreases	Increases

(Hemingway & Marmot, 1999; Orth-Gomer, Rosengren, & Wilhelmsen, 1993). Moreover, social isolation has been shown to predict mortality in Type A men, and high levels of social support in such people are related to lower levels of coronary artery disease. Thus, strong social support appears to exert some protective influence over the potential long-term health consequences of the Type A Behavior Profile (Blumenthal et al., 1987). Finally, strong social support has even been shown to buffer the development of the common cold after the infectious agents are in the body (Cohen, Doyle, Skoner, Rabin, & Gwaltney, 1997). Many believe that social support is perhaps the most important psychosocial buffer of stress (Cohen & Wills, 1985; Ornish, 1998). Perhaps one of the reasons that social support positively affects health and functioning is because social support allows an avenue to express emotion; it provides listeners to whom one can disclose.

Self-expression of emotion. Disclosure itself is considered a form of emotion-focused coping. Disclosure through writing (e.g., journaling) or verbal avenues (e.g., talking to someone) leads to improved functioning in many areas. These improvements include multiple signs of an enhanced relaxation response, such as decreased blood pressure, muscle tension, and skin conduction. Writing about upsetting or traumatic experiences has also shown heightened immune function, generally improved health, as well as better work and school performance measures, including absenteeism (e.g., Esterling, Antoni, Fletcher, Marguiles, & Schneiderman, 1994; Francis & Pennebaker, 1992; Pennebaker, 1993, 1997; Spera, Buhfriend, & Pennebaker, 1994). These improvements are likely a result of the fact that active inhibition of thoughts and emotions works the autonomic nervous system overtime, which can negatively affect immune functioning, the action of the cardiovascular system, and the biochemistry of the brain. In other words, the internal process of inhibition becomes a stressor itself. Disclosure in a safe context can eliminate that stress. The emotion-focused approaches of self-expression and social support can thus be helpful in changing one's response to a stressor. (See Table 17.1.)

Physical and Cognitive Strategies

Another set of strategies designed to help strengthen the ability to respond to a stressor differently include the physical and cognitive strategies. Included within the physical and cognitive strategies are physical activity–exercise, massage therapy, somatic and cognitive relaxation techniques, as well as cognitive reframing strategies.

Physical activity–Exercise. A review of the literature indicates that exercise has a positive impact on multiple indexes (Freeman & Lawlis, 2001), including mood states (Goldwater & Collis, 1985; Gronningsaeter, Hytten, Skauli, Christensen, & Ursin, 1992; Martinsen, 1990; Martinsen, Hoffart & Solberg, 1989; Martinsen, Medhus, & Sandvik, 1985; Simons & Birkimer, 1988), immune system functioning (Hoffman-Goetz, Simpson, Cipp, Arumugam, & Houston, 1990; Severs, Brenner, Shek, & Shephard, 1996), cardiovascular responses, stress reactivity (Blumenthal et al., 1990), and even reported job satisfaction (Gronningsaeter et al., 1992). Considering these findings and, in light of the well-documented association between stress and cardiovascular disease, exercise needs to be considered a key strategy aimed at countering the negative effects of chronic stress. To this end, individuals should be encouraged to establish a regular exercise regimen. Although exercise is typically pursued outside of the workplace, moderate physical activity can be a stress management strategy even on site. For example, even brief walks throughout the day can serve as appropriate outlets for frustration and provide decreases in overall muscle tension.

Massage therapy. Another well-documented avenue to decrease overall muscle tension is massage therapy. Massage therapy has become a widely used form of alternative treatment, surpassed only by relaxation techniques and chiropractic care (Eisenberg et al., 1993). Although the research on the benefits of massage is somewhat equivocal, the mechanisms and outcomes of massage appear to include stimulation of sensory receptors in the skin; increased circulation; reduced muscle soreness; increased joint mobility and flexibility; enhanced immune functioning (Zeitlin, Keller, Shiflett, Schleifer, & Bartlett, 2000); and evocation of the relaxation response by stimulating the parasympathetic nervous system. Freeman's (2001b) review of the research indicates that massage has been shown to be beneficial in the treatment of anxiety (Zeitlin et al., 2000), depression, as well as acute and chronic pain among other things. Even brief massage interventions in the workplace appear to be useful. Shulman and Jones (1996) found that a six-week course of 15-minute on-site chair massage resulted in a significant reduction in employee anxiety when compared to a control group that was given 15-minute breaks.

Relaxation techniques. Herbert Benson coined the phrase "relaxation response" to describe the "bodily changes that decrease heart rate, lower metabolism, decrease the rate of breathing, and bring the body back into what is probably a healthier balance" (Benson & Klipper, 1975). The development of skills designed to evoke the relaxation response provides individuals with the ability to down-regulate their physiology. When practiced routinely, these skills have been shown to result in health benefits.

There are several techniques–strategies that yield health benefits that can be categorized into what Freeman (2001d) referred to as either somatic relaxation or cognitive relaxation strategies. Somatic relaxation strategies emphasize muscle relaxation through observations of the body's kinesthetic sensations (i.e., systematic tensing and relaxing of muscles). Cognitive relaxation strategies incorporate the use of a mental device–mechanism (e.g., word, thought, sound, breathing) while maintaining a passive attitude. Although there are a variety of techniques to evoke the "relaxation response," Benson argued that all relaxation techniques produce a single relaxation response, suggesting that no one strategy is superior to another (Benson & Klipper, 1975). In light of methodological issues, it is difficult to determine which of these techniques is most effective.

Somatic relaxation techniques. Progressive muscle relaxation (PMR) techniques were originated by Edmund Jacobson and later abbreviated and manualized by Wolpe, as well as Bornstein and Borkovec (Bornstein & Borkovec, 1973; Freeman, 2001d; Jacobson, 1938;). PMR techniques have been shown to reduce hypertension, reduce chronic pain in a variety of medical conditions, and help manage mood states of anxiety and depression (Cruess, Antoni, Kumar, & Schneiderman, 2000; Freeman, 2001d; Syrjala, Donaldson, Davis, Kippes, & Carr, 1995). This skill is easily used at the work place to disengage from the stress of the day and reduce the general level of sympathetic arousal. PMR is the most common relaxation technique used in the peer-reviewed stress-management literature; of 64 work-site based, stress management studies, 13 used muscle relaxation training alone and another 30 used muscle relaxation training in combination with cognitive–behavioral skills training (Murphy, 1996). The results indicate that this approach demonstrates the strongest impact on physiologic outcome variables.

Cognitive relaxation techniques. Other methods of increasing autonomic balance (turning down the sympathetic fight or flight response and increasing the relaxation and recuperation response) include cognitive forms of relaxation such as a simple focus on the breath, meditation, imagery, and self-hypnosis.

- *Focus on the breath.* Breath work is fundamental to most forms of relaxation. The beauty of the breath has to do with its relative simplicity and its ever-present access. Using proper breathing techniques, one can learn to down-regulate the sympathetic nervous system. In other words, the breath may be the shortest distance between the stress response and the relaxation response (Fahri, 1996; Freeman, 2001d).

- *Meditation.* The practice of meditation has become more main-stream and recognized as a valuable stress management strategy in part because of the research that has demonstrated benefits with respect to medical and emotional states (Kabat-Zinn, 1990; Shapiro, Schwartz, & Bonner, 1998; Speca, Carlson, Goodey, & Angen, 2000). Although some authors disagree, the general findings regarding the physiologic effects from the research on meditation include reduced oxygen consumption, decreased heart and respiration rates, diminished blood lactate levels, elevation of mood states, improved immune functioning, changes in brain-wave activity, and positive changes in hormone levels. The form of meditation used most often in work-setting stress management programs (Murphy, 1996) has been Herbert Benson's Respiratory One Method (Benson, 1976). In this approach, a person sits quietly for 20 minutes twice per day repeating a neutral word (e.g., "one") with each outbreath while maintaining a nonjudgmental and passive attitude toward intruding thoughts (Benson, 1976). Another frequently used and similar technique that has gained exposure and support in medical communities is Jon Kabat-Zinn's adaptation of vipassana, or mindfulness meditation (e.g., Kabat-Zinn, 1990). Unlike other relaxation practices, regular meditation practice has also been found to lead to positive behavior change outside of the meditative state (Freeman, 2001c; Kabat-Zinn, 1990), and appears to produce the most consistent results across physical and psychological outcomes in worksite based programs (Murphy, 1996).
- *Self-Hypnosis.* Although self-hypnosis has not been used much in work-site stress management programs, the health psychology literature suggests that it is a viable alternative to consider. Hypnosis has been defined as a state of attentive, focused concentration with suspension of some peripheral awareness. (Spiegel & Spiegel, 1978). The use of clinical hypnosis is another example of the powerful mind–body connection that has been shown to be effective in the treatment of conditions including negative mood states (Whitehouse et al., 1996), pain (Spiegel & Bloom, 1983), and multiple medical disorders (Freeman, 2001a; Spiegel & Spiegel, 1978). Whether guided by a clinician or done independently, all hypnosis is self-hypnosis. The individual in trance is always in control. Although in this state of focused concentration, one can use motivation and suggestions to achieve some desired goal, such as greater confidence when faced with challenges, reduction of pain experience, or a more adaptive response to stress. Autogenic training is often considered as a form of, or ingredient in self-hypnosis. Individuals learn a set of suggestions (e.g., my arm is very heavy, warmth is radiating over my stomach) aimed at specific autonomic sensations (Linden, 1994). Autogenic training has shown positive effects with a variety of issues, including migraine headaches, insomnia, angina, and hypertension (Linden, 1994). When used during self-hypnosis, these sug-

gestions result in measurable physiologic changes that enhance relaxation and help deepen the trance state (Lichtenstein, 1988).

- *Imagery.* Imagery is the mental process that is at the core of mind–body medicine, and is fundamental to PMR, meditation, and hypnosis. Simply put, imagery is thought with a sensory focus. Imagery has been shown to have positive effects in the treatment of various disorders, including headaches, breast cancer, diabetes, skin ailments, arthritis, and severe burns (Freeman, 2001d; Syrjala et al., 1995). The use of imagery for the purposes of stress management or relaxation has been referred to as end-state imagery (Freeman, 2001d). End-state imagery is intended to produce a particular physiologic or biologic change. In the case of stress management, the end state would be the reduction of sympathetic nervous system arousal. The actual practice of imagery for the sake of relaxation invites individuals to use their "mind's eye" to visualize–imagine a place of comfort, relaxation, safety, and serenity to which they have been. By accessing all of the senses associated with that memory, individuals can reexperience the calming effects desired.

Cognitive Reframing: Changing Perception and Beliefs

Using the transactional model of stress, distress is a function of appraisal and perceptions. In other words, cognitions can determine how one feels about any situation and whether one sees that situation as a stressor. A quote from Shakespeare captures this notion nicely: "For there is nothing either good or bad, but thinking makes it so" (1936, p. 748). Training in cognitive reframing techniques helps individuals recognize that their thoughts, values, and beliefs influence their appraisal of situations. Through cognitive reframing or restructuring, individuals learn to reinterpret situations in a manner that reduces stress. Over time, individuals begin to rethink or reframe the ways they habitually perceive things as well as reformulate their general belief systems. Many authors have identified the impact of beliefs on health and happiness and described the use of cognitive skills in improving outlook, uplifting mood, and thus regulating stress (Beck, Rush, Shaw, & Emory, 1979; Burns, 1989; Ellis & Harper, 1975; Friedman & Ulmer, 1984; Seligman, 1991). It is the use of cognitive reframing, challenging thought distortions, and restructuring beliefs that is fundamental to Stress Inoculation Training (Meichenbaum, 1985), described earlier.

Conclusion

The cost of work-related stress to individuals, organizations, and society as a whole is staggering. With continued technological advances and the ever-changing face of the work environment, the need for prevention has never been greater. As business and industry work to reduce occupational stress through primary intervention strategies, individuals as well as organizations still need to recognize the role of the individual in the development and reduction of work-related stress. Secondary prevention strategies focus on increasing workers' awareness of the individual phenomenology of the stress response physically, cognitively, emotionally, and behaviorally. This increased awareness allows individuals to make a thoughtful, informed decision on how to best intervene to perhaps prevent, or at least counteract, the negative consequences of the stress response. These decision options are diagrammed in Figure 17.1. In the face of stress, individuals are encouraged to consider three broad response categories: avoid the stressor, change or influence the stressor, or change one's personal response to the stressor. Each of these approaches calls for the use of coping skills dependent on the response category chosen and the particular domain impacted by the stressor. Behavioral coping strategies include avoiding the stressor (short-term strategy) when appropriate and efforts to influence the stressor (i.e., solution-focused coping). If the stressor cannot be avoided, or the stressor is out of one's control, individuals need to change response patterns and develop alternative modes of responding. Emotion-focused coping through disclosure (e.g., journaling) and social support; physical strategies of exercise, massage therapy, and somatic relaxation; and cognitive strategies (including cognitive reframing and cognitive relaxation techniques such as meditation) have all been shown to be effective secondary prevention strategies.

References

Abernathy, A. D. (1995). The development of an anger management training program for law enforcement personnel. In L. R. Murphy, J. J. Hurrell, Jr., S. L. Sauter, & G. P. Keita (Eds.), *Job stress interventions.* (pp. 21–30). Washington DC: American Psychological Association.

Alexander, D. A., & Walker, L. G. (1994). A study of methods used by Scottish police officers to cope with work-induced stress. *Stress Medicine, 10,* 131–138.

Barefoot, J. C., & Schroll, M. (1996). Symptoms of depression, acute myocardial infarction, and total mortality in a community sample. *Circulation, 93,* 1976–1980.

Beck, A., Rush, J., Shaw, B., & Emery, G. (1979). *Cognitive therapy of depression.* New York: Guilford Press.

Benson, H. (1976). *The relaxation response.* New York: William Morrow.

Benson, H., & Klipper, M. Z. (1975). *The relaxation response.* New York: Avon Books.

Berkman, L. F., & Syme, S. L. (1979). Social networks, host resistance, and mortality: A nine-year follow-up study of Alameda County residents. *American Journal of Epidemiology, 109,* 186–204.

Blumenthal, J. A., Burg, M. M., Barefoot, J., Williams, R. B., Haney, T., & Zimet, G. (1987). Social support, type A behavior, and coronary artery disease. *Psychosomatic Medicine, 49,* 331–340.

Blumenthal, J. A., Fredrikson, M., Kuhn, C. M., Ulmer, R. L., Walsh-Riddle, M., & Appelbaum, M. (1990). Aerobic exercise reduces levels of cardiovascular and sympathoadrenal responses to mental stress in subjects without prior evidence of myocardial ischemia. *American Journal of Cardiology, 65,* 93–98.

Blumenthal, J. A., Jiang, W., Babyak, M. A., Krantz, D. S., Frid, D. J., Coleman, R. E., Waugh, R., Hanson, M., Appelbaum, M., O'Connor, C., & Morris, J. J. (1997). Stress management and exercise training in cardiac patients with myocardial ischemia. Effects on prognosis and evaluation of mechanisms. *Archives of Internal Medicine, 157*, 2213–2223.

Blumenthal, J. A., Sherwood, A., Babyak, M. A., Thurston, R., Tweedy, D., Georgiades, A., Gullette, E. C., Khatri, P., Steffan, P., Waugh, R., Light, K., & Hinderliter, A. (1999). Mental stress and coronary disease: The Smart-Heart study. *North Carolina Medical Journal, 60*(2), 95–99.

Booth-Kewley, S., & Friedman, H. S. (1987). Psychological predictors of heart disease: A quantitative review. *Psychological Bulletin, 101*, 343–362.

Bornstein, D. A., & Borkovec, T. D. (1973). *Progressive relaxation training: A manual for the helping professions.* Champaign, IL: Research Press.

Brodsky, R. (1989). Identifying stressors is necessary to combat potential health problems. *Occupational Health and Safety, 58*, 30–34.

Burns, D. D. (1989). *The feeling good handbook.* New York: Plume.

Cohen, S., Doyle, W. J., Skoner, D. P., Rabin, B. S., & Gwaltney, J. M. (1997). Social ties and susceptibility to the common cold. *Journal of the American Medical Association, 277*, 1940–1944.

Cohen, S., Tyrrell, D. A., & Smith, A. P. (1991). Psychological stress and susceptibility to the common cold. *New England Journal of Medicine, 325*, 606–612.

Cohen, S., & Wills, T. A. (1985). Stress, social support, and the buffering hypothesis. *Psychological Bulletin, 98*, 310–357.

Cooper, C. L., & Cartwright, S. (1997). An intervention strategy for workplace stress. *Journal of Psychosomatic Research, 43*, 7–16.

Cooper, C. L., & Payne, R. (Eds.). (1988). *Causes, coping, and consequences of stress at work.* New York: John Wiley & Sons.

Cruess, D. G., Antoni, M. H., Kumar, M., & Schneiderman, N. (2000). Reductions in salivary cortisol are associated with mood improvement during relaxation training among HIV-seropositive men. *Journal of Behavioral Medicine, 23*, 107–122.

Cummings, N. A., & VandenBos, G. R. (1981). The twenty years Kaiser-Permanente experience with psychotherapy and medical utilization: Implications for national health policy and national health insurance. *Health Policy Quarterly, 1*(2), 159–175.

Diener, E., & Lucas, R. (2000). Subjective emotional well-being. In M. Lewis & J. M. Jones (Eds.), *Handbook of emotions* (2nd ed., pp. 325–357). New York: Guilford Press.

Eaker, E. D. (1998). Psychosocial risk factors for coronary heart disease in women. *Cardiology Clinics, 16*, 103–111.

Eisenberg, D. M., Kessler, R. C., Foster, C., Norlock, F. E., Calkins, D. R., & Delblanco, T. L. (1993). Unconventional medicine in the United States. *New England Journal of Medicine, 328*, 246–252.

Ellis, A., & Harper, R. (1975). *A new guide to rational living.* Englewood Cliffs, NJ: Prentice-Hall.

Esterling, B. A., Antoni, M. H., Fletcher, M. A., Marguiles, S., & Schneiderman, N. (1994). Emotional disclosure through writing or speaking modulates latent Epstein-Barr virus reactivation. *Journal of Consulting and Clinical Psychology, 62*, 130–140.

Farhi, D. (1996). *The breathing book: Good health and vitality through essential breath work.* New York: Henry Holt.

Folkman, S., & Lazarus, R. (1991). Coping and emotions. In A. Monat & R. Lazarus (Eds.), *Stress and coping* (3rd ed., pp. 207–227). New York: Columbia University Press.

Francis, M. E., & Pennebaker, J. W. (1992). Putting stress into words: The impact of writing on physiological, absentee, and self-reported emotional well-being measures. *American Journal of Health Promotion, 6*, 280–287.

Freeman, L. W. (2001a). Hypnosis. In L. W. Freeman & G. F. Lawlis (Eds.), *Mosby's complementary and alternative medicine: A research-based approach* (pp. 225–259). St. Louis: Mosby.

Freeman, L. W. (2001b). Massage therapy. In L. W. Freeman & G. F. Lawlis (Eds.), *Mosby's complementary and alternative medicine: A research-based approach* (pp. 361–386). St. Louis: Mosby.

Freeman, L. W. (2001c). Meditation. In L. W. Freeman & G. F. Lawlis (Eds.), *Mosby's complementary and alternative medicine: A research-based approach.* (pp. 166–195). St. Louis: Mosby.

Freeman, L. W. (2001d). Relaxation therapy. In L. W. Freeman & G. F. Lawlis (Eds.), *Mosby's complementary and alternative medicine: A research-based approach.* (pp. 138–165). St. Louis: Mosby.

Freeman, L. W., & Lawlis, G. F. (2001). Exercise as an alternative therapy. In L. W. Freeman & G. F. Lawlis (Eds.), *Mosby's complementary and alternative medicine: A research-based approach* (pp. 424–454). St. Louis: Mosby.

Friedman, M., & Ulmer, D. (1984). *Treating type A behavior and your heart.* New York: Fawcett Crest.

Gold, P. W., Goodwin, F. K., & Chrousos, G. P. (1988). Clinical and biochemical manifestations of depression. Relation to the neurobiology of stress. *New England Journal of Medicine, 319,* 348–353.

Goldwater, B. C., & Collis, M. L. (1985). Psychological effects of cardiovascular conditioning: A controlled experiment. *Journal of Psychosomatic Medicine, 47,* 174–180.

Gronningsaeter, H., Hytten, K., Skauli, G., Christensen, C. C., & Ursin, H. (1992). Improved health and coping by physical exercise or cognitive behavioral stress management-training in a work–environment. *Psychology and Health, 7,* 147–163.

Hafen, B. Q., Karren, K. J., Frandsen, K. J., & Smith, N. L. (1996). *Mind body health: The effects of attitudes, emotions, and relationships.* Boston: Allyn & Bacon.

Hemingway, H., & Marmot, M. (1999). Evidence based cardiology: Psychosocial factors in the aetiology and prognosis of coronary heart disease. Systematic review of prospective cohort studies. *British Medical Journal, 318,* 1460–1467.

Herbert, T. B., & Cohen, S. (1993). Stress and immunity in humans: A meta-analytic review. *Psychosomatic Medicine, 55,* 364–379.

Hoffman-Goetz, L., Simpson, J. R., Cipp, N., Arumugam, Y., & Houston, M. E. (1990). Lymphocyte subset responses to repeated submaximal exercise in men. *Journal of Applied Physiology, 68,* 1069–1074.

Jacobson, E. (1938). *Progressive relaxation.* Chicago: University of Chicago Press.

Jiang, W., Babyak, M., Krantz, D. S., Waugh, R. A., Coleman, R. E., Hanson, M. M., Frid, D. J., McNulty, S., Morris, J. J., O'Connor, C. M., & Blumenthal, J. A. (1996). Mental stress-induced myocardial ischemia and cardiac events. *Journal of the American Medical Association, 275,* 1651–1656.

Kabat-Zinn, J. (1990). *Full catastrophe living: Using the wisdom of your body and mind in everyday life.* New York: Delacorte.

Keyes, J. B. (1995). Stress inoculation training for staff working with persons with mental retardation: A model program. In L. R. Murphy, J. J. Hurrell, Jr., S. L. Sauter, & G. P. Keita (Eds.), *Job stress interventions* (pp. 45–56). Washington DC: American Psychological Association.

Kiecolt-Glaser, J. K., Glaser, R., Strain, E., Stout, J., Tarr, K., Holliday, J., & Speicher, C. (1986). Modulation of cellular immunity in medical students. *Journal of Behavioral Medicine, 9,* 5–21.

Kiev, A. (1987). Managing stress to achieve success. *Executive Health, 24,* 1–4.

Kolbell, R. M. (1995). When relaxation is not enough. In L. R. Murphy, J. J. Hurrell, Jr., S. L. Sauter, & G. P. Keita (Eds.), *Job stress interventions* (pp. 31–43). Washington DC: American Psychological Association.

LaPerriere, A. R., Antoni, M. H., Schneiderman, N., Ironson, G., Klimas, N., Caralis, P., & Fletcher, M. A. (1990). Exercise intervention attenuates emotional distress and natural killer cell decrements following notification of positive serologic status for HIV-1. *Biofeedback and Self-Regulation, 15,* 229–242.

Lazarus, R. S. (1966). *Psychological stress and coping.* New York: McGraw-Hill.

Levi, L. (1981). *Preventing work stress.* Reading, MA: Addison-Wesley.

Lichtenstein, K. L. (1988). *Clinical relaxation strategies.* New York: Wiley.

Linden, W. (1994). Autogenic training: A narrative and quantitative review of clinical outcome. *Biofeedback and Self Regulation, 19,* 227–264.

Martinsen, E. W. (1990). Benefits of exercise for the treatment of depression. *Sports Medicine, 9,* 380–389.

Martinsen, E. W., Hoffart, A., & Solberg, O. (1989). Comparing aerobic with nonaerobic forms of exercise in the treatment of clinical depression: A randomized trial. *Comprehensive Psychiatry, 30,* 324–331.

Martinsen, E. W., Medhus, A., & Sandvik, L. (1985). Effects of aerobic exercise on depression: A controlled study. *British Medical Journal, 291,* 109.

McKinnon, W., Weisse, C. S., Reynolds, C. P., Bowles, C. A., & Baum, A. (1989). Chronic stress, leukocyte subpopulations, and humoral response to latent viruses. *Health Psychology, 8,* 389–402.

McLeroy, K., Green, L., Mullen, K., & Foshee, V. (1984). Assessing the effects of health promotion in worksites: A review of the stress program evaluations. *Health Education Quarterly, 11,* 379–401.

Meichenbaum, D. (1985). *Stress inoculation training.* Elmsford, NY: Pergamon Press.

Mencken, H. L. (1920). *Prejudices: Second series.* New York: Alfred A. Knopf.

Morgan, W. P. (1984). Physical activity and mental health. In H. Eckert & H. J. MonToye, *Exercise and health* (pp. 133–145). Champaign, IL: Human Kinetics.

Morin, C. M., & Kwentus, J. A. (1988). Area review: Sleep disorders—Behavioral and pharmacological treatments for insomnia. *Annals of Behavioral Medicine, 10,* 91–98.

Munz, D. C., Huelsman, T. J., & Craft, C. A. (1995). A worksite stress management program: Theory, application, and outcomes. In L. R. Murphy, J. J. Hurrell, Jr., S. L. Sauter, & G. P. Keita (Eds.), *Job stress interventions* (pp. 57–72). Washington, DC: American Psychological Association.

Murphy, L. R. (1996). Stress management in work settings: A critical review of the health effects. *American Journal of Health Promotion, 11,* 112–135.

Newman, J. E., & Beehr, T. A. (1979). Personal and organizational strategies for handling job stress: A review of research and opinion. *Personnel Psychology, 32,* 1–44.

Novaco, R. W. (1977). A stress inoculation approach to anger management in the training of law enforcement officers. *American Journal of Community Psychology, 5,* 327–346.

Ornish, D. (1998). *Love and survival: The scientific basis for the healing power of intimacy.* New York: Harper Collins.

Orth-Gomer, K., Rosengren, A., & Wilhelmsen, L. (1993). Lack of social support and incidence of coronary heart disease in middle-aged Swedish men. *Psychosomatic Medicine, 55,* 37–43.

Orth-Gomer, K., & Unden, A. L. (1990). Type A behavior, social support, and coronary risk: Interaction and significance for mortality in cardiac patients. *Psychosomatic Medicine, 52,* 59–72.

Pelletier, K. R., & Lutz, R. (1988). Healthy people—healthy business: A critical review of stress management programs in the workplace. *American Journal of Health Promotion, 2,* 5–19.

Pelletier, K. R., & Lutz, R. (1989). Mindbody goes to work: A critical review of stress management programs in the workplace. *Advances, 6,* 28–34.

Pennebaker, J. W. (1993). Putting stress into works: Health, linguistic, and therapeutic implications. *Behaviour Research and Therapy, 31,* 539–548.

Pennebaker, J. W. (1997). *Opening up: The healing power of expressing emotions.* New York: Guilford Press.

Perlis, M. L., & Youngstedt, S. D. (2000). The diagnosis of primary insomnia and treatment alternatives. *Comprehensive Therapy, 26,* 298–306.

Post, R. (1992). Transduction of psychosocial stress into the neurobiology of recurrent affective disorder. *American Journal of Psychiatry, 149,* 999–1010.

Quick, J. C., Murphy, L. R., Hurrell, J. J., Jr., & Orman, D. (1992). The value of work, the risk of distress, and the power of prevention. In J. C. Quick, L. R. Murphy, & J. J. Hurrell, Jr. (Eds.), *Stress and well-being at work.* Washington, DC: American Psychological Association.

Quick, J. C., & Quick, J. D. (1984). *Organizational stress and preventive management.* New York: McGraw-Hill.

Quick, J. C., Quick, J. D., & Horn, R. S. (1986). Health consequences of stress. *Journal of Organizational Behavior Management, 8,* 19–36.

Rodin, J., & Salovey, P. (1989). Health psychology. *Annual Review of Psychology, 40,* 533–579.

Russek, L. G., King, S. H., Russek, S. J., & Russek, H. I. (1990). The Harvard Mastery of Stress Study 35-year follow-up: Prognostic significance of patterns of psychophysiological arousal. *Psychosomatic Medicine, 52,* 271–285.

Sapolsky, R. M. (1998). *Why zebras don't get ulcers.* (Rev. ed.). New York: W. H. Freeman.

Sauter, S. L., Murphy, L. R., & Hurrell, J. J. (1990). Prevention of work-related psychological disorders. *American Psychologist, 45,* 1146–1158.

Schulman, K., & Jones, G. (1996). The effectiveness of massage therapy intervention on reducing anxiety in the workplace. *Journal of Applied Behavioral Science, 32,* 1–9.

Seamonds, B. (1983). Extension of research into stress factors and their effect on illness absenteeism. *Journal of Occupational Medicine, 25,* 821–822.

Seligman, M. (1991). *Learned optimism.* New York: Alfred A. Knopf.

Selye, H. (1976). *Stress in health and disease.* Boston: Butterworths.

Severs, Y., Brenner, I., Shek, P. N., & Shephard, R. J. (1996). Effects of heat and intermittent exercise on leukocyte and sub-population cell counts. *European Journal of Applied Physiology and Occupational Physiology, 74,* 234–245.

Shakespeare, W. (1936). The tragedy of Hamlet, Prince of Denmark. In *The complete works of William Shakespeare.* Garden City, NY: Doubleday.

Shapiro, S. L., Schwartz, G. E., & Bonner, G. (1998). Effects of mindfulness-based stress reduction on medical and premedical students. *Journal of Behavioral Medicine, 21,* 581–599.

Simons, C. W., & Birkimer, J. C. (1988). An exploration of factors predicting the effects of aerobic conditioning on mood state. *Journal of Psychosomatic Research, 32,* 63–75.

Speca, M., Carlson, L. E., Goodey, E., & Angen, M. (2000). A randomized, wait-list controlled clinical trial: The effect of a mindfulness meditation-based stress reduction program on mood and symptoms of stress in cancer outpatients. *Psychosomatic Medicine, 62,* 613–622.

Spera, S. B., Buhfriend, E. D., & Pennebaker, J. W. (1994). Expressive writing and coping with job loss. *Academy of Management Journal, 37,* 722–733.

Spiegel, D., & Bloom, J. R. (1983). Group therapy and hypnosis reduce metastatic breast carcinoma pain. *Psychosomatic Medicine, 45,* 333–339.

Spiegel, H., & Spiegel, D. (1978). *Trance and treatment: Clinical uses of hypnosis.* New York: Asic Books.

Syrjala, K. L., Donaldson, G. W., Davis, M. W., Kippes, M. E., & Carr, J. E. (1995). Relaxation and imagery and cognitive–behavioral training reduce pain during cancer treatment: A controlled clinical trial. *Pain, 63,* 189–198.

Whitehouse, W. G., Dinges, D. F., Orne, E. C., Keller, S. E., Bates, B. L., Morahan, P., Haupt, B. A., Carlin, M. M., Bloom, P. B., Zaugg, L., & Orne, M. T. (1996). Psychosocial and immune effects of self-hypnosis training for stress management throughout the first semester of medical school. *Psychosomatic Medicine, 58,* 249–263.

Williams, R., & Williams, V. (1994). *Anger kills: Seventeen strategies for controlling the hostility that can harm your health.* New York: Harper Perennial.

Williams, R., & Williams, V. (1997). *Lifeskills.* New York: Random House.

Zeitlin, D., Keller, S. E., Shiflett, S. C., Schleifer, S. J., & Bartlett, J. A. (2000). Immunological effects of massage therapy during acute academic stress. *Psychosomatic Medicine, 62,* 83–84.

Part IV

Methodology and Evaluation

The volume concludes with a three-chapter part addressing issues of epidemiology, program evaluation, and socioeconomic cost–benefit analysis. Epidemiology is the science underlying the study of disease epidemics and is the core science for public health as well as the basis for preventive interventions. In any kind of prevention or treatment intervention program, it is essential to conduct evaluations to know if the results of the interventions are as intended as well as to evaluate the cost–benefit ratios for the programs. Therefore, these three concluding chapters are essential for understanding the science of occupational health risks and disorders as well as the science of prevention and intervention to enhance health in occupational settings. These chapters help people working in occupational health psychology answer the question: Does it work?

Chapter 18 by Kasl and Jones develops the epidemiological perspective on research in occupational health psychology, with emphasis on design, measurement of exposures, and surveillance strategies. The authors come from a classical occupational epidemiology tradition, which offers knowledge and insights potentially alien or viewed as inappropriate in a psychologically dominated discipline. Thus, Kasl and Jones build on the classical occupational epidemiology tradition, discussing modifications and elaborations of strategies needed to make the methods they discuss more suitable for the study of psychosocial work exposures. Their perspective reflects the belief that examining the impact of work environment on health calls for interdisciplinary efforts, and that epidemiology has a valuable role to play in occupational health psychology.

Chapter 19 by Adkins and Weiss addresses the evaluation of occupational health psychology programs. As the authors note, even carefully designed, targeted, implemented, and tracked programs may fail to achieve their intended or expected results. The approach to program evaluation set forth in the chapter is a multidimensional process that goes beyond inputs, such as financial costs and personnel time, and outputs. Their model links these to expected program outcomes and to desired organizational goals. Based on their model, the authors set for an approach to the effective design and implementation of a program evaluation strategy for occupational health psychology.

Chapter 20 by DeRango and Franzini reviews the theory and literature on economic evaluations of occupational health interventions. The authors make a distinction between three types of economic evaluations, which are cost-effectiveness, cost–benefit, and cost–utility types. Economic evaluation addresses the question of the alternative use of resources to the intended use for the occupational health psychology intervention. The authors emphasize that an efficacy evaluation and effective evaluation should precede the economic evaluation. Although the basic tasks of an economic evaluation are to identify, measure, and compare the costs and consequences of the alternatives considered, the three different types of economic evaluations considered differ in the measurement of consequences.

18

An Epidemiological Perspective on Research Design, Measurement, and Surveillance Strategies

Stanislav V. Kasl and Beth A. Jones

In this chapter we intend to address a number of methodological issues that we view as important to studies of the impact of the work environment on health and well-being. Because this is the only chapter in the handbook that has a primary focus on methodological issues, we are somewhat concerned that the framework and the perspective we use—that of *occupational and psychosocial epidemiology*—may be seen as somewhat alien or inappropriate in a volume in which psychology is the dominant discipline. Accordingly, we wish to offer our epidemiologic commentary in ways that are both selective and modified to make the comments optimally compatible with, and useful for, occupational health psychology. Frequently, our procedure will be to describe the strategy used in classical occupational epidemiology and then to discuss modifications and elaborations of strategies needed to make the methods more suitable for the study of psychosocial work exposures. Specific topics to be covered include study designs, measurement of exposures, and surveillance strategies.

We certainly do not believe that epidemiology has come up with unique or superior methodological solutions to problems that persistently trouble social and behavioral scientists working in occupational health psychology. Nor do we believe that excellent studies that deal with physical and chemical exposures in the workplace, and focus on biomedical outcomes, should automatically be viewed as the suitable research models for studies of psychosocial work exposures affecting psychological or behavioral outcomes. However, we do believe that examining the impact of the work environment on health and well-being calls for a broadly interdisciplinary approach—more so than most other topics in psychology—and that epidemiology has a valuable role to play.

Even though study designs and measurement of exposure are topics discussed in separate sections, it needs to be recognized that methodological strengths or potential weaknesses in one domain may be linked to, or contingent on, strengths and weaknesses in another domain. For example, the impact of limitations in measurement of psychosocial work exposures may vary depending on the method used, such as laboratory-based biological data compared to self-reports of symptoms of distress. Similarly, cross-sectional designs may increase our concern about measurement shortcomings, whereas prospective designs may lessen some concerns, such as the influence of the outcome on measured exposure. Conversely, inappropriate analysis of data may undermine a particular study strength, such as a prospective design. And, of course, availability of specific additional variables, which can be included in analyses as controls for potential confounders, can dramatically alter uncertainties about the proper interpretation of findings, resulting from design or measurement limitation.

It is not clear to what extent methodological concerns are also contingent on the kind of theory (if any) that has guided a study. Obviously, the use of a particular theoretical approach in designing a study, such as the demand–control–support model or the effort–reward imbalance model (Bosma et al., 1998; Karasek & Theorell, 2000; Peter & Siegrist, 2000; Siegrist & Peter, 2000; Theorell et al., 1998), can be undermined by the omission of a crucial variable or the inadequate operationalization of an important construct. Problems also arise when a theory is marginally appropriate to a particular occupational setting, such as the use of the demand–control model when studying physicians: In this case, very high levels of decision authority in fact represent high levels of demand and responsibility (Calnan, Wainwright, Forsythe, Wall, & Almond, 2001). This may lead to inadequate analyses and to inappropriate interpretations of findings. But beyond that, it would seem that guidelines about good research designs and strong measurement are not particularly altered by the kind of theory that underpins a study.

Study Design Considerations

The broad objectives of studies in occupational epidemiology can be characterized as follows: (a) to demonstrate the etiological role of an exposure variable; (b) to show that this role remains after adjustments for necessary confounders and control variables; and (c) to learn as much as possible about the underlying mechanisms and the moderating influences involved in the etiological relationship.

The classical design in occupational epidemiology, frequently used and still serviceable, is relatively straightforward: establish differences in disease-specific morbidity or mortality by occupation and place of work, and then search for environmental agents in the workplace, the exposure to which might explain these differences. This strategy works well enough when certain conditions are near optimal: (a) self-selection into occupations (e.g., because of health status or personal characteristics) and company selection policies are minimal, and any selection that exists either does not produce confounding or can be controlled statistically; (b) type and extent of exposure can be pinpointed and quantified; (c) identification of cases and noncases is complete and without bias (e.g., not contingent on seeking or receiving treatment and not influenced by knowledge of exposure status);

(d) latency between exposure and detection is relatively short, an ideal that is more likely to be met for injuries and musculoskeletal disorders than for many cancers; (e) the disease is rare and the relative risk of disease, given exposure, is high; and (f) the disease has a simple etiology in that work setting and moderators of the exposure–disease relationship are weak or nonexistent. The original story of angiosarcoma of the liver and exposure to polyvinylchloride (e.g., Creech & Johnson, 1974) illustrates these optimal conditions admirably.

This classical design in occupational epidemiology is a useful reference point for studies conducted within the domain of occupational health psychology, but is not an adequate study design model because many of the conditions listed earlier are not satisfied. In other words, studies of physical and chemical exposures in relation to occupational cancers or workplace injuries are not enough of a model for the study of the impact of the psychosocial work environment on health and well-being. (A similar point will be made later when we consider the applicability of classical surveillance strategies to occupational health psychology.) However, the identification of the particular conditions that make the study of some exposure–disease link relatively uncomplicated is still quite valuable when we face a research problem that is more intractable. Most often, the problems we encounter in occupational health psychology have to do with (a) identifying the correct or relevant exposure variable(s) and measuring it (them) appropriately; (b) taking sufficient account of the influence of moderators, which may include a whole host of personal and trait characteristics, as well as behavioral and psychological processes taking place over time; (c) studying outcomes that have a complex etiology, that develop gradually, and where the relative risk of disease, given exposure, is rather weak. Other issues, such as self-selection concerns or biases in the detection of an outcome, would not seem to be a priori more troublesome in occupational health psychology than in classical occupational epidemiology.

Because the vast majority of studies of the health impact of work exposures use observational (nonexperimental) designs, it is useful to identify and discuss elements of observational designs that represent strengths. In our opinion, these elements are suitable targets for implementation at the point of designing a study of psychosocial work characteristics and health.

The Environmental Condition (Exposure) Is Objectively Defined and Measured

Admittedly, this is a position that, although completely noncontroversial in occupational epidemiology, is a subject of considerable debate in occupational health psychology, more so in the context of the narrower topic of "work stress" and somewhat less so when tied to the broader topic of "psychosocial work conditions." This debate, often using the uncomfortable and inadequate terminology of "subjective vs. objective" measurement, is not uncommon in other areas of psychology, such as the work that has dealt with the residential environment (e.g., Archea, 1977; Taylor, 1980; Wohlwill, 1973). We have previously elaborated on the reasons for anchoring the study to the objective assessment of the exposure conditions (Kasl, 1998; Kasl & Jones, 2001) and will deal with it separately in the section below on measurement.

Mediating Processes Are Studied, and Vulnerability or Protective Factors That Interact With Exposure Are Included

The intent is to include all the relevant psychological and behavioral variables that are emphasized by those who use primarily psychological formulations of the process (e.g., Perrewé & Zellars, 1999) or who have come out on the "subjective" side of the measurement debate (e.g., Vagg & Spielberger, 1998; Williams & Cooper, 1998). However, unlike the psychological formulations where the first step in the (presumed) causal process is the subjectively defined work exposure and there is no assessment of the objective features of the work environment, in the occupational epidemiology perspective that we are recommending, the first step is the objectively defined exposure and the mediating psychological and behavioral processes are anchored to it. Of course, this point is part of the overall debate about exposure measurement, and we return to it below. It might also be noted that a second controversy awaits our attention: whether negative affectivity is to be viewed as a vulnerability factor (a true moderator or even a true independent causal influence) or as an undesirable response set that inflates associations among self-report measures of stress, strain, and distress (Payne, 2000; Spector, Zapf, et al., 2000).

The Cohort Is Identified Before Any Exposure, Self-Selection Into Exposure Conditions Is Minimized, and the Cohort Can Be Followed Through the Transition and for Short-Term and Long-Term Effects of Exposure

This is perhaps the most idealized (i.e., difficult to achieve) design strength in our listing, but it is one that is especially pertinent to occupational health psychology. In studies of the health impact of physical and chemical exposures, the start of exposure may be relatively easily established (e.g., by date of the person's entry into the particular work setting or by the date of introduction of a new industrial process). The quantification of exposure may also be reasonably straightforward (e.g., the cumulative duration of radiation exposure by level of radiation). Using medical records to establish that individuals in the cohort are initially free of disease, such as cancer, is also relatively easy. Similarly, innovations in the field of molecular biomarkers (McMichael, 1994) can facilitate the measurement of internal exposures and of early biological response, such as precursors to cancer or early pathologic changes.

The contrasting situation in occupational health psychology is frequently more difficult, more complex. First, the field seldom uses the strategy of studying newcomers into a job (e.g., Saks & Ashforth, 2000), a design that would seem to hold considerable promise, particularly for the study of early adaptation and coping. Second, opportunities for using "natural experiments," with changes in the work setting that generate comparable groups of exposed and unexposed workers and that allow for baseline, prechange data collection, are relatively rare. Some exceptions include (a) studies of effects of job loss based on finding unexpected factory closures where all the workers lose their jobs (Morris & Cook, 1991); (b) studies of effects of job insecurity based in companies involved in downsizing and planned mergers (Ferrie, Shipley, Marmot, Stansfeld, & Smith, 1995); and (c) studies of unexpected changes in job demands and work environment (Kittel, Kornitzer, & Dramaix, 1980). These "natural experiments" provide baseline data and establish temporal sequence of changes, thus improving our ability to argue for a cause-and-effect relationship.

These comments are meant to sensitize the future investigator to the danger of setting up a longitudinal follow-up of a cohort of workers where often the best one can do is observe small changes in a cohort that is in a steady state. The beginning and the end of follow-up are relatively arbitrary points in the lives of the workers. The measurement of exposure is a particularly troublesome issue, given the presumed importance of the mediating psychological processes: Length of tenure in a particular job is a poor substitute for measuring the previous history of these psychological processes at various points in the past. The assumption that the respondent's position on these dimensions (e.g., psychological demands) at the arbitrary start of the follow-up is representative of the whole tenure in that job would seem somewhat dubious. This suggests that the steady-state cohort that is being studied during an arbitrary temporal window on their working lives will consist of three (hypothetical) types of individuals: those who are studied "too early" to observe any effects, those who are studied "too late" because the effects have already taken place, and those for whom the temporal window is "just right" to reveal effects. Unfortunately, most of the time we do not have external criteria for identifying these three (hypothetical) subgroups. By way of contrast, in prospective studies of incidence of physical disease outcomes, such as myocardial infarction, we delete those with history of the disease at baseline from the cohort. And we try to choose the age range for the study cohort to maximally reflect the period of risk for first events. However, when studying psychological and behavioral processes, and assessing exposures and outcomes with continuous measures, we do not set up a truly prospective design (before disease occurrence) but merely a longitudinal one—in other words, changes measured from one time point to another.

The comments in the previous paragraph are linked to the assumption that there is a standard and preferred way of analyzing such longitudinal data. The statistical model that is normally set up examines the outcome at Time 2 in relation to exposure at Time 1, controlling for the value of the outcome at Time 1 (among other control variables). It is inappropriate to fail to control for the value of the outcome at Time 1 (e.g., Niedhammer, Goldberg, Leclerc, Bregel, & David, 1998) or to predict the outcome at Time 2 from the average of values of exposure at both Time 1 and Time 2 (e.g., Cheng, Kawachi, Coakley, Schwartz, & Colditz, 2000). Because this standard way of analyzing the longitudinal data means predicting changes net of the baseline (cross-sectional) association of exposure and outcome, the cohort needs to include enough individuals for whom the effects of exposure have not yet played themselves out to be an informative design.

Special Study Designs in Occupational and Psychosocial Epidemiology

Elsewhere (Kasl & Jones, 2001) we listed a number of traditional designs in psychosocial epidemiology and discussed associated strengths and weaknesses. These designs were (a) random assignment to exposure or beneficial intervention; (b) prospective designs in which some cohort members change exposure status; (c) traditional prospective cohort designs; (d) cross-sectional population surveys; and (e) case-control retrospective designs. This is a textbook classification and is not as useful as grouping studies in an ad hoc fashion according to types of approaches actually used in occupational epidemiology (Kasl & Amick, 1995). We comment on three interesting varieties of design approaches.

Studies With Limited Information Using Occupational Titles

Typically, these are studies of total mortality (e.g., Fletcher, 1991) and selected morbidities, such as myocardial infarction (e.g., Bolm-Audorff & Siegrist, 1983) and major depressive disorders (e.g., Eaton, Anthony, Mandel, & Garrison, 1990). The studies do not tell us more than they seem to—namely what occupations have high and low rates, given the methodology. We cannot identify the specific aspects of these jobs that contribute to the differential rates, confounders remain uncontrolled, and what segment of the total etiology (risk factor differences, differential incidence given risk factors, case fatality) is reflected by these rates remains unclear.

Some studies have adopted the supplementary strategy of imputing values for the demand–control model dimensions, based on data from separate surveys of individuals (e.g., Hammar, Alfredsson, & Johnson, 1998; Schwartz, 2000; Steenland, Johnson, & Nowlin, 1997). Although this is an inventive bootstrap strategy, the concern is that the imputation is too narrowly based in a single theoretical model and alternatives are not usually explored. Furthermore, because occupational titles explain a fair amount of variance in some dimensions (physical demands, decision latitude) and relatively little in other dimensions (psychological demands, supervisor support; Bultmann, Kant, van Amelsvoort, van den Brandt, &

Kasl, 2001; Karasek & Theorell, 1990), this imputation strategy seems appropriate for some dimensions and not for others.

Intensive Studies of Single Occupations

The occupational health literature contains many studies of single occupations. Earlier work tended to focus on such occupations as air traffic controllers, bus drivers, police officers, and health care personnel (Kasl & Amick, 1995). The more recent work continues the interest in drivers and transportation workers (e.g., Gustavson et al., 1996; Peter, Geibler, & Siegrist, 1998; Piros, Karlehagen, Lappas, & Wilhelmsen, 2000) and health care workers (e.g., Bourbonnais, Comeau, & Vezina, 1999; Kirkcaldy & Martin, 2000; Williams, Dale, Glucksman, & Wellesley, 1997). The study of a single occupation would seem inappropriate when we are still at the point of trying to show that it is associated with high rates of some adverse outcome, or if we are worried that any association between exposure and outcome may not be generalizable to other work settings. Aside from these considerations, the primary question about this approach is, What is the payoff from this research strategy, other than finding out more about a particular occupation? If earlier work on many occupations points to these as high stress occupations, or if they have high rates of a particular health problem, will this strategy advance our understanding of the health impact of the work environment? The answer is that it depends. If the difference in the level of exposure to some hazard that describes the original difference across many occupations can be made even bigger and clearer or more precise by studying only individuals within a single occupation, then we learn more. If, for example, the presumed hazard among bus drivers is a result of bad traffic conditions on the bus route (Netterstrom & Juel, 1988; Winklebly, Ragland, Fisher, & Syme, 1988), then finding bus drivers on rural routes with very little traffic would be a good contrast that may control for many exogenous variables. If, on the other hand, the presumed hazard is uniformly high for most of the job occupants, then the risk factors for an adverse health outcome will be primarily related to individual differences in perceptions, responding, coping, and personal characteristics. Moreover, these predictors may be unique for that setting and will not account for the high rates of some health problems in this occupation, compared to other occupations, which was the original observation in search of explanations. Thus the work setting for air traffic controllers in high density air traffic areas seems fairly homogeneous, and some of the risk factors that have emerged reflected individual characteristics, such as Type A personality, amicability, and conscientiousness (Lee, Niemcryk, Jenkins, & Rose, 1989). We might also note a dilemma faced by investigators who study single occupations: whether to use a generic instrument for measuring psychosocial workplace exposures in any occupation (Landsbergis & Theorell, 2000), which may not be sufficiently appropriate for that particular work setting, or develop a tailor-made instrument, which will make it difficult to generalize findings to other occupations.

Designs That Describe Acute Changes in Biological Variables

The monitoring of acute effects of work stressors on biological variables is a research strategy that has become quite popular. The designs include 24-hour monitoring, changes during the working day, and comparisons of working and nonworking occasions, such as before work day begins, after work day ends, during sleep, and during vacation. The biological indicators most often used are blood pressure, cortisol, and catecholamines. It is unlikely that self-report measures of stress, distress, and symptoms would be suitable in these designs because the frequent data collection over a short period of time would have reactive effects.

A simple approach is to measure the increase in some biological indicator from the start of the workday to the end, and to relate the magnitude of the increase to type of job and to work conditions. The presumption is that larger increases will be observed in more demanding or hazardous work settings. For example, in a study of blood pressure in a prison setting, work-related increases among guards were greater in maximum security than in minimum security prisons (Ostfeld, Kasl, D'Atri, & Fitzgerald, 1987). Among other correctional personnel, those involved in treatment had higher increases than service and clerical workers, particularly for women. In interpreting these findings, one has to assume that a change during the day, such as a small decline, is a function of a relatively non-stressful work setting, rather than reflecting strong anticipation effects of coming to a difficult work setting, so that the values at the start of the day are already quite high.

Studies of increased reactivity during the work day have been significantly enriched by also examining changes that cross the work and nonwork boundary, the studies of so-called "spillover" or "unwinding" (e.g., James & Bovbjerg, 2001; Luecken et al., 1997; Sluiter, Fringo-Dresen, Meijman, & van der Beek, 2000; Steptoe, Lundwall, & Cropley, 2000). The measurement of failure to recover from putative work-linked high levels of catecholamines and cortisol comes close to the ideal of studying acute biological changes that have great promise as risk factors for adverse health events: Repeated occasions of such patterns of acute reactivity appear likely to translate into irreversible changes with clinical significance. However, one must not forget that the link to specific disease outcomes is yet to be securely established (Sluiter et al., 2000). It should also be noted that the spillover studies must be able to account for the possible contributing influences of nonwork demands and stressors. Failure to recover from high levels at work is presumably indicative of a stressful job only if the nonwork situation is relatively low on stress. Otherwise, such failure to recover is ambiguous, perhaps reflecting the impact of several role domains.

Some Issues in the Measurement of Psychosocial Workplace Exposures

One of the most persistent issues in this area of measurement is the debate concerning the proper place for "objective" versus "subjective" measurement strategies. The recent illuminating and helpful exchange between Perrewé and Zellars (1999) and Frese and Zapf (1999) is a testimony to the undying nature of this controversy. As we indicated earlier, the perspective that we use for this chapter—that of occupational and psychosocial epidemiology— puts us solidly aligned with the position enunciated by Frese and Zapf (1999): The objective measurement of the environmental condition (exposure) is a crucial component of an occupational health study and its omission is likely to limit the interpretability of its findings. Over the years, we have maintained this position (Kasl, 1978, 1987, 1991, 1998); the opposing viewpoints from the two sides of the debate continue to be formulated in similar ways. Hurrell, Nelson, & Simmons (1998) have provided an excellent and balanced overview of this continued debate.

We find it illuminating that although the argument of Frese and Zapf (1999) is essentially quite pragmatic, based on accumulated research experience, the position of Perrewé and Zellars (1999) is closely derived from theory, the transactional model of the stress process (Lazarus, 1966). It is from this model that they derive "a research agenda for the study of the organizational stress process that focuses on the appraisal of objective stressors, attributions regarding the felt stress, and the subsequent affective emotions" (p. 740). There is nothing wrong with this statement, except that it truncates the phenomenon that needs to be studied, and the research strategy that needs to be applied to it, in two crucial ways. It leaves out the objective stressors and it omits a variety of outcomes, both proximal and distal to the "affective emotions." The latter concern is important, because the transactional process may differ substantially, depending on the outcomes being studied. For example, outcomes such as sickness absence, heavy alcohol consumption, and lower back disorders may involve additional appraisal and attribution processes that should also be studied. Other outcomes, such as biological risk factors and clinical outcomes may necessitate the inclusion of other transactional steps, such as health-care seeking and adherence to medications.

The various considerations in favor of "objective" versus "subjective" measurement strategies may be summarized as follows (Kasl, 1998).

Arguments in Favor of Objective Measurement Strategies

(a) We will have a clearer linkage to the "actual" environmental conditions and will know much better what aspects of the environment needs changing, should that be the contemplated next step. (b) We will have a clearer picture of the etiological process, because the complete set of important antecedent influences on the subjective measures will be otherwise unclear. (c) There will be less potential measurement confounding when the outcomes linked to the exposure are psychological and behavioral. (d) There will be a clearer separation of where the independent variable ends and the mediator or dependent variables begin. With subjective measures describing the transactional process, the components (e.g., appraisals and attributions) in actuality may not be separate steps and may not take place in the theoretically predicted order.

Arguments in Favor of a Subjective Measurement Strategy

(a) The psychological meaning of exposure, and the experience of it, varies substantially across individuals. (b) Cognitive and emotional processing strongly moderates the overall etiological process and the subjective exposure clarifies the etiological mechanism. (c) Environmental manipulation is not possible, only differential reactivity of individuals can be addressed, thus making the appraisals the better target of any contemplated interventions. (d) Objective measures are irrelevant or hopelessly trivial or outside of any possible causal chain (in Lewin's terminology, not part of the life space but in the "foreign hull"—i.e., that part of the environment of which the person is not aware).

There would seem to be several possibilities for fine-tuning the debate so that it is less polarized. For example, there are some outcomes, such as musculoskeletal disorders, where there appears to be an exquisitely complex interplay of biomechanical and ergonomic factors with psychosocial variables (e.g., Devereux, Buckle, & Vlachonikolis, 1999; MacFarlane, Hunt, & Silman, 2000; Smedley, Egger, Cooper, & Coggon, 1997), so that the need for objective measurement of work dimensions seems essential. On the other hand, the accumulated evidence linking psychosocial exposures in the workplace to cardiovascular disease is rather impressive (e.g., Schnall, Belkic, Landsbergis, & Baker, 2000) and yet this research domain has not generally used objective measures.

Pragmatic considerations have also been part of this debate. Fundamentally, self-report measures tend to be more easily available, cheaper, and more convenient. Moreover, it is not difficult to develop generic instruments that can be used across many occupations. On the other hand, objective measures for assessing dimensions of the work environment are seen as expensive, clumsy, difficult to obtain, and with their own set of limitations. In addition, they tend to be specific to a few jobs, and generic approaches are difficult to develop. However, these are somewhat polarizing perceptions. Although the proposed methodology by Hacker (1993) does indeed seem complicated and labor-intensive, there are settings in which objective measurement appears less challenging. For example, Greiner, Ragland, Krause, Syme, & Fisher (1997) have been able to develop a useful objective measure of occupational stress for urban transit operators. In certain settings, such as jobs involving human computer interactions (e.g., Smith, Conway, & Karsh, 1999), many features of the job setting are relatively easy to assess objectively and may even be part of ongoing recordkeep-

ing: technology breakdowns, technology slowdowns, and electronic performance monitoring. And objective measures that are based on data provided
by informed personnel managers seem quite feasible even in large epidemiological surveys such as the Whitehall II study (Bosma et al., 1997). In
general, considerable methodological work continues to be carried out that
explores the validity, reliability, and usefulness of self-reports versus alternative data collection strategies for measuring work exposures. Studies
have targeted chemical exposures, biomechanic and ergonomic task demands, and psychosocial work dimensions (e.g., Benke et al., 2001; Fritschi,
Siemiatycki, & Richardson, 1996; Hansson et al., 2001; Ostry et al., 2001a,
2001b; Stewart & Stenzel, 2000; Waldenstrom, Josephson, Persson, &
Theorell, 1998). Investigators who keep up with this literature may find
useful new measurement strategies.

The strategy of examining data by job titles or job classifications represents a minimal concession to the argument for objective measurement. It
was noted earlier that occupational titles explain a fair amount of variance
in some dimensions (physical demands, decision latitude) and relatively
little in other dimensions (psychological demands, supervisor support;
(Bultmann et al., 2001; Karasek & Theorell, 1990). Such variation in
strength of associations is surely informative and represents an opportunity
to learn more about the meaning of our measures. It is interesting to note,
for example, that a similar variation was observed in a methodological
study using experienced job evaluators in a sawmill industry setting (Ostry
et al., 2001b). The evaluators were able to reliably estimate the job control
dimension, but for job demands the reliability was poorest of all the dimensions assessed.

The situation in which job titles explain a very small amount of variance
in a particular dimension, such as job demands, raises a number of challenges: Are the job titles too crude a classification schema to pick up variations in job demands, and do we therefore need smaller units of analysis,
which will more accurately reflect the actual tasks for that particular respondent? Or is it that more refined classifications will not explain more
variance in job demands because these are highly subjective assessments
not linked to the objective work situation? Does the meaning of high job
demands differ by occupations so that analyses of it as a risk factor, such
as for coronary heart disease, need to account for this in statistical model-
building instead of ignoring job titles altogether? Does the weak association
between job titles and job demands pose problems for developing work-
based interventions? Does such a weak association mean that job demands
simply reflect preexisting traits such as neuroticism or affective negativity,
or are they truly perceptions of the work situation, however idiosyncratic?

The last sentence is an obvious segue into the controversy over negative
affectivity (NA) and what role it plays—and should play—in occupational
health psychology studies. The original concern raised in the context of
work stress studies (Kasl, 1978) dealt with the potential triviality of reporting cross-sectional stress–strain relationships, given the conceptual and
operational overlap of measures of these "independent" and "dependent"
variables. This issue eventually refocused on the role of NA (Watson, Penne-

backer, & Folger, 1987), a presumed individual difference variable that reflects a general tendency to experience and report negative emotions and negative evaluations and distressing symptoms. The primary questions are, Does NA affect the measurement of subjective exposures and indicators of strain and distress in a way that creates a biased inflation of the observed association, which then needs to be partialed out statistically? Or does NA have "a substantive role" (Spector, Zapf, et al., 2000) and controlling for it distorts the true etiological relationships?

A number of observations can be made regarding this debate: (a) Most studies measure NA with symptom scales reflecting anxiety or neuroticism. We do not have any direct measures of NA as a *dispositional* tendency; we only have measures based on actual reporting of symptoms. (b) The issues raised are not relevant when a study uses objective measures of exposure and biomedical outcomes. For associations between subjective work exposures and biomedical outcomes, the issue of biased inflation of associations still does not apply, but the issue of a proper interpretation of the exposure variable can be raised. (c) We do have empirical evidence regarding the issue of how much difference it makes if we partial out the influence of NA: (i) relatively little (Spector, Chen, & O'Connell, 2000a), particularly if biomedical outcomes are involved (Bosma et al., 1997); (ii) quite a bit (Burke, Brief, & George, 1993); (iii) depends on what pairs of variables are involved in the adjustment (Brennan & Barnett, 1998; Chen & Spector, 1991). (iv) Payne's (2000) suggestion that there is no harm in comparing results without and with the partialing out of NA effects is eminently sensible, because knowing more is better than knowing less, and such additional information is fully in the spirit of carrying out sensitivity analyses. It does not oblige us to choose a particular interpretation. (v) The Spector, Zapf, et al. (2000) paper flows entirely from the initial hypothetical premise "if indeed NA has a substantive role," (p. 79), but empirical support for the premise is not easy to obtain. It is interesting to note that the discussion of how one could investigate this premise empirically drifts inexorably toward the suggestion that one would have to do this in the context of also having objective data on work exposures.

We end this section with a few comments on the need to go beyond existing, established instruments (e.g., Landsbergis & Theorell, 2000) and need to develop additional measures as new work issues emerge. For example, there is an increasing importance of the theme of precarious employment (Benavides, Benach, Diez-Roux, & Roman, 2000), downsizing (Kivimaki, Vahtera, Pentti, & Ferrie, 2000), job insecurity (Domenighetti, D'Avanzo, & Bisig, 2000), and lean production teams (Jackson & Mullarkey, 2000) that would seem to call for additional instruments. New developments in the workplace, such as computerization, seem to demand not just assessment of new dimensions of work but may also require paying attention to the associated changes in the whole organizational structure (Burris, 1998). The accelerating change from a manufacturing economy to a service economy may put strain on our theoretical models that are more tied to the former than the latter (Marshall, Barnett, & Sayer, 1997).

Surveillance Strategies for Psychosocial Work Hazards

Medical surveillance in the workplace has been described as "the systematic collection and evaluation of employee health data to identify specific instances of illness or health trends suggesting an adverse effect of work exposures, coupled with actions to reduce hazardous workplace exposures" (Rempel, 1990, p. 435). The primary prevention strategy is based on industrial hygiene *exposure* assessment, and secondary prevention is based on early and rapid detection of adverse health *outcomes* associated with particular work settings (Rempel, 1990). The primary prevention approach presumes that one has good documentation of the health risks associated with an exposure. Secondary prevention is often linked to the strategy of sentinel health events (Rutstein et al., 1983): Such events represent a disease, or disability, or untimely death that is related to occupation and the occurrence of which signals the need for epidemiological or hygiene studies and prevention intervention. The July–September 1990 issue of *Occupational Medicine* and the supplement to the December 1989 issue of the *American Journal of Public Health* provide useful overviews of the many issues and strategies.

Most surveillance strategies are based on monitoring selected adverse *health outcomes* that are linked to research in traditional occupational medicine, not occupational health psychology. For example, a recent Pan American Health Organization (PAHO) expert panel (Choi, Eijkemans, & Tennassee, 2001) selected three sentinel events for surveillance: occupational fatal injuries, pesticide poisoning, and low back pain. In general, the successful state programs for occupational disease surveillance concentrate on conditions that have a short latency period, are easily diagnosed, and are easily linked to a workplace hazard (Henderson, Payne, Ossiander, Evans, & Kaufman, 1998). Surveillance is often based on very specific existing databases, such as insurance claims for disability in a specific industry (Parks, Krebs, & Miner, 1996) or hospital emergency department records for work-related inhalations (Henneberger, Matayer, Layne, & Althouse, 2000). Broader and more systematic surveillance may need outreach efforts, often under state sponsorship and funding (Davis, Wellman, & Punnett, 2001; Forst, Hryhorczuk, & Jaros, 1999; Rosenman, Reilly, & Kalinowski, 1997). Nationwide data are often based on analyses of cause-specific mortality rates by occupations (e.g., Aronson, Howe, Carpenter, & Fair, 1999) or on linkages of two or more national data sets (e.g., Leigh & Miller, 1998).

Surveillance efforts that emphasize workplace *exposure* are considerably less frequent, often limited to a specific industry, such as construction (McKernan, 2000) and nuclear weapons facilities (Ruttenber et al., 2001). At the national level, the National Institute of Occupational Safety and Health (NIOSH) has been the source of several hazard surveillance surveys dealing with chemical, physical, and biological agents (Boiano & Hull, 2001). Monitoring of psychosocial work exposures is quite rare (e.g., Houtman et al., 1998). However, such "monitoring" is no different from surveying workers in many occupations and industries and administering one or more of the established instruments. These data may then be used to impute exposure to other workers in those occupations who were not surveyed (Schwartz, 2000).

Although epidemiology does not usually include the putative etiological factor with the diagnostic criteria, the diagnosis of "occupational disease" in occupational medicine comes from a more clinical tradition. Such a diagnosis can be quite a complicated exercise (Cherry, 1999; Palmer & Coggon, 1996), and its use in surveillance may involve additional pragmatic but nonmedical considerations: union-company contracts, workers' compensation guidelines, insurance reimbursement, judgment of referring clinician, and so on. The monitoring strategies noted tend to both oversimplify the diagnostic issues as well as focus on conditions (short latency, simple etiology, easy link to workplace hazard) where the diagnosis is reasonably justifiable. This is done in the service of detecting hazards that can be eliminated, not for the purposes of conducting an accurate epidemiological study of prevalence.

In trying to develop surveillance strategies for psychosocial work exposures linked to a variety of biomedical and psychological outcomes, we may not be able to borrow much from traditional occupational medicine (Kasl, 1992). It is very difficult to translate surveillance strategies, developed for chemical–physical–biological exposures and for health outcomes that are relatively easily linked to work hazards, into ways of monitoring psychosocial work exposures and health outcomes with complex etiologies. Consider the strategy of sentinel health events. We might choose some rare but notable outcome such as suicide (Sauter, Murphy, & Hurrell, 1990). Presumably, we would pay attention to suicides that occur in the workplace, but this does not make it an "occupational suicide" the way an injury at work does. Suicides occurring elsewhere could still be related to work but these would be missed. Because there is little evidence that suicides are sufficiently often work-related, one might end up doing a large number of psychological autopsies to detect the one that seems to have a primarily work-related etiology. Of course, nothing prevents us from linking cause-specific mortality data (i.e., suicide) to occupational titles to identify jobs with high rates, but this is no longer the sentinel health events strategy. We can also note that surveillance in occupational medicine uses a variety of sources of data to provide health outcome data: occupational health clinics, law-mandated physician reporting, registries, Occupational Safety and Health Administration (OSHA) 200 logs, workers' compensation data, and so on. However, none of these would be suitable for dealing with psychological outcomes or common diseases such as coronary heart disease.

Surveillance based on identifying workplace hazards runs into a different set of problems. Because some of the psychosocial work exposures, such as job demands, are very poorly linked to occupations, we cannot use job titles or expert raters to identify this hazard. We are primarily looking for individuals who report high demands; this is not surveillance, this is conducting epidemiological surveys. Even for work exposures that are more closely linked to occupational titles, such as decision latitude, identifying jobs alone is a relatively poor strategy given the additional importance of psychosocial characteristics of individuals that moderate the etiological picture. Thus the task is really to identify combinations of psychosocial work exposures and personal vulnerabilities of job occupants, rather than only exposures, which again moves us beyond the simple notion of surveillance. For many chemical and biological hazards, on the other hand, psychosocial moderators tend to be unimportant.

If surveillance is seen as a short-cut to identifying hazard–disease linkages that bypasses the traditional epidemiological cohort surveys that are more expensive and labor-intensive, then it would seem that occupational health psychology offers very few worthwhile possibilities for such shortcuts. Mostly, we need to fall back on traditional research strategies to provide us with additional information on the impact of the psychosocial work environment on health and well-being. Fortunately, as this handbook demonstrates, the accumulated evidence is considerable and provides a sound scientific basis for identifying work dimensions that are likely to represent health hazards.

Conclusion

In this chapter, we have dealt with three methodological topics: study designs, measurement of exposures, and surveillance strategies. Our mandate was to use the perspectives of occupational and psychosocial epidemiology to discuss and elaborate on these methodological issues. The procedure we adopted was to describe the specific strategies and practices used in classical occupational epidemiology, and then to discuss the modifications and elaborations of such strategies needed to make the methods suitable for the study of psychosocial work exposures and psychological outcomes typical of occupational health psychology. In this approach, our implicit assumption has been that neither a purely psychological approach nor a purely biomedical one will be adequate to tackle the complex research issues that characterize this field. We believe that epidemiology can provide the best framework for the broadly interdisciplinary approach that is needed.

References

Archea, J. (1977). The place of architectural factors in behavioral theories of privacy. *Journal of Social Issues, 33,* 116–137.

Aronson, K. J., Howe, G. R., Carpenter, M., & Fair, M. E. (1999). Surveillance of potential associations between occupations and causes of death in Canada, 1965–1991. *Occupational and Environmental Medicine, 56,* 265–269.

Benavides, F. G., Benach, J., Diez-Roux, A. V., & Roman, C. (2000). How do types of employment relate to health indicators? Findings from the Second European Survey of Working Conditions. *Journal of Epidemiology and Community Health, 54,* 494–501.

Benke, G., Sim, M., Fritschi, L., Aldred, G., Forbes, A., & Kaupinnen, T. (2001). Comparison of occupational exposure using three different methods: Hygiene panel, job exposure matrix (JEM), and self-reports. *Applied Occupational and Environmental Hygiene, 16,* 84–91.

Boiano, J. M., & Hull, R. D. (2001). Development of a national survey and database associated with NIOSH hazard surveillance initiatives. *Applied Occupational and Environmental Hygiene, 16,* 128–134.

Bolm-Audorff, U., & Siegrist, J. (1983). Occupational morbidity data in myocardial infarction. *Journal of Occupational Medicine, 25,* 367–371.

Bosma, H., Marmot, M. G., Hemingway, H., Nicholson, A. C., Brunner, E., & Stansfeld, S. A. (1997). Low job control and risk of coronary heart disease in Whitehall II (prospective cohort) study. *British Medical Journal, 314,* 558–565.

Bosma, H., Peter, R., Siegrist, J., & Marmot, M. (1998). Two alternative job stress models and the risk of coronary heart disease. *American Journal of Public Health, 88,* 68–74.

Bourbonnais, R., Comeau, M., & Vezina, M. (1999). Job strain and evolution of mental health among nurses. *Journal of Occupational Health Psychology, 4,* 95–107.

Brennan, R. T., & Barnett, R. C. (1998). Negative affectivity: How serious a threat to self-report studies of psychological distress? *Women's Health, 4,* 369–383.

Bultmann, U., Kant, I., van Amelsvoort, L. G. P. M., van den Brandt, P. A., & Kasl, S. V. (2001). Differences in fatigue and psychological distress across occupations: results from the Maastricht Cohort Study of Fatigue at Work. *Journal of Occupational and Environmental Medicine, 43,* 976–983.

Burke, M. J., Brief, A. P., & George, J. M. (1993). The role of negative affectivity in understanding relations between self-reports of stressors and strains: A comment on the applied psychology literature. *Journal of Applied Psychology, 78,* 402–412.

Burris, B. H. (1998). Computerization of the workplace. *Annual Review of Sociology, 24,* 141–157.

Calnan, M., Wainwright, D., Forsythe, M., Wall, B., & Almond, S. (2001). Mental health and stress in the workplace: The case of general practice in the UK. *Social Science & Medicine, 52,* 499–507.

Chen, P. Y., & Spector, P. E. (1991). Negative affectivity as the underlying cause of correlations between stressors and strains. *Journal of Applied Psychology, 76,* 398–407.

Cheng, Y., Kawachi, I., Coakley, E. H., Schwartz, J., & Colditz, G. (2000). Association between psychosocial work characteristics and health functioning in American women: prospective study. *British Medical Journal, 320,* 1432–1436.

Cherry, N. (1999). Occupational disease. *British Medical Journal, 318,* 1397–1399.

Choi, B. C. K., Eijkemans, G. J. M. & Tennassee, L. M. (2001). Prioritization of occupational sentinel health and hazard surveillance: The Pan American Health Organization experience. *Journal of Occupational and Environmental Medicine, 43,* 147–157.

Creech, J. L., & Johnson, M. N. (1974). Angiosarcoma of liver in the manufacturing of polyvinylchloride. *Journal of Occupational Medicine, 16,* 150–151.

Davis, L., Wellman, H., & Punnett, L. (2001). Surveillance of work-related carpal tunnel syndrome in Massachusetts, 1992–1997. A report from the Massachusetts Sentinel Event Notification System for Occupational Risk (SENSOR). *American Journal of Industrial Medicine, 39,* 58–71.

Devereux, J. J., Buckle, P. W., & Vlachonikolis, I. G. (1999). Interactions between physical and psychosocial risk factors at work increase the risk of back disorders: An epidemiological approach. *Occupational and Environmental Medicine, 56,* 343–353.

Domenighetti, G., D'Avanzo, B., & Bisig, B. (2000). Health effects of job insecurity among employees in the Swiss General Population. *International Journal of Health Services, 30,* 477–490.

Eaton, W. W., Anthony, J. C., Mandel, W., & Garrison, R. (1990). Occupations and the prevalence of major depression disorder. *Journal of Occupational Medicine, 32,* 1079–1087.

Ferrie, J. E., Shipley, M. J., Marmot, M. G., Stansfeld, S., & Smith, G. D. (1995). Health effects of anticipation of job change and non-employment: longitudinal data from Whitehall II study. *British Medical Journal, 311,* 1264–1269.

Fletcher, B. (1991). *Work, stress, disease, and life expectancy.* Chichester, UK: Wiley.

Forst, L. S., Hryhorczuk, D., & Jaros, M. (1999). A state trauma registry as a tool for occupational injury surveillance. *Journal of Occupational and Environmental Medicine, 41,* 514–520.

Frese, M., & Zapf, D. (1999). On the importance of the objective environment in stress and attribution theory. Counterpoint to Perrewé and Zellars. *Journal of Organizational Behavior, 20,* 761–765.

Fritschi, L., Siemiatycki, J., & Richardson, L. (1996). Self-assessed versus expert-assessed occupational exposures. *American Journal of Epidemiology, 144,* 521–527.

Greiner, B. A., Ragland, D. R., Krause, N., Syme, S. L., & Fisher, J. M. (1997). Objective measurement of occupational stress factors—An example with San Francisco urban transit operators. *Journal of Occupational Health Psychology, 2,* 325–342.

Gustavsson, P., Alfredsson, L., Brunnberg, H., Hammar, N., Jakobsson, R., Reuterwall, C., & Ostlin, P. (1996). Myocardial infarction among male bus, taxi, and lorry drivers in middle Sweden. *Occupational and Environmental Medicine, 53,* 235–240.

Hacker, W. (1993). Objective work environment: Analysis and evaluation of objective work characteristics. In *A Healthier work environment: Basic concepts and methods of measurement* (pp. 42–57). Copenhagen: World Health Organization Regional Office for Europe.

Hammar, N., Alfredsson, L., & Johnson, J. V. (1998). Job strain, social support at work, and incidence of myocardial infarction. *Occupational and Environmental Medicine, 55,* 548–553.

Hansson, G. A., Balogh, I., Bystrom, J. U., Ohlsson, K., Nordander, C., Asterland, P., Sjolander, S., Rylander, L., Winkel, J., & Skerfing, S. (2001). Questionnaire versus direct technical measurements in assessing postures and movements of the head, upper back, arms and hands. *Scandinavian Journal of Work, Environment & Health, 27,* 30–40.

Henderson, A. K., Payne, M. M., Ossiander, E., Evans, C. G., & Kaufman, J. D. (1998). Surveillance of occupational diseases in the United States. *Journal of Occupational and Environmental Medicine, 40,* 714–719.

Henneberger, P. K., Metayer, C., Layne, L. A., & Althouse, R. (2000). Nonfatal work-related inhalations: Surveillance data from hospital emergency departments, 1995–1996. *American Journal of Industrial Medicine, 38,* 140–148.

Houtman, I. L. D., Goudswaard, A., Dhondt, S., van den Grinten, M. P., Hildebrandt, V. H., & van der Poel, E. G. T. (1998). Dutch monitor on stress and physical load: Risk factors, consequences, and preventive action. *Occupational and Environmental Medicine, 55,* 73–83.

Hurrell, J. J., Jr., Nelson, D. L., & Simmons, B. L. (1998). Measuring job stressors and strains: Where we have been, where we are, and where we need to go. *Journal of Occupational Health Psychology, 3,* 368–389.

Jackson, P. R., & Mullarkey, S. (2000). Lean production teams and health in garment manufacture. *Journal of Occupational Health Psychology, 5,* 231–245.

James, G. D., & Bovbjerg, D. H. (2001). Age and perceived stress independently influence daily blood pressure levels and variation among women employed in wage jobs. *American Journal of Human Biology, 13,* 268–274.

Karasek, R., & Theorell, T. (1990). *Healthy work.* New York: Basic Books.

Karasek, R., & Theorell, T. (2000). The demand-control-support model and CVD. *Occupational Medicine, 15*(1), 78–83.

Kasl, S. V. (1978). Epidemiological contributions to the study of work stress. In C. L. Cooper & R. L. Payne (Eds.), *Stress at work* (pp. 3–38). Chichester, UK: Wiley.

Kasl, S. V. (1987). Methodologies in stress and health: past difficulties, present dilemmas, future directions. In S. V. Kasl & C. L. Cooper (Eds.), *Stress and health: Issues in research methodology* (pp. 307–318). Chichester, UK: Wiley.

Kasl, S. V. (1991). Assessing health risks in the work setting. In H. E. Schroeder (Ed.), *New directions in health psychology assessment* (pp. 95–125). New York: Hemisphere.

Kasl, S. V. (1992). Surveillance of psychological disorders in the workplace. In G. P. Keita & S. L. Sauter (Eds.), *Work and well-being: An agenda for the 1990s* (pp. 73–95). Washington, DC: American Psychological Association.

Kasl, S. V. (1998). Measuring job stressors and studying the health impact of the work environment: An epidemiologic commentary. *Journal of Occupational Health Psychology, 3,* 390–401.

Kasl, S. V., & Amick, B. C. (1995). The impact of work stress on health and well-being. In J. C. McDonald (Ed.), *The epidemiology of work related diseases* (pp. 239–266). London: BMJ Press.

Kasl, S. V., & Jones, B. A. (2001). Some methodological considerations in the study of psychosocial influences on health. In A. Vingerhoets (Ed.), *Advances in behavioral medicine* (pp. 25–48). London: Harwood Academic.

Kirkcaldy, B. D., & Martin, T. (2000). Job stress and satisfaction among nurses. *Stress Medicine, 16*, 77–89.

Kittel, F., Kornitzer, M., & Dramaix, M. (1980). Coronary heart disease and job stress in two cohorts of bank clerks. *Psychotherapy and Psychosomatics, 34*, 110–123.

Kivimaki, M., Vahtera, J., Pentti, J., & Ferrie, J. E. (2000). Factors underlying the effect of organizational downsizing on health of employees: Longitudinal cohort study. *British Medical Journal, 320*, 971–975.

Landsbergis, P., & Theorell, T. (2000). Measurement of psychosocial workplace exposure variables. *Occupational Medicine, 15*(1), 163–171.

Lazarus, R. S. (1966). *Psychological stress and the coping process.* New York: McGraw Hill.

Lee, D. J., Niemcryk, S. J., Jenkins, C. D., & Rose, R. M. (1989). Type A, amicability, and injury: A prospective study of air controllers. *Journal of Psychosomatic Research, 33*, 177–186.

Leigh, J. P., & Miller, T. R. (1998). Occupational illnesses within two national data sets. *International Journal of Occupational & Environmental Health, 4*, 99–113.

Luecken, L. J., Suarez, E. C., Kuhn C., Barefoot, J. C., Blumenthal, J. A., Siegler, J. C., & Williams, R. B. (1997). Stress in employed women: Impact of marital status and children at home on neurohormone output and home strain. *Psychosomatic Medicine, 59*, 352–359.

MacFarlane, G. J., Hunt, I. M., & Silman, A. J. (2000). Role of mechanical and psychosocial factors in the onset of forearm pain: Prospective population based study. *British Medical Journal, 321*, 676–679.

Marshall, N. L., Barnett, R. C., & Sayer, A. (1997). The changing workforce, job stress, and psychological distress. *Journal of Occupational Health Psychology, 2*, 99–107.

McKernan, J. (2000). Development of a hazard surveillance methodology for residential construction. *Applied Occupational and Environmental Hygiene, 15*, 890–895.

McMichael, A. J. (1994). Invited commentary—"Molecular epidemiology": New pathway or new traveling companion. *American Journal of Epidemiology, 140*, 1–11.

Morris, J. K., & Cook, C. G. (1991). A critical review of the effect of factory closures on health. *British Journal of Industrial Medicine, 56*, 557–563.

Netterstrom, B., & Juel, K. (1988). Impact of work-related and psychosocial factors on the development of ischemic heart disease among urban bus drivers in Denmark. *Scandinavian Journal of Work, Environment & Health, 14*, 231–238.

Niedhammer, I., Goldberg, M., Leclerc, A., Bugel, I., & David, S. (1998). Psychosocial factors at work and subsequent depressive symptoms in the Gazel cohort. *Scandinavian Journal of Work, Environment & Health, 24*, 197–205.

Ostfeld, A. M., Kasl, S. V., D'Atri, D. A., & Fitzgerald, E. F. (1987). *Stress, crowding, and blood pressure in prison.* Hilldsale, NJ: Erlbaum.

Ostry, A. S., Marion, S. A., Demers, P. A., Hershler, R., Kelly, S., Teschke, K., Mustard, C., & Hertzman, C. (2001a). Comparison of expert-rater methods for assessing psychosocial job strain. *Scandinavian Journal of Work, Environment & Health, 27*, 70–75.

Ostry, A. S., Marion, S. A., Demers, P. A., Hershler, R., Kelly, S., Teschke, K., Mustard, C., & Hertzman, C. (2001b). Measuring psychosocial job strain with the Job Content Questionnaire using experienced job evaluators. *American Journal of Industrial Medicine, 39*, 397–401.

Palmer, K., & Coggon, D. (1996). ABC of work related disorders: Investigating suspected occupational illness and evaluating the workplace. *British Medical Journal, 313*, 809–811.

Parks, R. M., Krebs, J. M., & Miner, F. E. (1996). Occupational disease surveillance using disability insurance at an automotive stamping and assembly complex. *Journal of Occupational and Environmental Medicine, 38*, 1111–1123.

Payne, R. L. (2000). Comments on "Why negative affectivity should not be controlled in job stress research: Don't throw out the baby with the bath water." *Journal of Organizational Behavior, 21,* 97–99.

Perrewé, P. L., & Zellars, K. L. (1999). An examination of attributions and emotions in the transactional approach to the organizational stress process. *Journal of Organizational Behavior, 20,* 739–752.

Peter, R., Geibler, H., & Siegrist, J. (1998). Associations of effort–reward imbalance at work and reported symptoms in different groups of male and female public transport workers. *Stress Medicine, 14,* 175–182.

Peter, R., & Siegrist, J. (2000). Psychosocial work environment and the risk of coronary heart disease. *International Archives of Occupational & Environmental Health, 73*(Suppl.), S41–S45.

Piros, S., Karlehagen, S., Lappas, G., & Wilhelmsen, L. (2000). Psychosocial risk factors for myocardial infarction among Swedish railway engine drivers during 10 years follow-up. *Journal of Cardiovascular Risk, 7,* 389–394.

Rempel, D. (1990). Medical surveillance in the workplace: Overview. *Occupational Medicine, 5*(3), 435–438.

Rosenman, K. D., Reilly, M. J., & Kalinowski, D. J. (1997). A state-based surveillance system for work-related asthma. *Journal of Occupational and Environmental Medicine, 39,* 415–425.

Rutstein, D., Mullan, R. J., Frazier, T. M., Halperin, W. E., Melius, J. M., & Sestito, J. P. (1983). Sentinel health events (occupational): A basis for physician recognition and public health surveillance. *American Journal of Public Health, 73,* 1054–1062.

Ruttenber, A. J., McCrea, J. S., Wade, T. D., Schonbeck, M. F., LaMontagne, A. D., VanDyke, M. V., & Martyny, J. W. (2001). Integrating workplace exposure database for occupational medicine services and epidemiologic studies at a former nuclear weapons facility. *Applied Occupational and Environmental Hygiene, 16,* 192–200.

Saks, A. M., & Ashforth, B. E. (2000). The role of dispositions, entry stressors, and behavioral plasticity in predicting newcomers' adjustment to work. *Journal of Organizational Behavior, 21,* 43–62.

Sauter, S. L., Murphy, L. R., & Hurrell, J. J., Jr. (1990). Prevention of work-related psychological disorders. *American Psychologist, 45,* 1146–1158.

Schnall, P. L., Belkic, K., Landsbergis, P., & Baker, D. (Eds.). (2000). *The workplace and cardiovascular disease. Occupational Medicine* (Vol. 15, No. 1). Philadelphia: Hanley & Belfus.

Schwartz, J. (2000). Imputation of job characteristics scores. *Occupational Medicine, 15*(1), 172–175.

Siegrist, J., & Peter, R. (2000). The effort-reward imbalance model. *Occupational Medicine, 15*(1), 83–87.

Sluiter, J. K., Frings-Dresen, M. H. W., Meijman, T. F., & van der Beek, A. J. (2000). Reactivity and recovery from different types of work measured by catecholamines and cortisol: A systematic literature overview. *Occupational & Environmental Medicine, 57,* 298–315.

Smedley, J., Egger, P., Cooper, C., & Coggon, D. (1997). Prospective cohort study of predictors of incident low back pain in nurses. *British Medical Journal, 314,* 1225–1228.

Smith, M. J., Conway, F. T., & Karsh, B-T. (1999). Occupational stress in human computer interaction. *Industrial Health, 37,* 157–173.

Spector, P. E., Chen, P. Y., & O'Connell, B. J. (2000). A longitudinal study of relations between job stressors and job strains while controlling for prior negative affectivity and strains. *Journal of Applied Psychology, 85,* 211–218.

Spector, P. E., Zapf, D., Chen, P. Y., & Frese, M. (2000). Why negative affectivity should not be controlled in job stress research: Don't throw out the baby with the bath water. *Journal of Organizational Behavior, 21,* 79–95.

Steenland, K., Johnson, J., & Nowlin, S. (1997). A follow-up study of job strain and heart disease among males in the NHANES1 population. *American Journal of Industrial Medicine, 31,* 256–260.

Steptoe, A., Lundwall, K., & Cropley, M. (2000). Gender, family structure and cardiovascular activity during working day and evening. *Social Science & Medicine, 50,* 531–539.

Stewart, P., & Stenzel, M. (2000). Exposure assessment in the occupational setting. *Applied Occupational and Environmental Hygiene, 15,* 435–444.

Taylor, R. B. (1980). Conceptual dimensions of crowding reconsidered. *Population and Environment, 3,* 298–308.

Theorell, T., Tsutsumi, A., Hallquist, J., Reuterwall, C., Hogstedt, C., Fredlund, P., Emlund, N., & Johnson, J. V. (1998). Decision latitude, job strain, and myocardial infarction: A study of working men in Stockholm. *American Journal of Public Health, 88,* 382–388.

Vagg, P. R., & Spielberger, C. D. (1998). Occupational stress: Measuring job pressure and organizational support in the workplace. *Journal of Occupational Health Psychology, 3,* 294–305.

Waldenstrom, M., Josephson, M., Persson, C., & Theorell, T. (1998). Interview reliability for assessing mental work demands. *Journal of Occupational Health Psychology, 3,* 200–216.

Watson, D., Pennebaker, J. W., & Folger, R. (1987). Beyond negative affectivity: Measuring stress and satisfaction in the workplace. In J. M. Ivancevich & D. C. Ganster (Eds.), *Job stress: From theory to suggestion* (pp. 141–157). New York: Haworth Press.

Williams, S., & Cooper, C. L. (1998). Measuring occupational stress. The development of the Pressure Management Indicator. *Journal of Occupational Health Psychology, 3,* 306–321.

Williams, S., Dale, J., Glucksman, E., & Wellesley, A. (1997). Senior house officers work related stressors, psychological distress, and confidence in performing clinical tasks in accident and emergency: a questionnaire study. *British Medical Journal, 314,* 713–718.

Winkleby, N. A., Ragland, O. R., Fisher, J. M., & Syme, S. L. (1988) Excess risk of sickness and disease in bus drivers: A review and synthesis of epidemiologic studies. *International Journal of Epidemiology, 17,* 255–262.

Wohlwill, J. F. (1973). The environment is not in the head. In W. F. E. Preiser (Ed.), *Environmental design research: Vol. 2, Symposia and Workshops* (pp. 166–181). Stroudsburg, PA: Dowden, Hutchinson & Ross.

19

Program Evaluation: The Bottom Line in Organizational Health

Joyce A. Adkins and Howard M. Weiss

The practice of occupational health psychology has flourished. Practitioners now perform a diverse range of functions across a wide variety of roles and organizational levels (Adkins, 1999). The acceptance and growth of occupational health psychology has been founded on the documented need and value of practices to organizations. This evolving tradition of data-based service delivery continues to exert a strong influence on program development and expansion, making evaluation measures and tools essential elements of practice.

In a highly competitive, global market environment, organizations, both private and public, have become increasingly attuned to the need for data-driven decision making. Resources are generally reserved for strategies and actions that contribute to business plans for cost-containment, improved productivity, and risk abatement and control. Occupational health psychology practices provide an opportunity to demonstrate the value-added nature of behavioral and psychosocial technology when applied to a workplace setting. To fully access that opportunity, practitioners must ensure that the technology they use is crafted to address the needs and context of their organizational clients while also maintaining solid roots in a scientific and ethical foundation.

Challenges in program evaluation and evaluation research arise out of the inherently applied nature of the activity. The dynamic context and numerous uncontrolled variables in a work environment create obstacles to effective measurement of organizational health interventions, whether those interventions come in the way of policies, practices, or programs. There is often little time and few dedicated resources available to conduct thorough literature reviews, carefully time and control program implementation, obtain a valid and reliable control group or randomize participants to selected exposures, and confront ethical concerns of withholding program availability from any individual or group of employees. All of these issues,

The views presented are those of the authors and do not necessarily reflect the official policies or position of the United States Air Force or the Department of Defense. The authors would like to thank Jack Needleman for his insight into the program evaluation process.

and others, contribute to the complex environment in which the practitioner works. Even if the work environment could be carefully controlled, the *influence* of individual differences and nonwork life spillover into the work-life domain (Hart, 1999) makes it difficult to draw firm conclusions about ultimate program outcomes. When confronted with these issues, a number of practitioners, unfortunately, may be tempted to avoid the situation by neglecting to design or implement an evaluation plan into their programs. Others may choose to restrict the value of evaluations by focusing on more easily obtained data such as program activity levels, utilization rates, or customer satisfaction ratings compared with implementation costs. In using either of these strategies, they sacrifice the opportunity to actively demonstrate the effectiveness of their work and to make a valuable contribution to science. Despite the obstacles, thorough and effective program evaluation strategies are vital to the sustained acceptance of occupational health psychology in the workplace and to its growth as a professional discipline.

Program evaluation involves the use of a variety of methodological strategies to collect and analyze information about a policy or program with the intent of coming to a determination about the relevance, progress, efficiency, effectiveness, and outcomes or impact of that policy or program. The strategies and procedures used in program evaluation are generally borrowed from the social, behavioral, and managerial sciences and the basic thrust of evaluation is central to the managerial process (Veney & Kaluzny, 1991), making evaluation a natural fit for occupational health psychology.

The purpose, origination, and conduct of the evaluation process can vary. Although systematic inquiry can provide valuable internal information for a program and an organization, not all evaluations are internally generated. Some are externally imposed on the program or on the organization in which the program functions. Often programs endowed by grants or other external or public funding sources are required to undergo systematic evaluation of both process and outcomes. In addition, programs may be evaluated from an upper layer of management within the same organization or from other sources. For many of these reasons, program evaluation has been viewed at times as mysterious, threatening, and political (Posavac & Carey, 1985).

Program evaluation is a multidimensional process that can legitimately focus on different facets of program design and implementation. First, needs assessment, also referred to as design evaluation, asks questions related to the relevance of the program as determined by the nature and extent of the problem to be addressed. As such, this program evaluation function focuses on defining the problem, the target population, and how the program fits into the overall organizational strategy. Other relevant needs assessment issues include an examination of alternative approaches to solving the problem and in fact whether the problem should be solved at all and if so how much attention and how many resources should be allocated to solving it (Veney & Kaluzny, 1991). Second, formative evaluations examine the program implementation process. Such evaluations serve monitoring and correction functions and tend to be conducted during ongoing program operations. Collection of these data can assist in fine-tuning program operations and ensuring that processes continue on-target. Third, summative evaluations look at overall impact or outcomes of the program or policy, both those that were planned and those that were unintended.

Thus, needs assessments generally accompany program planning; formative or process-oriented evaluations provide feedback for management of program implementation; and summative, or impact-oriented evaluations, examine the final outcomes of the program or policy. Although many program evaluators attempt to categorize techniques and strategies to one part of the evaluation or program life cycle, in practice the boundaries of design, formative, and summative evaluations tend to blur. Each provides important information and warrants consideration in an overall evaluation strategy. Needs assessments provide information to enable effective program component selection and to target groups of beneficiaries based on identification and clarification of organizational needs. Nevertheless, even the most effectively planned program can fail to fulfill intended objectives without attention to correct and consistent implementation and continuous feedback concerning program delivery over time. Even carefully designed, targeted, implemented, and tracked programs and policies may fail to achieve their intended or expected impact or may produce unintended outcomes. Program evaluation strategies provide valuable decision-making data to answer the when, who, what, how, and—importantly—why questions of program success or failure.

More effective program evaluation strategies tend to examine not just inputs, such as financial costs and personnel time incurred in program implementation, but also examine impact on desired outcome states or conditions. As depicted in Figure 19.1, inputs and outputs constitute only the beginning of the process in evaluating occupational health psychology programs. These variables are then linked to expected program outcomes and ultimately to desired or targeted organizational goals or outcomes. Because programs and practices are not implemented in a vacuum, mediating, moderating, or competing variables can exert a substantial influence. Organizational intervention programs that are multifaceted rather than focused on a single, isolated process have been found to be more effective in meeting organizational objectives (Halverson & Bliese, 1995; Ivancevich, Matteson, Freedman, & Phillips, 1990; Schurman & Israel, 1995). Evaluation strategies, therefore, often look at the combined effect of multiple programs and tease out individual program effects whenever practical through clear designs, specific measures, and strategic data analysis.

To effectively design and implement a program evaluation strategy, the links associated with inputs, outputs, outcomes, and the expected role of extraneous or contextual variables is determined by the assumptions associated with the theoretical model of the practitioner or evaluator (Bickman, 1987). Unfortunately, many evaluations, both internally planned and externally imposed, lack clear theoretical and conceptual underpinnings. In addition, the assumptions underlying the work often remain implicit and unspecified, providing little in the way of explanation and rendering data amassed less meaningful. The term *black box evaluations* has come

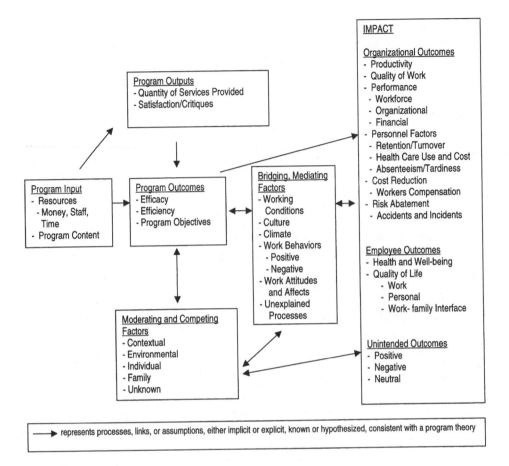

Figure 19.1.   Program evaluation process elements.

to signify the process of looking only at the inputs and outputs of a program, without a clear understanding of how the program works. Identifying or constructing program linkages moves the evaluation "inside the box" and generally falls within the scope of program theory. Program theory refers to a plausible, sensible, or logical conceptualization of how a program is expected or presumed to work (Bickman, 1987). It is different from, but relies clearly on, the scientific theory, orientation, or perspective of the practitioner. When fully developed and articulated, the program theory allows for increased certainty that the results of the evaluation accurately represent the program. A clearly specified theory or model also allows for either program replication or adjustment of the conditions to achieve a different result.

Lack of clearly specified theoretical assumptions is neither new nor restricted to occupational health psychology. A study of 119 evaluations (Lipsey, Crosse, Dunkle, Pollard, & Stobart, 1985) found that 20% of the programs could be classified as black-box evaluations, having no more than nontheoretical program descriptions. Two thirds were classified as subtheoretical, providing only descriptions of the program strategy or principles and intervention techniques with no information about the proposed outcomes or the assumed relationship between program activities and outcomes. Only 9% demonstrated an integrated theory. Sadly, these findings cut across disciplines and applied equally to academic evaluations and program-developed evaluations.

The lack of an effective program evaluation component carries over to occupational health psychology programs (Donaldson, 1997; Ilgen, 1990). A specific look at workplace health promotion programs found that only a third of organizations routinely recorded potential outcomes such as absenteeism or retention–turnover rates, and only 7% noted job performance changes. Evaluations that were conducted were routinely restricted to program utilization rates and customer satisfaction (Davis, Rosenberg, Iverson, Vernon, & Bauer, 1984). The links between program components and both proximate and distal outcomes have been rarely addressed. Yet program planners and evaluators who clearly identify, fully develop, and explicitly describe their guiding theory produce evaluation strategies that yield more satisfying and useful results.

Anatomy of an Organizational Health Evaluation Strategy

Evaluation measures provide a means of documenting the initial need, ongoing implementation, and subsequent impact of implementation of new programs as well as changes in existing practices, policies, or procedures. As so aptly stated by Light and colleagues (Light, Singer, & Willet, 1990, p. viii), analysis cannot fix what design bungles. Evaluation strategies are most effective when designed in advance as an integral part of the initial program design.

Clarify the Question, Problem, or Issue

To begin any data collection, a clear purpose, target, or question is fundamental. Increased ambiguity in the beginning will only lead to vague results. An initial design or needs assessment can provide relevant information that would lead to the development of an evaluation plan during program development. In an ideal world, an evaluation component would be a natural part of all programs and we would advocate for an increase in program-generated evaluations. However, the world is not always ideal and externally conducted, after-the-fact evaluations may be frequently encountered. In such cases, the evaluator will likely need to assist in clarifying the evaluation question and operationalizing constructs to develop meaningful measures and evaluation strategies. Consultation with program staff and other stakeholders can assist in developing a shared understanding of the essential elements of the program, generally improving the evaluation results (Bickman, 1987). By allowing input from and educating stakeholders about potential uses of the information, the evaluator is afforded the opportunity to identify obstacles, build consensus, and engender ownership of the evaluation and subsequent results (Posovac & Carey, 1985). Although developing a cooperative working relationship with relevant stakeholders assists in understanding the program objectives and implementation process, external evaluators are best served by going beyond the objectives of the program staff to look for both positive and negative effects that might not be expected by either the designers or implementers so that an effective and comprehensive program theory can be identified and developed (Bickman, 1987; Scriven, 1980).

Conceptualize the program theory. The program theory, also referred to as the program logic model, begins with a clear description of the program, including the content, process of implementation, goals, objectives, and expected outcomes. The description allows for additional conceptualization and mapping of a networking model or set of links between program components and expected program outcomes and ultimate organizational outcomes. The assumed links between program components and expected outcomes may be based on the tested or untested theoretical framework of the evaluator, past literature and empirical evidence, or past experience of the evaluator and the organization.

Each discipline approaches a situation differently and will likely explain the outcomes and assumptions based on their own worldview. Occupational health psychology, as an interdisciplinary field, draws measures and methods from multiple fields. Each component discipline, whether psychology, public health, organizational behavior, medicine, or others, holds a different piece of the strategic puzzle. Efforts have emerged to integrate the pieces into a single picture (Murphy & Cooper, 2000). However, many of the underlying foundations still lie with each puzzle piece. It is up to the practitioner to collect the puzzle pieces and fit them together in a way that makes sense to the organization or evaluation and is in line with the program logic model. Use of multidisciplinary teams or committees can assist in reducing potential for disciplinary partisanship in both program development and evaluation (Quick, Quick, Nelson, & Hurrell, 1997). Fortunately, many valid approaches and models can be used as the basis for an evaluation. The key is clarifying and documenting the theory and its assumptions so the results of the evaluation can be clearly understood. Only those assumptions that can be subjected to assessment will assist in program replication or correction.

Not all programs succeed even when implemented precisely as planned. Lack of success may also occur when the underlying assumptions of the program model fail to hold true. Even when assumptions are supported by scientific theory and empirical evidence, some, if not many, of the assumptions may remain implicit. Nevertheless, these assumptions warrant the scrutiny that comes with explicit specification. Pretesting or piloting is often helpful to illuminate black box or implicit assumptions in the program design and can serve the same purpose in the evaluation design. If the assumptions of the program theory associated with the evaluation design are faulty, the evaluation results can be questionable. If the evaluation fails to find successful outcomes, it may be a result of the program or it may be a result of a flawed theory or flawed assumptions. For example, Rog and Bickman (1984) reported an evaluation of a stress management program that assumed employees experienced stress primarily associated with home and family. They designed their program around that assumption and implemented the program with fidelity. Unfortunately, the evaluation data found that employees experienced stress on the job, not at home. Regardless of implementation, established programs are not likely to achieve their objectives if the underlying conditions or assumptions are flawed. If the program does succeed, it may not be possible to replicate those results if the program logic was faulty.

The program theory also drives the selection of measures and the strategy used in measurement. Individually oriented models hold that improving organizational health is achieved through assisting employees to expand personal resources through training or to manage strain through increased support. Criteria of success would likewise rely on individual changes that presumably result in overall organizational benefits. More organizationally based models rely on making changes in organizational structure or processes and focus on organizationally based measures. Some models take a systems view and seek to examine an integrated measure of both individual and organizational predictors and outcomes. In fact, the concept of organizational health hinges on the intersection of organizational effectiveness and personal well-being, with research aims focused on identifying factors that predict both individual and organizational health outcomes.

Determine Measurement Strategies

The presence of an occupational health psychology practitioner, whether an employee or an external consultant, can create change of some level or degree. The act of measurement itself may in some cases serve to create the beginning ripples of change. Therefore, taking preintervention measures whenever possible provides a foundation from which the direction and magnitude of change or program impact can be assessed.

Organizational Health Risk Appraisals

The concept of an organizational health risk appraisal (OHRA) is extracted from individual health management (Adkins, Quick, & Moe, 2000). Individual health risk appraisals (HRA) provide an overview of individual health risk factors and protective factors and generally tend to be behaviorally oriented. Following that reasoning, OHRAs provide a basic evaluation of psychosocial or behavioral risk factors and protective factors found within the organization. Depending on the question that requires attention, the OHRA can be either general and broad-based or more focused and targeted on discrete behaviors or conditions. This information is collected primarily through self-report measures such as surveys, questionnaires, or other methods designed to query attitudes and opinions from the workforce. Self-report data can provide a baseline snapshot of the preintervention organization and can also assist in looking at changes that take place over time and across employment groups.

A variety of processes have relied on questionnaire data to provide information for planning, targeting, and evaluating stress reduction and management programs, under a variety of labels (e.g., Cartwright, Cooper, & Murphy, 1997; Griffin, Hart, & Wilson-Evered, 2000; Kohler & Kamp, 1992). In fact, the link between work and health has largely been associated with epidemiological survey research. The 1974 report, *Work in America,* reported results from a national survey designed to examine the association of work with safety, health, and well-being of the workforce. The report recommended changes in work conditions as an important method of reducing mental and physical health costs, increasing productivity, and improving quality of life for workers. Since that time, a foundation of information linking work conditions and processes with health outcomes and organizational effectiveness has been generated through cross-sectional survey or questionnaire methods (Quick et al., 1997). Epidemiologic methodology can provide a wealth of survey data, but it can also entail a tendency to minimize the importance of theory. In addition, although useful in capturing a significant amount of data from a large group in a short time, questionnaires provide only a snapshot of the organization; the results can be misleading if used as the sole piece of information.

Organizational Health and Safety Assessments

Just as a complete physical or psychological evaluation of an individual provides a more complete and in-depth picture than can be seen with an HRA, a comprehensive organizational health assessment (OHA) provides a more complete view of the organization. The underlying concept associated with OHAs can be seen in a variety of workplace stress and organizational diagnosis processes.

The diagnostic process begins with a question, issue, or target area. The question is best posed through consultation with organizational and program leaders to facilitate a partnership approach, thus increasing the usefulness and acceptance of the results. A strategy is then formulated to develop measures that will illuminate the issue in question. In general, the strategy includes use of a standardized questionnaire in conjunction with supplemental questions targeted at the particular population(s) and target issue. The use of a standardized questionnaire provides an opportunity to benchmark or compare with established norms. Targeted questions fill in specific information that may be unique to this population or issue under study. Once the written data are obtained, more in-depth information is gathered through semistructured interviews with individuals and groups. Those data are then qualitatively analyzed to add depth and detail to written information. Additional details are gleaned from behavioral observations and relevant organizational records. Information about resources available for support and intervention along with current and past programs used to address relevant issues is also obtained. A multidisciplinary team is used to collect and analyze the data and develop recommendations, to minimize the potentially myopic view of a single practitioner. The information is then integrated into a composite report that is presented to the relevant decision makers.

Organizational assessments can provide a foundation for an overall organizational intervention and evaluation strategy. The process can provide a comprehensive needs assessment and paint a detailed picture of the organization preintervention. In doing so, it pinpoints targets of high leverage opportunity, populations at risk, and level of risk. As a general evaluation strategy, the use of a combination of quantitative, qualitative, self-report, historical, and current documented factual information provides a rich database. In addition, using multiple measures from a variety of sources provides a means of building convergent validity. Results can provide insight into both the design and the on-going implementation of change programs and policies. Repeated measures across time can be used to assess the direction and magnitude of the change in indicators used. As a systemic assessment, the OHA promotes systemic interventions and thus calls for systemic, interdependent strategies.

Craft an Evaluation Design

Technical issues are as fundamental to program evaluation as to any other field of scientific inquiry. Certainly, programs can fail because of a faulty theory or poor implementation. However, a poor evaluation design can also produce findings that mask the success or failure of a program. Despite the complex, applied nature of the evaluation process, scientific rigor is critical because of the practical implications of program delivery in affecting individual and organizational health and well-being. Therefore, technical issues associated with design and analysis require concentrated attention in program evaluation efforts.

The evaluation problem is generally straightforward: How can a decision maker determine whether an intervention, such as an occupational health psychology program, policy, or practice, is needed, functioning as intended, and producing the intended outcomes. At its core, the problem is no different than any other research question. In more basic research paradigms, comparison conditions are created to test implications of theory. In the applied research paradigm of program evaluation, comparison conditions are created to test the efficacy of interventions, even though the interventions may be rooted in theory. In both cases, the critical concern is the level of confidence in judgments about the differences between conditions associated with program exposure or participation and nonexposure or nonparticipation. Issues of internal validity and statistical conclusion validity (Cook & Campbell, 1979) apply in both circumstances, as both involve judgments about confidence in inferences that group membership (program participant versus nonparticipant) makes a difference in the dependent variable of interest, whether that variable is individual, organizational, or systemic health and well-being.

Although the core problem is equivalent, the contextual differences between the two problems are substantial and important. In program evaluation, operations are never arbitrary. They are the essential reason for study. The independent variable is the program. The dependent variable is the individual or organizational issue of concern. Effect sizes are essential to the judgment of efficacy. Nothing at the operational level is arbitrary. Unfortunately, the ability to implement designs that provide maximal confidence in inferences about the causes of group differences can be severely constrained by practical considerations. All these problems enter into program evaluation context.

Despite contextual issues, the true experiment (Cook & Campbell, 1979) remains the design of choice in all feasible situations. Effective experimental design provides a high level of confidence that group differences are a result of the program being evaluated. Such confidence is maximized when alternative reasons for group differences can be logically eliminated. Two sources of alternative explanations for group differences are generally identified: differences in the nature of the members in the participant and nonparticipant groups and differences in experiences between participants and nonparticipants other than the program of interest.

Random assignment is intended to rule out the first problem. However, random assignment does not necessarily produce group equivalence in the sense that individual members of groups are equivalent on all key variables. It can only produce average equivalence across conditions. Even here, randomization is not foolproof. Its logic will produce expected average equivalence, not necessarily actual equivalence in any particular case. Mean levels of measured and unmeasured variables will be equal, on average, for participant and nonparticipant groups (West, Biesanz, & Pitts, 2000). However, given small samples and single studies, it is likely that participant and nonparticipant groups in any particular program will still have initial differences that may be important for causal inference. This point is important but is not intended to justify the use of weaker designs by arguing the flaws of random assignment. Rather, it emphasizes that the characteristics of research design enhance or reduce confidence levels in inferences about the final program outcomes. Such confidence may be maximized with random assignment, but causality is in no way assured, even with textbook-design precision.

Random assignment also fails to account for group differences that can occur once the program is implemented. Differential drop-out rates for participant and nonparticipant groups are common occurrences in the field. This attrition has the effect of biasing causal inferences unless it can be assumed that factors associated with attrition are equivalent across groups. Examining condition-specific drop-out rates and characteristics of stayers and leavers in both conditions can aid in judgments about the severity of the problem, but neither are foolproof.

Random assignment also does not ensure control over whether the participant does or does not experience the program intervention and at what level. When programs are implemented across groups in the same organization, members of one group can become aware of the experiences of another group and their behavior may be affected. Program effects can leak to nonparticipant groups and that diffusion of the program intervention masks inferences about effects made from the examination of group differences. In addition, members of participant groups often differ in the extent to which they actually experience or are actively involved with relevant program elements, with some members themselves not complying with procedures and others receiving weaker exposure through procedural flaws of implementation. These programs are even more problematic when broad changes are made at the organizational level with the intention of affecting a large group of people but exist clearly even in individually focused programs such as stress-management training programs. Methods exist for estimating causal effects in the face of noncompliance (Little & Yau, 1998), but such methods are limited in scope and have methodological assumptions that may not always be defensible. These problems exist in spite of an evaluator's ability to assign participants to conditions at random. Of course, doing that simple task is sometimes difficult in program evaluation where participants are often assigned based on need or other considerations.

Practical problems with the implementation of true experiments have led to the use of a number of different quasi-experiments in program implementation. In general, these designs involve control over program exposure but lack random assignment. Their relative strength is found in the ability to rule out alternative explanations and thereby provide confidence in judgments about program efficacy. Such designs range from the elegant, such as regression-discontinuity designs, multiple-baseline designs, time-series designs with control groups or replications, to the inelegant, such as nonrandomized control-group designs with or without pretests (see the classic discussion by Cook & Campbell, 1979, or the more recent discussion by West et al., 2000). Elegant designs allow for strong causal inference. The irony is that this inference strength is precisely because of either the evaluator's knowledge of who gets the intervention, when assignment is controlled but not random (Kenny, 1979), or the evaluator's strong control over the timing of the intervention for multiple groups at multiple times. Such knowledge and control is generally as problematic as random assignment; so these elegant designs are mostly associated with infrequent demonstrations and textbook illustrations.

Inelegance is the norm, as most program evaluation uses the common design of assigning people to the extent possible to participant and nonparticipant groups and then trying to control for group differences statistically. Analyses of covariance controlling for initial differences are frequently used despite a tendency to underadjust. Newer methods based on structural equation modeling and multistage modeling carry assumptions that may be severe (Lipsey & Cordray, 2000), but are promising tools for occupational health psychology program evaluators.

Analyze Program Usefulness

Although both basic and evaluation research share the same design objective of maximizing confidence in causal inferences, that similarity should not hide the important differences in the broader objectives. Basic research serves the master of theory. Its structure is deduction and its aim is examining the credibility of theoretical propositions. Program evaluation serves the decision maker, who is interested in the usefulness of a specific program or intervention, particularly as compared with alternative courses of action. Therefore, the criteria used to evaluate the reasonableness of an underlying theoretical proposition are not the same criteria used to evaluate the effectiveness of an intervention. Yet the basic research criterion of statistical significance remains the most used criterion of program effectiveness (Lipsey & Cordray, 2000).

Statistical significance has come under attack (Schmidt, 1996), but its logic rests on a deductive model that is defensible for judging the results of basic research studies. As such, it is a useful tool to help gauge whether a theoretically driven expectation is supportable. It is also an important tool for gauging program effectiveness and outcomes, but it is not enough. Decision makers need information about usefulness and efficacy. They must judge gains against costs. They must be able to compare programs in cost–benefit terms. (See also chapter 20, this volume, for a discussion of economic evaluation.) They must be able to simultaneously look at multiple outcomes that programs will affect. The criterion of statistical significance examines the effects of program outcome against the alternative explanation of chance. This is necessary but not sufficient for program evaluation.

Outcroppings of significance tests are statistics gauging effect sizes, or the strength of the effects of the independent variables, and these are now being incorporated into program evaluation efforts (Lipsey & Cordray, 2000). Different methods exist for assessing effect sizes, but generally they attempt to express the size of an intervention effect in terms of standardized mean differences, or standard deviation units, between participant and nonparticipant groups. Essentially, the question is how much of an increase (or decrease) in standard scores on the selected outcome measures can be expected from the program or intervention?

Use of effect sizes allows different interventions to be compared in the same units, allows for multiple studies to be cumulated, and allows for moderators of program effectiveness to be identified through these cumulations. Because effect sizes are influenced by such things as the strength of an intervention and the variance in the participant population, they are of less use in examining results for basic research. However, in the context of evaluation, these factors are part of the core of the program itself. Will this intervention work and for whom? As a consequence, effect sizes have more meaning for program evaluation.

Although the examination of effect sizes is an advance over relying entirely on significance tests, it still does not get to the issue of usefulness directly. In addition, program objectives are seldom well-captured by single outcomes. In such cases, multiple effect sizes will exist, and some reasonable method for summarizing effects across outcomes within single studies is needed. In response to these and other issues, recent attempts have been made to examine the usefulness of programs using multiattribute utility analysis.

Boudreau (1991) provided an excellent summary of utility analysis. Multiattribute utility analysis essentially requires that the multiple outcomes of interest be scaled, usually by expert judges, on equivalent metrics of utility. For many organizational programs, that metric is dollar values; but dollar value need not be the only way to judge utility. In gauging program effectiveness and outcomes, utility estimates for standard deviation changes in the various criteria of interest are generated, and the utility of a program can be assessed by combining such estimates with effect sizes and summing across outcomes. An added advantage is that these utility estimates can be compared to costs for implementing the program. Finally, multiattribute utility analysis requires evaluators, program managers, and decision makers to carefully think through the nature of the desired outcomes and their importance, which also speaks to the importance of the collaborative design of a comprehensive program logic model for the evaluation.

Focusing on the importance of technical issues is not intended to discourage program evaluation efforts. Just as occupational health psychology falls on the border of psychology, public health, and organizational science, program evaluation lies at the intersection of the scientist–practitioner model. The occupational health psychology practitioner must balance perspectives of multiple disciplines, and the program evaluator must balance the realities of the program with the technical requirements of scientific inquiry. Just as a multidisciplinary team is an effective strategy for developing and implementing occupational health psychology programs, a consultative relationship or evaluation team that blends strengths of practice and science can serve to build a technically sound and practically useful evaluation strategy.

Value Added: Using Evaluation Results

Information obtained from program evaluation studies, regardless of validity and reliability, must be applied for the usefulness to be realized. The value of an evaluation lies in the utility of the results in informing policy or improving programs (Leviton & Hughes, 1981; Weiss, 1973). Use can take many forms. In general, the stated purpose is to provide information for decision making or problem solving, to validate or change the program under study. Rarely, however, do evaluations result in dramatic changes. Evaluation information is often used less for concrete decision making than for its capacity to empower users of the information (Patton, 1978). Insights from the evaluation feed the program evolution. Resultant information can reduce uncertainty, confirm results from other sources, control implementation schedules, or trigger modifications in implementation or direction of an existing program or policy.

In addition, the broader conceptualization of use extends beyond a specific issue. Both the evaluation process and results may be used conceptually to influence thinking about an issue without actually resulting in an immediate concrete change. In addition, organizational advocates or critics can draw on evaluation evidence to persuade others to support or oppose an issue or policy change. All information gathered becomes background information for conceptual changes that may prove to have a later impact on policy or program development (Caplan, Morrison, & Stambaugh, 1975; Rich, 1977). Overall, results can also become part of an integrated body of information that is accumulated and used over time in the evolution of programs in general, eventually effecting changes in attitudes and ultimately affecting policy, programs, or practices on a larger scale than in a single organization or industry, as has been the case in the development and growth of occupational health psychology.

In a meta-analysis of evaluation research, Leviton and Hughes (1981) identified a number of factors, described next, that increase the probability of use of evaluation results.

Relevance

Information that is perceived as relevant to policy or program concerns and that address decision-maker needs is more likely to be used. Developing relevant information requires an integration or partnership of the occupational health psychology evaluator with the organization and program being evaluated. The occupational health psychology practitioner is grounded in both organizational operations and behavioral science, creating an important role as a knowledge broker and translator of psychosocial or behavioral science information to organization and program managers. To be effective in that role, the practitioner may be required to formulate the findings from the evaluation in language that is practical and actionable and to integrate seemingly contradictory pieces of information that may arise from the process. Development of an effective program logic model will aid in this process. When a needs assessment is conducted, practitioners are afforded the opportunity to become familiar with the business objectives, culture, and language of the organization. Both the goals of the program and the objectives of the evaluation can then be tied to the overall organizational short-term and long-term goals and objectives, increasing the likelihood that all products will be perceived as a part of and therefore relevant to the business plan. The questions formulated from that assessment set the stage for the development of answers that are relevant and applicable to the situation. In addition, relevance is affected by the timing of results. Windows of opportunity in decision-making processes occur in every organization and in every program. Data that are realized in the window become imminently more useful. Increasing knowledge of organizational processes will likewise increase awareness of windows of opportunity.

Communication and Involvement

A flow of undistorted and unbiased communication between the potential user or consumer of evaluation information and the producer of that information results in both a better understanding of initial needs and a more effective method of dissemination of accurate information. In addition, as the level of user involvement increases, ownership of the process and the resultant information also increases. Information flow in organizations tends to be impeded by those who may feel threatened by potentially negative findings. Identifying and involving those individuals with a stake in the outcome of the evaluation can help to minimize resistance and facilitate the crafting of results in a format that is palatable. Presentation of the information is also critical. Clearly established goals, explicit recommendations, and easy to understand written and verbal communication will obviously enhance the probability that the information will be used. Clarity and specificity can also assist in reducing potential misuse. The addition of qualitative information and relevant examples, such as those obtained in an organizational assessment, can help evaluation consumers to visualize the more quantitative findings (Caplan et al., 1975). Sensitive communication of negative or unanticipated findings combined with direct communication with organizational leaders and managers can reduce the amount of organizational censorship or distortion that can take place when program personnel or other affected groups feel threatened by the evaluation process, as may be the case in any evaluation but perhaps most significantly in evaluations that are either externally required or imposed from higher levels within the organization.

Credibility and Quality

An evaluation is not the only source of information available to decision makers. It is therefore generally taken in context with preconceptions, day-to-day experiences, and other sources of information, often serving as a source of corroboration. Knowledge of that context will assist in developing information that fills informational gaps. Obviously, the results of the evaluation cannot be predicted in advance. However, information that is completely out of line with expectations or with other sources of information is likely to meet with skepticism. Such information would require extensive explanation and justification of the quality of the work. Surprisingly, quality has not been found to exert a strong influence on overall use (Patton et al., 1977). Rather, the importance of quality increases when findings must be persuasive or in situations posing a high potential for information misuse. Credibility of information increases when the source is seen as fair and impartial with no specific stake in the outcome. Therefore, for practitioners who develop evaluation components to their own programs, high methodological quality and well-developed perceptions of credibility in the organization will become increasingly important.

Commitment, Advocacy, and Politics

Evaluations are conducted in the political context of an organization. Advocates of multiple positions battle for and against issues that correspond with their own interests. Understanding that context is critical. In the end, results generally are used by specific individuals rather than a group or an organization as a whole. The presence of a champion for the evaluation will increase the likelihood of the results being heard and used. The emotional investment of that champion and their position in the organization can have a substantial impact on the advocacy of both occupational health psychology programs and evaluations. To ensure effectiveness, advance marketing and building solid relationships in the planning and implementation phase will set the stage for a receptive attitude once the results of the evaluation are completed. Building relationships within the organization is a critical but often neglected activity of both program managers and evaluators. Targeting information to key users and marketing the importance of that information to decision makers promotes meaningful use of evaluation results.

Ethical Considerations

Evaluators have obligations to diverse groups, including the client organization, stakeholders in the program, program managers and staff, program beneficiaries, and other professionals in their discipline. These obligations include conducting evaluations with fairness, objectivity, and professionalism. Evaluations must begin with realistic objectives and questions that the evaluator or evaluation team is capable of answering. Valid constructs and measures followed by skilled data collection and thoughtful analysis lead to results that can be relied on to guide policy or program decisions. In the process, it is important that individuals and the organization are protected from harm. Protection involves a respect for confidentiality and may require informed consent from those who participate. Ethical challenges arise when it appears that the project cannot be accomplished as defined. There may be questions about how much data is enough to answer the question; how much analysis is required as opposed to straight presentation of the information; or when causal inferences are appropriate to the data and methodology of the evaluation. Requests may be made from a variety of factions to present the findings in the best possible light. Information can be misused by clients or by individuals within the organization to support their own ideas or interests. Finally, findings can result in harmful action taken against participants in the evaluation, participants in the program, or employees in the organization if the findings fail to support health-engendering practices. Because of the potential for harm, it is incumbent on practitioners to consider the potential consequences of the evaluation process and to ensure that a process is established that will protect the participants, the organizational client, and the professional integrity of the evaluation itself.

Conclusion

The landscape of occupational health psychology practice is in flux. To continue to grow and adapt to a dynamic workplace, it is important to know what works and to be able to understand as fully as possible why it works, creating an effective core technology. It is critical for practitioners to envision the future and to find, develop, and acquire skills to implement alternate strategies to meet the needs of their client organizations. Effectively designed, conducted, and well-documented program evaluations provide the cornerstone for future development of the discipline.

References

Adkins, J. A. (1999, June). Promoting organizational health: The evolving practice of occupational health psychology. *Professional Psychology: Research and Practice, 30*(2), 129–137.

Adkins, J. A., Quick, J. C., & Moe, K. O. (2000). Building world class performance in changing times. In L. R. Murphy & C. L. Cooper (Eds.), *Healthy and productive work: An international perspective.* Philadelphia: Taylor & Francis.

Bickman, L. (Ed.). (1987). Using program theory in evaluation. *New Directions for Program Evaluation, 33,* 5–18. San Francisco: Jossey-Bass.

Boudreau, J. W. (1991). Utility analysis for decisions in human resource management. In M. D. Dunnette & L. M. Hough (Eds.), *Handbook of industrial and organizational psychology, Vol. 2.* Palo Alto, CA: Consulting Psychologists Press.

Caplan, N., Morrison, A., & Stambaugh, R. (1975). *The use of social science knowledge in policy decisions at the national level.* Ann Arbor, MI: Institute for Social Research.

Cartwright, S., Cooper, C. L., & Murphy, L. R. (1997). Diagnosing a healthy organization: A proactive approach to stress in the workplace. In L. R. Murphy, J. J. Hurrell, S. L. Sauter, & G. P. Keita (Eds.), *Job stress interventions* (pp. 217–233). Washington, DC: American Psychological Association.

Cook, T. D., & Campbell, D. T. (1979). *Quasi-experimentation: Design and analysis for field settings.* Boston: Houghton–Mifflin.

Davis, M. F., Rosenberg, K., Iverson, D. C., Vernon, T. M., & Bauer, J. (1984). Worksite health promotion in Colorado. *Public Health Reports, 99,* 538–543.

Donaldson, S. I. (1997). Worksite health promotion: A theory-driven, empirically based perspective. In L. R. Murphy, J. J. Hurrell, S. L. Sauter, & G. P. Keita (Eds.), *Job stress interventions.* Washington, DC: American Psychological Association.

Griffin, M. A., Hart, P. M., & Wilson-Evered, E. (2000). Using employee opinion surveys to improve organizational health. In L. R. Murphy and C. L. Cooper (Eds.), *Healthy and productive work: An international perspective.* New York: Taylor & Francis.

Halverson, R. R., & Bliese, P. D. (1995). (1995, Sept.). *Using multi-level investigations to assess stressors and strains in the workplace.* Paper presented at Work, Stress and Health 95: Creating Healthier Workplaces, Washington, DC.

Hart, P. M. (1999). Predicting employee life satisfaction: A coherent model of personality, work and nonwork experiences, and domain satisfactions. *Journal of Applied Psychology, 84,* 564–584.

Ilgen, D. R. (1990). Health issues at work: Opportunities for industrial/organizational psychology. *American Psychologist, 45,* 273–283.

Ivancevich, J. M., Matteson, M. T., Freedman, S. M., & Phillips, J. S. (1990). Worksite stress management interventions. *American Psychologist, 45,* 223–239.

Kenny, D. A. (1979). Correlation and Causality. New York: Wiley.

Kohler, S., & Kamp, J. (1992). American workers under pressure. St. Paul, MN: St. Paul Fire and Marine Insurance.

Leviton, L. C., & Hughes, E. (1981). Research on the utilization of evaluations: A review and synthesis. *Evaluation Review, 5*(4), 525–548.

Light, R. J., Singer, J. D., & Willet, J. B. (1990). *By design: Planning research on higher education.* Cambridge, MA: Harvard University Press.

Lipsey, M. W., & Corday, D. S. (2000). Evaluation methods for social research. *Annual Review of Psychology, 51,* 345–375.

Lipsey, M. W., Crosse, S., Dunkle, J., Pollard, J., & Stobart, G. (1985). Evaluation: The state of the art and the sorry state of science. In D. S. Cordray (Ed.), *Utilizing prior research in evaluation planning. New directions for program evaluation, No. 27.* San Francisco: Jossey-Bass.

Little, R. J., & Yau, L. H. (1998). Statistical techniques for analyzing data from prevention trials: Treatment of no-shows using Rubin's causal model. *Psychological Methods, 3,* 147–159.

Murphy, L. R., & Cooper, C. L. (2000). *Healthy and productive work.* New York: Taylor & Francis.

Posavac, E. J., & Carey, R. G. (1985). *Program evaluation.* Englewood Cliffs, NJ: Prentice Hall.

Patton, M. Q. (1978). *Utilization-focused evaluation.* Beverly Hills, CA: Sage.

Patton, M. Q., Grimes, P. S., Guthrie, K. M., Brennan, N. J., French, B. D., and Blyth, D. A. (1977). In search of impact: An analysis of the utilization of federal health evaluation research. In C. H. Weiss (Ed.), *Using social research in public policy making.* Lexington, MA: Lexington Books.

Quick, J. C., Quick, J. D., Nelson, D. L., & Hurrell, J. J. (1997). *Preventive stress management in organizations.* Washington, DC: American Psychological Association.

Rich, R. F. (1977). Uses of social science information by federal bureaucrats: Knowledge for action versus knowledge for understanding, in C. H. Weiss (Ed.), *Using social research in public policy making.* Lexington, MA: Lexington Books.

Rog, D., & Bickman, L. (1984). The Feedback Research Approach to Evaluation: A method to increase evaluation utility. *Evaluation and Program Planning, 7,* 169–175.

Schmidt, F. L. (1996). Statistical significance testing and cumulative knowledge in psychology: Implications for training of researchers. *Psychological Methods, 1,* 115–139.

Schurman, S. J., & Israel, B. A. (1995). Redesigning work systems to reduce stress: A participatory action research approach to creating change. In L. R. Murphy, J. J. Hurrell, S. L. Sauter, & G. P. Keita (Eds.), *Job stress interventions.* Washington, DC: American Psychological Association.

Scriven, M. (1980). *The logic of evaluation.* Inverness, CA: Edgepress.

Veney, J. E., & Kaluzny, A. D. (1991). *Evaluation and decision making for health services* (2nd ed.). Ann Arbor, MI: Health Administration Press.

Weiss, C. H. (1973). Where politics and evaluation meet. *Evaluation, 2,* 37–45.

West, S. G., Biesanz, J. C., & Pitts, S. C. (2000). Causal inference and generalization in field settings: Experimental and quasi-experimental designs. In H. T. Reis & C. M. Judd (Eds.), *Handbook of Research Methods in Social and Personality Psychology* (pp. 40–84). Cambridge: Cambridge University Press.

Work in America. (1974). *Report of a Special Task Force to the Secretary of Health, Education, and Welfare.* Cambridge, MA: MIT Press.

Economic Evaluations of Workplace Health Interventions: Theory and Literature Review

Kelly DeRango and Luisa Franzini

Economic evaluation asks the question, Is this program worth doing compared to other things we could do with these same resources? For example, when deciding whether to introduce an ergonomics program, an economic evaluation of the program would provide a firm with information on the costs and the benefits of the program. Drummond, O'Brien, Stoddart, & Torrance (1997, p. 8) defined economic evaluation as "the comparative analysis of alternative courses of action in terms of both their costs and their consequences."

Economic evaluation is only one of the evaluations useful when deciding whether to implement a program. It is always recommended to have economic evaluation preceded by an efficacy evaluation and an effectiveness evaluation. The efficacy evaluation is concerned with how effective the program would be if there is full compliance with the program's recommendations. The effectiveness evaluation asks how effective the program is considering both the efficacy and the acceptance of the program by those to whom it is offered. It takes into account the less than perfect compliance associates with most interventions. To continue our example of an ergonomic intervention, the program may have efficacy (it reduces job-related injuries for workers who comply with all its recommendations), but may not be effective in that most workers adopt some and not other recommendations and sustain a larger rate of job injuries then without the program.

The basic tasks of an economic evaluation are to identify, measure, and compare the costs and consequences of the alternatives considered. Although the identification and assessment of costs is the same across evaluations, economic evaluations differ in the measurement of consequences. The next section will address the different types of economic evaluations.

Different Types of Economic Evaluation

Economic evaluations can be categorized into three main types: cost-effectiveness analysis, cost–benefit analysis, and cost-utility analysis. They

Table 20.1. Economic Evaluation and the Measurement of Costs and
Consequences

Type of economic evaluation	Measurement of cost	Measurement of consequences
Cost-effectiveness	Dollars	Physical units (examples: life years gained, injuries averted)
Cost-utility analysis	Dollars	Utility-weighted health outcomes (expressed by quality-adjusted life years; utility measured by (a) time trade-off, (b) standard gamble, (c) rating scale)
Cost–benefit analysis	Dollars	Dollars

differ in how the consequences of the intervention are measured (see Table 20.1).

Cost-Effectiveness

Cost-effectiveness analysis is used when comparing programs with the same outcome, for example a worksite cholesterol screening program versus a worksite dietary intervention. Percent serum cholesterol reduction is the natural unit in which to measure the programs' effectiveness. The advantage of this approach is that no value judgments are involved assessing the program's consequences. The disadvantage is that the comparisons that can be made are limited to interventions with similar outcomes, and cost-effectiveness analysis cannot be used to compare programs with multiple outcomes or across interventions with different outcomes, for example an ergonomic program and an on-site cholesterol screening program. It is sometimes possible to reduce outcomes of interest to a single effect common to both alternatives, for example life years gained or workdays missed, but some interventions have more than one outcome and can therefore not be thus reduced.

Cost-effectiveness analysis comparing two programs identifies a dominant program (one program that is both more effective and has lower cost) or it computes the cost-effectiveness ratio that measures the incremental cost of an extra unit of outcome (life year gained, injury prevented).

In the special case in which two or more programs have demonstrated equivalent consequences, cost-minimization analysis is appropriate.

Cost-Utility Analysis

Cost-utility analysis allows broader comparisons across programs by measuring program outcomes in quality adjusted life-years (QALYs) or some variant like healthy years equivalent (HYEs; Johannesson 1995). QALYs combine several health outcomes into one measure by attaching a "utility" or "quality weight" to each health status. In this context, the concept of utility is of a measure of preferences that is not transformed in money. Drummond et al recommended using cost utility when comparing programs in which the health-related quality of life is an important outcome or when the programs being compared need a common unit of outcome but have different kinds of outcomes, for example they affect both morbidity and mortality or have a wide range of different kinds of outcomes (for example, a worksite nutritional intervention and a back injury prevention program).

The introduction of weights attached to health status introduces value judgments into the economic evaluation. Although cost-effectiveness analysis provides value-free information and requires the decision maker to use his or her own value judgment in choosing which programs to implement, the information provided by a cost-utility analysis has embedded into it value judgments on the desirability of health outcomes. This raises several questions: How should the utilities be measured and whose utilities should be measured? The classical method of utility measurement is the standard gamble that is based on the fundamental axioms of utility theory derived by von Neumann and Morgenstern (1944). The time trade-off, developed specifically for use in health care by Torrance and Sackett (1972), can also be derived from fundamental axioms of utility theory and is easier to administer. The rating scale methods is straightforward to use but is not based on economic theory (see Drummond et al., 1997 for an excellent review of these and other methods). Although economic theory guides the measurement of utilities, it provides no help in deciding whose utilities should be measured. Empirically, the utility weights obtained differ if they are elicited from individuals at risk of a condition, individuals with the condition, or the public at large. Once utilities have been assigned to different health status, cost-utility analysis is very similar to cost effectiveness analysis.

Cost–Benefit Analysis

Cost–benefit analysis measures all outcomes in dollars and is appropriate to compare programs with multiple outcomes of interest (for example onsite exercise programs may affect heart disease, hypertension, and depression) or programs across different sectors (for example, comparing an ergonomics intervention with a prenatal care program). The results of cost–benefit analysis are usually stated as a simple sum (can be positive or negative) representing the net benefit (loss) of one program over another. The difficulty of this approach is valuing health outcomes in monetary terms. The approaches that economists have taken to translate health outcomes into dollars can be grouped into three categories: the human capital approach, the willingness to pay approach, and the compensating differential (or revealed preference) approach.

Human capital. The human capital method uses market wage rates to assess the value of healthy time. The monetary value of a program is the present value of future earnings made possible by the program. This approach has been used in evaluating health interventions, both as the sole basis for evaluating health improvements and as part of the benefits of a health program. Although the human capital approach has been widely used, it has some measurement limitations. First, there is the difficulty of valuing the health of those not employed in the labor force, for example pensioners and homemakers. Shadow prices for healthy time have been used by considering the opportunity cost of time (for example, homemaker time would be valued by the wages he or she would be making if working in the labor force) or using a replacement cost approach (the cost of hiring someone to provide the services performed by the homemaker). Both these methods leave much to be desired in valuing health. Second, there are often imperfections in the labor markets, such as gender and race discrimination, that prevent wages from reflecting marginal productivity. The human capital approach has also been criticized for not being consistent with the principles of welfare economics that underlie cost–benefit analysis. In particular it limits the utility consequences of a program to its impact on labor productivity (Mishan, 1971). The notion of value embedded in welfare economics focuses on what resources the participants in a program are willing to sacrifice to have the program in question. This principle forms the basis of the willingness to pay approach discussed next.

Willingness to pay. Willingness to pay studies use surveys to ask respondents how much they would be willing to pay for a program or benefit. Respondents are required to think about a hypothetical scenario (for example, having the program implemented) and about the contingency of an actual market existing for the program. They are then asked to reveal the maximum that they would be willing to pay for such a program. This technique can be thought of as an attempt to replace a missing market because it allows measurement of underlying consumer demand and valuation for a good that does not have an explicit market. The methodology is also known as contingent valuation because respondents are asked to think of the contingency of an actual market existing. Depending on whether the program is being introduced or removed, the questions asked are about willingness to pay (WTP) or willingness to accept (WTA). In the case of the introduction of a program, we need to find out the maximum amount that can be taken from the beneficiaries of the program to keep them at the same utility level as without the program. That amount is called the compensating variation and represents the willingness to pay. In the case of the removal of a program, we would ask the minimum amount that must be paid to the users as compensation to forgo the program and keep the utility at the same level as it was with the program. That amount is the equivalent variation.

The difficulty is in actually measuring compensating variations and equivalent variations. What questions should be asked, of whom, and how? When asking willingness to pay questions, it must be made clear to the respondent whether to include the intangible benefits of health, the future health care costs avoided, and the increased productivity resulting from improved health. This is to avoid double counting in computing the value of a program. As in cost-utility analysis, the question of whom to ask is crucial. Different answers are obtained depending on whether those who are certain to benefit or those who may benefit in the future (the general public) are asked. The uncertainty of the health outcome inherent in many programs further complicates the valuation.

Revealed Preferences and Risk in the Work Place

A number of wage–risk studies attempt to examine the relationship between risks, in particular health risks, associated with a job and wage rates that individuals require to accept the job (Herzog & Schlottmann, 1990; Viscusi, 1979). These studies are grounded in economic theory and are based on Adam Smith's recognition that if workers are mobile and information on working conditions is widespread, labor markets would generate compensating wages for undesirable working conditions. Most studies, focusing on compensating wage differentials that reflect job hazards resulting in death or serious injury, have found such compensation to exist. Compensating differentials have been estimated in models (called hedonic wage models) that assume that firms and workers exchange wage–job risk bundles in an implicit market. The estimated required compensation for increased risk is used as an estimate of the value of decreasing risk.

The advantage of this approach is that it is based on actual consumer choices versus hypothetical scenarios used in the willingness to pay approach. The weakness of this approach is that labor markets are imperfect and so is the information regarding risk available to the workers. Therefore the observed wage–risk trade-off may not accurately represent a worker's valuation of risk. Economists have pointed also to methodological and statistical problems in much of this literature (Bartik 1987).

How should costs be estimated? Although economic evaluations differ in measuring consequences, they all measure costs in monetary terms. The choice of which costs to include depends on the purpose of the analysis and the viewpoint taken. If the analysis is done from the point of view of the firm, only costs paid by the firm are relevant. So, for example, participants' costs, such as out-of-pockets costs, would not be included. Often cost evaluations are done from a societal perspective and therefore an attempt is made to include the cost of all resources used in the program. Ideally, resource costs should measured from the economic notion of opportunity costs—that is, the value of the resources used in the program if those resources were used in the best possible alternative. In practice, market prices are used when available. In perfectly competitive markets, market prices reflect opportunity costs. When markets are not perfectly competitive, market prices may not reflect opportunity costs but are still used for convenience. When there are externalities (effects that spill over to other persons), market prices are poor indicators of opportunity costs. Techniques of willingness to pay are more appropriate in quantifying values in the presence of externalities or for other kinds of incomplete markets.

Difficulties arise when markets do not exist for some of the resources used in a program, for example, volunteer time. Values for nonmarket items are usually imputed using replacement values if available. For example, volunteer time can be valued at the cost of hiring professionals to provide the services provided by volunteers.

The allocation of overhead, capital costs, and shared costs (cost of resources used in more than one program simultaneously) is sometimes problematic, but methodologies have been developed to allocate those costs (see Drummond et al., 1997). Finally, all costs should be discounted based on the rate of time preference.

Statistical issues. Economic evaluations can be used with data that are generated from experiments (like randomized clinical trials) or observation (for example, comparing before and after legislative changes). In the case of data generated in observational studies, biases may arise because of omitted factors confounded with the program, selection bias (individual self-selecting into a program), difficulties in controlling for case-mix differences, and measurement errors and latent variables. The latter concern applies also in experimental studies.

It is also important to remember that cost-effectiveness ratios are based on estimates of costs and effectiveness, not on population parameters, and are therefore point estimates with a degree of sampling variation. Recently, methods have been developed to estimate confidence intervals for cost-effectiveness ratios (Briggs, Wondering, & Mooney, 1997; Gardiner et al., 1995).

Another type of uncertainty present in cost evaluations is the uncertainty associated with the assumptions made in the process of estimating cost or effectiveness, for example the discount rate used or the expected compliance rate. Sensitivity analysis deals with this type of uncertainty by varying the assumed parameter values and recomputing the cost-effectiveness ratio. We would put more trust in an economic evaluation whose results are robust to reasonable changes in assumptions.

Lessons From the Current Literature

This section of the chapter examines the empirical literature on the cost-effectiveness of workplace health interventions. Although there is a growing literature on the efficacy of worksite health interventions, the number of studies that report cost data is still relatively small. As Warner noted in his 1988 review of the cost-effectiveness of workplace health promotion programs,

> Despite these qualifications, the literature as a whole does not substantiate the widespread belief that workplace health promotion programs

> are cost-saving or even cost-effective. The analysis necessary to evaluate
> the premise simply does not exist. (Warner, Wickizer, Wolfe, Schildroth,
> & Samuelson, 1988, p. 111)

Unfortunately, the current situation in the literature is similar. For most, if not all, types of worksite health intervention, there are simply not enough published articles to reach a definitive conclusion regarding their cost-effectiveness.

In contrast to Warner's comprehensive review of the literature, this section reviews a small number of studies in depth. The purpose of this type of review is not to assess the state of the literature per se but to address some important methodological issues that are common to much of the research in this area. The methodological issues highlighted include

1. Research findings that the cost estimates of different worksite interventions respond differently to variations in the participation rate, suggesting that the relative ranking of these interventions by a cost-effectiveness criterion may not be stable outside of the circumstances unique to the study environment.
2. Research findings that show that the estimates of annual per person benefits from worksite interventions vary with the time span of the study. In particular, the longer the time frame of the evaluation, the more the benefits tend to outweigh the costs. These results suggest that the relatively short time span of two to three years typically found in most studies of worksite health intervention may lead to a substantial downward bias in estimates of benefits.
3. It is not uncommon for researchers to not include the costs of foregone labor in their calculations of worksite health interventions. Including such costs is especially important when considering the cost-effectiveness of different interventions that require varying amounts of worker time.
4. Society's perspective and the perspective of corporate management are not identical. Cost–benefit analysis that asks whether or not corporate interests are served by a worksite health intervention should not be used to determine if the same serves the interests of society. Specifically, the failure of a worksite health intervention to reduce medical costs and sick leave days sufficiently to offset the cost of the intervention does not imply that the intervention represents a net loss to society.

The case studies that correspond to the methodological points given in this list follow.

The importance of participation rates in the cost-effectiveness analysis of a cholesterol screening program. Wilson, Edmunson, and DeJoy (1992) examined the cost-effectiveness of five different worksite cholesterol screening programs using a nonrandom sample of workers from 37 worksites at Georgia Pacific. The impact of each intervention on blood cholesterol levels was measured by retesting each study participant six months after the intervention. The 5911 research participants were divided among five intervention groups:

1. A control group;
2. One-month education program with materials distributed all month;
3. One-month education program with an associated outcome incentive;
4. One-month education program followed by three-month reinforcement program; and
5. One-month education program followed by three-month reinforcement program with the same incentive as in group 3.

Administrative costs were allocated equally between the groups (one fifth of the total cost each) but screening costs and the costs of the interventions themselves were kept separate for each intervention. Cost-effectiveness was measured by calculating the per person cost of reducing the blood cholesterol levels of high-risk or borderline high-risk individuals by 10% or more. This calculation simply involved dividing the total costs by the total number of high-risk or borderline high-risk patients who (a) chose to participate and (b) conditional on their participation, realized a 10% reduction in their serum cholesterol. Using this criterion, groups 3 and 4 demonstrated the best effectiveness ratio.

In addition to the cost-effectiveness measure, a sensitivity analysis was performed that estimated the per participant cost savings associated with a 1% and 10% increase in each programs' participation rate. This exercise was motivated by the observation that participation rates varied substantially between the different program groups. Furthermore, this variation in participation rates accounted for a substantial portion of the variation in costs between the groups—the least effective interventions also had the lowest participation rates. In effect, high participation rates lowered costs and raised the cost-effectiveness of the most successful interventions, and low participation rates had the opposite effect for the least successful interventions.

This simulation exercise shows that although increasing participation would moderately lower the costs of the most effective groups (3 and 4), the per participant costs for the least effective groups (2 and 5) would fall dramatically under similar increases. These results suggest that the relative ordering of different health interventions may be sensitive to not only the relative effectiveness of the interventions themselves but also to the participation rates realized at different worksites. In general, if the researcher has reason to believe that participation rates are related to the parameters of the program interventions themselves, then variation in participation rates should not undermine the ability of managers to correctly interpret the reported results. However, if variation in participation rates is primarily a function of idiosyncrasies unique to each worksite, then the ability of managers to generalize research findings to a broader context is quite limited. In fact this concern seems validated by the report in Wilson et al. (1992) that program participation is closely related to the size of each worksite.

Ergonomics, smoking cessation programs, and the effect of longer time spans on benefit estimates. Aaras (1994) studied the effect of introducing ergonomic workstations on the health of primarily female employees of a Norwegian telecommunications company from 1967 to 1984. The workstations were designed to reduce static load and allow variations in work position. The health outcomes of interest were the relationship between postural load and the development of musculoskeletal illness. The design of the study did not include randomized selection into control and treatment groups. Rather, the researchers observed the incidence of load-related musculoskeletal injuries and the incidence of sick leave related to these injuries at the company before and after the introduction of ergonomic workstations. Both were reduced over time as a result of the introduction of the new ergonomic workstation.

Aaras performed a cost–benefit analysis at the end of her paper from the company's perspective of profit maximization. She tabulated the costs of the workstations themselves, as well as the cost of the new lighting installed at the factories. Against this cost she balanced reductions in costs associated with lower turnover rates and lower incidences of sick leave. High turnover leads to higher recruitment costs, lower on-the-job productivity from new trainees compared to the more experienced workers they replaced, and higher labor costs for training instructors. Aaras did not estimate the cost reductions associated with lower medical expenses.

The benefit–cost ratio implied by the size of the cost savings and investment reported by Aaras was more than 9:1. Besides the large magnitude of this return, perhaps the most striking aspect of these results is the distribution of the cost savings. Approximately 80% of the cost savings were generated by reductions in turnover. If one ignores the cost savings associated with turnover, the benefit–cost ratio is reduced to 1.9:1.

At 18 years, Aaras' study has an unusually long time frame that allows her to study the effect of her intervention on turnover rates. Yet the typical study of worksite health interventions spans one to three years, making it impractical to consider the cost savings from reduced turnover in firms where little turnover would be observed—*even without the intervention*—in this time frame. Yet if this one study is any indication, ignoring the effect of a health intervention on a company's turnover rate may lead to a substantial downward bias in the estimation of the potential benefits.

Similar findings come from Warner, Smith, Smith, and Fries (1996), which used a computer simulation model of worksite smoking cessation programs. The simulation allows for labor turnover, which leads to benefit leakage from the company and to society as a whole. The cost of the hypothetical program is set at $150 per participant. The accrued benefits included reductions in medical expenses, reduced absenteeism, increased productivity (the researchers assume that nonsmoking workers will have 5 more minutes a day to devote to work because they no longer take smoking breaks), and reduced insurance premiums. Although labor turnover causes the company to lose about one half of the benefits of the smoking cessation program, the remaining benefits still provide the company with a profitable investment.

Perhaps the most striking result of the paper is that the cumulative benefits of the program grow substantially over time. In the first three years, the program had a cost–benefit ratio below 1, indicating that the company lost money on its investment. By year 5, the cost–benefit ratio had become 1.74, indicating a net corporate gain. By year 10, this ratio had grown to 5.10, and by year 25 it had increased to 8.89. It is not difficult to imagine researchers conducting a three-year study of a smoking cessation program with a similar company erroneously concluding that the program is not profitable. Clearly the program does enhance profits, just not within three years.

Measuring foregone labor costs in a hypertension screening program. Ellis, Koblin, Irvine, Legare, and Logan (1994) examined whether a program run jointly by a voluntary health organization and the public health unit can result in a preventive strategy that is both clinically significant and cost-effective in controlling hypertension in small- to medium-sized worksites. They conducted a randomized study with a one- or two-stage screening protocol. Stage one participants were asked to see a physician within one month or one year (depending on blood pressure level). Stage two participants were called back again after two weeks and offered assistance. In all, 71 companies in Toronto were used to find 545 participants for initial screening and retest after one year.

The authors use cost-effectiveness analysis to evaluate the two different screening methods and protocols. The outcome measure is blood pressure reduction. The cost measure used includes the costs of screening, recruiting workers for the study, and the medical costs of each worker over the one-year study period. Their primary finding is that there was no statistically significant difference between groups in terms of diastolic blood pressure at year-end assessment and no clear pattern of one option being more expensive than the other. However, screening costs were 11 to 37% more for the stage 2 group in large part because of costs of foregone labor incurred during the second stage of the screening process for group 2 participants. Many researchers do not factor in the costs of foregone labor when evaluating the relative cost-effectiveness of various worksite health interventions (see, for instance, Wilson et al., 1992). Thus, had the researchers followed the lead of many research papers on worksite health interventions and not factored foregone labor into their cost calculations, it is likely that their quantitative analysis would have reflected similar levels of cost-effectiveness for both the single- and two-stage screening processes. The absence of estimates of foregone labor costs is somewhat puzzling because, as Ellis et al. (1994) demonstrated, the calculation is relatively straightforward. Simply multiplying the wage rate by the amount of time spent screening or visiting a doctor is a reasonably good approximation. If actual wage rates are not available, using an estimated wage based on information about local labor markets would be preferable to ignoring the costs of foregone labor altogether.

Distinguishing perspectives when valuing the benefits of worksite vaccination programs. Bridges et al. (2000) examined the effect of the worksite influenza vaccine program through a double blind, randomized, placebo-controlled trial over a two-year period of time. The economic costs considered in this study were the costs of doctor visits, drug costs and hospitalizations, the costs of lost workdays and lost work hours to physician visits, and the cost of the vaccine. In the first year of the study the total costs for the vaccine group were $124.21 per person compared to $58.62 per person for the placebo group. In the second year per person costs for the vaccine group were $51.43 compared to $40.26 for the placebo group. The authors concluded that "influenza vaccination of healthy adults is unlikely to result in a net cost savings to society" (p. 1663).

This assessment was echoed in the popular and medical press. Writing in *Pulmonary Reviews* (2001), Hughes wrote, "Although vaccinating healthy adults may reduce flu-related morbidity, it does not provide an economic benefit to society." An article in *Science News Update* stated that Bridges and her colleagues' work shows that "giving influenza shots to healthy individuals under the age of 65 years did not result in net cost savings to society."

It is important to note the costs and benefits considered by this study reflect the interests of the employer and the health insurance provider and not those of the employee. They certainly do not reflect those of society at large. When employees are sick, the company incurs costs associated with sick leave, additional health care costs, and reduced productivity. In contrast, when an employee is sick, she suffers lost income, lost leisure time, and in addition endures the difficult to quantify but nevertheless real cost of pain and discomfort. Furthermore, from the perspective of society, when an individual chooses to get vaccinated, she not only reduces the probably of becoming ill herself but also reduces the probability of transmitting influenza to those around her.

Thus, a full accounting of the costs and benefits to society of a vaccination program would include not just medical expenses and the costs of foregone labor, but the monetized value of the pain and suffering associated with influenza, lost leisure time, and the reduced likelihood of transmission of the influenza virus to others. Another way to consider the same question is to ask whether the benefits of vaccinations not considered by Bridges and her colleagues are smaller or larger than the $58 and $11 in net costs to the corporation reported in years one and two of the study. In effect, ignoring the value of leisure costs, pain and suffering, and decreased viral transmission undermines any basis for the concluding that "influenza vaccination of healthy adults is unlikely to result in a net cost savings to society" (p. 1661).

Conclusion

There are several methods that may be used to evaluate the benefits of the program when conducting a cost–benefit analysis, each with its advantages and disadvantages. This chapter has emphasized the human capital approach because it is the most commonly used methodology. However, researchers may want to consider two approaches to valuation found in the economics literature—the willingness-to-pay survey method and the revealed-preferences approach. Furthermore, researchers should not be confined to cost–benefit studies of workplace health interventions—cost-effectiveness studies measure the benefit of the intervention in terms of physical units (such as diastolic blood pressure reductions). Cost–benefit analyses measure the benefit of the intervention in dollars and cost-utility analysis measures benefits using utility-weighted health outcomes.

To calculate the net benefit of different types of worksite health interventions, a researcher must identify the actor who incurs the costs and benefits, the time frame in which these costs and benefit flows will occur, and then thoroughly account for all benefits and costs that will occur. Identifying the actor is crucial in distinguishing the costs and benefits applicable to a corporation and those of society at large. Programs that lower profits can conceivably increase social welfare, and conversely programs that raise profits can conceivably lower social welfare. Researchers should explicitly state whether the cost–benefit analysis is being conducted from the point of view of the firm or society as a whole and then confine its conclusions to the same realm.

Furthermore, researchers should carefully distinguish between the time frame of the study and the time frame in which costs and benefits result from the intervention in question. Focusing on costs and benefits directly observed during the course of a study is understandable but in many cases may lead to a downward bias in the estimate of total benefits. This concern is especially important when an intervention involves the purchase of durable goods that are expected to last for more than a few years. Moreover, a more explicit treatment of the relevant time line in future studies may lead to a new and beneficial line of research on the timing and duration of benefits. Questions such as, How long do benefits last after an intervention occurs? and, At what rate do benefits decay over time or grow after an intervention? are rarely asked in the literature but may be a fruitful area of research in the future.

In a similar vein, explicit modeling of the participation rate of research participants should be considered in research projects where the incidence of voluntary participation affects the size of per person benefits and costs. Simulating the hypothetical cost-effectiveness of various interventions conditional on different participation levels allows the researcher to separate issues of effectiveness from the effect of idiosyncratic variations in the participation rate.

A full accounting of all costs and benefits is essential for any study of workplace health interventions. Although the identification of benefits may vary depending on the type of evaluation considered, the process used to identify costs is the same regardless of evaluation method. It is important for researchers to include costs that may not be easily quantifiable. Lost work time is just one example of an easily overlooked expense that is common to many different workplace health interventions. Administrative data on the actual wages of participating employees is the most preferred source for this cost information. However, if no such records are available to the researcher, estimated wages are preferable to an assumption of zero cost. This strategy can be applied to other costs as well—if actual costs are difficult to obtain, researchers are better served by estimating the relevant costs than ignoring them altogether.

References

Aaras, A. (1994). The impact of ergonomic intervention on individual health and corporate prosperity in a telecommunications environment. *Ergonomics, 37*(10), 1679–1696.

Bartik, T. J. (1987). The estimation of demand parameters in hedonic price models. *Journal of Political Economy, 95*(1), 81–88.

Bridges, C. B., Thompson, W. W., & Meltzer, M. I., Reeve, G. R., Talamonti, W. J., Cox, N. J., Lilac, H. A., Hall, H., Klimov, A., & Fukuda, K. (2000). Effectiveness and cost-benefit of influenza vaccination of healthy working adults: A randomized controlled trial. *Journal of the American Medical Association, 284*, 1655–1663.

Briggs, A. H., Wondering, D. E., & Mooney, C. Z. (1997). Pulling cost-effectiveness analysis by its bootstraps: A non-parametric approach to confidence interval estimation. *Health Economics, 6*, 327–340.

Cost benefit of flu shots for healthy working adults questioned. (2000, October 4). *Science News Update*. Retrieved July 3, 2001, from http://www.ama-assn.org/sci-pubs/sci-news/2000/snr1004.htm

Drummond, M. F., O'Brien, B., Stoddart, G. L., & Torrance, G. W. (1997). *Methods for the economic evaluation of health care programs* (3rd ed.). New York: Oxford Medical Publications, Oxford University Press.

Ellis, E., Koblin, W., Irvine, M. J., Legare, J., & Logan, A. G. (1994). Small, blue collar work site hypertension screening: A cost-effectiveness study. *Journal of Occupational Medicine, 36*(3), 346–355.

Gardiner, J., Hogan, A., Holmes-Rovner, D., Griffith, L., et al. (1995). Confidence intervals for cost-effectiveness ratios. *Medical Decision Making, 15*, 254–263.

Herzog, H. W., & Schlottmann, A. M. (1990). Valuing risk in the workplace: Market price, willingness to pay, and the optimal provision of safety. *The Review of Economics and Statistics*, 463–470.

Hughes, D. (2001, Jan.). Should healthy adults and children get flu shots? *Pulmonary Reviews.com*. Retrieved April 3, 2002, from http://www.pulmonaryreviews.com/jan01/pr—jan01—flueshots.html

Johannesson, M. (1995). Quality-adjusted life years versus healthy-years equivalent: A comment. *Journal of Health Economics, 14*, 9–16.

Mishan, E. J. (1971). Evaluation of life and limb: A theoretical approach. *Journal of Political Economy, 79*, 687–706.

Should healthy adults and children get flu shots? Pulmonary Reviews.Com, 6(1) (2001, Jan.). Retrieved May 15, 2001, from http://www.pulmonaryreviews.com/jan01/pr_jan01/flushots.html

Torrance, G. W., & Sackett, T. W. (1972). A utility maximization model for evaluation of health care program. *Health Services Research, 7*(2), 118–133.

Viscusi, W. K. (1979). Job hazards and worker quit rates: An analysis of adaptive worker behavior. *International Economic Review, 20*(1), 29–58.

von Neumann, J., & Morgenstern, O. (1944). *Theory of games and economic behavior.* Princeton, NJ: Princeton University Press.

Warner, K. E., Smith, R. J., Smith, D. G., & Fries, B. E. (1996). Health and economic implications of a work-site smoking cessation program: A simulation analysis. *Journal of Occupational and Environmental Medicine, 38*(10), 981–992.

Warner, K. E., Wickizer, T. M., Wolfe, R. A., Schildroth, J. E., & Samuelson, M. H. (1988). Economic implications of workplace health promotion programs: Review of the literature. *Journal of Occupational Medicine, 30*(2), 106–112.

Wilson, M. G., Edmunson, J., DeJoy, D. M. (1992). Cost effectiveness of work-site cholesterol screening and intervention programs. *Journal of Occupational Medicine, 4*(6), 642–649.

Author Index

Numbers in italics refer to listings in reference sections.
References to footnotes are indicated by "n" after the page number.

Subject Index

References to footnotes are indicated by "n" after the page number.

About the Editors

James Campbell Quick is internationally recognized for his influential and groundbreaking theory of preventive stress management. He has more than 100 publications in refereed journal articles, books, invited book chapters, and encyclopedia entries, including a clinical monograph. His recent research and scholarship has focused on occupational health psychology and executive health. He was founding editor of the American Psychological Association (APA) *Journal of Occupational Health Psychology*. He is a Fellow of the Society for Industrial and Organizational Psychology (Division 14 of the APA), the American Psychological Society, and the American Institute of Stress, and he has been awarded an APA Presidential Citation. He has received more than $235,000 in funded support for research, scholarship, and intellectual contributions. He was APA's stress expert to the National Academy of Sciences in 1990. He is the recipient of numerous research and teaching awards, including a 2001 Minnie Stevens Piper Professorship nomination. He is listed in *Who's Who in the World* (7th ed.) and was awarded The Maroon Citation by the Colgate University Alumni Corporation. His professional work as a senior U.S. Air Force reserve officer (colonel, retired) led to numerous awards and decorations, including The Legion of Merit. He is currently director of the doctoral program in business administration at the University of Texas at Arlington.

Lois E. Tetrick received her doctorate in industrial/organizational psychology from Georgia Institute of Technology in 1983. On completion of her doctoral studies, she joined the faculty of the Department of Psychology at Wayne State University and remained there until 1995, when she moved to the Department of Psychology at the University of Houston. She is an associate editor of the *Journal of Occupational Health Psychology* and has served as an associate editor of the *Journal of Applied Psychology*. She is on the editorial boards of the *Journal of Organizational Behavior* and *Advanced Topics in Organizational Behavior*. Her research has focused primarily on individuals' perceptions of the employment relationship and their reactions to these perceptions, including issues of occupational health and safety, occupational stress, and organizational commitment. She is a Fellow of the APA, the Society for Industrial and Organizational Psychology, and the American Psychological Society. She is currently the chair of the Human Resources Division of the Academy of Management.